p 91, 93, 94-9
96, 98, 101, 106,
109, 113,

Leadership
in Higher
Education

Views from the Presidency

Leadership *in* Higher Education

Francis L. Lawrence

With a foreword by Kenneth A. Shaw

Transaction Publishers
New Brunswick (U.S.A.) and London (U.K.)

Library of Congress Catalog Number: 2006040362
ISBN: 0-7658-0328-3 (cloth); 1-4128-0590-2 (paper)
Printed in the United States of America

Library of Congress Cataloging-in-Publication Data

Lawrence, Francis L.
    Leadership in higher education : views from the presidency / Francis L. Lawrence.
        p. cm.
    ISBN: 0-7658-0328-3 (case alk. paper)—ISBN: 1-4128-0590-2 (pbk. alk. paper)
    1. College presidents—United States. 2. Universities and colleges—United States—Administration. I. Title.

LB2341.L247   2006
378.1'110973—dc22   2006040362

For my grandchildren, Josh, Ben, Beth, Jeremy, Jeffrey, Gary, Kelsey, Michael, Mark, Lucas, Isabel, Jacob, and Marisol. Your play has shown me that learning should be joyful; your love has taught me that it must be inclusive; your presence has reminded me that it continues through the generations.

Contents

Acknowledgements

The people to whom I owe the most are, obviously, the twelve university presidents and chancellors who generously agreed to be interviewed for this volume—three of whom now head national higher education organizations. They are all tremendously busy people with heavy responsibilities and tightly scheduled days in which they must confer, plan, and consult with people who have a far greater right to their attention than I do. Nevertheless they each allotted a large slice of time, three hours or more, to answer my questions about their successful careers. Whatever merits this book may have belong to them, to the lessons and insights they offered in their own frank, revealing stories of their leadership in higher education. For the transcriptions of the taped interviews, I want to acknowledge the work of Domingo Duarte.

I am grateful to Brent Ruben for convincing me that I ought to write about presidential leadership and for all of the excellent advice he offered as the project took shape, as well as his generosity in reading and commenting on the introduction and the Rutgers chapter. I have also imposed on a long list of people, chief among them Joseph J. Seneca, Nancy Winterbauer, John Wolf, David Scott, Rob Heffernan, and Carol Koncsol, asking them to delve back into their memories and records in order to check facts and interpretations of the twelve years of my tenure as Rutgers' president. They can be credited with the accurate passages in my account. Any mistakes should be attributed to me.

I need to share credit for this project with my wife, Mary Kay, the love of my life and my best friend. The book could not have been written without her patience, understanding, and encouragement, as well as her research, editorial assistance, and painstaking work filling in the blanks and correcting the mistakes in the original transcriptions. We are indebted to our siblings, who listened patiently and cheered us on through the countless iterations of transcription and correction of the interviews as well as the experience of reliving my presidency. I want to thank Juliette Bernier, Madeleine Nasuti, and Sr. Theresa Lawrence. Mary Kay leaned on the support of Alice Froeschle, Joanne Long, Carol Long, and Suzanne Reichert.

Finally, I must thank Transaction Publishers, particularly its scholarly leaders, Irving Louis Horowitz and Mary E. Curtis, as well as their staff, for their invaluable guidance in bringing this book to press.

Foreword

Leadership in Higher Education: Views from the Presidency offers a vivid mural of a richly varied group of universities and university systems painted by the leaders who have shaped them, the presidents and chancellors who have, by their own accounts, devoted every waking minute (and no doubt a few sleepless nights) to wrestling with the problems of their institutions and planning for their advancement.

In an introductory chapter, Lawrence has provided the national and international context of the new conditions and challenges that these leaders faced:

- the explosive growth of the demand for higher education in the new information economy,
- the impact of information technology on higher education,
- the unique claims of American higher education to distinction for both excellence and access,
- the pressures coming about through American demographic changes,
- the new rules of the game in the financing of public higher education,
- the results of the nexus of funding, demand, and selectivity,
- enrollment pressures and cost sharing,
- market forces in American higher education,
- institutional costs and prices and their effects on students and parents,
- diversity in academe,
- and even a coda on the conundrum of college athletics.

The interviews are remarkably candid and revealing, personal and direct in their tone. What emerges from them are stories of tremendous power and appeal. They depict some of the most distinguished and effective institutions of higher education in America—a total of twenty-three universities, state university systems, and national university associations over which the thirteen presidents and chancellors have presided, ranging from the Massachusetts Institute of Technology on the East Coast to Xavier University of New Orleans in the Deep South, and the University of California, Berkeley on the West Coast, and from the NCAA to the AAU.

xi

The time period that this portrait of American higher education treats is one of considerable economic and cultural stress, from the recession of the early 1990s through the shock of 9/11. The interviews reveal the ways that the leaders of these institutions, in collaboration with their boards, their faculty colleagues, their administrative staff members, and their external constituencies, have charted successful paths that have not simply kept their institutions functioning at the same level in times of fiscal stringency but have taken them forward to new heights of academic achievement in both teaching and scholarship.

With great energy and ingenuity America's higher education leadership, the interviewees and their academic communities, have continuously improved the bedrock teaching, research, and service missions of our institutions of higher education and have done so in circumstances of severe economic stringency. They have brought about this miracle by what in other circles might be termed entrepreneurial means, which are ably described in this book.

A conclusion sums up the salient common aspects of the leadership styles of the presidents and chancellors in this volume and ends with a passionate plea for action on the federal level to ensure that affordable access is available to the new more numerous and more diverse cohorts of young people coming of age and eager to enter higher education.

If anyone doubts the common perception that America has the best system of higher education in the world, Fran Lawrence has produced a casebook of leadership stories that will convince all skeptics. These are histories that students of leadership, their teachers, and prospective presidents alike will read with interest and great profit. I found myself unable to put this book down. It is not unlike reading a really good mystery novel. But here the mystery is in the way in which each story is told—unique but with common threads that soon become apparent to the sleep-deprived reader. I plan to read Lawrence's book several more times, and I expect the same from students in my higher education classes.

Kenneth A. Shaw
Chancellor Emeritus and University Professor
Syracuse University

Introduction

"Perhaps there never was a time when the opportunities for presidential leadership were so extraordinary or the consequences of presidential failure so great."
        —*Frank H. T. Rhodes*[1]

This collection of interviews, in which the presidents and chancellors of some of America's most respected universities reflect on their careers during the decade leading up to the turn of the century and immediately following it, provides a portrait of American higher education at what one could quite legitimately term a "leadership moment."[2] In another era, these men and women might have functioned primarily as skilled and beloved caretakers of the patrimony of knowledge, but around the turn of the century, when the growth of the information economy and the role of knowledge in creating a good quality of life for individuals and nations became universally acknowledged truths, the leaders of higher education were offered the opportunity of entering the pantheon of those who have had extraordinary roles thrust upon them by the circumstances in which they were called to serve, with all of the hazards that accompany such a distinction.

In the 1990s, as universities competed with other priorities for a share of state and federal budgets, enterprising public and private institutions issued economic impact studies in order to convince the public, the media, and legislators that their thousands of workers, their scores of construction projects, the practical applications of their research, their public service efforts, and their billion-dollar budgets played such vital roles in their regions that they deserved much greater attention, respect, and support. An observer with a wicked sense of nautical humor might say that higher education whistled for a breeze to fill its sails and reaped the whirlwind. As our colleges and universities have become increasingly important to society, the role of the university president has changed dramatically.

During the search for the successor to Penn president Judith Rodin, *Philadelphia Inquirer* business section columnist, Andrew Cassel argued that while the mayoral race was important, "you can make a good case that picking the next president of the University of Pennsylvania is just as big a deal for our region."[3] He pointed to the comparative statistics for the city and the univer-

1

sity: a municipal workforce of 25,000 versus Penn's 28,000 employees; a city budget of $3 billion, a university budget of $2.6 billion; and the extensive real estate holdings of both the city and the university, which make them important landlords and developers. He cited Penn's health care system, the second largest in the area, as well, but according to the *Inquirer*'s top expert on the economy, the university's most important contributions to the future of Philadelphia are: "Young people, particularly those with brains and skills. Facilities for lifelong learning. 'Knowledge-based' businesses. Cutting-edge research, particularly in areas with strong growth potential, such as biotechnology and the life sciences." As Cassel noted, "Decades ago, it might have been enough for a university president to have good academic credentials, with perhaps a flair for fund-raising on the side.... But these times and this region are clearly going to need a lot more."

It could be argued that Rodin set the bar for the next president very high. After announcing her resignation, she was chosen as the winner of the 2004 Philadelphia Award for "her unwavering commitment to elevating the economy of West Philadelphia and the quality of life for its residents...."[4] In the past the award went to such political luminaries as Pennsylvania governor Ed Rendell and Philadelphia mayor John Street. In accepting the award she acknowledged that the award recognized her use of her leadership of Penn to benefit the community "through a host of programs and initiatives to help spur economic development, educational opportunity, business growth and quality-of-life enhancements." In other *Philadelphia Inquirer* coverage of the president's resignation, it was noted that one of the challenges for a new president might be that Penn had been living beyond its means, with $1.4 billion in debt, a heavy load in relation to its endowment and a burden that it took on, at least in part, in order to restore its blighted urban neighborhood with new housing, and attractive sites for entertainment and retail stores.[5]

The devotion to community development that earned Penn's president high praise had a less happy outcome for Connecticut College president Claire Gaudiani, despite her success in raising the endowment from $31 million to $166 million during the twelve years of her tenure.[6] The college trustees chair praised Gaudiani's "visionary and ambitious contributions to higher education," but students and faculty grew increasingly critical of her management when shortfalls and cutbacks affected the college community.[7] In the wake of her resignation, with a generous severance package, the college lost $2 million on redevelopment loans and loan guarantees and remained obligated to pay $500,000 a year for fifteen years on a building for which it had not yet found a use.[8]

The line between success and failure in the public, politically sensitive arena of urban development is obviously a tightrope not easily negotiated and the penalties for a misstep are painful for presidents and their institutions alike.

The Global Information Economy

Although in 1990 state governments were still wringing their hands over the decline in the U.S. manufacturing sector, the transformation of the engines of production was already under way. In 1987, the Hudson Institute's *Workforce 2000: Work and Workers for the 21st Century* predicted "The Integration of the World Economy, The Shift of Production from Goods to Services, [and] The Proliferation of Advanced Technologies."[9] The report was prescient in its treatment of digital communication as a driving force in our economy: "By the year 2000, the nation will be blanketed by a digital telecommunications network that will connect most businesses and many homes with fiber optic links of enormous capacity. Most homes will have some sort of home terminal (in addition to a traditional telephone) for accessing this system. This network will make realities out of current dreams such as home shopping and banking, working from the home, and even dial-up music or video entertainment."[10] By 1992, the CEO of one of New Jersey's thriving drug companies, like other business leaders across the nation, hailed the advent of the new Age of Information. Now it is universally accepted that we have shifted from the Industrial Age, in which natural resources and manufacturing were the keys to progress and prosperity, to the Age of Knowledge, in which the wealth of nations depends not upon their factories and mines, but on their intellectual capital and their production of knowledge-intensive goods and services.

Higher education has been thrust into a new position of prominence as an indispensable engine of economic advancement. It provides students with the training and credentials essential to remunerative careers in our time. In fact, it has been called the new passport essential to the American dream of a comfortable middle-class life. It produces the basic and applied research that plays an essential role in creating new products and services and expanding business opportunities. It often spins off companies directly based on medical or technological advances. Along with the greatly increased, fundamental importance of higher education for individuals (as well as the economic development of the state and the nation), the new prominence has brought increased scrutiny and sharp public criticism. Universities are no longer viewed with the smiling indulgence that could once be accorded to moss-covered ivory towers. The traditional university missions of research, teaching, and service have put our institutions of higher education at the forefront of our society as gatekeepers for the knowledge, creativity, and invention that can guarantee economic security and advancement.

Information Technology

The rapid evolution and dissemination of information technology has connected us at a dizzying rate. Over the past decade, the burgeoning power of the Internet has increased a thousandfold and brought millions of people across the globe into instant contact. In doing so, it has made possible everything that such promiscuous juxtaposition of different cultures can accomplish. It has multiplied not only our ability to increase business efficiency, person-to-person communication, humanitarian understanding and good will, but also our opportunities to disseminate raw hatred and images of catastrophic conflict. At the same time, it has continued to fill the function for which it was created when, in the 1960s, academic visionaries foresaw the potential of a worldwide network of computers sharing information on research and development. Funded and controlled by the government through the Defense Advanced Research Projects Agency (DARPA), the roots of the Internet (ARPANET, 1969) were firmly planted in research. It was used primarily by scholars: scientists, engineers, and librarians until the National Science Foundation expanded its use, first by distributing grants for Internet connections to be made available to all qualified users on campus (1985), later by urging its regional users of academic networks to lower their users' subscription costs by expanding their networks to serve commercial customers, and, ultimately, by constructing a backbone of high speed networks and encouraging the commercialization and privatization of the Internet (1988). As the collapse of the dot com boom in 2002 illustrated, the discovery of business models for the profitable use of the Internet was not as simple and obvious as was once thought. Nevertheless, its use for communication among researchers continues to be extremely valuable, expanding communication and speeding discovery, particularly at the crucial initial levels of scientific investigation into complex medical questions. For example Rutgers University's Wise Young, director of the W. M. Keck Center for Collaborative Neuroscience, facilitated a worldwide network of scientists willing to share research that pertains to the search for cures for spinal cord injury, a holy grail that he hopes may be reached through stem cell research.

On a more mundane level, information technology has had profound effects on the multitude of service processes that all organizations, including colleges and universities, must perform for those they serve. It also enables a number of online teaching resources:

- online presentation of syllabi and course material to supplement the traditional classroom;
- easy, convenient e-mail communication between professors and students that allows questions to be answered outside the traditional limited contact of office hours;
- posting grades, notes, presentations, articles, and handouts online;
- presentation of text, tables, graphics, and links;
- linking students to Internet resources;
- access to an integrated online calendar;
- facilitating class discussion and group work outside the classroom with integrated e-mail, chat, and threaded discussion tools;
- listserv and online discussions;

- online testing; and
- online course rosters to which all students with university e-mail addresses are automatically added from the university registrar's office database.
- Even more ingenious Internet teaching resources include:
- interactive online text service. An instructor can post a document, such as an author's text or even a student's essay on a web page and everyone in the class can visit the site in order to make notations and comments on the posted text; and
- the web log or blog, an online running diary that can be used as a teaching tool to facilitate discussion or employed in order to encourage students to make comments over the term and track their own development, along with members of the class, while the instructor is able to view the discussion document at any time.

As these examples demonstrate, in the traditional domains of the university (i.e., the communication of knowledge, the development of skills, and the certification of competence), information technology has facilitated the growth and multiplication of asynchronous learning opportunities within traditional academe, as well as in the more widely publicized for-profit enterprises outside it, such as the University of Phoenix. Of course even this litany of effects sketches only the barest hint of what information technology is bringing about in our universities. It does not even touch upon the web-based resources that enrich our traditional campuses with virtual science laboratories, virtual field trips, math and foreign language exercises, and online reserved readings, to cite only a few offerings.

Demographic Changes

The change in American demographics is also profound. The long-predicted tidal wave of the baby boom echo is upon us and the new college cohorts are more diverse than those of the past. In California, Texas, and Florida, groups traditionally regarded as minorities are now the majority of the population and, not only in those states but throughout the nation, institutions are striving to serve larger proportions of ethnic groups historically underrepresented in higher education. According to the predictions of the U.S. Census Bureau, the balance of our population is shifting steadily: the white majority will become a minority sometime between 2050 and 2075. Sooner than that, by 2050, more than half of the traditional college-age cohort of eighteen to twenty-five year olds will be comprised of groups now considered minorities. Because access to high-quality preparation for college is still very unevenly accessible and the best preparation has always been available to students with the highest family incomes, the new cohorts present a tremendously diverse distribution of preparation for college. Immigrants and minorities, who are the most likely to be in the lowest income quartiles, have the least opportunity to attend very well funded elementary and secondary schools, and consequently are usually the least well prepared to succeed in postsecondary study.

Increased Demand for Higher Education

Our new campus cohorts are not only more diverse, they are much larger than they were in the past. The college-going rate has increased tremendously. From 1960 through 1980, the college-going rate fluctuated between 45 percent and 55.4 percent of those who completed high school. In the 1980s, it began to climb, topping 60 percent in 1990, rising to 67 percent in 1997, and remaining in the 60 percent plus range through 2001.[11] The total fall enrollment in postsecondary education has nearly doubled between 1970 and 2000, rising from 8.5 to 15.3 million. Demand for higher education has demonstrably increased and the forces that propel it show no sign of abating at any time in the near future: projected enrollment for 2013 is 18.2 million.[12] This burgeoning demand has produced what the National Center for Public Policy and Higher Education in 2004 termed a crisis in college opportunity, pointing out that by some estimates at least 250,000 aspiring students were unable to enroll in colleges and universities in fall, 2003 as a result of more selective admissions, reduced course offerings, and increases in tuition. Opportunity delayed is often opportunity denied for young people who, denied college entrance, may enter the workforce in low paying jobs and take on the responsibilities of marriage and children, making it a great deal more difficult to return to school later on.

The Financing of Public Higher Education: The New Rules of the Game

The issue of college opportunity is linked with the growing problems that surround the financing of higher education. The assumptions underlying the pact between the states and their public institutions of higher education are changing. For roughly the last two decades, the states, hard-pressed to meet even the needs of their entitlement programs, have pursued a policy of disinvestment in their state systems of higher education. State support for higher education budgets is classified as discretionary and it is the largest category of non-mandatory spending in the state budget. In crass practical terms that has meant that, when it came up, as the last priority to be considered in state budgets stretched to the limit by mandatory funding, higher education had to scramble, applying what public pressure it could, just in order to scoop up a share of the change left on the table. Institutions that formerly received as much as 50 percent of their budgets from their state's coffers now consider themselves fortunate to receive 20 to 30 percent of their operating budgets from the state. For institutions with medical schools, the percentage of state support of operating budgets has fallen even further, into the teens or even single digits.

In New Jersey, one of the "creative ideas" that the acting governor floated for solving the state's mounting budget deficit ($4 1/2 billion in 2004-2005) was to exclude higher education's annual $2 billion subsidy from the state spending plan, forcing its colleges and universities to find their own resources, possibly by floating bond issues to fund construction and operating expenses.[13] In effect, the proposal was that the state should consider abruptly privatizing New Jersey's entire public higher education system. Interestingly, this extraordinary idea resulted in no immediate outcry from the public or even from the public institutions that would have been affected. It is difficult to know whether that was because the proposal was too outrageous to be taken seriously or because, like other East Coast states in which public higher education is a latecomer, New Jersey lacks the emotional connection with its state colleges and universities strongly manifested by states in the Midwest and on the West Coast.

Increasingly, the burden for supporting state universities and colleges throughout the nation has been switched to tuition and the responsibility for funding higher education shifted to students and their parents. At the same time, the federal government has changed its emphasis in student aid from grants to loans. The Pell Grant program has been routinely under-funded, becoming proportionately less and less adequate to meet the basic expenses of the lower income college students it was intended to support. As for the loan programs, it must be kept in mind that what parents and children from comfortable, middle class backgrounds might regard as a manageable, albeit somewhat daunting debt load takes on the dimensions of an unthinkable, insurmountable obstacle to a low-income student. Research on the economics of education bears out the anecdotal evidence that high tuition sticker prices have a very negative effect on college enrollment.[14]

The Nexus of Funding, Demand, and Selectivity

When these pressures of diminished funding and increased need for higher education are combined with the demands placed on institutions by the rating game (e.g., the *U.S. News and World Report*-style ranking of colleges and universities based very largely on the SAT scores of their first year students), the effect is to push those on the lowest socio-economic rungs off the ladder. At precisely the moment when we have increased numbers of immigrants and minorities who need and aspire to take the traditional American path through education into a prosperous future, it is becoming more and more difficult for them to find their way. As James M. O'Neill, higher education reporter for the *Philadelphia Inquirer* pointed out, in recent years three of Philadelphia's local urban universities, Temple, La Salle, and St. Joseph's—all three with historic missions of serving students from economically disadvantaged Philadelphia areas—are becoming more selective. They are admitting larger numbers of students from suburban schools that equipped them with superior college preparation. They are even beginning to offer merit aid designed to attract students who are highly qualified academically but do not come from families with incomes low enough to qualify them for need-based aid. The titles attached to the Inquirer story epitomized the problems: "Lower-Income Students Feel the Squeeze" and "Education-Poor Get Poorer as Colleges Become More Selective."[15]

That is bad news for the students and their families, of course, but it is also very bad news for the nation as a whole. As one nonpartisan research group, pointed out, increasing our investment in need-based student aid would yield dramatic benefits to the nation in a number of ways, including higher tax revenue, lower unemployment, greater productivity, reduced need for public assistance, increased volunteerism, decreased crime, better health, and higher voting rates.[16]

On the issue of the growing selectiveness of urban colleges, O'Neill gathered some striking quotes from other organizations whose job it is to track and try to influence the formation of good higher education policy. Patrick Callan of the National Center for Public Policy and Higher Education said flatly, "As social policy, it's just a disaster. We're changing the mission of these schools without much public debate." Tom Mortenson of the Pell Institute for the Study of Opportunity in Higher Education declared, "The nation's flagship public universities are becoming exclusive, gated communities consisting almost entirely of rich kids." Of course that is an exaggeration, but it is true that it requires sustained, conscious effort by the leaders of our state land-grant flagship universities in order to keep their institutions on the path of broadly based access. The temptation is strong to yield to the siren call of greater selectiveness, to play the ratings game, and to become precisely the kind of institution that Mortenson describes.

Excellence and Access

We need to keep in mind the fact that our entire American system of higher education is repeatedly described as the best in the world not simply because our premier institutions offer superb graduate education, but also because we have what is certainly the most accessible system of tertiary education on the planet. It is our combination of access and excellence that distinguishes American higher education and, to be perfectly frank, our distinction is based at least as much, if not more, on our accessibility as it is on our quality. It is the successful marriage of the two that makes American higher education a model that the rest of the world is trying to emulate now, as governments around the globe have realized that the time for elitism is past. The future of nations depends upon their success in expanding educational opportunity.

This is the moment when America ought to be able to offer the world an invaluable model of accessible higher education. Now is the time when we should be able to let the world profit from our example of the expanded opportunities for advancement that we fought so hard to establish throughout our struggles with the improvement of access and our championship of the value of diversity. Ironically, this is also the moment when these hard-fought gains at home are threatened by the issues of inadequate college preparation and inadequate financial assistance for low-income students. And this is the time when we are having great difficulty in simultaneously funding our programs adequately and keeping tuition affordable, as state support dwindles.[17]

Higher Education in the Spotlight

These are momentous problems that are becoming acute and pressing. They affect not only our institutions and our nation but the world at large and they indicate a new frame of reference for higher education. Colleges and universities are no longer, as they once were, the exclusive province of the elite and of those who preferred white-collar occupations to what, in the Industrial Age, were equally well-paid blue-collar jobs. Advanced learning has become the *sine qua non* of progress, of employment, of social equity and mobility, and of economic competitiveness. Higher education is regarded as essential for a good quality of life, not just for individuals, not even for our country alone, but for nations around the world. That's the good news and, at the same time, that's the not-so-great news. Like the rich and famous, institutions of higher education are now the objects of intense societal interest and have been subjected to the white-hot glare of media attention. Like all absolutely necessary services under government control, public universities are regarded with suspicion, their operations minutely examined, and their failings subjected to scathing criticism by those whom they serve.

Private universities are not exempt from searching critical examination. In the 1990s, several private universities underwent rigorous audits by the IRS, in order to determine whether they were in complete compliance with federal tax regulations. The non-salary benefits received by their presidents came under particular scrutiny and at least one president of an elite private institution moved out of his university-owned residence when it became likely that the market-rate rental value of the house would henceforth be regarded as part of his taxable compensation (despite its heavy use for university events designed to strengthen the bonds of academic community and cultivate donors). On the broader stage of media attention, it is the cost of private higher education that grabs headlines and inspires panic in parents, who may mistake the sticker prices of Harvard, Yale, and Princeton as typical of college costs throughout higher education. In recent years, the cost issue has also attracted the attention of Washington politicians. A House bill slated to come before Congress as part of the 2005 renewal of the Higher Education Act stipulated that colleges which increased their tuition and other costs by more than twice the rate of inflation for three years in a row would have to provide a justification for the increases and submit a plan to slow the rate of their climb. The penalties for failure to comply included: placement on a government watch list; the requirement of a detailed accounting of expenditures to the Education Department; and an audit by the department's inspector general.

The Global Perspective: Enrollment Pressures and Cost Sharing

The problem of inadequate state support for burgeoning enrollment is not unique to the United States. There is a worldwide pattern of increasing demands on the public purse by the needs for growing public expenditures in such essential areas as health, welfare, pensions, policing, prisons, external defense, and primary and secondary education. In the past, the modest demands of a relatively small higher education sector could be supported by the government as a free benefit to a few highly qualified students. That privileged flight below the public radar is impossible now, as both public policy and citizen demand drive the change from an elite system of tertiary education for the few to a system that is expanding to meet the growing demand for higher education from students of traditional college age and adults.

In the higher education systems of Sweden, Denmark, Finland, and Norway, instruction is still cost-free, but room and board is not. Students finance their living maintenance through government-subsidized loans. Great Britain began charging tuition in 1998, the first country in Europe to do so. Currently annual tuition is a flat rate of 1,150 pounds, but that is, according to government sources, about one-fourth of the actual cost of providing the education, a figure that matches almost precisely the current ratio of tuition to the real cost of education at first-rate public universities in the United States. To increase the resources available to universities, the government made plans to raise the maximum fee to 3,000 pounds a year while offering government subsidized grants and loans, as well as small scholarships to be provided by the universities. At the same time universities must satisfy the new "access regulator" by showing that each institution has policies that will increase the admission of students from the most disadvantaged groups. Australia introduced higher tuition fees and income contingent student loans in 1989 and in Canada, where undergraduate tuition was deregulated, British Columbia's undergraduate tuition rose 30 percent in 2004 and there were student protests across the country. Still, as defenders of the new government policy pointed out, tuition provided only one-fourth of the total revenues of Canadian higher education: taxpayers contributed most of the remaining three fourths, and "the benefits to an individual from a university degree are so great that even if tuition rates [were to] become much higher than they currently are in Canada, the investment still is sound."[18] However the individual investment benefits of higher education failed to pacify Quebec's activist students, who went on strike on February 24, 2005 in protest against plans to switch student support from grants to loans. In mid-March, students occupied the office of the newly appointed Education Minister to protest not only the deregulation of tuition and the cuts in spending but the $103 million reduction in student grant funding enacted in 2004. The strike ended on April 1, when the provincial government pledged to reinstate $84 million in student funding next year. In Germany, as in the United States, university funding was cut as the states struggled to balance their budgets. The first steps toward demanding that students pay for their education were taken in the south of Germany in 1998, when students who had been undergraduates for six years or more were charged 1000 marks (about $550) a semester. In 2002, the federal government forbade the imposition of tuition, but on January 26, 2005, the Federal Constitutional Court ruled federal control over state-mandated tuition unconstitutional, clearing the way for the states to decide on whether or not to introduce fees. In France as well, proposed higher education reforms were feared likely to lead to the imposition of fees. The threats of budget cuts and the introduction of increases in student fees sparked student protests in the UK, Germany, France, Belgium, Ireland, Italy, and the Czech Republic in November and December of 2004 and January and February of 2005. In Israel, where the government cut its funding to higher education by a sixth over a four-year period and Tel Aviv University announced the elimination of ten departments, students held public rallies to demand an increase in the 2005 budget (and to accuse the university administration of mismanagement).

In Russia, higher education was a high priority under the Soviet system, but transition of the state from a command administrative economy to a market economy has meant a dramatic reduction in state funding. Formerly the state supplied funding for wages and stipends, construction and maintenance of student and faculty housing and academic facilities, as well as student stipends. As much as 10 percent of the national budget was earmarked for higher education. Now higher education receives less than 2 percent of the state's annual budget: most of that must be used for wages and student stipends. The new budget stringency made it prohibitively expensive for the universities to continue to provide housing, catering services, transportation, construction and repair, and medical services—as well as the spas and holiday resorts that some offered.[19] Universities eliminated most of the activities extraneous to education, including student dormitories, often leasing university buildings to private businesses. Unfortunately their resources have become so tight that Russian institutions have been unable to maintain essential academic facilities and equipment, or even to meet their utilities bills as needed. They have scrambled to raise money, primarily by a few easily available means. The first is offering fee-based education to students who have not passed their entrance exams and have not been accepted within the number of "budget students" whom the government is willing to subsidize.[20] The second option is divestiture, passing the responsibility for university housing on to private service providers or to the municipality. The third option that universities are pursuing is the rental of university buildings, in whole or in part, to private businesses, with less than optimal results in many cases: "The universities are now faced with rising crime and violence on their campuses. To stay in a dormitory which includes its own bars, restaurants, goods storage facilities—and a growing number of criminal ventures—is not always the best and safest place for studying."[21] These two sources supply as much as 10 to 20 percent of the institution's budgets and research activities for the government and industry may bring in another 10 to 20 percent.[22]

As this rapid survey shows, the shift in the responsibility for financing higher education from the government to the individual citizen has not simply been a U.S. trend; it is a fast-growing fact of life in tertiary education around the globe.

Market Forces in American Higher Education

The Futures Project, under the direction of Frank Newman, has presented a case for the argument that powerful forces are channeling the American system of higher education—and, it can be argued, higher education throughout the world—into a new, market-driven shape.[23] Some of the forces cited in the book based on the Futures Project include, as we might expect, the pressures already cited here: the explosive growth of the demand for higher education in the global information economy; the demographic changes in the United States and elsewhere that are expanding the range in ages, academic preparation, and diversity of the students who are entering higher education; and the impact of information technology on higher education, including the growth of asynchronous virtual courses available from both non-profit and for-profit universities. Newman, Couturier, and Scurry contested the argument that state funding for higher education has been declining, asserting that the states' share of higher education budgets has diminished only because institutions have pursued and increased other sources of revenue. However, at the same time, the authors acknowledged that governments here and abroad, squeezed between the need to expand enrollment to previously underserved populations and their other pressing public funding priorities, have encouraged institutions to shift the burden of support to tuition and other means of financing their operations (pp. 41-43). As Patrick Callan, president of the National Center for Public Policy and Higher Education pointed out, "Over the past three decades, governors and legislators have relied on a standard response to recessions: steep cuts in state higher education budgets and replacement of state funds with sudden, large and repeated increases in student tuition and fees."[24]

Moreover, at the same time as they cut funding to higher education, governors, along with state and federal legislatures have used carrots and sticks for the purpose of exerting pressure upon institutions to keep tuition increases low. New Jersey's governor Jim Florio offered relatively small but attractive bonuses to public institutions that held down their tuition in the early 1990s. In 2003, Senator Howard McKeon proposed an elaborate system of mandatory reporting, surveillance, and consequences in order to penalize institutions that raised their tuition beyond a certain percentage. Even though the states may have allocated more funding to higher education in the improved economic climate around the turn of the millennium, the extra funding was required just to keep up with the instructional costs for increased enrollment and the escalation in the costs of other educational expenses, such as the huge new expenditures for technology—and of course funding was slashed again in the economic downturn that followed the dot com crash of 2002.

The institutions themselves have been publicly excoriated in the more sensational media coverage for heedless spending and ruthless price-gouging while, in their own view, they have in reality been faced by inadequate resources for their growing needs and forced into a relentless downward spiral of price-cutting, compelled to reduce expenses by every means possible: repeatedly deferring maintenance of physical facilities; cutting budgets for any and all non-academic functions through staff and service reductions; relying on part-time adjunct teachers rather than hiring full-time tenure-track faculty to teach a growing percentage of classes; shifting the funding for non-academic costs, such as recreation centers, from the central operating budget to fees that can be levied only with student approval; and "freezing" positions, that is, delaying hiring for empty slots in the faculty, staff, and administration. Permanent cut-backs in the administration are common, not because the administrators are not earning their keep, but because it is necessary to make visible sacrifices in order to counter what James Duderstadt describes as "one of the great myths in higher education…that university administrations are bloated and excessive."[25] In institutions pressed to maintain their missions at the highest level possible while becoming more efficient and cost conscious, the universal mantra is that cuts must be made in non-essential areas: central academic functions must be held harmless.

Institutional Costs and Prices; Individual Deterrents and Incentives

As a veteran of long service at both a private and a public university, I am naturally more keenly aware than most that the pricing practices of higher education fly in the face of common sense and business practice. As economist Gordon Winston has repeatedly pointed out in his writings on college costs, prices, and subsidies "while colleges do sell their 'products' (educational services) to 'customers' (students), they always sell it at a price that fails to cover the costs of its production."[26] According to Winston's data, derived from IPEDS finance surveys, the average educational cost per student in U.S. colleges and universities is $12,779 a year, while the average price paid by the student is just $4,058, an incredible price reduction made possible by an average subsidy of $4,721. When the sectors are broken down into public and private higher education, the bargain is even more marked. The top public research universities, which have the highest sticker prices, also offer the largest general subsidies: their students pay just twenty-three cents for every dollar's worth of education they buy. In the private sector, it is again the most highly regarded research universities that give students by far the highest subsidy, resulting in a price-to-cost ratio of thirty-eight cents on the dollar. So when we speak of higher education as "market driven" and engage in passionate rhetoric about the influence of market forces on higher education, we need to keep in mind the fact that we are applying the concept of the market in a very special sense, one that no capitalist would recognize and any competent business person would reject out of hand.

With that caveat in mind, it is true that cost is a matter of tremendous concern to students and their parents. Although the price of tuition for public as well as private institutions is always lower than its true cost to the institution and, after grant aid and low-interest government subsidized loans have been subtracted, the immediate cash payment required will be substantially less than the sticker price, still the current outlay and the debt load together may very well be daunting enough to deter many academically qualified low income students from enrollment. Even for those brave enough to take on the debt, it may be a powerful incentive to reject the allure of a vocation in teaching or some other area of public service with a relatively modest level of financial return and to choose instead a less fulfilling and socially useful line of work that offers the advantage of higher compensation that will make it possible to repay school debts without significant strain and personal sacrifice. Everyone in academe has encountered and can recite a litany of examples in this vein, young people with real talent for teaching who, after brief experience (and often after notable success) working in the schools, have returned to the university in order to enroll in professional schools, having taken the measure of the kind of material return they can expect from careers in teaching.

The Privatization of Public Higher Education

When the University of Virginia announced its new $3 billion campaign for private donations, President John Casteen explained that the university was compelled by a 31 percent cut in state funding to redouble its efforts to secure funding from other sources.[27] The senior vice president for development and public affairs remarked that UVA was committed to becoming the first privately funded public university. That declaration was hardly surprising, given the fact that the university's Darden School of Business Administration and its School of Law were already ahead of schedule in implementing the goal of relinquishing their public funding in return for greater independence in setting their tuition and managing their resources. In the 2003-2004 Law School Foundation Annual Report, Dean John C. Jeffries, Jr. announced the beginning of the school's third year of self-sufficiency, comparing its financing to that of Harvard and Yale, "We, like they, depend primarily on tuition and secondarily, but crucially on private giving."

The University of Virginia has declared that it is voluntarily taking flight from a thinly feathered nest of state support, but in Massachusetts, the initiative to privatize state higher education came from Governor Mitt Romney, who, in 2003, proposed withdrawing funding from the UMass Medical Center, the Massachusetts College of Art, and the Massachusetts Maritime Academy over a four-year period, while allowing the institutions to remain in state buildings. Looking back with nostalgia on the federal government's massive post-World War II higher education initiatives (the GI Bill of Rights and the investment in basic scientific research fostered by Vannevar Bush's *Endless Frontier* report) and bemoaning state authorities' willingness to substitute tuition increases for taxpayer support, Robert Zemsky asked plaintively, "Have We Lost the 'Public' in Higher Education?"[28] In state after state—including Oregon, Colorado, Michigan, South Carolina, Texas, and Maryland—institutions proposed that the trade-off for budget cuts ought to be a greater level of independence that would allow them to make more of their own decisions in order to meet their challenges in innovative ways while continuing to perform at a high level of excellence. In Texas, where tuition was deregulated in 2003, undergraduate tuition at UT Austin rose almost 37 percent by 2005. Obviously if tuition must continue to increase at that rate in order to cover operating expenses no longer supported by the state, it will have a significant effect on access, unless public institutions adopt the Robin Hood mode of tuition pricing now practiced by private institutions, where the full tuition price charged students who can afford it finances need-based scholarships for those who cannot.

To illustrate the role of tuition increases in scholarship funding at private institutions, it is possible to cite an exhaustive study of three universities (Chicago, Duke, and Harvard) and one liberal arts college (Carleton) which revealed that increases in financial aid spending were responsible for a substantial part of the rising tuition charges at all four institutions.[29] Over a sixteen-year period, from 1976 to 1992, the proportion of the tuition increase devoted to financial aid was 14 percent at Harvard, 21 percent at Carleton, 31 percent at Duke, and 34 percent at Chicago. The study also reveals interesting facts about the other uses to which these four institutions put their rising tuition charges. Although increases in the market prices of standard expenditures, faculty compensation, and administrative costs account for between about 20 and 34 percent, most of the escalation in tuition, was expended on efforts to offer new programs and raise academic quality, making good institutions even better. State institutions, particularly the top tier flagship state research universities, are subject to all of the same standard expenditures that private institutions must meet and they have precisely the same imperatives for updating academic offerings and raising academic quality as the elite private institutions included in this study. If the current trend in the withdrawal of state support continues—and we have no reason to anticipate that it will do anything but accelerate—we can expect that the difference between the tuitions of public and private institutions will continue to narrow and, inevitably, access will suffer.

In fact, an analysis of IPEDS data for 1986-87, 1990-91, and 1995-96 performed by Gordon Winston revealed that access to the top public institutions has already been restricted in response to the tremendous enrollment increase and the simultaneous drop in state subsidies.[30] Public higher education expanded 15.2 percent between 1986-87 and 1995-96, while the public sector's per-student subsidies decreased significantly, down 3.8 percent during that period. The public research universities responded by keeping their enrollment growth down to 3.6 percent and raising their tuition (which they devoted primarily to increased per-student spending). The enrollment results in the top public universities could be summarized from two points of view: a home run for quality, measured by the qualifications of academically privileged entering students and the resources devoted to educating them, but a double whammy to access, measured by the diminished opportunities available to price-sensitive students who have had access to less well funded and less academically competitive secondary schools.

It was the two-year public colleges that absorbed much of the enrollment increase: their student population grew 26 percent. That disproportionate increase in the two-year sector of public higher education seems to have been anticipated and facilitated by state policy, which left public subsidies per student for two-year colleges almost the same. Tuition in the two-year sector increased by about $530, and the schools were able to use the money to discount the price for low-income students by increasing financial aid. To date, then, it is primarily the research universities in the public sector that have been encouraged to become more like private institutions in their increasingly restrictive merit-driven enrollment practices and their ever-more-aggressive pursuit of non-public resources to subsidize their expenses. Winston went so far as to characterize the contest among the wealthiest colleges and universities as "a competition for limited student and faculty quality—for 'institutional excellence'—and that competition has increasingly taken on the characteristics of a positional arms race." Although the difference between current saving and future wealth projections in the top decile of the public sector and the same level in the private sector are large—the ratio is 1 to 6 in current saving, slightly less than 1 to 5 for projected wealth in thirty years— the race is on, and since, as Winston points out, the prizes are the limited supply of the very best students and faculty (and the goal of excellence is a platonic ideal), "it is a race without a finish line." Unfortunately, this is a race that is likely to affect not just the institutions that are competing, but the students who will become collateral damage while access narrows and tuition rises. As Jane Bryant Quinn of *Newsweek* noted, "Rising costs and funding cuts are resegregating higher education, not by color but by class."[31]

Diversity in Academe

As good as our intentions were and as enthusiastically as higher education embraced the commitment of America to equality and non-discrimination, that high road became increasingly rocky in the 1990s and the opening years of the twenty-first century. In the heyday of affirmative action, institutions of higher education across the country gave special attention to the recruitment of students from underserved segments of our society, conducting outreach programs to encourage minorities to consider applying not only to our colleges but to our professional and graduate schools and directing financial aid programs to their support. It was essential that we make this aggressive, sustained effort. In the 1960s, only 5.4 percent of African Americans between the ages of twenty-five and twenty-nine had graduated from college; African-American students comprised just 2.2 percent of the nation's medical students (three-fourths of them in historically black institutions); and only 1 percent of law school students (one-third enrolled in historically black schools).[32] By 1995, there was some concrete evidence of success. The percentage of African Americans between twenty-five and twenty-nine years old who had graduated from college rose to 15.4 percent. The representation of African Americans among medical students increased to 8.1 percent and the proportion of African Americans in law school to 7.5 percent. Between 1970 and 1995, the number of Hispanic Americans with college degrees grew from 4.5 to 9.3 percent and their proportion of professional degrees almost doubled.[33] But by the mid-1990s, the courts and the public made it clear that affirmative action, as it was originally constituted, was in disfavor. A scholarship program for black students at the University of Maryland was struck down in 1994. In March of 1996, racial preferences in admissions were banned by a federal court decision in Texas; in November, Proposition 209, an amendment to California's constitution that barred the state from using preferences based on race or gender was passed with the support of 54 percent of the voters. Two suits challenging race-conscious admissions programs were filed against the University of Michigan, one against its undergraduate procedures, the other against its law school practices. Undergraduate applications and enrollment of underrepresented minorities decreased markedly at the selective institutions in the states directly affected, despite their best efforts in both recruitment and alternative approaches to affirmative action.[34] Emblematic of the impact on professional education at the national level was the effect on medical school applications: "Between 1996 and 2001, a period of legal and institutional assaults on affirmative action, the percentage of underrepresented minority applicants fell by nearly 21 percent, and during that same period the total number of minority students enrolled in medical school declined from a high of 8,254 to a low of 7,394."[35] In 2000, the U.S. Census Bureau reported that racial and ethnic minorities comprised 27.8 percent of the nation's population, but, according to

American Medical Association statistics, only 2.4 percent of practicing physicians were African American, 3.3 percent Hispanic, and 0.05 percent Native American.[36]

Finally, in June, 2003, when the long-awaited Supreme Court rulings on two affirmative action admissions programs at the University of Michigan, Ann Arbor were issued, their answer to the questions about affirmative action was yes—and no. At first there was great rejoicing from champions of racial preferences because the court upheld the law school's holistic, individual consideration of applicants in pursuit of student diversity, and, in doing so, accepted the argument that the educational benefits of diversity justified race-conscious admissions policies. However, in the case on undergraduate admissions, the court ruled against Michigan because the policy, which relied on a point system, put too much emphasis on race by arbitrarily treating whole groups of applicants as a class based solely on their color. In addition, the law school opinion projected the need for an end point to racial preferences in admissions, saying that in twenty-five years their use should no longer be necessary.

The happy mood did not entirely dissipate, but it was tempered as university legal counsel reviewed the decisions and organizations opposed to racial preferences, such as the Center for Equal Opportunity, the American Civil Rights Institute, and the National Association of Scholars, contacted colleges to warn them that they risked legal action unless they opened their race-based scholarships and programs to all students and ended racial favoritism in admissions. The effects were chilling. By March, 2004, when the *Chronicle of Higher Education* sampled the results, some seventy colleges had opened their minority programs to non-minority students, some under pressure, others on their own initiative.[37] The Department of Education's Office for Civil Rights had received complaints about racially restricted programs at other colleges and those were under investigation.

Conditions surrounding minority preferences in admissions and financial aid following the Supreme Court rulings on the Michigan cases were clearly just as contentious and complex as they were before—if not more so. From one side of the debate, Roger Clegg observed with satisfaction that an Office for Civil Rights investigation into a scholarship program for minorities in Wisconsin made the state back down on its race-restrictive policy and Virginia was currently under investigation for its admissions preference policies.[38] Martin Michaelson fired back, maintaining that, despite the machinations of its opponents, affirmative action did have a future, one not as severely restricted as its critics might wish, but he went on to point out that the court's criteria, which he called "neither pellucid nor self-executing" would have to be examined and thoughtfully interpreted by institutions.[39] William Bowen entered the debate from a different angle, urging that selective institutions adopt admissions preferences for the poor, while stipulating that such preferences could not replace preferences for underrepresented minorities because that would cause minority enrollments to drop by almost half in the group of highly selective colleges he studied.[40] Jonathan Alger, who was assistant general counsel at Michigan when its case went to the Supreme Court and is now vice president and general counsel at Rutgers University, sorted carefully through the key points of the court decisions to indicate the questions to which institutions will have to seek answers, the analyses they must conduct, and the efforts they will have to make to apply to race-based programs in financial aid, academic support, and outreach the principles articulated by the court for racially conscious admissions.[41] The College Board released a second, updated edition of its *Diversity in Higher Education* manual to help colleges work through the problems they face in interpreting the court's decision as it can be applied to admissions, outreach, and, in particular, financial aid—a subject not specifically addressed by the Court, but an increasingly vital issue for all college students and thus a fertile field for complaints concerning racial preferences.[42]

Nevertheless, what emerged from all of this careful legal sorting of questions, analyses, and reviews was pure, academically certifiable gold. The Court's imprimatur was firmly stamped on the concept of the educational benefits of diversity, and the model of the Harvard Plan for admissions, which Justice Powell described as a foundation for his opinion in *Bakke,* was cited by the Court as instructive. Given the fact that, like Harvard, all selective colleges and universities receive many times over the number of applications than they have places in their entering classes and most of those who apply are academically qualified to succeed should they be admitted, the selection process has always depended not simply on academic achievement but on the qualities of students who represent many different talents and experiences—baseball players as well as pianists, aspiring politicians as well as young scientists, students of various racial and ethnic backgrounds and students from different economic circumstances—for the excellent reason that they contribute to a stimulating, varied educational experience because they bring with them a variety of points of view that a class composed entirely of prep school valedictorians with perfect SAT scores could not furnish. As the framers of the Harvard Plan put it, "The belief has been that if scholarly excellence were the sole or even predominant criterion…the quality of the educational experience offered to all students would suffer."[43] Conveniently, while this prototype plan abjured quotas, the bête noir of affirmative action planning, at the same time it asserted confidently, "the Committee on Admissions is aware that there is some relationship between numbers and achieving the benefits to be derived from a diverse student body and between numbers and providing a reasonable environment for those students admitted." Thus, while abstaining from setting any "minimum number" for a category of students, the Harvard Committee enfranchised itself to devote "some attention to distribution among the many

types and categories of students." The Court's solution of individualized review for admissions applications (which can number in the tens of thousands
at public institutions the size of Michigan or Rutgers) Alger characterized
with understated irony as "challenging," and proposed an uncomplicated solution to a towering problem: "Colleges do not need to give every application
equal time and attention, however, as long as they do not give automatic,
mechanical weight to race as a factor in admissions."[44] Race-conscious programs will have to meet several tests: sound educational rationales for a diverse student body, flexible and limited consideration of race, minimal impact
on non-beneficiaries of race-conscious policies, and rigorous periodic reviews.[45]
Nevertheless, thanks to the Supreme Court rulings, while it will not be simple
or altogether easy, neither will it be impossible to create an educationally
optimal environment of varied experience and diverse viewpoints in our institutions, if we are willing to make the good faith efforts necessary to do so.

Coda: The Conundrum of College Athletics

College athletics offer wonderful benefits to higher education: they encourage a strong emotional bond between alumni and their institutions; they
instill the citizens of a state with great pride and create political support for the
needs of higher education; and they allow students to enjoy events that inspire pride and loyalty to their universities. College athletics constitute a
terrible burden on higher education: they divert financial resources and energy away from institutions' academic missions; they tempt athletic staff and
sports boosters to violate the rules of the National Collegiate Athletic Association and the standards of fair play in order to assemble winning teams; and
they undermine the academic integrity of institutions by creating conditions
that can lead to admissions preferences and failure-proof courses and majors
for athletes.

Unfortunately both statements are absolutely true. They create an inescap-
able dilemma. Few things can create a larger, nastier, more media-worthy scandal than athletics; however nothing can provide a more attractive lifelong
focus for attention and allegiance not only from alumni but the general public,
including potential students. At any rate, for most of us in academe—both
those who love games and those who despise them—whether or not the institution will have an intercollegiate athletics program and at what level it will
be played is a true Hobson's choice: the die has long since been cast. For
university presidents, the only real choices are whether they will try to dis-
charge the responsibility of overseeing the administration of athletics within
their institutions and whether they will choose to become involved on the
national level in the efforts of the NCAA to provide a framework of rules and
oversight for collegiate athletics. For example, the recent efforts of the NCAA
to ensure that athletes enter college prepared to do college level work and that
they make steady progress toward a degree were shaped within the framework

of new vision and mission statements for Division I athletics crafted in 2002 by the same presidential Task Force that presented the academic reform measures to the Division I Board of Directors:

Board of Directors Task Force
NCAA Division I Vision Statement

NCAA Division I is dedicated to providing student-athletes with an exemplary educational and intercollegiate athletics experience in an environment that recognizes and supports the primacy of the academic mission of its member institutions. Division I institutions are expected to maintain athletics programs that set rigorous standards of performance for both academic and athletics achievement by a diverse community of male and female student-athletes; that exemplify the highest level of sportsmanship and amateur athletics performance for the larger community; and that, in sum, are a source of pride for students, faculty, staff, and alumni.

Division I Mission Statement/Guiding Principles

The NCAA Division I governance structure, the Board of Directors and the NCAA President and staff are committed to formulating and evaluating NCAA Division I regulations, policies, actions and consequences in accordance with the following guiding principles:

- Recognize and support the primacy of the academic mission of member institutions;
- Advance the highest standards of amateur college athletics, fostering ideals of exemplary academic achievement, sportsmanship and service to the community;
- Inculcate among all of the components of the NCAA Division I community—including governing board members, students, faculty, alumni and booster organizations —the awareness and the commitment necessary to achieve these high standards of quality;
- Increase access to higher education for a diverse body of male and female student-athletes within the context of institutions' academic and admissions standards for all students;
- Set an expectation that each member institution will establish and maintain an environment that values cultural diversity and gender equity among its student-athletes and intercollegiate athletics department staff;
- Ensure that Division I student-athletes are encouraged by their training and competition schedules and by their coaches and advisors to benefit from a well-rounded college experience that strikes a proper balance between athletics and academics;

- Motivate, support and recognize student-athletes in taking full advantage of their college education as it prepares them to become exceptional leaders and citizens;
- Present national championships on a basis that supports the academic, athletics and budgetary integrity and interests of Division I institutions.
- Protect Division I athletics from the undue influence of commercial interests;
- Require responsible budgetary practices and financial stability for intercollegiate athletics within the context of institutions' missions and general financial controls, thereby ensuring that athletics budgets do not compromise the integrity of overall university resources.

These are high principles built on a sound foundation of presidential experience and firm resolve. Unfortunately the highest principles and most zealous resolve will fortify and bind only those who honor them: good rules like good laws cannot prevent bad behavior or criminal abuses. Some of our most ethical, greatly respected leaders in higher education have unwittingly presided over their great universities during periods when egregious violations were underway in their athletic departments that became public knowledge and created scandals only long after the fact.

The cynicism that greets each new effort to reform college athletics is not wholly unwarranted. As perennial college sports critic Murray Sperber pointed out in a sharply worded critique not long after new academic progress guidelines were issued in 2005, even scholarly work, created at the heart of academe, is no stranger to cheating and plagiarism. In any area of endeavor where there is tough competition and the stakes for winning are high, there will be people who cheat. Indeed, the butts of Sperber's most vigorous criticism are his own professional colleagues, certain faculty members whom he calls "jock sniffers" and blames for the existence of "jock majors and blow-off courses [that] will only lead to athletes receiving slipshod educations and meaningless degrees."[46]

Nevertheless, the reform of college athletics took significant, principled steps forward in 2005 with two important innovations: the implementation of new academic progress requirements based on a clearly articulated set of principles that assert the primacy of the academic mission of our institutions, and the appointment of the first university president to be selected as the head of the NCAA, Myles Brand. This fortunate conjunction of academic reform with the ascent of an NCAA leader famous for his principled, hands-on administration of athletics as a university president is as golden an opportunity as we are ever likely to get for achieving the vision the NCAA Division I guidelines propose: intercollegiate athletics programs that are, without reservation, "a source of pride for students, faculty, staff, and alumni."

Notes

1. *The Creation of the Future: The Role of the American University* (Ithaca & London: Cornell University Press), 2001.
2. A term borrowed from the title of Michael Useem's classic collection of nine case studies that illustrate the ways in which individuals respond at challenging moments that call for extraordinary leadership. (*The Leadership Moment* [New York, New York: Three Rivers Press], 1998.)
3. Cassel, Andrew, Presidency at Penn is a Post Worth Watching, *Philadelphia Inquirer*, October 12, 2003, p.E1.
4. Cuser, Frederick, *Philadelphia Inquirer,* April 30, 2004, p. B 8.
5. O'Neill, James M., No Easy Time for Penn's Next Leader, *Philadelphia Inquirer,* October 2003, p. B1.
6. Basinger, Julianne, A Promoter of Town-Gown Cooperation Finds Development May Be Her Undoing. *Chronicle of Higher Education,* 46, no.39, June 2, 2000, A39.
7. Basinger, Under Fire from Students and Professors, President of Connecticut College Quits. *Chronicle of Higher Education,* 47, no.9, October 27, 2000, A9.
8. Basinger, Connecticut President's Golden Parachute Angers Faculty Members. *Chronicle of Higher Education,* 49, no.13 November 22, 2002, A31.
9. Johnston, William B. and Arnold H. Packer, *Workforce 2000: Work and Workers for the Twenty-first Century.* (Indianapolis, Indiana: Hudson Institute), 1987, pp. 1-37.
10. Johnston et al, p. 34
11. NCES Digest of Education Statistics, 2003.
12. NCES Projections of Education Statistics to 2013, October 2003.
13. Gurney, Kaitlin, Assets Are Focus of Budget Debate, *Philadelphia Inquirer,* February 4, 2005, B 2.
14. Heller, Donald E., The Effects of Tuition and State Financial Aid on Public College Enrollment: An Update to Leslie and Brinkman. *The Journal of Higher Education,* V. 68, no. 6, November-December, 1977, pp. 624-659.
15. O'Neill, James M., Lower-Income Students Feel the Squeeze, *Philadelphia Inquirer,* April 25, 2004, p.C1
16. Institute for Higher Education Policy, The Investment Payoff: A 50-State Analysis of the Public and Private Benefits of Higher Education, Washington, DC, February 2005.
17. Callan, Patrick, Editorial: A Different Kind of Recession. College Affordability in Jeopardy: A Special supplement to National Crosstalk, Winter 2003.
18. Hepburn, Claudia R., The Increasing Cost of University: Is it Fair for Lower-income Families? *Fraser Forum,* March 2004. <http://www.fraserinstitute.ca>
19. Beliakov, Sergei, Mikhail Lugachyov, and Andrei Markov, Financial and Institutional Change in Russian Higher Education. *Centre for Economic Reform and Transformation.* Department of Economics, Heriot-Watt University, Riccarton, Edinburgh.
20. Johnstone, D. Bruce, The Economics and Politics of Cost Sharing in Higher Education: Comparative Perspectives, *Economics of Education Review,* V.23, no.4, August 2004.
21. Kodin, Evgenii, The Reform of Russian Higher Education: We Had, We Lost, We Gained, *Center for International Higher Education.* August 1996. <http://www.bc.edu/bc_org/avp/soe/cihe/newsletter/News05/text5.html>

22. Butovsky, Ruslan, The Russian Federation Higher Education System: Current Development Priorities. Russian National Tempus Office. January 2004. <http://eu.daad.de/tempus/download/2004_jahrestagung/tempus_russia.pdf>

23. Newman, Frank, Lara Couturier, and Jamie Scurry *The Future of Higher Education: Rhetoric, Reality, and the Risks of the Market.* San Francisco: Jossey-Bass, 2004.

24. National Center for Public Policy and Higher Education, Responding to the Crisis in College Opportunity, Supplement to Winter *National CrossTalk,* January 2004.

25. Duderstadt, James and Farris W. Womack, *The Future of the Public University in America: Beyond the Crossroads.* (Baltimore and London: The Johns Hopkins University Press, 2003).

26. Winston, Gordon C., Higher Education's Costs, Prices, and Subsidies: Some Economic Facts and Fundamentals, Study of College Costs and Prices, 1988-89-1997-98, V.2.: Commissioned Papers. National Center for Education Statistics, December 2001.

27. Strout, Erin, U. of Virginia Unexpectedly Opens $3-Billion Campaign to become a 'Private' Public University, *Chronicle of Higher Education,* V. 50, no.42, June 25, 2004, p.A33.

28. *Chronicle of Higher Education,* V.49, no.13, May 30, 2003, p.B7.

29. Clotfelter, Charles T., Buying the Best: Cost Escalation in Elite Higher Education, *National Bureau of Economic Research Monograph Series.* Princeton: Princeton University Press, 1996.

30. Winston, Gordon C., Differentiation among US Colleges and Universities: *Review of Industrial Organization,* V.24, 2004, pp.331-354.

31. Quinn, Jane Bryant, Colleges' New Tuition Crisis, *Newsweek*, February 2, 2004, p. 49.

32. Bowen, William G., and Derek Bok, *The Shape of the River.* (Princeton: Princeton University Press, 1998), p.5.

33. Bowen and Bok, p.10.

34. Tienda, Marta and Sunny Niu, Texas' Ten-Percent Plan: The Truth Behind the Numbers, *Chronicle of Higher Education,* V. 509, no. 20, January 23, 2004, The Chronicle Review, B20.

35. Missing Persons: Minorities in the Health Professions, A Report of the Sullivan Commission on Diversity in the Healthcare Workforce, September 20, 2004, p. 53.

36. Total Physicians by Race/Ethnicity, 2002, AMA, 2004, in the Sullivan Commission Report, p. 49.

37. Schmidt, Peter, Not Just for Minority Students Anymore, *Chronicle of Higher Education,* V.50, no. 28, March 19, 2004, p. A17.

38. Time Has Not Favored Racial Preferences, *Chronicle of Higher Education,* V. 51, no.19, January 14, 2005, The Chronicle Review, B10.

39. Affirmative Action Has a Future, *Chronicle of Higher Education,* V.51, no.23, February 11, 2005, The Chronicle Review, p. B17.

40. From "Bastions of Privilege" to "Engines of Opportunity,'" *Chronicle of Higher Education,* V. 51, no. 25, February 25, 2005, p.B18.

41. Putting the Michigan Rulings Into Practice, *Chronicle of Higher Education,* V. 51, no. 25, February 25, 2005, p.B28.

42. Coleman, Arthur L. and Scott R. Palmer, Diversity in Higher Education: A Strategic Planning and Policy Manual Regarding Federal Law in Admissions, Financial Aid, and Outreach, Second Edition: Updated following the U.S. Supreme Court decisions in the University of Michigan cases, CollegeBoard, 2004.

43. Final Report of W.J. Bender, Chairman of the Admission and Scholarship Committee and Dean of Admissions and Financial Aid (Cambridge, 1960) in Coleman, Arthur L. and Scott R. Palmer, 2004.
44. Alger, 2005.
45. Coleman and Palmer, 2004
46. Sperber, Murray, When 'Academic Progress' Isn't, *Chronicle of Higher Education,* V. 51, no. 32, The Chronicle Review, p. B14.

Robert M. Berdahl

As the eighth chancellor of the University of California, Berkeley, Robert Berdahl served from July of 1997 to June of 2004. He came to UC Berkeley from the University of Texas at Austin, where he had served as president since January 1993. As UT Austin's president, Berdahl worked to establish a stronger sense of community on the campus, brought faculty together to articulate a set of core values, and created a master physical plan for the evolution of the campus. Prior to his presidency of UT Austin, Berdahl was the vice chancellor for academic affairs at the University of Illinois at Urbana-Champaign from 1986-1993. On the national scene, Berdahl served as chair of the board of directors of the Association of American Universities.

Born in 1937 in Sioux Falls, South Dakota, Berdahl received his bachelor's degree from Augustana College, his master's from the University of Illinois, and his Ph.D. from the University of Minnesota. A historian, he is the author of one book, has co-authored another, and has written several articles on German history. He was a member of the history faculty at the University of Oregon from 1967-1986 and was dean of the College of Arts and Sciences at Oregon from 1981-1986.

At UC Berkeley, Berdahl created a master plan to renew the physical infrastructure of the campus, with major emphasis on its seismic upgrading. He also initiated a long-term academic planning process and worked to rebuild the library collections. He emphasized increasing the numbers of women and minority faculty members and was a strong voice in support of the educational benefits of a diverse student body. Taking over midway the responsibility for the completion of a $1.1 billion major fund campaign, he completed the effort by overshooting the campaign's goal.

After stepping down from the Berkeley presidency, Berdahl taught for a semester at the university. In the spring of 2006, he succeeded Nils Hasselmo as the president of the Association of American Universities.

Francis Lawrence: As you know, this interview will be one of a dozen with outstanding leaders in American higher education. You have headed two quite different, very distinguished research universities. Could you describe what you feel is the essence of leadership?

Robert Berdahl: I think that leadership is ultimately a moral endeavor. It involves two things. It obviously involves creating a vision and securing support for that vision of where you want to go, but it also involves the identification of the principles that inform that vision and undergird the enterprise that you're involved in. Those principles and adherence to those principles is where the moral issues come in. I found, in dealing with each crisis, that what helped me the most was trying to think through, usually with the help of other people, what principle we were trying either to follow or educate people about. Those principles ultimately had to be our guide.

FL: I'd like to begin our conversation on your career by asking you to talk a little about your family background and your education. How did they contribute to shaping your values and your development as a leader in higher education?

RB: I grew up in Sioux Falls, South Dakota. My father was reasonably well educated for his generation. He was a farm kid from South Dakota who went off to the First World War. The war transformed his whole life: it liberated him. He didn't go back to his Norwegian-American community; he didn't go back to the farm; he didn't marry a Norwegian or a Lutheran. After returning from France, he went to the University of South Dakota and graduated in 1922. Then, ironically, he came to Berkeley to graduate school. He only spent a year here, was then drawn back to South Dakota to become a superintendent of schools in the community where he grew up, largely because he was the only one in the community who had gone to college. He met my mother, who was teaching there. They both had a reasonably good education, so that I don't ever remember there being a question about whether my brother and I would go to college. It was always assumed. My parents were also victims of the Great Depression. I was born in 1937, the tail end of that hard time, but my dad didn't have a job when either my brother or I was born. My parents never quite got out of the Depression mentality, but they managed by frugality, so that we were never really poor when I was growing up. We had a moderate middle-class life. My father had a great influence on the formation of my values growing up. He laid a heavy stress on integrity and honesty and hard work. I took away from that a respect for those fundamental values that I associate with the Middle West.

We couldn't afford for me to go away to college, so I lived at home and went to the small Lutheran liberal arts college in Sioux Falls, Augustana College. There I got a good, though not an absolutely first-rate education. I had a couple of outstanding professors who challenged and guided me. I thought at one point that I might be a minister and, even though I didn't ultimately choose to do that, the humane value system that was implicit in my education was important. And so those were some of the influences that shaped my early life.

FL: What personal attributes do you feel have contributed most to your success as a leader?

RB: I would hope that they are some of the values I derived from that background. I've always been very conscious of making it a point to be forthright and tell things as they were. I've always insisted on telling people bad news directly. I could write good news, but I wanted to tell people bad news directly. Candor and openness are the personal attributes I value.

Another experience that helped me was that I was very active in intercollegiate debate and forensics in high school and college. Those activities cultivated personal skills that have helped me tremendously. As you know, as a chancellor or president of a university, you give speeches constantly, literally dozens of them a month. Being able to extemporize, think on my feet and respond to questions in a coherent manner are things that I learned through being active in scholastic and intercollegiate debate and forensics. I think that has been as important to whatever success I have had as anything else. It has been especially valuable in my work with the university's external constituencies.

FL: What do you regard as your first leadership position at any level—not necessarily a post in academic administration?

RB: I always was active in high school and college, so I was president of a number of organizations. As I mentioned, during the first few years of college I thought about going into the ministry. I was in a Lutheran College, but I wasn't a Lutheran. I had been active for a couple of years in the Methodist Church and I was asked if I would become the lay minister of a couple of rural churches outside of Sioux Falls. I worked my way through college by preaching in these two little country churches. That had a leadership component because I was doing more than just preaching. I had to spend time with the people and I learned to appreciate people with different perspectives. One church was a wonderfully harmonious community and the other church was fractured. Together they taught me how to deal with people from a position of leadership.

As far as academic administration is concerned, I took an associate deanship, when I came back from a sabbatical in 1977. The dean asked me to become an associate dean and lead a curricular reform effort. I was just back from sabbatical, trying to finish a book, and I didn't want to do it. He persuaded me by saying that he'd let me go back to Germany for six or eight weeks in the summer and still draw summer salary. As you know, having summer salary is very attractive for a humanist, especially when you have children who are nearly ready to go to college. So it was an attractive bribe that initially got me into it. Then I also led a curricular reform, which was a very mixed success, but furnished my first academic leadership experience.

FL: In addition to your father, who were the people that inspired you and acted as your mentors?

RB: I had an uncle who was a professor at the University of Michigan. He took a great interest in both me and my brother and encouraged us to go to graduate school. My doctoral advisor, Otto Pflanze had a great influence on me. I first got interested in German history in graduate school. He took me on, despite the fact that at that time, my command of German left a lot to be desired. He also taught me to write. Like all faculty, he had an innate suspicion of administrators. When I became a dean in 1981, his reaction was, "I didn't raise you up to be a dean." But he forgave me and we have remained close friends throughout my career.

In 1967, I went to the University of Oregon as a young assistant professor. Between 1967 and 1969 there were more jobs available in history than there ever had been previously or ever have been since. I was born at the right time. Several historians, one of whom is my closest friend and a colleague here at Berkeley now, were hired by the University of Oregon in 1967. Three of us were about thirty at the time, but they also hired a senior person, Tom Govan, who was sixty. He was an American historian but he took a great interest in younger faculty and was enormously supportive of our development. He became a father-like figure in that academic setting. He was a man of enormous principle. He had been at Sewanee, the University of the South, and in May of 1953, without having another job, he resigned because they refused to integrate the seminary. He is the only person I have ever known who has resigned on principle without having another job to go to. He was inspiring. The dean who recruited me to be an associate dean, John Baldwin, was also a man of genuine integrity and I admired him very much.

The person from whom I probably learned the most about academic administration was Paul Olum, who was the president of the University of Oregon while I was dean. Paul held that university together during extraordinarily difficult times just by the force of his determination, of his integrity. You could disagree with him, but you could never disrespect him, because you knew he was a person who always acted out of what he regarded to be the best institutional interests and he always told it like it was. If I learned the virtue of integrity generally from my father, from Paul I learned it specifically as an administrator.

I got involved in full-time academic administration when John Baldwin stepped down as dean in July and Paul asked me to fill in as an interim dean during July and August. He told me that during July and August nothing happens, so it would be easy. On July 3rd, the governor announced a huge budget rescission that, for the college of arts and sciences, demanded the equivalent of eliminating an entire department—with only two months remaining before the academic year began. My laid-back summer interim deanship became a very intense two months of planning, budget negotiating and dealing. The rumors about what we were doing were legion. I decided that, if people are going to act on whatever information is available to them, they ought to have accurate information. I published a document entitled "Who Got Cut, How Much" that told exactly how much every department got cut. This had never happened before. The consequence was that people were so astonished at this that the next year when they were searching for a dean, I ended up on the list simply because I had been willing to publicly announce the cuts. It put an end to rumor mongering, at least to the extent that is possible in a university. People might disagree with the decision, but at least they knew that they were acting on accurate information. My final mentor was Tom Everhart, who recruited me to be provost at Illinois. We only worked together for a year, but Tom was a person of integrity; he gave me a great chance and helped me grow into it.

FL: Has there ever been a time in your life when you have had to overcome a fear in order to continue and succeed in what you wanted to accomplish?

RB: That is an interesting question. I don't know if fear would be the right word. I first got involved in academic administration when I was a faculty member of the University of Oregon and ultimately became dean of arts and sciences there. That was a comfortable place. I had been there for years. I knew the faculty; I knew the issues. When I left Oregon to go to the University of Illinois, I was scared. It was a much bigger and better place. I didn't know whether or not I could cut it in that different environment. That scared me. Each transition has been filled with fear. It is more a fear of failure than a fear of anything terribly concrete and you have to sort of grit your way through it. When I left the University of Illinois after six and a half years to go to be president of the University of Texas, my brother couldn't understand it. He also lived in Illinois and didn't want me to move away, but he is fundamentally a more cautious person than I as well. He said, "You've done a good job. Why are you leaving a good job to go into an unknown?" Texas really was an unknown, and being non-Texan presented obstacles. I was worried about whether I could handle that and he thought I was crazy. Then when I came to Berkeley, he thought I was even crazier.

FL: What were the challenges that UT Austin faced at the time when you became president?

RB: UT Austin is almost the opposite end of the spectrum from Berkeley. Berkeley is a faculty-driven culture; UT Austin was an administratively driven culture. It is an institution or was an institution, more then than now, which was heavily top-down managed, with very little shared governance. The university senate was composed exactly 50/50 faculty and administrators and had no real authority. For a variety of reasons, there was a serious division between the administration and the faculty. It was, in part, this structure that left faculty feeling disempowered and alienated. And the division was, in part, just the natural antipathy that exists toward university administrators on the part of the faculty: deep suspicion and distrust. I think that the fundamental structural problem played out in many, many ways across the campus. It affected staff. There were no labor unions because public employees were not allowed to organize in Texas, so there was no form even of staff representation and no forum in which the staff could present their points of view. It was a very large university that had very little sense of community. That is true of a multitude of universities, but for different reasons than at Texas.

The division was compounded by the fact that there had been virtually no new money coming into the university from the state and, during my time there, no new money that came for salaries. We had to carve out all the salary increases by internal reallocation. Texas looks to the outside world like a very rich university because it has what is always listed as an endowment that comes from the oil money, but really is simply a substitute for state money. Texas had roughly half the dollars per student that Berkeley had when I moved here, so there was a lot of financial stress. Texas did have a fabulous physical plant because for many years the permanent university fund could only be used for capital projects. That had been changed before I got there, so it was used for the excellence fund, for supporting research, specialized institutes and libraries that added excellence to the university. It was a situation with financial stress and stress that was derived from the structure. Those were the primary challenges that I faced when I got there.

FL: When you took office at UC Berkeley, Proposition 209, the ban on affirmative action admissions, had been approved by California voters and the Federal Appeals Court had upheld the amendment to California's Constitution. You had just come from Texas where Hopwood had ended affirmative action in college admissions in 1996. Did your experience in Texas prepare you in some measure for dealing with the problem in California?

RB: Yes—and no. It probably was one of the factors that caused my appointment here. What you have to take into account is that the Board of Regents of the University of California had passed a ban on affirmative action before the state passed Proposition 209. So it was the regents that initiated the ban on affirmative action. Ward Connerly, as a member of the Board of Regents, had led that action of the Board and then led the statewide campaign to pass 209. That sequence is important to remember because the majority of the Board, as it was then constituted, opposed affirmative action. Ward Connerly was on the search committee. I made no bones about the fact that I supported affirmative action. At lunch, after I had come, he admitted to me that he knew that I couldn't be chancellor at Berkeley and oppose affirmative action. He's not an unrealistic man. He also knew that I had been living with that reality in Texas and that we had been devising ways of living with it and working to enhance diversity in the absence of affirmative action. I think that was one of the factors that played in favor of my appointment as far as he and the other board members who were involved in the search were concerned.

What I hadn't appreciated was that there was a huge difference between the end of affirmative action coming as a result of a court decision and it coming as a result of the regental and voter action. Texas' motto was "Don't mess with Texas." There was a strong sense that the courts had messed with Texas, even though public opinion in Texas was probably as strong, if not stronger, than California in opposition to what Ward Connerly referred to as racial preferences. When I spoke about the issue of Hopwood in Texas, there was a sense that it had been the courts that had imposed integration in the South and now the courts were messing with us again. Even though Texans may have approved the decision, they didn't like the way it came, because it was again a federal court action. If I gave in California the same speech that I had given in Texas about why I believed affirmative action was important, that speech had a different ring to it and evoked different audience responses in each state. I don't think that my Texas experience really prepared me completely for the California situation.

FL: In a 2002 piece, your former director of admissions, Bob Laird observed that in 1998 underrepresented minorities dropped from 19.1 percent of the class down to 9 percent. He characterized Berkeley's outreach program and its new policy of admitting the top 4 percent of each high school graduating class as limited tools and pointed out that underrepresented minorities were just 15.9 percent of the admitted students. Has that improved?

RB: It improved a little bit until this last year, then it dropped back roughly to where it was in 1998. It has been very, very difficult to deal with. I think that it is the single most difficult issue that the University of California faces. We are an extraordinarily selective campus. Between one in four and one in five, roughly 23 percent of the in-state applicants to the university and one in ten of the out-of-state applicants are admitted. The competition for admission is extraordinarily intense. We are forbidden by Prop 209 from taking race into account in that admissions process. On the other hand, we have a court settlement that occurred after 209 as a result of a case in which Berkeley was sued by MALDEF (the Mexican American Legal Defense Fund) and the legal defense fund of the NAACP. They wanted to ensure that our admissions process didn't have a disproportionate impact on minorities. Thus, Berkeley is uniquely caught between a rock and a hard place, with a legal agreement on the one hand that requires no disproportionate impact on minorities and 209, which disallows any consideration of race in admissions, on the other.

In our experience, there is ultimately no surrogate for race in achieving racial diversity. You can use economic disadvantage as one of your criteria in admissions. But the fact of the matter is, at least in California, there are as many poor whites or poor Asians as a percentage of the population as there are poor Hispanics or African Americans, so if you look at economic disadvantage as a factor, as we do, it doesn't really yield a more diverse student body. During the past year, we have been under assault by a number of members of the Board of Regents for our practice of comprehensive review, according to which many factors are taken into account in admissions, trying to admit students who have shown extraordinary drive and determination, regardless of the odds.

Although academic criteria still weigh most heavily in the admission process, other factors are also considered, except for race. Anybody who looks closely at our comprehensive review (we have had careful analysis of it being done by statisticians here) will find that there is virtually no impact of race on the admissions process. Depending on how one wants to look at it, there can be some statistically significant differences in expected admission rates and actual admission rates, but we are talking only about a difference of a few individuals. That is, based on the factors we use, you might expect there to be a certain percentage of minority students admitted, but our minority acceptance rate is slightly higher than the expected rate. It is probably due to some of the factors we consider other than race. Pat Hayashi, who was involved in admissions here, said that his rule of thumb is that all changes help Asians. Anything we do to change the admission process has assisted Asian admissions more than anybody else. We have in our freshman class this year, a freshman class of 3,800 students. There are fewer than fifty African-American males, over half of whom are student athletes, who are in a special admissions pool. I feel that it is devastating for our future as a public university to see this enormous disparity, then to see the ways that it has come about.

I delivered a talk dealing with the issue of university admissions at the Commonwealth Club in San Francisco when I first arrived. We did a lot of research prior to that talk. I attribute a lot of what's happening to the fact that obviously there are some very poor and very ineffective schools in some of the major urban districts in California. However there is also an awful lot of consistent tracking of minority students away from college prep courses going on here. I think that this is a violation of 209 to which nobody ever pays any attention. In one of the Southern California districts that has a fairly diverse population, the students who qualify for the mathematics track leading to the college-level are comprised of 100 percent of the district's Asian students, something like 91 percent of the Caucasians, around 51 percent of the Hispanics, and 44 percent of the African-American students. All of these students qualify for the college-bound track, but a disproportionate percentage of minority students are not given access to it. There is clearly racial selection going on in the process of tracking students into college preparatory courses in the high schools. No one seems to be concerned about that violation of 209. I raised this whole issue in the Commonwealth Club speech and suggested that, if people really wanted to enforce 209, they shouldn't look exclusively at college admissions, they ought to look at school tracking. But college admissions is the big prize, where middle class angst is most manifest, so it's the only thing that gets attention.

FL: What effects have the demands of each of these leadership posts had on your family life? How do you maintain a balance?

RB: When I was a dean, my oldest daughter had just left for college. When I left for Illinois, my second daughter was in college and my oldest daughter graduated. My youngest daughter was a junior in high school and leaving Eugene with two years of high school left was a very hard adjustment, so I have more guilt about that than any other impact on my family. I think that the fact is you can't balance easily personal and professional responsibilities in these jobs, because there are so many demands on your time. But I don't think I could have done either presidency with children still at home, I wouldn't have wanted to try.

One thing that we haven't discussed but relates to this is the changing role of the president's spouse. I know that Peg and I have been criticized at times for the fact that Peg cannot be at every event. But I simply have said that Peg is not an employee of the university; I am. She comes to a number of events and there are a number of sort of must-do events, but I've tried not to demand of her that she act as a full-time university employee. With a few exceptions, she has been able to choose what kinds of events she would participate in and what she wouldn't. More recently our daughter's illness has taken her out of town for much of the time. She spent about 40 percent of her time helping with our daughter's family and people have been kind in understanding that. Unless the spouse really loves being a president's spouse—I think that is probably true of only half of the AAU presidents' wives—there is always a tension created by the demands of the job on the spouse and the spouse's sense of being exploited. That certainly has been true for us. It has really at times been a difficult set of balancing acts that we have had to deal with.

FL: In addition to finding a solution to the ban on affirmative action, what did your internal constituencies, governing boards, administrators, faculty, students, staff in each of these presidencies expect of you? What did you feel you owed them? Each of these groups can make some very strong demands.

RB: Each of the groups believe that they own all of your time and each of them believes that, if the university does not precisely exist for their benefit, certainly they are the major stakeholders in the university. The expectations, however, have been somewhat different in California than in Texas.

The University of California is a very flat system. Even though I would say that Berkeley is the flagship and Berkeley, UCLA and San Diego are probably the standout institutions in the system, six of the eight are AAU universities and are truly fine institutions, so the system operates with the same ostensible expectations of faculty and the same funding formula for each of these institutions. They may disagree. Some may feel that there's more money in Berkeley than there is elsewhere and we sometimes feel there's more money in San Diego or UCLA than here. It is a system in which, if Berkeley is the first, as I would say that it is, it is the first among equals.

The University of Texas had a very different system. It ranged from UT Austin, which is a research university, to UT Brownsville, a community college that was growing into a four-year institution. It had a huge spectrum of institutions and Austin was the prize or the focal point. The UT System was justifiably very proud of the medical centers in Dallas, Houston, and San Antonio because they were outstanding, but Austin was the University of Texas. That's one fact. The second fact is that there are twenty-six regents of the University of California, eighteen of whom are appointed by the governor. They are appointed for twelve-year terms. There were nine regents in Texas appointed for six-year terms. Virtually all of the regents in Texas were Austin graduates. Virtually none of the regents in California are Berkeley graduates. So the relationship with the regents is very different and the president of UT Austin interacts with the UT regents much more regularly than does the chancellor in Berkeley. The expectations are quite different. I have not had to interact with regents on a constant basis here, as I did there. That makes the job easier in some respects.

The same is true of the legislature. In Austin, we were just four blocks away from the state capital. Legislators read the student newspaper, the *Daily Texan,* right after they read the *Austin American Statesman* or the *Dallas Morning News.* So I was constantly getting calls from legislators asking what was going on there. It is a heated political environment with a very conservative legislature in Texas and they naturally focused on what they saw as a liberal, permissive university. The interaction with the legislature was constant in Texas. Also, because of the structure that gave faculty no forum to deal with their issues internally, an enormous number of the problems that came up in our interactions with the legislature originated with the faculty. Minority faculty went to minority legislators to complain about X, Y, or Z. Conservative faculty (we had a big American Scholars group there) went to legislators to complain about some liberal outrage on campus. In California, the legislature is in Sacramento and is a full time legislature, very professional in its style. Legislators are concerned about the university and the issue of access is critical, but they are not intrusive in the way they were in Texas.

On the other hand, the Berkeley faculty owns the university. As I said, this is a faculty-driven culture—there is no major decision that can be made at Berkeley that does not involve substantial faculty input—and the faculty senate is very powerful. The faculty senate appoints the budget committee, which reviews all promotions, and all merit reviews, so it has a voice in individual faculty merit raises. That puts limits on what you can do as an administrator. The role of the faculty in the governance of this university is extraordinary. I have come to believe that, because the faculty has historically been so protective of excellence and so willing to make very hard decisions in merit evaluations, promotions, and tenure decisions, it is the role of the faculty in governance at Berkeley that makes Berkeley the outstanding university it is, despite the fact that we have considerably fewer resources than the private institutions with whom we compete. Administrators, no matter how powerful, cannot build a great university alone; building a great university requires investing trust and responsibility with the faculty and the faculty taking that responsibility seriously. Even though it at times is conflicted, awkward, and cumbersome, I believe that the role of the faculty governance in maintaining excellence in this university is really critical.

The student constituency here is one of the hardest things to handle because this is a university that has a long, sacred tradition of student activism. Students have historically come to Berkeley because they have social concerns and feel that this is the place where you can act them out. That was true in the free speech movement at Berkeley in the 1960s. If you examine the videos of Berkeley in the 1960s and pick out the people who were the leaders of the free speech movement, you find that a lot of them were not California residents. They are students from other states who came to Berkeley because this was where it was happening. That still is the case, though to some extent it's less so, partly because of the enormous growth here in the number of Asian-American students, who are very goal directed and career oriented in their education and less involved in activist causes. But the fact is that, even in Berkeley's most activist times, it was a small minority of students who were activists. It doesn't take very many to create a difficult situation. That aspect of the job has been much more difficult here than it has anywhere else that I've been. We are much better equipped to deal with protests and demonstrations than most places, but it is still difficult. People here are experienced in dealing with demonstrations and the police are very efficient in arresting students when that's necessary, but it remains one of the hardest issues for any chancellor.

FL: I found that out at the beginning of my presidency at Rutgers. As everyone told me, the university was known affectionately, but not without reason, as the Berkeley of the East.

RB: During the divestiture conflicts of the 1980s, only about half of the demonstrators were students. The demonstrators had an encampment on campus that police finally had to move in to break up. Demonstrators responded by lighting fires in dumpsters and rolling them at police. This place can blow up in your face. My second year here we had a very difficult demonstration around ethnic studies. It was related to declining minority enrollments and to Ward Connerly's proposal that we get rid of ethnic studies departments. A number of faculty in the Department of Ethnic Studies had left and not been replaced, so the students as well as some faculty believed we were getting rid of the department by slow attrition. The unfilled vacancies in the department resulted from the division in the department, its inability to agree on a plan for replacements that was acceptable to the Faculty Senate Budget Committee, which reviewed all FTE allocations to departments. So the student protest was fueled and supported by the Ethnic Studies faculty. It was, I would say, the most irresponsible behavior of faculty that I ever witnessed as an administrator. We had a hunger strike and a huge encampment and demonstration that went on for over a week, despite numerous arrests. We ultimately resolved it by allowing the department to fill the vacancies according to a plan that was to be developed with the help of faculty intervention from outside the department. To many, it looked as though we merely caved in; others believed the department should be dissolved. No resolution was possible without inviting criticism from some quarter of the campus. It was the most difficult thing I had to deal with since I've been here and my first exposure to what Berkeley demonstrations can be.

FL: How have you managed the different, sometimes conflicting expectations that you run into in these jobs?

RB: One thing about Berkeley that is different and that is that there is a high level of tolerance. I have said to people, and it's true, that the great thing about Berkeley is that it is the most tolerant place I've ever lived. The bad thing about Berkeley is that it doesn't always understand the difference between tolerance and license. That's true of the city and, at times, it is also characteristic of the university. During my inauguration, there were three simultaneous demonstrations going on. A man protesting animal rights abuses was camped out for about six or seven days on a platform that he had somehow gotten up the Campanile. Donna Shalala spoke and the very activist Bay Area AIDS awareness community protested because of a controversy in Health and Human Resources about a needle exchange program. Then there was also a demonstration about affirmative action. My brother came for this inauguration and he, of course, was appalled at all this going on, but the Berkeley faculty and alumni just shrugged and said, "That's Berkeley." I don't know how to say that I managed these, other than trying to understand them. I think much of what our jobs involve is interpreting the university to the external world and the external world to the university. Depending on the issue, that's harder or easier.

FL: What has been your greatest challenge as a leader?

RB: It's hard to rank order them because they're very different. In a very real sense, the biggest challenge any chancellor of Berkeley faces is making certain that it remains the top-ranked public university that it has been for the last half-century or more. How do you protect greatness in the face of ever increasing competition from the leading private universities and an operating budget that isn't keeping pace? Beyond that is the question of making certain that the university is prepared for the rapid changes in research calling for new equipment, facilities, and greater opportunities for cross-disciplinary collaboration.

I think that the most concrete challenge as a leader that I have faced at Berkeley has to do with the physical infrastructure in the campus, which is a kind of prosaic need. We discovered about two months after I arrived, thanks to an analysis that was being done by structural engineering firms, that 27 percent of the buildings on the campus were rated poor or very poor seismically. The Hayward Fault runs through the edge of the campus, passing right under the football stadium. There are predictions that it is highly probable that a major earthquake will take place on the Hayward Fault in the next twenty-five years. I was concerned about the possible loss of life a major earthquake might cause. I was also concerned about how we could maintain ourselves as a research center if the laboratories and libraries were inaccessible because of damage.

Seismically retrofitting the campus does not inspire great thoughts, yet it is the most fundamental need of this campus because if these buildings are out of commission for a period of years because of earthquake damage, Berkeley ceases to be Berkeley. Realizing the urgency of the problem, I formulated what we called the SAFER Project to retrofit the campus and we spent over three quarters of a billion dollars doing it. Unfortunately we don't get much state money for renewing the infrastructure, so we have to raise money for renovation as well as the seismic retrofitting. Insofar as the renovation is visible and the faculty can appreciate it and benefit from it, that's fine, but an enormous amount of our capital expenditures are not even visible. You are always asked about your vision for the campus. To say my vision for the campus is not to have it fall down in the next earthquake is not an inspiring vision, yet I think it's a fundamental need for the campus. Without the seismic retrofitting, people would die in a major earthquake. I don't want to leave this job feeling I haven't at least done everything I can to protect human life. The disparity between what I think to be the manifest needs of this campus that I have been intent on addressing and the kind of inspiring vision that commands excitement among the faculty has been my biggest challenge in a way. I have had a lot of crises to deal with but I don't consider them fundamental challenges in the way that this is a fundamental challenge.

FL: How have you recruited and structured your leadership teams in each post? Could you tell me something about any restructuring you have done in your administration?

RB: My view has never been to come in, clean house, and get all my own people in. Both here and in Texas I have always tried to get to know the people who are in the administration and make changes only after I've felt it necessary or found the need to do it. I try to play to people's strength. If I had to identify some of the mistakes that I've made, they were that I did not move fast enough to make changes in some administrative posts. That's partly because, coming in as an outsider in Texas and here, I didn't know the players, so I made changes gradually. Other presidents make changes immediately so they have their own team in place from the start. That can also produce some unintended consequences. Somewhere between those two extremes of moving very slowly and moving terribly fast, I think would probably be the right tone.

The restructuring that we have done here has been the consequence of my own view of this office: that is that the chancellor and the executive vice chancellor and provost are two in a box. I want a provost who knows everything I know and I want to know virtually everything he or she knows about what's going on in the institution so that we're interchangeable. We structured it so that all of the vice chancellors report either to the provost or to me, or to both of us. So the chancellor's office is constituted of a chancellor and the executive vice chancellor and provost. Obviously I make the final decisions if there's a tough call but my philosophy is this has got to be a team effort. Then finding the right person for that team is not easy. I have succeeded here with Paul Gray, who is probably the best academic administrator I've ever known. I think that having a division of labor that's strictly between internal and external duties isn't the way to do it. I think you have to have somebody who can stand in for you on the road too. I see Paul and me as virtually equal partners. It is like a marriage. You've got to have real trust, you've got to have real affection, you've got to be willing to share everything and, if you have that, then who is number one and who is number two is strictly a matter of title.

The other reorganization that we have done here has been to accommodate the strengths or weaknesses of people. It's been, to some extent, an effort to accommodate individual strengths and weaknesses, which each of us has.

FL: Can you tell me some of the specific qualities you look for in people that you choose to work with or depend upon?

RB: I want them to be smarter than I am. That is the basic quality I look for. Some might say, that's easy in my case! I'll never forget a comment by Pierre Bourdieu, who was a good friend of mine. We spent a year at the Institute for Advanced Study in Princeton, where our families lived next to each other, and we spent a lot of time together. I later visited him in Paris, where he had built the Center for European Sociology, which struck me as a very harmonious and productive group, so I asked him what criteria he used to choose people. He told me that obviously you want the very brightest people you can find, but beyond that, you ought to look for humility (Pierre was a person who had genuine humility). I asked him why. He told me that a person without humility at twenty-five is going to be a person without ideas at forty. I thought it was a really interesting insight and, subsequent experience has proved it to be largely correct. I look for people whom I think have a fundamental sense of human frailty, including their own—people who are nevertheless smart and decisive, and I think that's the best combination.

FL: How did you formulate a vision for the future of either Texas or Cal-Berkeley?

RB: I tried to assess what I felt to be the needs, the fundamental needs of each campus when I arrived. The vision that I tried to create at Austin involved building a sense of academic community and uniting the disparate parts of that campus with a sense that they were all a part of a single, ambitious goal. We did that in a number of ways, many of them community-building kinds of things. We also restructured the faculty governance. I worked with a faculty committee to change the university senate by getting rid of the administrators who comprised 50 percent of it. I told them that it didn't make sense: administrators controlled every vote and, as a consequence, the faculty had no consultative power. The

regents were very nervous about this change and my boss, who was my predecessor, didn't like it either. He thought I was turning the asylum over to the
inmates. Yet it did build a much stronger relationship between the faculty
and the administration. My successor, Larry Faulkner, has been able to
continue that, because he has much the same kind of value system.

We also brought in a consultant who led us through a weekend retreat with
a group of faculty. This was preparatory to a capital campaign, but it was
focused on identifying the core values in the university, discussing them, and
formulating them. We had faculty, staff, a few students, some alumni and donors, and some administrators gathered for this retreat and people really threw
themselves into it. We came out with what I think was a wonderful definition
of the core values that still persist there and provided the value structure for
the campaign that ensued after I left.

When I thought about that exercise here, I knew it wouldn't work. Nobody
at Berkeley wanted to talk about core values because they knew what their
core values were. This is more than a self-confident campus; in many ways, it's
an arrogant campus. Even though we worked on community building here as
well, the faculty were not going to be interested in the collaborative effort we
had in Texas because they already had it structurally in place. They knew their
place in the governance and they shared the governance structure, so there was
no need to try to change that. The vision thing here was really much different.
It was centered on what Berkeley needed and it was related to what we ended
up calling "renewing the foundations of excellence." The library was in terrible trouble when I came here. It had slipped from third place to sixth place
among research libraries. It was somewhat dysfunctional: I got more complaints about the library than anything else. So we put a lot of effort and a lot of
money into the library. The creation of a vision here really grew out of trying to
take an assessment of the needs of the campus and then trying to articulate it. I
don't think anyone ever found it a soaring inspiration, but we did accomplish a
lot in terms of renewing the physical infrastructure at Berkeley.

FL: How did you transform your understanding of each university together with the external realities into a long-range plan for change and
improvement?

RB: We did not do an academic plan at Texas because Texas was terribly
large, decentralized, and the role of the faculty made it difficult to do a comprehensive academic plan. Academic planning was done school by school,
college by college. However one of the things I felt that the campus needed
was a comprehensive plan for its physical evolution. Up to that point, it was
dropping structures into open spaces, without a plan or vision about how they
fit together. So we actually created a master plan for the physical evolution of
the campus with the help of some outstanding architectural consultants. It
pulled people together in an important way and created a physical vision for
what the campus needed to be. We've done the same thing here, to a lesser extent,

but here we also made a major academic plan, which was done closely with the faculty. It was co-chaired by the chair of the faculty senate and the vice provost. It identifies ten areas for research and academic investment, all of them inter-disciplinary. We have begun the process of committing faculty lines to it.

FL: How did you link the changes you wanted to make in this kind of plan with the financial budgeting process of the institution?

RB: Here, we decided, with some pressure from the state and from the office of the president, that we would grow a bit. There was considerable resistance to the notion that Berkeley can afford to grow at all. It's a small, landlocked campus and we have a lot of friction with the city over growth, but, given the way in which we are structured and given the pressures of the Tidal Wave II population boom coming, there was a lot of pressure to grow. So we said that over this decade we would add 4,000 students to the enrollment and go from about 29,000 students when I got here to 33,000. That growth will, we hope, yield ultimately around 240 new faculty positions because we're funded basi-cally on a population model. The whole purpose of that plan was to think long term, over a decade, about how the growth would take place, where it would take place, where those resources would be applied, and in what order they would be applied. We're on track with that, although this current fiscal crisis has set us back because we have not been able to grow the faculty this year at the rate that was projected for this year. But it means that, in addition to the regular hires of about fifty replacements a year, we are going to add another twenty-five a year over the decade, so we will be hiring about seventy-five faculty annually. That will allow the full time enrollment to increase in the departments that have been designated for growth and new initiatives.

FL: The natural follow-up question on long-term planning is, "How did you get faculty on board and enthusiastic about the changes?" However, if you were planning to add 240 new faculty positions, I would imagine that you didn't have to work very hard to do that.

RB: No, although there were a lot of faculty who appropriately were skep-tical about whether or not we would get the students and not the faculty. I think that they had a point. They were very concerned about that and remain concerned. This was all done in really good times. Given the downturn in the economy and the slowing of the hiring, there is some validity in that skepti-cism. So to say we had complete buy-in is not true, although it was a wonder-ful collaboration with the faculty senate that produced that plan. Then, as we identified the new areas, we brought in an external review team to review the proposals that came from the faculty for the addition of faculty in these areas and that external review team really helped enormously. It was an outstanding team of people, so we got some exciting initiatives on the way to resolving it.

FL: Making changes is often not synonymous with making friends. Can you describe one or more critical incidents, how they arose and how you dealt with them? The job isn't fun twenty-four hours a day, seven days a week.

RB: One of the hardest things I ever had to do occurred when I was a dean: that was to fire my best friend. It ruptured the friendship. We've barely spoken since then, but it was one of those things that you have to do if you're going to do the right thing by the institution. I don't think that ultimately you can think about making friends.

You don't have friends in this kind of job. In Oregon, I had friends because I grew up in the faculty there. I lost some, like the one I mentioned; others remained friends. But when you come in from the outside in one of these jobs, you do not make friends. It is one of the things that I miss the most about the job because as you get older in life, it's harder to make friends anyway. I don't think you can worry about friendship. You can worry about collegiality; you can worry about whether or not what you do will perturb working relationships in ways that are not easily fixable or that make them dysfunctional. Friends cannot be the measure.

I had two friends on this faculty when I arrived. One died just as I was arriving. The other is still probably my closest professional friend, a historian. We're going to team teach. He, to his great credit, told me that he would never talk with me about university affairs. He said, "We'll talk history, we'll talk politics." I was his chancellor for seven years, his dean for five years. Never in those twelve years has he ever asked me for a favor, but that's a rare friend.

FL: Accountability and outcomes issues have been on our doorstep to stay for at least a decade. What methods have you used internally to assess the outcomes of your initiatives and your progress toward your long-term goals?

RB: The accountability that we're talking about as being on our doorsteps is particularly to legislatures and boards of regents and is always measured by a prescribed menu of metrics. But measuring success and achievement of our initiatives and goals within the institution is also very important. There our mutual friend Brent Ruben has been extraordinarily helpful because at the beginning of each academic year, we have defined in very broad categories the goals of my administration: enhancing the research opportunities, improving undergraduate education, these very broad categories of things that we want to achieve, then specific goals within those categories. There is a point person on each of those and, throughout each year of cabinet meetings, periodically we update the progress that has been made so that every person knows at the beginning of the year what their objectives are for that year or beyond (because most of these are multi-year projects) and what precise steps are going to be taken in the course of that year. I'm not as systematic a thinker as this. I'm a historian and, happily, Paul Gray is an engineer. Engineers are great at process, mapping out timelines and all of those things that are not part of my tool kit. Paul has been a fabulous component of that effort and Brent has been extraordinarily helpful.

FL: What importance have you placed on the role of UT Austin and UC Berkeley in their communities?

RB: If we're talking about the local communities, I have to say that the two universities were very different. Austin occasionally had friction about expansion, but the president of the University in Austin was seen as a major player in the community and the university was seen as a major asset to the community. Ironically, that's much less the case at Berkeley, though it's a much smaller community. They might blame me personally for that, and it may be that that's a legitimate blame, but the friction between Berkeley and the university, the town-gown relations, are probably as difficult as they are in Cambridge Massachusetts and maybe a few other places, like Palo Alto. However Berkeley's has got to be about as difficult a town-gown relationship as any that I know. It goes back to half a century or more, with the expansion of the university in a landlocked community, and the problems of an urban university in a very small town. Berkeley has 110,000 inhabitants. The university is a very big elephant in a little place and is resented. Of course I have to say that I have not been good at this. I once commented to some of the council members that if it wasn't for the university, Berkeley would be an insignificant suburb of Oakland. That was not the politic thing to say, but the fact of the matter is it's true, so town-gown relations have occupied far more time here than anywhere that I've ever been.

FL: What do they want you to do?

RB: Basically they want us to bail out their deficit. They see the university as costing the city enormous amounts of money. They've just presented a study where they concluded that the university is an $11 million a year burden to the city, which coincidentally is just what their deficit is.

There's no question that the neighborhoods around the university are impacted by the university. We don't have enough parking. They want us to provide more parking so there's no parking on the street and they want us to provide less parking so that fewer people can drive. These are no-win dilemmas. I think certainly for anybody considering one of these jobs, do not underestimate the amount of energy and time and frustration that can be drained by the town government relationships. It was a surprise to me because the university-city relationship was productive and harmonious in Austin. The city got excited about the master plan that the university did and decided that they could do a master plan that would also draw on things like the creek which wound itself through the campus and create a much enhanced continuation of that creek from the campus on into the community. There was a synergistic relationship with the city there; here it has always been much more conflictive.

FL: How have you allocated your time in these different posts? What have been your top priorities?

RB: When I arrived here, we were halfway through a capital campaign to raise $1.1 billion. Chang Lin was a renowned fund raiser and my great fear was that we'd just lose ground and the steam would come out of the campaign, so

I spent an enormous amount of time in the first two or three years on the road getting acquainted, trying to raise money and make certain that we met the goal. We ultimately over-realized the goal and raised one and a half billion dollars, which was the most at that time any public university or any university without a medical school had ever raised. We also are a major player in Asia, and so in those first years I was making three trips a year to Asia.

FL: Do you have good financial support from Asia?

RB: Yes. Of course that was truer when Chang Lin was chancellor because he had so many contacts in Asia, but we do have very good friends there and thousands of alumni. Every other year we host an Asian leadership conference. We bring some of our faculty and some of our foundation people. Then about 150 to 200 Asian alums who are leaders in industry, in academia, and in government gather someplace in Asia and we have a three-day conference. That has been enormously successful. Because of the end of the campaign and personal circumstances, my travel and fund raising focus in the last two years has been a lot less than it was in the first five. Obviously the budget has also become a much more major issue to deal with. There is an ebb and flow with these things and you adjust your time allocation accordingly. I begin my workday by getting to the office at about 8:00. Between 8:00 and 9:00 I meet with my executive assistant to go over the day or clean up whatever is left over from the day before, give her the mail that I've been through the night before, and meet with my chief of staff. I meet with him multiple times a day because he has no real portfolio. He is basically chief troubleshooter and follow-through person. Then the calendar starts at 9:00 A.M. and is packed through the day. I take home my mail and read it at night. Peg and I have tried to save two evenings a week for ourselves and have tried to save one weekend day a week. That's harder. In fact, Peg got really upset because she was concerned about me in my second year here. She called the chief of staff and she said, "I just want you to tally the scheduled hours." He did, and we found that I had been scheduled for over eighty-five hours a week. Then even he realized that this could not continue. Peg really put her foot down. That was the year she insisted on my getting away for a month. We then restructured the time and we now also have calendar meetings that involve the alumni association, the development office, this office and the house staff. At the beginning of each semester we go through the events of the semester to decide how we schedule, how we allocate time. I think that's important.

FL: What part of your work have you enjoyed most?

RB: I would say three things. I think that academic planning, trying to reposition or position the institution, is ultimately the most important and interesting kind of thing that you do. That involves a whole lot of conversations with faculty and the recruitment and retention of faculty. I meet with most senior faculty we're trying to recruit. I meet with every faculty member that we're trying to retain, if I can. Trying to position the university for the future is interesting. The other things that I find very interesting are some of the knotty problems. A case in point is the problem that arose from a project that is partly an art practice project and partly an engineering project. We have mounted on the Union Building a video camera that observes Sproul Plaza. You can access the camera feed from your computer, zero in on somebody, and get about a ten foot-by-ten foot profile. You can do all kinds of things with it, then these things are posted and people make comments about the pictures. The Whitney Museum in New York is interested in it as a new form of art, a new use of photography. It is also an invasion of privacy: people don't know they're being photographed. There have been cases where obviously they've zoomed in on attractive young women. There is just an enormous nest of legal issues related to technology and what it can do, what we can do, and the posting of these things, the use of people's images. We had a two-hour discussion yesterday with some legal experts and the faculty involved. At issue was, were we supporting a new technology in a cutting edge intellectual experience or were we allowing our students' privacy to be invaded and potentially putting someone at risk of humiliation or worse. In fact, it appeared we were doing both; the problem was to support the first without encouraging the second. It's a fascinating intellectual kind of problem. It has been a liberal arts education being in this job and I have loved that. The other thing that I've enjoyed enormously is the interaction with the external world. It reshapes the prejudices about the business community and that external world that you may pick up as a faculty member. As I said, one of my strengths has been public speaking. I do enjoy that and I have enjoyed the alumni, the people who care about this institution, and contribute to it. It's quite amazing the number of people who give many, many hours a year and a lot of money to the institution just because they care about it and don't care whether their names are on buildings or anything else. That has been a civic education to me. I wish that every faculty member could really come to understand what that is. It happens because they had good experiences here as undergraduates. (Our graduate students don't make enough money as a rule to contribute unless they happen to start up a business.) I expected the Berkeley alumni to be laid back, kind of cool, not necessarily rabid Berkeley fans or CAL fans and I expected the fact that this university has always had been the center of protests would turn off an awful lot of people. It doesn't. It's a wonderful thing, and I've enjoyed that.

FL: Every leader experiences planned and unplanned events that escalate to time-consuming crises. Among these are fiscal challenges, contract negotiations, and PR challenges that pop up unexpectedly. Are there any crisis management stories that you would like to share?

RB: I had one big crisis at Texas which involved a donor. He was, truth be told, not a huge donor to Texas and was thoroughly disliked in Austin. Some of our faculty became incensed because one of his company's international operations had a security force that involved the nation's army and people were killed there. Some of our faculty got very active in protesting the gift and the naming of a building for the donor. Then, when he threatened the protestors with a lawsuit, a situation that was initially of interest to a limited number of faculty became an issue of free expression and of interest to the entire faculty. I was caught between my boss, my predecessor, who was a close friend of the donor and the faculty. It was one of those situations where the faculty felt utterly disempowered and threatened. It's a long story that has many, many comic aspects. The donor was working to get me fired, so I had to go and meet him in another city. When I was running out the door early in the morning in the dark to catch an early plane to fly there, I tripped, fell and broke my wrist, but I didn't know it was broken at the time. I realized it was broken somewhere en route to the meeting but I spent this whole day in terrible pain with the donor and a broken wrist. I didn't get fired. I had to speak out on behalf of the faculty in defense of academic freedom, but of course the faculty were employees as far as he was concerned and if he had employees that criticized the university, why he'd fire them.

The big crisis at Berkeley was the Ethnic Studies demonstration that I mentioned. I had never before dealt with large scale demonstrations and, during this one, we had to arrest a number of students. The third crisis was one that involved a teaching assistant in the English department here who was a member of the Students for Justice in Palestine. Our course descriptions are now mounted on the web and were not monitored at that time. In the freshman rhetoric class, they teach writing by subject matter, presenting a little seminar on a subject. This teaching assistant decided to teach his section on Palestinian literature. He talked in his course description in very inappropriate ways about the Israeli-Palestinian crisis and concluded it by saying conservatives should seek other sections. This was picked up by Roger Kimball in a column. I learned about this because of the column in the *Wall Street Journal* and then, of course, the follow-up at Fox News. We have a very strong support group from the Jewish community and very strong representation on the board of regents. Handling this as an issue of academic freedom, mentoring this student, who is very bright, and threading the whole matter through with a lot of board attention and criticism was very difficult. It was important to define and defend the principle of academic freedom despite the fact that others, who normally would be staunch supporters of academic freedom, in this case did not see it that way. We got through it, but nobody who has not had one of these jobs can appreciate the amount of time that is consumed by that sort of crisis. It can mean weeks on end when half of your day is spent in meetings, on telephone conversations, or flying. I flew to Los Angeles and met with Jewish leaders there. I spent time with the Anti-Defamation League folks here in the Bay Area. The Jewish- Palestinian crisis really played out on this campus with big Palestinian demonstrations, large counter-demonstrations by Jewish students, and a lot of friction. And I worked very hard to try to keep these groups within bounds. We've had our share of crises, although I had an easier run than a lot of my predecessors.

During the issue of the Palestinian literature course, I spent a lot of time with one of our brilliant lawyers talking about academic freedom. He had been a lawyer with the AAUP and had spent time thinking through the very nuanced set of issues about academic freedom: what its limits were and what were the basic principles that we had to defend. I think that ultimately people get into trouble and fail to provide leadership when they lose sight of those principles in trying to deal with an issue in an expedient fashion. In dealing with an issue to dispose of it, you are trying to move in a direction and build consensus around something that doesn't have that kind of fundamental core of principle. When we had the conversation at Texas about core values, we defined a core value, as something to which you adhere, even when it costs you. Leadership is knowing what your core values are so clearly and firmly that, even when it costs you, you know who you are and what you must do. You asked me earlier what I enjoyed. All of education is self-discovery. I have learned more about myself, what I really believe, what I find critically important, what is central and what isn't central in my life and my value system through being in these jobs than I ever would have without that experience.

FL: More than if we had remained in our academic specialties?

RB: Yes, you have principles in those circumstances but you're not called upon to put them on the line in the way that you are in these kinds of jobs. It's one of the reasons that there's a high level of stress and it's one of the reasons that you're subject to a lot of criticism. I would say the other thing that's important in leadership is the capacity to tolerate ambiguity, because by the time you get to a job like this, no problem that lands on your desk is easily soluble. If it had been it would have been solved before it got to you. If you have to have a black and white world, you should find other work.

FL: What are the most important qualities for a university president today? What advice would you give someone coming into this job for the first time?

RB: I think I'd go back to saying knowing what you stand for, because I think that that's where you get tested and where leadership falls down. At UT Austin, Martin Myerson (not the Martin Myerson who was president of the University of Pennsylvania but a man associated with Ross Perot) gave a wonderful lecture about leadership. His point was that ultimately nobody is going to follow a leader if they don't feel that he knows what he stands for. I think that's terribly important.

FL: How have the role and demands of the presidency changed over the past few decades in response to the disinvestment of the states in public higher education?

RB: It has put tremendous strain on the role of the president because it has increased the demands on and the demands from external constituencies, whether they are students who must pay much higher fees or legislatures that cut your budgets and simultaneously demand that you continue to provide maximum access and may even put additional constraints on how you spend or raise money. The decline in public support for higher education has really put higher stress on all of its constituencies: parents, students, and donors, so all of those constituencies now believe they have a larger stake in the direction of the university and the decisions of the university. Their pressure on the leadership of the university has increased as a consequence.

FL: What has been the effect of the technological revolution on the demands of the presidency?

RB: There are two aspects of it. One is to implement it in the university. Keeping pace with it is terribly difficult and terribly costly. The second aspect is the kind of legal and moral implications that it brings with it, whether students' file sharing and theft, which has become a big issue, or the kind of privacy issues that I mentioned. The preeminence of science and technology have displaced and rendered peripheral so many of the traditional academic disciplines. There are very few university presidents left who are humanists. I was the only non-scientist among the chancellors of the University of California system. Now, with my replacement by a physicist, there will be no non-scientist in the president's office or in any of the chancellorships. The voice of the humanities within the university whether from faculty or administrative leadership has been marginalized by the advance of science and technology. I think that this ultimately has consequences for education.

FL: What effect have the growing roles of private support and commercial application of university research had on the responsibilities of the presidency?

RB: We've had the big test case here with the Novartis agreement that attracted so much attention. All of the issues related to intellectual property are very complex and have become more complex as whole new disciplines have come into play. As faculty have become involved in research that could potentially make a lot of money, questions arise about what that means in terms of their commitment to the institution and the conflicts of interest that can develop. The fact that universities will have to seek support from commercial enterprises in the development of intellectual property is a very knotty problem. We've had careful study of the Novartis agreement done internally and externally. The external review concluded that it had no impact on the direction of research and had no impact on academic freedom. Nevertheless they concluded that we shouldn't do it. I think ultimately universities will have to craft these agreements, as we did, so that there is no adverse impact on the freedom of the university, but they are difficult.

FL: Presidencies were once measured in decades—Derek Bok at Harvard, Frank Rhodes at Cornell—but now presidential tenure is typically limited to four or five years. Do you believe that the changes in the role have brought that about or are there other reasons for the high rate of attrition?

RB: No, I think it's the changes in the role that have caused that. I've often said you start these jobs with a full bank account and you spend it down with every decision you make because you never replenish the account by creating goodwill. You only draw it down by creating ill will with decisions. And the fact that many constituencies now have much more claim on the university simply means that you spend it down faster. I've enjoyed really wonderful support, but there also comes a point where you feel like you've done what you can do, and I think that comes faster. I spent four and a half years at Texas and I think that was too short. I left with a sense of unfinished business. I felt that I had accomplished something but I wasn't sure it would last. I think the seven years that I've been here, or a tenure between seven and nine years is about the right amount of time. If you stay less than seven years, you probably aren't going to get done what you can get done. More than nine years is probably too long.

FL: How would you characterize your leadership style?

RB: Consultative. I try always to talk with people about the principles that ought to guide us in what we're trying to achieve and, in that sense, try to mentor them, as well as drawing from them advice on what those basic principles are.

FL: What do you feel have been the most critical capital investments made under your leadership? Was it the seismic refitting of campus structures?

RB: Yes, it is the effort to renew the physical structure of the campus.

FL: What do you believe were the most significant legacies that you left to Austin and Cal-Berkeley?

RB: At Austin it was a stronger sense of community and shared responsibility for the direction of the university. At Berkeley, it is probably two things, first the effort to renew the physical infrastructure of the campus, and second the long-term academic plan that we inaugurated with the decision to grow in size.

FL: How did your decision to step down come about and how did you make your decision about what you would do after the presidency?

RB: I've been thinking about it for some time. I'm sixty-seven. I had been here only five years when I was sixty-five and I didn't think that was long enough, so I thought I might spend seven or eight years doing this. When my daughter's health got so bad and Peg had to be away, I decided that I had done what I could do here and I needed to give what time I have now to my family, so it was really a personal decision.

FL: What advice would you give to new presidents?

RB: The best advice I ever got was from Paul Olum as I was leaving the deanship at Oregon to go to be provost in Illinois. I went into his office just before I left and asked, "Well, Paul, what advice would you give me?" He said, "Never forget that you're faculty."

FL: What is the most critical skill or set of skills that a president will need to succeed in the future and how are those skills different from the skills needed in the past?

RB: The appreciation and understanding of the scientific revolution that we're engaged in and launching is a critical skill: I think that's the reason that fewer and fewer presidencies are going to humanists or others. As the university becomes more a center of science than it ever has been in the past, the ability to understand and guide it in that vital area is essential. Just in terms of disciplinary skill I think that is important. A second thing that is going to be important as we struggle with resources is increased reliance on data-driven management. Universities have never been very good at driving decisions by accumulation of data, but we're gradually getting there, in part because of issues of accountability and in part because of constrained resources, but also because the kind of leadership that we're drawing on is more accustomed to data-driven decision making. I think it's an absolutely essential direction for universities to go. The other essential skill set would be the ability to communicate. Ultimately all things come back to that. If you can't communicate clearly, if you don't appreciate the importance of communication and consultation, you are going to fail.

FL: What has been at the core of your work in higher education? What are the underlying purposes that you have worked to accomplish?

RB: That's a hard question to answer. Community is a core value to which I have given a high premium because I think our universities have become so disjointed. Even though interdisciplinary research, cross-disciplinary research and all of those things that have brought faculty out of their disciplinary silos are critical for their research, we have lost a sense of what an academic community is and can be. Maybe I'm a romantic, visualizing academic community in ways that it may never have existed, but I certainly think that a university with a sense of community was a stronger place. I've studied the history of the University of California Berkeley. When I think about the community that was built by Lawrence and the physicists I am sure that there was a lot of tension and competition, but it was an incredible place that produced seven or eight Nobel Laureates who came here as students and stayed as faculty or came here and became a Nobel Laureate scientist. Now the university is so large and we are so intently engaged in our local activities that we don't have that sense. Berkeley is the multiversity that Clark Kerr talked about in some ways. So the core efforts that I have launched, whether through the construction of the first big $172 million interdisciplinary science building on this campus as part of the renewal of the infrastructure or through various efforts at academic planning and shared governance, all have had as their leitmotif the effort to renew and restore academic community. I hope that I've had some success in doing something in that regard.

FL: As states reduced their funding of higher education while state legislatures and governors tried to cap tuition, how can institutions resolve their budget problems to continue to build both access and excellence?

RB: They can't. I just don't think that equates. You can't cap revenue, whether it's from tuition or from the state legislature, and hope to maintain both access and excellence.

FL: Is it the responsibility of our state institutions to solve the problem of access?

RB: It is the responsibility of the state to solve problems of access, not necessarily of the institutions. The institutions haven't created the underlying problem of access which is, at least in California, the result of constrained enrollment and high prices. We haven't created the economic disparities that exist. I think we have to work to solve the problem of access, but the limitations on access have been largely a result of state actions, whether it is access that is derived from some form of affirmative action or access that's derived from some form of financial support or the lack of financial support. We are going to be criticized for restricting access, as a place like Berkeley is constantly, with only one out of four applicants getting in. But if I have to choose between access and excellence, if these two are incompatible, given the circumstances we are granted, we have to choose excellence because once you lose excellence you can't restore it. Access could be restored with an infusion of funds from the state. Excellence isn't going to get restored that quickly.

FL: Is there any realistic hope that state and federal government will take on more of that responsibility or do you think that's more than a long shot?

RB: I think it's more than a long shot given the predilection to reduce taxes and the impending fiscal crisis that the federal government and the states are facing with social security and health care costs. I tend to be fairly glum about the capacity of this country to respond to these crises in a rational fashion. At the same time, I believe strongly in the need for this country to invest in education. Aside from the security of its citizens, there is no activity in which we collectively engage as a society that is more important than preparing the next generation of students. I believe we must invest in this vital public good.

FL: Can partnerships between state universities and community colleges offer partial solutions? Let me use Rutgers as an example. Our enrollment rose on all three campuses during my tenure as president, but the bulk of the increase was in New Brunswick. We found ourselves in a situation in which we had applicants who were admissible, but we had no room for them. We created partnerships with all nineteen county colleges to offer what we called a dual admissions program. Good students for whom we had no room could attend their local community college, take a prescribed curriculum of core courses and prerequisites for their intended major, earn a B+ grade point average, and be assured of admittance to Rutgers as juniors.

RB: We have crafted a very similar plan here at the initiative of the governor to reduce the funding for the enrollment growth. We offered a guaranteed transfer option to students, to community colleges. In the California system of higher education, the community colleges were meant ultimately to be feeder schools. According to the master plan, 60 percent of our enrollment is to be upper division. We have achieved that because we admit about 3,800 freshmen and about 1,800 junior transfers, mostly from community colleges in

California. The difficulty with that solution is that the community colleges themselves have a fiscal problem and, for a variety of reasons, many of the community colleges don't offer the right transfer curriculum or the students don't go to them for that. As a consequence, although we may have as many as 100 community colleges and city colleges in California, we probably get transfers from less than fifteen to eighteen, those that are known to be the feeder campuses for community college transfers. The State of California has one of the highest percentages of college-going populations in the United States and one of the lowest percentages of students acquiring a baccalaureate degree which means that a lot of students are going into community colleges, but no further.

FL: You have worked with more than one governing board. Could you outline what you feel are important characteristics of good governing boards and some of the problems that one can encounter in dealing with governing boards.

RB: I think that the biggest problem that arises with governing boards ultimately is distrust of the administration: the sense that the administration isn't being straight with them, that we're not providing them with all the information they need in order to govern, or that we're giving them partial or incomplete information. This has certainly been exacerbated following Enron and other corporate collapses that have been a consequence of poor governance. The advice I would give to a new president about a governing board is to be sure to keep the governing board as informed as possible, without, however, inviting the governing board to engage in administration. This is the hard dilemma because there can be an inclination on the part of the governing board to begin to make the administrative decision rather than the policy decisions. A good governing board knows the difference between policy and administration.   Now, in order to make policy, they have to be well informed but if they take the information and then try to make administrative decisions, they cease to be a decent governing board. It's a very hard balance it seems to me between those two.   It depends upon trust and it depends upon the university offering and the members of the governing board being willing to attend a good orientation. We should spend three or four days with new board members orienting them about what their responsibilities are. They don't usually want to give the time. My impression on this is that private universities may be better situated in this regard.   That is partly because you're drawing from a somewhat different pool of people who are more familiar with the corporate world and how it operates, people who are accustomed to delegating authority to an executive committee within a larger body. The difference between policy and administration doesn't get nearly as confused as it does in public universities.

FL: In the past few years there have been several instances in which the governor of the state has gotten involved directly with policy issues or even personnel decisions in the state's flagship university or the system itself. Do you think this is a trend about which we should be concerned? How can chancellors and presidents deal with these kinds of issues, given that the governor is usually the most powerful person in the state?

RB: The governor is a constitutional member of the board of regents at the University of California. It was Ronald Reagan who, as a board member, moved the firing of Clark Kerr when he was governor: the governors have been intrusive at times. Certainly when Governor Pete Wilson wanted to run for president, he was able to push hard as a board member of the University of California, and to get the issue of affirmative action approved. I don't think there's any way in which that issue can be dealt with effectively: if the governor wants to intrude, the governor will. Again it does come back, to some extent, to the issue of trust. Dick Atkinson had fantastic relationships with Pete Wilson and with Gray Davis, so he was able to work with both of them effectively. But for the president of a public university who is engaged in negotiations with the governor, the relationship with the governor has to be carefully cultivated and maintained. If it's lost, I think the president should renew his vita because, unless the governor is a real short timer, ultimately if the governor gets crosswise with the president of the university, the university is going to suffer.

FL: You have served as president of two NCAA Division I schools. What's your take on the current very public damaging perceptions of serious problems in recruiting, admission, retention, graduation, student athlete conduct, and funding of athletics including the huge escalation of the compensation of successful Division I coaches in revenue sports? Can we solve these problems?

RB: The problems are soluble but the will to solve them doesn't exist. I have been to many meetings where presidents have talked about the arms race and the expenditures on intercollegiate athletics. We have lamented the cost, the professionalization, all of these things, then we all go back to our campuses and do the things that make the situation worse.

FL: The latest suggestion I have heard was the imposition of an NCAA cap on expenditures, not an institutional cap on salaries, but a cap imposed by the NCAA on the amount that any Division I intercollegiate athletic program could spend.

RB: That could probably be challenged in court as an action in restraint of trade and I don't know whether it would survive a legal challenge. Certainly the thing is out of hand and I am as guilty as anybody in creating the out of hand situation. We had to compete to maintain a football coach who is now winning, so we're paying him an obscene salary and if anything it was worse at Texas. It is trite but true to say that football is a religion in Texas. I don't have a solution to it. I think that a reduction in the number of football scholarships would be a huge step toward cutting back expenditures. Why do we need eighty-five scholarship football players? If you cut it back to fifty, or forty-four, that would be enough for four teams and would solve so many of the problems of runaway costs and of Title IX issues. I would like to see freshman eligibility eliminated again because I think that runs counter to the ultimate goal of being a student athlete. We've put enormous emphasis in the last three years here (as a result of some scandals to be sure) on the role of student athletes as students and who we recruit and what kind of students they have to be. We've worked very hard on this issue. The other thing I would say is that, if you are a new president at a Division I school, you have no idea of the amount of time that you are going to spend on intercollegiate athletics and the kind of box that it puts you in. I've said this to Bob Birgeneau, who, from his experience at MIT and the University of Toronto, naturally doesn't have a clue about the problems. For example, we have a football stadium under which the Hayward Fault runs. To retrofit that stadium would cost in excess of $100 million. Not to retrofit it means that everybody who is working in it is put at risk, but I couldn't justify putting it high on our list of priorities because we don't have many people working there. If you are looking at it in comparison with other academic buildings, and it is occupied for just 24 hours a year as a stadium, what are the odds of an earthquake happening during a football game?

FL: How have your universities responded to the widespread criticism that research universities don't care about undergraduate teaching?

RB: First of all we do care. I think we have demonstrated that and we have put a lot of effort into it. The criticism of research universities and undergraduate education, I think, may have been valid fifteen to twenty years ago. I believe that it's not valid today.

FL: I agree with you. We talked about your efforts to diversify your student body through admissions. How have you managed to diversify your campuses in terms of faculty or administrators and staff?

RB: The staff is quite diverse just because we live in the metropolitan area and you have a very large employment pool to draw from. We put a big emphasis on hiring women faculty. It had dropped down. At the time I came to Berkeley, we were down about 22 or 24 percent in that year and the year after. We got it up to about 46 percent last year, in terms of new hires. So far as African-American and Latino faculty are concerned, we have just held our own. We've replaced the ones that we've lost, but we have not grown. Our numbers of Latino faculty probably have grown a bit, but our number of African-American faculty is absolutely flat.

FL: What do you see as the strongest forces driving the need to change in higher education over the next ten to twenty years? What are the most important changes you expect to see take place? What will higher education leaders need to do or do more of in the future to help their institutions succeed, given the rate of change in the environment?

RB: I think that the strongest forces driving the need for change are going to be a combination of budgetary expectations and technological innovations. The online universities are going to provide higher education access for a lot of people. Maintaining the quality and consistency of that higher education is going to be a huge challenge, but I think there will be some growth in that, although it hasn't taken off like I thought it might. People still like to come to a residential campus, if that's possible. But the budgetary constraints are going to be enormous and my feeling is that universities are going to have to make terribly hard choices, choices they've never had to make, about areas in which they're going to be excellent. It's going to be very hard for a place like Berkeley which is probably the only public university that has virtually all of its humanities and social science departments ranked in the top ten. Those are the departments that have been sustained at private universities because of the resources that they have had, but most public universities have not been able to afford that.

Sustaining excellence across the board is going to be very hard and making choices about where you don't do that is going to be difficult. Clearly we're going to have to become more understood as private entities and more appreciated as such. We will have to compete with the privates in fund raising. Berkeley has a pretty good fund raising operation. We raise somewhere between $150 and $250 million a year, but Stanford is raising twice that, with a much smaller student body. I don't know how to depict all of the strongest forces, but they will be essentially budgetary and technological.

The other thing that's going to happen and is happening already is the drying up of the huge influx of excellent foreign graduate students. We have been heavily dependent on foreign graduate students for the sustenance of graduate programs. They are declining in part because of the recent problems and anybody who has traveled extensively in China knows that their universities have been transformed. When I first went to China in 1987 and visited the major universities in Shanghai and Beijing, it was like stepping back into the early twentieth century in terms of equipment and classroom capacity and research resources. Now some of them are more modern than we are: they have state-of-the art stuff. I don't know how many million Chinese take the college entrance exam in China but two or three universities get their pick of the very best. They're brilliant students. We're not going to be getting graduate students from many of those places in the future and many of the graduate students elsewhere are going to be going to China to do their graduate work. So the competition from abroad is going to be substantial and this great export industry in American higher education isn't going to be a great export industry anymore.

Myles Brand

Myles Brand is the president of the National Collegiate Athletic Association, a post he assumed on January 1, 2003. He is the first university president to serve in that role.

Born May 17, 1942, Brand attended Rensselaer Polytechnic Institute and graduated in 1964 with a bachelor's degree in philosophy, then went on to earn his Ph.D. in philosophy from the University of Rochester in 1967. His professional background includes service as provost and vice president for academic affairs at Ohio State University, president of the University of Oregon (1989-1994), and president of Indiana University (1994-2002). At the University of Oregon, he alleviated a funding crisis by making selective cutbacks based on faculty recommendations. His recruitment of out-of-state students established a new source of revenue, increased program quality, and positioned the institution as a national university. At Indiana University under his administration research funding tripled, leadership in fields such as biomedicine improved, the endowment increased sixfold, substantial capital improvements were made, the university took a greater role in state economic development, the School of Informatics was founded, and the university's hospitals were combined with a private institution to create a new private hospital system named Clarion. Throughout his administrative career, he continued to teach and do research in philosophy.

On the national level, Brand has served as chair of the board of directors of the Association of American Universities (AAU) in 1999-2000, a member of the executive committee of the American Council on Education (1994-97), and a member of the board of directors of the National Association of State Universities and Land Grant Colleges (1995-1998). He was also a member of the board of the umbrella organization of Internet2, the University Corporation for Advanced Internet Development.

At the NCAA, Brand has implemented a Division I athletics reform agenda that is designed to improve the pre-college preparation of student athletes and keep them on the path to progress toward a degree. In addition, the NCAA has established standards for student athlete graduation rates and penalties for institutions that fail to meet those standards.

Francis Lawrence: Myles, could we begin by talking about your background, the people in your life who influenced you, and the personal traits that have contributed to your development as a leader?

Myles Brand: I was born in Brooklyn, New York and had a very ordinary education in the public schools there and on Long Island, where my family moved when I was a teenager. I enjoyed school, but my high school years were spent looking forward to a more challenging time in college. Since my parents were pragmatic people and brought me up in a vocationally oriented atmosphere, I started out at Rensselaer Polytechnic Institute in engineering and spent two years in that curriculum. Then I encountered a teacher who literally changed my life by opening up possibilities that I didn't know existed. He was a philosophy faculty member named Robert Whalen (long deceased now). He was not a particularly high-level researcher, but he knew the history of philosophy and he introduced me to a world of abstract ideas that just thrilled me and excited me to a degree I had never experienced. He gathered around him a small group of students and, remarkably, three of us became professional philosophers. That was a turning point in my life. It has stuck with me because it made me realize how important teachers are and what faculty members can accomplish in working with young people. So I ended by earning my bachelor's degree in philosophy. Then, having picked up the habit of hard work, I finished my Ph.D. at the University of Rochester in about two and a half years.

Among the personal attributes that contributed to my success, people would probably point out my willingness to work hard, as well as to listen to people and take their concerns into consideration, the ability to put matters in context, to see the bigger picture, look beyond the moment, and take personal responsibility.

FL: What were the challenges that the University of Oregon faced when you became president?

MB: It was at a time when it looked as though Oregon's economy was really booming. They were moving into the early stages of information technology (IT) development and the state had good tax revenues, so it looked like the challenge was to build a good Association of American Universities research university into an even better one. There had been some conflict between the former president and the governor; but when someone new comes in, you get the benefit of the doubt, so that didn't prove to be a problem. Things looked bright for about a year and a half.

FL: Then there were some issues, weren't there?

MB: After about a year and a half, there was a property tax revolt of major proportions and the state passed Measure 5, which was comparable to California's Prop 13. The income tax was already regressive and people felt that they were really paying the maximum amount they could be expected to pay in state taxes. There is no sales tax in Oregon. In effect, the people of Oregon made the decision that they didn't want to support certain services, like higher education, at the level they had been funding them. In a three-year period, we lost about 75 percent of our state funding.

Those were extraordinarily difficult times. We formed a blue ribbon committee of faculty and administrators to make recommendations on what should be done. My only advice to the committee was not to cut across the board because that would degrade the institution to an intolerable level, since it had not been well funded even before this drastic budget reduction. Naturally, they gave me a menu of choices, since no committee wants to take direct responsibility for cuts. I understood that I had to make the final decisions. I worried a lot about it and then I made what I considered to be the best possible choices. Oregon operates in a town hall meeting environment with no faculty senate, so to announce the cuts we reserved the largest space on campus: still it was overflowing. I told the assembly that we would close a college, the college of physical education, which housed a number of programs, including geriatrics. I also closed all of the Ph.D. programs in education except special education and cut back on arts and sciences, but the major thrust was closing the college. A thousand people were going to be put out of work and a large number of degree programs reduced or closed. The dean of the college of physical education, whom everyone knew was dying of cancer, stood and made the case for his unit, telling his colleagues that though it was his college that was being closed today, their college could be next. I had to reply that this was the decision; it was what we had to do to preserve the institution. That was a tough time and a depressing year followed it.

We lost several thousand students when we made the original cutbacks. One day before Measure 5 was to be enacted, in a meeting with students who were very upset because we had cancelled a Grateful Dead concert, I told them that the concert ought to be the least of their worries because Measure 5 was going to affect their tuition drastically: it might even double. I was wrong about that: it tripled.

Then, over the next year, a solution emerged that I was able to develop. As the state reduced the budget to a single digit percentage of expenditures, we began to operate as if we were a private institution, recruiting out-of-state students. Frankly, that was the key that turned the situation around. What we did was to turn the University of Oregon into what was essentially a semi-private institution. Within two years not only did the enrollment come back up, but the quality of the programs improved. Students were wearing tee shirts that said "The University of California at Eugene Oregon." It was a difficult time, but when I left the institution I was able to go feeling that we had not only turned around the problem but positioned the institution so that it would be better in the future. Of course that doesn't mean that everyone liked what I did: the departments that were cut were unhappy and some of the students graduating from programs that were closed refused to shake my hand at graduation, but the most important fact is that what we did was a success, not merely in terms of rescuing but improving the institution during hard times.

FL: That is a remarkable example of leadership in a difficult situation. You made the hard choices because you had to do the right thing for the institution. Certainly you paid a price as the focus of the pain and anger of the people who were adversely affected by the cuts, but in the end, you were able to see that you had made the right choices for the university. Indiana, with its eight campuses and nearly 100,000 students, presented new challenges. What were the major issues you needed to tackle when you assumed that presidency?

MB: Indiana was, as Midwestern Big Ten universities tend to be, on much firmer ground. The people of the state of Indiana were committed to the success of Indiana University and, along with Purdue, it is regarded as one of the jeweled crowns of the state. The great challenge was the complexity of the institution. It wasn't a single campus but eight, including a medical school, and the most serious problem was how to resist the normal academic desire for so much autonomy that the institution spins apart. How do you sustain the unity, purpose, and identity of a single institution that complex? It's not a system in the way that California and New York have state university systems, and it's not a major campus with some small regional campuses like the University of Michigan. In addition, the complexity and size of the Indianapolis campus, combined with the medical school, made it a serious competitor with the more traditional Big Ten campus in Bloomington. The challenge was to make all of these units work together.

FL: What effects did the role and demands of each of these leadership posts have on your family life?

MB: I think that you identify with the university—you become the university—when you are the president. Not only do you internalize the values of the institution, but the successes and failures of the institution are yours personally. You take on the role of being the institution. That happens whether you like it or not and my philosophy has always been not only to accept it but to embrace it. These presidencies are not jobs. They are lives. The institution becomes your life. I never thought I was off. I'm a bit of a workaholic, but when I got finished with the dinner meetings about seven or nine o'clock at night, I'd start on my paperwork and I would do the paperwork until I fell asleep at 11:30 or so and then be up for my breakfast meeting to start all over again, seven days a week. To my great benefit, my wife Peg understands this as well. She's a faculty member but, within the context of her own academic work, she was willing to devote the time necessary to be very supportive and she understood what was required. It's all consuming and there were some family stresses, but probably not more than one would find at any other high-level job.

FL: What did each of your internal constituencies—governing boards, faculty, students, staff, and administrators—expect of you at each of your presidencies?

MB: All of the multiple constituencies, internal and external have their own different interests, and they don't always coincide. I always thought that it was extremely important to work well with the university's board. In public universities, board members are chosen not necessarily because of their leadership potential for the institution, but rather because of their connections with the political party in power or the governor. Sometimes they're chosen because they have been critical of the university and they have their own agendas. I felt that communication with the members of the board was critical and I worked hard at it. Before our monthly board meeting, I would call every board member and spend enough time on the phone with each of them to make sure not only that they understood the issues coming up, but understood them in relation to their specific concern. I would also visit them once or twice a year in their own offices. I would listen very carefully to what they had to say. That doesn't mean that I always agreed with every board member, but they knew that I was listening and when we disagreed, I acknowledged that. My relationship with the board was always good, and that's not always true for presidents in public universities.

The faculty have different interests, and their interests vary according to their academic disciplines. At Indiana, I saw that they were in the Stone Age in terms of information technology. I think that it is impossible to be a successful major research university today unless you have a leadership role in IT, so I conducted an international search, hired a very strong chief information officer, and we undertook a strategic plan in IT. We were able to move into the top institutions in the area of information technology in a short period of time.

A great many faculty members were excited about that, but not all of my friends in the humanities were. Some humanists thought that we were neglecting the traditional studies, even though that was where I came from and where I taught every year at both of my presidencies. I tried to support my faculty colleagues in the humanities by addressing their needs, for example, by providing research funding when various foundations stopped supporting humanities research. That helped, but still they thought that their interests were not well served.

Faculty politics, independent of discipline, is always very interesting. On one hand, faculty are creative and ground-breaking in their fields. On the other hand, they're very conservative in protection of their individual rights and prestige. That is independent of their political views, conservative or liberal.

FL: Would you like to say anything about what students expected of you?

MB: With a hundred thousand students at Indiana University, it was hard to know very many of them personally. I tried. I met with student groups, such as the student newspaper staff. I became friends with those I got to know in the student leadership, but it was very difficult to become familiar with individuals in the general student body. I think that's one of the difficulties of the presidency of these very large institutions.

FL: I experienced the same frustrations. I could get to know the student leaders and I went to the dormitories every year for fireside chats, but my best efforts were just a drop in the bucket so far as getting to know a student body of some 52,000 was concerned.

MB: I did continue to keep clearly in mind that one of the key purposes of the university is the education of undergraduates. That's a principle drawn from my own undergraduate experience.

FL: What did you feel you owed to all of these constituencies? What did you feel that you needed to do in response to their needs and demands?

MB: My philosophy of leadership is based on my perception that, to oversimplify considerably, there are at the extremes two kinds of presidential leadership. The first type is interested in communication and good feelings. They're not necessarily decision makers. They're very personable. Warm and fuzzy is the term that comes to mind. When there is a hard decision to make, they tend to postpone it or get someone else to do it for them. The second type is more focused on future directions. Of course, these are extremes. Real presidents fall somewhere on the continuum between the two end points. I feel very uncomfortable with the first type of leadership. Having identified with the institution, I have always wanted it to get better and I'll make the hard decisions. I will take personal responsibility for my decision and, if it's a tough one, even though I've consulted widely, I don't blame it on the people I consulted. I'll take the heat for any decision I make. I have a responsibility to the institution's constituents to act in the best interest of the whole university. My obligations to faculty members and other constituents were to support them in their academic efforts and to make the institution as a whole a better institution.

FL: What do you feel was your greatest challenge as a leader?

MB: The crisis in funding at the University of Oregon. I was pleased and proud that it turned out in the end as I had hoped and predicted it would. That was very hard, but another difficult time was at Indiana with athletics. That is a situation I cannot discuss because of pending litigation.

FL: Let's talk a little about organizational structure. How have you recruited and structured your leadership team in each institution?

MB: Some people come into a presidential position, listen carefully to the board, and say that we have to clean house and start all over again. I have never accepted that. There has always been some initial turnover of people who weren't working at a high level of performance, folks who retired early but were still in office, but it was usually very few. By and large, the people I found in place at my presidencies were very good. They were a high level team that just needed to be reoriented and had the ability, as good professionals, to be flexible, open, and change their loyalties. I never worried about the restructuring as much as I did about being sure we had the right people in the right positions. I tend to assimilate myself to the structure that exists rather than make massive changes.

FL: What was the highest-level position on each of the several campuses of Indiana University?

MB: Each campus has a chancellor. On the two larger campuses, Bloomington and Indianapolis, the chancellor is like a provost with additional powers to look after student affairs, for example. Other functions were carried out by my leadership team of vice presidents. My leadership team and I couldn't get around to every campus, so we depended upon the chancellors of the six smaller campuses to do the vast majority of the work, including community relations. Any time that external constituents were involved, particularly governmental constituents, I worked together with all the chancellors. I told them that sending separate individual messages to legislators was a hanging offense and that we had to stay together as a team, even if the budget favored one campus over another. As a result, I never had any issues on this score.

FL: What are the some of the specific qualities that you look for in the people that you choose to work with and depend upon?

MB: The most important attribute is how smart they are. I want to work with smart people, people who get it, who don't have to be told twice. I want to work with people who are self-starters, who can initiate action. We agree upon the goals that we need to accomplish. I don't micro-manage. I want them to keep me up to date on what they're doing, but I expect them to work through it. I want people who understand loyalty—not in the sense of concealing wrongdoing, if there is any—but loyalty to the team and the university. They must have the ability to work together and feel good about each other. They don't have to go off and party together; they don't have to be the best of friends on Saturday night; but they have to be a good working team, mutually supportive of each other, self starters and again, very smart.

FL: I know that in each post you've been expected to spend a lot of time away from the university. As a president you are the chief representative of the university to the alumni and the public and the primary person who solicits major gifts. In each of these posts, have you had someone in your administration who stood in for you, handling the day-to-day work of the university while you were gone?

MB: No. The fact is that in this day and age, you can always be in contact through Blackberries, telephones, and other communication devices. Fortunately I don't have to lug around my laptop anymore.

FL: I want to talk a little bit about the vision. How did you formulate a vision for the future at each of the institutions that you served?

MB: Visions can't be imported. They have to be homegrown. I always found that it took about a year, one cycle, to really understand the depth and the subtlety of an institution. Even though in some ways public research universities may look alike, there are very important, subtle differences in terms of their traditions and their aspirations, as well as their strengths and weaknesses. I always spent the first year going through a planning process. It was good for the institutions to have that exercise in self-reflection, but it was essential for me in order to understand what each institution was about. Once I understood what its aspirations were and what was possible in terms of its strengths, then I would let a vision emerge. I would constantly test and retest that vision. I'm a philosopher and philosophy is mostly done through dialectic debate, so I would formulate a position that I thought might work and I would go into a group to try it out. I wanted people to argue with me. Could I defend this position? Did this make sense? Did they have objections? That's the process. It just takes some time and you have to be patient with it. But at the end of the process, there emerges a future vision of the institution that is consistent with and indeed underlies what its members want it to become but is more than they are currently able to reach. The vision of the future has to be a stretch, something more than they had in their minds when they started.

Let me go back to information technology for an example. Even though we started from nowhere, the vision was to make Indiana University a leader in information technology in absolute terms nationally and internationally. We had the wherewithal to do it, but the university was not organized to accomplish it. When I said that, people didn't have a clue what I was talking about and weren't willing to accept it, but we accomplished what we set out to do. I'll give you another example, this one in the area of fund raising. Indiana University was at the bottom of the Big Ten in numbers of chairs and professorships. I worked with the foundation board (which as you know is different from the governance board in public institutions) and said that we were going to have a campaign and when we finish this campaign, we'll be number one in the Big Ten in chairs and professorships. They thought I was from Mars. The fact of the matter is that we did it and we had an extraordinarily successful campaign. That was what we needed at the institution, that was what the people wanted, but they were not willing to say that was where we were going. They needed someone to stand up and say that this is our goal, we're going to focus on it, we're going to put our energy, our people on it and we'll get it done. That's what it took. Of course everyone was happy when it was accomplished, but they didn't believe it was possible when we started.

FL: What strategies did you use to communicate and create buy-in to the vision by the academic community, as well as the external constituencies, such as alumni and friends?

MB: I tried grassroots planning in the first year. I would meet with departments and colleges, cross sections of faculty, and department heads. I never got complete buy-in from any group of faculty. Their interests are more focused in their disciplines. I think campus politics plays a part there too. I did get more buy-in than when I started and I got enough buy-in to get it done, but there were always those who were skeptical and some who were cynical. In this day and age, if you let that control your actions as president, you're not going to get anything done.

FL: You mention the sometimes narrow disciplinary focus of faculty scholars. Do you foresee that one day departmental barriers will be broken down and we will manage our faculty in a different kind of structure?

MB: I don't believe so, because, given all the increased communication opportunities, faculty members no longer identify with the institution, at least faculty in big research universities. They identify with people in their subdiscipline on a national and international basis. They don't talk to the people in the same department down the hall. They talk to people half way across the country and that is their support group, not their local colleagues. The barriers are no longer local, institutional barriers that you have a hope of breaking down by bringing people together at your house for dinner. You can't do that any more because the identification of faculty members is in a much more dispersed fashion and doesn't rely upon institutional connections. At least in the foreseeable future, I don't think we'll break down those barriers.

FL: You are probably right about the fact that faculty find their colleagues and support groups in their highly specialized subdisciplines, which are national and international in scope. As you know, that was true in research universities even before we had a greatly expanded communication network. But in some cases you do see people bringing together disparate disciplines to focus on a problem. A Rutgers neuroscience faculty member came in and immediately started working with people in computer science, anthropology, and other areas on a multifaceted problem so, all of a sudden, a cluster of people who would never have spoken to each other were working together on key projects. He explained that he was a scientist, but many large problems require bringing in other disciplines in an effort to reach a solution. Of course many of our interdisciplinary research and teaching centers and institutes are set up to serve just that purpose.

MB: We are seeing the growth of disciplines in a much more rapid fashion than we've ever seen before. People from certain fields are coming together to create new disciplines. They may not be long-lived, but those multi-disciplinary attempts or the invention of new disciplines, once they get a foothold, begin to look at relationships across campuses, across states, across countries, and they too then become insular. It's exciting for that period of time when new constellations are coming together, but as soon as they form and are productive, they're not going to be unique. There will be similar constellations across the country and those will become the lines of communication among faculty.

FL: How have you strategized translating your understanding of each university together with the external realities into a long-range plan for change and improvement?

MB: I believe in grassroots planning. I think you have to go through data gathering and then it falls to leadership groups to figure out the future focus. You start very early getting a fix on it, scanning the institution to pick out the strengths and weaknesses, trying to be as factual as possible, and often involving external consultants to give some validity to the claims and simultaneously working to create the long range, global vision. Then, in planning, you bring the two things together. I think that's a healthy exercise. Probably presidents have an opportunity to do it once during their tenure unless they happen to be there for twenty years. Then they have to reinvent themselves and the institution. But, as you know, most of these presidencies last five to ten years, so you only have one opportunity to do long-range planning, and it's best to do that early in your presidency.

FL: How did you link the changes you wanted to make to the financial budgeting process of each institution?

MB: You always have to make clear that it's the plan that drives the budget, not the other way around. But the fact of the matter is that there are so many fixed costs at these universities and so many reasonably good directions you don't want to pull back from, that your flexibility is within a 5 to 10 percent level. It's within that 5 to 10 percent margin that you can make changes. I always found that the best way to promote the goals of the plan is to identify new revenue sources and use those to provide incentives for the plan. As I mentioned in the case of private fund raising for endowed chairs and professorships, you can provide them to the areas you want to develop. We went out and raised external funds rather than trying to reallocate. I think you can do that to motivate the changes and once you get that momentum going, then you can begin to shift budgets around. But even if you're successful, the redistribution will be just five to ten percent.

FL: How have you gotten faculty on board and enthusiastic about changes?

MB: I haven't always been able to do that. I think there are some faculty who are open to change and looking for new ways, so of course you work with them. Then there's a good middle group who see not merely that the money is there, but there's some intellectual excitement and new opportunities. What you've drawn out in the plan is actually their tacit aspirations. But there will be some faculty members who are either so focused on their own narrow work or their own personal lives that you're not going to bring them along, and then there are always the cynics. If we wait to see if we can get eighty or ninety percent of the faculty headed in the same direction, I think that we'll never get anything done. At the same time you can't have a successful plan with just ten or twenty percent of the faculty behind you. You have to have a good critical mass.

FL: Making change often is not synonymous with making friends. Can you describe one or more critical incidents, how they arose and how you dealt with them?

MB: For the most part, in Oregon or elsewhere, in the other hard decisions that I had to make there was reasonable acceptance. But I have learned how not to take personally the concerns and sometimes the statements of those virulently opposed to decisions I have taken for the good of the institution.

FL: In instances like the Oregon situation in which you took actions that displeased many people, what was the media reaction? How did they deal with the issue? Were you a villain or were you a hero?

MB: Externally I got credit for doing the hard work. While Measure 5 was being debated, I was very vocal. Interestingly, Oregon has a law that prohibits the heads of agencies, and that includes the presidents of the universities, from speaking about any issue pending before the state legislature. Obviously I was on a stump to try as best I could to prevent this measure from passing. I and other opponents of the measure failed in that, but even so I would give speeches in which I would tell people that you must understand that I can't say anything about this, but if I were to say something.... I filled the newspapers with op-eds. At the board level, the chancellor level, the legislative and the gubernatorial level, I think there was appreciation that I was willing to make the hard decisions. The newspapers sometimes were interesting. They wanted to know how many people were going to be fired, the names of everyone, and when. I said that these were personnel issues and we weren't going to talk to them about it. There was a little conflict with the newspapers, but by and large, the external reception of this rather hard-nosed approach, combined with a plan for the future, was well received.

FL: Let's go on to monitoring progress and celebrating success. What methods did you use to assess the outcomes of your initiatives at each of the institutions?

MB: At Indiana, we set specific goals and we measured ourselves against peers. We did not use *U.S. News and World Report* and other such measures, but we looked more carefully, for example, at the amount of private funds we raised each year, at the standing of our information technology among peers, at the number of faculty members who won awards, and the placement of our graduating students. We looked at a number of concrete measures, set up specific goals, and met them.

Of course in regard to any of these goals, there can be conflicting opinions. For example, Indiana is a rather homogenous state and seven of the eight Indiana University campuses draw students almost exclusively inside the state. However the Bloomington Campus has an opportunity to recruit nationally and internationally, which gave us a real opportunity to increase the diversity of the campus, thereby providing a better education for all the students. That caused us to measure our admissions criteria in ways other than simply SAT scores. Some faculty members wanted to measure principally in terms of SAT scores. I have always thought that greater diversity creates a better environment for all students and that diversity is a positive measure. So there can be disagreement about whether you are making progress based on disagreement about the metrics, but, for the most part, we had clear metrics.

FL: What importance did you place on the roles of the University of Oregon and Indiana University in their communities?

MB: In the case of Oregon, particularly given the financial situation, we were mostly inwardly directed, but in the early 1990s we did some external outreach and started a research park. At Indiana University, I made it a major initiative, part of our strategic plan, that we would be engaged with our communities and the state. It seems to me that for public universities, the most important variable in their success is not the president or even the governor: it's the economy of the state. A public university engaged in the economy of the state will create a greater partnership with elected officials and business leaders as well as helping itself.

I worked very hard in Indiana to improve the economy of the state and made it a major issue, particularly my last few years there. Indiana had a Rust Belt economy, a basic manufacturing economy that needed to change dramatically. In one instance, we needed some start-up funding for transferring research activity to the private sector and for some partnerships between university faculty and the private sector. I went to the lieutenant governor who was the head of the department of commerce and told him that we needed a research fund of about $25 million a year, a relatively small amount compared to our neighboring states. He turned ashen. I went around the entire state and hired a couple of people to help me to connect with various constituencies. I talked to every Rotary Club, talked to all of the fraternal organizations, the Lions, the Elks, and so on, had articles in all the newspapers, got the professional associations and the business community on board, had industrial leaders testifying before the state senate and so on. We got the funding we needed from the state. That was a breakthrough. It seemed to me that Indiana University had a real opportunity in the biomedical fields. It has the only medical school in the state and that offered us a leadership opportunity to change the economy. The school of medicine faculty were good researchers; they were also entrepreneurial and they were open to this approach. So I went to the Lilly Endowment, which is Indianapolis based, and asked them for very significant dollars. It turned out that over a several year period they gave us almost $250 million. The Lilly Endowment had rarely given money to public universities and had never provided funds for life sciences and medical studies, but they gained trust in us and made a major investment. Right now the state is entering a new economic era with an interest primarily in biomedical research, some information technology as well, and, with Purdue, in advanced manufacturing. I think the state's economy is turning around. The universities, and Indiana University in particular, have gotten very significant credit for that.

I saw my role at IU differently than I did my role at Oregon. In Indiana, the need to engage the university in the future of the state was primary, so I spent a lot of time with business leaders as well as elected officials. You've got to adjust yourself to the situation. In Oregon, that wasn't the right approach. In Indiana, it was the required approach, so we made it part of our strategic plan. When I started to do that, shortly after I arrived at Indiana and before the economy really went into the tank, people on campus didn't understand what I was talking about, but over time, they embraced it. We created a new college called the School of Informatics. We expected about 150 majors in the first couple of years. In the first year we had 1,200 majors. There was enormous capital investment by the state in new university research facilities. That had never happened before; they had never supported research facilities. It was a dramatic turnaround in the relationship and partnership with the state because the times and the environment demanded it, not for some abstract reason.

FL: What did the alumni expect of you?

MB: It's interesting. Indiana has a basketball team that does well. Some—perhaps many—alumni were more interested in this than in our intellectual accomplishments, so part of my job was to present the intellectual strengths of undergraduate education and research. Towards the end of my tenure there, alumni were much more alert and supportive of our engagement activities with the state.

FL: What part of your work have you enjoyed most?

MB: That's a hard question. I think the part I enjoyed most was working with the leadership team in formulating our goals and working together to get it done. It made me feel good to be part of a team aimed in the same direction, working hard, and being able to enjoy some of the successes. I probably enjoyed that more than the point when the final success was reached, when we met our metrics, when we became first in the number of chairs and professorships. That was nice and got a lot of notice but the fact of the matter I think is that I just enjoyed working with these people towards a common goal.

FL: How many chairs did you have and what was the level at which they were funded?

MB: We started with under a hundred and within five years we had 350 to 400, funded at approximately one to one and a half million each.

FL: Every leader experiences planned and unplanned events that escalate into time-consuming crises. Among the most common are fiscal challenges or contract negotiations and PR challenges that crop up unexpectedly. Do you have any crisis management stories that you would like to share, other than the funding crisis in Oregon?

MB: When *Time* magazine named Indiana University as the number one undergraduate institution in the country among public universities, we were very proud of that and it was quite unexpected. They just sent teams to each of the leading campuses. We weren't able to prompt it, it just occurred. Of course after we were so designated we put it on billboards—I mean that literally—and it was a big boost. Apparently that had caught the eye of the *Princeton Review* (which has no connection with Princeton University) and the *Princeton Review* then labeled us the leading party school in the country the following year. The way they undertake their research is by standing outside of bars on

Friday and Saturday nights (I'm not making this up) and interviewing students who leave the bars about whether or not they had a good time. We had gotten a lot of publicity from the *Time* magazine report and we got a lot of publicity from the *Princeton Review* party school designation. Once we were labeled a party school, we had additional notice. *Girls Gone Wild* came to campus to film our coeds and bars, then a California pornography company came into one of our dorms uninvited, and possibly illegally, to do some filming with actresses and volunteer male students, so it was a crisis of some proportions. TV shock commentators took up the criticism. We went from being able to boast that we had the greatest undergraduate program to dealing with all of these bottom feeders who came in and tried to take advantage of the publicity they could generate. We had a crisis management team and I had on staff a person who was a media chief of staff, so we did as much as we could to answer things directly and, when necessary, put the president up front. I think we handled it as well as we could, but these crisis management situations become very time consuming.

FL: Just one more set of questions before we get into the National Intercollegiate Athletic Association. Is there anything more that you want to say about how you would define leadership? You gave two excellent examples of your own leadership.

MB: I think leadership consists of the ability to see ahead and put things in global context, to identify with the aspirations and the values of the institution, to take personal responsibility, and, frankly, to work hard.

FL: What are the most important qualities of the university president today?

MB: I think you have to understand the context in which you're working and realize that various constituencies or individuals will press you for this or that, but that you have to make the right decisions, not the politically expedient ones. Don't be deterred by the negative comments of those whose positions you did not adopt. There are some presidents who have been in office for a long time in various institutions who were beloved by their institutions and have managed to make few decisions during their tenure. I would expect that the campus has good feelings about them, but I wouldn't consider them strong leaders. It isn't necessary to have conflict to be a leader but it does come sometimes with the position. I think you have to be willing to take strong positions when you understand that it definitely benefits the entire institution.

FL: How have the role and demands of the presidency changed over the past few decades in response to the following factors, first the disinvestment of the states in public higher education?

MB: It has made presidents much more committed to finding other sources of funds and in some, though not all cases, has caused them to redistribute funds on campus. It has made the job much more externally directed than it has been in the past. The bad news is that that's a trend that has not abated.

FL: The second factor is the technological revolution.

MB: I think it's changed the way the presidency is conducted. The technological revolution now allows you to be in communication all the time. It increases your workload dramatically. It gives you more opportunity to understand the detail, but it is enormously time consuming.

FL: The third factor is the growing role of private support and commercial application in university research.

MB: I think the intersection between universities and the state or community in all research institutions is now such that the boundaries between what is the university and what is not the university have been blurred, even broken down. I personally think that that's good. Some would like to keep the ivy-covered walls between the university and the external community. I think that in the future, we're going to see a greater blurring of those boundaries. I think it's healthy from the university's point of view, as we become more engaged in the rest of the world's activities and local activities, and it's of great benefit to those who help to support the institution, particularly the taxpayers.

FL: And the last factor is the increasingly strident demands of students and politicians for high quality and accountability in both expenditures and results.

MB: I think we're all accountable in much more explicit ways that we have been in the past. Rather than resist that, it's always been my view that what presidents have to do is make sure you use the right metrics and then be held accountable to it, not just you personally, but the institution. That is a change that puts more pressure on the office and the institution, but I think it's a healthy change.

FL: Presidencies were once measured in decades but now are more typically limited to terms of four or five years. Do you believe that the changes in the role have brought that about or are there other reasons for this accelerated rate of attrition?

MB: Let me tell you a story. William Bryan was the president of Indiana University for almost forty years, starting before the turn of the twentieth century. This is what his day consisted of. After rising and having breakfast, at about 9:30, he would take his horse and buggy and he would drive over to the other part of the campus where his office was. He'd hold meetings from about 10:00 to 12:00, no more than ten minutes a meeting, and then he would go home for lunch. He would spend the rest of the day in his home office with handwritten correspondence or writing lectures and papers. He had built into his contract that there would be no social events. No president has that luxury today.

FL: No one could survive.

MB: It would be a short tenure. The time demands, the pressures for decisions, the dealing with far more vociferous constituency groups make that impossible. The job has changed dramatically.

FL: How would you characterize your leadership style?

MB: I think I'm aggressive. People sometimes think that when I try out an idea, I'm really settled in it. They don't understand the dialectic. I want to put things out tentatively, get feedback and understand all of the points of view, so the dialectic is very important to me. I'm value oriented. I'm a long-range thinker. My strength lies in thinking of strategic context and global positioning of the institution as opposed to details. I'm not a particularly warm and fuzzy guy and that may grate on some people but that's something I've learned about myself and I'm no longer upset about it. I'm a strategic thinker. I'm demanding and sometimes impatient with those who just don't get it.

FL: What do you feel have been the most critical capital investments made under your leadership at each university?

MB: I think that at IU, we made very significant investments in research facilities and laboratories, both in the medical school—often in partnership with the private sector—and on the Bloomington Campus. At one point we had, proportionally, the most construction in the history of the institution. We made several billion dollars worth of capital investment during my tenure. It was quite a remarkable transition once we got the state to understand the importance of research facilities, especially laboratories, and facilities in the performing arts. So that turned out to be an important part of our goal. Here the public institutions do have one advantage over the privates. That is, when the times are good, when the economy is strong, you can convince the legislature to make investments of a capital nature. After all they don't pay for it now. They may bond it for the next thirty years, but they're feeling good about the budget and they will undertake those obligations. So I think IU has been advantaged in that regard.

FL: What do you believe is the most significant legacy that you left to the University of Oregon?

MB: My legacy is probably the repositioning and rethinking of what it needed to do to succeed, that it needed to reach out beyond its borders in terms of attracting non-resident students. It needed a different kind of budgetary approach than the traditional one that the system imposed. It needed to be a national university and I think that came out as a realization in the process of solving the budget cutback problems.

FL: Why did you leave Oregon to accept Indiana?

MB: I felt I couldn't leave Oregon until we were well on the way to solving the budgetary problems. Then there was this wonderful opportunity to go to a major Midwestern public university. I've always believed that the heart of public education in America is in the Big Ten group. There are wonderful public universities elsewhere of very high stature, from the University of Washington and Cal Berkeley on the West Coast to Rutgers and the University of North Carolina at Chapel Hill on the East Coast, but the heart of public education always seemed to me to be in the Big Ten institutions and when I had an opportunity to play a leadership role in one of those institutions, I decided to move on.

FL: What do you see as your most important legacy to Indiana University?

MB: I think Indiana has made some dramatic improvements in several areas. It's so big and complex I can't say that there's one legacy. The research funding tripled. The endowment I think has increased sixfold. The quality of the students is high, the capital improvements are substantial, the role in state economic development has increased dramatically, so there's a whole bunch of metrics that have improved.

FL: Certainly the university has improved in regard to its technology infrastructure.

MB: The university has improved its technology, its engagement with the state, and its leadership in certain fields, such as biomedicine. The hospitals associated with the medical school were facing some very serious financial problems about six or seven years ago and I led an effort to consolidate those hospitals with a private institution, Methodist Hospital, to create a new hospital system named Clarion. That was the largest privatization ever undertaken in the state. I can't overestimate how important the medical school is. Particularly during that transition, the medical school took up a quarter of my time, and I don't think you're going to see any great public universities in the future unless they have research-oriented medical schools. Over 50 percent of the research funding now comes through NIH and there's going to be a differentiation between those that can really engage wholly in the life sciences and those that cannot. I would say that generally the institution is much better positioned for the future than it was in the past. It's ready for the rest of the twenty-first century.

FL: How did you make your decision to leave Indiana University to head the NCAA?

MB: Life's an adventure and, if you allow me, I have a chunk theory of careers. My chunk theory is that about every five years, plus or minus a year, you have to ask yourself and your family if you want another chunk. You could say yes, that's great we'll do another chunk here, but if you say I've done as much as I can here and maybe we should look elsewhere, that's fine, but I think you need to have that assessment. After five years with Oregon, we sat down, asked ourselves if we wanted another chunk, and thought that we'd see what opportunities came up. At Indiana, I was in my second chunk. After the first five years we decided that we'd like to go again. I was already beginning to think about whether or not I wanted to do a third chunk when I was contacted by the NCAA. I was thinking of another university or more likely a third chunk at IU, so I threw out the initial inquiry. My wife said, "Wait a second, why don't you look at this?" We did. It was fortuitous and unplanned, but that's why I feel that life is an adventure. You have to be willing to take interesting opportunities when they arrive and take the risks that come with them.

FL: What advice would you give to new presidents?

MB: Even if you come from the institution, you still have to take a year to listen and learn. Don't jump to conclusions. Really try to absorb the aspirations and traditions and subtleties of the institution. So don't act too quickly, don't go in and fire the senior staff, don't go in and say you've got a plan that you're going to impose upon the institution. Don't make quick decisions on the people who work for you or with you. Give it time; be patient.

FL: Is there anything that you would choose to tackle first?

MB: In each institution, there are a few little things that are very annoying. For example, it may be that people are just not happy with the janitorial service, or the staff salaries may be incredibly low. There will be some little things that really don't fall into a large-scale plan. You can go fix those immediately. Take care of the odds and ends, but don't put yourself in a position that would force you to foreclose any major new directions.

FL: What is the most critical skill or set of skills that presidents will need in order to succeed in the future and how do those differ from the skills needed in the past?

MB: I think the job is so complex, particularly at the large research universities, public or private, that you have to know how to keep many things in the air at the same time rather than doing them sequentially. You must be capable of focusing on a wide range of issues simultaneously. I think that in the past, there was far less need for crisis management, far less necessity for working with the media: you could take your time and do things as they came up. You don't have that luxury anymore.

FL: What has been at the core of your work in higher education?

MB: It's all about the students. It's all about the future. It's all about others. Work in higher education is altruistic, when it's done well. It's about the students getting a good education in the way that my undergraduate teacher, Robert Whalen, taught me the virtues and values of intellectual thought. In the large public universities, it's also about the people in the state. It's about the next generation—and it's about social change: these institutions are the instruments of social change.

FL: What are the underlying purposes that you have worked to accomplish?

MB: My purposes have been to leave the institution better than I found it; to reposition the institution so that it is a positive force, particularly in the state, but also nationally and internationally; and to make the institution a valued part not just of the intellectual climate but the social and cultural climate.

FL: Let's move on now to national policy: the NCAA. All of the presidents I know have found that, in recent years, higher education has become the focus of intense public interest, with all that entails, both good and bad. Of course college athletics has always been a focus of public interest, to the extent that politicians have sometimes tried to exert influence over it. What has been your experience as president of the NCAA? How has media and political attention helped or hurt you and the organization and your attempts to get your agenda before the public for a full and accurate hearing?

MB: One of the differences between being a university president and being president of the NCAA is the amount of media attention and visibility. Certainly a president, especially a public university president, gets a lot of media attention within the state and he or she is subject to newspaper and TV interest all the time. But it shifted to a national forum when I became associated with the NCAA. I don't seek it and sometimes it's not helpful but there is no avoiding the media attention. I have some very good help at the NCAA. I work with superb people and to the best of our ability we try together to manage it so that our message gets out in the best way possible. But media attention comes with the office and that's been a learning experience.

Let me turn to politics, because I think it really opens up a much deeper and important question. What I think we're beginning to see on a national basis is an attempt to federalize universities. One of the key strengths of American higher education is the diversity of the kinds of institutions and the autonomy that they have held from the state and federal government. That is under attack. We see attempts in the Congress to regulate tuition, for example, as well as to influence research much more than in the past, and to control policy through student financial aid. All of these are wedge issues to get the federal government into higher education. Potentially the biggest wedge issue is athletics. The NCAA has been involved in more and more congressional hearings. Some of it is just because certain elected officials would like to get re-elected and they can help make their case back home by showing that they're standing up for their school, no matter what violations the institution committed. But it's also true that, at least covertly, people feel that if you can get into intercollegiate athletics at the federal level, then you can you use it as a wedge issue to get into all of higher education at the federal level. I would not be surprised to see an increase in federal pressure.

My own experience with intervention in either athletics or academics at the state level has been minimal. As a university president I did see a few local legislators on the far right side of the political spectrum who wanted to close down the Kinsey Institute in Indiana University or who made anti-gay statements, but they were just making points at home. None of it was very threatening and I never experienced a gubernatorial intervention. Some politicians suffer from the desire to show that they are arguing in favor of their constituents and for a particular coach or a particular team against the school administration. We've seen that on a number of occasions, but I don't think it has increased, and I believe that a good president can deal with it. I think the federal trend is much more important.

FL: You hit the ground running at the NCAA. You were able, on coming in, to take off on the basis of your January 2001 speech to the National Press Club on "Academics First: Reforming Intercollegiate Athletics." As you know, the NCAA was already in the process of formulating and trying to bring to its board of directors a full program of academic reforms to increase the entrance requirements for student athletes, to strengthen progress toward degree requirements, lay down guidelines for more accurate graduation rate collection, and formulate graduation rate expectations, with penalties for failing to achieve them. Your coming coincided so beautifully with the reform movement that there was real hope that we would be able to get these things done. Nevertheless, in talking to some of our colleagues, I have found great skepticism among leaders in higher education about our ability to take control and clear up problems in recruiting, admissions, retention, graduation, student athlete conduct, and in the funding of athletics including the huge escalation in college coaching salaries, football and basketball in particular. One leader's opinion was that the only way out of the recurring scandal would be for the professional teams to institute farm teams, especially in basketball and football, in order to develop the talents of young people who really have no interest in higher education but are forced into it in order to prepare for professional careers. Do you think that farm systems in those sports would be a good idea and would relieve the universities of some of the pressures associated with athletics today?

MB: I think if you started minor leagues in the key sports that generate all the revenue, basketball and football, you would destroy college sports as we know it. I think that is throwing up your hands and saying it doesn't work. Once you rent out the stadiums, license the logos and start to pay the players, the fan interest will disappear. You can fill a stadium with a hundred and five thousand people because students are playing for Michigan or Ohio State. You can't fill the stands with some minor league club that has no relationship between the players and the institution at all. Minor league clubs tend to lose money and fail: college sports as we know it would simply go away.

FL: What would happen to the other sports?

MB: You would have no money to support them. As you well know, the way it works is that there is a redistribution of funds. College basketball and football subsidize all the other sports. In these very difficult financial times, universities would have to put in an enormous amount of money to support the non-revenue sports, given the loss of revenue that would occur if basketball and football moved to a farm team system. College sports as we know it would disappear.

FL: Returning to the earlier subject of academic reform, perhaps you could talk a little bit about what you feel will happen as a result of the measures now being enacted by the NCAA.

MB: The two primary problems facing college sports today are the needs first for academic reform, and second for fiscal responsibility. The need for academic reform began to be discussed in earnest about a decade or more ago, in the first Knight Commission Report, issued in 1991. Many good people worked on it. In response to the latest Knight Commission Report, the NCAA put together a very strong committee of presidents, which you chaired, and the Group of Six athletic conferences put together a group of presidents on which I served from the very beginning. All that good work was going on in advance of my taking over at the NCAA. Some very strong and appropriate legislative changes were put in place. I was able to bring that to fruition.

I think that we have passed all the legislation we need to meet the academic reform goals that were set out, standing on the shoulders of others in doing this. We do have to implement these measures, but I think for all intents and purposes, we have finished this academic reform cycle: we got it done.

In many ways, as important as academic reform is, it is the easier of the two problems to solve. The tougher problem is fiscal responsibility. The cost of athletics operating budgets, the cost of facilities for athletics, and, most importantly, the autonomy that athletic departments have with respect to the rest of the institution raise the risk of scandals and frauds. How do we deal with the whole complex set of issues?

Here the NCAA's hands are not as free as in the case of academic reform. We cannot pass any national legislation to change the fiscal situation because of anti-trust laws. The only way we're going to solve this problem is if institution by institution takes responsibility for managing their affairs in a better way. In particular the presidents, who are the most important players, are going to have to step up and take full control on their campuses and reintegrate athletic programs into the academic missions of the institutions. We're at the very beginning of that. We're not even at the stage where we were when the first Knight Commission Report came out. This is going to be a very hard second step for us to take because the presidents, who must be in control for this to be successful, are under enormous pressure, not just from boosters and others, but from their boards. Those factors constitute a tough set of problems that make fiscal responsibility a very difficult issue to resolve. But I think the academic reform movement has really come to fruition and I couldn't be more pleased about that.

FL: Those who were closely connected with it, as you and I both were, felt very good about it. My worry is that there may be presidents and universities in the country that haven't taken the time to understand and plan for the implementation of the reforms. Is it possible for the NCAA to find ways to communicate directly with the presidents in order to ensure the success of the reforms?

MB: I think that most presidents actually do understand it, certainly those in Division I. I meet with presidents of each conference as much as I can. There's a good understanding of what needs to be done. Some are not entirely happy with the current approach. It's a small minority, but some are not pleased that we're raising the standards. You also have some critics who think that the problems can't be solved, but I think a very large majority of presidents are fully on board, and that goes for Division II as well. Division III, on its own, has gone through a very dramatic reform effort, particularly at the last NCAA convention, and those presidents are also well informed. So I think that the presidents do understand and I think that, through the legislation, the NCAA has sufficient authority to enforce these standards. I'm optimistic that we'll get all of that done.

FL: You've clearly been on the side of the angels in your championship of Title IX and the strong stand that you've taken on the need to improve hiring practices and increase the numbers of African-American and Hispanic coaches in all sports. Have you seen any results from your advocacy and from your other efforts to identify and train more candidates?

MB: In Title IX, we've seen a very important victory. If you believe, as I do, that intercollegiate athletic participation in college sports has educational developmental value, if you believe that education involves more than just textbooks and lectures but also character building and goal-setting, and that intercollegiate athletics plays a role in that development, then why would you offer those opportunities to men and not women? The fact of the matter is that Title IX gives educational opportunities as well as athletic opportunities to women and that's critically important. When Secretary of Education Paige, under the White House's direction, reexamined Title IX recently, there was great concern that they would overturn Title IX. The fact of the matter is it was reaffirmed and even strengthened. So I consider that a victory.

FL: That was a very significant victory.

MB: With respect to hiring of coaches, coaches of color in particular, we have two issues. One is the issue of having a search process that allows the best talent to rise to the top and the second is making sure that assistant coaches are prepared to move into leadership roles. I think we've made progress on both of those. The NCAA has started what we call Coaches' Academies to ensure that promising young coaches of color will have an opportunity. We're starting a new one this year for women coaches. One of the problems we've had is that it used to be that the majority of the people who coached women's teams were women. Now a large majority of those who coach women's teams are men, so some of our best women coaches haven't had the opportunities they need. We'll also begin to look at that. The numbers have changed modestly, but I think the effort is in place now to see some changes in the next few years.

FL: Speaking of coaches, we pick up the newspaper almost daily and find that we have coaches who have gotten off the straight and narrow in one way or another. Of course that reflects badly on all of the programs including the 99 percent that are playing strictly by the book. Is there anything that can be done about that?

MB: I think that the athletic directors play a critical role. As you integrate athletics back into the mainstream of the institution, the athletic directors become much more important and become, as it were, key administrators within the institution rather than administrators simply running an auxiliary enterprise. They have the responsibility of working with the coaches. We expect these coaches to do three things. First, we expect them to have competitive teams. Winning comes with the territory. Second, we expect them to respect the academic mission of the institution as, for example, measured by graduation rates. Third, we expect them to represent the institution well. Going to a strip bar in a very visible way is not representing the institution well. In the past, coaches were able to do some of these things, live normal lives, if you like, but that's no longer true because the market has driven up the coaches' salaries, with about two dozen of them earning seven figures a year. It has reflected upon the behavior of all the coaches. Coaches in major programs are now under the same scrutiny as high elected officials. It comes with the territory, even if they're not one of the two dozen making those large salaries, so they have to understand the level of scrutiny, the level of visibility that they have, and what they need to do to represent the institution well. The AD plays a key role in that.

FL: You mentioned in one of your earlier comments about athletics the problems that can be connected with the active involvement of board members. What can be done to educate boards about the potential danger in which they put the institution by yielding to the temptation of being closely connected with the athletic director and encouraging the athletic director to move in certain directions?

MB: The Association of Governing Boards (AGB) came out with a white paper recently in which they made an important statement on that topic. They said the policy of overseeing athletics is the proper role for governing board members just as they oversee every other part of the university, but the administration and management of athletic departments, including hiring and firing coaches, is entirely in the hands of the president. That is a very important principle to the extent that, if that principle is ignored, the institution is placed at great risk and the president is placed at enormous risk. If someone gets fired, it's not the board members; it's the president. There is temptation, and even precedent in the traditions of some institutions, for some board members to be directly and actively engaged in the hiring and firing of coaches in the athletic program. There are some institutions that still have a separate 501C3 for the athletic department. The president has no real control over it. We've got to be able to move to a situation in which the presidents are in charge in athletics and the board members understand that. No one person may be able to create that change. It is going to take an agreement, a movement—and the NCAA may be able to play a role here—that helps people better understand what is the proper administration of athletics. I consider that an insidious problem on some campuses.

FL: I was pleased to see that you had directed committees to use a "student athlete first" or "kindler, gentler" approach in regard to academic waivers and eligibility appeals. I'm sure that its implementation is not without controversy. How is it working out?

MB: I think it's working out very well. We're not all the way there, but we're getting there. The key idea is that the students come first. The only reason we have intercollegiate athletics is because of the students. Unfortunately, even though our policies and our large book of rules said that students come first, our practices had been that competitive equity took precedence, particularly in the NCAA membership committees. I've tried to reinsert that key understanding that the students come first. It took some work to do it with the staff because they had been focused on the issue that if it looked like there was competitive advantage, even if the student was inadvertently harmed, we would take action. Now if the student is inadvertently harmed because of a situation or because of the rule, we give the student the benefit of the doubt. Minor changes in competitive equity frankly didn't matter much and it didn't affect every case, but it does affect some. Certainly the principle that the student comes first changes the attitude, the way we look at each case. Some of our membership committees are still getting comfortable with it, and we'll have to make some legislative changes. Change comes hard. Coaches and others in the athletic programs are very competitive people and they focus on what happens in the competition, but I think we're moving in the right direction.

FL: What do you see as the major issues on the horizon for the NCAA and its members?

MB: I think the major issues are implementing the academic reforms that have been passed and then beginning to address fiscal responsibility and the integration of athletics into the academic mission of the institution. The only way you're going to be able to control cost in athletic departments is if the decision-making process for athletics is just the same as the decision-making process for the school of business and for liberal arts and sciences.

FL: I know that you've asked Reverend Edward Malloy to head a task force to analyze the results of the NCAA gambling study and make recommendations. What do you think will be the major issues of the next ten years for the organization?

MB: I think that issues like gambling and alcohol abuse or drug abuse and scandals are issues that are very visible and noisy, but not deep. We're never going to solve them completely, given human nature. We can make progress, but look outside of athletics. We have all the laws in the world about violence, felonies, and so on, but people still commit the crimes. Having rules and enforcing them is not enough to stop everyone from committing crimes, but I think that we can make some progress. I think that we can make sure that students understand at a very early age that participation in athletics is compatible with and mutually supportive of their education. Many students understand that, but in certain sports, men's basketball in particular, that understanding is not complete. Implementing the new academic standards and rules which we put in place is a long-term matter; the other mission we need to accomplish is fiscal responsibility and the integration of missions. We're at the very beginning of that. As I mentioned, that is a bear. It is going to be a very tough problem to solve. If we can do that over the next decade, implement sound athletic academic standards and arrive at integration of missions and fiscal responsibility, I'll wave the flag and say we have reached a major accomplishment.

FL: There are just a few issue-oriented questions on which I'd like to get your opinion. One is in regard to funding. As states reduce their funding of higher education and state legislatures and governors try to cap tuition, how can institutions resolve their budget problems and continue to build both access and excellence?

MB: It is important for institutions to become very mission directed, not try to be all things to all people and for presidents particularly not to fall into the trap of always trying to move to the so-called next level. Understand what your mission is and succeed in that area. Even for research universities, I think one has to choose very carefully what areas to emphasize, not to starve the others, but to decide where the investments should be made. My prediction is that, over the next decade or two, we will see greater mission differentiation among types of institutions as well as among research institutions themselves. The ambitions of the faculty are broad, deep, and all encompassing. You know you've got a good institution if the ambitions outstrip the resources, but the fact is some decisions must be made and focus is going to have to be greater. I think we'll have to accommodate ourselves to more restrictive budgets than we have in the past. There are some opportunities for private fundraising and there are certainly opportunities for engagement with the private sector, but they're limited. For public universities, the major source of resources is tuition, which is not going to go up as fast as it has in the past and state funding, which is limited. We are just going to have to learn to be more focused in what we do.

FL: Is it the responsibility of our state institutions to solve the problem of access?

MB: It depends on which state institution you're talking about. I think if you look within a state as a whole, taking all the public institutions in the state, the answer is yes. But if you're looking at a research campus, it's not necessarily good for the research campus to solve the problem of access because what you want to do is to create a very high level intellectual environment. You want access across gender and across different population groups, African Americans, Asian Americans, and so on, but you don't want access in terms of those who are just barely able to go to college. Other institutions in the state need to be more focused on diversity. So in terms of the system within a state, the answer is yes, but you have to differentiate between institutions.

FL: Do you think then, having said this, that partnerships between state universities and community colleges can offer at least a partial solution to this?

MB: Perhaps, but I have some serious concerns. It depends on what a community college is. In some instances, a community college is a competitor of research campuses or other four-year institutions, where the community college sees itself as offering the first two years of a four-year education. The way you operate a public university is through cross-subsidization. Freshmen and sophomores tend to subsidize juniors and seniors and everyone subsidizes the graduate students. The most productive course in the university is always Psych 101 because that's where you gain the greatest revenue, which is then used to cross-subsidize the classics department. So if the community college perceives itself as two years of college, then what you're doing is taking the revenue sources for cross-subsidization out of the control of the institution and the problems we talked about before, the lack of state support becomes exacerbated in the extreme. If the community college, on the other hand, sees itself mostly in terms of workforce development activity, as many of them do today, then I think it is complementary. I think that the statistic is that a quarter to a third of the enrolled members of a community college have baccalaureate degrees. They are not there to get their first degree or their first two years of college; they're really there for improving their careers or switching careers. If that's the case, then the community college can be supportive of the economic development activities in the state and can remove some of that burden from the four-year state institutions.

FL: Getting back to the question of access. Is there any realistic hope that the states and the federal government will take on more of this responsibility of providing students from low-income families access to quality education?

MB: They can do that through improved need-based grants, Pell Grants in particular. We've been moving away from that direction. It may take a new approach by this administration or the next administration in order to go back to greater emphasis on need-based grants. The institutions themselves and the states have been moving away from need-based grants. Take the Hope Scholarship Fund in Georgia, which is a superb idea, except that it tends to support those who succeed well in high school and those tend to be upper middle class. The greatest correlation between SAT scores is with zip codes, a socioeconomic surrogate metric, so it depends on where you went to high school and what your high school experience was whether or not you're going to get a Hope Scholarship.

FL: It also produces serious budget problems for the state.

MB: In Georgia, they started to finance the merit grant programs by using gaming money, but they have outstripped gaming money at this point. Institutions too are moving more towards merit-based scholarships and away from need-based scholarships. I understand that we certainly want to have some merit-based scholarships. Athletic scholarships are merit based. But unless we put more funds into need-based scholarships, access problems will increase. I think it is possible to make some headway in the financial aid issues at the federal level, but it will need a change in the direction of federal policy.

FL: You've had the opportunity to work with more than one governing board. It might be helpful to the readers of this book if you could outline what you feel are the important characteristics of good governing boards and what are the problems one can encounter in dealing with governing boards.

MB: Good governing boards have good communications with the president and understand that the president was hired to set the direction and to administer the institution. A good governing board provides good leadership in policy, advocates for the institution, and avoids letting end runs take place around the president and the administration. I think I've been very fortunate in both Oregon and Indiana to have outstanding boards. In general, I would think that one of the most significant problems facing the presidents of public universities is the quality of boards. It's incumbent on governors and state legislatures, if the governing board members are appointed through them, to make sure that the people who are appointed to these boards have the experience to do a good job. It's important to have some members who have large business experience, given the complexity of the universities, people who are not only good friends of the institution because they're alumni or donors, but are committed to the future of higher education.

FL: In the past few years, there have been several instances in which the governor of a state has gotten directly involved with policy issues or even personnel decisions in the state's flagship institutions or the system. Do you think this is a trend about which we should be concerned?

MB: I don't think it's a trend. I think it depends upon the individual governor. I didn't personally experience any of those problems and most governors understand that a certain level of autonomy is necessary for higher education. It's always important for the president of a major public research university to have a good working relationship with the governor. That can prevent some of the problems. In the extreme case, and sometimes it happens, the president has to say no. You can't keep your job at any cost. There are certain points of principle and situations where one has to recognize that it is time to go back to teaching. You can't stay in the job if the governor or someone else is leading the institution in a path that's detrimental to its future.

FL: How important do you think it is for presidents and chancellors to participate in national associations and join in the work of discussing and formulating solutions to current problems?

MB: I'm highly in favor of it and I have found that there were very few presidential meetings I attended—whether it was the Association of American Universities, the National Association of State Universities and Land Grant Colleges, or the American Council on Education—where I didn't learn something. That was always my criterion of whether these meetings were worth my time: did I learn something? I'm not so focused on my own accomplishments that I won't borrow a good idea, wherever it comes from. I have imported and made workable within the context of the university many ideas that I've gotten through those meetings. There's a secondary effect too, that never should be underestimated and that is that presidents are really alone. They have a few people in their higher-level administration teams they can talk to and who will say no to them about certain issues. But it helps a lot. I think, to spend some time, even if it's only a couple of weekends a year, with people who are in similar situations, who are facing similar personal issues, such as the impact of time on family, and to be able to talk to them and get to know them. So I have always found that secondary effect important as well.

FL: I agree with you. I've felt that I learned something at all of the meetings I attended and colleagues are always willing to give you an honest response. Now you've mentioned undergraduate education, but I'd like to give you an opportunity to add something if you wish. Your institutions responded very clearly to the criticism of research universities not caring about undergraduate teaching. Certainly being cited by *Time* magazine for the quality of Indiana University's undergraduate education was a clear sign that your university was doing wonderful things.

MB: It's all about the students. These institutions are very complex. The good ones will have ground-breaking research and creative activity in the arts, discover new drugs in the medical school, will be engaged with their states and help the economy and the cultural life of the state, but if they're not doing their job very well in undergraduate education, they're a failure. Undergraduate education only took up 20-25 percent of my time among all the things I had to do as a president, but that was a very important 20-25 percent. And of course it's quite possible to do it well at a research university. Just as some people are better at research, others are better at teaching and you have to be able to differentiate the workloads to some extent along those lines. I think that we'll see more and more people working with undergraduates who are on long term teaching contracts as opposed to the normal tenure track that requires research as well as teaching, but you've got to design the institution and make understood through rewards and praise the importance of undergraduate education.

FL: In regard to affirmative action, aside from the admissions issues, how have you managed to diversify your campus in terms of faculties, administrators, and staff?

MB: Well I think in attracting high level administrators, the president can do a great deal. It becomes a matter of what you bring to the table when you hire a high-level administrator, whether it's a dean or a vice president. One can have a clear and open search and aggressively seek out outstanding people, maybe take some risks if necessary in terms of someone not having all of the prior experience possible, as long as they have the natural abilities. You can do that on the administrative side and, on the faculty side, I think that programs that provide incentives and encouragement through resource allocation work.

FL: Yes, money talks in higher education as it does in other fields. The last question is about the future. What do you see as the strongest forces driving the need for change in higher education over the next ten to twenty years?

MB: I think the economy is going to drive it. It has become clear to everyone that one needs a college education to succeed. I think the reaction to the federal government in terms of its intervention into the traditional autonomy of institutions is going to be a factor. I think that, given the pressure from economic concerns and fiscal constraints, conditions are going to favor those institutions that become more focused in their efforts. Those institutions that understand the need to break the boundaries between the university and its community, its state and corporate America will be most successful. That's going to be very hard to manage. There's a great tendency, certainly among some folk on the faculty, to be rather inward looking and there are dangers in terms of crossing the line into non-academic partnerships. They have to be managed very carefully. But those institutions that can see their way through it are going to be most successful. There are some who think that what you should really do is to build the walls higher and stronger. I believe that's an error. The institutions that oversee those changes in ways that are protective of the intellectual honesty and freedom of the institution while contributing to the general well being of the rest of the state and the nation are going to be the most successful ones.

FL: What do you think are the most important changes that are going to take place?

MB: Because of the changes in the demography of the country, we are going to see a greater number of ethnic minorities engaged in undergraduate education. We want to make sure that there are adequate faculty role models and administrators to support that. I think fiscal constraints will be prominent in the foreseeable future. I think there will be great exciting opportunities in research, especially biomedical research, and those institutions with research capabilities will prosper. What I call the Ponce de Leon effect is in action, namely that those who make governmental decisions about supporting research would like to live forever, or at least have their families live forever, so the biomedical revolution is good for another decade or two.

FL: And finally what would higher education leaders need to do or do more of in the future to help their institutions succeed, given the changing environment?

MB: I think they're going to have to be leaders, not just in their institutions, but on a broader set of issues. They're going to have to stand up more in corporate circles, in community circles, and on the state level. We're starting to see that more and more. There was a time when presidents were very inward looking because that's what their institutions asked them to do, but I think we're seeing more and more presidential leadership on a broader scale, addressing social issues and addressing the economic issues. I think that's what it's going to take to be a leader among presidents.

Molly Corbett Broad

Molly Broad served for eight and a half years (1997-2005) as president of the University of North Carolina, where she was responsible for the supervision and representation of sixteen campuses and their affiliated enterprises. A native of Pennsylvania, Broad earned her bachelor's degree in economics from Syracuse University, her master's from Ohio State University. Before becoming the president of the UNC system, she served in several high administrative posts from coast to coast, including vice president for government and corporate relations at Syracuse University (1971-1985), chief executive officer for the university system of Arizona (1985-1992). She came to UNC from the Califirnia State Univeristy system, where she served as senior vice president for administration (1992-1993) and as executive vice chancellor and chief operating officer (1993-1997).

On the national level, she has chaired the National Association of State Universities and Land Grant Colleges (NASULGC) and presided over the International Council for Distance Education and the Internet 2 Corporation. She has also served on the Business-Higher Education Forum, the executive committee of the Council on Competitiveness, the advisory board of the Mellon Foundation, the Association of Governing Boards Presidents' Council, and the Parsons Corporation Board of Directors, as well as other state and national organizations.

In her leadership of the University of North Carolina system, Broad stressed expanding affordable access and improving student retention, increasing managerial flexibility for campuses and fortifying the state's historically black institutions, diversifying the system's sources of revenue, setting strategic directions, building partnerships with K-12, investing in information technology, building an enrollment growth formula and securing its funding, documenting the condition of the university's buildings, and mounting a successful campaign for the passage of a $3.1 billion bond referendum.

Francis. Lawrence: Molly, I was impressed by your inaugural address in North Carolina. You did a splendid job of outlining important issues that are still on the higher education agenda so you were looking forward, not just for North Carolina but for the whole area of higher education in the United States.

Molly Corbett Broad: The University of North Carolina is the oldest public university in America and I believe it stands as one of the finest. Within the sixteen-campus system, we have a rich diversity of distinctive missions that, in many ways, reflects the full range of public universities in our country. Our strategic priorities align very well with the challenges and opportunities facing public higher education in America. I am pleased that you found my inaugural address conveyed the important national themes.

FL: Could we start by talking about your family background, your education and how they contributed to shaping your values and your development as a leader in higher education?

MCB: I was born and raised in a coalmining town in Pennsylvania, Wilkes-Barre. My father and mother were both schoolteachers. In those years if you were a woman, you could not be a schoolteacher and be married, so my mother retired from teaching school when she was married and had, relatively late in life for that time, four children, one right after another. I was number three and the first girl in the group of four children. All of my grandparents were born in Ireland and came to the United States as young children. My grandfather Kelly, who had a third grade education, went to work in the mines and in due course became superintendent of the mines. My mother was the tenth of thirteen children and remembers vividly "moving into the big house," where the superintendent of the mines lived and where she recalled "there was a wonderful library." She went to college and became a schoolteacher. My grandfather Corbett, who also had just a third or fourth grade education, went to work in the mills. I think ours is a very typical American experience in a family that placed a priority on education. In the space of a generation, it was possible to move from working in the mill or in the mines to a leadership post in a great university.

FL: It is important to be able to describe the early background of leaders in higher education, many of whom have had experiences similar to yours, because today we continue to have many first generation college students enrolling in our universities. It is vital for them to realize that such stories are not unique, that they can be replicated.

MCB: Absolutely, I agree with you. There are a lot of immigrants from other nations who, I believe, exhibit exactly the same characteristics of the American dream that we think of as part of our own personal history. The only difference is that they may be coming from Vietnam or from Mexico rather than from Ireland or Germany.

FL: What are the two or three personal attributes that the people who know you best might say have been key to your success?

MCB: I had a meeting earlier this morning with the director of our office of federal relations. (J.B. Milliken, the senior vice president to whom he reported, has become president of the University of Nebraska this month, so we're in the midst of a transition.) He said to me that J.B. told him that working with Molly Broad is like drinking from a fire hose everyday. I think that may not be entirely positive, Fran. I do think that people who know me well think of me as industrious, a strategic thinker, hardworking, a marathoner, somebody who is persevering. I think they see me as a person who is mostly modest, but with a sturdy constitution. I'm resilient, like those toys that you knock over but they bounce right back up. The thing that I hear from others that pleases me the most is that I am a person of integrity, with enough courage to live out that integrity. So I pray every day that it is true and that God helps me to continue on that path.

FL: What do you regard as your first leadership position at any level?

MCB: I'm not sure I can remember, but somehow when I was a little girl, in the context of my siblings, I took responsibility for family things and in some ways I think that is where the seed of leadership sprouted within me. I may not have known it then but, as I think back about it, I can't remember a time when I wasn't, to some degree or another, willing to assume responsibility for some larger goal or objective.

FL: I believe it would almost be impossible simply to develop leadership skills as you take over an organization. It's got to be there before. It's got to grow somehow. And you're right, responsibility and accountability as well.

MCB: I have also been blessed at many points in my life when other people saw things in me that I didn't see in myself and invited me to take on some new leadership responsibility. I have benefited enormously from folks who urged me and then supported me and provided mentorship. I have been very fortunate in my life that other people who were leaders themselves, have wanted to support me in advancing my leadership opportunities.

FL: Who were the people who inspired you and acted as your mentors?

MCB: I think as a young child, God was my inspiration. I'm Roman Catholic and was influenced profoundly as a young woman by the writing of Teilhard de Chardin, theologian, scientist, and philosopher of the mid-twentieth century. I had some wonderful mentors, teachers in school and a couple of professors in the university. Arguably the most important experience in my life was when I had the opportunity to go to Syracuse University. I was a freshman, taking economics 1A, in one of these huge lecture halls and when the professor gave back the bluebooks from our examination, he called out the names of several students and asked that we report to the department. He was chairman of the department. I said, "Oh no, what did I do?" And he said, "I think you have a flair for economics and I think you should seriously consider changing your major. And I would be very pleased to serve as your faculty adviser and to assist you in selection of courses and faculty members." I was blown away and needless to say I became a major in economics. He was my great adviser and mentor and friend for many, many years after that. I'm sure that there are thousands and thousands of kids just like me, students in a university whom some professor, not thinking he was doing anything special, managed to influence in a way that changed their lives. That department head was a great mentor and I have had more than my share of people who helped me.

Ron Brady completed his service in higher education as the senior vice president for finance in the University of California system, but I met him when I was a first-year graduate student at Ohio State, newly married and farther away from home than I had ever been. He told me later that when he met me I looked like a deer in the headlights. Ron mentored me and we became fast friends over many years. Our paths crossed in various institutions. The course of my own career is deeply impacted by the mentorship that I received from Ron Brady. I feel the same way about Barry Munitz. By the time Barry recruited me to come to California State University, I was already a fully developed, very mature person, but I felt enriched by the opportunity to work with him and to learn from the way he saw the world and the way he organized the institution and his own thinking. Those are just a few of my mentors.

One of the most remarkable experiences I had was when the dean of the Maxwell School of Syracuse University at the time, Scotty Campbell, called me in one day in 1977. I was a young professional. He told me that the state was creating a Blue Ribbon Commission on the future of higher education in New York. The City University had been closed down by the fiscal crisis. Hugh Carey, the governor and Abe Beam, the mayor, didn't know exactly how to frame a solution, so they created a commission to study the policy and budgetary issues. "They're looking for somebody to lead the staff of that commission," Scotty Campbell said, "and I think you ought to do it." It was an amazing opportunity. I had two young children and I had moved right from my parents' house to my husband's house when I graduated from college, but I did this. For the first time in my life I lived alone. I commuted from Syracuse to Albany every Monday morning on the overnight train from Chicago and came back to Syracuse at the end of the week. I had been a director of institutional research and had been working in budget management and data information systems — all "back of the house," number- crunching kinds of work. Then I found myself interacting with governors and legislative leaders and the board of regents of New York. It was an amazing opportunity for me to see how rational, analytically strong policy can intersect with politics. It showed me that when you're successful at developing such a policy strategy that is also politically smart, you can really change the policy direction of an institution or even a state. It was a remarkable experience, something I never would have thought of on my own. Somehow Scotty Campbell saw that potential in me. It was a fabulous experience.

FL: I was struck by your comments about faculty mentors. We don't celebrate the importance of that mentorship enough. While I was fund raising for Rutgers from coast to coast, many, many alums came up to me to ask, "Is professor so and so still there? He/she is the reason why I decided to do what has become my career."

MCB: Yes, and how many dozens and dozens of alumni events have you and I attended where you're honoring an alumnus or an alumna who has achieved great distinction and they get up there when you give them that award and they become very emotional. "If it weren't for professor so and so, I never would have...." It always inspires me. Individuals who have won the greatest awards and acclaim that their profession gives, when faced with reflecting on their university experience inevitably become very emotional and connect where they are today to some members of the faculty who made it possible by opening up their minds to something new. It's one of the most wonderful parts of being in an institution like a university.

FL: Do women who are leaders of higher education need to have different or superior skills and leadership qualities than men who are leaders? Of course, that's a different question in 2004 than it would have been in 1964.

MCB: I think women are viewed differently in leadership positions and in higher education. There may be a different set of standards. I think it requires great sensitivity to understand that most of the people in leadership positions with whom you interact or to whom you report see you as the other, not one of them. I think that's a fact of life and that to be effective you need to find a way to build the bridge, to build rapport, if you will, even while acknowledging to yourself that you probably aren't going to be the one that they invite to go out and play a round of golf or to grab lunch together when they have a free moment. The relationships are probably going to be more formal and more professional.

Now I think that's different from whether, in my observation, women use a different set of skills at leadership. I do think that there is something to this hypothesis that throughout history the role of women in the family has been what we might call today multitasking. Whereas men went out to hunt and their sole objective for the day was to be successful in the hunt, the role of the women was to look after the babies and to pick the berries and to weave the baskets and to cook the meals. So I do think that there has been a culture passed on through many, many generations that makes our little girls and women think about success in a different way, in a multi-pronged way as contrasted with excellence in a single direction, which is the way I think sometimes how men see themselves. It may be akin to the difference between "command and control" management and collaborative management styles

FL: It's a tough question. In academe, the glass ceiling for women in administration has just begun to yield. In 1990, when I first attended the Association of American Universities as Rutgers' president, their membership included just one woman president, Hannah Gray of the University of Chicago. Now there are several women who preside over AAU institutions and their number is continuing to grow, but we are not yet where we should be.

MCB: I don't think you find the tenure of women presidents is as great as it is for men. I think we're developing an old girl's network, a counterpart for women to the system that has been in place for men. Experienced women leaders in higher education now nominate other women for presidencies, advise and mentor them and prepare them for the interviews. But you and I have both watched a lot of very bright and able women who just didn't know how that game was played and ended by being unsuccessful even though they may have been very well qualified to be a president. I'm the first woman to serve as president of this university in its 211 years of existence.

FL: On the other hand, what you've done paves the way for women to rise to the highest posts in academic leadership.

MCB: I hope so.

FL: Change is occurring, not as quickly as it should, but....

MCB: But at an amazing rate. When I was in Arizona and led a commission on the Status of Women, we worked toward defining some policies that helped women who found themselves in the child bearing years and the tenure bearing years simultaneously. We addressed building policies that wouldn't force women to choose between those two parts of their lives. At that point, when we did some projections, given the path we saw before us, it looked as though it would be 2020 before we would be able to see any significant increases in the number of women who could make their way through the ranks to full professor, department chair, dean, and chief academic officer. It has happened much faster than that. I look at the pools of candidates when we do searches for chancellor within the sixteen campuses of the University of North Carolina and they are now filled with extraordinarily well-qualified women.

FL: That is good for all of higher education. I'd love to talk about this question longer because it's one that's always concerned me, but I have other questions and I know that your time is limited. What were the challenges that the University of North Carolina faced at the time that you became president? As good as the North Carolina system has been, and it has been considered as one of the best in the country, I am sure that there were things that needed to change.

MCB: You're exactly right. The University of North Carolina has for a long time been a fine university. As I have reflected on why the search committee and the board of governors selected me to serve in this role, I have concluded that the most significant of those reasons was to bring best professional practices to the operations of the university and to build organizational capacity behind the university's vision. As a new president, I did my homework on the history and condition of the University – the strengths and weaknesses, opportunities and threats – before setting priorities. I consulted widely and then brought to the assignment experience from other regions and kinds of institutions. Those priorities have driven a lot of what we have tried to accomplish. Some of those priorities were new initiatives to capitalize on the universities' great strengths, while other priorities were playing defense, trying to address deficits. One of the major deficits was the condition of our capital facilities and the backlog of deferred maintenance. We did an assessment of the buildings and infrastructure across the entire university and found that the accumulation of deferred maintenance was rendering this university at serious risk if we didn't make major investments in capital. North Carolina is not much different than many other states where capital planning and capital financing are not tied together. The balance sheet and the operating statement don't come together in most major public universities. As you know, we were successful in securing the overwhelming passage of a $3.1 billion bond package in 2000 and that funding is transforming the physical character and quality of our campuses.

Another challenge was the decline of our five historically black universities that are part of the University of North Carolina. They had gone through a period in which their enrollments and the academic levels of achievement of incoming students were both declining. In general, the condition of their physical facilities was nothing short of disgraceful. We had a real but quite understandable problem because these campuses were developed when they were the only opportunity for a university education for African-American students in the South. However, after some very difficult years when the university was negotiating with the Department of Health, Education, and Welfare (HEW), a Consent Decree was issued that led to opening access to all UNC campuses. Then, African-American students were admitted to Chapel Hill, NC State and other historically white campuses, providing very attractive alternatives to attending one of our historically black universities. Yet these HBUs are so critical to the landscape of North Carolina and to our history and tradition. Addressing their future well-being had to be right up there at the top of the priority list. We are proud to tell you that the condition of the public historically black universities in North Carolina has been transformed in every way, as evidenced in our recent five-year report. You will not find stronger or higher quality public historically black universities anywhere in the country today and they are getting better with every passing year.

When I arrived, I also thought we were at risk on our affirmative action practices. Higher education was in the midst of a number of propositions and legal cases across the country that certainly made it look as though the great public universities in each of the judicial districts were being identified for legal challenge to their practices in affirmative action. Our practices in North Carolina were a direct derivative of the Consent Decree, even though the Consent Decree had long since expired. We promptly scrubbed our policies and practices in admissions and financial aid to insure that they would pass legal muster if we were the institution chosen to test that law.

I have just described the sorts of activities, issues, and challenges that I saw right at the outset of my presidency and we began to address them. There were others, of course. How should information technology fit into the future of the institution? Since it is increasingly becoming the scaffolding on which modern science and research are being conducted, we knew that we must also insure that our robust networks and high performance computing remained state of the art.

Another of the issues that we identified as something that needed to be fixed was the issue of managerial flexibility. The bureaucracy in North Carolina from the state to the campuses of the university is very strong and very rigid. As the university transformed itself, those regulatory and bureaucratic practices became like handcuffs on the capacity of the university to be nimble, to be responsive, to be opportunistic, and to think about change at a rapid rate, so we embarked upon efforts to try to fix that. I am pleased to report that here too we have been able to make impressive progress and the results are reflected in campuses that are more nimble, that are increasing efficiency and that are able to manage projects in a timely and cost effective manner.

FL: All of them very important issues that were not simple or easy to resolve.

MCB: They take many years of continuing effort. Then there were some important opportunities for new initiatives which the University of North Carolina had not fully pursued. One of those—that is also a personal passion for me—is extending affordable access. This university has been a wonderful institution for many generations but it didn't serve a large proportion of North Carolinians. Throughout the history of this university, our college going rate has never met the national average. I'm really proud to say today that we have a college going rate in North Carolina that is in the top five of the largest states.

FL: Do you remember what the percentage was and what it is now?

MCB: Of course it all depends upon how you calculate this, but for the university itself, which of course is a component part with the community colleges and the other private institutions, our share went from less than 25 percent to now 31-32 percent, which is a huge difference. We've grown by 25,000 students in the last four years and will continue this path because we do have the population, but also because we have set different expectations for ourselves about extending affordable access to North Carolinians.

FL: It's also so much more important whether in North Carolina or New Jersey or any other state for students to have the opportunity for college education. At least in my generation, you could get a good job without a college degree. Now that isn't possible.

MCB: North Carolina is a perfect example of that. In the past, you didn't even have to graduate from high school to get a great job in a furniture manufacturing or textile manufacturing plant or working on a tobacco farm where the revenue per acre is the highest of any agricultural product that we have ever known. Those jobs in manufacturing are gone and they aren't coming back. We've lost 100,000 manufacturing jobs in those industries over the course of the recent period of time. Consequently, we have a huge assignment in front of us to raise the level of educational achievement in North Carolina.

FL: It's a very important goal. When it comes down to it, increasing access to higher education may be one of the most important goals that all of us face and you have an excellent team to work with you to accomplish it.

MCB: Increasing affordable access is what we think of when we wake up each morning. In this university that goal is of pre-eminent importance. We have some of the most talented people I've known in my career on the team in the Office of the President. There's nothing like establishing a lofty goal and making it a mandate to expand the creative juices. But our team has just been phenomenal in laying out the kinds of programs and strategies that have helped this university raise the college going rate. It's not the only opportunity; there are many opportunities for us to strengthen and enhance the University of North Carolina.

Another initiative under way is to diversify our sources of revenue. It is my belief that even if the robust economy that was in place in 1997 when I became president stayed forever, given our aspirations about enrollment growth, the State of North Carolina would be stretched to sustain the level of support for the university. That means we are going to have to work harder at generating other revenues through private fund raising and through expanding our sponsored research. We have set about in each of those areas to help build the capability of each one of our campuses and it is working. For the last fiscal year 2003-2004 this university will have received over a billion dollars from sponsored research in competitively awarded grants and contracts. It's just phenomenal and we have more capacity for that growth to continue. We're also building the fund raising infrastructure on every one of our campuses. Chapel Hill is very far along in a 1.8 billion dollar capital campaign. Ten years ago, Chapel Hill was just beginning to do fundraising. There are a number of initiatives like this that I think we need to take if we are to continue to serve the state and the people of North Carolina in a very different global economy.

FL: As you mentioned earlier, you are from Pennsylvania and you have served in high administrative posts from coast to coast. How did the culture of each state where you served differ and what effects did the differences have on your work?

MCB: Culture is central to understanding the people, the state, the institution, and the press... I could go on and on. Nobody told me that when I moved from upstate New York, where I was a vice president of a private university on a single campus, and went to Arizona, to a public institution that happened to be a public system, not a single campus. The cultural changes between public and private and the cultural difference between the northeast and the southwest as well as the culture that governed the way the legislatures worked were notable and difficult to negotiate. In New York, getting to meet with the governor or the speaker or the president of the senate was a very challenging assignment and it took weeks before you could bring it about. In Arizona, I could have coffee with the speaker at seven o'clock in the morning in his office almost any day. New York was a very complex culture and bureaucracy.

Arizona, on the other hand, is a great place for broken field runners. Nobody is going to stop you, but nobody is going to necessarily help you either. It's an every-man-for-himself sort of culture. I learned a lot through the school of hard knocks until I finally figured out that the culture of New York wasn't going to be readily, completely, or successfully transferable into the culture of Arizona.

Then I had to make the transition to California, a big complicated bureaucratic state but still a part of the West, a culture where everybody leaves the office at five o'clock to go to the beach and surf. Finally somebody said to me, "You know, these folks want to leave at five o'clock but they won't go as long as you're here unless you tell them it's okay for them to go. So if you keep staying here at your desk till seven o'clock at night, you're going to have a lot of really unhappy people."

In North Carolina I have found yet another, profoundly different culture. Of all the challenges that I have faced, not being a North Carolinian has to be right at the top of the list. It's a state that has great pride in its history, in its tradition, in its culture, in its sense of community, in Southern hospitality and the level of civility — all just wonderfully attractive traits. But being a North Carolinian and understanding how North Carolinians think and act is a very important part of understanding how to accomplish things in this state. This question really goes to one of the key ingredients for any individual who wants to take on a leadership position in a new institution: you must learn the culture, be a good student of the culture.

In North Carolina, people will listen to you very courteously and if you're not from North Carolina you'll think that they're agreeing with you, but you learn not to mistake courtesy for agreement. Changing cultures is very tough.

FL: What effects have the role and demands of the job had on your family life and how do you maintain a balance? You mentioned earlier staffing a New York commission while you had two young children. As you've gone through your career, how has this worked out?

MCB: I am so lucky, Fran. I have an amazingly supportive husband and we say that we're on a twenty-year plan. The first twenty years I followed him and the second twenty years he is following me. And during that first twenty years is when our children were born and raised. They were moving out of the nest by the time the second twenty years led to a move that I initiated. When we left Syracuse for Arizona that was my move, whereas the previous ones had been Bob's moves. In addition, my Mother lived with us from the time our children were young until her passing in 2000. What a gift for our children and the whole family. By the time I was in a position of demanding leadership, the child rearing activities were pretty much behind us. And it seems to me that the family stresses you mention have as much to do with the children as with the spouse. By the time I became president of the University of North Carolina, my husband was semi-retired, still working part of the time. He is in the hospitality industry, so he has been able to take on the role of working with the caterers and the operations of the President's house, the menus and all of the things that typically you think of the wife as handling. It's just fortuitous that I have a husband who knows an awful lot and has been willing to take on those support roles. But, as you know, the presidency of a large sprawling university system is bone-crushing work. It's unrelenting.

FL: Whether your appointment letter spells it out or not, you are president seven days a week, 365 days a year, plus that added day in a leap year.

MCB: Yes, and I think it's easier for the person in the presidential role to understand that than it is for the spouse, who sees the cumulative impact of the stress. As you suggested earlier, it is difficult to find any time when you are able to truly relax. The headlines in each morning's newspaper bring a new surprise and a new crisis in some area that affects your job, whether it appears on the sports page, the financial page, the first page, the city or state page. There is so much about this work that you cannot predict that you can never be very far away from the job mentally, even when you are physically far away. It isn't healthy, but I don't know what you can do about it. I have great admiration for the university leaders who have succeeded in carving out a month to simply remove themselves from the university and go away to think and to read and to soak up a little rest. I haven't figured out how to do that, but I keep trying.

FL: My wife solved that problem by telling me I couldn't accept the presidency unless I promised to take the yearly one-month vacation that my contract stipulated. I had never taken a sabbatical or even as much as a one month vacation while I was at Tulane, but I honored that commitment to her.

Let's go on to the topic of organizational structure. How did you recruit and structure your leadership team here in North Carolina? Did you find it necessary to restructure the administration to some extent?

MCB: The administration that I inherited was comprised mostly of individuals who were well into their sixties, not far from retirement, so there was inevitable turnover. Moreover, the vice president who handled government relations decided to resign in order to run for the United States Senate. The circumstances that presented the need to recruit people to fill those positions also allowed me the freedom to reorganize and to reframe the administrative structure of the university. I did that in a way that was consistent with the historic structure but eliminated several vice presidential positions, combined some of the others, and created new positions to fill the needs I saw. For example, we had no chief information officer and no office of federal relations at the university when I arrived. We did have a vice president for student affairs, yet in a system office you have no responsibility for direct supervision of students, so student affairs may not be a vice presidential level position. I made a number of changes that were evolutionary, but they occurred within the first three years I was here. Virtually every vice presidency turned over for one reason or another.

FL: Can you tell me some of the specific qualities that you look for in the people you choose to work with and depend upon?

MCB: Integrity is right at the top of the list because the way that you behave in a crisis, when things are really tough, derives from your integrity. I look for people who are good strategic thinkers and who see the relationships and interconnections among the various parts of the university. My personal philosophy of leadership inclines me toward a team approach that I like to call interchangeable parts. What I want to create is an open, collaborative, consultative way of thinking and acting. Some of us have special expertise in a given area, but all team members are able to translate their expertise and to connect it to the other vice presidential areas. I look for individuals who see those relationships, whose style of leading and managing is open and consultative, people who can think strategically, and who know how to create organizational capacity in support of our vision. Those qualities are the most important to me.

FL: The kind of teamwork you describe is essential, because otherwise you develop a group of self-contained silos.

I know that in your post, you've been expected to spend a great deal of time away from this office. You are the chief representative of the University of North Carolina in the general assembly, to state officials and to the federal government. In addition you must spend a good deal of time visiting the 16 campuses of the system on a regular basis. Do you have to continue the day-to-day business of the system while you're on the road or do you have someone who fills in for you if you decide to spend the next four or five days visiting different campuses? Is there someone on the scene here who acts for you or must you stay in constant communication?

MCB: We do not have a chief operating officer. I have a team of five executive officers, any one of whom is fully capable of handling something unforeseen or some emergency in my absence. We have good connections and with cell phones and all of the other handheld devices, we are able to be in regular communication. So except when I might be in some remote part of the world, they can get me anytime they need to.

FL: How did you formulate a vision for the future of the university that took into consideration the specific circumstances of the whole system, its history, its virtues and its needs?

MCB: There's nothing quite like prior experience to help you to know what the questions are. The benefit of having been at many different places, public and private, big and small, northeast, southwest, and developing an awareness of the differences in culture has helped me in understanding the questions that need to be asked and in laying out a vision that gives us a strategic direction. I think that answering those questions is the most important homework that a president has to do. Happily for me, the University of North Carolina has had a long-standing capacity to do long range planning. What we have tried to do is transform that into a strategic plan by identifying a small number of strategic directions that the board of governors understands, reviews, approves, and modifies once every two years. It's a five-year plan but with a biennial update. Every member of the senior staff in this office has on their desks the six strategic directions that guide this university. All of us have the clear understanding that if the way we are spending our time today doesn't advance one or more of those strategic directions, we ought to keep thinking about how we're going to alter the way we invest our time. There are many enticing ways in which one could spend time in a university and do so productively, but because we are lean in our staffing, we focus, focus, focus on these broad strategic directions.

FL: What strategies did you use to communicate and create buy-in by the entire system once you had developed these strategic directions or as you continue to work on developing them? How have you gotten every campus, whether it is Chapel Hill or North Carolina State, or any of the other institutions, to be fully supportive of these directions?

MCB: As you know, that is easier said than done. I'd like to think that if you woke any one of our experienced chancellors in the middle of the night and said, "Tell me what the strategic directions of the university are?" every one would be able to tell you what they are. We organize the agenda for our board meetings and our board committee meetings in a way that's linked to our strategic directions and we organize the agenda for the monthly meeting that I have with all of the chancellors in that way. But, having said that, what the implementation of that strategic direction looks like at Chapel Hill is very different than what it looks like in the implementation at Asheville because the mission of these institutions is profoundly different. Of course one of the great challenges of providing leadership to a university that has so many diverse campuses with missions that are quite distinct and quite different is not having a cookie cutter mentality and being open to see that the manifestation looks quite different at North Carolina A&T than it may look at UNC Wilmington.

FL: How did you go about transforming your understanding of the university system together with the external realities into a long-range plan for change and improvement?

MCB: One of the results of studying North Carolina, its history, its culture, its tradition with respect to the university was a fuller realization of the extent to which the people of North Carolina believe in this university. North Carolinians believe that what North Carolina is today is in some part defined by the quality of the great university they developed. They believe this even if they have never set foot on a campus of the University of North Carolina. The University has a phenomenal connection to the people of North Carolina. One of the most important ways of communicating and tapping into that well-spring of support is to understand their belief in the institution. That is why my passionate commitment to extending access affordably resonated with the people of this state. They have come to believe that the University of North Carolina would provide an opportunity for their children or their grandchildren to have a university education. The people in this state know that a university education now is much more important than it may have been for the parents of the current generation. The communications strategies that have worked the most effectively have been to spend time to meet the people, to become acquainted with businesses of today's economy, and to help build the bridges to the university so we can assist and support their efforts. Several years back we embarked on a major effort in economic development to redefine what we mean when we say public service/ outreach. We want our outreach mission to mean transforming the economy of North Carolina so that its citizens can be prosperous in a global economy—an economy that looks very different than the economy that made North Carolina strong and prosperous in the second half of the twentieth century. North Carolina in a sense lured the manufacturing jobs from New England because our wage rates were lower than the wage rates in New England. When Franklin D. Roosevelt was president of the United States he made a speech that is seared in my brain. He announced that the greatest problem the nation faced was the South, its poverty and joblessness. Today more jobs are created in the South than any other part of the nation and it has been in some measure the universities in the south that have helped in this transformation. Communication about the mission and goals of the university really becomes effective when you're able to go to the people and their businesses, to tap into their concerns, and help to build the connection between them and the efforts of the university.

FL: How did you link the changes you wanted to make to the financial or budgeting process of the system and of each institution? I find it interesting that a lot of places think more about the big ideas but don't link them to the financial part, therefore at some stage they have real problems.

MCB: If we went about achieving expanded access to the university only through what I consider to be extraordinary outreach efforts and we didn't have the resources to back up every one of those students, it would be a pretty hollow success. We have gone very systematically about building an enrollment growth formula that reflects differential costs of delivering different academic programs and differing levels, undergraduate, master's, Ph.D. So we have a funding formula that is a twelve-cell matrix, four groupings of academic departments and disciplines, three levels — undergraduate, master's, and Ph.D. We have a dollar amount in each one of those cells that determines the new funds to be allocated for every additional student. Securing full funding for enrollment growth has been on the top of my priority list as we lobby for our budget.

I am happy to say that, despite the suffering that North Carolina has and is continuing to experience from the downturn in the economy and the decline in state revenues, the governor and the legislature in both houses have ultimately fully funded that growth formula. I was at the mansion the other night. The governor was going around a group of assembled leaders and connecting what he has been working on with them or their organization. He said to me, now I have fully funded every bit of Molly's new enrollment growth every year that I have been governor. She keeps pressing me to make that an automatic part of the continuation budget escalation, but I can't do that because I need everything I can muster to negotiate with her over the university's budget. This was said in a mostly humorous vein, giving himself the legitimate and appropriate credit he deserves, but it also reveals that he knows he can't have a conversation with me about the budget in which the full funding of that enrollment growth doesn't come up. We've been tenacious about the things that we consider to be foundational requirements to achieve the goals of the university. This year we received an increase in state funds for our basic operating budget of 9.25 percent. We're also very opportunistic in pursuit of support when we sense the time is propitious. For example, we came out of this legislative session with $388 million in new health related research and facility projects. It was an amazing result in this environment and it was an example of a lot of hard work and a lot of good strategic thinking and a lot of excellent support from politicians in an election year. We do seek that kind of funding, but not at the expense of what we consider to be the priority foundational requirements for resources.

FL: How have you gotten the public and the institutions on board and enthusiastic about these different initiatives that you have going forward? I know it's hard work. I know you must spend many hours talking to politicians, but what are the other aspects of your communication and commitment plan?

MCB: If you think I never experienced University of North Carolina chancellors and hospital chiefs and other CEOs sitting around the table shaking their heads and muttering here comes another unfunded mandate from the president, you're wrong. I have great sympathy for our chancellors, who are spread as thin as any other major university leaders and are trying to do everything at once. So, for example, when we launched this major new initiative to connect this university to the economic transformation of North Carolina and made economic development a high priority, I know that a lot of them just shook their heads about it and wondered how we could add all of these goals to our present priorities. But I think that we have been successful inside the university in communicating that our ability to secure the resources to support them is now, and will in the future, be based on the belief of the public that what the university is doing is creating the workforce of the future, supporting the technology and research that is going to create new jobs and new products, and that we are committed to extending the expertise of the university out into our communities, urban and rural. Money is a very important incentive in any university and I think even modest amounts of money can induce faculty who are innately curious and interested in exploring new areas. If you can find a way to tap into that passion about what they do and you have a little bit of money to help them do it, you really can accomplish a lot of things that I don't believe the private sector could possibly accomplish with three or four times as much money.

FL: Making change is often not synonymous with making friends. Can you describe one or more incidents and how you dealt with them?

MCB: In public universities it has grown increasingly difficult to align the interests of the various constituencies whose support of the institution is a prerequisite to success and to maintaining your ability to lead. In my professional lifetime, and especially in the last decade, we have had to deal with problems in accomplishing needed change, not only in a culture that doesn't easily adapt to change, but in situations where there are multiple constituencies whose interests are aligned with the way things used to be. I don't know anybody who has been able to succeed as a change agent without accumulating barnacles. I have a sort of conceptual metric of the "accomplishment to resistance" ratio and if I'm not pushing the limit on that, I feel as if I'm not accomplishing enough. I believe there is a great sense of urgency about fulfilling our mission in the context of twenty-first-century requirements, but the resistance to transformational efforts will grow if we aren't respectful of the reasons for that resistance to change. And of course in a public university system you are bound to have board members who have a special interest in the campus they attended as students, people who may be avid athletic fans, others who may have a particular policy interest that is their personal passion, some who have political aspirations, and politicians who are trying to accomplish their agendas. There are many ways in which public university leadership jobs are very complicated. If you make a hundred decisions and ninety-eight of them are ones in which some key leaders—whether board members or politicians, government leaders or business leaders—were in full agreement with the decisions you made, they forget about it. But if there are two in which the decision you made was not aligned with their interests, those are the decisions that are etched in their memories. Arguably the greatest challenge to leadership in public higher education today is the issue you've defined: how do you accomplish change and maintain the support of all the constituencies that are central to the life of the university?

FL: The way in which you responded to that question I think is ample proof that you are an experienced and successful leader. As you and I know, you can't win them all. You have to understand the turf very well, know when to hold firm, and when to yield gracefully. As you learn about the culture, you begin to have in advance an idea of the way that you can tackle the issues that are worth taking on and going the distance to support.

MCB: Yes. You can't compromise on your values and sometimes the price you pay for that is a very high price. You have to wake up every morning knowing that today may be the day that you pay that price.

FL: One of the nicest things a couple of board chairs told me was that they felt that I was tough because I was willing to make difficult decisions on issues that involved values. Of course, that doesn't mean I don't have scars.

I can't leave the topic of vision and planning without asking you about your stunning success in persuading the legislature, the governor, and the public to support a huge public bond issue. It was $3.1 billion to finance construction and renovation of facilities for the whole university system and the community colleges. How did you pull off this miracle?

MCB: It was a two-year process and between year one and year two, I said to my colleagues, more times than I care to count, that everything looks like a failure when it's only half done. We began the effort by documenting the condition of more than 800 buildings in the University of North Carolina. We pulled together teams from all of our campuses under the leadership of a consultant to accomplish that. We did our homework. We knew what was needed. We developed threshold requirements for every classroom and every laboratory in the universities that told us what it would cost to bring every campus and every building up to twenty-first-century standards. It took us a lot of time and a lot of hard work to compile the report that we made to the general assembly.

FL: Did you have some people from the different campuses with you when you went before the assembly or was it just you and your staff making the presentation?

MCB: Throughout the entire process we tapped everybody who was part of the university, but the result of our study showed that we needed to make an infusion of capital of $7 billion in order to meet the ten year enrollment projections, to have enough space to accommodate the enrollment that we projected, and to bring old buildings up to modern standards. I will go to my grave remembering the look of shock on the faces of the chancellors when I said I think we ought to go for at least half of this right now. We got some very quick support from the senate. I should have known better than to believe that you could accomplish something this big so easily, but the senate very quickly turned this into legislation, passed it through the committee, and it looked as if it were sailing through. Then we hit a wall. Election politics were heating up. The House leadership had recently become Republican for the first time since reconstruction. Three billion dollars would have doubled the debt of the State of North Carolina throughout its history. It was the biggest bond issue ever in American higher education anywhere and there was no history of North Carolina being willing to issue debt on the full faith and credit of this state in an amount even approaching what we were asking for. It became a very big election issue that turned on fiscal responsibility and the matter of whether or not it was right for the legislature to take this action without a vote of the people. Our friends and supporters in the senate didn't think we needed a vote of the people. I think Senate leaders thought we could never get a bond approved by the voters because it was so huge. The house passed a bill that was closer to one billion than to three and required a vote of the people. This result reflected election politics, but it also reflected the historic dynamics between the house and the senate. All of this happened late in the session when everybody wanted to go home. The differences were so great that the conference committee never even met and the session adjourned without taking any action on our proposal.

What we asked them to do in the final study bill was to give us a legislative study commission to take a look at our report, examine our proposal and come back with a recommendation. I made it clear that I was fully prepared to take a bond referendum to a vote of the people. We spent five to six months bringing that legislative commission around to campuses of the university and showing them the condition of our laboratories and other facilities. We took a big risk by revealing labs with inadequate wiring, leaking ceilings, lab equipment that was antiquated or being cannibalized to repair other equipment. We believed that the citizens did not want our students—their kids—to study in second-rate facilities. In the visits of the legislative commission to our campuses, things happened that none of us could have orchestrated or predicted. A young professor teaching chemistry expressed to the commission, in a most professional way, the challenges she felt in protecting the safety of our students in an antiquated laboratory. As she spoke, all of a sudden she was overcome by emotion. You could have heard a pin drop in that room. There were many "poster children" –facilities that were unsatisfactory to meeting our standards for academic quality – that we showed the members of the study commission. The public television network, which is a part of the university but operates with complete editorial independence, picks a theme every year, in order to focus on an important North Carolina policy issue. In that year, they selected the condition of the physical facilities of higher education in the state because they thought that it was such a significant, if controversial topic. They did documentaries that were shown on public television over the course of a year. It helped!

It was a long and very busy year that I will summarize in short. Within the first week after the general assembly reconvened the following year, they introduced and passed legislation unanimously authorizing the university to seek support of the people through a bond referendum in the amount of $3.1

billion. There were lots of people, including the smartest politicians, who thought we should not go to the ballot in a presidential election year. It was also a year in which Jim Hunt, with sixteen years as governor of the state of North Carolina, was leaving office. We were electing a new governor for the first time in a very long time. They thought that we would never get the attention of the voters with so many other major issues on the ballot. There were many newspaper cartoons during the months leading up to and following the election. One of my favorite cartoons shows one person saying to another "Was there anything else on the ballot this year besides the bonds?" The response was, "Oh yeah, I think we elected a president this year." It turned out that the bond issue provided coattails. Once the political pollsters learned that there was lots of support for the bond issue, it was endorsed by people who were running for election.

I think we ran a good campaign. We raised money to run it. The North Carolina Citizens for Business and Industry, which is our state version of a chamber of commerce, served as the independent intermediary to oversee the campaign. We were able to deposit with them the money that we had raised to run the campaign in order to make sure that we were operating within the legal guidelines because there are strict limitations on how you can use funds within a public institution. We visited Rotaries for breakfast, Kiwanis for lunch, and local chambers of commerce for dinner. At one point we put together a little piece that characterized our campaign as stretching from barbershop to board-room. It was both grassroots and grass tops. The students and faculty on every one of our campuses were out in the grocery stores and in the barbershops. I think we had a good strategy on our campaign. We invested our money in the right kinds of TV and radio, but most importantly what we were able to do is to connect with those people in North Carolina who fervently believed in the university and wanted their kids and their grandkids to have an opportunity to go to the university. The bond issue passed in all 100 counties with the support of three out of four voters. Some of the highest positive voting rates were in the counties with the lowest educational attainment. In the poorest, most rural parts of North Carolina, the citizens came out and supported this bond referendum. It was a clear and ringing statement of how North Carolina sees itself as a progressive, forward-looking state.

We came out of it feeling pretty good, but, as all the chancellors and my colleagues know, the ultimate success depends upon how we execute the projects funded by this bond. The single phrase we most often hear re-quoted is my comment that this is a marvelous career-ending opportunity, because we pledged that we were going to implement this on time and within budget. Amazingly there are more than 300 capital projects underway today within this university. We are essentially on time and within budget. We have had a lot of good luck. The interest rates have been so low with the economy down, that the cost of capital is the lowest in forty years. Moreover, the economic downturn has meant bids on the construction have been under budget. We have almost 90 percent of the construction under contract and we are witnessing an amazing physical transformation of each of our sixteen campuses. The results are extending the university's ability to serve more students, enhance the quality of instruction, expand our research capabilities, and create aesthetically beautiful environments. The potential is truly inspiring.

FL: You created your own luck.

MCB: You're kind to say that.

FL: What methods have you used to address the outcomes of initiatives in the system as a whole and the needs of the sixteen campuses?

MCB: We are serious about accountability and in our strategic plan and strategic directions we try to identify metrics that we can use to monitor our progress. One of the things that the North Carolina system had been doing, long before Molly Broad arrived, is a series of student satisfaction surveys. Now we've expanded our accountability efforts. For a long time we have used the National Survey of Student Engagement, a Pew Foundation initiative which I think is a terrific way of measuring the quality of the academic experiences of students. The results are sent to the chancellor each year. We don't do comparisons from one campus to another but we look at the pattern over time on individual campuses and when we sit down with the chancellor and his or her team, we talk about where there have been changes, where there have been improvements, and where there is an indication that perhaps efforts need to be invested. But when we say, for example, that we're committed to affordable access to the university and people ask why we are raising tuition if we want it to be affordable, we have some pretty serious metrics about how we achieve affordable access. They're not complicated, but we say if our college going rate continues to go up, if the amount of debt the students are graduating with is not going up and if unmet need based upon financial aid requirements is not increasing, then we feel as if we are providing affordable access. It's that kind of metric we use to be accountable so that people know we're not just engaging in hyperbole or wishful thinking.

FL: How did you measure progress towards your long-term goals? Do you do that as well?

MCB: We do. And so we monitor some fairly straightforward metrics. For example, we report the academic performance of athletes. I bring in all the athletic directors, and we report to the board of governors on these key issues. They're not high stakes in any sense but the public character of those reports is a pretty significant incentive for campuses to want not to be embarrassed by the results. So in each of the areas that we have a strategic direction, we report every year to the board of governors.

FL: And how do you celebrate that success? Is there some kind of report that goes out so that the public, beyond the people that you're meeting with, will understand that you are successful?

MCB: Yes, but I believe most universities tend to hide their light under a bushel, in part because our role as "critic" of ideas gives us discomfort in claiming bragging rights. The University of North Carolina does not communicate our successes as well as other universities. We have only one person who has responsibility for communications. We communicate our achievements in our public reports to the board of governors.

FL: What have each of your internal constituencies expected you to do for the university system, for each individual university, and in response to their particular needs? For example, what are the expectations that the members of your governing board have of you?

MCB: There are thirty-six members of the board of governors. They are all elected by the general assembly, half in the house and half in the senate. They have four-year terms, so every two years, they are either up for reappointment or we get new members of the board of governors. It is a very large board and is inevitably comprised of individuals who have served in campus roles. We also have boards of trustees on each of our campuses to whom certain areas of authority have been delegated. Many of the members of the board of governors were presidents of their alumni organization or were on a campus board of trustees. They come with deep knowledge of and commitment to a single campus. What the experienced members explain to new members is that they are now a body corporate on behalf of the entire university and not the advocates of individual parts. One of the important challenges faced by every public university system is that the board is inevitably comprised of constituents of given individual institutions.

FL: Is there anything specific that they expect of you or is it just everything that falls under the rubric of being head of the system?

MCB: The code of the university spells out very clearly the duties and responsibilities of the president and those are well understood.

FL: What are the individual expectations of the administration of each of the sixteen universities, short of giving them all the money they need to run their campus?

MCB: They expect me to give them support in their major priority areas. One of the essential roles that can be played by individuals in a central office is to know the most important goals that each campus is trying to accomplish. It is our job to do blocking for them and help them to make it happen. On the other hand, we need to hold each institution to high expectations. The central university administration must know when to do everything it can to help individual campuses make innovative and worthwhile projects possible, but it must also know when to say no. Our responsibility to the social compact between the university and citizens is to balance the aspirations of the university and its faculty with the needs of the people of the state.

FL: What does the faculty expect of you?

MCB: The faculty of the University of North Carolina is a terrific group of individuals who believe deeply in the university and there is a level of civility in this faculty that you don't see in very many places. We have a faculty assembly that's comprised of faculty representatives from each of our campuses. I meet with them on a regular basis. They ask hard questions and take on big, important, tough issues, but our faculty is grateful for the efforts that have been undertaken and the resources we have been able to find in the budget for the new buildings. They rise above the inconvenience. We have had only modest salary increases in the past several years and it would be quite understandable if they were grumpy. Yet the faculty assembly is very supportive of our efforts on the university's behalf. I don't know very many university presidents who get standing ovations from their faculty senates for what was secured in last year's budget. They nominated me for the prestigious AAUP Meiklejohn Award for Academic Freedom, which I was honored to receive last year. It is a great privilege to work with this faculty. Our faculty senate is an amazingly dedicated, civil, and high-minded group.

FL: What are the students' expectations of you?

MCB: We meet with the student body presidents. They are all members of their campus boards of trustees and I meet with them on a regular basis. I set part of the agenda; they set part of the agenda. We close each year by asking them to identify issues they have come to learn need attention. We invite them to make presentations to the university officers focused on policies, programs, and problems where we can help the next generation of students. These sessions have been very productive in areas such as improving orientation of student leaders to their trustee responsibilities, addressing student advising, dealing with campus safety, or whatever other issues emerge from these discussions.

FL: Do the staff have particular expectations of you?

MCB: We do not have collective bargaining but we do have staff councils that have been put in place in the last few years. We consult with these staff councils and listen carefully to their ideas and concerns. In my experience, staff members at universities, from groundskeepers to vice presidents, take pride in the institution they serve and have a strong belief in the value the university provides to students and society at large. They are a central component of the university community and contribute importantly to keeping it a community.

FL: And finally, what do the alumni of the University of North Carolina expect? You probably encounter them in different venues.

MCB: We do see in them in different venues and we have an organization of all the alumni associations. It is quite helpful to us on lobbying and other efforts in advocacy. At one meeting of the board of governors each year we receive a report from the alumni and have an opportunity for some interaction with them, promoting good relationships with the alumni. On major initiatives, such as the bond campaign, we have mobilized the alumni networks of the campuses of the university to great success. They can be our most ardent advocates.

FL: How do you manage the different, sometimes conflicting expectations of some of these constituencies? Are there any particular incidents or issues that you would like to talk about concerning those conflicting expectations?

MCB: As you know so well, one of the great challenges of university leadership is the multiple constituencies whose interests must be balanced. Those interests may not be aligned. Trustees and students may have very different views about increasing tuition. Legislators and the press may have their own ideas about tuition. The faculty views of the role of athletics may not be perfectly aligned with the interest of alumni and sports fans. And so it goes. At our campuses that participate in Division I athletics, the amount of time and attention the chancellors invest in intercollegiate athletics is disproportionate. The chancellors receive more email, telephone calls, and letters on matters relating to athletics than any other single issue that faces them.

FL: Historically you have had very good athletic teams in many sports, both men's and women's teams.

MCB: That's correct and we have historically had the reputation of running a first-rate program where students graduate and where the values of the university are front and center. For example we're now going through a very difficult public exchange over whether or not Chapel Hill will permit businesses to put up billboards inside the previously pristine athletic arenas. Chapel Hill is reaching the point where the cost of its athletic program is prompting them to look for sources of revenue like this and it has caused an uproar in the newspapers.

FL: What importance have you placed on the role of the North Carolina system in the state and upon the role of each individual university in its community?

MCB: We expect university campuses to be front and center in a leadership role in economic growth and development in each of their regions and they are. However, what we've been trying to do is to articulate the fact that we are no longer a group of institutions each of which owns a certain part of the state's geography. In a world of e-learning and distance education, the marketplace is open and competitive. There are institutions coming into North Carolina— the University of Phoenix to name just one—that are expecting and striving to grow their enrollments. So we no longer believe that a given campus owns its region of the state but that it must be competitive to attract students from everywhere and can use its expertise to help in other communities and regions.

FL: What have been the two or three major groups outside the university system that you have needed to work with and what have these groups expected of you personally as head of the system? I assume that one of the major groups would be the legislature.

MCB: Of course. The general assembly is our banker. They provide the resources. This is a state where the authorities of the governor are relatively speaking limited and the authorities of the general assembly are very great, very powerful. Securing their support in funding but also in legislative policy requires us to work very closely with the legislature. Over the long sweep of history, the general assembly of North Carolina has been very supportive of this state's university. Their track record is very strong. The political dynamic has become complicated in recent years because of the dramatic political shifts occurring in the South. We also work closely with the North Carolina Citizens for Business and Industry and our connections to the businesses of North Carolina are very important. They work with us and support our legislative agenda.

FL: So support is not a one-way street, it's a two-way street for the business community and the University of North Carolina.

MCB: Exactly.

FL: In dealing with the day-to-day realities of your presidency, with so many responsibilities, how do you allocate your time and what have been your top priorities?

MCB: The allocation of one's time is very important, so we audit our calendar. When we do our self-appraisal, we identify how we distributed our time and effort last year and what changes we're proposing to make in how we distribute our time next year. It's a simple but illuminating way to engage with vice presidents about where they see their division going and how they might find it useful to alter how they are allocating their time. Certainly the way I allocate my time is very different today than the way it was when I first arrived, when I was spending a lot more time outside the university getting to know the state and the major constituencies, creating an office in Washington, and establishing a presence of the University of North Carolina in major national higher education associations. But I do think it is an important issue. Our schedule and our calendar run our lives and if we delegate that to somebody else without managing it, then we have nobody to blame but ourselves when we conclude that we've allocated our time inappropriately.

FL: Would I be correct in saying that your top priorities are those six issues that that sit on your desk as well as everybody else's desk in order to remind you of your focus?

MCB: Absolutely. That's the acid test of how we're spending our time. These six strategic directions guide our action plans and they guide how we organize the work of the university.

FL: What part of your work have you enjoyed the most?

MCB: Hearing students talk about what their university experience has meant to them. It's another version of our earlier conversation about how alums, when they come back and are recognized, reflect on what the university has meant to them. Realizing the impact of the university on the lives of students is the most wonderful part of what we do. It is a way for us to feel part of something that is so much bigger than any one individual. Moreover, we're part of something that has stretched across generations and that has changed the lives of people.

FL: I'm going to go from the sweetest to the most difficult. Every leader experiences planned and unplanned events that escalate to time consuming crises. They can be fiscal challenges. They can be contract negotiations. Among the most common are PR challenges. Are there any crisis management stories that you can share with us?

MCB: One thing of which you can be sure is that there are going to be many crises. You don't know where they're going to come from or what they're going to be about, but you can be absolutely certain that they will arise. The example that comes to my mind at the moment is the freshman reading assignment, which was a book on Islam at Chapel Hill the year before last. It became a cause célèbre in the state and around the nation, as people with heightened concerns after 9/11 saw it as an inappropriate act to study the religion of those who were responsible for 9/11. Yet we are a university and if there is any place in society where differences of viewpoint ought to be able to be addressed civilly and openly, the university ought to be the place where that can happen. However this had many different manifestations and there were some moments in which, over this single issue, our budget was being held hostage, with the risk of deep and major cuts. Sometimes people behave in ways that are completely irrational when you have touched issues that are emotional and this is just one example. But we have all lived through such situations. Sometimes the emotional issues are ones that happen in the minds and hearts of students when the sun is out, spring is just around the corner, and their passions run high. They pick issues that brew a crisis overnight, when students mobilize, take over buildings, and call on their peers to strike from attendance at their classes. It is just inevitably a part of our life. Balancing individual freedoms with civility and respect for others— not to mention good taste—is, however, a matter of growing concern on American university campuses.

FL: Those are excellent examples. The attack on the freshman reading assignment was a crisis that spoke to our raison d'être as universities. Briefly how would you define leadership?

MCB: I think of leadership in the context of the university—an open and highly consultative organization. It is very important to acknowledge that there are many definitions of leadership. The one that means the most to me is the ability to create organizational capacity behind the mission and goals of the institution. That can't happen without vision; it can't happen without strategy. It can't happen without building a strong team to make it happen. It can't happen without good management, and they all are interconnected in my view of what leadership is.

FL: What are the most important qualities for a university system president today?

MCB: A deep knowledge of the university and an abiding commitment to the values of the university, a robust constitution, an appreciation for complexity and ability to keep the long-run welfare in mind. The events of today, while they may eat you alive, cannot totally define who you are and what role you are playing. You must keep the longer-term welfare of the institution always in focus.

FL: How have the role and demands of the system presidency changed over the past few decades in response to the disinvestment of most of our states in public higher education?

MCB: Because higher education is a discretionary part of most state budgets, it has been subject to pressures from the economy, the devolution from Washington to the states of responsibility for health and welfare, as well as the rising cost of prisons and other criminal justice activities. All of these factors have forced public university systems to operate in an increasingly competitive environment for state dollars.

FL: What changes have occurred in response to the technological revolution?

MCB: It is my belief that information technology is today a fundamental part of every aspect of our mission. Information technology is the scaffolding upon which modern science and research are conducted. The price of involving information technology in the university is a very high price. It is very difficult to make the investments necessary at a time when resources are so strained, but in my view it is the responsibility of the system president to ensure the future welfare of the institution. While you may not be at the cutting edge of the use of technology, you must be at the proven edges of its impact and its contribution to the university.

FL: How has your role changed in response to the need for access to quality higher education for much larger, more diverse cohorts of students?

MCB: We know unequivocally that a university education is the single most important factor in determining lifetime income and we believe it plays an equally important role in the quality of life. We are the bottleneck institution through which success and failure must go and it is our duty in my view as public institutions to make sure that the university reaches out and serves an increasingly diverse group of potential students. Achieving this diversity is a social, educational, moral, and economic imperative.

FL: How can a president function in response to the increasingly strident demands of students and politicians for high quality and accountability in both expenditures and results?

MCB: Pray and practice yoga.

FL: How would you characterize your leadership style?

MCB: I think my leadership style, and here I am playing back what I hear from my colleagues, is a very hands-on, open, collaborative style. They always tell me that I am leading from 50,000 feet, that is, at a relatively high level of conceptualization, strategy and abstraction while delegating the implementation to individuals within the organization. Because I have spent my entire career in universities and have served in each of the major university divisions, I also have a deep understanding of the details. I believe it is a good combination—leading from a vision and managing from experience and understanding.

FL: What do you believe will be the most significant legacy that you leave to the North Carolina system?

MCB: I certainly hope that the legacy, if there is one, is directly connected with those priorities that I identified to you at the beginning of our conversation:

- that our historically black campuses are strong and vital in fulfilling their mission,
- that we have invested wisely in information technology,
- that we can maintain quality and competitiveness in teaching and in research,
- that we have extended access to North Carolinians,
- that we have been able to sustain our college going rate at the most competitive levels in the nation.
- that we have improved our retention, and
- that we've succeeded in diversifying our sources of revenue in a way that builds on our state support but provides that margin of excellence that can only come from private grants or from federal grants.

My personal experience as a university student had such a profound effect on my life and my aspirations that I am sure it shaped my desire to make the university my life's work. One of the most important things in the earliest stage of my life in the university was the oath to the Athenian State that is etched in the wall of the Maxwell School of Citizenship at Syracuse University where I was a university student. It essentially laid out the goal of making the city (substitute "the university") better and more beautiful, so that you can pass it along to your successor in a way that is stronger and better than the institution that was passed to you when you accepted this post.

FL: What advice would you give to new presidents? What should they choose to tackle first?

MCB: Tackle first the issue that is a combination of most important and achievable.

FL: What is the most important skill or set of skills that presidents will have to have to succeed in the future? And how are those skills different from the skills most needed in the past?

MCB: To be successful in a public university presidency you have to be able to operate in different frames. What do I mean by that? These are frames that are quite different than the one in which a faculty member is successful as a solo contributor where the rational frame plays the most important role. To be successful as a president, you have to be able to function effectively in the political frame and the symbolic frame, as well as in the rational frame. That is easier said than done and, in my judgment, it is worth getting some help from a place like the Center for Creative Leadership or an executive coach or someone who is experienced. Advice is especially important if you are moving into a presidency for the first time from the very different kind of role that a faculty member or a dean plays.

FL: And finally, what has been at the core of your work in higher education? What are the underlying purposes that you have worked to accomplish?

MCB: I think the university is arguably the most important institution in our society and it is the institution that both conserves the best of the past and envisions what is possible in the future. It is an institution that transforms the life of individuals and if we don't keep that at the core of what we do everyday, if we permit ourselves to get caught up with any set of difficult and complicated problems and forget what the ultimate purpose of the university is, we cannot be fully successful.

FL: Now we turn to issue oriented questions. As states, squeezed by entitlement programs and revenue shortfalls, reduce higher education funding, how can public systems resolve their budget problems and continue to build both access and excellence? Is it the responsibility of our state systems to solve the problem of access? Is there any realistic hope that the states and the federal government will take on more of the responsibility of providing students from low-income families access to quality education?

MCB: I do think that declining state support is a challenge but a very important one for us to face and not ignore. We must connect the future of the university with the needs of the state today. I believe if you can make that connection, you are going to be in a better position to insure that access to higher education is extended. Otherwise I think higher education as a discretionary part of the state budget will face stiff competition from entitlement programs like health care for limited state dollars.

FL: You have had the opportunity to work with more than one governing board in your experiences. It might be helpful to the readers of this book if you could outline in general terms what you feel are the important characteristics of good governing boards and what are some of the problems one can encounter in dealing with governing boards.

MCB: The most important characteristic of a good governing board in my opinion is one that behaves like a body corporate, one that understands that it has a collective responsibility for the welfare of the entire institution and resists the temptation to focus its energies and its interests on any single part or any single issue.

FL: Do you want to talk about any of the problems that presidents might encounter when members of their boards do become focused upon certain issues?

MCB: Yes, the danger is that boards may become the vehicle through which political leaders wish to accomplish their goals. There are obviously personal and special interests that we read about or see getting acted out in public universities. In America we see individuals who view their board membership as an opportunity to advance their personal ambition. The *Chronicle of Higher Education* is filled with stories and you and I know colleagues who have found themselves in very challenging governing circumstances.

FL: In the past few years there have been instances in which the governor of a state has intervened in policy issues or personnel decisions in the state's flagship public university or in the system. It is more the exception than the rule, but it is disturbing, particularly if it marks a trend toward politicization.

MCB: I hope it is not a trend. I certainly think we can find examples of many different sorts. The finest exemplar that I have known was Bruce Babbitt, the former governor of Arizona who, when he named the members of the university's board of regents seemed to have a grand master plan in his mind. He envisaged that a great university board should have people with certain skills and experience, leaders of large complex organizations, hospitals, corporations, utility companies, experience with major athletic teams, persons of color and so forth. He would invite people into his office to interview them before he asked their permission to nominate them to the board of regents. He would tell them something to this effect: "I'm naming you to this post because of your experience, your judgment, and your commitment to the state and the university. I don't want you to second guess or try to figure out what I want you to do. I want you to exercise the good judgment that led me to appoint you. Whenever I have an issue that I want you to give special consideration, I will come to the board, I will lay it out. If you agree with me, support me, if you don't agree with me, vote against me." While this is not the typical example, it is the sort of leadership philosophy that can make a huge difference in the quality of the governance. Inevitably board members may question whether the individuals or the organization that put them in this role did so expecting the board member to help advance their interests.

FL: What is your take on the current very public and damaging perceptions of serious problems in recruiting, admission, retention, graduation, student athlete conduct or misconduct and funding of athletics including the huge escalation in the compensation of successful Division I coaches in revenue sports? Can we solve these problems or are they just insurmountable?

MCB: I'm not very optimistic about it. Although I hasten to say that in the University of North Carolina one of the authorities that is delegated to the campuses and to the board of trustees is athletics and I am very judicious about observing that delegation. Having said that, I am a sounding board and adviser to the chancellors and I do my level best to help them accomplish what they want to accomplish within the framework of the board policy. I believe the arms race in athletics is completely out of control. The consequence of placing the chancellors or presidents with direct responsibility for athletics has the effect of making the chancellor or president the focus of all the constituencies of influential individuals in the state who then lean on the president or the chancellor when the chancellor depends upon their good will and their philanthropy and their political support. I think presidents and chancellors are in a very difficult position and if I were Czarina for the day in athletics, I would put the idea of a spending cap on the table for serious consideration.

FL: How important do you think that it is for system leaders and university presidents to participate in national associations and join in their work of discussing and formulating solutions for current problems and issues in higher education? And what do you think have been the most important contributions that you have been able to make on the national scene.

MCB: I think it is our duty on behalf of the larger higher education community to contribute to shaping the national policies that impact higher education, not just today, but much more importantly downstream. So I believe that it is one of our inherent responsibilities to give back to the profession that supports us. I also see this as an opportunity to shape policy directions in ways that advance the mission of our institution and in a way that allows you to write on a much larger screen than your state or your institution. The areas in which I think I personally have contributed the most include work on the role of the university in economic growth. I am very active in the Council on Competitiveness on the new innovation initiative. I am very active in the Business Higher Education Forum and I led an effort that produced the report "Building a Nation of Learners," which talks about transforming the learning process and the role of information technology in accelerating the pace of academic achievement. I am deeply committed to the work of the National Association of State Universities and Land Grant Colleges (NASULGC), in particular its efforts in the areas of information technology and redefining the meaning of outreach and engagement, as well as its goal of serving the states, which is the primary mission of NASULGC.

FL: How have the universities in the North Carolina system responded to the widespread criticism that research universities do not care about undergraduate teaching?

MCB: Our campuses have been quite responsive. Every year we gather and report the data on the interaction of tenure track faculty and full professors with undergraduate students and on average class size. A number of initiatives have been undertaken on our campuses, including very small class sections, classes in interdisciplinary areas team-taught by full professors. Those efforts are very much a part of the freshman year on many of our campuses. I think they are great examples of our concern about undergraduate education.

FL: In the area of affirmative action, what steps has the University of North Carolina system taken to encourage diversification of its campuses in terms of student bodies, faculty, administrators, and staff?

MCB: Because North Carolina is a state that went through the era of segregation and then desegregated under a consent decree, we are in a different circumstance historically than states in other parts of our country. What we have done in North Carolina has been to scrub our policies and practices relating to admission and to financial aid to ensure that they meet the legal tests so that this university does not get mired down with the cost and the lack of progress that comes from a major legal case against our practices. We've done all of that at a time when we also actively increased diversification of our enrollment. In terms of faculty, I think we still aren't there yet. We are continuing to work hard to diversify our faculty, but it is more challenging now that target of opportunity approaches are not warmly welcomed by the courts, so it requires us to reach out more effectively and more creatively to bring nontraditional candidates into the pipeline.

FL: The last question is on the future. What do you see as the strongest forces driving the need for change in higher education over the next ten to twenty years? What are the most important changes that you expect to see take place? Finally what will higher education leaders need to do or do more of in the future to help their institutions succeed, particularly given the rate of change in the environment? If you have to look above the trees, what do we need to do, what are going to be the big problems that are looming around the corner?

MCB: The first is a global change and the most important challenge we face in the future; the explosion of knowledge, the expansion of information technology into every part of our life, and the transformation of our economy from one that depended on land and natural resources, then to an industrial manufacturing economy, and now to one that relies on intellectual capital to be productive. The creation of intellectual capital is the most critical ingredient in the global economy of the future. Those are all powerful forces of change that are occurring globally. Our universities must play a central role in addressing these forces of change and responding to them.

John T. Casteen III

John Casteen became president of the University of Virginia in August of 1990. An alumnus of the university, he taught at the University of California, Berkeley and the University of Virginia before becoming the secretary of education of the state of Virginia in 1982. In that post, he supervised reforms in higher education and in secondary education, directed the desegregation process for higher education, and initiated state support for research.

From 1985 to 1990, Casteen was the president of the University of Connecticut. There he worked with the university community to formulate an ambitious vision for the university, set goals, and build several major programs. Under his leadership, the university built important research and teaching facilities as well as a basketball facility that played a role in positioning the university as a national institution.

At the University of Virginia, he has restructured the university's administrative structure and governance, overseen improvements in academic programs, and undertaken major physical improvements, including structures for the Darden School and the Law School, as well as for American Studies and a special collections library. He successfully completed one of the largest capital fund campaigns ever undertaken, ending with $1.4 billion, and has announced a new campaign with a goal of $3 billion.

Among the national leadership roles he has taken have been membership on the boards of directors of the American Council on Education and the National Collegiate Athletic Association, as well as trustee and chair of the College Entrance Examination Board, commissioner of the Education Commission of the States, chair of the Association of Governing Board's council of presidents, and chair of the Association of American Universities.

A writer of short fiction, as well as scholarly papers in medieval literature, bibliographical contributions, and papers on public policy, Casteen received the 1987 Mishima Award for a collection of his short stories.

Francis Lawrence: John, you've had a career that has taken you into the top ranks of higher education leadership, serving as Virginia's secretary of education for three years, as president of the University of Connecticut for five years, and, since 1990, as the president of the University of Virginia. What has been at the core of your work in higher education? What are the underlying purposes that you have worked to accomplish?

John Casteen: I see my career in education as a series of accidents. I never intended to be a professor. I never intended to be a dean. I never intended to be a president. I have been fortunate in the time in which I've lived because it's been possible to build my life around issues that matter to me. One of the chief among those issues has been opening up this university to all of humankind, helping it to be not a boy's school, not a white boy's school, not a rich, white boy's school, but helping it instead to embrace the entire population. Finding ways to allow the university to serve broadly has been a big part of my relationship with the University of Virginia because I grew up in a place where I saw people of varied educational backgrounds achieve wonderful things. There are very few pleasures quite like watching what happens when a skilled artisan, say a boat builder, puts a boat into the water and the thing does what it's supposed to do. In the culture where I grew up, that was a big deal. You really admired people who could accomplish things with their hands. That has something to do with what you are asking me. Universities free people to be the best they can be. I talked the other night to the man who designed the hull of my boat. He is actually a marine architect, a superbly educated man. He asked me which boat I was talking about and I told him. He said, "Oh yes: those wonderful arc sections." I asked him what he meant. He said that every line you can draw through the hull is a perfectly regular arc. This man spent a couple of years circumscribing the hull from every conceivable angle to make sure that there was no hostile angle to be seen, and he remembered the boat in terms of mathematical exercises. To admire his product from his learned perspective was wonderful.

FL: Could we talk a little more about your roots, about the ways that your family background and your education contributed to shaping your values and your development?

JC: I grew up in Portsmouth Virginia, a shipyard town, where my father and all of the men in my family worked in the shipyard. My father is a retired sheet metal worker and my grandfather was a storekeeper who processed ship supplies. In those days, the culture of the town was very much a blue-collar culture. Typically boys finished high school, spent time in the navy, as my dad did, enrolled in an apprentice school, as my brother did—I have a brother who is an outside marine machinist—and then spent careers that typically extended up to about age sixty working in their specialties at the shipyard. For boys, career progress consisted of the military period, the apprentice period (a very structured and rigorous-four year introduction to the marine trade), then a skilled trade rate called journeyman, the first kind of licensed mechanic, up through various intermediate grades. At one point, my dad was a layout man: he devised the drawings necessary to put together a complicated job and later became a foreman in his specialty. As the industry changed, he and my brother made the transition from their original areas of specialization to something else. My dad became the superintendent of an entity called the naval reactor plant, which was primarily a maintenance facility for the reactors that drive nuclear submarines. My grandfather's original education was just through the eighth grade level, but in midlife, he attended the Wharton School. My dad had a high school education, followed by the apprentice school, and then more advanced education. One of the things that always struck me about the people in my family was that they returned to schooling regularly rather than simply disappearing from schooling after their initial formal years of education ended. My grandfather was in his forties when he went to the Wharton School.

Girls in the town where I grew up tended to be brighter and to work harder in school than boys. They took more advanced courses in high school and tended to go further in school. As I remember it, the classes were about half and half divided between boys and girls, but the girls occupied about two-thirds of the seats in the advanced courses and were usually the valedictorians and the salutatorians of their classes. About twice as many of the girls went on to college as did the boys, and the girls were the great achievers in the group. My cohort stayed fairly close to one another. We mailed newsletters that have kept this community intact, even though people have wandered all over the world. The occupation of choice for girls was to be a schoolteacher, either as a life-long occupation or for part of a lifetime.

What does any of that have to do with my history? My father and grandfather both had the notion that any child in the family, girl or boy, ought to be able to choose to be any kind of professional that the person wanted to be. There was no pressure to go to college but, if one wanted to go to college, the family message was that one had to be prepared at the point of finishing high school. So we really did not have the option of electing not to take the hard subjects. We took mathematics, science, and foreign languages. Our choices were driven not so much by ambition as by a statement frequently made in the family that you had to be qualified to make a choice. If you didn't prepare, you wouldn't have that option.

Another factor in my education was that I was in high school at the time when this university and others in the region first began to pay attention to SAT scores. Twice during my schooldays an unexpected success in a standardized test, a success that seemed to surpass my performance in school, attracted attention that was healthy. When I was in the fifth grade, my teachers made me retake a statewide IQ test. They suspected that I was cheating because the score was too good. I sat in a room with a number of adults monitoring me while I took the test over again. My score was better the second time, of course, because after seeing the format of the test once, I had worked out some of the things that had delayed me the first time around.

My teachers were ambitious for me. From about the fourth grade on, they told me that I really had to go on with my schooling and most of the ones who expressed an opinion about where I should attend college said that I should go to the University of Virginia. The area where I grew up literally had no colleges. We had a regional division of the College of William and Mary in Norfolk, but other than that, the closest college was William and Mary, which was about an hour and a half by car. The University of Virginia seemed like a long way away—it was about a four hour drive in those days—and Virginia Tech was a lifetime away, a full day's drive to the west.

The other test on which my performance singled me out was the SAT. Admissions travelers from Princeton and Harvard, who did not ordinarily visit schools like mine, came and were very kind about explaining how financial aid worked and what the options were. The admissions traveler who made a difference, though, was a man named Marvin Perry, who was the admissions dean at the University of Virginia and subsequently became president of Agnes Scott College in Atlanta and Goucher College in Maryland. Because he had daughters, Marvin had a passionate interest in the education of women. However, he had been a friend of Edgar F. Shannon, Jr., the president who made the University of Virginia a major university, and Edgar persuaded Marvin to spend four or five years finding a way to build a strong class of students. (Edgar's father was a Chaucer scholar at the turn of the century and published a significant book on Chaucer and the Roman poets, probably when his son was a little boy.) My dad and I went to the college night program at the school and met Marvin, who said he'd like to come to the house to have a talk with my parents.

I remember watching Marvin, my dad, and my mother sit in our kitchen at our sheet metal table with pull-out leaves on springs while Marvin jotted down numbers on a sheet of paper, showing my dad how it worked. What impressed me was that college recruiters came at all, because it was a humble community. People did not see themselves as having large claims on the world, but here was this man from a totally different civilization who came to explain to us that this is the way this child can be educated. Nobody ever said I had to do it, but Marvin laid out the way to accomplish it. Earlier in my schooling, I had contacts with the University of Virginia because many of my teachers came here for master's degrees and a couple of UVA professors became interested in me. One collected the papers that I wrote from about the ninth grade on. I would come to Charlottesville and he would sit down and talk to me, going through the papers with me. He was doing some work related to Julian Stanley's project on mathematical precocity in young children, but he was also just a very benign sort of man. From the time I was about thirteen or fourteen years old there were people at the University of Virginia who were in touch with me or with the family. I felt sought out. In some respects, the attention puzzled me: I was not a great student. I think that the reason they were interested was, first of all, because at that time people were beginning to realize that there were kids who didn't fit neatly into the holes. In my first year at the University of Virginia, I struggled with the mathematics and science requirements while doing pretty well in other subjects. Some things changed for me in the second year of college, and a lot of what I had learned previously came together for me. Nevertheless, I think that at the end of my time here, I probably had the thinnest margin for election to Phi Beta Kappa in the history of the university.

I really treasure having grown up in a blue-collar place that was committed to families, to hard work, and particularly to caring for children. The character of that community interests me, partly because I cannot remember a case of abuse of a child in that place. The community pressure for raising children in benign ways was very powerful. It was in many respects a very simple community composed primarily of people with English surnames who had done what their parents had done and lived in the same houses, on the same streets. It has retained a good bit of that character even into very modern times. The school I attended is gone now and the ethnic make-up of the community has changed: it's a wonderfully multi-racial area now. When I go back there, I still get the sense that people really cherish the integrity that was part of the way of life when I was a child.

FL: That's an interesting and extraordinary story.

JC: It has changed now, but it was a marvelous way to grow up. You could move around at night with no fear of being hurt. The biggest threat was the possibility of stepping on a snake.

FL: What personal attributes do you feel have contributed most to your success as a leader?

JC: One is that I learned how to deal with setbacks and adversities slowly. The early setbacks were painful and frightening. I learned how to live with uncertainty. Keats' letter to his brother George and his brother's wife Georgiana about negative capability comes to my mind fairly often because, as he discusses the making of a poet, he says that the state of mind has to be one in which you can live with uncertainty, not needing to have absolute answers to questions. There is a great deal that you can never know if you are operating at the top of an organization like this one, with the long range horizon and the strategic horizon in front of you. I didn't have personal mentors in the way in which Martin Meyerson was so good to people like Donald Stewart at Penn, but I did have good models to watch. When I was an assistant professor at Berkeley, a man who had retired as dean of the business school started meeting with me once a month over coffee: he would simply talk through what was involved in running the university. He had opinions based on his experience that got me thinking in an analytical way about what was involved. In 1975, I was quite happy at Berkeley: I had found a way of life that I enjoyed.

When Frank Hereford, whom I had admired a great deal when I was a student at UVA, succeeded Edgar Shannon as president, I was here as a visiting professor for one Berkeley quarter. A professor who had taught me in graduate school called to say that Frank needed an admissions dean but had not found anybody, so it might be interesting for me to talk to him. I knew nothing about admissions. In those days, the tradition here was that the admissions dean was a tenured faculty member: no titles as dean were assigned to anyone who was not a tenure-track or tenured person. I told Frank very candidly that I knew nothing about it, but, if the idea of working for him was what we were talking about, that would be attractive. We discussed it for a couple of hours and the next day a friend called me to tell me that Frank wanted me to do the job and to ask if I could start on a certain date.

That's where my administrative career started; I taught half time in the department and oversaw the admissions office. The university went out into the labor market and hired a veteran admissions officer from an historically black institution to help us begin the process of desegregating the student body. I had told Frank that one of the things I would want to do was move vigorously on desegregation and another was complete the process of becoming a coeducational institution, processes that had been started under court orders that occurred over about a twenty-year span. We had been making good progress on co-education and slow progress on desegregation. Frank used my new position to show me how the university worked. So I was invited to sit in on issues such as reform of the curriculum and was assigned research tasks that had to do with the relationship between secondary school preparation and freshman performance in our courses, as well as performance in subsequent courses. Mathematics interested me because I discovered that you could develop a powerful negative predictor of attendance at the University of Virginia simply by looking at what course turned up on a high school student's eighth grade transcript in the math category. Students who didn't take algebra in eighth grade didn't come here. It was that simple. It was such a powerful negative predictor that later on we used it in trying to restructure the state's school curriculum. I did the admissions job for six and a half years. It was hard and good work. I had to learn everything from scratch. I had to travel; I had to oversee staff; I had to do my academic work. I was doing a good deal of writing in those days: I published a book during that period and was heavily involved in my academic role.

In 1981, Edgar Shannon, who was close to Chuck Robb, called me and said that the governor-elect wanted to talk to me about some things I had been writing on what ought to be done to improve the curriculum in the public schools. I had been doing some work for the Southern Regional Education Board as a guest speaker and a consultant, looking at high school transcripts.

We had assembled an enormous bank of transcripts and were beginning to realize that course selection, particularly in the eighth and ninth grades, was a powerful predictor of what students would or would not be able to do. It seemed to me that this information had to do with preparing students to make a choice, and, there again, I can see the influence of my family's views on education. I talked to the governor-elect for about an hour. Later that night, his assistant called to tell me that the governor wanted me to serve as secretary of education. I took a leave of absence from UVA, and the board agreed to a four-year leave, so that I would be able to serve out the whole term. The work in Richmond turned out to be useful because it taught me how to manage the Washington process at the time that the federal government was giving block grants to the states. I was involved in the negotiation of the block grant for health care and education, but also for library support services and a lot of the research money. I was heavily involved with the schools. In that period, I got to know people like Ted Bell, Doc Howe, Pat Graham, Jerry Murphy, and other people who became mentors in various ways and degrees. Sid Marland, who was head of the College Board, and I became convinced (or to put it differently, he taught me) that good public universities have powerful obligations in regard to the general quality of education in the state.

Unfortunately, a lot of what has happened subsequently is not particularly well guided. In Virginia and in some other states, the fad of using tests to prove that the kids are dummies and the teachers are bad has become more important than the ongoing process of building the curriculum and sustaining enrollment in the curriculum. Teachers have been made scapegoats in very bad ways, especially in the last fifteen years. The current governor is actually quite interested in education, but there was a series of governors who were alarmed about the schools but had no meaningful remedies to offer, so they attacked rather than asking the harder questions about why the schools did or didn't work.

I was persuaded early on that it is the business of schools and teachers at every level to define standards in such a way as to provide open options for students and that the earlier the student drops out of the hard courses, the lower the student's horizon becomes. We did some studies while I was in Richmond that became important to my later thoughts on schooling. One was a set of studies done largely by Charlotte Scott, a prominent economist who was associated with our undergraduate business school here. Others were done by a man named John Knapp, who has recently retired, an economist who studied indicators that persuaded us that there is ultimately no real difference other than the course choice between the performance of the least advantaged and the most advantaged students in the schools. For example, at the point when black students in southern schools are tracked out of mathematics (largely by the advice that they get from their schools), their performance in mathematics is essentially the same as anyone else's performance: the statistical deviations are so small that they don't pop up as significant. These studies turned me into a kind of missionary. I see tracking too early as a means to diminish choice, and that as a very powerful form of disenfranchisement.

I got interested in international systems at that time. One parent, I think a CIA agent who had his children enrolled in schools in France, went around the classrooms and collected information that was used to teach parents how to make good choices for their children as they moved through school. One device we used with some success in Virginia, and actually won some prizes for it, was a large wall chart that was posted in every classroom in the state to show children what each choice meant in terms of future choices. It was a multi-color, elaborate visual aid, adapted shamelessly from a chart then used in French classrooms. The value was really in having parents see it because it helped parents to understand, first of all, that there are choices that end-stop the progress, but second that there are, almost all the way through the system, ways to go sideways and move forward again. If the determination to move exists, there really is no such thing as a dead end.

FL: That was an important initiative because parents have a very significant impact on their children's choices.

JC: My concerns about providing multiple avenues for students to go forward moved me to become very much engaged with community colleges, as I still am. I was convinced that the great hope for the region in which I had grown up was community colleges, though new developments in higher education have emerged in that area of the state in recent years. The 1890 historically black Land Grant institution, Virginia State, which is in Ettrick, Virginia, developed a branch college in Norfolk and created an important urban campus there that has been successful over time. The other new option is that the Norfolk Division of William and Mary was put under its own board and became a regional university called Old Dominion: that has made a difference. A third opportunity emerged when the Methodist Church developed a Wesleyan College at Norfolk after my time. I'm still convinced that the community college is an important driver in that region, but it has all sorts of allies there now.

FL: How did your transition from Virginia's secretary of education to a university presidency come about?

JC: My movement into being a college president was the result of a couple of accidents. I had written something that was of interest to a member of the search committee at a liberal arts college in the Northeast. The person chairing the search called me and asked me to talk to the search committee. I had frankly not thought about being a college president. My wife and I spent three consecutive Saturdays and then several days on the campus thinking it over. We had some doubts about it. In the end, they chose another candidate, but they passed along my name to the University of Connecticut. The chair of the UConn search called me one Sunday night at home and asked if I would be interested in talking with them. After we talked about it in the family a little bit, I called him back and said that I would. I was very interested in what I saw at the liberal arts college, but it wasn't a good fit. I was interested in looking at a different kind of place. The search chair described UConn as a blue-collar place, saying, "Our kids are children of immigrants. It's a very rich mix of people but, from what we know of you, this is the kind of place where you could flourish." With relatively little prior knowledge of the institution, after interviewing and due diligence, I took the job and had five really wonderful years there. It's a place that one learns to love quickly, largely because it stands at its best for hard work, for determination, and for accomplishment that is not driven by prior prestige. When I went there, UConn had an institutional ego problem and was building a number of major programs. The one that the nation probably knows best is the basketball program, but the building of programs that would be points of identification in which people could take pride was a matter of conscious strategy. We sat down and figured how to do it. One of the satisfactions of my attachment to UConn over the years has been that it has accomplished everything that it wanted to and many other things: it has been an important piece of my life and work.

Coming to the University of Virginia was almost accidental. The board had been conducting a search but had not found what it wanted. A very fine president had left after a fairly short tenure and there was doubt in the air about the university's intentions. I came here expecting to have considerable difficulty because everything I had heard during the search told me that the university was in trouble and there were problems. Something like $35 million had been subtracted from the base budget within about three months following the time when I arrived. We were forced into a very early beginning of a capital campaign that we had intended to be a small one. It turned out to be a very large one instead, and, in the process, we learned that there was a way to run the institution without the state support that had previously been fundamental to the base budget. The state now provides about eight and a third percent of the total operating budget of the university. We generate from private sources about double the amount that the state provides now. But although I came here expecting it to be a hard grind, it has been a superb place to be.

FL: Looking back on your life, what do you regard as having been your first leadership position at any level?

JC: I was elected to school offices when I was in high school. I was the president of my class and that sort of thing, but there were leadership positions I didn't win. I lost the election to be president of the student council. Then, frankly, I had to run so hard to stay in place when I was an undergraduate that I couldn't describe it as a time when I had much to do with leadership. Coming to the UVA from my high school, catching up with boys who had been educated at Andover, St. Paul's and other college prep schools was quite a run.

In the professional sense, probably my first leadership position was the dean's job that Frank Hereford gave me, but before that I was asked to be an assistant dean in the college during my dissertation year and I did that. The university was experimenting with having non-tenure track faculty in the administration: I was the experiment. That post probably had something to do with my interest in leadership. I became very much involved with the process of bringing women into the university as a student. I also was one of the authors of a report that led to the appointment of student members to the boards of visitors, which are the governing boards of Virginia's colleges. There was a chair of the board (or a rector, as they are called here) who, for some reason, thought that I had ideas about student representation that were worth hearing and had me write a report. Edgar Shannon and his wife, both now deceased, thought that qualities they saw in me had some bearing on what ought to happen to the universities and talked to me about those issues. I wrote periodic feature columns for the student newspaper when I was in graduate school. My purpose, frankly, was to raise the level of discourse because, at that time, there was a lot of screaming and not much logic in the student newspapers. That may have had some bearing on my aspirations to leadership.

At Berkeley I had the usual junior faculty assignments. I was chair of English 1A for a while and that sort of thing. I'm not sure why, but my colleagues elected me to the faculty senate at Berkeley, and for a while I chaired a section of the course committee, which was the operating entity of the senate that actually exercised control over the curriculum. I remember having accepted those responsibilities because I was really interested in what I learned about how things work. It was fascinating to discover that when you start an issue, you think you know which side has the good guys and which one has the bad guys, but when you get into it, you discover that there are good and bad guys on all sides. I remember one controversy in which I went to meet with the chancellor because we thought we had discovered that the chancellor was raking off money from substandard courses that were being offered with our name on them in distant towns. The chancellor sat down with me and explained to me in about an hour that one of the things the university does is reach out to its community and that courses like the ones we had targeted are among the ways that is done. That type of slow learning about what really matters in universities was one of the benefits of the kind of work I was given to do.

FL: That is an uncommonly insightful summary of an apprenticeship in higher education administration. You have already addressed the topic of mentorship, but was there anything you wanted to add on the subject of the individuals who inspired you and interested you in the choice of your career?

JC: Probably for most people in our business, high school would not matter as much as it does for me, but the teachers in the town where I grew up were really a remarkable bunch. I stay close to those who are still living and admire them enormously. In addition to the two UVA presidents I knew well, Shannon and Hereford, I had a close relationship with a prominent renaissance scholar named Fredson Bowers, who from time to time, would decide to teach me something about how universities worked and would take me along to watch him do something as an administrator. I dealt with people who had well informed notions about how universities work, and I was very fortunate there were people who were willing to talk about issues other than those that were the normal subjects in the faculty coffee breaks.

FL: What were the challenges that the University of Connecticut faced at the time that you became president?

JC: People often talk about UConn as an example of a place with union problems. The truth is it did not have union problems. The unions were the heroes. They protected faculty compensation because virtually everyone except the medical faculty and the law faculty belonged to the unions. The unions had tremendous influence which they used very well. A major challenge was the historic under-funding of infrastructure. One of Phil Austin's great accomplishments has been the alliance that was struck in the commitment of first one and then two billion dollars in bond proceeds to fix the infrastructure.

At the University of Virginia, one may have few or different reasons to think about infrastructure because of the presence of beautiful old buildings that are properly maintained and running perfectly. UConn needed tremendous investments in its buildings, and the state was simply not tuned in for much of my time there. A second challenge was that, by and large, the assumption was that UConn was somehow not as good as its private competitors, particularly Yale, which was a benign neighbor. (Bart Giamatti used to go to budget hearings to testify for UConn.) I came from a place where there was no private competitor. In Virginia, you don't think much about private institutions because, just by corporate history, quality in state higher education resides in public institutions. It took me a year to realize why everybody was moping around: some of our folks were embarrassed about Yale. I wasn't, frankly. I felt that the alliances with Yale were tremendously beneficial to us. We were linked through our land grant functions because Yale has the land grant for forestry. There is a Connecticut Agricultural Station at New Haven that Yale and UConn share. The research collaborations and the clinical collaborations were a lot more important than the differences. Colin Campbell was at Wesleyan in those days, and Colin actually came and spoke at my inauguration. Another major issue for UConn was that it was going through the process of deciding what to do with its branch campuses. The university also had problems in athletics. When I went there, UConn had one major sport that had not graduated a player in six years. I became very interested in what it took to graduate players because I had learned in Virginia that, when access is increased, the goal has to be to provide conditions in which students succeed. When I talked to coaches,

I learned that that was not a value for some of them: they saw players as expendable. At the same time, Eastern Connecticut is a different kind of place and there's a tremendous sense of certainty about UConn's future in that region of the state. I was surrounded by people, political leaders in small towns, who had absolutely no doubt about the functions of the land grant university in a changing state. I worked with good people in the governor's office, and we had a very fine commissioner of higher education. Not many people in our business acknowledge that good commissioners make a big difference, but Commissioner Glasgow knew when to meddle and when to refrain. She was a good advocate in the general assembly; I felt lucky to have that sort of backing.

FL: Could we apply the same question about challenges to the University of Virginia, as you came in as president? In a way, it had to be a great homecoming, but home has its problems too.

JC: There were some very hard things. One was that the state had done a faulty job of projecting revenues. When I was in state government, one of the things I did was to work on revenue projections. Leonard Sandridge, who is the executive vice president of UVA and chief operating officer now, was at that time the chief financial officer. He came to see me in Connecticut and told me that I needed to be very skeptical of the Virginia governor's revenue projections. I did the numbers, and we had the numbers done by personnel in the Darden School. Then we communicated with the governor and told him that his numbers appeared to be suspect. He told us that we should stay out of things we didn't understand, that Virginia was bulletproof, there would not be a recession, that he knew what he was doing, and he resented our intrusion. Three months later, the state collapsed financially and the governor wanted to lay off thousands of state workers. He wanted to retrench the universities: to close them down or cut back their offerings. He tried to give the impression that if the universities hadn't failed the state, the recession wouldn't have happened. He went on a real tear, and we—the institutions that were most damaged by the state's poor budget controls and revenue projections—were set up to be the bad guys. The damage done by gutting the instructional budgets was enormous. We have calculated the cost to individual faculty members of the market-price salaries that were abandoned. The salaries were forced down for about a twelve or thirteen-year period. It's an amazing set of numbers. If you aggregate the entire state, the lost income to families is in the billions of dollars. You have to project the losses out over a lifespan in order to take into account the effect on the faculty's defined-contribution retirement benefits. One of the hard things was that the governor simply didn't get it. In prior times, he was a friend, someone I've always admired, but the economic challenges were just too much for him. Sad to say, he left office having accomplished nothing except gutting basic functions of government, transportation, health care, and particularly higher education, but also K-12 education and library services. Those things have not recovered completely.

FL: What effects have the role and demands of each of these posts at Connecticut and Virginia had on your family life? How have you maintained a balance? It can be difficult to resist the pressures to work twenty-four hours a day in this kind of job.

JC: There was a time when I probably did overwork, way back in the years when I was in admissions. By the time I had been at this for ten years, I was not working nights. I was no longer skipping vacations or going to see the family on weekends, while they vacationed and I stayed at the university. I learned I couldn't do it, and I began to take time to relax. My ways of enjoying private time aren't necessarily what would please others. For example, I can't sit and watch television, but surfing on the Internet I find a very relaxing activity. I have been a sailor since I was very young: that is the leisure time activity that has been most valuable to me. I'm also a walker.

I had a serious illness that required a series of operations about fifteen months ago. A lot of people told me that I needed to change my way of living and slow down my activities. Two very wise doctors advised me instead to do exactly what I have always done, but to do more walking and sailing. Frankly, given the pleasures of those activities, I feel better now than I ever have. Another thing that I've always enjoyed is the nexus between the things archeologists turn up and literary culture. I was trained as an Anglo-Saxonist, so the cultures I know well, roughly the period from the sixth to the eleventh centuries, happen to be current targets of a great deal of archeological exploration and discovery. Following the field, even though I'm not actually contributing to its scholarly literature, has been more than relaxing. It has been a constant source of pleasure.

I continue to be involved with the lives of my children. We have found various ways to maintain family continuity. When I began the capital campaign that occupied the second half of the 1990s, my daughter took to traveling with me and learned how to stand in a receiving line at the door of the room and greet people. We had wonderful times. As they grew older, my children sometimes remembered having met at our dining table people whose names they recognized in the newspapers. For some reason that I no longer recall, Gerald Ford had dinner with us one night in Connecticut. Every time Gerald Ford appeared on TV for the four or five years after that, one of the children would point at him and say, "He was really a nice man." That contact with significant people, causes, and movements had meaning for the children as they grew older.

FL: Could you tell me a bit about the recruitment and structuring of your leadership teams in Connecticut and Virginia?

JC: My thesis is fairly simple: the institution's business is academic work and the academic work is divisible in two or three pieces: UConn is a land grant university, so its work is in three pieces; the University of Virginia's work is essentially two pieces. Everything is organized to support and sustain the academic enterprise. I use a chief operating officer arrangement in which there is a chief officer whose business is to deal with the resources and support the provost. I delegate to the greatest degree possible. I look for administrators who are not control freaks, realistic people who understand the importance of setting real targets, maintaining real metrics, and acknowledging shortcomings as well as successes, and for people who treat those around them with dignity. I once had to pull two very talented senior vice presidents to this room and tell them that if there was any further squabbling between the two of them, they would both have to go. I couldn't make a choice about which one started it. They resolved their differences. I need an environment where people respect the people around them. I have found that persons who come from parts of the population that were historically denied places in top institutions are a tremendous source of talent, so my administration is fairly heavy with women. I find that a lot of minority people are extraordinarily well prepared because for so many years they understudied somebody and are overdue for advancement. You see very few failures.

I organize in teams. I chair the senior management team. The teams reorganize, depending on what the issues are at a specific time. For example, when it is time to develop and test the budget thesis, the chief operating officer heads a team with the vice presidents and other persons with special expertise at the table, and they work out the budget parameters. There is a team that has to do with legal issues involving students. There are teams that have to do with faculty benefits, faculty wages, and faculty careers. While the people at the table will change, the style is that whoever has the greatest competence in a given area is in charge, and I sit on the teams when I'm not the leader. I sometimes sit on teams where the real expert, someone whom I may see only once or twice a year, is presiding and devising the solution to the problem. I have tried to insist that the university has to speak with a rational, unambiguous voice and, to the extent possible, in terms that cannot be interpreted, so the standards imposed on written communication and oral communication are fairly high. You have to fight bureaucracies all the time in any organization, but I thought that in the university, the fight was especially important because bureaucracies are so good at freezing out those who are not inside them.

Much of the work here has involved fund-raising. Because we are still relatively immature in that, in order to raise money I have to get into the field and talk to people. We don't have the kind of network of super-productive senior staffers that Princeton or Yale or, for that matter, Michigan or California may have. They're simply larger and better deployed. So we have to work harder. Much of our work is organized around guaranteeing that the revenue stream required to support the academic mission flows predictably and regularly. We put a lot of emphasis on conserving resources. The way we structure our endowments and the way we manage them follow from our thesis that our business here is to support the academic enterprise and everything else is subsidiary.

FL: In each presidency, you have been expected to spend quite a bit of time on the road, away from the university. You are the chief representative to the alumni and to the public as well as the primary person who deals with major gifts. Have you had someone in each of these administrations who stood in for you, handling day to day matters?

JC: Yes. As soon as I realized that the way of life was going to be so much outside work, I began using a chief operating officer model. It's not a flawless model. I think in the best of all worlds, you would have provosts who are also experts on facilities management, long range planning, short range planning, and cash management resource allocation, but that isn't possible. You have to fragment the job rather than having the provost personally do all that.

I think that the necessity of traveling constantly is, in many respects, the thing that breaks presidencies, first of all because of the isolation that it involves. This year, for the first time in about a decade, I have begun to stipulate that when I travel, I need staff along on the trip. For a long time, because I get along all right when I travel, I thought it was better just to be on my own and let staff carry out their work here. Then I realized that I was having trouble with the feedback. No matter how many emails I wrote or memos I dictated over the phone, the messages were not getting through. Right now we work with a list of about 170,000 names. To maintain the documentary database requires constant staff attention to record keeping. I dislike the idea that the president comes in with a retinue and acts as though he's some sort of general. My whole background is organized in the other direction. I prefer toning down leadership to the point where it becomes a natural part of a collaborative process rather than creating a hierarchy in which somebody sits at the top and gives orders, although there are certainly times when you have to give orders. I've also thought that the chief operating officer model has value because it empowers other people.

There are college presidents in various places around the country who started that part of their lives working with me. They tell me that they take away things from their work here that they use elsewhere. There are several of those people whom I talk with regularly. One is struggling about when to retire. He has pretty much done all that he can do in his place so he's thinking about stepping aside. He actually came here about two weeks ago and we spent the better part of the day talking over his life. I don't have a lot of daily contact with him. The one to whom I'm closest by telephone is probably Dick Byyny at Colorado. Dick has been dealing with issues there, especially the athletics problems, that are like the issues we were dealing with when he was at the University of Virginia a decade ago, so there is a natural reason to be in touch. The chief operating officer model has served pretty well in terms of developing leadership. Staff people have gone on from here to other posts. Jay Lemons, who is the president of Susquehanna University in Pennsylvania, started out as a senior assistant here after his Ph.D. When we had a sudden resignation in a small liberal arts college that the UVA operates in the coal fields, I had nobody to put in there, so Jay agreed to go down there as a caretaker. He stayed for eight years and had really a very good run there. I think that, in that case, the model worked well. He had never thought of himself as a college president before suddenly the responsibility was his, and he has become very, very successful in two quite different institutions. We have talked pretty often, when I have a difficulty of some sort and need his views, and vice versa. The family alliances with people like that are important too. I almost feel that Jay's children are mine. When I was single, Jay and others who had spent time here and become close friends had keys to my house, and when they came to Charlottesville, knew which bedroom was theirs.

FL: How did you formulate the vision for the future of each institution and the plans to implement the vision?

JC: I use a planning model that consists of phased planning. I'll start at the long end of it. The conception of long range planning that I use says that the plan is not resource-bound and is not bound by a defined time frame. It's the far horizon. It has to do with determining aspirations as to institutional rankings or program mixes or whatever might be the purpose: long-range development of a campus, physical development, and long-range development of faculty talent and academic work. In the case of UVA, as we've gone from public to private funding, it has involved long-range planning for finance. Then there is a series of exercises that can be seen on the website, the project called Virginia 2020, which is an effort to relate long range to strategic plans, which is to say plans that exist in real time and acknowledge monetary and other practical limits. This process initially involved the identification of four large weaknesses, then the formulation of a set of plans envisioned as progressing by steps. At the beginning, they were not resource-bound or time-bound, and then as time passed and the plans developed, they became increasingly constrained, so that at a certain point you get down to the place where you have to make choices. We have ten dollars on the table, we have fifty dollars worth of work: how do we allocate the ten dollars to achieve as much of the fifty dollars worth of work as we can? Then where do we regroup and secure the resources to keep moving toward the fifty dollars goal? That has been the long-range piece of the planning.

Then there's a regular process of annual planning driven forward by the strategic plans. The purpose of linking the two is to make sure that annual planning is not business as usual, not simply incrementation and justification, but instead that it is always directed toward the goals in the strategic plan. We have modified annual planning recently by adopting process quality assurance systems based on some of those used in Europe as part of the European Union's emphasis on quality assurance and constant improvement. We are requiring all of our leaders now to identify best-in-class comparators, to provide running analyses of how best in class differs from what we do, and to devise short-term strategies to achieve whatever aspects of best-in-class practice make best sense, so that our annual reports, like our assessment cycles, are now being driven off that analysis. We also have begun to require movement upward to the next class as a quantitatively assessable target for each unit in each year. For twenty years we have been somewhere in the second tier among the top twenty-five. We have lurked at or near the top of the publics, but always with the oddity that we are not the kind of research powerhouse that Berkeley and Michigan are. We are stronger in humanities and social sciences or law or business than in physics, and we've been trying to develop good metrics to let us index ourselves, not against the best in this class, but against the best in the next class up. The strategy for the capital funds campaign that we are putting together now is to finance a major step up. That has to do with the range of faculty expertise that we bring in, our quality expectations of faculty, research productivity, and, in particular, making a massive step forward in science—the kind of commitment that Yale has made with new research facilities or Michigan has made with the North Campus development.

FL: You have consistently linked the changes to the budgeting process. How have you gotten faculty on board and enthusiastic about these directions?

JC: I can't explain that, except that I have always felt I had an obligation to be absolutely straight with faculty about where we were, what we knew about our situation, what we could predict, and what we were determined to do that was not predictable. We always lay out targets to the senior management group, to the faculty senate, and the board. I have always given faculty leaders (the senate) my confidential annual reports to the board so the faculty knows exactly what the board knows about what we think and what we're doing. I feel the way I do about the faculty partly because I came to the UVA as a very young person, a student, and came up through the ranks here to some extent. The faculty are the peers who ultimately judge you, and what you owe them is an absolutely open and uncompromising picture of the way it is. Faculty here have realized over time that the state's decision to abandon them wasn't the end of the world and, indeed, they are better off because we have begun to learn institutional self-sufficiency. There is a diligent group trying to put together a union in the hospital and having very little success because hospital employees don't see the state, whose right to work law is the logical target of the union's activities, as the savior any more. Our people have come to know that the university will accomplish things on its own, and that elected leaders have other priorities.

The other thing I can say about faculty is that the rapport with them is in large measure the result of the fact—and I'd contrast it with Berkeley in my years there—that both at UConn and here, the faculty senates have been strong, effective, and vision-driven. They've had their own view of how things ought to go, and the work with the senate has lifted us rather than dragging us down.

The Berkeley Senate is a large, complicated organization. Frankly I learned a lot being in it: I admire it. But the senates I've worked with subsequently have been better focused in their work. The one at UConn is fascinating. It is a university senate, not a faculty senate. Faculty members more or less dominate it, but employees who cut the grass, students, and even some representatives of the town have seats on it. It's like the council of a European or Asian university. It handles the grievances. I've attended grievance trials by the senate at Storrs when there was a controversy that required some kind of adjudication. It is, at least in my experience of it, a responsible, self-sacrificing, and determined organization. Here we don't have a faculty union, but at UConn a symmetrical relationship between the senate and the union was one of the university's great strengths. People would serve in a position in one entity and then go over to the other entity, so there was constantly interchange between the two. Harry Hartley, who followed me as president, had served as both senate chair and union president before becoming the chief financial officer. I've never seen a system like this one elsewhere, but it worked then, and it still works.

FL: Making change often is not synonymous with making friends. Can you describe one of more critical incidents, how they arose and how you dealt with them?

JC: Sure. Let me make sure that I don't tell you incidents where I think that necessarily I got it right. When we began to realize that the state was not going to finance the university, and we had to have another means to do it, a number of the deans who were in place were convinced that the university had a pot of money somewhere and that we were hiding the money. In a couple of cases, I simply lost persons I admired and respected when I said, "Look, your job has changed. We will do the core of the work, but you're going to do a great deal of what's involved in financing your school." When I put responsibility for financing the schools primarily on the deans, about five or six years ago, we had another round of departures. What we are trying to do is distribute the work so that each person in the organization knows what part of the work he or his area has to do. Some academic officers simply do not accept the concept of financing the academic enterprise as a part of their work. It's a problem sometimes in hiring people. I'm talking to someone now who strikes me as a wonderful prospect, but he comes out of an institution where he's been a department head, and he's convinced that he doesn't have or want responsibility for financing what he wants his faculty to do. He wants a commitment that we will spend a half billion dollars over six years to achieve what he wants, but he wants it from the central bucket that he imagines is hidden somewhere here.

FL: Those days are gone forever.

JC: I think so, and I think that the linkage between planning, especially the long range and the strategic plan, and actual work, including the work of raising necessary dollars, is a necessary one to forge. I've sometimes just plain lost fights, and sometimes I think it's just as well: I was probably wrong. Currently the board is really spectacular, but the most difficult thing here was getting prior boards to realize that they had to leave their political alliances, their personal business attachments to one another, and so on at home. I would say that it is not so much that I succeeded as that we have had people come onto the board with knowledge of where prior boards perhaps got into trouble and a real determination to fix it, to make the board an effective fiduciary and governing body. We've seen statespersons emerge as board leaders. When I first began to evolve the thesis that the business of the university is to feed the provost, I worked with a provost who did not accept the concept. He wanted to be the financial officer's boss despite his lack of experience with financial planning and financial markets, not to mention fund-raising, rather than a member of the team working hand-in-glove with the financial officer. I never resolved that. I don't know what happened to that provost, but were he still here, he would go to his grave angry about that, because he was sure that when he became provost, he owned all the money.

FL: I think that the first option you gave him would have been one that most provosts would be very happy to accept.

JC: Maybe so, but the provost's position really is, in my view, the hardest of all the administrative positions. I think all the pressures come to bear right there, and persons going into the position often make the assumption that the provost is enormously powerful. I think that when one hears administrators talking about their power, that is a signal of a problem. People can talk about responsibility or something of that sort—I can parse that—but when they tell me about their power, I get nervous.

FL: A softball question in a way but an important one: what methods have you used to assess the outcomes of your initiatives at each university and how did you measure the progress toward your long-term goals?

JC: Something we stumbled across at UConn is the value of a published checklist. We list the goals we're trying to achieve, we have target dates for each one, and there's a spreadsheet. Anybody who wants to go to the library or look at the website can read it, and judge it. Regular updates—progress reports—are very important because they keep bosses honest. Now that management metrics have emerged as a respectable science, we're using a lot of European Union management material. We do follow-up reports, so there is a regular cycle of reporting on what we've accomplished and where we have fallen short in one area or another. In 1990, with the board's support, I set the target of becoming, if not the top ranked public university, equal to the best, so that there would be a target, a definable end result. I said that for the purposes of this exercise, we're going to accept the public metrics. We're going to stop saying that *U.S. News* doesn't know what it's doing. We're going to say that, by the metrics that *U.S. News* uses, here is where we are, but we're not going to argue the metrics. People accepted the conceptual value or unvarnished, external metrics, and that acceptance generated achievement, especially achievement of the goals everyone knew were out there. One thing we do constantly is set public targets for fund raising and endowment. Faculty members know where we're trying to go, and when we make it, they know that. When we fall short, they know that too.

FL: How do you celebrate and communicate the success when you've reached these goals?

JC: I don't know that we do celebrate some of it because by the time you reach a goal, you have another goal to pursue. The important work is never finished because its end is the beginning of something else, which is the academic realization of the vision that has driven the work. If you're working on a five-year planning cycle, as we do in some regards, and it rolls forward in the third year, the successes are billows but they're not raging waves. The successes that matter more are measured in terms of the accomplishments of faculty with students, of faculty in laboratories, of faculty in the scholarly press. We do a lot of celebrating about that.

Our senior administrators are reasonably secure in their own capacities. We have been together a long time: fifteen years is a run. There's been some changeover, but people who move in from outside find the depth pretty quickly. It takes about a year before you have a good fit. We brought in a new chief for the hospital, a professional who formerly ran the University of Iowa's hospitals. I've been talking with him about where we are in the last several days because I learn by listening to people debrief on what they've been doing. I am struck with the fact that he has found his place and has momentum—all in about two years. His next round of targets is a lot more dramatic than the ones I gave him. He has learned how to push the organization toward the five-year horizon so that every year we know how far out it is. I think a lot of what we do or I do is teamwork, but to talk about celebrating something is probably not the style of the place. When you walk into a room in this place, you walk in from the back, you go through the crowd, you say hello, shake hands, and start in a quiet way.

FL: What have each of your internal constituencies expected you to do for the university and/or for them? What have been the expectations on the part of the governing board, the faculty, students, staff, and alums?

JC: We have many boards. The board that would be the closest to what we call a governing board is actually an accountability mechanism: it's called the board of visitors. In Jefferson's time, visitor meant auditor, and that board is the board that holds us to account. The relationship is collaborative. What they expect is the truth. I have found that, especially in the last seven or eight years, they deal with failings as effectively and thoughtfully as they do with successes. They are well beyond the point where they expect to need to pat me on the back and say this is great. It's a very professional and sympathetic relationship. Their daily working relationships are much more with the chief operating officer than with me because the board works through a strong committee system. The topics that interest them in their committee roles more often drive them to him than to me. We have a custom of using the copy lines on memos to make sure that everybody knows what's going on. So the rector, the chief operating officer and I have all the same knowledge on almost any issue. The COO perhaps has less information on fund raising. He knows everything I know about political relations. He knows everything I know about planning. I use a planning coordinator who works with me instead of having a chief planning officer and the vice presidents are charged with generating most planning documents, although Virginia 20/20 was actually structured by a non-university entity. We put together think tanks. For example, Donald Kennedy came in to help us reason. The think tanks put together the priorities, and then faculty committees amended them, fleshed them out and made them realistic. The governing board accepted those plans as valid statements of the work we needed to do over about a twenty-year period in order to address long-term weaknesses in sciences and various other university areas.

What I think faculty members expect from me is, first of all, the straight story. As a group, they cherish the independence that they have had within their spheres in the departments and schools. I'm about to have to get involved in a search for a dean because this search is not going as it should to replace a dean who's leaving earlier than we would like. When I have to get involved in a faculty issue—this is one—I try to make clear why I'm involved, how long I'll be involved, and what product I'm trying to generate. I make sure that everybody knows my email address, that everybody knows my number is in the phone book. Very few people ever bother me. Those from whom I hear typically have something constructive to say.

Students, I'm convinced, look first of all for ethical leadership and treatment. It seems to matter to students that I make a point of speaking to them. There will be students I have seen for years around here, young persons with whom my relationship is no more than a hello, good morning, how are you, who at some point will stop me and start debriefing about what has been going on in their lives for years. This is a place where you walk and, since I go out walking the dogs and Betsy and I go walking together, we are visible and have relationships with students that, in 99 percent of the cases, never come to anything. We pass one another. Some smile or nod or speak. Some do not. What is striking is that some feel the need at some point to stop me to talk about what are, typically, profound issues. I pay attention when a student begins to talk. Students don't usually tell me their complaints; they know how to solve their problems. They generally want to talk about where they go from here, and what it means that they have accomplished whatever they have accomplished.

The alumni are a somewhat different story. Our alumni feel a tremendous sense of ownership. We have known one another for a long time. My relationship with them is more a servant relationship than it is anything else. I did not belong to a fraternity in a place where fraternities were very important. I had jobs while I was a student. I didn't have time or money for some of the things that I know add value to student life. I was doing something different from what most students were in those days. So I treat alumni as equals, and in truth many are friends with whom the acquaintance stretches back almost as far as I can remember. I invite alumni into our planning processes, and they take part, they wrestle with the problems. We have so many boards that there is a place for almost anybody who wants to work.

The larger state constituencies are fairly complicated. Northern Virginia is the most volatile part of Virginia. Leadership turnover there occurs with lightning speed. Leaders rarely have long experience in state affairs. Some come to me because they want to learn what's going on. Some come because they don't like what they see, and they want to change it. A few have become close friends; but most of them are more at the level of professional acquaintances. Despite the financial realities, the legislature has been pretty benign in strange times. The worst one might say is that they have more or less accepted the financial assumptions in the governors' budgets rather than driving dynamic policy. The policies tend to be very static; the governor defines them.

FL: How have you managed the different, sometimes conflicting expectations of these constituencies? Are there incidents that you can relate in which you have encountered particular challenges?

JC: I am working right now on a conflict among the families of our African-American students. At the moment, some families of students who are athletes and some families of students who are not athletes are pitted against one another on matters having to do with student conduct. To take part in the conversation, I have to acknowledge the limits of what I know and understand, and try to help people who know more than I can know enter into a process of negotiation that will lead to a resolution.

There have been times when I have had to draw a line in the sand. We bus students all over the place. A board member about a decade ago objected to the fact that black students were all (or all as he saw them) standing at one bus stop. I let him talk for a while and then, at a certain point, I said it seemed to me that where people stand at bus stops is pretty much their business. I had gone and stood at the bus stop and discovered that there was a very interesting dialogue there: it was a constructive gathering place, a forum. But until that member left the board, he complained about the students standing at the bus stop. When you encounter something like that, you really have to say that people have rights. There are always, on every day, freedom-of-expression issues in universities. I've got one going now. An organized group of parents don't like it that a Michael Moore film is on the schedule of films to be shown in the student theater today. I have had to tell these folks that, as far as I can tell, showing this film is lawful. I've also had to remind them that I didn't hear their objections when the fraternities were showing *Deep Throat* and using ticket sales to raise money and that it seems to me that they are oddly selective in their objections.

FL: What importance have you placed on the roles of UConn and UVA in their communities?

JC: Quite a lot. Public flagship universities must set the standards, especially with regard to what is taught in the schools, what is valued in the civilization, what work is supported to improve life and its quality.

FL: Who are the major groups that you work with?

JC: In Connecticut, I worked directly with the State Board of Education. I wrote Connecticut's standards of quality: I was a co-chair of a commission that was set up to do that. In Connecticut, I had a lot of contact with agricultural groups. You don't think of Connecticut as a farm state, but in fact the university extension groups are all over the state.

In Virginia, I make an annual or biennial round of speeches to the major civic clubs, and nowadays also to our major alumni clubs, to describe a legislative agenda for education. I don't argue the University of Virginia's case: the topic is education in general. Sometimes, I have opportunities to discuss larger public policy issues. Many Virginia cities have municipal forums to which people are asked to come in order to discuss issues of large concern. I got worried several years ago about the lack of new investment in high technology enterprises in parts of Virginia localities where traditional industries had died: furniture making and fabric making, for example. That put me into direct contact with county boards of supervisors and other local administrators.

Our own alumni organizations are powerful forums. The commentary there nowadays is more on the general issues than it is on the old tired issue of when the state last did a major round of budget cuts. The General Assembly took $52 million out of the base budget last year—2003. I went to eight of our alumni clubs. In one case, the turnout was about two thousand people. We had more people who were better informed about the state's budget problems than any other group in the state. The legislative leadership in both parties asked for my talking points and wanted to know what the sentiments of the audience were. We weren't saying the state can't do this to us. It was pretty clear that the state had again miscalculated its revenue projections, the setting of tax rates and so on. So we tried, first of all, to explain where we are as a state. That had impact on the tax reform bill that passed last year. People who watched it acknowledge that. I think we talked to 10,000 people in the course of a week before the assembly did the budget. We kept our notes and videotapes of our audiences, took the material to legislators and said, "Here's what we learned." One senate committee met specifically to get a debriefing on our results. It's not something we would do every year, but this was a case when our alumni organizations gave us a means to inform people.

FL: Do you also connect with the community in Charlottesville?

JC: Yes. After you leave, I've got to go home and change into work clothes because I'm meeting our new mayor, the city council, and the city manager. We have a city and county that are totally separate jurisdictions, so there's a three-way conversation. The chief operating officer, who is a native, usually attends these meetings. We have an entity called PAC, which is an intergovernmental cooperation unit. We get involved with the city on matters having to do with student welfare. I have a meeting tomorrow morning with a group of landlords because we began looking last year at abuses reported by students and discovered some that were pretty bad. There were fire code violations. Landlords were overselling their parking lots, paying or licensing towing companies to remove student's cars when they were parked on the grass, and then letting the towing companies charge the student whatever the student looked like she or he could pay. The towing companies had been very hostile to the students. Last year, students took me into apartments to show me that their kitchens were totally non-functional. One took me to her apartment to show me that the ceilings had all fallen. So we work with the landlords. They're coming tomorrow to make peace, and we will make peace, both because there is another narrative about students abusing apartments and failing to live up to their leases and because the property managers want to move beyond the current conversation. I have a direct relationship with parents because I meet with them twice each year and also invite them to local alumni events. Tomorrow afternoon is the year's first speech to parents. The landlords want to talk to me before I talk to the parents because they say that every time I talk to the parents, it costs them money. The system works.

FL: How have you allocated your time in the different posts? Is it possible to do that?

JC: I used to let the work drive me. I don't now. I set my own priorities. I delegate to good people when there's something I can't do, don't have time to do, or should not do. When something really messes up, I usually can't fix it. We have serious problems right now with construction job management. We have about $700 million worth of construction in progress and, as always, there are things that are going wrong. I don't know how to manage a construction project. So we use a professional manager and task the manager with fixing problems and driving jobs through to successful conclusions. I can't micromanage functions that I just don't understand.

FL: What parts of the work do you like the most?

JC: I like the planning. I like the fund raising. I like the direct work with faculty who are doing extraordinary things. We have 2000 faculty members; I've realized there's no way in the world to know all of them. The ones I know will come and show me what they're doing and invite me to their lectures or other events. I am asked to speak at faculty funerals; that is a moving thing. It used to be very hard emotionally, but I realized that if the final remarks address the work accomplished, the enduring components of the work, and acknowledge the human attachments to colleagues and family, then a statement that's simple, honest, and direct is the appropriate salute to a human life lived well. A wonderful man, Andrew Somlyo, who took pathology here from nowhere to the top ten in the course of thirty years as chair of the department, died last spring. Andrew and his wife also owned a major collection of Asian art, and moreover (and in fascinating ways) Andrew was a lifelong émigré or perhaps refugee. He had lived in something like five countries because he kept having to move on, until he came here. Speaking at a funeral of that sort and having a chance to acknowledge that this work and this life are important is an honor. I derive pleasure from memorializing the accomplishments of women and men of this quality. In Andrew's case we published a booklet containing a bibliography. Robert Kellogg died last fall. He was my teacher. Colleagues here and in Iceland are assembling a substantial endowment to support graduate study in fields that interested him. This work to preserve memory of his accomplishments and temperament provides a kind of comfort despite the loss of one of my oldest and dearest friends.

FL: How would you define leadership?

JC: I'm not sure I know how to do that, but I would say that, as I see universities, leadership has to have an ethical core. It has to stand for values that are not constituent driven or politically driven. The values have to be as close to timeless as you can make them be. Universities are peculiar in our culture in that they live in historical time and not in political or economic time. Historical time requires the long view of how we got here and where we're going. I think that leadership, in addition to having an ethical component, has to be driven by an impulse toward service rather than an impulse toward exercising power. Universities by their nature are collaborative, collegial institutions. When they don't function consistently with these qualities, they don't function well. If leaders perceive their role as the exercise of power, even the making of large decisions, then the institution cannot function as a university. Every decision that is worth making begins with a collegial process. There may be a point when someone has to decide whether or not to move, but before you get to that point, a lot of people have participated in the preparation for the decision. I always admired Frank Hereford. Frank had a way of dealing with ethically impossible propositions (of which one hears a fair number). I admired him because he had an amazing certainty or clarity about right and wrong—an intuitive moral compass. He was not a talkative man, but when he heard something outrageous, his reaction was always, "Good God, no!" That's all he would say. That variety of ethical clarity that enables one to make a judgment and to accept that, while this may not be what I like, it is what is right, then to articulate and defend the necessity of taking the right position, has profound value. Leaders are responsible. Maybe leadership is, in part, the exercise of large responsibility.

FL: Do you think these are also the most important qualities for university presidents today?

You have to have a certain measure of intelligence and what the kids call street smarts. At the same time, situational flexibility and situational ethics just do not work when the institution itself lives in time that exceeds a human lifespan. I'm a bank director; I've been involved in banking for close to twenty years. Running a university is very different from running even a major bank because all corporate entities are engaged in processes of transition toward being something other than the current corporate entity—mergers, acquisitions, profit-loss cycles—and those organizations tend to be driven much more by the identity of the CEO than universities are. Many banks are for sale when the CEO hits age fifty-nine. Everyone knows that. It's just a different kind of enterprise. Leaders of universities are, in the ultimate sense, trustees as opposed to owners. Their mission is to define, preserve, improve, perhaps above all to preserve, and then pass on to someone else.

FL: How have the role and demands of the presidency changed over the past few decades in response to the disinvestment of states in public higher education?

JC: In the places where I have worked, two things have happened. In Connecticut, the university devised a way to receive large sums from the state by way of bonds. Here the bonding mechanism has not been available. The state was not willing to accept the responsibility inherent in the obligatory assumption of long-term debt. Connecticut has the CSU system, the UConn system, the community colleges, and that's it. In Virginia, we have fifteen senior institutions and twenty-three community colleges, with many separate boards and governance schemes. We knew in 1991 that either we would find a way to raise money as major private universities raise money or we would crumble. There was no middle ground. We decided to find a way to raise money.

FL: How would you characterize the changes in the role and demands of the presidency in response to the technological revolution?

JC: We have had to make hard decisions, often resource decisions, and make new kinds of personnel decisions. We decided in 1991 to invest heavily in digital technologies for the humanities. We have become one of the largest electronic publishing houses in the world—an enterprise in which we have had a lot of support from the Mellon Foundation. The electronic imprint was a major financial decision and a major personnel decision: we reorganized the library and the press to support it.

FL: How have the growing roles of private support and commercial application in university research affected the presidency?

JC: I'm watching a particular commercial application right now because a patent that we have exploited successfully for a long time is about to expire. I am struck by the fact that so far no university known to me has been successful in building a steady stream of patent revenues. It's always boom and bust. Somehow, universities fall down on planning and execution. If you get it right you succeed, if you don't you fail. American universities in general do a less than good job of developing and exploiting intellectual property. By contrast, the German universities, despite the much-discussed inefficiencies and slippages in the national system, do a good job of capturing and capitalizing on intellectual property. Australians do that too.

FL: What have been the effects of the increasingly strident demands of students and politicians for high quality and accountability in both expenditures and results?

JC: Those are not exactly the demands I get here. The demand I get from politicians is to let their constituents in. The demand from students is largely for a more responsive system of advising, for a curriculum that gives them the credentials they need when they move out of here. Our graduation rate right now in the undergraduate schools is about 93 percent over six years, so there's not much slippage. Students used to be focused primarily on graduate school. I can remember a time when the big issue was the demand for help with getting into the top graduate schools. The current fad for being in the economy for two or three years (working at a ski lift, a car wash, an internship), then going back to school is making it difficult to read what they expect. Students tell me that they want some credential in addition to the traditional baccalaureate degree in liberal arts fields so we are now offering larger numbers of our students the chance to get basic business credentials—accounting and that sort of thing—while majoring in art history or whatever they choose.

FL: Presidencies were once measured in decades, but now are more typically limited to four or five years. Do you believe that the changes in the role have brought that about or are there other reasons for the rate of attrition?

JC: I think there are other reasons. The job itself has changed, and frankly it is not what most people think it is when they get into it. I think that searches are run in a really terrible fashion. The covenants that ought to exist between boards and presidents often do not exist: neither side has presence of mind to enter into the right agreements. I have never had a contract, but at various times when the board here was particularly fractious and political, I felt that they ought to provide one. At one time they refused to do it. I quit asking. The current board is not like former boards sometimes were. The old boards used to deliver mandates to me. If you don't appoint this person or that person to some job we're going to fire you. That's not the way it is anymore. I think that getting beyond the tenth year is a liberating experience. I live with my own set of inner fears about what constitutes failure or what defines not holding up my end of the bargain. .

The current chair of the board is thoughtful and collaborative. He knows exactly what I think about, fret about, and feel good about, but that's unusual in my experience. And it may be that a basic reason for my longevity is that I took on a job I wanted to finish, and the only way to finish it was to stay at it and finish it. It's blue-collar thinking. That's the way my dad dealt with sheet metal: you've got to get this done.

FL: How would you characterize your own leadership style? .

JC: I hope that what matters in my style is that the institution, the faculty, and, where relevant, the student body, are more important than I am. I hope that I have moved through the world with a fairly light touch because I don't mean to come in and have somebody banging the gong, saying here he is. I hope that the leadership is exercised more through the quality of concepts, ideas and actions than through a set of demands, but I have to acknowledge that I don't know the answer. Leaders I have known rarely understood at a deep level how they did their work.

FL: What do you feel have been the most critical capital investments made under your leadership in Connecticut and Virginia?

JC: In Connecticut, there were basically three. One was the development of a laboratory facility for engineering at a time when engineering was in danger of slipping. Another was a patho-biology building that ironically came in as an unexpected earmark arranged by Senator Chris Dodd. The patho-biology building provided a necessary point of linkage between the medical center at Farmington and the Storrs campus. Developing the basketball facility there was also important because basketball had a role in positioning the university as a national institution.

At the University of Virginia, the major capital accomplishments have to do with finding ways to build significant structures that are physically beautiful without the state's assistance. The Darden School and the Law School replacements, which are off to the west of the campus, are an example. We are just completing an above-ground structure for American Studies and a below-ground special collections library. Most of that money is private money, the greatest part of it from two donors, but there is a state element to it. The two replacement school buildings were financed with massive investments of private money to produce more viable schools. We've tried to build structures that are modern in form and function and consistent with the general architectural themes of this campus. We have built about a hundred buildings since I've become president but the majority of them are the deans' projects or the chief operating officer's initiatives. We decided several years ago to begin constructing parking garages that would be adequate to store vehicles off the street, which resolves some of the traffic problems. The COO has taken the brunt of the not-in-my-back-yard opposition to those projects and he has done it very well. He has also done some great things to improve traffic in the town.

FL: What do you believe have been the most important legacies that you have given the University of Connecticut and the University of Virginia?

JC: I hope that at Connecticut it was the awareness that an aggressive and ambitious vision was good for the institution and that the institution has a future that is limited only by what it imagines. Among the things I admire about Phil Austin is the way that he has taken that as the first point and then moved dramatically beyond it. What I hope that I'm doing at the University of

Virginia is putting together a resilient institution that has the sophistication and means to protect itself against the bad things about being public, but also to function consistently with its origins, with its deeply public obligations. In our time, it seems to me crucial that this place, of all places, be a public university. On the other hand, if being a public university means starving, being academically inadequate and weak, that's not what I'm talking about. I'm talking about an institution that is really an instrumentality of the state as opposed to an agency of the state, a university that accomplishes large public purposes and does it on a resource base which protects the public interest against political treachery.

FL: What advice would you give to new presidents?

JC: Don't be afraid of serving the vision. Most of us fail at something at some point and it's just as well to fail at something big as at something little. Acknowledge the large target and move to it. I think that I would encourage any president to pursue the life of the mind and not simply become a management functionary. I would urge presidents to realize that the quality of sympathy for the work that people do throughout the institution is crucial. Any work, any job done well, deserves acknowledgment in our culture.

FL: What is the most critical skill or set of skills that presidents will have to have in the future to succeed and how are they different from the skills needed in the past?

JC: At least in a place like this, a president needs the skills involved in mobilizing large numbers of people to do more than they intended. That's important. Sophistication with regard to the life cycle of assets is more important now than it was when I started. There is a skill involved in setting aside one's own ego and realizing that what universities do is empower academics to achieve. The most important thing that a president does in the course of a day is likely to be providing funds from a gift account to see to it that a faculty member can complete a project. Today I'm going to take some steps to protect us against losing a sociologist who has had a very attractive offer from an Ivy League institution. I doubt that I'll ever meet her, but I've read her work, and I know we need her. I will do something this afternoon that is going to drive her dean crazy. I am going to double her salary. The dean will come over next week and tell me that I need to do that for everybody he knows. The answer is going to be that in the case of the sociologist whose salary is being doubled, there is a threatened institutional asset that I can define. I can't define all these others. Show me the asset, and we will figure out how to protect it.

FL: What has been your greatest challenge as a leader?

JC: Early on, it was the fact that I had no background to do what I was doing, that I had simply fallen into something that fascinated me, but it was the last thing I knew how to do. Later, simply the realization of the scale of the problem, once the state started pulling out in the financial sense. We actually had a serious discussion here for six months on whether we ought to scale back, to say we're not AAU level, we're not playing on that field, we're going somewhere else. We made a conscious decision that we would not do that. We studied the whole proposition of retrenchment and realized that what retrenchment involves, if the university is at all well regulated, is not cutting away dead wood, but cutting out hard wood, then waiting to restore something that takes an incredibly long time to grow back. So we did some strategic cutting, but it was cutting in areas where we simply were not strong and areas that had let themselves become academically isolated. The hardest thing was to figure out how to maintain life flow at a time when the entity that was supposed to sustain us had simply said, "We don't care about you any more." They were very clear that it wasn't anything personal: they just didn't care any more. Voters were older. The issues had changed. The imperative to make sure the university was well supported was gone from the neighborhoods that elected the legislators. The politicians were wrong about that. The voters' support is coming back in a way that I think is going to bring the state back to the table eventually. But at that time in the early 1990s, when things were really tough, our elected leaders were saying that nobody cared about universities any more, that they were irrelevant.

FL: That's a frightening thought.

JC: You asked me earlier about the pleasures of the presidency. Since so much of my attention has been focused on this state and I grew up in a part of it that is not a power center, I always felt that I was on the margin of the power center. Now I have reached the point where I have the impression that I understand at least some of what goes on in the state. People who make major decisions about things other than education sometimes call to ask what I think about issues and what I think might happen if they did this or that. I have the chance to get involved in things that fascinate me because they have to do with the lifeblood of the state, for example the issue of how deep the channel to Baltimore ought to be. That is a major issue in the state because of the Atlantic shipping commerce. Do we put another highway in the roadbed of Interstate 81 and, if we do, how do we finance it? What do we do about the traffic jams around northern Virginia? We know that political misfeasance and malfeasance and gross dereliction of duty caused these problems, but how do you fix them once they exist? Or, to go to a totally different issue, what is the public posture on healthcare in regions that we know are about to be depleted of population because the productive industries have left? There is one region that UVA has taken on as a kind of personal project: the far southwest, the coalfields. We now provide the public health system down there as a public service exercise of the university's medical outreach. We literally move the services down there, and the doctors see thousands of people in the course of two or three days' activity. It is a source of enormous pleasure to realize that there is a tangible problem that may not be our direct responsibility, but we can have a role in ameliorating it.

FL: Service of that kind is an important and immensely satisfying aspect of a state university's mission of service. Let's turn to the issue oriented questions. You had the opportunity to work with more than one governing board. It might be helpful if you could outline what you feel are the important characteristics of good governing boards and what are the problems one can encounter in dealing with governing boards?

JC: The UConn board when I was there was, in the words of its chair, a yeoman board. He said that it was a board of people who worked for a living and that what they had in common was that the university empowered them to do the work. The chair was Andy Canzonetti, who is an enormously important figure in Connecticut's modern history. He was right. That board was extremely competent. The individual members knew exactly what they were doing, and I never had a second's conflict with them. They taught me constantly. When we tackled the hardest issues, I could introduce the problem or they might, we would sit through one or more discussions of how to do something and then we'd do it. I learned a lot from them.

I have seen several different kinds of boards here because the boards change as the governor changes. At its best, the UVA board is magisterial in dealing with the hard problems. The board decided last year that the slow disappearance of students from the lowest income groups from the top tier universities was not tolerable. They decided that on their own. We had done some analysis of average family incomes in the top twenty-five universities and we had shown them the numbers, which are dismal. They said, find a solution. To do that, we have broken away from the federal system of allocating financial aid. We're using our own system and it works a lot better than the federal system. The board has had the same attitude toward equity and diversity issues in recent years. It has, in a sense, defined the best the university can expect of itself.

Board members are human beings. The worst boards have venal board members, who tolerate conflicts of interests and get involved in side deals so that the discussions at the board table are not the operative discussions. I worked once for a board that regularly excluded me from the room when they wanted to do something they knew was wrong. It was hard, but we talked our way through that issue. Over a period of time, we came to terms.

I rely on board members to be critical when that is appropriate. I especially rely on them to tell me when a strategy or purpose that we are developing doesn't ring true. It's easy to be persuaded by your own rhetoric; board members have just enough distance to hear the false notes. I admire the ones who are my constant critics. Because he has completed his eligibility, we are losing one this year who has been, in a sense, a constant critic, but I have to say the man has been right more often than he has been wrong. When he has been wrong, he's been really wrong. Eighty percent of the time, by listening to him criticize something I wanted to do, I have learned how either to change what I want to do or do it better. Board chairs are the critical players. The chair in Connecticut was the same man the whole time I was there. He was amazing—a straight, disciplined, selfless public servant, which is what you pray for. I have seen several chairs here because they have term limits. The current one is the very best. He is the managing partner of a large law firm, has seen everything and has done it all. He has the great quality of objectivity, as well as depth of knowledge, and he is fair.

FL: Let's switch now from university governance to the related matter of state politics. During the last few years there have been several instances in which the governor of the state has gotten directly involved with policy issues or personnel decisions in the state's flagship institutions. Do you think that this is a trend?

JC: It's a trend but it's not a new trend. In the 1890s one of Virginia's governors tried to make his assistant the president. I think it's just the way it goes. It seems like a trend in any one person's time, but it goes on all the time. Virginia's governors include people I consider close personal friends, but also people I probably would criticize if I got into a discussion about them. Some have had bad ideas about education or about higher education, and some have done harm, but others have had excellent understandings. The strangest relationship I've ever had with a governor was with one who died a decade ago. His name was Mills Godwin. He was the only governor in Virginia's history to serve two terms. He served four years and sat out four years, then came back. He is the most complicated political figure I have known because he was an architect of massive resistance, a strategy in which Virginia seized and closed local public schools rather than desegregate them after Brown. The state got rid of its compulsory attendance law. In jurisdictions where the local school boards complied with the federal orders to desegregate, including Charlottesville, the state seized the schools and closed them. Mr. Godwin was in the thick of that. On the other hand, although he never quite came to the point of explaining his role in massive resistance, he went through a remarkable process of atonement: I wish that he had come to terms in public with the sinister part of the story, but he did not. Yet Virginia's community college system was his one-person creation. He was convinced that if we were to be equal, the equalizer had to be education, and specifically the local community college: for this state, he got it dead right. I knew him for about 20 years and we had never had a personal conversation, but one day in the 1990s, we were both pallbearers at a funeral. It was a cold winter day and we were both freezing. The then-governor had been chewing me up in the newspapers. Mr. Godwin looked at me across the casket and said "John, don't you back up one inch." The great institutions of the state all have his marks on them but, in the end, what mattered to me was that one quiet remark.

FL: You have served as the president of two NCAA Division I schools. What is your take on the current very public and damaging perceptions of serious problems in recruiting, admission, retention, graduation, student athlete conduct and the funding of athletics, including the huge escalation of the compensation of successful Division I coaches in revenue sports? Are these problems ever going to be resolved?

JC: I think the problems are always going to be there. To some extent, solutions to some of them are in process. Some problems, such as the compensation of coaches, are going to be resolved only if a powerful government agency like the IRS begins to look at disproportional benefits from non-profit sources as an issue. The IRS is now starting to examine what is paid to CEOs in non-profits and to threaten intermediate sanctions in particularly serious instances of abuse. That's interesting, and I'm glad they're looking at it. If the IRS applies the same logic to coaches, it could address the problem without incurring the liability that universities acting together would have. We cannot form a cartel to put a limit on coach's salaries: it would be in restraint of trade. The IRS can treat excessive salaries for coaching as betrayal of a public trust, and so the IRS may be able to do some good that we can't do.

Many of the academic issues are, first of all, the fault of presidents who are not prepared to stand up for meaningful standards. One thing I know about athletics is that when misbehavior occurs, if the president does not confront it head on, call it what it is, and take action, the institution's moral fiber atrophies very quickly. I went through a hard set of violation reports here in the early 1990s. Dealing with these issues was hard. I assumed that I was a dead duck when I realized what I was dealing with. What I had to do and did was call these violations by their real names, treat them honestly, and take the difficult high road by discharging people I had known and liked all my life. Then we spent five years defending my actions in the federal courts. I didn't know that we would win. One of the things about fights you fought and finished is you forget that there was always the prospect of losing. I'm convinced that if a president doesn't deal with issues of that kind directly, personally, and swiftly, it doesn't get done.

FL: Excellent advice.

JC: Finally I think that in any athletics department, at least in all the ones I know, there's a certain amount of anti-institutional fervor, a boys' club atmosphere that you have to combat.

FL: Do you think it is useful for presidents to be involved in national associations and participate in the work?

JC: The ones in which I have been involved have taught me a great deal. I've served on their boards and have chaired some of them. I have taken a lot more out of those relationships than I put into them. Talking to the president of the Association of American Universities, Nils Hasselmo, once a week is one of the best ways of getting information that I know. I have always thought that in my next life I'd like to do the kind of thing Nils does because the pieces that interest me come together there: it seems to me that one learns a lot more than one gives. I chaired the College Board once; that was a great educational experience. It really gets you into the nitty-gritty of what's going on in schools and how they connect to colleges.

FL: How has the University of Virginia responded to the criticism that research universities don't care about undergraduate teaching? That was a greater issue in the early 1990s, but one still hears the accusation.

JC: It is not as great an issue here as it may be at other places because we were so late in developing the character of a research university. This university is, probably to a greater degree than any other major institution, built on its undergraduate program. We were slow to develop the Ph.D. as a terminal degree. We kept the number of Ph.D. programs pretty strictly controlled. We developed strength in the humanities, the social sciences, and law and business long before we got good in any scientific area, and that pushes you toward an undergraduate orientation.

FL: How does the proportion of under-represented minorities in the student body of the University of Virginia compare to their percentage in the state of Virginia? Was the relative proportion the same at the University of Connecticut? How have you gone about diversifying the campus, the student body, the faculty, and the administration?

JC: When I was at Connecticut, the undergraduate student body there was about 20 percent minority. The growth population at the time happened to be Hispanic because of the migration of people from Puerto Rico to East Hartford, Willamantic, and other towns. African-American students were actually less numerous in those days than Asian-American students.

At the University of Virginia, the minority population of the undergraduate student body is currently in the range of 30 percent, with African-American students making up 11 or 12 percent, Asian and Asian-American students I think this year were about 15 percent. The Hispanic component in Virginia's public school population is less than 5 percent and they are not evenly distributed in grades one through twelve. Hispanic children currently in Virginia schools are a younger cohort. We know that that cohort will move up and will come to us over the next five years, so the admissions people are working systematically at that. The growth population is Asian and Asian American. We have a vigorous program of reaching out to what was thought to be a relatively small Native American population. We have been the host for a series of summit meetings among the Virginia tribes and have discovered that a number of Virginia tribes are not recognized as tribes because of the eugenicist history in the state's records division. For about fifty years the state refused to record on a birth certificate that a child was an American Indian. American-Indian parents had to choose whether their children were black or white. The tribes are reforming themselves and doing so with a good bit of success. We're in the thick of it. Is it going to produce a large number of students? Probably not, but it will have some impact.

The early emphasis here on remedying the damage done to the African-American population by the state's laws against integration is now phasing toward a more mature emphasis on equity in a broader sense. Our statistics look a lot like those you will see elsewhere. Looking at the whole population, African-American, Hispanic and Hispanic-American, and Native-American students are underrepresented and, by most calculations, the population of Asian and Asian-American students is somewhat overrepresented. There's one other quirk here: under a court order issued in 1983, we do not count any non-citizen student as a minority person. The court order required the state to remedy the problem of underrepresentation with regard to Virginia's population, rather than some imported population. This year, for the first time, we will report two numbers, the total number of minority students and the number of minority students who are citizens. That will cause our proportion of minority students to go up by about 5 percent in the number that reports all students.

FL: Are you increasing the number of minority faculty?

JC: Slowly. The barriers are largely within the departments, which is to say that we have had failures on the part of our hiring committees and hiring officers. The board became seriously concerned about this last year. The provost has set a performance program involving the deans to begin to remedy the problem. The problem is concentrated in certain areas. Some of our departments and some of our schools do beautifully, but I don't think all of them have yet understood the message.

FL: Have you been more successful in hiring minorities to work in the administration?

JC: I don't think we're a model for the world, but we have been more successful in hiring minorities in the administration. Our vice presidents include three women. There is one African-American vice president. My staff includes three or four women and one African-American man.

FL: The presidents whom I've interviewed for this book have expressed great concern about the problems of higher education access and capacity, which will become exacerbated in the next five years as growing numbers of students seek to go on to higher education. Shirley Jackson spoke about the huge demographic shift coming in this country. She called it a coming perfect storm in which the underrepresented minority, if it does not become the underrepresented majority, will certainly become the underrepresented plurality. She feels that much greater efforts must be made to prepare students for college, perhaps by means of summer academies. David Ward pointed out that the uneven geographical distribution of immigrants will create huge problems as Florida, Texas, the East Coast corridor and California run out of capacity in their higher education systems. The University of Virginia has traditionally been small and highly selective. At the same time, I know that you've always been keenly aware of the principles of Thomas Jefferson, its founder, who believed that the common good, the good of the people, is the first good and education is its foundation. Under your leadership, the UVA has just adopted loan free financial aid for needy students, capped need based loans for middle income students, and has committed to meet 100 percent of need for all students. So within your traditional mission, you are taking steps to increase access. Do you want to share your thoughts on this issue?

JC: Part of the background for what we're trying to do there is that we are in the fourth circuit and the fourth circuit has had a long history of rejecting remedies to patterns of disadvantage that have anything to do with race. The Podberesky Case in Maryland, for example, is a fourth circuit case. So when universities in other parts of the country were looking at affirmative action as a way to deal with racial inequity, we had reason to look at other patterns of inequity because, so far as we can tell, the largest issues in Virginia subsume all racial groups. Many of our policies on equity are built on Virginia concerns, as opposed to national concerns.

This state's economy changed in the 1990s in important ways that the state missed completely. There are only two planning districts in Virginia that showed positive economic numbers for the whole period of the 1990s: northern Virginia and the corridor that runs down to Charlottesville. Net job creation, tax capacity, all the other measures were negative in the entire remainder of the state. Virginia was pulling itself apart. It still does this, but northern Virginia has some of the best public schools in the country. One high school in Fairfax County, the Thomas Jefferson High School for the Sciences and Technology, produces more merit scholars than the rest of Virginia combined. It's an important phenomenon. The Northern Virginia counties have been willing to tax themselves. They have replaced state money with local money as the state has scaled back its contribution. Their impulse as a region is toward investing in children. Other parts of the state lack the means and may sometimes lack the vision as well. They may not be dealing with parents who have the same take on what education is all about, or they may not have the money. A lot of centers of prosperity that we recognized when I was a boy—Danville, Martinsville, Roanoke—are now places in a recession. They're not seeing job creation. The Charlottesville area has just published a ten-year report on job creation. All of the job creation in this region over a decade has depended upon UVA: everything else is negative. My view is that we're building up a problem that you can define in economic terms. The local schools able to educate children are increasingly likely to be in places where well-educated parents earn substantial incomes and believe in investing in their children. The less affluent are going to be more and more isolated and trapped in an economy that they can't work their way out of.

The current governor, I believe, understands the problem, but the solution is baffling. Frankly, the solution may be beyond what a governor serving under a four-year term limit can hope to do. The solution is twenty-five years of reinvesting in schools, plus remedial programs for people who were trapped in the period when the state was doing nothing. Beginning in 1990, the state began bailing out on its young people. What we have done at the University of Virginia, and we hope the state and other institutions will do it as well, is determine that we're simply not going to let economic disadvantage be the barrier that keeps a student out of here. We are systematically making pledges to parents of small children that the policy is here to stay, that we're going to do what we promised to do. That's the only remedy I know for a top tier public flagship institution that wants to serve its state with regard to access on a systematic and general scale. Now, ironically, we are being faulted for recruiting poor students. I had to deal with a phone call from a legislator yesterday who said that his local college president had come and said that we were stealing all the poor kids. I thought about that a little bit and told him, "Well you're right. Watch; we're going to do it." That is exactly what the board wants to do.

I think part of our motive here is understandable only in a local context. You quoted Jefferson and referred to his notions about the common good: that's all but a religious belief here. We live with a history that includes every permutation on the theme, including a lot of bad permutations. It's very hard to praise this place for the way it behaved in the generation after the Civil War, for example, or, for that matter, the way it came kicking and screaming into an era when equity was of value. But if you live in the shadow of somebody whose words define a political culture, as Jefferson's words do, and learn to live with all the warts and wrinkles involving his personality, in the end it's very, very hard to think or talk about what it is to be an American university without hearing his words because he was so systematic in defining the purposes of the university as providing the tools of freedom to individual people. I have watched the board work on this: that is the language, the rhetoric and the belief system that drives where we go. I admire them.

FL: It is also an issue which every state is going to have to face.

JC: Yes, Virginia has broken into a bunch of fragments, due to a lack of state willpower to deal with the problems.

FL: It hasn't happened in Virginia alone. I was publicly pilloried when I talked about the capacity issue in New Jersey a few years ago. The legislature and the governor's office were very upset about it.

As states reduce their funding of higher education down into the single digit proportion of their universities' budgets, while state legislatures and governors cap tuition, how can institutions resolve their budget problems and continue to build access and excellence? I know that the University of Virginia has been able to fund its budget in part by charging out-of-state students 100 percent of the cost of their education, just as Rutgers does. Is it the responsibility of our state institutions to solve the problem of access? Do you feel that there is any realistic hope that the states and the federal government will take on more of the responsibility of providing students from low-income families access to quality education?

JC: In the end, the solution to the problem, if there is a solution, lies with the institutions and not the state or federal government. I don't think that the political will power to solve the problems exists right now in the states or in Washington. Yet we have the option of getting serious about raising money from a very affluent and widespread alumni population. The amount we raise varies from year to year, but it is somewhere between $175 and $250 or $260 million now. To do that, you have to have a message that makes good sense to people who came here in prior times, when the priorities were different.

The message also matters to state officials. I have developed a standard message that I deliver to state officials in public meetings when they say either that they like what we've done about financial assistance or that, by doing it, we are creating some kind of embarrassment for somebody else. The message is that, in my view, this is really their job. The state should be providing those dollars. State officials should be the ones realizing that, unless we get rid of the barriers that make the economy the chief obstacle, they fail as public officials. I don't have the rhetoric down pat yet because I am still driven by something like outrage that they let this happen. The good news is that the governor gets it, and the principal leadership in the legislature gets it.

Virginia used to be a one-party state, but Virginia Democrats were, by and large, Republicans in sheep's clothing. Now we have a multi-party state. We have Democrats, who are, in a way, the demoralized minority. We have about five different factions who are Republicans, but from the opening up of opportunity to Republican leaders, who used to be denied committee chairs and positions of power, we now have a brilliant bunch of strategists running the legislature. I love talking to them. They think uncommonly well. They have to function at the level where politics finally gets done, and it's not always a pretty level, but the quality of their concepts and their understanding of the problem I find very encouraging. If they can get any kind of popular mandate at all, I think they will do some good. Of Washington, frankly, I just despair. I don't think they get it up there.

FL: As a fund raiser, you are in a class by yourself, not only in regard to what you have done, but what you are planning to do. Do you think that the University of Virginia is unique in its prospects for success in the goal of becoming the first privately funded public university? Or is that a realistic goal for other public universities, for example, Cal-Berkeley, which, like the University of Virginia, draws its students from the very top academic achievers in-state and out-of -state?

JC: Fran, we are an unusual case because we had such enormous untapped assets in the form of the alumni base when we realized that we were in trouble. Knowing Berkeley as I do, I guess I have to say that I think Berkeley faces a different set of issues. California, being younger and more complex, lives different realities. The taxpayer revolt in California seems about to wear itself out. The actions taken by the new governor, the restoration of funds to the University of California make me believe that California's Land Grant College Act/populist approach to public education is likely to survive. Virginia is a different story. Virginia didn't have statewide public schools till 1900. This state has a wonderful rhetoric about education, but the history is a one-man history. It was Thomas Jefferson and then nothing. The bill that created statewide universal public education in Virginia was introduced by Jefferson in 1774 and systematically rejected until 1900. My take on it is that we face a different culture, a different set of issues here. I don't think that everybody has quite the assets that we have going in. I do think that many more have the assets than realize it and that persons who become university presidents may in some sense resist the task of financing the institution by finding donors. Raising money is not what people think it is: I don't play golf, I don't play tennis, I don't hang around bars, I am not a good shmoozer. I deal with people who want to see solid propositions about change. I have never found a donor of any consequence who was prepared to pay for the status quo. What people want to pay for is a better university. What I have to do is to finance the core operation out of the revenues that remain after we subtract what the state took away from us. The financing of the future is what I can do with the help of the private donor. To do that, you've got to be able to demonstrate value.

FL: I think you're going to see a lot of imitators attempt to follow you because the need is great, if you look at the cuts in public education funding throughout the country.

JC: The odd thing is that in Virginia there have not been many other major fundraising attempts. Virginia Tech does a good job, William and Mary has launched a campaign that I think will succeed, but relatively few of the others are prepared to test the waters.

FL: What do you see as the strongest forces driving the need for change in higher education over the next ten to twenty years? What are the most important changes that you expect to see take place? And, finally, what will higher education leaders need to do in the future considering the rate of change in the environment?

JC: The curriculum has to go through another set of reforms. I like the direction that Larry Summers is taking at Harvard. I think that we have gone where we needed to go with regard to learning to learn and it is time to get down to the substance of what we are learning. That is a timely readjustment. The curriculum ought to leave options open until later in people's lives. That is important because people will drop out and drop back in for further education from now on.

The access issues that Shirley Jackson and David Ward talked about earlier are dead on. I think that they are absolutely right. Traditional universities, while aggressive about one kind of affirmative action, have really not taken on the larger set of issues that have to be addressed. If I'm right in believing that the cross-cutting issue is an inequitable economy, then one of the changes that has to occur involves opening up access to higher education by way of a radical reform of the financial aid system. That is part of the reason for my skepticism about Washington. I see no sign of interest there in dealing with what Congress did when it decided that poor people ought to borrow. It is just a bad way to finance education within that part of the economy where debt delimits opportunity. Educational debt is a great mechanism for the middle-income class, but it makes no sense at all for the poorest Americans.

I am convinced that research is going to suffer for a while because I think that NIH and other constant fountains are going to back down some. The political magic of Homeland Security appropriations is going to hurt traditional research enterprises. I'm persuaded that we are missing the boat on economic policy as a factor in research. That's going to have to change, but we will suffer first. U.S. trade negotiators in general don't understand that intellectual property is a tangible, exchangeable value.

Finally I think that the managerial reforms that we have not talked about in this interview are crucial to what I've seen here. Those reforms have got to continue. We have to control the unit cost of what we do outside the classroom and we have to get better at quality assurance with regard to what goes on in the classroom. I'm hoping that it will happen because we figure it out and not because the government imposes it on us, but the resistance in the economy to quality assurance is the core business of accreditation. It strikes me as self-destructive. I don't understand it because, of all human enterprises, teaching and learning must be the most process-intensive.

Mary Sue Coleman

Mary Sue Coleman assumed the presidency of the University of Michigan in August, 2002. Before coming to Michigan, she served as the president of the University of Iowa for seven years. At Iowa, she led the institution in a successful effort to increase the national recognition of the quality of the university, raised private funding for construction that transformed the campus, and worked with the faculty to improve the undergraduate experience. Prior to that, Coleman was provost at the University of New Mexico from 1993-1995, vice chancellor for graduate studies and research at the University of North Carolina at Chapel Hill from 1992-1993, and associate provost and dean of research at UNC Chapel Hill from 1990-1992.

Coleman earned a bachelor's degree in chemistry from Grinnell College and a Ph.D. in biochemistry from the University of North Carolina at Chapel Hill, then went on to do postdoctoral work at Chapel Hill and at the University of Texas at Austin. She was a faculty member at the University of Kentucky in Lexington for nineteen years, including eight years during which she served as the director for research of the Cancer Center.

At Michigan, she is focusing upon initiatives that encourage interdisciplinary teaching at the undergraduate level, the development of a center for ethical issues in public life, and the alignment of all the elements of the health system to develop a model for health care. She is also initiating an examination of residence systems in order to improve the atmosphere for undergraduate education by integrating academic and residential life.

Elected to the Institute of Medicine of the National Academy of Sciences in 1997, Coleman is also a fellow of both the American Association for the Advancement of Science and the American Academy of Arts and Sciences. She has served on the board of trustees of the Universities Research Association, the ACE Task Force on Teacher Education, the AAU Task Force on Research Accountability, and the Business-Higher Education Forum. She has also served on the board of trustees of Grinnell College.

Francis Lawrence: Do women in higher education need to have different or superior skills and leadership qualities than men who are higher education leaders? You've been part of the generation that broke through barriers, certainly at the beginning of your career in science.

Mary Sue Coleman: I've thought a lot about that question because I am often asked that. As you know, these are tough jobs. I think it's equally difficult for men and women. I don't subscribe to the notion that somehow that this is tougher for women than it is for men, or easier, for that matter. I think it's hard for everybody; there are so many external forces that are outside your control that you have to learn to roll with the punches. One of the things that I've tried, and has worked for me, is that I try to be calm no matter what is happening. Even if I'm outraged, I try to be calm. I see this quality in men too, so I don't think that it is gender specific. I never burn bridges. Even with people who have given me very difficult times, I have tried not to say that the relationship is cut off forever. I have discovered that there may always be some necessity to get back and it is best to know that you can do that. I try not to take things personally. I understand that when you're in a position of president that sometimes it's not about you personally but about wanting the figure of authority to acknowledge and recognize that these voices are there and want to be heard. It is not easy and it doesn't get any easier over time, in my view. When we have students who protest, the protest is almost more important than the outcome for many of them. They can do that and it's okay. I remember what it was like growing up and wanting to make my point. Students need to have that opportunity. I just try to keep in mind all the time that this is the way it is. I try to be as calm and rational as I can be, but still stand up for what I think is important and believe in. Of course that is not always easy.

FL: You have to agree, though, that in the last decade that we have seen more and more women becoming presidents of major institutions: that is a change.

MSC: I think more women are being given a chance, just as I was. I am very grateful to the regents at the University of Iowa, who gave me a chance. I think that probably many of them felt as though they were really going out on a limb. As more institutions do select women as presidents, more boards are seeing that this is something that they can consider. And sometimes women fail, just as men fail. As I said, these are tough jobs and there are some things that can happen to you that you had no part in: they just happen.

FL: There is no real recipe for total success.

MSC: I don't think so, because circumstances change so much, governing systems change so much, and many issues are totally out of your control. I'm just delighted that more and more women are being given the opportunity because I do think that women have a lot of capacity. Women as individuals are as well suited as individual men to the job. I find it hard to think that there are some gender specific characteristics that make men or women better suited.

I always look at it as a blending of the two: individuals are stronger in some areas than in others.

FL: It would be interesting to hear about your background, your family, your education, and the people who influenced you in shaping your values and your development as a leader in higher education.

MSC: I am the middle child in a family of three daughters. My parents were very much focused on education and on the notion that you must never depend on anybody else to provide a living for you. I remember as a very young child being aware that you have to do something very significant that makes you financially secure through your own efforts. My dad's family came out of the hills of Kentucky and his parents understood the value of education. My mother came from South Georgia. She was very self-directed. Her family didn't particularly value education, but she went to college and took courses toward a master's degree. My father earned a Ph.D. in physics education with the help of the G.I. bill and he taught physics and chemistry at the University of Northern Iowa for many years. My mother was first a high school teacher, then an elementary schoolteacher. Both my sisters and I were encouraged to strive toward academic achievement. My older sister is a physician, my younger sister an attorney, and I became interested in science at a very young age. I think I was fortunate because my interest was piqued in 1957, just at the time when Sputnik caught the attention of the nation. I remember it very clearly: the nation was obsessed with the notion of catching up in science. There were lots of programs in the summers. It was fortunate for me because everybody was so desperate that they didn't care whether you were male or female: if you were interested in science, you were in. Before and after the Sputnik phenomenon, women's interest in science was not so readily accepted. In high school I was interested in science fairs and earned several awards for my projects. I was also very fortunate because I went to the laboratory school at the University of Northern Iowa, which was very innovative and let me do anything I wanted. My fellow students thought it was really special that I was doing things in science and I was rewarded for that with the kind of recognition that athletes or musicians usually receive. It was an interesting environment and, I think, an unusual one. I was lucky to attend a school in which my interest in science was not regarded as odd and I wasn't made to feel like an outcast.

Then I went to Grinnell, a liberal arts college in Iowa, which was quite radical politically but very tough academically. I was a chemistry major and I had fabulous instruction. In fact I had a particular professor there, Luther Erickson, who was very influential in my life and in encouraging me to go to graduate school. I met my husband at Grinnell and we married right after we graduated. We both applied to graduate schools across the country and decided that we wanted to go to Chapel Hill. I felt that I could get a good biochemistry background there and he knew that they had a good program in his area, political science and Latin America. Again, it worked out well. I had a wonderful mentor in graduate school, Mary Ellen Jones, who wasn't my Ph.D. adviser but became my postdoctoral mentor. She was a distinguished scientist, a member of the National Academy. Unfortunately she's passed away, but she molded me and gave me aspirations for doing things that I didn't even know existed. Because my parents had come out of an education background, they had not had the experience to know what you could do as a research scientist, so it was important for me to have these excellent teachers as mentors who told me that I could strive for whatever I wanted to achieve.

I had one year of post-doctoral experience at Chapel Hill while I was waiting for my husband to finish his Ph.D., then, in 1970, we moved to Texas. The academic job market just closed up at that time, so my husband accepted the job at Southwest Texas State University in San Marcos. I got a post-doctoral position at Austin because I felt that I wasn't ready for a faculty career; I wanted to do more post-doctoral work and improve my lab skills. It worked out well: that year our son was born. Then my husband took a job at the University of Kentucky in Lexington, so we went off, baby in tow. I had an NIH post-doctoral fellowship that I could transfer to Kentucky, so I didn't have to worry. I just showed up in the biochemistry department and said that I could fund my own salary: all I needed was a lab. Since I was free, they were happy to have me. I decided to work for Fred Bollum, again an excellent scientist, very rigorous, and, again, an important mentor for me. I had advanced from being a post-doctoral fellow to a research associate and the department gave me some teaching responsibilities. There were no women scientists on the faculty, but the department was going to double in size, from eight to sixteen faculty. Fred told me that I should apply for a job because I was a good scientist and my work was going well. I had grant money by then; I was funding myself. He really did push and encourage me.

Ultimately, they did offer me a position. They hired me as an assistant professor. Basically that was all I needed; I just wanted to have the opportunity. We were at Kentucky for nineteen years and I advanced pretty rapidly. I was five years an assistant professor, five years an associate, then advanced to full professor. My work went well and I was well funded by the National Cancer Institute. I did a lot of things across the campus. What was really interesting to me was my involvement with university-wide committees. For example, I served on several search committees hiring administrators. That experience was important because I was in a medical school and I needed to see how the larger institution worked.

I think that the turning point for me was when I was invited to be part of a Cancer Center administration, just after I'd become a full professor. In the early 1980s, the Cancer Center director left, so they asked me to come in on an interim basis. I ended up staying with the Cancer Center for eight years in an administrative role as the director for research. I learned how to build programs, do fundraising, and develop the skills that you need as an administrator. It was fun and interesting. I was having a great time. Then in the late 1980's, I was selected to be on the search committee for the president of the University of Kentucky. This was a truly eye opening experience for me, Fran, because I had always thought about presidents as being superhuman people. But while I was on the search committee I looked at the resumes and thought to myself that I could do it. It was a fascinating process for me because it gave me the first glimmering that this might be something that I could aspire to do. During that period, I had another very interesting and informative experience: I was elected by the Kentucky faculty to be the faculty representative to the Board of Trustees. That was invaluable because I sat on the trustee's side and could see the interaction with the president. We hired a wonderful president, David Roselle, who is now at Delaware. There was a basketball scandal and unfortunately Kentuckians didn't want to hear about the scandal. David did the right thing and stood up to the power brokers in the state.

When President Roselle left and our son went off to college, my husband and I realized that we could have other options. We looked around and we got several offers. The one we decided to take was at North Carolina. I was first hired as Associate Provost and Dean of Research and my husband had a job in political science and Latin American studies. Then I was promoted to vice chancellor for graduate education and research. We were there for three years; it was an enriching experience because I learned so much about that side of the institution. Then I realized that, in order to be credible as a president at the kind of institution I wanted, I needed to have an experience as provost, so I applied to several places. We went to New Mexico because my husband liked the Latin American studies program there and I thought it would be a very different experience. It was. New Mexico is a tough place because it's relatively resource-poor and yet it does fabulous things. I have tremendous admiration for the University of New Mexico. I learned a great deal in each of the administrative posts I had before I accepted the presidency of the University of Iowa.

FL: What personal attributes do you feel have contributed most to your success as a leader? I think that each president has certain strengths that are very helpful in accomplishing the job.

MSC: I try very hard—and I think this is important—to shape what the questions are that need to be decided within the institution. It has always seemed to me that if you don't somehow shape what the debate is going to look like, then you are open to the debate getting off the essential points. I try to get input and then to make a decision. One of the things that I found the most frustrating during my career were leaders who decided by not deciding, by never really making sure that people understood what the decision was. When a decision was made, even if it was one that people couldn't agree with, they were glad to have the matter settled. I have made every attempt to get input, and listen to people before making a decision. I'm willing to change my mind. I'm not so focused and convinced I'm right all the time that I'm unwilling to listen to arguments. I'm also a competitive person. I want the institutions to thrive and do well. That competitive spirit has been part of my life. In every single thing that I've ever done I have felt that it is important to do well and to be respected for what you do.

FL: You have already mentioned people who inspired you and were your mentors. Were there any others you would like to cite?

MSC: You find people at almost every place whose opinions you respect, so you go to them for advice. In Iowa, I was very fond of a person who was on the board of regents when I was hired. His term was limited so he went off the board about a year after I was there, but he's remained a friend for a long time. I called on him for advice. Particularly at Iowa, there were major donors to the university whom I got to know quite well. Many of them were corporate leaders, so when we were going through some terrible budget cuts, I asked them to draw on their experience in business in order to counsel me about how to anticipate things like employee reactions to the university's budget cuts. They were very helpful. Here I have a presidential advisory group that comes in twice a year. I talk to them about issues around the university and they give me input that I find fascinating. I view all of those people, not as mentors in the formal sense of the word, but as knowledgeable individuals willing to exchange with me information and opinions that I have sometimes found enormously helpful.

FL: What were the challenges that Iowa and, later, Michigan faced when you became president?

MSC: Iowa had gone through a period of intense strategic planning during the seven to eight year period before I got there. It was the classic case of groups that assembled, produced a thick report, everyone looked it over and everyone was happy with it, since it recommended more for everyone. Then they would put it on the shelf and that was the end of it. When I came in, I was handed the latest version of it and wondered what I could do with it. I started out by saying that sometimes it's better and easier to decide how we're going to make investments if we know what our deepest principles are in this institution. I started a process to get people to think about the issues and how we could go about defining the university's core values. That was a long process that initially met with a certain amount of cynicism from the faculty, but we worked through it and ended by developing a list of core values. Then I said that what we needed to do, once we had distilled our core values, was to develop some measures to allow us to track our progress on this plan. Again it was a process that we had to work through. The first thing that the group produced was 300 measures. I said that if we have 300 measures, nothing will mean anything. We have to have a few that we can focus on. We whittled it down to about thirty and we did a report once a year. I was doing it for two purposes: first for the institution to understand that we could change and make progress, and second because I wanted the legislature to understand that I was very attentive to this issue. Otherwise the legislature is always likely to say that it is impossible to say whether or not the university is successful, since it cannot produce any measures to prove it. The measures provided tools that we could use. One of the things that surprised me was that, in the midst of budget cutting problems, having those tools was really helpful to us in deciding what we were going to keep and what we weren't going to keep.

FL: It is always helpful to have clear priorities that everybody knows in those difficult situations.

MSC: Everybody knew the things on which we focused attention: that worked very well in Iowa. When I came to Michigan, the affirmative action case was front and center and that took all of my time the first year. The second issue was the culmination of the case dealing with student athletes in basketball who had accepted money. It was a very complicated case and despite the fact that it was ten years old, the evidence really didn't come out until right before I got here. So I had to take some actions that were really tough in the athletics program, but both of the measures I took worked. Those were the two major issues I faced on coming to Michigan.

FL: What effects have the role and demands of each of these leadership posts had on your family life and how have you managed to maintain a balance in your life?

MSC: One of the very tough aspects of this job is that it is so consuming. The university owns you, twenty-four hours a day, seven days a week. I have a terrific partnership with my husband. He was a faculty member until we went to Iowa. Then he decided that he wanted a change, largely because when you're the president's spouse, it's hard to be a faculty member in the institution. So he has embarked on a totally new career and works with a private company nearby the university. It's a market research firm. He had done public opinion research as a professor, so this was a natural second career. We try hard to make sure that sometimes during the summer we get completely away We probably don't do it as much as we should, but I love the work and I love to be in a university environment, going to lectures and concerts and all of those things that I enjoy in a university community. One of the things that really centered me and was very helpful in Iowa was the presence of my husband's father, who lived to past 100. All the time we were at Iowa, he was either in a retirement apartment there or, during the last two years, in a nursing home. My husband went to see him every day, took him out, and did things with him. I think that was very good because it gave us another focus: he was important and our lives weren't just about our jobs. My mother, who is ninety, now comes to visit us twice a year for five or six weeks. When you go home and your ninety-year-old mother is there, you have to think about other things and that re-centers you. So those are two good family focal points that helped us to keep ourselves sane and mindful that this job is not the be all and end all of our existence. You need something outside. Our son is married and happily situated. We enjoy visiting him and his wife and participating in their lives.

FL: What did your internal constituencies—your governing board, faculty, students, and staff—at each of your presidencies expect of you, and what did you feel that you owed them in response? Each constituency sizes you up and presents you with a list of their wants and needs as you come in.

MSC: Of course the nature of constituencies is to feel that their concerns are more important than the concerns of anyone else. You have to balance the time that you spend with each one. It is particularly hard at Michigan because we have almost 500,000 alums. I don't spend enough time with the alums; I don't spend enough time with the faculty; I don't spend enough time with the students. Yet I try my best to balance the time I devote to each. We have calendar meetings where considerable thought is put into the matter of how I try to reach out and what I do. Of course you cannot completely satisfy all the demands, but you just have to keep trying to do the best you can.

FL: I think that's probably the best answer that can be devised for that issue. You just can't make everybody happy: you must simply do your best. How have you managed the different, sometimes conflicting expectations that your constituencies have of you?

MSC: Ultimately I am who I am and I can't make myself into something that I am not. I always like to get out and learn, so I'll push myself a little bit to go to a lecture, even though I might not completely understand the field. I think it's important for me to do that because every time I attend something, it gets back to a lot of people that I've gone and people are pleased about it. In the end, all you can do is try to plot out a course, stay to the course, have as many interactions that you can with the various groups, and ultimately be confident in yourself that you're doing the best you possibly can. As hard as you work, you must understand that you cannot be all things to all people.

FL: It's frustrating because, like most flagships, Michigan is a very large place.

MSC: It is a huge place. Once a month I have a meeting that is open to students. We invite students randomly because we want to make sure that enough students know about it, but any student can come to these meetings. These meetings last for about an hour and a half. We have them all over the campus so that students aren't always obliged to come across campus to one place. When I go in, it's usually the end of the day. I'm tired and I wish I didn't have to go to yet another meeting, but when I come out of it, I'm always energized. The students bring up different topics and broach issues that they want to talk about. I enjoy that a lot. I think that you derive real pleasure out of those interactions and it keeps you going.

FL: It's also a reminder of what got us into this in the first place. What was your greatest challenge as a leader?

MSC: At Iowa and at Michigan I experienced very challenging situations that were really quite different. At the beginning of the last year I was at Iowa, we were, of course, very much affected by September 11. Shortly afterward, the brunt of the budget crisis started hitting Iowa and we had two major campus tragedies as well. A highly respected executive dean in the medical school was killed, then, a few days later, in a construction accident, the golden dome of an iconic building on campus burned. It felt as though the world was falling apart. I had to keep the morale of the campus up. I knew that I had to be out there talking about the future, saying that we're going to rebuild, that it's going to be okay. All of this happened in a two-month period and was emotionally draining.

When I came to Michigan, the team around me was extraordinarily nervous about a new president coming in because the affirmative action cases had been developed and led by Lee Bollinger. He left before the Sixth Circuit Court ruled in our favor, as a matter of fact. We thought it would probably go to the Supreme Court, but we didn't know for sure. I had to come in and keep it all going in a very public and high profile way. It was very tough, but in the end enormously rewarding

FL: How have you recruited and structured your leadership teams in each of your presidential posts?

MSC: At Iowa, the team was pretty much in place and they were very good people. The only person that I really had to recruit was a provost. I did some reshuffling of the other people who were there but that worked. It was a cohesive group that worked well together. When I came here, there were five major vacancies that I had to fill right away. That was a big challenge. I made appointments from the inside for two posts. For the other three I conducted national searches that went on for quite a while. That uncertainty of having interim appointees was an unsettled feeling because you weren't working with a team that you are certain will continue to be there. Building the team takes work and takes time. It's not something that you can do overnight. It's a bigger group, ten or eleven people here, than it was in Iowa, where there were only five or six people. Bigger is more complicated, but what we are doing is working together to make sure that we've got shared goals we understand and we can depend on each other. Those are issues that I think you have to work out and we've been doing it.

FL: Can you tell me some of the specific qualities that you look for in the people you choose to work with and depend upon?

MSC: Smart. If they're smarter than I am, it's great. I want people who have good judgment. Sometimes I look for qualities that are different from mine because I think that it is good to have people who are willing to engage in a fruitful debate and bring different ideas to the table, who aren't afraid to push back and say, "Wait a minute you know I'm not sure I agree." Of course, ultimately, when the decision is made, you need them to be team players and go out and support it. I want people who are prominent in their own right, who are recognized nationally either for their discipline or for what they do administratively. I want that recognition to be there; I think it's important. For decades, Michigan has been a place from which leaders are recruited. Many presidents have been through here as provost or vice president. That's a great point of pride for the university and it's one I tell people I am recruiting: they can use Michigan as a launching pad.

FL: In each post you've been expected to spend a lot of time out of the university, on the road. As a president, you're the primary representative to the alumni, to the legislature, to the general public, and soliciting major gifts. Have you had someone in your administration who stood in for you, handling the day-to-day work of the university?

MSC: When I was at New Mexico, they actually had a procedure in place so that, whenever the president was out of town, I was named the acting president officially. I've never experienced quite that level of designation. In Iowa I relied on a couple of people to let me know what was going on, convene things and be decision makers, though I was never gone for that long a time. Here it's much more collaborative. I have three executive vice presidents: the provost, the executive vice president for finance and the executive vice president for medical affairs and those three, since they are so much involved in the money part of the institution, keep the ship going, but I don't designate a single person to do it. We have dispersed functions here. What that requires is that people work together: it's a great group.

FL: How did you formulate the vision for the future of each institution?

MSC: At Iowa, there had been a lot of work done before I got there on what the aspirations of the university were. They were to raise its profile, particularly in the sciences and the arts. There were several areas of real strength in the university. I always felt that people in Iowa were far too modest about what the institution had achieved and that we really needed to find ways to promote, to document, and to talk about the extraordinarily rich history of the institution. We worked on that and we made a lot of progress while I was there in terms of making sure that candidates got promoted for membership in the National Academies. We were very deliberate about it. We were in the Midwest, we were in a small state, and I just felt that people were not paying any attention. On the arts side we worked hard on having great architects come in and do the buildings so that we constructed things that we could really point to.

I was also very focused at Iowa on the undergraduate experience and making sure that we provided special things for our students. One of the things that is not well known about Iowa, but really does enrich the institution, is that almost 40 percent of the students come from out of state. We had that astonishing percentage because the population of Iowa has declined and the population of the high school graduates has declined, so the university had unused capacity. We recruited a lot of students from surrounding states; for example we brought in many students from Chicago and its suburban areas. Those young people, as they rightly should, had certain expectations of the institution. We worked hard to develop private resources to get real interaction within our living learning centers and other special programs for our students. I was really obsessed with the notion of having very good career counseling for students because I thought it was so important. I got a donor to provide a major gift for a big facility to make career counseling available early on in the students' careers, so that they could start thinking about it when they were freshmen and sophomores, not just as juniors and seniors. We worked on hard on these things and we made good progress in Iowa.

Michigan is a vast institution with extraordinary breadth and depth. People can come here and study anything that they can possibly think about. It's an unbelievable place. It's also a place that is decentralized, much more decentralized than Iowa, even though I thought Iowa was pretty decentralized. All of the colleges have their aspirations. The other interesting thing about Michigan is that if you look across the colleges and departments it is extremely impressive to note the number of them that are in the top ten in the nation in their area. If you go to top twenty, that would include almost every unit in the university.

We have four presidential initiatives that we are getting underway at Michigan. We do an excellent job at this institution in interdisciplinary and multidisciplinary research in graduate education. We don't do it quite so well at the undergraduate level, so I want to start a program that will encourage joint development and team teaching of courses by faculty from different disciplines in order to bring that power of interdisciplinary research and teaching to the undergraduate level. I think that it would be an enormous strength for the university.

The second initiative is an investigation into developing a center for ethical issues in public life. I've been alarmed by what is happening nationally. I think that the area of ethical issues in public life is an important one in which we could productively do research and create curricula. It is an important area for institutions to investigate and teach at this time when everything else seems to be falling apart in society.

The third area relates to our enormous strength in the health system. We own a hospital. We own a practice plan. We own an insurance company. But, until this past year, we were really treating those as separate entities, as though they didn't relate to each other. I want to align the interests of all of those entities, use the strength of our health policy experts (many of whom are prominent on the national scene), and use the power of our health sciences colleges to develop some models for health care that will be affordable and sustainable for society in the twenty-first century. We want to launch a major effort: I'm excited about that.

The fourth initiative relates to something that is going to be a twenty- or thirty-year project. That is to look at all of our residence systems that are in great need of examination and change, even though we now have some excellent living learning centers. I want to use this as an opportunity to integrate academic and residential life much more closely in the university and to get faculty involved in some of those designs. It's a marvelous opportunity to do it right now because I think it could change the face of undergraduate education in this university. Along with these, we have major facilities improvements underway across the campus. We are also focused on access and financial aid for needy students.

FL: What strategies have you been using to communicate and create buy-in to these plans by all of your constituencies? Are there any new methods that you are trying out?

MSC: Certainly when I was developing the ideas, I worked with executive officers, worked with deans, and had meetings with faculty groups to explain the initiatives to people, to ask what they thought about them. We're putting together groups now that are going to carry out the initiatives. It's a constant effort to devise ways to help people to understand how they could participate.

FL: How have you strategized translating your understanding of each university, together with the external realities, into a long range plan for change and improvement?

MSC: This has been, as you might imagine, topic number one because of the budget climates of both states. Iowa has long been committed to education at all levels, in K through 12 as well as higher education, but the state budget was devastated and the higher education budget was subjected to the same slash and burn process. We had to develop really aggressive tuition policies there just to make up the difference. These tough budget situations always offer an opportunity to stop doing things that you'd like to cut, but can't in good budget times. We certainly used that strategy. We also went on to consolidate, focus, and combine departments in order to produce some administrative savings. In Michigan the budget problem hasn't been as severe because the university has a rich diversity of funding sources that Iowa didn't have. Still we have had to make some tough decisions. This has forced us to be much more efficient in our business operations and to examine whether there are things that we do that could be done by an outside entity. We've done modeling for our region based on budget scenarios for the state. It's difficult because you don't know what is going to happen, but it has also been a very good exercise in planning. Budget planning and fund raising have been a major focus of our attention.

FL: You've touched on this, but I'd like you now to focus specifically on the link between your strategic directions and your budgeting. How did you link the changes you wanted to make to the financial budgeting process of each institution? Often presidents are accused of neglecting to make that strategic link very well, so it would be helpful if you could furnish some good examples.

MSC: First of all, we established principles and we disseminated them broadly. We pinpointed the things that we were not going to cut. We did not cut financial aid: in fact we increased it so that people could see that was what we were doing. At Iowa, we did not cut library collections. We had two or three things that we weren't going to cut and everybody knew it. We also had a four-year graduation contract that guaranteed students the courses they needed at the time they needed to graduate and we said we're not going to cut that: we'll cut in other areas. You have to decide and publicize the things that you are not going to cut and you have to tell people the principles that you are using. We told people that we were going to make sure that we put our academic quality above all else. Let me give you an example. In the first round of cuts we made changes in our custodial staff that people didn't like because it meant the custodians weren't around all night. It was cheaper for us just to have them there during the day because we didn't have to pay shift differential charges. When people complained, we told them that it was either that or we would have to cut some classes. We are not cutting the grass as often as we used to. We're not replacing equipment as fast as we used to. We took all kinds of economy measures we could explain to people because our first goal was to make sure that we didn't reduce the number of freshman seminars or that we didn't increase our class sizes above a certain point. We had a list to show people why we made our cost-cutting decisions. I think that is the best you can possibly do. You are always going to have arguments from people because you have a constituency for every single thing within the university, but it has worked for me to be able to go back, point to our principles and point out that the cut in question aligns with those principles.

FL: How have you gotten the faculty on board so that they understand and support the difficult changes that you have had to make?

MSC: The only way that I know how to do that is to get out as much information as you possibly can and keep repeating it over and over again. One of the things I've learned in this job is that saying it once is not enough. It takes people three or four hearings to let it sink in. You must just keep at it, explaining over and over again. One of the things that has helped is that most universities are facing these kinds of problems: we're not alone. They can look at their colleagues at other institutions and see that everybody else is having problems, so it's not as though our faculty alone are being picked on. They have been remarkably good natured about it.

FL: You and I both contributed to my friend and colleague, Brent Ruben's book, *Pursuing Excellence in Higher Education*. I've read your piece on implementing a strategic plan and I know that you have a terrific answer to my questions on that topic.

MSC: It was important for me to get people to understand that this wasn't something that you just put on the shelf, whether it was a plan that was handed down or whether it was a new one that was being crafted. We had to find ways to measure whether we were making any progress. Does this make any difference for us to have this vision? So the first thing we had to do was to establish what our shared values were, the second was to say how will we measure ourselves to see that we're making progress, and the third was to be very public about it, to get out once a year and say yes, we made progress in these areas, or no we didn't make progress in these areas, but here's why. Sometimes what you learn in that process is that the things that you're trying to measure aren't very good indicators, so you throw them out. That's fine. You don't need to make progress in every area because if you did, people wouldn't think you were serious. You have to stretch yourself. You have to do some things that are going to be tough; you have to do some others that people can feel good about. You find that people start aligning their behaviors to help make progress on the carefully selected things that you measure so that you can really say yes, our institution is better off than it was five years ago because these things have happened. I can give you some simple examples. You know that we measured the number of faculty elected to National Academies. That is an important indicator that grew enormously during the time that I was at Iowa because we started putting people up for election. There hadn't been a deliberative process about putting people up for nomination. Once we did that, they were recognized. The other thing that I did at Iowa had to do with the issue of broadcasting the excellence of the university. I told our public relations people that I wanted a measure every month of how many times we were mentioned in the top twenty newspapers in the country. I told them that we were going to track it and we were going to have goals for increasing by 20 percent the times we were mentioned. That had an astonishing effect on the publications people because they knew they were going to be measured on it. They started cultivating relationships with reporters at the national newspapers so that they could get in their stories about good things happening at the University of Iowa. It was a simple device, but it changed the behaviors all the way up and down the line. Then the faculty members were delighted because they were called upon to be experts and we were able to publicize it when professor so-and-so had a book review in the New York Times. It was things like that that people could focus on. We also measured the number of members in the alumni association. As a result the alumni association did a big program to increase membership and made real progress in that area. Those were some of the things that people could see were having an impact and it helped to get the buy-in.

FL: It's interesting that in higher education each faculty member works in a separate, highly specialized subfield. The specialists in our own field know our work well. For example, my field was seventeenth-century French literature. My disciplinary colleagues in the United States, France, and around the world knew my work, but my colleagues in the college and even in the department didn't know anything about it. Without an effort like yours, the university may have hundreds of distinguished scholars on the faculty, each one of whom is well known and respected by international specialists in the field, but whose achievements have little impact or recognition in the home institution.

MSC: That's right, and I felt that gaining recognition for its distinguished faculty was critical to the University of Iowa at that time.

FL: These questions about assessment of the outcomes of your initiatives at the university and measurement of progress toward long term goals are, I think, very important. Recently I gave a keynote address at a forum on distance education. Over the whole weekend, from Friday to Sunday, we talked about assessment. It may not be the kind of issue that excites large numbers of faculty, but the rest of the world is interested in seeing means of measuring progress.

MSC: I agree. In fact, when we did our outcomes and measures, something like 80 percent of them were outcomes not inputs. One of the things that really bother me about the *U.S. News and World Report* rankings is that they are entirely based on input. How much money did you spend per student? How selective are you?

FL: And how large is your endowment?

MSC: All of those inputs are fine, but what do you produce? The outcomes were what we needed to focus upon. In the sciences particularly, we used things like the citation index (how many people were referring to the work) and what we discovered at Iowa was that there was much more impact than people might have thought, given the relatively small size of the faculty. It was clear that the faculty was doing extremely well. I went out and talked about this to alumni groups and donors. They were always delighted to hear about it because I could tell them how many books emanated from faculty at the university and who got into the *New York Times* best books of the year: it was something like fifteen from Iowa. When people saw that, they were just astonished. The other helpful aspect of our outcomes measures was that I could always use them with the legislature. If they complained about, say, the number of senior faculty teaching undergraduates, I could tell them we actually measured that and about 85 percent of the freshman and sophomore classes are being taught by senior faculty.

FL: Isn't it also important that the faculty who are celebrated in this way feel even better about what they're doing? It's one way to let them know how much we care about their work and how important it is.

MSC: I agree, and telling stories is very important.

FL: Is there anything else you want to talk about as far as celebrating success? Are there any other approaches you have used?

MSC: I think that it can be done in many different ways. One of the things Michigan is wonderful about is designating faculty every year as university professors, an honorific title. The thing I love about the Michigan program is that the faculty member being honored gets to name the professorship for somebody that they admire. It's a way for the faculty member being rewarded to honor a person who perhaps was a good colleague or mentor and give a lecture in his or her honor. Those ways of recognizing people are, I think, extremely important.

FL: Turning toward external constituencies, what importance have you placed on the roles of the University of Iowa and the University of Michigan in their communities?

MSC: Both universities are in relatively small towns. Iowa City is smaller than Ann Arbor. I think that the relationships improved during the time that I was there because rather than fighting with each other and not letting each other know when we were planning this road or this building or this parking structure, we worked hard to try to cooperate with the city. In Iowa City, we did a wonderful thing there jointly with the city that was a sort of re-streetscaping. Since writing is so prominent at Iowa due to the Writers' Workshop, we did a project in a street that was right next to the university, a sort of front door of the university. It was a writers' walk with bronze plaques that were uniquely designed to honor writers who had been either at the University of Iowa Writers' Workshop or in Iowa City or in Iowa. We had thirty or so of them, all in the sidewalks. The university put in a couple of million dollars and I think the city put in a couple of million for this whole streetscape. It was a huge success and those sorts of things I think can be very successful joint projects and people were working pretty well together.

We try to work with the city here too. We don't always agree because sometimes we have differing needs and differing expectations, but I think the communication is absolutely critical because we are totally dependent on each other. The university is dependent on having a nice city. The town is depending on us to draw people here. Even though we are a tax exempt organization and don't pay property taxes, all the people who work here and live here do pay local taxes, and they make this a thriving town.

FL: What have been the major groups outside each university that you have needed to work with?

MSC: All the donors, particularly when you are in a capital campaign, as well as the legislators, and the governor.

FL: Did they have specific expectations of you at each place to start off with? You knew what you wanted to do with them but they also had things that they wanted from you.

MSC: I think that certainly there's always a period of getting to know each other. It takes several years before you get to know people, so the donors and legislators are probably trying to size you up to see what you're like, but both in Iowa and here, I didn't spend a lot of time personally at the capitol. We had lobbyists to do that because the philosophy at Iowa was—and I think it is here as well—is that if the president goes to the legislature, it must be for a specific reason.

FL: I want to ask some questions on day-to-day realities of the presidency now. For instance, how have you allocated your time in different posts and what have been your top priorities? This place is huge, Iowa may not be as big, but both of them have made certain demands on your time.

MSC: They do. First of all you have to spend enough time every week with the people who are really carrying out the work of the institution, the executive officers, to make sure that you're in good communication with them and it requires several hours every week just to be up to date on everything. Donor issues now are pretty daunting for us. We've just announced a two and a half billion-dollar campaign for Michigan

FL: Over a period of?

MSC: Five years. I'm spending a lot of time meeting with people and talking to people. I also need to spend time with the regents. We have monthly meetings with our regents, but I spend time outside of those monthly meetings with regents to make sure that they have enough information. I apportion the rest of my time working on the campus with students and faculty. In the summer it's a little bit different because I don't do much work with students in the summer. Every day is different, as you know, but any given week, I would certainly touch all of those areas. I'll be spending time on athletics as well, because it's not something you can ignore. Though I have very good people in athletics, still the issues demand your attention.

FL: Doesn't a two and a half billion-dollar campaign mean that you will be on the road multiple days of the week?

MSC: I will be traveling almost every week.

FL: I'm sure your constituency is coast to coast; it's not just located in Michigan.

MSC: You're right. Nearly every week I'll be doing development work of one kind or another.

FL: Did you have a campaign at Iowa?

MSC: We did. I launched our campaign there and got it through it up to the public phase. It started out as a $750 million campaign and they upped the goal to a billion. They have extended the time. It's a little bit smaller campaign than Michigan's but Iowa is a smaller institution

FL: Every leader experiences planned and unplanned events that escalate into time consuming crises. Among the most common are fiscal challenges, contract negotiations, and P.R. challenges. Do you have any crisis management story that you'd like to share with people who aspire to be presidents?

MSC: There are some I can't share, but the one I want to talk about is the burning of the old capitol dome in Iowa while I was there. It was a construction accident. The dome itself was being refurbished and a team was removing asbestos. Even though they had been warned not to use heat guns they did it anyway. It caught fire and burned. The building was built in the 1830s and is a classic building. The only reason that it didn't go up in flames was that back in the twenties, the thrifty Iowans had built a concrete dome as fire protection underneath the concrete cap beneath the dome itself. The burning wood just fell onto the concrete and didn't get into the building and burn it, though we had tremendous water damage. That was a big crisis. People were upset about this accident and were asking if the university was liable in some way, whether the university had done something wrong. So it was a big task just managing the information.

On the day of the fire, I announced that my husband and were making a $5000.00 contribution to the restoration of the dome. I did that within hours because I wanted people to understand that we were going to fix it, it was going to be fine, and the president and her spouse were going to be the first donors. I got students involved in raising money for it. It turned out that insurance covered most of it because it really was an accident and we were not liable. It's very important to have a good team around you who can get out the information, respond to the questions, get talking points, and keep people on message. I have a superb communications team, the best I've ever seen. We prepare for these things all the time and we have crisis management groups. If something's coming up, they get together and decide what we're going to do and what the message is going to be. I think that we do a pretty good job.

FL: One of the recurring issues in crisis management is having a student on campus die in a suicide or of some other cause on campus. That is unbelievably difficult to deal with.

MSC: It's very tough. Right before I came to Iowa, there had been a death of alcohol in a fraternity: an eighteen-year-old had gotten drunk, vomited, expiated the vomit in his lungs and died. The university had started a whole process that I had to come in and manage and we had town hall meetings, we got Robert Wood Johnson money to try to effect a change in behavior with alcohol consumption. It was just brutal because Iowa City has a huge binge-drinking problem. People don't realize that it has the highest density of alcohol outlets within a mile of the campus of any place in the country. I worked at this incessantly for all the seven years that I was there, against much public criticism. I've noticed just recently that the city has gotten serious about addressing the problem. They're beginning to have some of the bars close. They've levied stiff fines now for underage drinking, and they're beginning to make the changes that are necessary to make a big difference.

FL: The final question in this category, before we go to issue oriented questions, deals with the issue of leadership. What is your definition of leadership?

MSC: I've always thought that it was important for the leader to be able to frame the issues in a succinct way, then get input and listen very carefully, and finally make a decision and communicate the decision. Under that general outline, I think that you can manage almost any situation, but you have to develop a level of trust. It is important that people trust you.

FL: What are the most important qualities for a president today?

MSC: Lots of stamina: feeling passionately interested in the work of the presidency and not just the ceremonial aspects. Being the president and doing the presidency are two very different things. You need to be able to live with ambiguity: there are very few black and white issues out there. Most issues are fraught with nuance. You have to be able to weigh the nuances and pick the solution that is best for the institution, knowing that it isn't perfect because nothing will be perfect.

FL: That's a thoughtful and nuanced response. In your view, how has the presidency changed over the past couple of decades in response to the disinvestment of the states in public higher education?

MSC: That's been a very discouraging trend because I think that it's important for presidents to speak up to remind the nation that one of sources of the great wealth in this country is the willingness to have public universities that are equal to private institutions. We have democratized higher education in a way that has brought great wealth to this country. I know that we may just be continuing to tilt at windmills in talking about it, but it's important. We need to try to change public opinion. This has become a topic that I talk about all the time, as my colleagues do as well, reminding our states and the nation how we got to this point.

FL: I think that may be the most important issue we can address: trying to recreate the understanding of the importance of the democratized system of higher education that the federal and state governments created in the industrial age. Ironically the government supported that system at a much higher level then than it does now, when it is needed more than ever, in our post-industrial age of knowledge.

How have the role and demands of the presidency changed in response to the technological revolution?

MSC: I think that our students come with totally different expectations. This requires huge investment on the part of the institutions and constant change. The change is much more rapid that it used to be. Our modes of learning differ. When I was an undergraduate, and later, as a graduate student, I loved going to the library and reading randomly in the stacks. They have at their fingertips much more information that we ever had, yet we still need to teach students how to vet information, because people aren't vetting it for them. They need to be more skilled now, not less. I think that it's much more difficult to fashion your arguments when you have unlimited information.

FL: One of the things I learned about the technological revolution is that it can be a good tool for active learning at a higher level and for increased communication, as opposed to sitting mute in the classroom taking notes. A Rutgers scientist who was one year from retirement learned how to offer a virtual laboratory online for his large introductory class, along with his lectures and more conventional kinds of assignments. He spoke about his experience with the online learning environment before the board committee on educational policy and was very emotional about it. He told them that students who practiced first in the virtual lab had far fewer accidents in the conventional laboratory. Then he went on to say that he had taught more than 300 students a year at Rutgers for almost forty years but this was the first time he actually had the opportunity to know all of his students, thanks to the online environment. I listened to that and I felt that there is a lot more that can be done. The library is never going to be unimportant, but technology has valuable things to bring to higher education.

Let's discuss the demands on the presidency that stem from the growing roles of public support and commercial application in university research. That's getting to be a very sensitive issue.

MSC: Yes, it is getting to be sensitive, and yet there is the pull and push because the states, particularly a state like Michigan, want desperately for the universities to help in economic development and to make these bridges with commercial entities because they see it as a way to diversify and change the dynamic in terms of jobs and companies. You have that pull on one side, while on the other side you have faculty members who don't want to have their research directed: they are concerned about the companies' motives, so it's something that is not going to go away. We can only work at it and make sure that we develop the right kind of policies. I just see it ever more important in the future. I think we've got to figure out how to do it right, but we've got to do it.

FL: There's also the issue of scientists who are doing research for pharmaceutical companies, but who are also serving as reviewers.

MSC: We've got to make clear policies about those issues.

FL: Then, finally, how has the presidency changed in response to the increasingly strident demands of students and politicians for high quality and accountability in both expenditures and results?

MSC: Yes, this is a fact of life that we're faced with. We know that students have lots of options and we need to make sure that the experience that they have at the university is good. Part of what I see now in terms of student activism is something that I don't think is necessarily bad because one of the things we should be doing within universities is encouraging students to try to take on an issue and have something positive happen. I think this gives them the feeling that they can go out and change the world. In a lot of ways, it makes me proud to see that students get passionate about an issue and want to do something about it. We need to find ways to help that happen.

FL: Presidencies were once measured in decades, now they are more typically limited to four or five years. Do you believe that the changes in the role have brought that about or are there other reasons for this high rate of turnover? You could look at this phenomenon in our AAU presidential seniority listing. When I was named president of Rutgers in 1990, I was at the bottom of the list. When I left in 2002, I was ninth in seniority. There were people who had become presidents after I did who were no longer doing the job. Why is this happening?

MSC: I don't know if there's a single answer. I do think that these jobs take a lot out of you emotionally, physically, and intellectually in a lot of ways as well. It may vary by discipline. Some people have disciplines to which they can return. I've talked to people who have been humanists or lawyers who feel that they can go back and, with some retooling, get into their field again and take right up where they left off. If we look at it that way, certain people may not want to continue as presidents, but they don't want to go back to being faculty members, so they leave to do something other than being a president of a university. That doesn't explain why it happens so often or why the tenures are getting so short, but I do think the demands are much greater. I'm sure there were some really rough times for presidents a century ago, but it's hard for me to imagine that they were in the sort of spotlight with the incessant pressure of events that attract attention and demand their immediate response.

FL: No, I think you're absolutely correct. When you say 24/7, that was almost in my letter of appointment. You're in the job all the time; you are president all the time. Even when you go out for a little time on you own, you must always be careful.

How would you characterize your leadership style?

MSC: I think that people would say about me that I'm open, direct, approachable, and easy to talk to. I consciously try to find things that I can talk to people about, whether they are professors or shopkeepers. I work on that all the time. I think people would say that I'm somebody who does listen, that I'm willing to give somebody a shot to come in and try to change my mind. I may not change it, but I'm certainly open to considering that. I also understand that, in the end, much of what happens in the university is going to come right back to me.

FL: What do you feel have been the most critical capital investments made under your leadership? What is your favorite capital project, one that you feel really good about?

MSC: We did a lot at Iowa and the reason that we did so much is that the institution had gone through the decade of the 1980s deferring capital expenditures when there were budget problems, so it was a crisis. We were building huge research facilities, and for undergraduate students, we constructed an honors center, and a career center. We built a journalism center and an art history building. We constructed building after building because we had raised the money. We changed the face of the campus: that was really important.

Here we are doing a lot of capital construction as well. The hospital and the medical school had not been able to make decisions about going forward with critical facilities: we've moved past that. We are on schedule in constructing a great number of facilities because we have to build for the future. The other significant project will be our big investment in student residences. I think that will be very important to Michigan.

FL: What do you regard as the most significant legacy that you left to the University of Iowa?

MSC: At Iowa, I would say that it was raising the profile of the university nationally. We worked very deliberately to do that. That was one of the things that were very important to me. I also spent a lot of time worrying about the undergraduate experience and making that more meaningful for students, both in terms of what happened outside of the classroom and what happened inside the classroom. In Michigan, we have a huge investment in the life sciences. I am absolutely committed to seeing that through in order to change the dynamic of the sciences at Michigan and make it far better. I said before, I want to align the interests of all of our medical sciences components in a way that will make them a dominant feature of the university. Then, if we can bring this interdisciplinary approach down to the undergraduate level, we will have taken a great strength of Michigan and transferred it in a way that will be extremely powerful.

FL: What advice would you give to new presidents? What should they choose to do first?

MSC: I think that it depends on the circumstance, but the key is quickly getting people that you can trust. I think talking to former presidents is sometimes a really good idea to give you a sense about the institution. That is one of the things I did in coming in here: I talked to Lee, I talked to some of the people who had been here, and I took a lot of notes. I've gone back recently to review those notes and found that they were absolutely right in terms of the issues that were out there and the people that I should really consult because they were going to give me good advice. I got lots of good information that way. I think that another thing you can do is to select some people who are donors to the institution or regents and ask their opinion to get some information so that you can triangulate opinions on issues.

Part of what you need to do at the beginning is simply to observe the institution until you begin to know the who, what, and where, of the things that you need to worry about. I think that using team-building methods for the people with whom you work most closely is a very valuable use of time because you learn a lot about each other that way, and you have to learn to trust each other. Just because people have been working at the same institution for years doesn't mean they trust each other. Therefore you have to find ways to break down those walls. Some people are just going to hang out there and not going to do what you want them to do. Sometimes you can make a change, sometimes the political realities are such that you can't, and you just live with it.

FL: That's right. You move on. What is at the core of your work in higher education? What is the underlying purpose that you want to accomplish?

MSC: At the University of Michigan, I want this to be a place where students and faculty can pursue the highest level of scholarship and intellectual and creative endeavor, a place that is endlessly exciting and ever getting better. Part of my responsibility is to bring in the resources to let them do that, then get out of the way and let them do it.

FL: As states reduce their funding of higher education, while legislatures and governors try to cap tuition, how can institutions resolve their budget problems and continue to build both access and excellence?

MSC: This decrease in state funding and how we can resolve it is one of the huge issues in higher education. The double bind created when the states reduce their funding and want to cap tuition is an impossible set of circumstances.

FL: It's a lose, lose situation.

MSC: That's why we need to keep educating people, talking about the problem, and building models showing people why this is such a disaster. We've focused on this in Michigan for about the last six months and the conversation has changed here, I'm not getting questions about why this is so expensive, I'm getting questions about whether the quality is going to be there. People can be turned on by the quality issue and they'll vote for quality every time. I keep talking to the state about ways that it can help resolve the problem.

I think that most of our financial aid should be based on need rather than merit, but for some states this is really hard because they've sold these middle-class programs based on scholarships for students regardless of their financial need. Michigan has traditionally pursued a high aid model based solely on need and I think it's something that we're going to have to continue to pursue in order to provide access. It's our responsibility as institutions to go out and look for students who are talented, yet whose families think they can't dream of coming to the University of Michigan. More and more institutions are going to be doing this. I made it a major feature of the capital campaign to raise money so that we can provide more grants and fewer loans.

FL: What worries me as I look into the future is the issue of access. The numbers of college applicants are increasing tremendously in New Jersey and therefore our enrollment went up during the last few years I was there. They were qualified to come and the prospect of turning them away was painful.

MSC: That's right.

FL: Of course, you can always do what some schools do, reduce the number of students you admit in order to raise your average SAT scores and increase the perception of quality for the magazine ratings game, but that does not seem to me what public institutions should do to fulfill their mission.

MSC: We don't have an overall higher education governance system in the state of Michigan. Each institution has its own board and that has created many interesting and good institutions, so we don't have limited capacity in Michigan. Our challenge is to encourage more and more people to pursue higher education. In fact Dearborn and Flint campuses of the University of Michigan have unused capacity, though we don't have any extra capacity in Ann Arbor. I think that there are a lot of ways that we can try to improve access and the notion that community colleges could be part of the solution is one that I think should be pursued. I think community colleges can play a very important role here and have been under utilized.

FL: You've had the opportunity to work with more than one governing board. What are the important characteristics of good governing boards and what are the problems one can encounter in dealing with governing boards?

MSC: I've worked with every kind of governing board, system boards and institutional boards, and there are multiple ways that states use to either appoint or elect. Here in Michigan they are elected; in other states they're appointed. You can get good people both ways. I don't think the method is critical. I think it's important to have people who understand the role and the responsibilities of the governing board, particularly its fiduciary responsibilities. It is important that board members put personal interests aside in making decisions.

FL: That's a key point.

MSC: Sometimes it's hard because people do feel so passionately about certain issues, but it's very important for the good of the institution.

FL: In the past few years there have been instances in which the governor of the state has gotten involved with policy issues or even personnel decisions in the state's flagship public university and the state's higher education system. How can institutions of higher education deal with that kind of political interference?

MSC: I think that politicizing the university is very dangerous. Fortunately I have not recently been in places where this has been an issue. The University of Michigan is a special case because it has constitutional autonomy. In fact before I was hired, they fought and won in the State Supreme Court, an exemption from open meetings in terms of presidential selection. They reconfirmed their autonomy in this issue. That has been a great strength for the University of Michigan and one that the regents jealously guard. That's not always the case in every state. Politicians can always express their opinion, that's fine, but determining the outcome is a very different thing.

FL: You have served as the president of two NCAA division 1 schools. You've been a member of the Knight Commission, served on the NCAA board of directors, and have chaired the NCAA task force that is recommending extensive academic reforms. What's your take on the current very public and damaging perceptions of serious problems in recruiting, admission, retention, graduation, and student athlete conduct? Can we solve these problems?

MSC: I hope so, or I wouldn't be willing to put all this time into the issues. I am pleased that we've gotten these reforms through. I do think that they'll have a positive impact. I've thought for a long time that it is important for us to be more explicit about our expectations, for us to align our expectations of coaches, for example and to put this on the table in discussions among presidents. I am pleased with the changes in the NCAA in terms of the way that it does its business. What is sometimes discouraging to me is the amount of time it takes to get what I think are important reforms through the association approval process. Clearly there's still tremendous divergence of opinion among the vast diversity of athletic conferences and the schools themselves in terms of their different missions and it is not easy to manage all of this. So I'd like to think that there's hope, but I'm not naïve about it: these are pretty daunting problems.

FL: I agree with you. I think that all these reforms are going to have an impact, at least if, as we move along, we can manage to assess whether or not they are working. I also think that it is going to be very helpful having Myles Brand at the head of the NCAA, a leader who has been a president and is very concerned about wanting to solve this.

MSC: I hope so. I certainly think that he's out there using the bully pulpit, which is really very important. It's clear that what we've done. perhaps unwittingly, is to create a system in which athletes don't think they're accountable and even some coaches, surprisingly enough, don't think they're accountable, which is hard to believe in this day and age but it's true.

FL: We just discussed one of the areas, athletics, in which it is very important for all presidents to get involved. How important do you think it is for presidents and chancellors to participate in national associations like ACE and AAU and in other national forums?

MSC: I do think it's important and I wouldn't limit it only to national associations. I enjoy the work of the AAU very much. I think the AAU is important and collective action in the AAU can bring about change. That's one of the reasons I don't think I've ever missed a meeting. In the last four years, I also have been working actively on the national problem that vast numbers of our fellow citizens lack health insurance. It is an area in which I've developed a lot of expertise. I have a bully pulpit here that I can use for that issue. I've gotten a lot of satisfaction out of that work. I think presidents can and should take the opportunities that they have to spotlight an issue about which they feel very passionately. It may be in higher education or peripherally related to higher education or, perhaps, another area of their expertise, but it certainly makes you feel like you're doing something valuable for the society in addition to the work you're doing for the institution. It has been extremely satisfying for me.

FL: We've already talked about undergraduate education but I'm going to give you one more opportunity in case there's something that you forgot that you would like to mention. Periodically, research universities, their faculty and their presidents are accused of neglecting undergraduate education. I have never felt that our undergraduate education was as bad as our critics claimed. There was some rhetorical exaggeration in their claims, but I did feel that there was some truth to the charges. I served on an AAU committee that surveyed our foremost research universities about what it was that we were doing and how we were changing, through providing opportunities for more students to do research with faculty, among other things. Is there anything else that you would like to say on that topic?

MSC: I think that it's extremely important for us to pay attention to undergraduate education. Consistently updating it, refreshing it, and thinking about it is important because society expects us, as great public universities, to offer great education for undergraduates. Research universities have the ability to promote research for undergraduates. I think it's an enormous strength, one that differentiates us, and we should use it as much as we possibly can. I was delighted when I came to Michigan and found out that apparently, in terms of numbers of students who get involved, it's one of the highest in the nation in terms of undergraduate research. I've seen students get excited about it: thousands of students are involved. The other thing that big research universities have the capacity to do and can do really well is to get students involved in service learning, get them out there in communities, get them to understand what it's like to have some of social problems that we face. Our large cities are laboratories that are wonderful learning environments. As public universities we're often called upon and its part of our DNA to do it. I always thought that the great distinction between public and private universities is that private universities can make the choice to get involved in their communities, but it's always a choice with them. For us it's not a choice, we must become involved because we are public institutions. It's that feeling, that sense that I think is so important and can be used in many ingenious and creative ways to help educate our students.

FL: If we want our young people to do a better job in their communities once they are grown up and working, there's no better way than to involve students in service learning over their four years of college, which are among the most impressionable years of their lives. When they leave college after having been active in their communities, they continue to be involved. Their universities know that because they keep track of their alumni. College, where students live and work in a diverse environment, is the optimum point for them to become involved in their communities.

MSC: That's right. It's often the first experience they ever had because of the re-segregation of the society.

FL: In the wake of the Gratz v. Bollinger decision by the Supreme Court, you said that you were confident that by the fall of 2004, the university could come up with a new undergraduate admission system that both complies with the Gratz ruling and continues Michigan's commitment to a diverse student body. Is that system in place now? Can you describe it?

MSC: Actually we had that system in place in 2003. We had it in place within six weeks of the Supreme Court decision, so we were ready. What we did was to put more money into our system and the reason that we needed to put more money is that we needed the higher, much larger number of people. So we redesigned our entire application. We ask many more questions now about income and about parental education. We're trying to get at these issues of first generation college attendance and socioeconomic status, in addition to racial and ethnic background. We put more essays on the application. The point was to make our review much more holistic. We hired about fifteen new people. We developed a system in which each application is read independently by two readers and they give it a score based, not on a point system, but just a holistic look at all the student's characteristics. If those two readers agree, independently, on reject or admit or wait, that's fine. If they don't agree, then it goes to a committee that includes faculty members. Then the application is read and scored a second time. It's a much more intensive process and we have been extremely pleased by the outcome. We did have a decrease in the numbers of applications, but because our yields are higher, it looks to us as though the students that we lost were the students who were applying to Michigan but weren't really serious about it, so they decided not to do it because the application is more difficult to fill out now. So we saved ourselves some work, but the quality of the class by every single measure that we can look at is as high or higher than it has been in the past. We have had a drop-off in our African-American students. We're worried about that because we think that, because we had to change the mechanics of admission, some in that community have interpreted it as having lost the case. We did not lose the case; we simply lost on the mechanics. So we have a lot of education to do about that.

FL: Do you have a communication plan for that?

MSC: We do. The other thing that faculty who are reading these essays tell us is that they're learning much more about the applicants than they have ever known in the past, and they are actually quite heartened about what they are learning. I think that there must be a way for us to use that information. We haven't quite figured out how to do that yet, but we know much more about these classes than we've known about any other classes in the past. So it's up and running. We are changing it slightly, tinkering with it for the next year, but we're very pleased. We had no delays and everything was on time. It was a heroic effort by the admissions staff but they did it very well.

FL: So now to the strongest forces driving the need for change in higher education for the next ten to twenty years. What are the most important changes that you expect to see take place? What will higher education leaders need to do or do more of in the future to help their institutions succeed, particularly given the rate of change in this environment, because the environment seems to grow worse every year?

MSC: It is worse every year. It's all about funding, making sure that we have enough. It's all about making sure that we're accessible to broad sectors of society and that we're not excluding people, we're not creating a permanent underclass, and it's about this technology that is just relentless. It is changing the way that we teach, the way that we interact with students, the way they access information, their expectations of us. It's a blindingly rapid process.

FL: Do you expect sea changes in higher education? We've talked in the past about breaking down the departmental structure. How do we do what we need to do in a changing environment so that we can continue to be effective, so we don't give away what works, but we also don't cling to the same thing we've been doing for 500 years, while the world passes us by ?

MSC: I like to believe that we could do that. There's a tyranny in the disciplines. We're hoping that with this mechanism that we're trying to use for curriculum development we will have some impact on that. I believe that, while a disciplinary study is really important because students need to be well grounded in their subject matter, the interesting issues are going to happen at the interfaces of disciplines. That's what we've got to get them more used to dealing with, and it's very difficult.

Here at Michigan we are creating an experiment with the life sciences, a large institute that has people from many disciplines and has no departmental structure, but, in order to create certainty for people, they still have an appointment in an academic department. The academic department is a very good construct for things like managing the teaching, managing the committee work, and other things that have to be done within the institution. The task for which the departmental structure is not so good is the challenge of being really innovative about what students need to know and thinking about launching fresh ideas. How do you marry those two and get rid of what is inhibiting about departmental structures, yet do it without losing what is good about them? This is a very tough problem. Michigan has done this better than any place I have ever seen and done it for a long time, but it's always at the research graduate level. Forty percent of the faculty in Michigan have appointments in more than one department. It's astonishing. The Institute for Social Research, which for sixty years has brought together people who are leaders in their fields to do surveys and develop data, has people from every discipline you can imagine. They have all joined departments and yet they do work in ISR. It's been extraordinarily effective but I don't think that you could give up, say the sociology department, the psychology department, the history department, or any of the departments that feed people into it. They still have a role. It's figuring out how to apportion those activities, manage them, and support them that is key here. We've toyed with the idea here of trying to merge basic science departments in the medical school with biology. Why should we have a biology department over here and have biological chemistry and pharmacology over there? Why do we do all that? It's difficult because the departments have different expectations and different cultures. These are conversations that are very hard to have. We're going to try to have them but I don't know if, in my lifetime, I'm going to see much change.

FL: When you talk about the technological change, I assume you're talking about the delivery of learning in some way, not just for traditional students, but for the rest of the world, which is getting more and more interested in higher education.

MSC: Yes. How are we going to deliver that education? How are we going to supplement what we do within the university with these new modes? We know now that our students are enormously facile at dealing with picking from here, picking from there, putting it all together. They do things in a way that we can't do.

FL: It's scary and exciting at the same time because you can't just adopt innovations for the sake of change. On the other hand, you can get outmoded very fast in this new world. Is there any question that I should have asked?

MSC: I think you've been unbelievably thorough. It's been a lot of fun.

Norman C. Francis

Norman Francis has been the president of Xavier University in New Orleans since 1968, the longest serving university president in the nation. A native son of Louisiana, Francis is an alumnus of Xavier, where he earned his bachelor's degree, and of Loyola University New Orleans School of Law, where he was the first African American to be admitted and earn a degree. Xavier, which was founded by Mother Katharine Drexel and her Sisters of the Blessed Sacrament, is the only historically black Catholic university in the United States. Francis was the first male and the first lay president of the university. Under his leadership, the university has more than doubled its enrollment, expanded its campus, acquired new property adjacent to the university, built attractive, functional facilities, and multiplied its endowment several times over.

Xavier is nationally recognized for its excellence in both the liberal arts and the sciences. It is ranked first in the nation in the number of African American students who earn bachelor's degrees in the life sciences, chemistry, and physics, and first in the award of Doctor of Pharmacy degrees to African Americans. Its premedical education is also extraordinarily successful in terms of the number of its applicants who are admitted to medical schools (77 percent) and in the number who complete their medical degrees (92 percent).

On the national front, Francis has served as an advisor to four administrations and has been a member of fifty-four boards and commissions. He has chaired the boards of the Educational Testing Service, the Carnegie Foundation for the Advancement of Teaching and the Southern Education Foundation. He has also served as a member of the board of trustees of Catholic University, as the president of the United Negro College Fund, and as chairman of the regional accrediting agency, the Southern Association of Colleges and Schools.

Francis Lawrence: You have had an extraordinary career in higher education leadership, one unique in its length and record of accomplishment. I
have been interviewing many of our colleagues who have held administrative posts in one or two universities, then gone on to accept the presidency at one or two more. You have been the president of Xavier since
1968, making you the undisputed champion of presidential tenure, the
longest serving university president in the nation. You have served on the
national level as well and have received a long list of honorary degrees,
including one from Rutgers, and, I understand, most recently from Harvard
and Dartmouth. Could we start this conversation by talking a little bit about
your family, your education, and their influence on your development as a
leader in higher education?

Norman Francis: Let me say what a pleasure it is for me to talk about the
issues that we're going to cover today. I haven't had the chance to sit down and
write. I've been cautioned by everybody to start writing before I'm no longer
able to remember, so this is a very great privilege for me. It is an opportunity to
put on record things that need to be recorded. Let me start with my family
background. It is an important starting point because many students and other
people I have met have asked me how I got to this position. They have wanted
to know if I was born with a silver spoon in my mouth, if I knew somebody, and
whether I prepared all my life to become the president of a university. The
answer to all those questions is no.

I grew up in Lafayette, a small town in Acadiana, Cajun Country, down in
southwest Louisiana. I was born in 1931, a Depression baby. My family taught
me all of the values that I know. My mother and my father did not graduate
from high school. I like telling that story because it says to students that it
doesn't matter what economic background you've come from, but what you
make of the God-given talents and the experiences and values that your parents gave you in those early years. None of us has the chance to choose our
parents but, at the same time, as I look at it, God gives each of us the parents
that we need for what we are supposed to do. Lafayette is an interesting town,
a Catholic city. In fact, the first ten of the twelve black Catholic Bishops
named by the Church came from an area within a fifty-mile radius of Lafayette.
It was a strongly Catholic area, but very segregated. The Plessy versus Ferguson
separate but equal decision was based on a law that was passed in Louisiana in
1892 and reaffirmed by a favorable U.S. Supreme Court decision in 1896.
Segregation was practiced in our churches and schools, but the people had a
common bond: besides being Catholic, most were poor. I lived on a street with
white youngsters. The children I grew up with did not see any differences
between us except the differences the law set down. Of course segregation
made those of us who were black feel that we needed to prove that we were as
good as anybody else and that we had to be better than some people at some
times. More importantly, God had to have given us a greater faith than he gave

most because we had to look past the laws on segregation and look past the religious leaders who were enforcing them.

My parents were like many good parents in Lafayette. Even though they had not graduated from high school, they knew more about the fundamental values of what one had to be and what one ought to be able to do than, I suspect, many Ph.D.s in our universities. They instilled in my brother, my three sisters, and me a set of core values: get an education: respect yourself, respect people, always value who you are. These are the fundamental things that have guided me, even to this day. My brother was a Catholic bishop, actually the fourth black Catholic bishop. Only one other time in the history of the United States have there been a black Catholic bishop and a black brother of that bishop who was the president of a Catholic university: the Healy brothers in the early 1920s. I'm told they had a black father and a white mother, both of whom were Catholic. One became the president of Georgetown University; the other rose to the bishopric.

FL: Your brother was a distinguished leader of the Church in New Jersey.

NF: My brother was auxiliary bishop in the Diocese of Newark and became a very hard worker for human rights and civil rights in the church. As time passes, I hear more and more about the kinds of things he did. That is the solid background I came from. As I sit here looking back at it, I could not have had a better foundation for where I am today.

FL: What personal attributes do you feel have contributed most to your success as a leader?

NF: Respect for people, respect for their talents, and the will to share with the excellent people who work with me the responsibilities for the work that we do. It happens that I've been in education, although I was trained as a lawyer. I believe that it has been fundamental in my work here at the university to share responsibilities, to respect people's abilities, and to believe in their willingness to do anything that they had to do. I have been given the credit for a lot of things I don't deserve in regard to where the university is today. Xavier's progress has been a true partnership. When asked what I would describe as the single most important element for success my answer has always been that I have shared the decision making with people who are smarter than I am, and then I have gotten out of their way and supported them.

I have had the good fortune of having worked with extremely able people. There are two people in particular who started with me in 1968. One was Clarence Jupiter, who was in charge of fund raising because as a small school with no endowment and very little money, we needed to have a development person. The second was Tony Rachal, who was executive vice president. Clarence had worked in volunteer tasks with the university and was a graduate; Tony worked very closely with me in my earlier days, prior to my presidency. He was a Xavier graduate who earned his master's from Ohio State in industrial arts and he was a builder. When we talked about Xavier, we talked in terms of building a new institution on the strong foundation of earlier years. These two men were both older than I was, but the three of us worked together for thirty years. They have both passed on now, but I think that the stability and continuity of working with these two men whom I respected so much provided the key elements for me.

FL: What would the people who know you best say about your personal attributes?

NF: I think the first thing they'd say would be that I was friendly, that I always had a smile when I met them even though it might have been tough times. Then I think that students, staff people, and faculty members would say that I was easy to talk to about matters concerning the state of the institution. I believe that they'd say I was fair in my treatment, even though I may have disagreed with them or had to make decisions at some times that might not have gone the way they wanted.

FL: What do you regard as your first leadership position at any level, even as a youngster?

NF: My earliest leadership roles were in high school, where I was the editor of the high school paper and coached the basketball team for the junior high school. I was also president of the senior class in my very small high school.

FL: Were there any people who stand out in your mind as having inspired you and acted as your mentors?

NF: There were so many people that I don't think I could single out one or two in particular. I have to say my mother and my father were probably the two people whom I would best describe as mentors, in addition to their roles as father and mother. Looking back today at all of the things I had to deal with in growing up, I know how much I depended on my rock of a father, who was very industrious. He had five children. As I recall it, he worked first on the railroad in a roundhouse, where he did maintenance and oiled the big wheels of the steam engines. Then he worked at the bus station, handling the buses. He did whatever he had to do to make a dollar because you must remember that I'm talking about having grown up in the Depression and World War II, when everything was rationed. In his next job, he worked his way up to being the head bellhop at the Evangeline Hotel, the number one hotel in that small town, where all of the political leaders stayed when they came through, the Huey Longs of those days. I remember sitting at the kitchen table and hearing him talk about his experiences, about people who were political figures and people who had businesses. He talked about their work ethic and the kinds of principles they used in their work.

I have vivid memories of that hotel. My brother left home very early, after the seventh grade, to go into the seminary, so he would come home during the summer. I would go with him to deliver my father's supper and I can remember walking into that big hotel holding his hand. My father and the other workers had to be in the segregated area in the back. We couldn't come through the front door of the hotel, so we came in the back entrances and had to pass huge steam furnace boilers on our way to the little room where my father sat, in the segregated area for the workers. I was frightened to death to hear those boilers roaring as we came through looking for my dad. That was my picture of the grand hotel where my father worked.

My daddy then decided he was going to be his own boss. He opened up a barbershop and I remember him best as a barber. I'd go bring his lunch sometimes and sit in that barbershop as I grew up. As I tell people today, I learned a lot about the world sitting in that barbershop and listening to him talk to the folks who came in to get their haircuts. You hear all kinds of things in a barbershop, but my father would say to people, "Well now I'm not sure that's right: here are some things that would challenge that." He had street sense and a work ethic that made an indelible impression on me. I can remember his coming home every night from the barbershop and keeping a little book where he wrote down how much money he made every day. He would hide it away, so one day I asked my mother to see what was in there. He wrote down what he made each day: $2.50, $3.00, $4.00. Of course on Saturdays he made more money, but he charged just twenty-five cents a haircut. That industry, that discipline, that knowing you had to feed your family impressed me. We were poor. We didn't know we were poor because we always had clothes that my mother had washed and ironed and we had food. In that small town, we had chickens, we had cows, we had a little garden, and all of those things helped to support us. I saw my father both in the role of an entrepreneur and of a person who made sure that he used all the resources he could put together to feed his family. I saw those qualities in a lot of different people, so in a way a lot of people mentored me, enhancing what I learned from my dad. My mother, as mothers are, was a negotiator between father and son. She also set an example that has helped me: she always saw a silver lining or a better time or a better day or something better that might come out of what could have been bad. She was patient, never raised her voice, and had a calming influence, so I had that great balance. My mother was the diplomat; she saw the best in people; she never uttered unkind words; she was truly a saint.

One of the unforgettable things that my dad used to tell me was that if you work with your hands, which he did all his life, you'll make a living, but if you work with your head, you'll make money. He did not mean that you had to choose to work with your head to make the money, but that you should have the capacity and the ability to choose whichever you wanted to do. If you wanted to do it, working with your hands was honest and important. All of us, and that included me from junior high school on, had to have a job. I had to work with my hands and I did. I started working by shining shoes on the main street of that little town during the war and after the war. Then I worked with a painting contractor. When I see workers around the university painting something, I'll stop and chat with them. I'll ask them if they've sanded it and what kind of paint they're using. The new painters will ask me how I know about painting and I'll tell them that I worked with a painting contractor and I didn't start by painting, I started by washing the brushes and cleaning up the place and worked my way up. I still shine my shoes today. I think I've gotten one shoeshine in my life. I was in the San Francisco Airport about twenty-five years ago and asked for a shine: the guy brushed my shoes, passed a little water over them, put on one coat of paste, brushed it, then tapped me and said. "$2.50."

I told him that when I shined shoes, they called that a lick and a promise: he was a little surprised. Working with my hands is something that I have done and I appreciate anybody who works with his or her hands.

FL: Before you became Xavier's president in 1968, you were an administrator at Xavier for eleven years. Those were tumultuous times, when protest marches, sit-ins and school integration were taking place throughout the Deep South. What part did Xavier and its students play in civil rights activism during this period. What role did the leaders of the Catholic Church take in the struggles over desegregation?

NF: First let me give you the background of the founding of Xavier and the impact that the university has had on New Orleans and beyond the city. The Catholic Church as an institution owes a great debt of gratitude to Katharine Drexel, our foundress. Her father, Francis Anthony Drexel, a wealthy banker and business partner of J.P. Morgan, left her an inheritance of $20 million. Little did he know that she, a blue-blooded Philadelphia socialite, would decide at the age of 30 that she wanted to be a nun, take a vow of poverty, and devote her life and fortune to projects, especially schools, for the benefit of Native Americans and African Americans. She came to New Orleans in 1915 in order to open a Catholic high school and a normal school to prepare teachers for elementary schools in Louisiana because, at that time, the opportunities for a quality education in Catholic elementary and high schools were not what they should have been. She first opened an elementary school, next a high school, now known as Xavier Prep, and then a normal school where she and her Sisters of the Blessed Sacrament began instructing young black people who went out to teach in rural schools all around Louisiana.

Katharine Drexel saw the talent of African-American students, a large number of whom were Catholics, and felt very strongly about the lack of a place for them to get a college education. New Orleans had no Catholic colleges that accepted young black Catholics. In 1925 she opened Xavier as a four-year college program and in 1927 added a college of pharmacy, both with the express purpose of educating black Catholic leadership for the future. She would have been pleased, but, I think, not surprised, if she had seen into the future and learned that not only was the first black mayor of the city, Dutch Morial, a graduate of the college that she established, but that one of her graduates, Alexis Herman, would sit around the table at the highest level of U.S. government as the secretary of labor, and graduates of her college would work in all of the professional fields. When it came to the question of civil rights, it was her graduates who gave leadership to the civil rights movement in New Orleans. To my memory, having lived this, the institutional Catholic Church was not involved in civil rights to the degree other religious faiths were. The Baptist Church produced the Reverend Martin Luther King and other prominent civil rights leaders who were Baptist clergy, but it was the graduates of Xavier, Katharine Drexel's college, who provided leadership, people like Raymond Floyd, who just died. A Xavier graduate, Llewellyn Soniat, led the strong youth movement of the NAACP. Xavier students and alumni were involved with CORE. All of the sit-ins were led by Rudy Lombard, our senior class president, with Aretha Castle Haley, who married the executive director of CORE. Vincent Roux, who later became the head of the Howard University Hospital Medical School, was also involved. Our Xavier students marched on Dryades Street with future New Orleans mayor, Dutch Morial, and were in the forefront of the struggle. I was not president at the time. I was handling development and was the executive vice president. I was also of counsel to the law firm of Collins, Douglas and Eli, which represented the Congress of Racial Equality (CORE).

I got involved in different ways. Going back to the 1950s, I was the first black graduate of Loyola's Law School and the three years that I spent there with my white classmates helped to lay the foundation for their civil rights activity. It was good for New Orleans because Mayor Chep Morrison chose many of the young Turks, like Moon Landrieu and Michael O'Keefe, to work with him. I became a bridge in those earlier pre-1960s days for white aspirants for political office who wanted to talk to blacks in their social clubs. Most white politicians didn't seek the black vote. In fact, during that era, it was better not to say that you were seeking it. New Orleans had very few black voters but many of my classmates and others in 1954 to 1956 were teaching people how to register to vote. In Louisiana, you had to fill out a card to vote and if you didn't literally dot every i and cross every t, or if you misspelled a word, you were denied the right to vote. Most public officials didn't seek the black vote when they ran for office, but the young Turks figured that they could put a combination of black and white supporters together. I provided them with an entrée. When they came to meetings in the black social clubs, they talked straight, they were not patronizing, and many of them did get elected with black support.

Then, moving from those days of the 1950s, into the 1960s, during the civil rights era, we were actively involved on campus. There was reluctance and a little fear at the beginning, but we got leadership from alumni. Rudy Lombard and Vincent Roux were in the leadership group that started the famous Freedom Ride from Washington to New Orleans. No one has yet written about something I'm going to tell you. I was intimately involved in the Freedom Ride preparations. Rudy Lombard, who was president of our senior class and Vince Roux, who was also a senior, came into my office one day and said they were planning a Freedom Ride. I asked them, "What's this? This is new. You're not marching anywhere?" They answered, "No, no, no, we are going to have a Freedom Ride. That means we are going to have a group of both black and whites together board a bus in Washington, DC, sit anywhere on that bus and ride to New Orleans." I kidded them, saying, "You'll never make it to New Orleans." They said, "There you go, you're conservative, you don't have faith." So they made a little bet with me. They said they knew I liked chocolate malts (which I did), so we bet a chocolate malt to a hamburger.

The ride started and before too long—two days at the most—they came into my office to tell me the bus was fire-bombed, outside Anniston, Alabama, but the activists vowed to make it to New Orleans anyway. I told them, "You win the bet!" They said "Yes, but we're here for another reason. We need a place for them to stay. We know that there is room on the 3rd floor of St. Michael's dormitory. Will you put them up?" I told them that was a big decision. Two floors of that dormitory were filled. We did have a third floor empty, but there were reports that the people who had fire-bombed the bus were going to come after the Freedom Riders wherever they went. I had a responsibility to the students in the dorm too. So I went to the president's office and told her what was being asked. She asked me what I thought we should do. I said that we had to put them up because nobody else wanted to touch housing the riders, they couldn't go to a hotel, and no public accommodations were available. I made the arrangements and set the ground rules. No one was to be informed that they were coming because the publicity and the possible violence would affect the students.

They did come, and I can still see those heroic people, black and white, bandaged and bloodied, getting out of the cars and standing on the porch of St. Michael's. The person who had been most badly beaten was a white minister who was slight of build. He filed a lawsuit that lingered at least twenty-five years, until he finally won the case. I think that he died only months later. The story of the Freedom Riders is a significant part of the history of civil rights, but nobody has ever written about the fact that they did get to New Orleans and stayed on the Xavier campus or the fact that the leadership came from Rudy Lombard who, in addition, was one of the leaders who sat in at the lunch counters to integrate them and was arrested. I had to go get him out of jail because he had already been awarded a fellowship to the Maxwell School of Urban Planning at Syracuse. That was a great thing for him, but there he was, in jail, missing classes. A couple of students came to me to tell me that Rudy was in jail and said that he was not coming out till everybody else was released. I told them that I was going to get him because everybody else was not in college and he had too much riding on completing his studies. So I did get him out of jail, he graduated, and went on to Syracuse.

If you look at the record of the institutional Church in New Orleans under Archbishop Rummel during the civil rights era, my judgment would be that the leadership was far from stellar. When I came here in 1948, I was part of a group of black and white students from Loyola, Dominican and Ursuline who founded an organization called SERINCO, South Eastern Regional Interracial Council. Father Joseph Fichter was teaching at Loyola then, along with Father Louis Toomey. Father Fichter had a grant from the Ford Foundation for a two-part sociological research study of the Catholic Church in the South under segregation, during the time when blacks had to sit in the back of the church. Archbishop Rummel banned that study, so Joe went back to teach at Harvard and the second book was never completed. He came back later to teach at Loyola and was run out again when he wrote about the police treatment of blacks in New Orleans. My personal opinion about Archbishop Rummel is that he delayed a number of decisions on integration because the White Citizen's Council under the leadership of Plaquemines Parish boss Leander Perez said they would cut off the schools' water if they were integrated. (The archbishop later excommunicated Perez and ordered integration of the Catholic schools.)

FL: We moved to New Orleans in 1959 because I had a National Defense Education Act (NDEA) Fellowship for graduate studies at Tulane. I remember how disappointed we were that the Catholic schools weren't integrated until 1962, two years later than the court-ordered integration of the public schools.

NF: Archbishop Rummel delayed drawing that line in the sand with the segregationists. Historians will write that he did not want to divide the church, but look at it from our perspective. We are talking about a man of the cloth and the principles of the church. This was a huge Catholic community and we were people created under one God. The leadership during the civil rights struggle, which was a very important time in the history of the South, did not come so much from the established institutional church hierarchy as it did from the black Catholic laity, in large measure from people educated by the university that Katharine Drexel founded. When historians write about the church as an institutional church and its role, they ought to name the lasting influence of St. Katharine Drexel and Xavier, the university she founded here in the 1920s. All of us who lived through that time know that to be true.·

FL: That is a very important chapter in the history of civil rights that de-serves to be told and I can't think of anyone more capable of telling it than you, who were so intimately engaged in those landmark events in desegrega-tion. You have given Xavier exemplary leadership since 1968. As we've said, that is remarkable for the length of your tenure, but we need to note that it is also remarkable in the context of the history of Catholic higher education. When you became president of Xavier, most Catholic colleges and universi-ties were still headed by members of the religious order that founded them. Why did the Sisters of the Blessed Sacrament turn over the governance of the institution to you at that time?

NF: That's a very important point. It's important for Xavier but it's also important for Catholic higher education. The sisters knew that Katharine Drexel had founded Xavier to create leadership. Mother Mary David was the president of the order at the time. The whole country was in a state of unrest. Kennedy had been assassinated in 1963; the civil rights movement had already started. In the summer of 1963, right before Kennedy was killed, I covered Jackson, Mississippi and Birmingham, in cooperation with Bobby Kennedy, the president's brother. Robert Kennedy had gone to Birmingham in the spring of 1963, talked to Bull Conner, and challenged Alabama about their segregation and employment discrimination policies. Bull Conner looked at Robert Kennedy and told him that in Alabama they would hire "negroes above the mop and broom level" in the state of Alabama the day the federal government did. Robert Kennedy reportedly said, "What?!" Conner said, "I will repeat that: we will hire negroes above the mop and broom level the day that the federal government does it." What may not have been clear to Robert Kennedy was that the people in federal jobs in Alabama, whether they were the head of the regional office of the agency of housing or the IRS, were the same people who ran the state of Alabama and they had the same racist beliefs. So what Bull Conner was saying was, "Before you come down here and tell us about what we should do in state government, you need to think about what you are going to do about your own federal branch of government." Robert Kennedy went back to Washington, apparently had a talk with his brother, and decided to send teams of people to the South to start recruiting blacks in all areas where the federal government's hiring record was less than equal and fair at high levels of appointment. Tony Rachal and I had been working with what was then called HHFA, the House and Home Finance Agency. Robert Weaver was the secretary of that agency, which later became HUD. We had been working with his staff in a number of areas. We got a call from him in late July and August. He told us that he wanted us to join the team. Our mission would be to go out and find blacks to integrate the federal government at level 12 and above. I was assigned to Birmingham, Alabama. I stayed in Gaston's Motel, a black-owned motel in the black section of Birmingham, just about six months after it was bombed and only a month before those four little girls were bombed in the black church. I met all the civil rights folks because the way to do the recruiting was to go underground, meet all the activists and tell them that you were here to recruit and what the qualifications were for the jobs you needed to fill. I was assigned to recruit for the FHA, so the candidates had to have experience in real estate. You could cut the tension in Birmingham with a knife that summer. I didn't realize that the black section of Birmingham was so near downtown Birmingham; I'd walk right into the downtown area.

After Birmingham, I was sent to Jackson, Mississippi. I got to Jackson right after Medgar Evers was killed and again I went underground. Medgar lived next door to a Xavier graduate, a pharmacist, who was at Xavier when I was in school, so I was able to get information. Jackson was a powder keg at the time. In addition to the fact that Medgar had just been murdered, his wife Marylee and the NAACP were boycotting downtown Jackson. Charles Evers had come to Jackson to take his brother's place in the NAACP. The South at that time was so divided with respect to Kennedy and what he was doing that he was hated. It was just unbelievable how much he was hated. The day he was assassinated, I was using my lunch hour to go and make a deposit in the bank. I was standing in the line behind a white lady talking with a teller, also white. She asked the teller if she had heard the news. The teller said no, then, told that Kennedy had been killed, she snapped "About time."

We were fighting in Vietnam. Everybody was challenging everybody else. Nobody wanted to respect authority, not even people who were part of religious organizations like the priests and sisters in the Catholic Church. The economist, John Kenneth Galbraith said that historians of the future who write about the 1960s will say that Americans didn't know exactly what they wanted. They only knew they didn't like what they had. That was so true. The sisters were caught up in the happenings of the time. They were running a Catholic university with the specific mission of preparing black leadership. Black students here, as I described, were active in the civil rights movement: demonstrations were taking place and demands were being made. Mother Mary David said to the order, "It's time to bring to fruition the purpose for which Xavier was founded. There must be someone ready to take a leadership role. Let's turn it over."

FL: And that was you.

NF: It fell to me. That was a major decision! All of the sisters might have agreed in principle but it's just like you and me. We have sons and daughters. Say that we have nurtured these youngsters, they're now twenty-one, and we are preparing to turn over everything we have to the twenty-one-year-old children: our house, our cars, everything. We'd probably say, "Oh I'm not sure they're ready." So not all the sisters thought we were ready, but Mother Mary David got the approval of the board. The board that ran the order was the same board that ran the institution: that was the usual arrangement in Catholic colleges. That board was a Pennsylvania corporation, so they decided to create a Louisiana Corporation: that's why it's called Xavier University of Louisiana. Their reasoning for doing it was that the university had reached the fulfillment of the rationale for the founding of Xavier. I met with the sisters, many of whom had been my teachers, and some of them might have thought that Xavier was going to "go to hell in a handbasket." I understood that: it was a major decision. I visited with Father Reinert in St. Louis when St. Louis University and Notre Dame were going through that same change. I went to talk to them about what the sisters had done, giving us carte blanche. The Jesuits and the Holy Cross Fathers created separate boards, but they still had, I think, five priests of the order who had overall jurisdiction of certain things, though I don't know if they ever used it. Not the sisters. The sisters told us here it is, created a board, and turned Xavier over entirely.

We had the opportunity to recreate an institution almost from scratch. In 1970, when I had been president for a little over a year, we created a Commission on Governance. We brought in a couple of consultants from the outside and we studied for a year and a half how Xavier ought to be governed. Then we made a recommendation to the new board, the board adopted it, and we have been operating under that governance structure since then.

FL: What challenges did Xavier face when you became president on April 4, 1968, the day that Martin Luther King was assassinated?

NF: The first one of course was fiscal, without question.

FL: And it probably doesn't change from year to year: one of the top challenges is always fiscal.

NF: I said the day we opened our doors that it was a miracle because we had an endowment of about $1.8 million. (I must note that when Katharine Drexel died in 1955, her use of the interest on the corpus of her father's estate ended. He died before she became a nun and in his will he named other beneficiaries. Xavier did not receive any of those funds.) In addition, we were charging much less in tuition than most schools because the sisters had always had the goal of keeping tuition low in order to serve students who couldn't have afforded college. Except for this building where my office is located and the library, all of the buildings were World War II barracks. We taught chemistry in an old army mess hall. Vic Labat, who taught industrial arts, built the industrial arts building and made all of the tables in the chemistry building. We were not operating in glorious buildings. This one, of course, was very nice, but we didn't have money to do many of the things we needed to do; what we did have was good people. We had dedicated people, the sisters and the lay people alike. I had the support of a lot of people because they admired and respected the decision of the sisters and the mission of Xavier.

However for the first fifteen years, there were some graduates and others who thought that, because for forty-three years the sisters had run the university so long and so well, it must still be run by the sisters and the president they had appointed was just a puppet, doing what the sisters told him to do. Xavier had received funds from the interest that Katharine Drexel had available until her death. After she built these two original buildings, she used it to recruit faculty members and to buy equipment that was needed. She knew that if you have the best people and equipment, you can do the best. For example, she established and equipped quality sports teams.

Some people were convinced, however, that because this was Katharine Drexel's university, the sisters continued to administer the school. It didn't bother me because under the guidelines we had adopted with the advice of the Commission on Governance, it was clear that I was going to be the president and I was going to manage the institution. The board was going to establish policies, I was going to carry them out and report to the board.

FL: And that is precisely what the sisters intended when they handed the institution over.

NF: Exactly. Now, what we did do was to say that for as long as it is possible we should have sisters on the board. We fixed the proportion of sisters at one-third, so on an eighteen-member board, the sisters would be represented by at least six members of the order. It was important not only to have the sisters as a historical, real, and continuing presence, but to do so out of respect for the enormous legacy that the sisters had created. It was, however, determined that at Xavier, as in all well-constituted universities, the governance function of the board would be to make policy. The sisters embraced this governance policy and process in its totality.

So the Sisters of the Blessed Sacrament turned Xavier over, gave me the responsibility, and never looked back. I kid them about it. At every board meeting, I say, "The first decision a board has to make about the president is whether to fire him or her or keep him. If the decision is to fire, fire him and get a new president. If it's to keep him, let's start the meeting." Then we talk about board policies.

We don't have many Sisters of the Blessed Sacrament teaching here now, six or eight at the most. I'm leaving tomorrow for Philadelphia because they are dedicating a Justice and Peace Building in Bensalem. They want the world to know about Katharine Drexel, not just to dwell on what she did, but to think about what ought to be done for the future. I worked with them when the building was going up. They're going to dedicate it on Saturday, so Blanche and I are going to leave tomorrow to attend the dedication and the Mass.

I should add that in the thirty-six years I have been Xavier's president, never once did I get a call from the Archdiocese to do something. I have to amend that: I got one call. When I had been in the office about three years, Archbishop Hannan called me. I picked up the phone, said hello, he told me who he was and asked how things were going. I told him that everything was fine and asked him why he was calling. He said that he just wanted to know how I was doing. I repeated that I was fine and Xavier was fine. He said, "Well that's great." I probed gently, "But didn't you call me for something?" He laughed and told me that a lady had called him to complain about something Xavier had done and she had asked him to call the president. "So," he said, "now I've fulfilled her wish: I have called the president."

FL: On the personal side, I know that you had a young family when you accepted the presidency. We often saw and talked with you at the Carrollton Playground, where your sons Timmy and David and my son Chris played baseball. How did you manage to strike that excellent balance between the heavy demands of the presidency and the issues that surrounded it and your family life? Is your answer going to be that what made it possible was that Blanche worked really hard, just as my wife did?

NF: You are not far off. You and I sat in the stands whenever we could find the time to be with our children, but we were fortunate to have wives who spent time getting our children to school and back, going to the games, and being at the performances. You and I worked it out by asking what time the game started and promising that we'd get there, hopefully in time. It could not have been done without that partnership. Timmy got married late and just had his first child and he asked me, "Daddy, how did you do all this, raising six of us?"

FL: I remember one night when Timmy slid into the plate and broke his foot. It was agonizing to watch.

NF: That night I wasn't at the game, but I was called and went to the hospital. They thought that the breakage might affect his growth, but it didn't, thank God. But when Timmy, with his one child, asked me how we managed to raise six, the answer has to be, no question about it, that without Blanche, it couldn't have been done. She was a gem. Her major was physical education and dance. She enjoyed all of the children's activities. We had an old red station wagon that carried football players, basketball players, baseball players to and from the playground and I'd meet her there. I tried to arrange my schedule, plus we lived on campus for the first twenty years and we had good support. For example, at the time the order made it an important issue to have young nuns finish their last two years at Xavier. They built what is now called the House of Studies and the young nuns stayed there, right on campus. Any time that we needed a baby sitter, those young nuns were happy to walk across the campus to our house and babysit for our kids. We also had Xavier's big football field available. On holidays or Saturdays, I could go out to hit baseballs in the football field and play pitch and catch. The fellows in the dormitory would come out and ask to play with me and my boys. When I speak to groups, I meet men who are lawyers or in other professions and they ask how the boys are, "How is that bowlegged one, how is he doing?" (They're talking about David.) I tell them that they're all doing fine.

It was a very important thing for them to grow up on a college campus. It shaped their relationships to people. They were the first black children at St. Rita's school: they didn't know anything about race. The majority of our faculty was white, so we had black and white people on campus. They didn't have any experience of race until they went to elementary school and their first experience of prejudice was at the Carrollton Playground. I look back and my admiration for Blanche grows. Carrollton had the big playground in our area, so two or three of the kids at school said to David and Timmy, "Man, you ought to be playing ball with us at Carrollton." So David and Timmy asked their mother to register them at the playground. Blanche, who was expecting, about six or seven months pregnant, brought David, Michael and Timmy to the playground. When they got to the playground, the other kids said, "Yea!" and they started playing ball. She went to a little house to register with the executive of the association. She asked for the registration form and he told her that our children couldn't play there. She pointed out that Carrollton was a New Orleans Recreation Department (NORD) playground. He said that was true, but it was operated by an independent association that leased it from NORD. She pointed to our boys playing with the other children and demanded that he go tell them they couldn't play together. He refused, so she took the boys, came home, and told me about it. She was angry and crying. The boys didn't understand it because the children on that playground were the children they played with every day. The future mayor of New Orleans, Moon Landrieu, my law school classmate, heard about it and Moon was mad. He came to the house and asked why I hadn't called him. He got in touch with the Carrollton Association executive and told him that if our boys couldn't register and play, the association would no longer be able to lease the playground. The rest is history. The boys played.

FL: When did all of that happen?

NF: It had to have been, it would have been about 1966 or 1967. Moon was a councilman, I think. He still talks about that episode. It was important for your children and mine to have that opportunity to play sports and for us to balance our time to be there with them and watch their success.

FL: What did all your university constituencies expect of you?

NF: Let me put it in context. They expected a lot because, in many ways, I was a pioneer in activities, organizations and a profession where there were not a lot of African Americans. I'm being honest about this: I did not feel the pressure. I knew there was pressure, but it never affected me. What prepared me for it was my entrance into Loyola's Law School as the first black student. I didn't fully appreciate at the time what a big thing that was, even though I was aware it was a momentous decision, a societal milestone because for so long, Loyola had passed over Xavier graduates who could have been admitted. There was an organization called the Catholic Committee of the South composed of white professors and black professors at Xavier, together with other interested individuals. They met after Mass on Sunday, once a month, and worked with Father Fichter and Father Toomey to integrate Catholic organizations and institutions.

One of their goals was the integration of Loyola's Law School. They decided that they were going to have one of our highly qualified Xavier seniors apply for law school admission starting in 1950 and continue this until Loyola admitted a Xavier applicant. The first Xavier senior to apply was Harry T. Alexander, who had been a serviceman and had graduated from Xavier. They turned him down. He went to Georgetown, eventually became a federal judge, and is still living. The second, in 1951, was also a serviceman, Richard Gumble, Bryant and Greg Gumble's father, who came back from the service, enrolled in Xavier, and was one year ahead of me. He too was denied entrance to the Loyola Law School. Richard also graduated from Georgetown and he became a judge in Chicago.

I was in the class of 1952, the third Xavier student to apply, and I was accepted. If I had failed, it would have confirmed in the minds of everybody in the city, especially black people, that it couldn't be done, but I never thought about that. I've met people many times who asked me if I realized what a big step forward that was. I knew that I had a Catholic college education equal to the education of students at Loyola. Most of the professors who taught at Xavier came from excellent schools in the East or the Midwest; so did the sisters, who were very well educated. Xavier was known for opera for years and years because one of the sisters had been on the opera stage in New York. I had twenty-four hours of theology and philosophy. I studied Thomistic philosophy taught by the Dominican Fathers. So I was ready. I must confess, however, that I was a math major, not a political science major, but I never thought that I was not going to succeed. I didn't fully appreciate the pressure that existed. Instead, I felt that this was another challenge and I was going to meet it. When I was named president of the university at thirty-seven years of age, again I figured I could do it. I had been in Xavier's administration for more than ten years; I knew where all the bodies were buried; I knew everything about the institution. I was going to a new level, but I was counting on a whole lot of people who were smarter than I was as well, so I accepted the challenge.

FL: You understood the institution and its culture.

NF: Yes. I knew what needed to be changed in the turbulent sixties. I understood why it hadn't been changed, but I knew that we were ready for change. I had worked with the students in civil rights and I had something going for me: I wasn't much older when I became president than some of the students. The seniors were twenty-one or twenty-two years old and I still related to them because I had lived in the dormitory and had been in student services. I could talk about anything they wanted to talk about. There weren't many black lawyers in the city when I graduated from Loyola's Law School. A.P. Tureaud, the dean of black lawyers, was meeting with Thurgood Marshall. Dutch Morial and I were studying at the old French hospital building where Attorney Tureaud had his office. Dutch had integrated LSU's law school. I tutored Tureaud's son in math so that he would be ready when his father filed to get the Louisiana State University to admit a black student. That was huge. He passed the exams, was admitted to L.S.U., and stayed one semester, then came to Xavier. So I felt comfortable.

Ken Ferdinand, the youngest of three brothers, was the president of the student body at Xavier. His brother Keith was at Cornell and is a cardiologist now. The oldest brother was at Southern. He changed his name to an African name: he's a poet. You may recall that at Easter break they closed Southern because the oldest Ferdinand brother took the flag down. Brother Keith was pictured on the cover of *Time* magazine standing at a microphone on the steps at Cornell with a gun in his hand and bandoliers strung over his shoulder. When the Xavier students decided they were going to protest, Ken Ferdinand, as student body president, came to tell me about it. I asked him how they wanted to do it. He said that they wanted to block the steps. I told him that they could block two on the side but they had to leave the center open. In fact if people came down the blocked steps the protestors needed to let them through, but if people wanted to come in, the protestors could tell them that they should come up the center steps. Ken said that they didn't have that much to protest about because they knew that I was in the civil rights movement, but they just didn't want to be left out of the protest movement.

We had already started to involve students in our governance at Xavier. Ken was on the Commission on Governance and the students opted out of sitting on the university's governing board. He said the board doesn't make the kinds of decisions we're interested in: those are made by the management side. The board, he said meets for a day and a half and only passes on what management is recommending: we don't want to be co-opted. We want to sit on committees that talk about curriculum and other student concerns. They achieved those objectives. They sit on all the committees, except tenure. Ken was smart and he was right: we still don't have a student on the board.

One day the students came in and told me that they were going to boycott Pepsi Cola. I asked them what they wanted me to do and they said that they wanted me to take all the Pepsi Cola machines out of the dining hall on campus. I knew Avery, the student who was leading the group. I told the students that I thought they didn't want me to have the powers of "kingship" that would allow me to make a decision and take away the rights of everybody to choose. They were nonplussed and asked me what I meant. I told him that if they wanted to give me this power, then when I took the machines out of the cafeteria and the whole campus, I would take away the right for everybody to choose whether they were going to drink Pepsi Cola or not. I said that I thought a boycott was a situation in which you believed that you could be persuasive enough to convince other people that the cause was good and they just ought to pass up that machine. Of course that is an individual choice that each person makes, and you have to be persuasive to do it. I said that they could probably get 100 percent to do it, but, I added that if they just got 25 or 50 or 75 percent to join the boycott, in taking the machines out of the campus, I would have taken away the right for the other 75 or 50 or 25 percent of the people to make a choice. They had been arguing with me about authority, but they seemed to want to give me much greater authority, the authority to take away the right to choose. If they wanted me to do that, I said that I had a lot of other things on which I would like to make decisions that way. They thought about it and told me that they had decided that I should just leave the machines where they were, not take them away.

About a month later, I went into a meeting of the student government as the new president. The room had one door and no windows. I walked in and saw everybody sitting around a long table with an empty seat at the front. I was about to sit down and one little guy on my left threw a paper in front of me. He said that it was a list of non-negotiable demands. I looked at him, handed it back, got off the chair, and started walking out. They asked me where I was going and I said that they had presented me with non-negotiable demands and that in the law non-negotiable demands are things that cannot be discussed. I got halfway down the room and the student on the other side of the table said, "Come back, let's talk." I said, "Oh, you mean they're negotiable? Fine." I sat down. There were a dozen points on the list; nine of them were simple things. By the time I walked out, there might have been three things that needed more thought, but most were the kinds of changes that needed to be made. So it made it easy for me at that point to do the kinds of things we needed and to work with the students in doing it.

FL: You took that opportunity to educate your students about the way to present problems to you.

NF: Yes. The situation I just described was one of the places where I could have drawn a line in the sand and said I'm going to teach these young kids who's the boss. Though I had the authority, that was not a battle that needed to be fought. The lesson I wanted to teach them was that before you start making demands, you need to talk about what the issues are and their respective meanings and consequences. So I didn't throw a presidential gauntlet down.

FL: How did you pick your battles? How have you handled the more controversial decisions that you have had to carry out?

NF: Let me tell you about one which came almost immediately thereafter, on the academic side. There was a group of students who felt that theology, in particular, and perhaps philosophy as well (they lumped both together) were not subjects that should be a part of the core curriculum. They wanted to get rid of them as a part of the core. I felt that they were part of our core, just like math, history, and political science. It is important in a religiously affiliated institution that theology be an academic subject. We had some very fine theologians. The theology department had a meeting and voted to recommend to the university that theology be made optional. There were about six people in that department, one or two older theologians and the rest young faculty members who were scared. One was a young faculty member who started his career at Xavier and later became a tenured professor at Princeton.

I met with the department to tell the faculty that I was there to support them. I said that theology was part of the core because we thought it was as important as history or political science. I didn't have political science professors, math professors, or chemists coming in and telling me that we ought to make their disciplines optional and I couldn't see why they would want to take their discipline out of the academic core. I told them that I just wanted them to know that I could not accept that recommendation and that, as far as I was concerned, I was going to recommend that it remain a part of the core. Some students said that they just thought that the number of hours required was too much. I told them that I was not against discussing with the faculty a reduction of the number of required hours in the core, but the hard-liners said no, they wanted it out completely. When I told them I wasn't going to do it, they said that they wanted to bring their complaint to the board. They made their presentation to the board. I told the board what I thought about it and the sentiments of others on the campus. The board voted that theology would remain in the core. The controversy had been going on for two and a half months, but after the board made that decision, there wasn't a peep of controversy from that day forward. In thirty-two years I have not heard any more discussions about that. So when you talk about picking your battles, this was one that I thought was substantive: it was a part of the institution, it was a part of the core, so we picked our battle on substance and mission

As you know, in this job there are certain people who have good ideas, some who just want to pester you to death, and some who are just bullies. You decide which of the bullies you take on. In this business, you have to listen to people, then make a decision based on your principles and try to be fair about it.

Another battle that involved both students and faculty developed when I had been in the presidency about two and a half years. We had about a hundred faculty members at the time. Two of them were activists of the take no prisoners school of thought. One was a young white mathematician and the other was a black female sociologist. We had developed a standard faculty contract, and they objected to one or two sentences in the contract that said something about respecting and fulfilling your obligations in keeping with the university standards or something of that nature. Ninety-eight of the one hundred faculty had signed the contract but these two refused. They were there on term appointments and had finished one year. They just refused to sign it; they said they wanted a special contract. I told them that we didn't write special contracts; this was the basic contract. They worked up students, saying that the university administration didn't like their political views and wanted to get rid of them.

Students started protesting. That went on about a week. I called all the leaders in and said to them that it was over. They had done their protests. I was not changing my mind. Ninety-eight other people had signed the contract; there was nothing untoward about it. I told them that tonight was the last night for the protest and if they showed up to protest tomorrow I would suspend them from the university. I tried to educate them about not fighting other people's battles, particularly if they did not know all the facts. I told them that they were being used by faculty who were flexing their muscles, challenging a new president. I said that I did not have to offer those two faculty members another contract because they were on term appointments, but I had offered them one. However in the next two days I was going to write to them and say that the contracts that I offered them were no longer on the table. They were null and void. I told the students that if they wanted to support those two faculty members, they could do that. I would respect their choice and commitment, but they would be out of school by midnight the next day. About two years ago, I met one of the protestors, who is now a dermatologist in Chicago. He told me that they went back to their dormitories, had a little powwow, and decided I meant what I said and that they would give up their protest. That was a battle in which I drew a line on the sand. There are battles which you choose to fight. You are educating young people about what those are and whether these battles are important enough for the consequences one must accept. Some are and some aren't.

FL: Did you ever imagine when you first came to Xavier that the university would become first in the nation in many significant ways, an institution nationally known and respected for the quality of its graduates? How did Xavier accomplish these remarkable feats?

NF: Xavier from its inception was a very strong academic institution. We were the best-kept educational secret in the United States. We had people prior to my time who were first in their professions. A Xavier grad named Bell was the first black to be admitted to the Ph.D. program in physics at Notre Dame. I knew that we were strong and that our potential was tremendous. We were getting some of the crème de la crème of Catholic high school kids from New Orleans and all over the country, so I had no doubt about our strength. We produced graduates who not only took and passed the Louisiana exam for licensed pharmacists, but also went to places like Los Angeles, Chicago, and Washington, took the national exam (NAPLEX), and passed it. I was in awe of the quality of education at Xavier. Taking pharmacy as an example, I met yesterday with the accreditation review team. There were initially two colleges of pharmacy in historically black institutions in the United States: Howard and Xavier. The first dean of the third college of pharmacy at a predominately black institution, Texas Southern in Houston, was a Xavierite. A year or two later, when the dean of the college of pharmacy was named at a fourth historically black institution, Florida A& M, that dean was also a Xavier graduate. I knew that we had the building blocks and that all we needed to do was to look at the needs down the road and plan how we were going to react to the new demands in jobs and in graduate and professional schools for the students whom we were educating. I was very much aware that there was an emerging need for our well-prepared graduates, particularly because I had spent some time in government recruiting.

As you know, President Kennedy under his Executive Order 1095 set forth in no uncertain terms the demand that the federal government and corporations with government contracts had to start hiring minorities in all areas and at all levels. The government needed minority employees. Corporations had to have minority employees in order to get government contracts. They started coming to recruit Xavier students. We had a strong liberal arts institution, but the need for young people in certain science areas (in which we were strong) and in research were new, emerging demands. I asked our faculty what we had to do in order to educate students who were qualified to get into graduate and professional schools or to get jobs after they graduated. We formed a fundamental policy: the Xavier undergraduate experience had to produce students who, whatever their discipline might be, would have the option, after college, to go to work or to graduate school. We based our goals on the principle that the things corporations were seeking in the people they hired were the same skills and competence that the graduate and professional schools wanted, namely graduates who were prepared to handle the demands for reading, writing and analysis and who were adaptable, capable of change when that was necessary. If we educated our students in those key skills and competencies, then students wouldn't have to turn around and complain that we prepared them for jobs, but now they wanted to go on for graduate study at Rutgers or would like to apply to graduate school at Tulane and Notre Dame, but did not have the preparation that they should have had. We wanted to make sure that our students had all of the necessary prerequisites for whatever path they wanted to pursue at graduation.

The watershed mark in our planning was around the latter part of 1965, when it was reported that, on the national level, the number of African Americans applying for admission to medical schools was dropping. It had never been high or what it should have been. We had a number of faculty in the sciences—J. W. Carmichael, who is still here, Jacqueline Hunter in biology and a number of others—who said that we could do something about that. Not that we didn't have Xavier graduates going into medical schools and graduate school, but they were not going in the numbers that we wanted to see.

We decided that we ought to enhance the high school experiences of students. Our faculty members went into high schools and did magic shows. They went into public schools and said to the teachers who taught science, particularly chemistry, "Could we come in maybe every month, twice a month or once a week and teach some of your chemistry classes?" The teachers said yes and those faculty members came with senior undergraduates, did magic shows, taught chemistry, and the high school students got excited about it. So our faculty asked the students if they would like to come to Xavier in the summertime and spend three weeks learning about science. We got foundation grants to finance summer programs and the rest is history. We saw some of the brightest students, young people who were not being challenged. They came in the summertime and we started with what I call the grandmother of all of the summer programs we have offered: SOAR (Stress on Analytical Reasoning). We offer about six programs for high school students now. If you think back twenty-five years, high school students, regardless of their race, weren't really being taught analytical reasoning in its pure form. We exposed them to the SAT with pretests and posttests. After four weeks these students were starting to add as much as 100 points to their SAT scores. When they came in, some tested at a combined score of 700-800 points, but they had not been taught how to handle standardized tests. This is a cultural influence, but an important factor. Because the black leadership and others were saying those tests are biased and they don't really test what you know, the black students started saying, "Well, to heck with the test."

FL: They felt, "Why should I pay attention to it?"

NF: Exactly, a self-fulfilling prophecy. St. Augustine High School where a number of our graduates taught, decided that they were going to prepare students to handle the SAT. They did it at St. Augustine; we did it for the public school students and others. I was on the ETS board at the time and they asked me what we were doing that improved these student's scores so much. I said that there were two things. There was a raging argument in which some people claimed that the SAT was an aptitude test. I felt that it was not just an aptitude test: it had achievement built into it as well. It was a combination of both, so what we were doing was teaching the students how to deal not just with simple academic aptitude, but also with the achievement side of certain aspects of it. We still have, roughly 1,200 students coming to Xavier for summer programs, bright kids whose parents are so happy when their children go back to do well in high school. Many of those high school students naturally come to Xavier for college and that's one of the reasons that 65 percent of our arts and science students major in the natural sciences

I spent two years on the commission that wrote *A Nation at Risk*. What *A Nation at Risk* revealed was that, in the late sixties, seventies, and going into the eighties, we were not holding kids to high expectations. Kids will give you what you expect of them.

We raised the bar for those kids who came to our summer school programs. They start at 8 in the morning, go to lunch at 12, go back to class, take a little time to eat dinner and at 6 o'clock in the summertime you can see these high school kids going back to the classroom or laboratory and spending two more hours there. We teach them that college preparation is serious, but there is another psychological part. For the seniors or rising seniors, who are graduating and going to college, we break the students into teams of twenty. We have six teams of twenty. The leaders of each team are a faculty member and two seniors from Xavier who have been admitted to graduate or professional school. Those high school students see a college senior not much older than they are saying, "Hey, I did it. You can do it." We have built a farm system of students ready to play in the big time. I get letters from the deans of medical schools and the deans of graduate and professional schools saying that they love to have Xavier students because they come with no chips on their shoulders: they come to school saying, "What is it I'm supposed to do? I know my strengths, I know my weaknesses and I'm not going to complain." Xavier students just step right up and take care of business. The medical school at the University of San Francisco is considered the Harvard Medical School of the West and they recruit some of our top graduates. When I spoke at an NIH session, the dean of that school came down from the stands to tell me how highly he thought of our graduates. These feats may seem now extraordinary now, but they were accomplished by doing basic kinds of things. We recognized what the problem was, we turned the light on for those students, and they said, "I can do this. You know that I can do this. Nobody said I could do it before, but I can."

It's a managed process; we still do it. For example, in the building we constructed in 1987, you walk into a little hallway leading to the elevators and on each side are glass cases. The only way you can get upstairs to the laboratories and classrooms is by taking those elevators. In the glass cases are the pictures of last year's seniors who have been admitted and are in medical schools. Then around April or May, they put up the pictures of the current year's graduating class who have already been admitted to medical school. As a matter of basic psychology, if you are a freshman, over a three-or four-year period you will pass that case every day and you will have to say to yourself, "One day my picture is going to be in that case and that's why I'm going upstairs to learn." I spoke at an affair on Sunday where there were several Xavierites present. They were talking to me and to one another about how grateful they were that we didn't allow them to get away with anything when they were eighteen and nineteen years old. We raised the bar, we held them to it, and we gave them support. That's how these remarkable feats took place.

FL: That is a marvelous institutional success story that reaches from pre-college preparation to the cultivation of high career ambitions.

NF: A lot of schools need to be doing this, but you have to have a passion and you have to be willing to work at it. We do that in their freshman and sophomore years of college so that when they graduate, they're ready. It's amazing to see them when they walk across that stage to graduate and then later, when I meet with them as they go on. This summer I was at a meeting in Washington, and a young woman who is one of our graduates was there. She was the captain of the women's basketball team when we won the championship six years in a row. She was also majoring in computer engineering. Her team practiced at 5 in the morning and they traveled to games out of town, but she had a 3.8 academic average. We get our students summer internships and this young woman worked for two years at Cal Tech in the summertime. She's now at UC Berkeley. She told me that kids who graduated from Xavier and went to medical school at Harvard were proud that, when they sat next to a Harvard student in the lab, the Harvard grad would ask them how it was that they already knew how to do a certain procedure and they would answer that they were taught that as undergraduates at Xavier.

FL: How have you linked all of the changes, the improvements you wanted to make at Xavier to the financial budgeting process of the institution?

NF: That's one part of what I call the miracle. Part of it has been that we have been able to raise money both in research projects that supported what we wanted to do, NSF funds, NIH funds, Title III funds that are dedicated to institutional development in part for historically black colleges and we've kept our tuition low. A college rating system published by Black Enterprise illustrates the fiscal challenge we face. This is the second year they have published the rankings. Xavier is in the top five of the fifty institutions they rate. If you look at the tuition charges of the four institutions above us and compare it to Xavier's tuition, ours is obviously much lower. Now if I had Morehouse or Spellman's tuition for each of the 3000 students I have, wow, what I could do with it! Last year Black Enterprise included an academic quality quotient in their rankings. We scored only two-tenths of a percent less than Harvard's academic quotient, according to the magazine's formula, and we had a higher academic quotient than the top four. Where we were downgraded was in comparison to the much larger endowments of Spellman and Morehouse. They also had a higher social score because we didn't have a good place for student activities, but now we have a university center that's very nice.

FL: Yes, I saw it. It's a beautiful facility.

NF: We've kept our tuition down, so we have to struggle to balance our budget. In most of the major things that we have done, we have tried to be very sophisticated and creative. We have sought money that would move the institution in the direction we wanted to go in our planning. If we decided we wanted to do more, for example, in encouraging young people to get into internships, graduate school and the like, what were the things that we needed to do? If an African-American youngster or any young person has undergraduate research opportunities, the chances that student has of being admitted to graduate or professional school increase 100 percent. We have just formalized and opened an official, systematized center for undergraduate research. To head it, we've recruited a woman who is bright as a whip and has boundless energy. She coordinates in every discipline what research opportunities that certain faculty want to offer, whether it's sociology, philosophy, or in the sciences, in particular. We applied and got a grant to create that office. Now the office is able to spin off and help faculty members in getting grants to support their work with students in research projects. I tell people there are some monies we don't want because it doesn't fit into what we can do and we don't try to do everything. That's why we've increased our partnership with Tulane immensely and why we have looked for other partnerships.

Dr. Shirley Jackson, the president of Rensselaer, sent people down here last Wednesday to talk about a partnership arrangement with Xavier. That's what we look for and we push for students to do these things. So in terms of trying to get the fiscal resources for our work, tuition brings in only about 50 percent of the total cost. We don't get a great deal of money in unrestricted gifts, but whatever we get is very helpful. From our alumni we've gotten up to $800 thousand in unrestricted funding. We get monies from the United Negro College Fund (UNCF) although it's falling short now, because it's harder for them to raise unrestricted money for thirty-nine schools when some do not offer the disciplines that some corporations want as a quid pro quo, i.e. if corporations give money, they want to know that we are educating workers and want to see those graduates come to their companies. Certainly there are institutions among us which are doing that, but there are others that are good institutions but are not focused on what corporations want and need. The long and short of it is that we have to go everywhere we can to bring in the funding we need, but our heightened recognition has allowed us to compete for grants that fulfill our mission and further our goals.

FL: I especially admire your steady commitment to teaching and learning as Xavier's central mission. That really is so important. You've never lost sight of it, even when other universities were grasping for higher status by directing their attention much more heavily to research as distinct from teaching. Now what you're doing with the students in undergraduate research is absolutely correct. That gives them a leg up on most other students.

NF: We send them in the summertime elsewhere to do the research because we can't accommodate all that research on campus.

FL: So in doing all of that, you have cultivated these links with other research universities. Are you adding other institutions, as well as Rensselaer, as a possibility?

NF: We're adding wherever we can. We have relationships with Duke and Emory. Certain labs are now becoming important parts of our future, not just individual researchers, but research labs in various parts of the country. You're making a point that I want to emphasize. We can't do everything for everybody, but we can find others who will do it and we can make arrangements for our students to get those experiences. Our partnerships have been extremely important in accomplishing that. We're trying to add to and extend those partnerships.

FL: I know that Xavier draws many students from New Orleans and Louisiana. What part of your student body is from other states?

NF: We do not get more than 300 freshman students from New Orleans. Our freshman class recently averaged 920 and this year is 1,001 overall. Steady numbers are coming from Louisiana, but we're drawing students nationwide. That's why we have to build so many dormitories. We held our enrollment down for a period of about five years until we could build those dormitories. We've got about 1,600 students on campus now and, as you know from your Tulane days, a lot of students, after their sophomore year, go out and find apartments in the city. That's fine with us because it gives us beds for freshmen.

More than 50 percent of our students come to Xavier from all over the country because they read about us. Some of them have come to our summer programs.

FL: And your reputation draws good students.

NF: Our reputation is well known now and it's a good buy for $10,000 a year in tuition. Many students qualify for Pell Grants and other forms of aid and we give a lot of institutionally financed aid as well. There are a lot of students whose family economic background is not a determinant of their academic potential. We attract a lot of very bright students on Pell grants who can make it here and are coming to us from outside the city. We also offer about $5 million in remission scholarships to students who need that support. We are investing in the future. I keep trying to tell the president of the United States and the Congress to invest in these young people because they are going to be the leaders, they're the ones who are going to be productive, they're the ones who will get jobs, and they're going to pay income taxes far greater than the amount we have given them to educate themselves.

FL: All indications are that the issue of access and the severe, continuing erosion of state and federal funding are going to get worse: our colleagues throughout the country are unanimous in asserting those facts as two of the ruling problems of our future. It has been a constant thread running through our conversations. You've seen that University of Virginia is launching a $3.1 billion campaign. John Casteen wants UVA to become the first privately funded state university. He is determined to accomplish it.

NF: I visited with the three editors of the *Chronicle of Higher Education* last Friday and spent hour and a half with them, I talked a little about Xavier, but I spent most of my time talking to them about the policy of ensuring access and choice in higher education that our country has yet to adopt. We need to make sure that we invest in the young people who are going to be the leaders of this country. That includes the ones that we have been talking about, young people who have not been well served by high schools, students who have not had the resources to allow them to go to colleges and universities where they will grow. Many times those will be private schools, although some state schools as well. There is this large group coming down the road, you can see the dust rising, they have been born and they're on the way, but we haven't come to grips with the necessity of spending money on human capital.

What I've advocated for years is hard for some people to accept, but my theory is that American youngsters ought to have access to higher education and the choice of where to go, be it a public or private school. The fact that they are poor should not limit their choices. They shouldn't be told, "Well, you met the criteria for admission, you're smart, but you ought to go to another institution."

FL: To a community college, where the tuition is lower.

NF: Or to a state four year college, because they don't have the money. My argument is that if they were children of the well-to-do, they'd have the choice of going to a private school or to a state institution. All of the citizens of the state help to pay for the children of people of means if these children choose the state college. These well-off young people have choices and access. Why should the sons and daughters of parents with means have greater choices than those who have less, yet are bright? That's a public policy issue that we haven't grappled with, but my point is, it's an investment issue because there are some students who would be better off in a private institution, some would be better off in a state institution, but they ought to have the right to choose. That's a tough argument public policy-wise, and I've been trying to make it.

FL: It's being made and it will be debated for years. You have a great store of wisdom to share with other presidents and administrators. For example, it would be helpful for you to explain what strategies you've used to communicate and create buy-in for your vision. You have many new initiatives. How did you get the faculty, Xavier's alumni and friends, as well as leaders in the city and state on board as you moved this university forward? How have you informed and persuaded people? New ideas and new directions are helpful to all institutions, but it is sometimes difficult to move them forward.

NF: Early in my administration I was ready to move the institution forward quickly. I had ideas and I thought there were things we needed to do. We wrote a proposal to the North Carolina Foundation and we got a grant to enhance the teaching of math, so I went to the math department and they said, "What do you want us to do with that?" I said, "Here's the money." They said, "It's your program, you do it." I got the message. I learned to talk first to the people who might have an interest in it, found those who said they'd like to do it, and gave the ownership over to those individuals. Then I said, "I'm right here ready to help you make it work. What do you need? You develop it." It's passing on ownership that is important. That lesson early in the game taught me to throw out things that might be good for Xavier, find out who was willing to bite, sit and talk with them, then say, "I'm going to be your biggest cheerleader." It was revolutionary the way that they did some of the summer programs and other initiatives. I supported what they wanted to do when it was in my purview. I didn't say they had to do it, but I told them that if they wanted to do it, I was going to support it: it doesn't hurt to have the chief executive supporting you and talking about it. The first principle was that ideas, however good they are, have to be accepted and put into action by the people who are going to carry them out. More than that, ideas should really be developed by the people who know in toto what the field is. All of the proposals that not only made sense but were competitive came from the people who knew what they were talking about. All they needed was information about how to go about the process of application and how you put together the proposal. We helped with that. The business of having phantom grant writers doesn't work. Competitive review teams can tell whether whoever wrote the proposal knows the discipline. So you have to have the buy-in of the people involved. My second principle is that I never pass up an idea that might sound crazy without hearing it out. Mine is a close working relationship with all of the vice presidents and deans. As you said earlier, I served on the Carnegie Foundation, on ETS, and on other national boards. From those I learned what the trends were, so I'd come back and talk to my faculty and administrators about what I had learned.

FL: It's a great advantage for the faculty not only to get this kind of information from you, but to have your support in dealing with it.

NF: We were then and we still are small enough that I can put all 260 faculty members in one room. Four times a year now I stand up and I tell them where we are on certain things in the university as a whole. I talk about what some of the national trends are and what I hope that they will think about in order to figure out whether they can, in fact, deal with the new developments and whether they will need help in doing that. I have my bully pulpit to talk about these things. I say, "You've read about this. It is coming down the pipe and I think we can do it. We're doing some of this." Communicating is so important in an institution because people will say, "Nobody tells me anything. I don't know anything about that. Nobody told me." In my sessions, I use the expression that Mayor Vic Schiro made famous: "Don't believe any rumors unless they come from me."

FL: And "If it's good for New Orleans then…

NF: "…I'm for it!" I say that and everybody in the audience laughs. I tell them that I'm here to tell them what's going on, so they can tell folks that they heard it from the horse's mouth. We put out publications, but what is important is communicating our mission, it is communicating and reminding people that we are here for the students and what the country is expecting of our students. Then it is also important for us to be able to congratulate faculty and tell them what I just heard of a student who has done such-and-such. If it's a student in math or history, I want to congratulate the department about what has happened and build that kind of ownership in their students' accomplishments. As I said earlier, I have totally delegated the authority for major decisions in academic matters, including tenure. However, though I can delegate the authority, I cannot delegate away the responsibility, so I remind the faculty that all of these decisions come home. I tell them that I go to court a lot, that Xavier gets sued and the interesting thing is that when that complaint and court order comes, it says John Doe versus Xavier University and Norman Francis, et al. It doesn't say Xavier University, Norman Francis, and the Committee on Tenure. I want them to know that I have to have great faith and confidence in their decisions. I want them to make those decisions that I'm going to have to answer for. I have great faith in our faculty and in my thirty-six years I have reversed no more than seven tenure decisions, because I know how tough our tenure committee is. I don't even appoint the members. The faculty elects them. All of the decisions, favorable or unfavorable, were made by their peers. I tell them, jokingly, that there were a large number of recommendations that I held my nose and signed. Then I get a big laugh. As we said earlier, it's a matter of communicating, letting people know they have a responsibility and that I have faith that they're going to do the right thing.

The same thing is true of administrative staff people. Sometimes I like to give people a colorful expression for what I need to get across. I tell them that, having delegated the authority in all of these areas for years, I sleep well at night, but I know that my deans, vice presidents, and other administrators who have to make decisions sleep like babies: they wake up every two hours. The reason they wake up is that the university community knows that they will make the decision the next day, not me but that I'll back them up. I do tell them, however, that I must admit that if they keep making certain decisions that I just can no longer approve, we will have to have a "Come to Jesus" talk and one of us is going to have to change. People start to see that it's their ownership and their responsibility. I tell them that the last thing that is important for me is that they are all smarter than I am in all of these areas, so I have to rely on them. They have to know I have that faith and all I keep asking them to do is the right thing.

FL: What are the qualities that you look for in the people whom you choose to work with and depend upon?

NF: The first one is the commitment to teaching and learning, whether they are administrators or teaching faculty. They must be committed to the belief that students can learn and be willing to work at helping them to make it. Not everybody is going to make it, but we must believe that there's a chance. That's number one. Then the second is loyalty to their profession and their jobs. I just gave that speech to the full faculty. In my opening remarks, I told them that the day that they cannot get out of bed in the morning and be happy and satisfied in their work is the day they need to come and say to us that they've had it. I was not talking about a few days here and there but about a constant condition. When they reach that stage, they are no longer good for themselves or for the institution. It is not good for Xavier to have somebody who is not fulfilling the job. They have to be committed and loyal and want to do it. And the next thing that is necessary is a total sense of professionalism, respect for people and honesty. That has been my good fortune in being at Xavier: 96 percent of our faculty and administrators have those qualities. The others, we happily separate. I have no compunction about people who come in and say that they don't like this place. That's fine.

FL: Making change is often not synonymous with making friends. Can you describe one or more critical incidents dealing with change and how you handled them?

NF: We had a faculty committee that we appointed to look at loads in terms of teaching and other duties. Its recommendation was that we cut teaching loads and raise salaries, but it didn't say how we could accomplish that fiscally. In fact the committee said, in effect, that's not our problem. At the time, we had never in the last 20 years failed to raise faculty salaries. Our starting point was low, but every year, I went to the governing board to recommend a 4 ½ to 6 percent increase. So I told the committee that they knew that we had a faculty advisory committee on salaries that studied the matter every year and made a recommendation, working toward raising our faculty salaries to the 50th percentile. They also knew that I went to the board each year to make the case for their raises. I said that I was just managing to balance the budget and asked how they thought I could go to the board with a request for a 25 percent reduction in teaching loads coupled with a 5 percent raise. I told them that there were just two alternatives, they could give up raises and teach less or maintain their teaching load and get more money. Before a meeting of the entire faculty, all 250, I told them that I just couldn't do it. The fact was that there were schools in Louisiana that had frozen salaries while we had gone to the board and gotten approval for raising salaries every year. The few people who had recommended the teaching load reduction continued to insist that they wanted the raises and the smaller workload, but the vast majority of the people said, in a sense, that they were willing to carry the same teaching load as long as they kept getting a raise.

Nevertheless, that was not a popular response. It hasn't come up again in the last four years although we've now appointed another committee to examine the workload. I have asked them to tell me how they propose that any recommendation they make can be carried out within our budget.

FL What have each of your internal constituencies – governing board, faculty, students, staff, and alums - expected you to do for the university and for them?

NF: Every group wants my assurance that we will maintain the excellence of an institution devoted to the highest degree of a total education. They want a quality education institution, and of course each one wants to be helped to grow in his or her professional life or work with the resources necessary to do that. That's what they expect and that's what I promise every year. I meet with the faculty and the staff at the beginning of each academic year and I tell both groups what the university expects from them.

At the opening of school in the fall, I said to the staff—the maintenance workers, the painters, and the security guards—that I was wearing the same blue suit and the same pink tie to all of my meetings. One of my administrators who sat in the faculty meeting told me that it takes a real secure guy to wear a pink tie. I said to him that I was wearing the same pink tie because I didn't want anybody to say I treated the staff of the university differently than I did the faculty.

FL: How have you managed the different, sometimes conflicting expectations of these constituencies? Are there any incidents that you want to relate?

NF: I try to explain to each the rationale for what we are doing. For example, when I go to the board to propose a building, I have to tell them why it is important for faculty and students, for their morale and the environment we need for teaching. The board will point out that we don't have the money to do that and I will say that I have found that we can use a bond issue for that purpose. Then, when they point out that there is a risk in issuing bonds, I can show them that, when I come to them, I have tried to anticipate everything that could go wrong and have come to the conclusion that we can take that risk. That doesn't mean that I'm just rolling the dice. I have had people whom I trust analyze the risk and assure me that it is a reasonable undertaking. Then it comes down to the point where we have to muster the courage to take that reasonable risk. In that context, we have been risk takers and entrepreneurs.

FL: What importance have you placed on the role of your institution in the community? Have you felt obligated or sometimes even pressured to undertake urban renewal projects or other community obligations?

NF: I think it's important to Xavier to be very much involved in its community, and we are heavily involved, the faculty as well as the institution, starting when we gave the land to build a swimming pool for Gert Town and the health center. Xavier received from NIH the third five million dollar award to create a fifty-million-dollar endowment for the enhancement of our Center for Minority Health Disparity, working in the St. Thomas Clinic and others. We've chosen to focus on hypertension and diabetes because these are high incidence diseases among African Americans. The population of New Orleans is almost 70 percent black. We have a College of Pharmacy, so we have devoted ourselves to that project.

But we are pressured sometimes to do things we are not capable of doing. Let me give you an example. The public schools in New Orleans are going through some really difficult times. We've worked with the school system in many ways. Aside from our summer programs, we've taken teachers in to instruct them in how to use technology in their classrooms. Among others, Senator Mary Landrieu has suggested that it would be good for universities to take over failing schools. I said from day one that Xavier could not take over failing schools. Our department of education is small; I don't have people who I can assign to run a school. If I took a school over, I would have to go hire people to do it and, once that happens, it's no longer Xavier that's running the school. The reason they're asking us to do it is because they say that we know how to run a good school because Xavier is good. It is, but here's an example of the reason why we will not take over failing schools. We have a very good pharmacy school. We are in the business of educating pharmacists, but our pharmacy school is not capable of taking over a failing Walgreen's Drug Store. That's a perfect example of what they're asking us to do and we're not going to do it: we can't do it.

FL: What are the other major groups outside the university that you have needed to work with?

NF: You know I can't think of any in particular that we haven't worked with. We've been open to public officials: we hold forums. We had a debate on the election for the U.S. Senate that was broadcast statewide and C-Span is broadcasting it nationally. We work with public agencies. At lunchtime the other day, the secretary of the city council told me that they wanted to thank Xavier for joining the workforce meetings. Xavier had representatives there. We work with almost all of the agencies in areas where we have some degree of competence or can offer to bring something to the table through the involvement of students and volunteer services. We consider ourselves citizens of the community and we should be ready to do whatever in our capacity we can do. We cover the waterfront.

FL: Turning to the day-to-day realities of the presidency, how have you allocated your time and what have been your top priorities?

NF: People think that the major responsibility or the only responsibility of the president of the university is to raise money. That's a major responsibility, but it's not the only responsibility. In my particular case, I have seen as my top priority assuring that Xavier keeps its eye on quality teaching and learning. I meet with everyone who reports to me to make sure that we all keep in mind the reason that we are in business. I do less fundraising than most presidents. Again we're smaller, we have trimmed our staff. We have increased our fundraising operations but my top priority is assuring my board and this community that Xavier is meeting its responsibilities for teaching and learning. When I do fundraise, I can look at a foundation or corporate executive and say, "I want you to invest in Xavier." I don't ask them to make a gift to me or tell them that if they make me a gift, I'm going to run back to New Orleans and develop this program. I say that I've got the program, it is working well, and it is doing great things, but I need your investment to keep it excellent and growing. Corporate people understand that. That's when our reputation and all the rest come into play. Like any investor, they are not going to invest in a failing operation or give their trust to somebody who doesn't know what they're doing. I ask for investments, so my top priority is first making sure that Xavier is in fact meeting its goals in teaching and learning, and secondly making sure that it has the resources to do it.

FL: Your service to the community and your work at the national level, which has involved serving on something like fifty-four boards and commissions, must require a good deal of your time away from the university. When you are gone for this period of time, do you have someone within the administration who makes the day-to-day decisions?

NF: In the first thirty years of my administration, I relied on the two people that I told you about, both older than I was, and I felt comfortable. The community knew that when Tony made a decision on administrative matters and the like, it was what I would have done. The same thing was true of the academic vice president. Though these folks had the authority, they would come into my office and talk with me, review our options, thrash out problems, and we would come to a conclusion. I could leave confident that these two people knew what I would do if I were sitting there and knew that I was going to count on them to do it. That allowed me in those first thirty years to go out like a scout, find out what was out there, come back home and tell people what I had seen on the horizon. That worked perfectly for me, because by delegating authority while I was away, I could also fulfill my responsibility for teaching and learning on the campus. I have very good people now as well, but they're younger and I'm spending more time with them. I'm doing a lot of things locally, but I'm spending less time nationally.

FL: What part of your work have you enjoyed most?

NF: My relationship with programs and initiatives that develop our students' capabilities and set them on the path to their careers. I stop and talk to students all the time, especially to seniors around the time of their graduation. Because I was a Xavier student myself, I have always been a student-oriented president. As an undergraduate I lived for years in the dormitory: all the maintenance workers know it because I talk about it. They know that if a boiler breaks in the dormitory and hot water is lost on a Friday at 4 P.M., they can't leave for home until they fix it. That has happened, and we've fired people for neglecting it. I've lived in dormitories and I'm not going to have a student taking a cold shower for three days while the workers responsible are enjoying home comforts.

I hold student forums whenever the students ask me to do it. I can tell you that I know most of the questions that are going to come up. It used to be complaints about dormitories and food, but we're now in good shape there. Parking is going to always going to be a problem. I do not talk about people. I let them know what the ground rules are in advance. I will not talk about Professor So and So who gave you an F in class. You probably earned it; if you didn't, don't ask me about it. Personnel complaints are out. If they want to talk about processes in the university not working, for example financial aid or registration, that's fine. We'll talk about it. I enjoy working with students, communicating with them to make them part of the university.

Last year one of our student forums lasted about three and a half hours. A couple of times, the student body president told a questioner, "If you had that problem, you should have come to your student government. Please don't answer that Mr. President." Sometimes I told them that I didn't know what they were complaining about was a problem. Then I asked them where they thought it belonged and what they thought we should do about it. They had a big squabble and I just stood at the microphone and let them argue among themselves. My point is that I want to let them identify problems and see what it takes to make things work in the institution. I enjoy creating opportunities to know what students are concerned about and to make sure that they're happy and getting what they want. That keeps me going.

FL: How would you define leadership? How would you characterize your own leadership style?

NF: I would define leadership as a condition of someone who's willing to serve as well as lead. You can't lead unless you're willing to serve, that is to do what others ask you to do. In assuming the responsibility of leadership you must also be willing to share it with others. You have to be secure enough to be able to do that. Leadership requires the willingness to share responsibility as well as the willingness to serve and respect others who have been given roles that involve leadership.

I would characterize my own leadership style as entrepreneurial in many ways. I feel that all of the issues that we face and any challenge that we meet can be an opportunity. I know that we have to be entrepreneurial to survive, and not just to survive, but to excel. I define an entrepreneur as someone who sees a challenge or problem as an opportunity and goes about to solve it without worrying about the resources available to him. An entrepreneur will not stop because somebody says that you might as well forget it, you don't have the money to pull it off. The answer to that is, when I solve it, the money will be there. As people will tell you, we started doing a lot of things when we didn't have a dollar. One example is the property that you see on Carrollton Avenue, where we now have a big parking lot. When Katharine Drexel bought in this area, they sold her the land where the old lumberyard had been but they stopped it at Short Street. There was no way to come to Xavier unless you came over the Pine Street Bridge. I always felt that Xavier should have a front on Carrollton Avenue and when I made the case to the board, a board member from New York pointed out that we didn't have the money. I told him that it was hard to explain it to him, because I was emotional about it, but I thought that the original sale of the land had been designed to keep us away from the Carrollton Avenue entrance. I thought that we needed to be there. About five years later, we still didn't have the money, but we bought the land through a gift/sale. Xavier does at last have an entrance on Carrollton (though we're still waiting for the city to solve traffic problems there). That's my style. If people say that we can't do that, I respond, "Let's see what we can do in time." I believe in constructive alternatives.

FL: Presidential tenure was once measured in decades but now terms of four or five years are more common. Do you think that the much shorter average tenure of contemporary presidencies is due to changes in the role in the last few decades or are there other reasons for it? Certainly your thirty-six-year tenure is unique.

NF: There are a few presidents who have been at it almost as long, but the fact is that the presidencies today have become extremely complex and demanding. I think five years is a little too short a time. It would be nice if one could do eight or ten years, but the problem is a combination of things. You have much more state and government interference into higher education: that is difficult. You also have demands for serving so many constituencies with so little resources: that is taxing. You have changes that are taking place in how the institution should conduct its business: change is one of the most difficult things to do in higher education. The various constituencies we've talked about and all of the university's stakeholders make demands on the chief executive's time and ability to be all things to all people. At every event, they want the president to be there. I prefer to have the people who are very important to the project or the effort there. However the organizers have a mindset that demands that the president be there.

Responding to all of these demands is taxing. I can understand fully why people who have served in presidencies are now leaving after five to seven years. If we look just at the colleges affiliated with the United Negro College Fund, the private black colleges, I have seen schools with four presidents in ten years, and three in six years. I'm seventy-three years of age now. I've been at this for thirty-six years and I can tell you that, although there's nothing completely new under the sun, it can be overwhelming for new presidents. I tell people that I've learned how to walk on water because I know where the stones are. You have to know what some of the shortcuts are. You have to make priorities about some things you can't or won't do and know which ones you'd better do. At least, given the length of my career, I have a road map that I have traveled before so, when I see new things I know which way I'm going to turn.

Let me just mention another thing about entrepreneurial leadership. I am very respectful of creative ideas that move the enterprise. When I'm in either a faculty meeting or a staff meeting and somebody says, "Look I've got an idea," I don't say that we've been there and tried that: it won't work. The reason I don't is that when we tried it fifteen years ago, that may not have been the time for it, but this time, it might work. I ask them to tell me more about the idea, and then I go into my lawyer mode and start asking questions. If they have the answers, I say, "Let's go for it." Old jokers like me could say, "Hey, I don't want to hear that, we've tried it: let's pass it up." But now may be the time for it.

FL: What do you regard as the most critical capital investments made during your tenure?

NF: There were several major ones but let me tell you about one that stands out: our decision not to get out of pharmacy, but instead to build the pharmacy building that ensured our reaccredidation. There were two schools of pharmacy in New Orleans: Loyola and Xavier. Loyola was not admitting blacks to their college of pharmacy. In 1967, both universities were told by the accrediting agency that if we didn't build a separate building for our college of pharmacy, we wouldn't be reaccredited. Xavier's school was on the third floor of the arts and science building: they said that was inadequate. It didn't make a bit of difference that our students were passing their state certification exams.

I was the executive vice president at the time. The president and I met with the chief fiscal officer and Xavier's lawyers on the matter. (Loyola had decided to drop pharmacy rather than construct a new building for it.) Everyone was advising the sisters that if Loyola couldn't stay in pharmacy, Xavier would have to get out as well: Xavier was going to announce it the next day. I felt that, considering the fact that Xavier was producing the largest number of African Americans in pharmacy, getting out of the field would be like Notre Dame announcing that they were dropping football. I asked the president not to make that decision and proposed that they give me a year to raise the money for the building. I told them that the School of Pharmacy was just too important for the black community for us to throw away that jewel. The president agreed to give me a year. Miracles do occur! I raised the money, was named president in 1968, and we dedicated the building in spring of 1969 and kept our accreditation. That was a significant capital investment and the most important decision an institution like this one could have made at that time.

FL: It is part of your definition as an institution and the student market is yours.

NF: When that decision was made by Loyola, the newspapers covered it. The *Times Picayune* wrote an editorial saying we have lost our college of pharmacy in New Orleans, ignoring the fact that Xavier, just a few blocks from the newspaper facility, had a fully accredited college of pharmacy. I went straight over to ask the editor, "What do you mean by saying that you have lost your college of pharmacy?" But just as Ralph Ellison wrote, African Americans were invisible people. Xavier was an invisible institution so far as that editor was concerned. Of course that only gave me more strength to accomplish raising the funds for the new pharmacy building.

FL: What advice would you give new presidents? What's the most critical skill or set of skills that new presidents need to have to succeed in the future?

NF: Perseverance is number one, plus determination and a total respect for the community in which they're working. A new president should not become enamored of the title of president. You have the corporate responsibility and the authority. However the real capability to lead comes from your colleagues. If you think as a new president that you can do it all, you're dead in the water. You have to recognize indigenous leadership. Identify the people who are committed, strong and talented. Align yourself with them, encourage them, and support them. No matter how many faculty you have, you will need a small, strong group who are loyal, mission oriented and understanding: they will do what is good for the institution and they'll bring others to it. Don't get overly enamored with your new title and power and don't fret when that first ill wind blows. It will blow many times.

FL: Good advice. What has been at the core of your work in higher education? What has been the underlying purpose that you have wanted to accomplish through your work at Xavier and your service at the national level?

NF: The bottom line, the vision of Katharine Drexel when she started Xavier was the desire to create a larger cadre of African-American leaders. That was her fundamental purpose; that was and is mine. If a Xavier did not exist today, I'd spend my time trying to found one because the need for people with higher degrees who can furnish leadership to the country, in particular minority communities, and specifically from the African-American community is as great today as it has ever been. For example, look at the number of percentage of African Americans in the professoriate. That number is about 5 percent.

FL: It hasn't grown very much in the last twenty years.

NF: That is exactly what I said to the group I spoke to on Sunday. I said it hasn't changed in twenty years and it isn't going to change in twenty more years unless a great deal more is done to educate African Americans at the undergraduate level and inspire them to go on to the graduate and professional level. If somebody asks "What is the need for black colleges, what is the need for Xavier at this time in history when everything is open?" my answer is that of the top twenty undergraduate schools that are producing the highest number of black undergraduates going to graduate or professional school, twelve of the top twenty are black colleges. For some time to come, obviously, we're going to have to keep up that productivity. It may not be in the numbers it ought to be, but it must be at least enough to keep furnishing more than that 5 percent. Fifty percent of our youngsters go on to graduate and professional schools in the arts and sciences. Sixty-three percent of our graduates in the sciences go on, and they make up the half of that 50 percent we send to graduate and professional school. If little Xavier is supplying this cadre of people going on to their Ph.D.s, but African Americans have still comprised just 5 percent of the professoriate for the last twenty years, where would it have been if we didn't produce the few that we produced? That's what I told the editors of the *Chronicle of Higher Education* when I met with them. I didn't want a story in the *Chronicle*. What I wanted was to educate them in the issues and destroy the myths, so that when their reporters write stories and they, as editors, read them, they will be aware that, according to that president from the black college in New Orleans, access and choice is important, black colleges are important. We need more African Americans in the professoriate, and we need to be concerned about where they're going to come from. Let me just throw out one thing, which comes within the same category. I'm convinced, Fran, that if Brown versus the Board of Education had been implemented as it should have been implemented fifty years ago, we would have reduced the amount of racial prejudice that we find now. If we had a higher number of minority teachers, African American or Hispanic or Native American in all schools, but particularly in elementary schools, we would have tackled some of the core problems which develop racial prejudices.

FL: You have served on the board of trustees of Catholic University and you've had your own twenty-member board of trustees at Xavier. What do you feel are the important characteristics of good governing boards? What are the problems that can be encountered in dealing with governing boards?

NF: Well the very first one is critical everywhere. It is a pledge that the boards understand the role they serve as policy makers and give their strong support for the management responsibilities of the institution. That's critical and I've found that to be the case in educational and non-profit boards that I've served on. Once you get that straight, you have a good board. But the second thing that I think is important is to have on boards people with different experiences and competencies. In developing policies and supporting policies, their knowledge can enhance the work of the institution. You need people with good marketing skills on the board. You need people with good fiscal understanding on boards. You need people who have expertise in human resources. You need people with all of these competencies and you want them to share their experience in the development of policies during their board service. At the same time, the danger is that a board member may move over the line and start to manage the administration of those policies or start to listen to people in the institution who are stakeholders who want to get around the administration of the institution and go straight to the board. Board members who do this have lost their standing and they've damaged the institution. In fact I was one of a number of presidents recently interviewed by Dick Aft, who was with United Way, about this very issue for an article that is going to appear in Trustee Magazine, the publication of the Association of Governing Boards (AGB). The question was how you can get help from a board member in some of the things that you have to do as a president without crossing the line into the management side. That can be tricky. My answer was that once you can establish an understanding with the board about the difference between policy and management, you can go to certain board members and say, "Look here's what we're dealing with. We have a problem that may eventually come to the board and I need your advice. Whom should I talk to about this?" You're not asking that board member to make the decision, because the decision is one that you're going to have to make with your staff, but that board member may have special expertise in the area or may know someone who does and could counsel you.

FL: Getting advice from people who work in related areas is always helpful. The more advice you get, the less likely you will be to make a mistake.

Moving on to matters of funding, private universities are often severely criticized for tuition increases that limit access and saddle parents and students with large burdens of debt. How have you managed to keep your tuition at a level that is reasonable enough to attract increasing numbers of students and at the same time continues to meet the needs of your university?

NF: It has been difficult, extremely difficult. As you well know, the question of tuition is a major issue before the Congress right now. It was pulled it off the calendar and is not going to be pursued now, but it will come back later. Much of what is in the House, in committee, are changes aimed at helping profit-making institutions. According to the media reports, the impetus for these changes has come from legislators who have received substantial contributions from those profit-making institutions. Unfortunately some of the proposed changes will impact non-profit institutions like ours, in particular.

The efforts to regulate tuition charges are alarming. At Xavier we have kept our tuition down all these years to make sure that we can serve a constituency that has been ignored by other institutions. Our tuition is significantly lower than other institutions. How can they now make regulations that would require us to keep tuition increases to no more than 3 ½ percent?

FL: Public institutions are also at a disadvantage because the states are cutting their support to higher education. As the states lower their contribution to public universities' budgets down to a smaller and smaller percentage of operating expenses, the institutions have little alternative but to raise tuition to replace at least a part of the lost funding.

NF: You know it's a popular political move for legislators to promise not to raise taxes so that they can be voted back in. It is like the homestead exemption in Louisiana. Don't touch it.

FL: Yes, if it were possible to institute a reasonable level of property taxes, the city and the state would be much better off

NF: No question about it.

FL: The last question is important because you've been in this business for so long. What do you see as the strongest forces driving the need for change in higher education over the next ten to twenty years? What are the most important changes that you expect to see take place? I would say, based on what we have discussed, that one of the great issues will be the issue of more minority faculty, in particular more Hispanic faculty and more African American faculty, because the population of those minorities is going to increase significantly.

NF: The growth in the minority population which will take place in the next ten years is tremendous. The need to have faculty members in higher education to meet that demand across the board is going to be a driving force in the challenges for higher education in the future. The second problem we face is that the federal government is going to drive changes, some of which are not going to be good. The question is whether or not higher education can make sure that it doesn't happen. The jury is out. I have spent a lot of my time on that. Governmental forces are going to try to force more and more change in higher education in the next ten years. I think that though some of the changes may be good, the vast majority will not be welcome. What are the most important changes that I expect to see take place? What I think ought to happen is that the government ought to focus a greater amount of attention on providing financial assistance to students across the board. Having fought to increase the Pell Grant to a higher level than it is now, I can't see how low income students, black, white, Hispanic, will be able to continue to borrow the amount of money that they are now forced to borrow for their undergraduate education. I think that's going to be a drag on our ability to get these low-income students, black or white or whatever color they may be, into graduate and professional schools. They will be so burdened by their undergraduate debt that they're not going to be able to go on. And to me that is a tragedy. It shouldn't happen. But let me tell you about another crisis that we have to deal with and I don't know how: the lack of African-American males in higher education. Their numbers are just not there relative to the number of eighteen-to-twenty-four-year-old males in the population. Take Xavier, for example. Do you realize we have three females for every male in this institution? You look at the graduation rates in high school. Look at who is graduating and graduating with the capacity to go on to college. It's not males among African Americans, it's females. America is facing a growing crisis in the lack of educated black males proportionate to their percentage in the population. It is a crisis. Part of the problem that causes kids to drop out is that people are not holding kids to high expectations. They're telling black kids that they can't learn, so they ought to be out there trying to find a job.

FL: What jobs are available?

NF: They are unfortunately turning to drug trafficking. The high murder rate that we have in New Orleans and in most urban centers is drug related, There are drug dealers killing drug dealers, and they're now impacting innocent individuals. A story was in this morning's newspaper about a young man who was killed right down the block from Paris Street, along the route I travel to go downtown. He was the father of three children and was about to apply for a job as bus driver for Greyhound. He went to the grocery store where he'd been going for years, just about a block from the St. Bernard project, and a gunman killed him last night. The victim had no police record. The violence is spilling over at an alarming rate. We must find solutions or lose another generation of young people. In higher education we have a terrible lack of black male students. African-American males are showing up in college sports, but not in the academic arena.

FL: They see that as a way for financial survival, a chance for a good life.

NF: This is a growing crisis. We're talking about it in the black community and now researchers are looking at it. I used to give a lot of high school commencement speeches. Lately I've haven't done many, but when I was doing so, even ten years ago, African American males were not in those classes.

At Xavier when we announce honors and there are some black males in the number everyone starts shouting and clapping because most of the names called are females. In the college of pharmacy, I'm sure it's three to one, three females to every one male.

Let me tell you the social aspect of it. Black women will tell you in a hurry, that there are just no black males out there for the large percentage of black females who are professionals. I have two daughters who are not married. They're professionals and they're doing very well, but there are fewer black males who are professionals out there for them.

FL: I have been looking forward to this conversation with you and it has exceeded even my highest expectations.

NF: I'll probably never get the chance to sit and write a book, so I am glad to have the chance to talk about some of the things I've seen and heard. Your interview was well structured and I'm happy to put these things on record. I have talked to young people about it as many times as I can. They just sit there google-eyed because as far as they're concerned, the world started yesterday. I've enjoyed this Fran; thank you for giving me the opportunity.

Nils Hasselmo

The former president of the University of Minnesota, Nils Hasselmo, became the president of the Association of American Universities in July of 1998. Founded in 1900 by fourteen Ph.D.-granting institutions, the AAU is currently comprised of sixty-two public and private universities (sixty in the U.S. and two in Canada) distinguished by their research accomplishments and their strong graduate and professional programs.

Membership in the association is by invitation. Its board of directors is composed of the chief executive officers of its member institutions. In cooperation with its members, the association furnishes Congress with information concerning higher education issues, in particular on matters pertaining to research, accreditation, and federal regulation. The association has also encouraged its members to establish institutional policies ensuring self-regulation.

Hasselmo's native country is Sweden, where he earned undergraduate and graduate degrees in Scandinavian languages and literature from Uppsala University. He came to the United States as an international student and teacher of Swedish in 1956-1957 and completed a B.A. at Augustana College. Later he returned to study structural linguistics at Harvard, where he was awarded a Ph.D. in 1961. His scholarly specialization is in the area of bilingualism, on which he has published a book and a number of articles.

Prior to becoming a member of the faculty of the University of Minnesota in 1965, he taught at the University of Wisconsin. At Minnesota, he taught for eighteen years and served as the chair of his department, director of a language and area studies center, associate dean of liberal arts, and as vice president for administration and planning. Recruited by the University of Arizona to fill the post of senior vice president for academic affairs and provost, he spent five and a half years in that position, then returned to Minnesota as its thirteenth president in December of 1988. At Minnesota, Hasselmo developed a strategic plan for the reform of undergraduate education, created a master plan for the campuses, reorganized the health sciences, and presided over the building of the Weisman Art Museum, designed by Frank Gehry.

Hasselmo has chaired the National Association of State Universities and Land Grant Colleges and the Big Ten Council of Presidents. He has also served on the boards of the National Merit Scholarship Corporation, the Universities' Research Association, the Carnegie Foundation for the Advancement of Teaching, and the American Scandinavian Foundation.

Francis Lawrence: Nils, you have had a successful career in university administration and policy formation, first as president of the University of Minnesota and now as the president of the Association of American Universities (AAU), which provides sixty American and two Canadian research-intensive universities with a forum to discuss a broad range of higher education issues and develop national policy positions bearing on research and graduate and professional education. Perhaps you could begin by telling me something about your family background, your education, and how they contributed to shaping the basis for your future as a leader in higher education.

Nils Hasselmo: As you know, I was born and grew up in Sweden. I came as an international student to the United States in 1956 on a one-year scholarship to Augustana College. It was a scholarship to teach Swedish, be kind of a junior faculty member, and take courses at the college, which I did. My parents were both teachers. I grew up in an environment that was very oriented towards education. I belong to the second generation who went on to higher education in my family. My father went to a teachers college and had a position as the organist in the church and a teacher in the public school system. The title for that position is "*kantor*," a good Swedish word! My mother was highly educated too. She did a degree in mathematics and science in Stockholm in the 1920s, which was rather unusual at that time. It was a program designed for women to get the equivalent of a master's education in mathematics and science and other subjects to teach in the public school system. I had a background where education was primary as far back as I can remember. There was no question that I was going to pursue education as far as it could possibly go. That was the expectation; I knew it without question when I was three years old. Fortunately I responded very well to that orientation. My grandfather on my father's side was an entrepreneur. He had left the countryside, gone into the city, and started a little furniture factory. My father did not go to secondary school. He finished 6th grade and worked as a gardener's apprentice. Then, when he was about eighteen, he decided to get an education and managed to get into the teachers college, but all his life he was hampered a little bit by the fact that he had gotten off what was then the very rigid educational track. He was determined that his son and daughter were not going to get off that track, and we didn't. My grandfather on my mother's side was a bookkeeper in a mining company up in a little town in Lapland and sent his daughter to Stockholm to get a degree. I was twenty-five years old when I came to the United States. I was beyond college age and hovered between junior faculty and student at Augustana College. I did not intend to stay for more than a year. I came out of great curiosity because I had grown up in the World War II generation, where America loomed very large on every horizon. I was very interested in American literature and grew up reading Fennimore Cooper and Mark Twain for fun. I read the great American realists, Steinbeck and that whole generation. But, the first 800 English words I learned were the 800 words that Hemmingway uses! I was also interested in jazz. There were all kinds of reasons why I wanted to go to America, but it was pretty much on a lark. I did have one serious interest because, while I was studying at the University of Uppsala, I became very interested in American linguistics. I was headed for an advanced degree in Scandinavian languages and literature, but that was in a traditional historical linguistic program. I wanted to go to America to study the new, exciting linguistics that had grown up partly out of the study of American Indian languages, and through linguists such as Franz Boas, Edward Sapir, and Leonard Bloomfield. A linguist named Gleason had just come out with an introduction to linguistics, a very fascinating approach to structural linguistics, I thought. So I had a serious interest as well. After coming here, I decided for two reasons to come back. First, I had met a very charming woman who later became my wife. I was married to her for forty-two years until she passed away in 2000. Second, I got a scholarship to go to Harvard to get a Ph.D. in linguistics. Actually there was a third factor. I discovered the Swedish language in America when I was here the first year. I decided that this was an interesting topic for a dissertation, an interesting topic to study. I wrote a dissertation, a number of articles, and a book about the Swedish language in America, a study in bilingualism and language contact, which became my major professional linguistic specialization.

I have been extremely fortunate and of course never could have anticipated that I was going to have the kind of opportunities that this country has given me to work, not only in an academic field but also in exciting administrative assignments.

FL: What personal attributes have contributed most to your development as a leader?

NH: I don't know that I have thought of myself particularly as a leader. In one way I have a certain amount of Swedish shyness. I have found myself in a way thrust into positions. I haven't really systematically sought out these opportunities that have come my way. I have been tempted enough, maybe adventurous enough, to say, "Okay, I would like to do that:" going to America, getting a degree in America, staying in America and getting drawn into faculty governance, being elected to the faculty senate at the University of Minnesota, then being asked to help write a report evaluating the functioning of central administration, of faculty governance, and writing the chapter on strategic planning for the university. Then the president came to me and said, "Why don't you do it?" All of a sudden I was vice president for administration and planning. I realized that academic administration really was quite fascinating, although I had not thought of myself in those terms. Then an opportunity came to become provost at the University of Arizona. I grabbed that opportunity, had a wonderful time, and then was contacted about presidencies. I ended up back at the University of Minnesota. In the same way, when I stepped down at Minnesota, I was retiring, and then got this wonderful opportunity at AAU, which I have enjoyed very much. It's really opportunities that—in the marvelous way that this country can operate—have been placed in my way, so to speak, and I have, I guess, grabbed the opportunity when it came.

FL: What do you regard as your first leadership position at any level?

NH: You know, in one sense I was a little resistant to leadership because I was very shy as a teenager. But, when I was in gymnasium in Sweden, I got elected to offices. I hated to get up and speak in public but being elected to these offices almost forced me into it. All of a sudden, this was my responsibility. I had to do this thing. Then, of course, eventually I started realizing that this was interesting. It got my adrenaline going. But, throughout my life I've had this feeling that things have been placed in my way. I have found myself in situations where I had to take responsibility and I have done that. Then, gradually, I have become more and more comfortable with it. I have realized that the interest of it, the stimulation of it, is an intellectual stimulation, but I have also enjoyed the wonderful human contact that you get with a range of very interesting people as you step into these positions.

FL: Were there people who inspired you, worked as your mentors and encouraged you to assume some of these leadership positions that you were not interested in pursuing?

NH: It wasn't that I wasn't interested in them. This is an interesting situation because I always thought of myself as a scholar. My interest was scholarly. I wanted scholarship. I wanted to sit in the library. I wanted to do field work in linguistics and I wanted to analyze and write. I love writing. I never thought of myself as an administrator but opportunities and circumstances took me in that direction. Now, when I look back, both of my parents were leaders in their community and in their professional communities. Although I didn't think of myself at all as a leader, I think that I absorbed something from my parents: in their particular communities, they were leaders, both of them.

FL: What were the challenges that the University of Minnesota faced at the time that you became president? How did they change over your tenure? What were the things you had to work on immediately as urgent necessities?

NH: Of course, when you take on the presidency, as you well know, you inherit the situation. You don't step in with a blank page. You have your own agenda, but that agenda is very quickly, by necessity, shaped by what has gone before, what the circumstances are, and, of course, what during your presidency is thrown in your way. Of course, a basic trait of leadership is to keep that sense of direction and purpose, of what it is you really have to accomplish. So much is driven by circumstances that you inherit and some circumstances may well be beyond your control during your presidency. There were two things in Minnesota. On the positive side, I had a predecessor who was a strong and creative leader: Ken Keller. He had established an agenda for the university that he called "commitment to focus." There were others involved in this too at the time, including the governor and the governor's financial officer, who later became my finance vice president. The issue was establishing an agenda for a university that tried to be everything for everybody and was gradually, over several administrations, trying to focus. Given the fact that there were sixty-four higher education campuses in the little state of Minnesota, it seemed evident that the university should not try to do what seven state colleges, nineteen community colleges, and thirty-four technical colleges could do. It was a hard political battle because it was the tradition that the land grant university was for everybody. The notion that every high school graduate in Minnesota should not have access to the university was politically hard to deal with. My predecessor established a very aggressive agenda and probably ended up in a situation where he had to resign, partly because he pushed that agenda very hard against strong political forces. I don't want to go into those circumstances, but that was the dominant feature: my predecessor had been forced to resign. There was a credibility gap at that point. The university was in trouble. I have a cartoon that was in the St. Paul newspaper at the time when I became president: there is a little, timorous Hasselmo standing down in the corner of the picture facing a big, ferocious dog sitting there with the tattered clothing of a former president in his mouth. The dog is labeled "Legislature" and little Hasselmo is saying, "Nice doggie, nice doggie." That was, perhaps, a good expression of this troubled situation: there was an immediate need to step in and reestablish relationships that had been somewhat tattered, especially with the legislature and the governor, and maybe with the state as a whole. That was really the overriding task ahead when I first became president. Mind you, I'd inherited an agenda that I subscribed to 100 percent. I give my predecessor credit for that agenda and, in a way, he broke the resistance at considerable cost. I was able to come in next and do many of the things that he had outlined in his agenda. But, I also had the problem that I could not be too explicit about the fact that it was the same agenda. First I tried to kind of bootleg these changes by not calling it anything, or calling it retrenchment or reallocation, which my wife said was so dull that people's eyes would glaze over immediately when they heard it. That was exactly what I wanted. I wanted to do the agenda, but not stir up any political turmoil about it. Eventually that became a problem: they said, "What's Hasselmo's program?" Then it became my program. Most of the elements were a continuation. I think that a key to leadership is to try to provide continuity, not just try to lead by coming in and saying, "Everything I do is brand new. This is my plan," but rather to say, "We have a sound foundation, we have some good things going on here, let's build on them. Let's not unnecessarily change the agenda, let's go on with the agenda," I think that providing continuity is a very important leadership responsibility. Under somewhat precarious circumstances, that was really my initial task: to provide some kind of continuity in a situation that had involved a good deal of political turmoil.

FL: What effects did the role and demands on the presidency have on your family life and how did you maintain a balance as you took over an operation that large?

NH: Fortunately my children were all off to college or beyond college so I did not have children to neglect at home. As a matter of fact, my daughter who was in Minnesota, although she went to a different institution, kind of enjoyed the life of the president's house and still misses it. I try to explain to her (as of course she well understands), that it goes with the job. My wife entered very energetically and fully into a partnership. We truly had a partnership as president and first lady and much of our life became a university-centered life. We tried to set aside some private times, but it was very hard to do, and I'm not sure that I can say that I struck a balance. That was a constant challenge, to try to keep some private space, but it was compensated for by the fact that she and I did things together, both at the university—university events, entertaining 4,500 people a year in our home—and traveling to see alumni around the country, as well as abroad, in China, Japan, Indonesia. If there was balance, it was a balance of a partnership in the presidency.

FL: What did each of your internal constituencies, governing board, faculty, students expect of you when you came in? Is there anything specific that they hit you with, saying, "It's got to be handled immediately?"

NH: It was very clear when the board hired me that they wanted the reestablishment of the relationship with the legislature. The situation was so precarious that the chairman of the board had gone to the legislature and had withdrawn the university's request to the legislature. We had to resubmit it. They were very clear about the fact that I had to reestablish credibility and working relationships with the state's leaders: the governor, the legislature, alumni leaders, business leaders and so forth. My predecessor had strong support in some quarters, but there were also some problems—undeserved problems, I think. The house and the remodeling of the house became the issue and lit the fire, set off the powder keg.

FL: Always a tough issue.

NH: It is always a tough issue, but there were underlying issues that had to do with his change agenda, too. Reestablishing key relationships was the most important thing. What I did immediately was to set up a kind of grading sheet which said "These are the issues that we have to confront." Then every board meeting, every month, I graded my administration on what we were doing on each of those things, and I think that helped. First of all, it kind of pinned it down. It wasn't just an amorphous credibility gap. It was: "These are the issues, this is the way we're addressing the issues; this is what we are doing; this is where we haven't been able to do anything, but will keep trying." We tried to be honest about the fact that we weren't immediately able to solve all of these things. At least there was some sense of having an agenda, of pursuing it, and of making an honest effort to evaluate progress on the issues.

FL: You've gotten into it a bit, but how did you manage the sometimes conflicting expectations on all sides? That's always a problem.

NH: It certainly is and, as you well know, the multiple constituencies that you have can be problematic because they have very different expectations. I can't generalize about my administration because at different times I had more credibility with one constituency than with another. But you know that first of all you have to have an agenda, give a sense of purpose, and give a sense that there are certain values that drive your decision-making. That takes a certain amount of explicitness. This is why I set up this grading arrangement. It may sound like a phony thing to do, but it was helpful because it pinpointed what we were trying to do and then made it possible to address each particular agenda. We also developed fourteen indicators because, as so often happens, the legislature passed measures concerning the university on the basis of anecdotes Somebody's son or daughter or they themselves had had a foreign TA who couldn't speak English when they took algebra or calculus at the university: this drove this perception that the university was not concerned about teaching. That is why we set up the fourteen criteria. I worked very hard on that.

FL: You were setting up accountability measures.

NH: That's right: accountability measures. We said these are the fourteen things that we are going to want to be evaluated on. I had a wonderful member of the faculty who for two years led this effort. The faculty member went out and talked to constituencies around the state, as well as to the faculty, and we reported to the board. The fourteen criteria became the substance of very extensive discussions with a whole spectrum of constituencies. It wasn't that we were, in the end, able to get complete agreement on the fourteen criteria, but it was again an opportunity to pinpoint what was important in the university. The university had a miserable graduation rate for undergraduates. I addressed that in my inaugural speech. That was really the main thrust of it, that we had to do something about this graduation rate. There were criteria, then, that had to do with the improvement of the graduation rates. Another criterion was participation by minority students. We adopted a whole spectrum of criteria, including how well we were doing in introducing contemporary information technology into the university's operation and how well we were managing our budgets. So we had both, not only academic outcome criteria but also management criteria. It helped because we could refer to this with the legislature. We probably still got legislation by anecdote, but those fourteen outcome measures were very helpful. I think that was one, probably the most important way, of dealing with constituencies. Then of course there was personal contact, the fact that you show up. I traveled around the state all the time. We had this wonderful extension service. In every county there were university people and I visited many of the eighty-seven counties in Minnesota. I was out on the hustings very often with alumni and with various civic groups.

I went to visit legislators in their districts and also set up a program where we invited to the university the representatives of major corporations such as 3M and IBM in Rochester and Medtronic. We invited the CEO to bring half a dozen people and we looked at the relationship between the university and those corporations. I tried to cover a whole spectrum of constituencies by personal presence and discussion of the university agenda.

FL: In regard to organizational structure, how did you recruit and structure your leadership team? Was there a particular plan that you developed in order to make sure you had all bases covered to respond to these issues?

NH: The organizational issues were and are difficult in Minnesota. The tradition was that my official title was President of the Board of Regents and Chancellor of the University. So I presided over the Board of Regents, although most of the work was done in committee of the whole where the chairman of the board presided. But I was president of this system, which at that time had five campuses. I was also the chancellor of the Twin Cities Campus, which has about 80 percent of the activities, at the same time as I was responsible, as president, for the Duluth, Crookston, Waseca, and Morris campuses. Morris had about 2,000 students, Waseca had about 1,000, Crookston had about 1,000, Duluth about 8,000. To be both the system head and the head of the main campus always presented the challenge of ensuring that you were being fair to these other campuses. There were various euphemisms used: they were not subordinate campuses, they were coordinate campuses. I understand they're going through this process in Minnesota right now and may actually go to a full-fledged system arrangement. So that organizational issue was always there. Then, because of the fact that you were both system president and campus chancellor, it presented problems with the academic vice presidents. The academic vice president was a systems academic vice president, but also a campus vice president. I experimented with different models of administration. You also had the fact that the health sciences had a vice president of their own for a number of years, with good reason, given the complexity of that enterprise. Then the agricultural interests got their vice president and the arts and sciences said, "You know agriculture and health sciences have their vice presidents, why shouldn't we have a vice president?" So, before my time, a vice presidency for arts and sciences and engineering was established. That left us the law school, business school, architecture, and education and some of the other professional schools free standing. So, we had free-standing professional schools, a vice president for arts and sciences and engineering, a vice president for agriculture, forestry, and home economics, and a vice president for health sciences. I gave more power to those vice presidents, for better or worse, because it was a large university. Especially with the heavy change agenda we had, you needed local leadership to drive that agenda. Of course, this made the academic vice president of the university on the Twin Cities campus more of a system functionary than a campus functionary.

FL: As a follow-up to that, while you're describing your organizational structure, what are some of the qualities that you look for in the people that you choose to work with and depend upon, other than the expertise needed in the position? Are there certain qualities that you think are important for working together as a team?

NH: You're looking for a lot of things. You are looking for competence in the particular field whether it be academic affairs or student affairs or finance. In areas such as finance, given the incredibly complex financial system that the university has, you need somebody who really has strong financial experience. You're looking for that strictly professional competence and you're also looking for people who understand what the university is about: that it isn't just a financial enterprise that has to be managed but an academic institution where financial management is simply an instrument for achieving certain academic goals. So even the finance vice president has to be comfortable with and understand the academic agenda and plan to be patient with the academic culture, which is a very participatory culture. Candidates must be comfortable with a decision-making mode that must be both decisive and consultative. It is, of course, no mean task to strike the balance between those two. I think loyalty is also essential. You are part of the team and you are honest and forthright. If you have a disagreement, you speak your piece, and then the decision is made by the person who is responsible for making the decision. You don't drive your own agenda against the president. You have to have that kind of loyalty. And if you cannot give that loyalty, well, then, get out. I had some extraordinarily able people who I can just give the highest grades in every respect. I also made some mistakes and I tried to correct them by terminating those appointments, which of course was hard to do. But those are the qualities: competence, proper understanding of the values, the ability to be decisive and consultative at the same time, and loyalty. I think those are the most important things that I look to.

FL: Clearly you made changes in the administrative structure but your system was so complex that, given everything else you needed to accomplish, that you had to do it with care at the same time.

NH: If you look at the University of Minnesota you will find that there has been this constant: there has not been a stable structure that has lasted for decades, but there has been experimentation. I think that is because of the complexity and the skewed character of the system. There is a certain time when certain issues are foremost and you need a certain structure. That doesn't necessarily mean that in the next stage the same structure is functional. I was driving a very heavy change agenda and I needed this decentralization of decision making to vice presidents, whom I ended up calling provosts under the academic vice president. But that structure is not necessarily transferable anywhere else, nor is it necessarily appropriate at other stages in the development of the university. So I think flexibility of structure is very important.

FL: How did you formulate a vision for the future of the institution? You indicated you had a number of accountability measures. How did you take that agenda and move the vision forward in the direction that you intended?

NH: As I said, I in many ways inherited the vision: it was the vision of focusing the university on what truly were the university's responsibilities in a very highly developed statewide system. The total system was probably overbuilt in certain respects. Focusing was the underlying vision. I had been the vice president for planning in the early 1980s, so I had participated in the early development of that vision, the vision to focus, which my predecessor gave explicit form and substance. When the pressure for a new, explicit plan became very strong, after I had been in office for about three years, we developed a plan that we called "University 2000." We started a planning process where we went out and met with a large number of constituencies and went through focus group hearings. In those hearings we asked, "What are the most important things that the university should contribute?" Then we tried to sift through and winnow the information. We tried to build credibility for that process. We formulated the "University 2000" plan, which was probably in many ways generic. I think university plans are often generic. You have to deal with the same basic set of goals, issues, and means. You can call it different things, but I've certainly been struck over the years just how generic this is. To be sure the local actors, the local circumstances influence it, but it is, in many ways, a common agenda. It was that kind of agenda that was my vision when I stepped in. Then, three or four years later, when I created something with a different name, "University 2000," it was a continuation of that vision. But, I did concentrate on a few things: the quality of undergraduate education, and the definition of undergraduate education at the University of Minnesota, was the Achilles heel. It was a wonderful university, very prominent in many areas of research, and had very effective extension service and outreach activities. But undergraduate education had been quite amorphous. The university was flooded with students and the graduation rate, as I said, was very, very low. There was very little evidence of a residential campus in the Twin Cities. On some of the other smaller campuses, there was more of that environment. We really needed to reduce the number of undergraduates so it was tractable. We needed to raise the entrance requirements in order to be sure that we didn't get saddled with unreasonable amounts of remedial education, which would drag down the whole thing. We needed to stress graduation, if not in four years, at least in five years. We also needed to create a more residential environment or at least an environment where we had smaller cohorts of freshmen coming into the university, getting to know each other, studying together, having contact with professors. We did all of these things. We actually wrote a plan for the reform of undergraduate education. I think there were seven steps. They ranged all the way from reform of general education to creating a residential campus environment. We did that in the residence halls by associating faculty members with cohorts of students. In the Institute of Technology, we had freshmen divided into groups of about a hundred students each. We had them take the basic engineering curriculum together, get to know each other, and have faculty advisers that they got to know. We tried to create a more intimate campus environment for students in a situation where there were 5,000 freshmen coming in every year. The constant complaint was the impersonality of the university, that you go there and you just drown in the sea of freshmen and never see anybody but the TA. We tried to aggressively counter that reality, as well as that perception. I think that what we did probably had some impact. My predecessor had started some of these efforts. My successor continued some of them, and I think the overall, sustained effort has changed the undergraduate experience at the university. The expectations are different.

We created some new honors programs. Because we raised admissions requirements, the best students in the state started competing to come to the main campus in Minneapolis/St. Paul. Earlier the perception had been, "well, you can always go to the old U. because they take everybody." Now it became a matter of competing to get into the university and I think that was a good thing. Of course, it flew into the face of good old egalitarianism in Minnesota. There's another area where I think leadership is very important. That is, how do you reconcile the need for selectivity, a certain kind of elitism, of meritocracy with democracy, access, and opportunity? It's a tremendously difficult and important issue and I think that's where leadership really has to be exercised.

FL: How did you communicate to the whole community that you were going through these changes and how did you gain support for them? As you defined it, the democracy and access versus meritocracy issue is a tough one internally as well as externally.

NH: I started in my inaugural speech, talking about the graduation rate. To some extent it was kind of a family secret that the graduation rate was so miserable. People were just shocked when in my inaugural speech I quoted the graduation rates.

FL: What was the rate when you came in?

NH: It was probably down in the twenties.

FL: For a four-year period, a five-year period?

NH: For a four-year and even for a five-year period. There was a tradition of working and going to the university at the same time. This is what universities in a big city have to fight, because there are so many opportunities to work. That is perfectly legitimate, in certain ways, but so many students came in and kind of dribbled away their education as far as I was concerned. Maybe I drove this too hard, but I was adamant on a four-year education. I had a member of the board who kept lecturing me on how a four-year education is only for the rich kids, so I had considerable very direct resistance to the very notion that graduation in four years was desirable. But I spoke about it all the time and I tried to put it in terms of the opportunities that this provided students. If they got their education, they could go and be active professionally in society. They could be more effective and make more money than if they kept dribbling out this education. Besides, the educational experience, I tried to argue, was better if it was a little bit more intense. It was something that I spoke about very often. I tried to avoid the trap of elitism because, of course, such accusations were flying. People were concerned, "If we don't admit these students, what happens to them?" They went to one of the seven state universities, to one of the nineteen community colleges or to one of the thirty-four technical colleges. There were plenty of opportunities there. I also tried very hard, Fran, to get the notion of transferability on the agenda: that you can go to a community college and complete your general education requirements in a community college, then be transferred lock, stock and barrel into the university. We started joint degrees with the community colleges. We started half a dozen applied bachelor's degrees in information technology management, in emergency medical services, and areas like that. So, at the same time as I was adamant on the admissions requirements, I tried to bridge the relationship especially between the community colleges and the university.

FL: How did you transform your understanding of the institution and of the external realities into a long-range plan to change and improve the institution? You talked about it in your inaugural, but somehow it had to be communicated to the whole community. Faculty, students, and alumni had to understand it; the state needed to know what was happening and why. Did you have a way of communicating with all of those constituencies?

NH: I talked about this in every speech I gave to the alumni. I tried to address it around the state in a way that depended on the constituency and how the plan reflected that particular constituency, including trying to emphasize the tremendous importance of the research agenda. Of course that was not difficult to do when it came to things like health or engineering, but I also stressed the importance of what the university meant to the cultural environment. I tried to draw examples of how the university, through its presence, its research, its scholarship, and the education that it had provided, had been the key to developing important aspects of the environment in the state. I cited examples like Medtronic, a direct spin-off from the university, and the introduction of the Taconite process that saved the mining industry in Minnesota for generations, but I also tried to show how the Guthrie Theater was an outgrowth of the fine theatrical tradition at the University of Minnesota and the way the artistic community in Minnesota was dependent on the university. I tried to use concrete examples of what the university had meant to Minnesota. I've always been a little bit resistant to highfaluting language about vision. I try to bring it down to something that is more concrete and specific. As a matter of fact, I've even been a little bit resistant to talking about a great vision in leadership. I think there can be a danger that you come in and here you are, the great visionary leader who's going to create this vision. You create the vision and then you go away to create a vision somewhere else, so somebody else is left picking up the pieces, because implementation is so extremely important.

I may have erred in the direction of not being aggressive enough in formulating in visionary language what the university was all about. I was more concerned with "We've got to do it, we've got to do something about it; we have fourteen criteria, let's do something about it." It is, I think, also to some extent by personal inclination and to some extent by circumstance that we have to decide when it is important to have really driving visionary language about institutions. When do you more quietly go about actually implementing change? I had to take the culture in Minnesota into consideration, too, a culture that is unusually suspicious of highfaluting visionary language. After all, it is Garrison Keillor's state. They apparently used my inaugural speech at a Harvard Seminar for new presidents and I was told by somebody that what they had emphasized was that here's a president who really is trying to gear his rhetoric to the audience. I talked about excellence and I said, "Of course in Minnesota you realize that, as Garrison Keillor has so often said, you know that we're pretty good and you know that we have to try to be pretty good...." That means, of course, that Minnesota is one of the places of extraordinary quality and excellence. That's what it really means in this understated fashion. I think you have to gear your rhetoric to the audience in that sense. I genuinely believe that Minnesotans have a desire for quality. They don't want exclusiveness, they don't want pretense, they want something that is, you know, pretty good, but it had better be good!

FL: Finally, on that point, how did you link the changes that you wanted to make, undergraduate education among others, to the financial budgeting process in the institution? Was there a link between the two?

NH: Absolutely, and I did use a lot of rhetoric about undergraduate education, but it was not until I reallocated very significant amounts of money that the faculty said, "Maybe he's serious about it; he isn't just talking about it." It was absolutely essential to make very visible investments in specific improvements in undergraduate education. I think that is generally true. As one faculty member told me, "Nils, you know that the only way a president can express love is through money."

FL: So you got faculty buy-in on this. They understood and agreed with what you were trying to do.

NH: We had a very aggressive retrenchment and reallocation process which we started before the financial crises of the early 1990s. Of course, these crises come with some regularity, as you know. We started an aggressive plan right away when I became president. We clawed loose about $60 million at that time for reinvestment. Unfortunately the state's budget crisis came and so we lost some of that money. But the important thing was that we could show the faculty leadership that yes, we're taking money away here and here and here, but we're taking money out of administrative services, not only out of academic programs, and we're putting the money here and here and here. There are benefits. Frankly we got wonderful buy-in for the reallocation plan when we closed a campus, which probably is something that doesn't happen too often in a public institution. It was abundantly clear that it was a campus that was duplicating what was being done elsewhere. This was one of the small, originally agricultural technical campuses that had grown out of an agricultural experiment station. Most probably it became a campus when the university was trying some decades ago to build credibility in the legislature by getting rural bastions because the strong support for the university came from the rural areas, not from the Twin Cities. The Morris Campus grew out of an Indian School that was way out in Western Minnesota. Waseca and Crookston were both fine institutions and served their purposes, but, especially as a technical college system and a community college system grew, they became duplicative of what the technical colleges and community colleges were doing. It was difficult for the university in this tight situation to provide a very expensive education in Waseca, for example, when it cost twice as much to educate a student at Waseca as it did in the College of Liberal Arts in the Twin Cities, and fourteen miles away there was a technical college that did pretty much the same thing that Waseca did. So we took the bull by the horns and closed Waseca. It was terribly unpleasant and there was a political uproar about it, but the board of regents and the chairman of the board of regents supported it, so it went through without any trouble, except a lot of rhetoric and cussing. Legislators could say, "The Board of Regents is in charge of the university and we can't help it that they're making this awful decision." Of course, some took me into their offices and privately said, "Nils, you're doing just the right thing," while others were beating up on me in committee!

FL: When you make changes, it often does not gain friends for you, as we well know. Can you describe one or two critical incidents, how they arose, and how you dealt with them? Of course closing down a campus must have been one of those situations.

NH: The Waseca situation was painful because I liked the people at Waseca and I had been down there. Of course, they threw in my face statements of support for Waseca that I had made when I was down there. Then I closed it down and had to go there to face 2,000 protestors and a blockade of farm equipment. I marched through this gauntlet. What is the saying?

FL: Run the gauntlet.

NH: Yes, I didn't make friends. I'm sure that that is a region of Minnesota where my name is still anathema. But the chairman of the board came from there. Eight of the board members are elected by congressional district. He came from that congressional district and he stood by this decision, an amazing profile in courage. He went with me down to the campus when I announced this closing. That was certainly a key, that the board chair would take that kind of personal leadership and that it was a unanimous vote by the board to close the campus. That was one critical incident. The other one was in the health sciences. It's an agenda that to some extent was mine when I came into the job. We had an excellent health sciences center, which was surrounded by some of the most prominent and best HMOs in the country. The health sciences center and the university hospital were just absolutely in a vise, in a situation where we had thirty-four medical practice plans. Some of them consisted of one member, where a faculty member of the medical school could decide whether he wanted to practice in the university hospital or not. You couldn't run an efficient, competitive operation under those terms. So the first week I was in office, I met with the clinical chiefs and said that we had to consolidate the medical practice plans, which didn't gain me a lot of friends at that particular time. We also had some severe regulatory problems in the medical school, especially in the surgery department, where some improper practices had been going on for twenty years, and I had to ask the chairman to step down. That didn't gain me friends either. I remember the letter I got from an irate citizen saying, "Dr. So and So should save lives and you should do the paperwork." The mail I got when I made some of these really tough and controversial decisions was quite interesting. I got phone calls and letters saying, "Thank you, thank you for doing this." You're sustained by the fact that there are people who will actually appreciate that action is taken and give you support. This is where the chairman of the board was just a tremendous force enabling me to make those decisions.

FL: I'm going to move to external constituencies and just ask you a few brief questions on that. What importance did you place on the role of the institution in the community?

NH: The University of Minnesota is such an integral part of the State of Minnesota that almost every aspect of life is touched by the university. I realized that the university has to have those connections, but at the same time you somehow have to try to sell the fact that the university is also very exclusive, world class both in its research and in its teaching, and that it is not egalitarian in any narrow sense. You must convey that this is exactly what the state needs and that the university serves every citizen in the state.

FL: Were there any major groups outside the university that you needed to touch base with, other than legislators?

NH: Absolutely: the business community. We had the University of Minnesota Foundation. Sometimes the Board of Regents can be driven by politics and individual ambitions to the extent that it begins to make governing a little shaky: I had that situation when I had different boards at different times. The foundation board was always a source of stability and good judgment. They had no formal role vis-à-vis university governance. They were strictly related to the University of Minnesota Foundation, but politically and perceptually and personally that foundation board was a tremendous strength. I don't know how common this is, but in Minnesota, the balance was very important between the sometimes politicized governing board appointed by the legislature and the foundation board, that was self perpetuating and had many of the community's corporate and civic leaders on it. The foundation board also gave me access to the business community. It gave me access to the civic leadership in the state and that was very important. I also spent a lot of time through the extension service with the grassroots and that was very important in Minnesota, too. I think that some of the things were possible to do because I was out on the hustings with the grassroots people often enough for them to say, "Well, you know he's raising these admissions requirements, but he isn't necessarily a bad guy because he's out there talking to us." And of course I loved doing it, too. You have to like the people you talk to. You can't go out and be effective with them if you don't like them. I liked the people I talked with, even when we disagreed.

FL: Did you find you had to allocate your time and you had to develop priorities otherwise you responded to everything at the same time or tried to, at any rate?

NH: When I came in, I read a book called *Why Leaders Can't Lead*. Of course it's the constant distractions that make it hard to lead. I tried to steel myself and say "What has to be accomplished?" Every day I had three things I wanted to get accomplished that day and by 5 o'clock in the afternoon, I might not have gotten to any of them because there were always other things that came up. Overall I think that I did accomplish some of the tasks I set myself, but I certainly spent an extraordinary amount of time on those things that were brought up by circumstances, especially the travail in the medical center and the tenure issue that flared up, quite unnecessarily.

FL: You spent a lot of time on the road throughout Minnesota for various reasons. When you were doing this for two or three days at a time, did you have someone back on campus who was running the campus for you, or were you always in touch and continuing to do it yourself?

NH: I kept in touch, but I'm pretty good at delegating. I used to say, "You know I'm hiring you not to have to tell you all the time what to do, but possibly to have to stop you once in a while, when you're doing something I don't want you to do. I would rather have to stop you than have to constantly urge you on." I was blessed with having both an academic vice president and a finance vice president who were self-starters. I had very good chiefs of staff. That was really the key. You could not operate as both system president and campus chancellor and expect to be involved with day-to-day operation all the time. You had to have people who would do it. Most of the time, I had people who were able to do that. That's what made it possible for me to be on the hustings.

FL: Every president experiences planned and unplanned events that escalate into time-consuming crises. .Are there crisis management stories that you would like to share, other than the ones you've covered this morning?

NH: I've mentioned the crisis of closing the campus, which was a self-induced one. The crisis in the medical school involved a number of regulatory issues, at a time when conflict of interest was just beginning to emerge as a problem area. The university had some policies, but clearly the policies and the processes were lagging behind the demands that were being placed on them. You had faculty members in the medical school establishing outside business activities that were related to their research. I had some nasty situations there that were hard to deal with.

And asking this very popular and very distinguished chair of surgery to step down—that was probably the toughest decision I've ever made. I had a situation where the health center leadership kind of folded and wouldn't do it, so I had to step in and do it, which of course made it even worse. That was hard. Here again I saw the way outsiders, corporate leaders, civic leaders were willing to take on tasks for the university. When I did major reform of the organization of the health sciences, the just retired CEO of Medtronic worked for a whole year pro-bono, full time, to help in that restructuring and did a tremendous job. I relied very heavily on that kind of civic leadership. There were others, such as another retired CEO of a company in Minnesota and the human resources vice president for 3M, both of whom worked for a year pro-bono to help reform the human resources system for the university. So I relied heavily on volunteers.

I tried assiduously in that human resources reform to stay away from the tenure issue.

The university had a rather Byzantine tenure code. It was a university-wide tenure code so, if you fired somebody in Crookston, they had tenure rights throughout the system. You could not lower anybody's salary. You could freeze the salary, but you couldn't lower the salary. There were also some other procedural issues, but I did not want to try to mess with the tenure code because I knew that it was the third rail. Then I got a chair of the board who insisted that Minnesota was going to lead the reform of tenure in North America. Bang, I mean everything just turned into a conflagration. In retrospect, I should have said immediately "No, we're not going to reform the tenure code; tenure is very important and on the whole this code works well"—just thrown my body before the express train, which I eventually ended up doing. I was probably a little bit too willing to say, "Well, there are some aspects of the tenure code that could stand some change, and we probably need some form of post-tenure review." So that kind of undermined, to some extent, my credibility with the faculty at least for a while, although I think when I eventually said no and laid my body on the railroad track that I regained some of that credibility. But that was a difficult, very difficult one

FL: And personally very difficult.

NH: Personally very difficult. Of course there was little understanding and appreciation of tenure in the legislature, and the governor did not seem to recognize the importance of tenure. Then, if things began to settle down and we began to get a handle on the issues, there was another board meeting and the thing would blow up again. We also suffered from the Internet gossip network, because rumors spread like wildfire. I got irate letters and resolutions from faculties at distinguished universities taking me and the university to task for abolishing tenure. The *Washington Post* had an editorial praising the University of Minnesota for taking the lead in abolishing tenure—which was, of course, never contemplated, even by those who pushed hardest for reform. It was a nightmare and finally did settle down, but it was one of the worst things I've ever been through in administration.

FL: What gives you the strength to keep going through good times and tough times? You had to have something to keep you going at that time. Where was that strength coming from?

NH: I think that when you take these jobs, you have to really believe that you know this is a good thing: "These are the values that are essential to me and that I think are central to our society. This is the most important thing in our society." And I have never had a second's doubt that universities are the most important force we have in our society.

It may sound phony, overly idealistic, but that is the belief that I have and that sustained me every morning when I got up. When I was going to go to the surgery department to announce that I was asking the chairman to step down, my stomach was all in knots, but then I said, "You know, that's what you have to do. It is essential to the values of this university that this be done. Just go and do it."

FL: And the values of the university are, I think, even more important today.

NH: Yes, I think so too. It is of course difficult because there are certain instances when, in order to make things work, people have to compromise a little bit. But, I was never comfortable doing that and not good at it, frankly. In the end, you have to have the basic belief that the action you take has a value and then you have to be stubborn.

FL: Because it's the right thing to do.

NH: Sometimes it becomes very important to be able to rely on inner satisfaction!

FL: We've talked all along about the issue of leadership. Could you define the term in a few words?

NH: I'm always a little bit uncomfortable talking about leadership and especially uncomfortable about talking about myself as a leader. It isn't only what some people consider the traditional Scandinavian false humility! I genuinely feel that way, and I think that there is so much false leadership. I mean Hitler, Mussolini, absolute maniacs who inspired the masses, had these enormous visions that caused worldwide disaster. So the word leadership is, in one sense, tainted. That's why I like to stress a much quieter mode of leadership. There are people whom I admire greatly who can articulate basic values, sometimes in a very quiet way, and by example and personality convey the sense that these are good things. Let's join together and do these things. That's the kind of leadership that I really look for.

FL: In your current role you should be the ideal person to answer my next question. What are the most important qualities for a university president today?

NH: I think it's getting more complicated rather than less. Traditionally we have looked to academics to be the leaders, and I think it's absolutely essential that the leadership of universities continue to be academics. The tension is that the management responsibilities that land in the lap of a president are enormous and are getting more complicated. That is partly because we get less and less money from the state. We have all of these entrepreneurial activities, all these multifarious ways of getting resources, and then we try to match the resources with university purposes. It is extremely complex and requires a strong foundation in academic values, but also an understanding of how the financial systems work, how you manage resources, and how you recruit the right kind of people to assist in the management of these complex institutions. Now, with information technology and the rest of the incredible technology that is developing, the president makes a decision that costs fifty million dollars or seventy-five million buying into a technology that is extremely complex and ever-changing. The demands are enormous. You need the academic leadership that has academic values; you need a leader who can handle the management responsibilities; you need someone who can handle the political role in order to maintain relationships with all kinds of constituencies; and you need someone who will try to reconcile all of these.

FL: It's not an easy job.

NH: It's not an easy job. At the same time, of course, it's the world's most fascinating job.

FL: It is. My next question is, how have the role and demands of the presidency changed over the past few decades? You started talking about that by citing the disinvestment of the states in public higher education and the technological revolution, and continued in your references to the growing roles of private support and commercial application of university research. In referring to the political role of the president, you touched upon the increasingly strident demands of students and politicians alike, for low tuition, high quality and accountability in both expenditures and results. Would you like to comment on the issue of the growing demands for low tuition and high quality?

NH: One of the difficulties is that you all too often are arguing your case in some kind of never-never land where the people you are arguing with have little or no comprehension of how it really works. You're not talking about the real issues. You're talking about some kind of fictitious issue.

Sometimes you run into sheer disingenuousness A governor's office may take the university budget, divide it by the number of students, and say, "You're spending a lot of money on those students!" Perhaps the state provided only 20 percent or less of that budget. The rest was money that the university generated through its own activities. Universities may get little or no credit for generating a billion or more a year to the benefit of the state. The attitude is often that universities are just feeding from the public trough at an enormous rate. Then maybe a governor will point out that the state university is the largest employer in the state. Yes, that may be so, but that is not because the state pays for all those employees. They are not feeding from the trough: many of them are people who are there because of the university's own efforts, its faculty members' efforts to bring in research money, the private donations that the university's donors provided, and the partnerships with industry that the university established.

The fact that there is sometimes so little understanding of how this really works gets to me, the sheer ignorance or disingenuousness that you are often up against, arguing, as I said, in never-never land. I see this now with the federal government's approach to tuition. The political messages are: reduce public support, don't raise tuition, don't enter into any relationship with business that might raise conflict of interest issues....

FL: And be an engine of the economy.

NH: That's right. I've run into these messages, both on a university board, occasionally, and in the political arena.

FL: Presidencies were once measured in decades but now they are more typically limited to four or five years. Do you believe that the changes in the role have brought that about? Perhaps the role has gotten so complicated that after five years people say, "I've had enough of this; this is not what I wanted to do the rest of my life." How do you account for what is happening? Did they get into something they really weren't interested in doing? Was it too stressful?

NH: When I got into the Big Ten, I of course had the least seniority; when I left eight and a half years later, I was chairman of the Big Ten conference, which was strictly by seniority. I don't know exactly what limits presidential tenure now. I think it's the pressures and sometimes it may even be that, if you're really pursuing a change agenda, there is a cycle to a presidency. There is some truth to the fact that presidents make two major contributions to the institution: when they come and when they leave. There's a life cycle to the presidency and that life cycle may be shorter or somewhat longer. I think that you can invigorate the institution when you arrive because it is a new start, although I also think continuity is very important. You also probably get worn out, not just in a physical sense, but you become too familiar, and then the university and the state need somebody else to come in and say what needs saying. It may be that the new person says the same things, but says it a little bit differently. I am becoming very aware of the life cycle of a presidency. That life cycle may be getting shorter because of the demands and the pressures and the controversy that swirls around the president almost all the time. Those things make the nature of the job difficult enough to induce more turnovers. President Northrop, one of the legendary presidents of the University of Minnesota, was president for thirty-four years. I remember reading in an old Minneapolis newspaper at one time that President Northrop took the train to Anoka, which is a suburb about ten miles from downtown Minneapolis. He took the train to Anoka and gave a lecture on Shakespeare. I thought about that. How idyllic; you go downtown, take the train, and give a lecture on Shakespeare. Then you go back, smoke a cigar and make a few decisions about the university!

FL: It was certainly a very different time. How did you decide it was time to step down?

NH: I was fifty-seven when I became president and I said, "The longest I must stay is sixty-five; I'm going to step down at sixty-five." I had that in mind. I was also getting tired and worn down. I had had a wonderful relationship with the board, but my relationship with the board at that time soured, especially with the tenure issue. I also recommended closing something called the General College, which was a good institution for students who could not get adequate background in a high school. In the past, when many high schools did not provide college preparatory curricula and there were no community colleges, they could come to General College and have access to the university. But in our situation, with almost all high schools providing adequate curricula and with nineteen community colleges as access points, General College was not an essential unit, in my opinion. When the board asked for a new round of dramatic cuts—we had already cut and reallocated about one fourth of the state-appropriated dollars during my tenure as president—I proposed closing it down. I probably didn't go about it in the right way, so I took a real beating on that particular decision. I had planned to stay till I was sixty-five, and I ended up staying till I was sixty-six. I had completed my work at the university by that time, so it was not a difficult decision. It was both a thing that I had planned and a thing that was logical at that particular time.

FL: How did you make your decision about what you would do after the presidency?

NH: This is where the discrepancy arises again between my self-image as a scholar who desires only to sit in the library all day and the reality that I am much more extroverted, that I actually love interaction with people and love the hurly-burly life of administration. I was going to go back and be a professor. I was going to do research, and I was going to teach again…

FL: This is what I'm doing.

NH: Yes, and you seem to thrive on it. But, just after I stepped down at Minnesota, the chair of the search committee for the Association of American Universities president called me and asked me if I would be a candidate for the AAU presidency. I said, "I don't know. I'll think about it." I went to Iceland, came back, and the search committee chair called again and said, "Would you be a candidate for the AAU presidency?" I said, "Okay, I'll come down and have an interview." The next day, the AAU chairman called and offered me the job. It was another one of these situations where an opportunity was placed in my way and I took the leap. I have been so happy in this job; I can't tell you what a wonderful job it is. Rather than my deliberately planning the next steps in my life, at several points in my life an opportunity has been offered and I have taken it. I think it was Kierkegaard who said that you can only understand your life backwards, but you have to live it forwards. As I look back at my life, it is obvious that I have had the opportunity to serve in a number of very interesting assignments; as I lived my life I was blessed by fortuitous circumstances!

FL: In a few words, how would you characterize your leadership style?

NH: The way I like to think of myself in a leadership position is that I have a commitment to certain basic values and that I'm willing to stand for those values and be pretty stubborn about doing what I think those values require. I like quiet leadership. I don't like the bombastic leadership style. I like a low-key approach. That's the way I would like to be and that's the way I strive to be. I think that's the best characterization I can give.

FL: What was the most critical capital investment made under your leadership at Minnesota? If you had to pick one thing, what had a major impact?

NH: Here again, you inherit things from your predecessor and you leave things to your successor. There were a number of building projects that were completed during my tenure that had their roots in my predecessor's activities or even farther back. There were also projects that were completed during my successor's term for which I was probably largely responsible. I think that if I had to pick one important project, I would pick the Weisman Art Museum. We built this museum with private money, including the $4.5 million that Frederick Weisman gave us; that's why we named the museum after him. It was important because it was the fulfillment of a dream that went back to 1934, when the president of the university said that this university needs an outstanding art museum. It was not until I was president that this came about, but my predecessor had laid the foundation for it. I have chosen it because it was the fulfillment of a long-standing dream, but also because it was done with such extraordinary quality. We selected, through a joint community-university selection committee, the California architect Frank Gehry, and he designed a very interesting structure. I don't know if you have seen it, but you know Frank Gehry's sculpted buildings. It is controversial, of course, but it's such an inspiring structure. It was done with such quality that the *New York Times* wrote in its review that the interior makes it one of the outstanding college museums in this country. The third reason I would choose it is that it immediately became such a focal point and such an inspiration to campus life. It is right in the middle of the campus. You have activity there all the time, not only exhibits but also other events every day: the colleges have events there, so do the student groups. It has become an inspiration to campus life. So for all three of these reasons, the history, the quality of it, and the inspiration to campus life, I would say the Weisman Art Museum was the most important capital investment.

FL: That's a very good example. What about your legacies? For one thing, you saved tenure.

NH: Well, I didn't. I just managed to clean up the mess that I had contributed to making because I didn't handle it right from the beginning. But, yes, I think that some faculty members will think about me as somebody who stood up for tenure at a critical time. Some of them will not think so. I think that, if you ask someone at Minnesota, my most important legacy is that I did something about undergraduate education. Not only did we have a vision of what undergraduate education should be, but we actually did take practical steps to improve it. We really completed those seven things that we said we were going to do, and it has had a rather profound effect on recruitment, on graduation, and on campus life. Of course these things evaporate very quickly; the students who are there now are probably complaining about the situation again. But, I think the undergraduate initiative probably is my most important legacy. There are some buildings that I was instrumental in getting: we have a new concert hall, we built a new business school, and we built a biomedical engineering center. We started the Alumni Center, although it was completed under my successor. We did master planning for all of the campuses: that was important. The third thing would be reorganizing the health sciences, actually turning the University Hospital over to a not-for-profit HMO and saving the patient flow and the financing of the health sciences center. Those are the things I would mention, but the undergraduate initiative is the one that I'm most proud of, the one least driven by circumstance, and the one that was directly driven by my own commitment and interests. I continued what I had started as provost at the University of Arizona, in a way.

FL: Now you're in a very different sort of post as president of the Association of American Universities, but there are undoubtedly a number of commonalities as well. So I'd like to focus first on the unique aspects of this role. During your presidency of the AAU, what have been the areas essential to higher education where you think that the AAU has been able to make the greatest contributions or to head off the most egregious potential problems?

NH: It's always very difficult to assess the impact because AAU's influence is very general and in some ways diffused. It's hard to know what is cause and effect in the political arena. There are six presidential associations that work very closely together, so it's hard to sift out what AAU has done as opposed to what the presidential associations or the higher education representation in Washington in general have been able to do. AAU works with the American Council on Education (ACE), the National Association of State Universities and Land Grant Colleges (NASULGC), the American Association of State Colleges and Universities (AASCU), the National Association of Independent Colleges and Universities (NAICU), and the Association of American Community Colleges (AACC). Of course, we also work through individual universities, as we did when you were president. We worked through your federal relations operation. When I went with you to Congress, that had much more impact on your New Jersey delegation than if I had gone up there alone. So it's a hard question because of the diffuseness. I think the most important aspect of AAU is that the public and private research universities have been able to band together in this voluntary fashion to create a quite distinctive group of universities with a distinctive agenda, a distinctive culture, and a distinctive role in society. I think that it is very important to focus on the special concerns of the research universities, universities that are leaders in terms of the quality, not only of their research but also the education they provide. We've been able to have a distinctive voice and force within the higher education community. I think that is very important.

It is interesting that in another week I'm going to the University of Leiden in Holland to meet with the League of European Research Universities, which is a new organization modeled on AAU. Europeans are trying to band together some of the leading research universities and are quite envious of our ability to do that with the commonality of values and agenda exhibited by AAU. I think that's been AAU's most important contribution.

Then, because of the excellence of the universities that we represent, and working through those universities, we've probably been able to have an influence both on the administration and on Congress. We certainly have access to the administration and to Congress because of the nature of the institutions that are represented here. As you know, having been one of those people we worked through, this has created an understanding of the importance of research. Many factors led to the doubling of the NIH budget: the general concern about health, some excellent leadership by Congressman Porter, Senator Specter, and others in Congress. But, I believe that the research agenda both in the administration and in Congress has been greatly enhanced by the fact that there has been a group of excellent universities that has been able to lobby for it and explain it. I think that AAU's influence has been greatest in regard to federal funding for research.

The AAU has also had a direct influence on federal regulations. Through our study of conflict of interest and the establishment of the new accrediting agency for human subjects protection (which really came about through AAU), the AAU has been able to build confidence in the administration and in Congress for self-regulation by research universities. I think that's a very important part of our system. The AAU has been a strong force for self-regulation in terms of research regulations and in terms of helping preserve the accreditation system. We have also turned to our own academic community to try to ensure that we meet the responsibilities that come with self-regulation. We have encouraged our member institutions to establish strong conflict of interest policies. We are trying to help reform the accreditation system and keep it on track, addressing its essential purposes of ensuring appropriate educational outcomes, rather than having it get into management issues that may not be its proper domain.

FL: Under your leadership, the AAU has also considered issues in regard to undergraduate education. In the early 1990s, when you and I both led our universities to increase their focus on undergraduates and reform undergraduate education, the quality of undergraduate education in research universities was a national issue, not just a Minnesota or New Jersey issue.

NH: Yes. The AAU is primarily oriented toward research and graduate education and the presidential cut on the issues that we try to emphasize, but we have gotten into the issue of undergraduate education in the research university because of the fact that there has been a credibility gap with the regard to that issue. How much impact we've had, I don't know. The main thing we have done—here I credit my predecessor and others in AAU because this started before I came—is a study of state graduation standards and of preparation necessary for entrance into AAU universities. Under what we call the "Standards for Success" project, we have sent to every public high school in the country an instruction book and a CD Rom that describes what kind of preparation is necessary for entry into undergraduate education in the AAU universities. We did also do a directory of public service programs in AAU universities. All our member universities, both public and private, do have substantial outreach programs, including cooperative programs with the surrounding communities.

FL: Years ago there were some concerns raised about what some felt was a growing perception by Congress that the AAU was just another lobbying organization. Is that an area of concern anymore?

NH: It is. Especially in this administration and in the Department of Education, we ran into that. We had people coming in who referred to us and the other presidential associations as the union or the unions. They wanted to go directly out to the universities and did not look upon us as legitimate representatives of those universities at all. We ran into this in a very sharp way in various respects when members of the Department of Education refused to even talk to us.

FL: How do you account for that?

NH: I think it was a combination of false expectations and the breach of personal contact that seems to take place with every change in administration. We've dealt with it by continuing to work with the Department and establishing personal relationships with their representatives, and it's working much better now. I don't think we run into that attitude in this administration any longer. That was the initial attitude: that we were just a bunch of paid lobbyists who had no connection with the real higher education that was out there somewhere. As administrations change, it's a constant battle due to the lack of continuity between administrations. We encounter it to some extent in the Congress too, but especially with successive administrations. You have to reestablish relationships. It occurs with the OMB too: we had to establish a relationship with the former OMB director; now we're seeking to reestablish that kind of relationship with a new director. It's a constant rebuilding effort that has to take place to maintain some kind of credibility for the association.

FL: Nils, how important do you think it is that presidents and chancellors participate in national organizations and join in their work discussing, formulating solutions to current problems and issues in our education? People often ask why presidents belong to all these associations. What good is it? Isn't it a waste of time that you could be using to do university business?

NH: Fran, without that participation, first of all we couldn't exist and we certainly would be totally ineffective, because it is the collective power of the public and private universities and the leadership that those universities have, that's where the punch of AAU comes. If presidents are not willing to participate actively in AAU and represent the research university community, whether under the label of AAU or in other ways, with the administration and Congress, we don't have much chance of having any impact. That relationship is absolutely essential. In the last meeting with the Executive Committee, I discussed specifically how we can continue to engage the presidents individually, but maybe also in small groups, in even more intense fashion in contacts with the administration and Congress. Beyond the meetings between presidents and representatives of the administration and Congress that we've tried to do in connection with our spring meetings, and calling on presidents in ad hoc fashion when we need somebody for a hearing, can we activate them in some other way? That participation is absolutely essential, and is a very important aspect of leadership by the president of an institution. Participation in federal relations is an important part of the many responsibilities of those presidents.

FL: It was one of the aspects of my job that I particularly enjoyed.

NH: You were good at it and very helpful in doing it.

FL: Now I have a few issue-oriented questions. The first one has to do with governance. What do you feel are the important characteristics of good governing boards and what are the problems one can encounter in dealing with governing boards?

NH: That's a rich topic and one that AAU presidents fairly often indulge in contemplating. First of all, let me say that I have come to really appreciate the importance of the governing board. Again, this is something that universities in other countries do not have. They are looking to establish something like governing boards that can link the university with society. I used to say that the role of the governing board is to direct and protect. The governing board helps the university to orient itself towards the needs of society and bring to bear the university's special expertise on the needs of society, not because universities are just utilitarian—they have a much broader function—but because it is important that they keep in touch with what the real issues in society are. The governing board's function is also to protect the university's autonomy and ability to operate in an intellectually honest and straightforward fashion under the political pressures that always build up. I think boards are very important and I think that what I call good and bad governing boards has to do with their functions, too. To what extent can they link the university's agenda with society without becoming narrowly utilitarian or political? To what extent can they rise above narrow political concerns, let alone personal ambition and personal issues? To what extent are they willing to stand up to protect the university when the winds blow hard? When somebody has done something, touched on some third rail, whatever the issue happens to be, will they stand up in order to protect free speech and academic freedom? It is quite amazing how citizens coming out of different walks of life can rise to that challenge and exercise what I consider really important leadership. It is also quite unfortunate the extent to which some people will use boards to further their own personal ambition, to deal with their own personal grievances, and try to muddle the roles between the president and the governing board. This is where the chair of the governing board becomes very important in maintaining a good sense of how to exercise the leadership that is appropriate to the governing board and not try to be the executive of the institution. I think that's a very important matter.

FL: That is a very wise comment. I know that many presidents and boards have had to struggle with those problems. In the past few years, there have been several instances in which the governor of the state has gotten involved directly with policy issues in the flagship public university or the state higher education system. How can chancellors and presidents deal with political interference in academic governance?

NH: To some extent we should be flattered because it just shows how important the universities are. I think that universities are seen as more and more important. Perhaps we exaggerate the quietness of earlier times, but it may have been that the attitude was that it was nice to have a university: students could get an undergraduate education and there was always a job waiting if they got their B.A degree. From that it has gone to universities being seen as absolutely, fundamentally important to the region, to the state, and to the nation. I think that's why we may have seen increasing interference in the university on the part of governors and other political leaders. They want to turn them to their own advantage, and they sometimes, from our perspective, misguidedly try to turn them into something that is more narrowly utilitarian than is appropriate. Yes, I think we've seen more interference and I think the reason is that we are becoming even more important. Governors see that universities are essential to the completion of their agenda. We are reaping, to some extent, the fruit of something we planted: the importance of the university to economic development. We played that card and maybe we have overplayed it, because they are playing it back to us now. They want to see the university as strongly focused on economic development, even to the neglect of the basic research and education that we provide in a much broader context. There is probably more interference because we are seen as more important. This is where the board becomes very important to protect the university, because our main contribution is due to the autonomy, the independence, and the objectivity in the public interest that we can provide. That has to be preserved. I see this as a major battlefront that we have to deal with, both federally and at the state level.

FL: On issues of funding, what is your take on the increasing problems that public universities are encountering as states reduce their funding in higher education while legislatures and governors try to gain political advantage by capping tuition?

NH: This is the never-never land situation that I mentioned. In my more facetious moments, I think that one of the favorite solutions to university problems is to spend money that doesn't exist. Of course another favorite thing is to do things that are illegal and the third one is, "Why don't you do such and such," when you've been doing precisely that for the last 30 years. Those sometimes seem to be the favorite solutions to problems. Spend money that doesn't exist. Do something illegal, or do what you're already doing. We have a major responsibility for explaining how university financing works. We have to try to educate so we can get out of never-never land and talk about the realities. If we don't get public support, how do we then finance the university? First of all, we have to try to manage more effectively. Even though we have always tried to do that, we can improve the operation. We have to make sure that we try and try and try to do that. We have to communicate better what we are doing and the relationship of outcomes to inputs, which we haven't always been willing to do in a very explicit way. We have the responsibility of transparency and explanation. There's a profound lack of understanding, and I see that as a very severe problem that we must address, not just complain about.

FL: Do you see how institutions can resolve their budget problems and continue to build both access and excellence? We have to find a way to do it.

NH: This is what you have to do. What we tried to do at Minnesota was to focus. You can't do everything. You've got to decide what it is you're going to do. A state university of course has a broad range of responsibilities that it has to address but it doesn't have to do everything. That's why we had to close a campus like Waseca. Somehow, as the states provide less funding, you have to try to negotiate with the state the ability to focus your activities and not do everything. You have to focus on those things that are essential to the flagship university and let other parts of higher education take on the other responsibilities. That gets you into the bind of elitism, but you have to try to resolve that, because I see no other way than that kind of focusing. Then you have to try to leverage your state's investment with other resources, such as from collaboration with industry. It's a complex situation, but it has to be done that way because it is a pipe dream that we are just going to have a flow of public funding. The demands from health care and from other societal needs are such that you're probably not going to see a dramatic increase. Maybe we can stop further erosion, but I don't think we're going get back to the good old days when the state funded 100 percent or at least 75 percent of the public university. So we have to negotiate the liberty, the ability to use the other resources.

FL: Is it the responsibility of individual state and private institutions to solve the problem of access?

NH: I think it's a shared responsibility between institutions and the public. The institutions themselves cannot do it. As far as private universities are concerned, I think that's what Harvard and others are doing, to use their endowments and use differential tuition rates to further access and to be need-based in a very fundamental way. I think this is a responsibility. But it is also very much a public responsibility through the Pell Grants and through other need-based programs. And, as much as I like merit-based programs in many ways, I think that it is necessary to focus on need-based aid because that's the only way we're really going to solve the access problem. It is not only a financial matter; it is also a cultural matter. The institutions have a responsibility to try to overcome the cultural barriers that are still very strong. The expectations that are built in for certain groups mean that institutions have to reach out at an early stage to get across the message that college is possible and college may be for you.

FL: Is there any realistic hope that the states and the federal government will take on more of the responsibility of providing students from low-income families access to quality education?

NH: It doesn't look very promising at this time, either at the federal or state levels. This is because of the general financial situation, which to some extent is self-inflicted because of what I consider unreasonable tax reductions, but also because of competing needs—social security, health care, all of these things that are demands on the state treasury. We have to continue to make the strongest possible arguments while we cast about within whatever leeway we have for ways in which we can help provide that access. The whole nature of American society hinges on our ability to do that. We could become a bifurcated society with an upper class that has access to education and an uneducated or low-educated mass, and the consequences of that are horrendous to contemplate. Besides it's a betrayal of the American dream, a fundamental betrayal of that dream.

FL: Do you think that partnerships between state universities and community colleges can offer at least a partial solution to the problem?

NH: Absolutely essential. The community college movement is one of the most important things that have happened in the last fifty years.

FL: They are better as institutions year after year. At Rutgers we initiated a dual degree program and transfer agreements with all New Jersey community colleges.

NH: They are and working with them to provide transfer through systematic programs is, I think, terribly important.

FL: Now one of our favorite topics: athletics. Recent years have seen a second highly critical report by the Knight Commission and a major effort by the NCAA to reform academic regulations in order to improve student athletes' preparation for college and their progress toward degrees as well as their ultimate success in earning degrees. What else can universities and their organizations do to solve the problems of college athletics? Are these problems with us to stay?

NH: Fran, it's a juggernaut and you know it is very difficult for presidents to deal with. Athletics can be, and is in certain respects, an asset to a university. It's one of those things that an American university has that really connects the university with the public. But it has come at a horrendous cost and of course it's the big time athletics that has crept into the universities that is the reason for that. I think the only solution is that we stop being the farm team organization for football, basketball and maybe hockey. Baseball has already taken the pressure off and, in some other sports, I don't think we have much of that pressure. But it has to be possible for somebody to become a professional football player without going through college, without having to crawl through that needle's eye where many of them don't want to crawl—and get stuck. I don't know how we can solve the problem if we are going to continue to have this funnel through the university system for professional football players and basketball players, in particular. In basketball now, we have what I regard as the fortunate circumstance that some can go directly from high school to professional basketball, but I think it requires a farm team organization to really make that route effective. And I know that in football it is argued that the players have to mature and this maturation presumably is going to have to take place on a college campus. I think this just puts us in a bind we cannot get out of unless we get that safety valve of the farm team organization taking the pressure off. It's hard for individual presidents to deal with this.

FL: I'd say it's one of the toughest issues.

NH: I have noted from time to time that you can only resign once. You can break your sword once. And to control a culture that is driven by these powerful financial and other motives is terribly difficult. You have a culture that has to be monitored and watched every step of the way because judgment is not always exercised where it should be exercised. We had one of those things at Minnesota in the basketball program, where we had a full-time monitor of compliance. Nevertheless we got this terrible situation in the basketball program there, which ripened after I left but really was started when I was there. I trusted some of the people who exercised singularly bad judgment. To have a system where you have to watch people who are in responsible positions is not a good thing. It's almost insoluble.

FL: Yes, and it has such profound effect on the institution when it happens.

NH: It undermines the values on which the institution is built. But Fran, I think that NCAA rules and all of this preaching and all these admonitions go only so far. A fundamental structural change to the farm team organization in football and basketball is the only way we're going to solve the problem. That's my private position, not an official AAU position.

FL: How did you manage to make progress in improving diversity of the student body and faculty at Minnesota?

NH: In Minnesota, where the total minority population I think was 7 percent at that time, you had to have pipelines. This became controversial because some people said you should serve only your in-state population. We could not get any kind of critical mass of minority students if we relied only on in-state recruitment of minorities. So we established pipelines, especially to Chicago, for African Americans and had a pipeline to our college of agriculture from agricultural high schools in Chicago. We got some good African-American students who came to the College of Agriculture and began to build up a critical mass. We probably would never have had an African American in agriculture if it hadn't been for that pipeline. We had some success with pipelines. We did have an influx of students of Asian background because Hmong and Vietnamese and others migrated into the state and some came to the university. The Vietnamese got into the university very quickly and established themselves. They probably came out of an educated tradition in Vietnam.

FL: I note that there's a new document issued by the Department of Education on race neutral practices of increasing diversity, but in places like California, where such practices had been used, they are reportedly ineffective. Is there currently much interest from the membership of the AAU in exploring answers to the questions of legal and policy issues raised by the Supreme Court's decision on the Michigan case?

NH: There is interest. We participated actively in the Michigan case in the Supreme Court. We took part in the amicus briefs. We have also taken an interest in following up on finding out what are the alternatives that can be used within the confines of the Supreme Court decision. Several AAU universities have addressed the need for socio-economic access, not as a substitute for affirmative action but as a supplement. As we evaluate our agenda, it's one of those issues that the association will need to continue to address. We're seeking a way where we can be meaningfully engaged. It certainly is a critically important issue, not because socio-economic access will solve the racial problem, but because both the lack of access for racial minorities and the lack of access for certain socio-economic groups, both of them are a concern. It has to do with the bifurcation of American society. I think it's a very difficult issue.

FL: What do you see as the strongest forces driving the need for change in higher education during the next ten to twenty years? What are the most important changes that you expect to take place?

NH: I think the central issue is how universities can continue to play their traditional role as producers of basic knowledge and as arbiters and guarantors of knowledge and information as well as their role in liberal arts education and educating people to an understanding of civic responsibility, while at the same time they are called upon to meet legitimate demands for utilitarian applied research development and education for specific competencies that society needs. How can we do both and how can we balance them properly? I think that maintaining that balance will continue to be a major issue, especially as these utilitarian and economic development pressures continue to build. I think that is a really fundamental issue. What are the changes that are going to come? It may be that we're going to see more spinning off of highly specialized forms of research into independent research institutes. I believe in the Humboldtian philosophy of having research and scholarship as a foundation for more advanced education but maybe there are some university-based research activities that will be spun off into more autonomous research institutes. Is it desirable or not? I don't know. I think it can be workable. It may be an illusion that certain facets of very highly specialized research are going to be meaningfully attached to an educational institution. Of course, we have many different instances of separation already and it may be that this will increase. I think also that for-profit education is going to continue to have more and more of an impact on public and private not-for-profit education. I think we're going see more and more programs that educate for specific competencies.

FL: More of the University of Phoenix kind.

NH: Yes. I think we're going to see more for-profit organizations offering that kind of training program and perhaps also digging more deeply into professional education, partly because there is interest in paying tuition for those kinds of programs. Probably those two trends, the independent research institute and the for-profit sector spinning off will make the funding of the university more difficult because research and professional education are two things that can generate resources for the university and can cross- subsidize other activities.

FL: Is there anything that I have missed that you would like to discuss?

NH: I think that you have asked awfully good questions based on your profound insight and experience. The only thing I can think of that we have not touched on is the international dimension. It is of course enormously important today. As you well know, all of our universities have a network of international contacts ranging from undergraduates coming here from other countries and our efforts to send our own undergraduates abroad to the enormous dependence we have on international graduate students as teaching assistants, graduate assistants, research assistants, post doctoral fellows, plus, of course, our international research collaboration. We have a whole set of issues here. How can we ensure the continuation of that flow of talent and contacts under the new security conditions? How can we continue to get more Americans into especially critical areas in mathematics and science, while we also encourage this international flow of talent and scholars? And are there new ways in which we can collaborate and compete with institutions internationally? There is a lot of collaboration among AAU universities as well as fierce competition among them. Even in the corporate world you see collaboration and competition in a kind of symbiotic relationship. Universities are in the same situation. Can we continue to expand to our own benefit such collaboration and competition on a worldwide scale? That's the only thing I can think of that we haven't touched on.

The AAU is involved in exploring what the role of AAU might be. This is why I'm going to interact with the League of European Research Universities, which was established after our international convocation in 2001. We recently had a meeting at Berkeley of the Group of Eight, which is a group of eight research universities in Australia, and we're exploring further collaboration with that group. I was in Berlin a few weeks ago at a meeting with the German Rectors' Conference. The trick is to be able to associate with research universities to get that commonality of interest that we have within AAU and that we potentially have with the League of European Research Universities and with the Group of Eight, rather than getting into organizations that have an enormous span of interests, where the AAU's specific agendas are only minor portions of the overall agenda. We are exploring to what extent AAU can serve as a broker and convener and possibly even tackle, with certain organizations in other countries, some of the specific issues that we face, especially issues related to security. Another concern, of course, are the new conditions created after 9/11 and the effects that strictures of security have on research and education, including visa regulations and other security-related regulations that have to do with select, potentially harmful, biological agents and with access of foreign nationals. The post 9/11 agenda is important not only in this international dimension but also as a force that is imposing itself on the university, including the civil liberties issues involved. It has been suggested that student concern over the civil liberties impact of security measures could be the next campus protest issue.

Shirley Ann Jackson

Shirley Jackson was appointed the eighteenth president of Rensselaer Polytechnic Institute in July of 1999. Prior to assuming the presidency, she chaired the U.S. Nuclear Regulatory Commission, a post she assumed in 1995. In that position she led the agency in the initiation of a planning, budgeting, and performance management system, introduced risk-informed regulation, developed a new reactor oversight process, and a license renewal procedure for reactors. She also led the international community in forming the International Nuclear Regulators Association and served as the first chairman of the INRA, leading officials from the United States, Canada, France, Germany, Spain, Sweden, the United Kingdom, and Japan in the examination of nuclear safety issues.

A theoretical physicist, Jackson earned her bachelor's degree and her Ph. D. from the Massachusetts Institute of Technology. She worked as a research scientist at AT&T Bell Laboratories from 1976-1991, leaving it in 1991 to serve as a professor of physics at Rutgers University. Prior to her professorial appointment, she had served as a member of the Rutgers Board of Governors.

At Rensselaer, she has led the institution in the development of a strategic plan that is linked to a performance-based planning and budget process, created a new senior leadership team, instituted new enrollment management approaches, and enhanced research with investments in biotechnology, information technology, nanotechnology, and other key fields. She has also initiated a building program that includes a Center for Biotechnology and Interdisciplinary Studies (which opened in 2004), an Experimental Media and Performing Arts Center, and athletic facilities, including a basketball arena, and a natatorium In fund raising, she has secured a $360 million unrestricted gift and launched a campaign with a goal of $1 billion.

Among her other notable accomplishments, Jackson has served as president of the American Association for the Advancement of Science and chaired its board, is a member of the National Academy of Engineering, a fellow of the American Academy of Arts and Sciences and of the American Physical Society, a life member of the M.I.T. Corporation (the university's governing board), and a trustee of Georgetown University and of the Brookings Institution, as well as an executive committee member of the Council on Competitiveness. She is also a member of the Board of Directors of the New York Stock Exchange, the Board of Regents of the Smithsonian Institution, and the Council on Foreign Relations.

Francis Lawrence: You have had a varied career as a scientist and a top-level administrator. At MIT, you were a student leader and the first African-American woman to earn a Ph.D. at that university. You went on to become a leading research physicist at Bell Labs. At Rutgers University, you became a member of the Board of Governors, a post you relinquished when you became a Rutgers faculty member. President Clinton appointed you to chair the U.S. Nuclear Regulatory Commission. Now you have entered yet another phase of your career as the eighteenth president of Rensselaer. It would be interesting to know what you regard as your first leadership position,

SJ: It is a question of how one defines leadership. In the context in which we are talking today, it might be formal leadership positions, but I have always believed that one leads in a variety of ways in a variety of circumstances. It can include mentoring young students and I did that, particularly at Bell Labs. We had a number of summer programs targeting women and underrepresented minorities in order to get them into science and engineering and encourage them to get Ph.D.s: I did that. I also was elected in my professional society, the American Physical Society, to the Governing Council. I chaired a number of committees and I continue to do things of that nature. As you might remember, I was a founding member of the New Jersey Commission on Science and Technology and I was one of the four public members who are private citizens. I was a co-chair of the Scientific Fields Committee, or vice chair of the Scientific Fields Committee. So I did a lot of committee-based governance, collegial leadership, early on.

FL: That is an excellent description of several ways to exercise leadership. Even though we are focusing these questions on leadership in higher education, you and I both feel that people in every field can and should develop their leadership skills at many levels.

SJ: For instance, I chaired the Physics Selection Committee, for the Council for the International Exchange of Scholars, which is the committee that made the main recommendations on Fulbright Scholars for a couple of years. That is all part of this process.

FL. Could you sketch your family background and your education and talk about their influence in shaping your development as a leader?

SJ: I grew up in Washington, D.C. in a family with my mother and father and three siblings. My brother, who was the youngest, actually passed away twenty years ago and I have two sisters, one older and one younger. My father was a postal worker in Washington, D.C. He worked his way up from being a letter carrier to being the superintendent of all of the vehicle operations for the post office in Washington, D.C. My mother essentially worked as a social worker. She was a caseworker in the Department of Human Services in Washington, so she worked for the city government. My father did not go to college. My mother did: she graduated. She actually taught for a short time before she went to work in Newark, New Jersey, in a factory during the war. But both of my parents believed very strongly in education and doing well in school and the value of education and its enabling capability. My parents, my mother in particular, were involved very much in the PTA and things of the school. My mother, in fact, went to high school. My mother was orphaned by the time she was thirteen. She was the youngest and her siblings took care of her, in particular her oldest sister. There were no high schools for Negroes in the part of Virginia in which they lived. So her siblings pooled their resources and sent her to a boarding school.

I am a child of transition: that is what I call myself. I think two events coalesced in the fifties that had a big effect on my subsequent development and career. The first was the Brown versus the Board of Education decision, whose fiftieth anniversary, as you know, we are celebrating this year, with lots of questions being asked about progress. The other was the Sputnik launch in 1957, which riveted the nation's attention on the space race, but really it was a scientific race with the Soviets. Because of that, the curriculum in many schools shifted to give more emphasis to science and math. Special programs were created to encourage people to study science in particular. Washington, D.C., coming out of the integration of the public schools following the Brown decision, created a tracking system. One was tested in the sixth grade and my class was the first one tested. It was essentially an IQ test and, depending upon how one did, one was placed in one of four tracks. I ended up in the accelerated track, called the honors track. That meant that I finished high school, the standard college prep curriculum, a year early and spent my senior year taking what today are AP courses and some college level courses. I was my high school's valedictorian and went off to MIT with two scholarships, one from Martin Marietta Corporation, which is now part of Lockheed Martin, and the other from a Masonic Lodge, Prince Hall Masons, which was the Washington branch chapter of a national black Masonic Lodge.

FL: Your parents played significant roles in your formation. Were there others who inspired you and served as your mentors?

SJ: Growing up in Washington, I had as teachers some unique women, African American primarily, who were good, well educated. I subsequently learned they were especially chosen to teach when the schools were integrated because they had certain backgrounds. They were actually uprooted from other parts of the country to come into the D.C. school system to be the first teachers in the integrated schools. They were women who, if they had been my age or of our era, may have been classic scholars. One of them was a mathematician who was my math teacher for three years running. There was also an economics teacher, a Latin teacher, and others. Two of them are still living and they had a very big effect, particularly my math teacher. Let me tell you how they had an effect. The effect had to do with the rigor, the intellectual depth, not bothering to do something if one is not going to try to be excellent at it, and their being very demanding. They were demanding of us, the students, and expected us to be demanding of ourselves. They also spent a lot of time talking about what it meant to go to college, what one could expect in the larger world, and talking about world events. Even though we were nominally having a Latin class, my Latin teacher would try to relate some of the stories we translated and read in Latin to world events. That was easier, obviously, for my economics teacher. My math teacher just introduced us to the beauty of mathematics and what it could do and was probably one of my primary influences among my teachers. My parents and this group of teachers I had beginning in middle school, but especially in high school, were great influences on me.

FL: What do you remember as the challenges that you faced as you became president of Rensselaer?

SJ: Rensselaer, as you may know, is the oldest technological university in America. It certainly is the oldest private technological university, having been founded in 1824, and had a great legacy. Some of the great builders of this country are Rensselaer alumni. It was founded to educate those who applied science to the common purposes of life. Because of that, it has always had a strong focus in engineering. If you look at it, it matches up in terms of some of the basic areas with schools like MIT or Carnegie Mellon, particularly when it was the Carnegie Institute of Technology. And it was always known as being innovative in terms of how it educated undergraduates in particular. That came out of the vision of the first head of school, a gentleman by the name of Amos Eaton, who helped to found Rensselaer with Steven Van Rensselaer. I'm sounding like a president, but this has had an effect on me. It has had different kinds of leaders over the years, but when I got there in 1999, there was only one president who people were talking about. That was George Lowe, who had been in charge of the Apollo Program to put man on the moon and was a Rensselaer alum, had been president for eight years and died in office in 1984. When I came in 1999, the school had had some financial challenges. It even had to have layoffs and voluntary separation programs for faculty. What I felt needed to happen was that we had to build a strong leadership team and stabilize the university, obviously improve its financial operations, and then begin to rebuild, but as a technological university and not to have it just remain as undergraduate centric as it was. Although it had always offered graduate degrees, masters' and Ph.D. degrees, it had moved away from that over a fifteen-year period and its reputation had suffered over those years. I felt I had several things to do, to do some very specific things with respect to finances, with respect to overall operational process and procedures, but more importantly to get people to look forward and not look back.

FL: That gave the university good direction from a president coming in with a clear sense of where the issues were. A quick personal question: what effects do the role and demands of the presidency have on your family life and how do you maintain a balance?

SJ: What balance? Well, it is hard, but there were two things that saved me. One is that our son was going off to college the year I began my presidency at Rensselaer, which meant that he was off, and so was I, not that he did not still need us, but it is a different kind of degree of attention on a day-to-day basis. The second is that my husband also is a physicist. At that time he was still working at Lucent Technology, the Bell Labs, which is where we met. And because of that, because we met there and I was a physicist when we met, he was always accustomed to the fact that I had my career. So we have always shared; we have needed to share things. He supported my decision to go and be the chairman of the Nuclear Regulatory Commission. In that case I was commuting from Washington. I would be there all week and at home on the weekends, primarily going to swim meets. Our son was a swimmer and captain of the swimming team.

In a certain sense, I never had a life to start with, particularly in being chairman of the U.S. Nuclear Regulatory Commission. But the real answer to your question is that I have an extraordinary husband and because we have at least had careers that have a similar route, he has understood how I worked and had to work. Then we were blessed that our child was healthy, well adjusted, and did well. And it just happened that when I started the presidency, he was going to college. I was actually named president in December of 1998, when I was in my last year as chairman of the NRC. I had been asked to continue as chairman, to serve another term, but I decided that I had made a contribution and it was time to move on. When I was asked to be the president of Rensselaer, I did say to the board that I could not start until the following July. First, because I was still in that last year as chairman and felt I had to fulfill my obligation to the President by serving out my term as chairman, and second because our son was in his senior year of high school and I was not going to move. They agreed, so I started in July. That was how it happened that my going there was essentially coincident to his graduation from high school.

FL: Timing is everything isn't it? What did each of your internal constituencies, governing board, faculty, students, staff, alumni, expect of you as you came in? When you are the new person coming on campus, everyone wants a piece of you today.

SJ: That is true. The board made it clear that they were bringing me in because I had high-level experience in government. They were hoping that I could use the leadership experience and prominence from that to help elevate the university, as they say, to take it to the next level. The faculty were hoping the same thing, but I think theirs translated into the hope that my prominence would help people appreciate the university and therefore help them, as well as help raise money. Everybody was very clear about that. It is not clear what the students' expectations were, other than the fact that they wanted the president to care about them, but also they were excited about having this person that everybody was fussing about. The alumni are interesting. Unless the new president is a graduate of the institution or has been there all the time as one of the faculty or as a provost, I think the alums are more inclined to wait and see. They were not quite sure what to make of me because I was so different from previous Rensselaer presidents in all ways, obvious and less obvious.

FL: How do you manage to address the conflicting expectations that these groups often have? They all think their demands are eminently reasonable and, from their point of view, of course, they are.

SJ: It was interesting having been chairman of the NRC before being president of Rensselaer. They are a nice isomorphic match. A government agency has career civil service and the professional career civil servants are like the counterpart of tenured faculty, so they're pretty empowered. In addition, in the government you have to deal with the Congress and the White House, because it is the president who has appointed you. Then an agency such as a regulatory agency has to deal with the public, with those who regulate the licensees, and the media, the high media. One has to balance the demands of those constituencies and do the right thing. I managed sometimes conflicting expectations by being clear on what my own expectations were of myself, of what people should expect from me and clear, from the beginning, about the direction that I was going to try to take the university, that I intended to take it, and not be namby-pamby, not waffle, not say one thing to one group and another to another group. Otherwise one gets torn apart and one cannot do that.

FL: That is a very good lesson in preemptive conflict resolution. You talked about organizational structure earlier, but how did you recruit and structure your leadership team?

SJ: I believe in the last word in your question, namely team. There had been some history of some people going around the president to the board and some history of people in conflict about what it meant to be an administrator and administrative leader versus being a faculty member or in some other position at the university. I had two key principles. One was that the group would operate as a team and that was how I structured it. I will explain more about that. And the second was that there were not going to be any end runs. Now when I say structured it that way, my model is not the COO model where the provost is the COO. That is very different in most universities I know. My model is closer to what one might call the Executive Officers' Group. The key individuals are the provost, the vice president for student life, the vice president for research, because I had a strong research agenda for the university, and the CFO. What I said from the beginning, in my inaugural address, was that students are the reason we exist as a university at all, our raison d'être, faculty are the academic heart of the university, and staff are the great enablers, so everybody matters. That was a key focus of mine, everybody matters, and I have espoused the term communiversity. I do not know where the word came from or where I may have seen it, but for me it meant a university as a community and the university being part of the larger community which exists.

FL: So your administrative structure is different than it was in the prior administration.

SJ: The previous president had what he called a president's council consisting of all of the VPs, the provost, and all of the deans. I separated the deans and I had a president's cabinet that consisted of these vice presidents and the provost. Two of the key new positions created as university officers, with the support of the board, were the vice president for research and a vice president for human resources. The latter had been under the administration division before then, but I wanted to make sure people understood that I meant what I said, that people matter. The university had been using external counsel exclusively, so I asked the board to create the position of secretary of the institute and general counsel. We hired the university's first permanent general counsel. Otherwise it was a question of changing some positions. My provost is new, the secretary of the institute and general counsel had done legal work for the university, but I brought him in from the outside, the vice president for human resources was a new position and a new person. The vice president for research had been away at the National Science Foundation for a couple of years, so I brought him back. I also moved one person laterally and some people left.

FL: Did you have this particular model in mind, short of knowing every position you wanted to change? As you went in, did you have a general idea of the way you wanted to structure it?

SJ: I think I have been blessed with one thing. I have always been able to read a situation pretty rapidly. I do a lot of homework and reading, trying to understand the history and culture and what is happening and so on before I get there, but I sized it up fast. The model was driven by my fundamental belief about what was important and necessary. What I mean by that is, if I believe that students are the raison d'être, then I cannot elevate one essential part of the university over the other: I have to have the vice president for student life and the provost as key players. I also knew that it was important to strengthen and rebuild the research mission and that no president is going to get along without a chief financial officer and treasurer. There had been some particular personnel issues, some fairly serious ones. That is why I moved the human resources function out from under the vice president for administration and gave him the vice presidential rank. It has made a tremendous difference.

FL: How did you formulate the vision for the future of the institution?

SJ: Again, I like to be a student of the history of an institution. I spent time at Rensselaer in the six months between the time I was named and when I started. I met with every existing vice president, every dean, plus some key faculty leaders, chair of the faculty and other faculty members, as well as some of the other people who had interviewed me. What struck them about me was that while they interviewed me, I was interviewing them. Once a month I would go to the university and people would come to see me. I had them tell me how they were organized, why they were organized that way, what the current situation was, and what they saw as the key challenges. I took all that and read the university's history, trying to understand why people were so focused on George Low. Between George Low and me, there had been three presidents and two acting presidents (one of the presidents had also been the acting president before he became the president). I felt that the institution needed to recalibrate itself, to look forward not back, to look up not down, that it had a lot of inherent strengths and very brilliant people, but they did need it to come together and move ahead. I felt, based on what the board had charged me with doing, that it was my job to move it into the top tier, so I formulated a vision that Rensselaer was going to become a top tier, world class technological research university with global reach and global impact. And, in so doing, it would live up to its history and the early legacy that it had been given.

FL: Were there any strategies that you used to communicate or to create buy-in by the different parts of the community, internal as well as external?

SJ: I know you are probably going ask me later about planning, but actually the two things go together for me. Many presidents, when they start, spend the first year or two getting to know everybody, the various constituencies, faculty, staff, students, alums, and community people. I felt two things. First, in a certain sense, I felt that de facto I had done a lot of that. I decided to use the planning process itself to get to know the university and for the university to get to know me and to get to know itself better. That required structuring a very complex strategic planning process, but that was what we did and I would be happy to describe it, if you are interested.

FL: I'm very interested.

SJ: It was really done in four parts. I had a leadership retreat with the vice presidents and the deans within weeks of when I got to the university. In fact I had to cut short a Harvard seminar for new presidents that I went to, in order to get back to my leadership retreat at Rensselaer. I got people to let their hair down and talk about the issues. I gave them feedback on the things they told me and what I had read. But the key steps were first, in my inaugural address, I laid out the vision, including putting certain markers down in terms of things that I felt we had to do. The second was that we created and initiated a document drawing these key things and markers from my inaugural address, plus things I had learned over the summer. We also laid out boundary conditions and an actual time line for getting the plan done. The third step was a very complicated planning process that occurred in three orthogonal directions, and I will explain what that means. I formed a steering committee heavily weighted with the faculty, but including staff from other parts of the university. That steering committee was chaired by the acting provost. The job of the steering committee was to have a series of public workshops where the rule of the road was that the workshops would be focused on each of the portfolios, a portfolio being an academic department or a major cross-university program (e.g., we have a program on IT, information technology), or a key administrative office. The rule was that the portfolio owner, meaning the given dean, vice president, or unit leader would not lead that session, preferably wouldn't attend and there would be an open discussion. Everybody was asked to answer the same five questions. The questions were, in each thing that you do, what is the intellectual core and if it is not purely academic, what is the core? Is it important and why? And the answer to why it was important could not be simply because you had always done it. The second question assuming you have answered the first, was: are we in a leadership position? Leadership was defined not just in terms of rankings but really having impact and being able to prove that. The third was: if we are not in a leadership position, do we have underlying strength such that, with the right focus and investment, we can be in a leadership position in a short period of time? The fourth, irrespective of the answers to the first three, was: are there certain things that are so vital and so important that we must do them even if we have no presence today? I had already posited one such thing, which was the area of biotechnology. And the fifth question was always the hardest one. What are we willing to give up, totally transform, or walk away from in order to create a platform for change? These twenty-some workshops, one chaired by the steering committee, occurred over a few months' span and were very intense. That was what we called the horizontal direction. The vertical direction was that each portfolio owner within his or her school or administrative division went after the same five questions with his or her own people. So it crosscut the horizontal, a vertical cut. Then the orthogonal was that we brought in some high end folks from the outside to look at us, particularly in the academic and research areas, but also certain administrative functions, in order to give us external assessments, their views of our strengths and weaknesses, and to give us their opinions on what it would take to move ahead. The external came as independent reports to me, each of the portfolio owners did a portfolio assessment structure around the questions, and the steering committee distilled all of the public workshop inputs into a series of key strategic issues that had to be addressed by the university. I divided the cabinet into the writers and the readers. The writers were (I am always consistent) the provost and the vice president for student life. And the readers were everybody else, because they had developed those portfolios. They started writing and we got a professional writer to help. All of this was done according to the schedule and the initiating document. We started this process October 1 (my inauguration had been on September 24) and by the middle of December we had the first draft of the plan done. Then we sent it out to all of our alums for whom we had addresses, key leaders in the community, including certain politicians, and industrial executives who worked with the university, and sent it to all the students. Everybody got it in the mail, but we also put it on the web. We posed some questions that we wanted people to answer for us relative to the plan, but they could say anything they wanted to say. Then the steering committee's job was to take all of these inputs. We put it out for comment for sixty days. It was originally to be forty-five, but we stretched it out. By the middle of February, the task before us was to have distilled all of those inputs into a series of recommendations as to how the plan should be changed. We did that, and then we rewrote the plan in a second draft. Following that, we had what we called the structured reviews where, in person, I would go to meet each of the groups—the key executives, the students, the faculty, staff groups and some outside people, as well as the politicians, the Rensselaer Alumni Association Board, and the alumni. I was there, but not in order to run the meeting. The meetings were run by the acting provost and the scribe was the vice president of student life. I was there to give them feedback on things that were pretty well formed and what was not about to change. Now you could say, "Where was the board all this time?" With the support and help of the chair of the board, I got the board to agree to a certain way of proceeding. The board had fallen off having executive committee meetings between board meetings, so the chairman reinstated those. A lot of the standard business got done in those executive committee sessions, so that when we had the board meetings, which occur four times a year, we would dispense pretty quickly with the standard board stuff. Then we would spend the bulk of the meeting on the planning and where it was going, what things were emerging, what were some of the key issues and so on. When we put out the first version of the plan, I had the board agree that they would comment on it as individuals, not as a board, because it was coming to them in the end for their review and approval anyway. They agreed to that. We had a big retreat in February of my first year. We brought in outside people who had the second draft plan and laid it on the line about Rensselaer: what it looked like, and where we were. At that point the board was ready to vote on it and I said, "Not yet. We still have this final structured review." In the interim, they did a straw vote, saying, "We approve the plan." At the same time, I reminded them that we had to get the final refinement. That was submitted to them in mid-April of my first year and it was unanimously approved by them at the meeting. We have been off to the races ever since.

FL: That is an impressive process. Did you link this strategic plan into a financial plan?

SJ: Absolutely. We have the whole performance-based planning and budget process that we have instituted since I have been there. We do every year what we call performance plans and they are structured to achieve the Rensselaer plan. This forces a rank ordering of everything, even new initiatives, against existing ones. It's funded according to the rank order. Extra largesse is allotted as a function of how well people have achieved their goals. The leadership team is evaluated in relation to their performance against the plan.

FL: Well, in the light of this outstanding planning success, my last question on this area has to do with the less happy aspects of change. Sometimes when you make change, you do not make friends. Do you have descriptions of critical incidents you would like to share, along with the way that you were able to handle them?

SJ: Interestingly enough, when I first met with the key executives, they had a certain vision of what they thought Rensselaer was and they were just pitching away at the plan. I finally told them, "You know, it either hangs together or it does not." The other challenging group was the alumni association. They had a different vision. I was positing research. What people worried about a lot was research versus teaching, so we had to talk through that.

We made a big change in our graduate tuition and student support policy about two years ago that caused a big brouhaha and there are still people who have some neuralgia about it. What it did was to put more onus on the faculty to support their graduate students. You know the support was not going to come just from centrally provided funds, but rather from competitive peer-reviewed, externally funded research contracts with research assistantships built into them for the graduate students. That is what research universities do, particularly in the sciences and engineering. That was a big issue.

FL: Monitoring progress, assessment, celebrating success: how do you monitor and track outcomes and progress on your goals and how do you reinforce and celebrate success?

SJ: We build metrics into our performance plans every year and we do quarterly roll ups to look at where we are relative to those metrics. You asked me earlier if we attached budgetary considerations to the plan and we absolutely do. We actually break our plans down into activities and we have activity-based budgets that are costed by activity. We monitor the expenditures versus accomplishments of certain goals. The metrics are both internal ones, in terms of relating to whether you did what you said you were going to do, but they also have external benchmarks that relate to our ranking and how we compare to others on the outside. All of that is part of this quarterly roll-up. We still have the retreat every year with the Board of Trustees (that probably is harder in a public university system). At the retreat we present the complete plan for the board every year. The person in charge of each portfolio presents a summary of his or her plans. The board gets big thick plans with each portfolio. We also send to the board an executive summary of a list of the key initiatives and a set of power point graphs that lay out the key elements of the plan and what each portfolio manager says he or she will deliver. We do that to make the board hold our feet to the fire, but it also helps the board to stay focused.

FL: The ability to hold a retreat of that kind is a great advantage. Rutgers is constrained by New Jersey's open public meetings act, so our Board of Governors can't meet in a retreat to talk about anything that pertains to university business. That is unfortunate.

SJ: Rensselaer's retreat is just the board and the cabinet. We have the deans hooked up by video conferencing. It works extremely well because people can let their hair down and get into various things. We also have a leadership retreat every summer with the internal leadership team. We try to look at what's happened in the past year, the good, the bad and the ugly. We examine what we have learned and, looking into the next year, what are the risks we see and how those risks relate to the risks overall for the university. We view all of it in relation to the Rensselaer plan. So we have a holistic leadership retreat, but we also have metric based and benchmark based performance reviews as well. As I said each dean and each vice president's actual performance review is linked to the plan, so when it comes time to consider them for merit increases or anything of that kind, they are judged according to goals that are linked to the plan.

FL: Could we talk now about external constituencies? What importance have you placed on the role of the institution in the community?

SJ: Very high, Fran, because of two things. I was a student of the formation of the New Jersey Commission on Science and Technology that had as its vision building strength in infrastructure in the four research universities in New Jersey, the two publics and two privates—Rutgers, New Jersey Institute of Technology, Princeton, and Stevens Institute, as well as the University of Medicine and Dentistry of New Jersey (UMDNJ)—in areas that were deemed important to New Jersey's economy and important for keeping the major enterprises in the state. That was the basis for the formation of the Center for Advanced Biotechnology and Medicine, a center for fiber optics, and others.

FL: The Center for Ceramics Research and CABM (the Center for Advanced Biotechnology and Medicine) are both right here on the Rutgers campus, in cooperation with UMDNJ.

SJ: That is right. These things were big deals. A microbiology lab was built at Princeton, an informatics center that was distributed among the schools. There was a Center for Hazardous Substance Management at NJIT. It went on and on. That led me to the two definitions of community. One has to do with universities as fundamental economic drivers in a state, that whole coupling in that way that the Commission on Science and Technology was meant to facilitate, I thought was visionary. A lot of states were doing various things, but the way New Jersey structured it, the amount of funds that were committed I thought, for the time, was significant, and the public-private partnership that went into it as well. The second thing was observing the impact as Rutgers grew and I was here. I was involved when Rutgers became part of the AAU. I saw the impact of the university's growth and development on New Brunswick, coupled with the decision of Johnson and Johnson to remain headquartered here. As you know, one need only look around to realize the fact that Rutgers has made large investments in the community. Among them, I remember building that combination residence hall and retail space across from the train station. Those are big commitments to the city.

FL: Yes, the Easton Avenue Apartments that you mention were built during my tenure. You may not be acquainted with another big project, the edifice in downtown New Brunswick that we built for the School of Planning and Public Policy together with the Mason Gross Visual Arts Department. We have also planned a new Rutgers Police Department facility on George Street and Commercial.

SJ: In the mid-eighties up to mid-nineties, I believe that New Brunswick's population was about 50,000. The population of Troy, New York is 49,000 and Rensselaer is the game in town. Unlike New Brunswick, Troy does not have much in the way of a real industrial base, so the university is a key driver of whatever will go on in the city. So communiversity then meant and continues to mean that the university has to be a partner with the city to bring about a renaissance, not only at Rensselaer but in the City of Troy, which was once a great industrial city. It sits on the Hudson, it is at the northern-most navigable point on the Hudson. It has what is called NYSSTAR. New York State has a New York State Science and Technology and Research Organization. It was not quite structured the way the New Jersey Commission on Science and Technology was structured, but there are programs that provide support to the universities in various areas. So we formed a strong partnership with the State Senate Majority leader, who is originally from Troy and has a very great interest in Troy and in Rensselaer County, where the university sits. We have things ranging from neighborhood revitalization programs, where we actually give people grants to fix up their homes or to address safety or code violation issues, to where we have actually done streetscape improvements putting in new signal lights, sidewalks, and lighting. We are training the fire department in biohazardous materials management, a training program for entry-level people. So the answer is that we think that the role of Rensselaer in the community is critical, because our destiny is inextricably linked to that city and the region.

FL: Have there been any major groups outside the university that you have worked with?

SJ: We have worked with the other universities in the greater capital region. We worked with the state legislators, particularly, as I said, the state senate majority leader, the speaker of the assembly, our own assemblyman and the State Senate. We have actually worked with our state's U.S. senators, Clinton and Schumer, relative to their vision for the economic revitalization of upstate New York. We have worked with various community-based groups, particularly in Troy. We have worked with the Chamber of Commerce and we are involved with what is called the Council for Economic Growth. We were part of the formation of a Business Higher Education Round Table that brings together presidents of the universities in the area and key CEOs of businesses in the area. So we have worked with all of these as well as with our neighbors, in neighborhood groups.

FL: How do you allocate your time and what are your top priorities? Your job is a seven-day-a-week job: how do you handle your scheduling?

SJ: I think that the key elements are always there, but the actual allocation among them can vary, depending upon what there is to do. I think one has to ensure that the campus is safe and functioning well, but that requires having the right leadership team and delegating to them, having high expectations and holding them accountable. I would say that I have a very good leadership team. That helps with the day-to-day activities. The second element (this is not in the order of priority, you know) is fundraising. A lot of my time, and increasingly more of my time, is spent in cultivating leadership gifts. The third, which relates to the second, is representing the university to the outside world, particularly in other arenas, with other major university presidents. We recently opened an office in Washington D.C. In the corporate arena, I have gotten involved with corporate boards and even the New York Stock Exchange Board. I do those because they link to what Rensselaer is about. For a technological university, the corporate linkages are even more important in some ways than they are for other universities. I am just very organized. I get good support and I delegate.

FL: You are truly the university's representative to the external world. You are out soliciting major gifts; you are on the road doing the work of Rensselaer. Do you have someone in your administration who stands in for you, doing the day-to-day business, or do you still have a great deal of contact and stay involved in decision-making while you are on the road?

SJ: It's both. I spent a lot of time at the beginning of our discussion talking about the team and each team member knows what he or she has to do. I also expect them to operate as a team, checking in with each other and they do that. I do delegate a significant part of responsibilities when I am away to the provost and to the Secretary of the Institute and General Counsel, but I also have a chief of staff whose job it is to stay in touch with all of the vice presidents and what is going on on the campus. She travels as well. In addition, in these days and times, it is possible to be a lot more tethered electronically, cell phones and PDAs, faxes and emails, so I am in touch every day whenever I am traveling. But I expect people to go ahead and make the decisions that are theirs to make. In addition, I always assign delegated authority when I am out. It is typically delegated to the provost, but I can vary it, assigning it to the general counsel at times.

FL: Whether at home or away, of course you have the ultimate responsibility for the institution. Every colleague I've known has experienced planned and unplanned events that escalate into time-consuming crises. Have you gone through any that you would like to share, along with your advice about how handling crisis management?

SJ: The nation-wide crisis that every president faced was 9/11. That was a crisis, not only from the point of view of worrying about terrorism, but being in New York State. We had a number of students who were from New York City, with families there, and at least one of our alums perished at the World Trade

Center. In addition, Rensselaer throughout its history has had a strong link with the military, so people were very affected by the deaths and by what happened at the Pentagon. I think that in such a case one really has to step in to assume a role that is more of a ministering role as well as leadership through ˙crisis. That taught me how much one has to be prepared to do that. Then we have had various eruptions: we have had rape on the campus; we have had students die. To me those are the hardest things. We have memorial services for each student, as well as an overall one for all who passed away in a given year. I don't know if you call them crises: these are life's challenges. We have had TB scares and things like that. But again, as I told you, much of what happens originates with the students and so we put a lot of attention on the whole student life area.

I think many people do not appreciate—and this is the great difference between online universities and universities like yours and mine—that we have a resident population of students. It is not like the University of Phoenix. Our resident university students have a lot of attendant issues and a lot of crises can arise as a consequence of that. They can sometimes escalate to something really big and embarrassing that has the potential to besmirch the institution, but the small ones hurt as well. With 9/11, of course, we had the whole issue of being part of the national crisis.

FL: How would you define leadership or, in a narrower context, what do you believe to be the most important qualities for a university president today?

SJ: To me, leadership begins with caring about individuals and the institutions that enable individuals to do things. That can be true whether one is working in the university or government and industry. Then caring has to be translated into a vision for what the institution should be and can become in the context of an increasingly complex and difficult world. The vision thing does not mean anything if you cannot make it happen. I call myself a visionary and a pragmatist. Those are what I would say are key leadership qualities. Caring about people is central, because universities are inherently very personal institutions, even when they are large. You have to deal with people and their idiosyncrasies, but you must ignite them. That is where the vision comes in, getting people to ignite. You know it is like herding cats. I call it the Brownian walk. [Brownian movement is a term from physics used to describe the irregular movement of particles in gas or liquid, caused by the bombardment of the particles by the molecules of the medium.] But what you want is a directed Brownian walk, so you have got to have something to try to get people moving along. About the Rensselaer plan, our strategic plan, I say that we are generally moving northeast, That is where the road is going, but there can be all kinds of bouncing around: back and forth, up and down, side to side. Still generally, that is the drift and what the president tries to do is to affect that drift velocity, to keep it moving along.

When we set out with the plan, it was like setting sail across the North Atlantic. We knew where we wanted to go, but we were building the ship, assembling the crew, and defining the roles all at the same time. That is pretty deep, when the icebergs are all around you in the ocean as you go. A president has to be a visionary and a pragmatist to really know how to make it happen. A lot of people can talk a good game about vision, a good game about strategic plans, and hire consultants. It is ironic that we never hired a consultant to do our strategic plan: we did it ourselves. A lot of it I envisioned; I had learned a lot from my previous experiences. Then we said we want to reduce this plan to real action to create performance or operational plans. So we hired a consultant and had him come to our leadership retreat the summer after the plan had been approved by the board. What he wanted us to do was to re-do the strategic plan. I think that is what all consultants know how to do—the vision thing, getting you to write down something. I do not believe most of them could ever have carried out as complicated a strategic planning process as we did and had it come to closure. That is what I am proudest of, that we actually had it come to closure. I did not just have some wonderful group sitting off in a corner somewhere to write the plan. It really was a participatory process and that is how you get the buy-in: you have a participatory process, but you have enough structure so that you can move people along. That kind of balance, I think, is critical. Then, in addition, I think you really do have to have high integrity. Nobody is perfect but you have to try to set a high ethical standard. I think that a leader and a university president has to be consistent and not be afraid to make hard decisions. To make them and to be able to pull them off, one has to be a good communicator and communicate, communicate, communicate in order to have people, if not agree, at least understand the rationale for it. And then one has to be consistent, because if one waffles, one gets into trouble, and in the end people lose respect. One has to be a networker and one has to be an excellent fund-raiser. As Frank Rhodes, the former president of Cornell and a prodigious fund-raiser said, fundraising is really friend-raising. That is what one has to do. And one has to have excellent time management skills and have an ability to build and shape a leadership team. Let me put it in a different way, if I can, Fran. People do not like the word CEO in relation to university presidents, but the truth is a university president ends up having to be a visionary, an intellectual leader, a politician, obviously a fundraiser. I always react to that and I will explain that in thirty seconds. But actually one has to have CEO qualities because a university is a complex organization, and it is only getting more complex.

FL: Let me piggyback on that, because you have covered some really wonderful points on this whole idea of leadership and presidents. How have the role and demands of the presidency changed as you have observed our colleagues over the last decade? Has it always been the same, or do presidents assume it is different simply because they are doing it?

SJ: I think there is a core running through it that has always been the same in terms of caring, being able to minister to the needs of people in the university, being a planner, but I think what is different are the following things. I think the role is much more public than it used to be, even for private university presidents. There are so many constituencies that no longer just accept certain things, and they come with clear expectations of their own for the president and the presidency. I think the pressures are a lot greater and I think that with the advent of the Internet and new media, it is not that presidents are media stars, but they have to be a lot more media savvy than I think they were in the past.

FL: Right. The media is in their back pocket daily, whether the university is private or public.

SJ: Exactly, so I think there is a lot less personal privacy for leaders of private as well as public institutions these days. I think obviously public university presidents saw it first, but private university presidents, many of them, are getting caught up short because of how public their lives really are. Then I think there is a whole coin of the realm having to do with how prodigious a fundraiser one is.

FL: That is the badge.

SJ: That is the badge. And if one just did that, one would obviously leave a legacy of having elevated the financial foundations of the institution, and yet probably not be thought of as a particularly great president.

I find that, because the pressures are so great, fewer presidents are being national spokespersons, even when they are the presidents of the great universities. Presidents used to assume the role of thought leaders as university presidents.

FL: Possibly that has changed because the pressures that current presidents face—precisely the things you talked about—occupy their time twenty-four hours a day. But if we look at the turnover among our colleagues, the average term is now, according to the *Chronicle of Higher Education*, four to five years. Do you believe that the changes in the role that you talked about are the reason why people leave after four to five years, or are there other reasons?

SJ: I think there can be different extremes. I think one has to do with the fact that there is a lot of pressure, but I think, interestingly enough, there is another factor which you could say is positive and negative. It is a much more complex job to lead a major university and, you could argue, any university today, so the universities are looking a lot more for seasoned people. So one observation I would have is that you seem to find more presidents who have multiple presidencies. Gordon Gee was at Brown for two years and the new president of Syracuse, Nancy Cantor, was at University of Illinois for about two years, so I think there's some of that as well. I do not know how widespread it is but among our local presidents in the Capital Region, I think one is in her second, maybe her third, but certainly her second presidency. So if you fold that in, it, by definition, shortens the tenure. My anecdotal impression is that there has been a change at least among a subset of the presidents. As opposed to having this one glorious ten to fifteen, in some cases twenty-year presidency, people have multiple presidencies. The question is, is that really true and how widespread is it? That would certainly contribute to the average tenure being a lot shorter.

FL: When I think of long tenures, I think of my friend Norman Francis, the president of Xavier University in New Orleans, who is in his thirty-seventh year in the presidency of the institution. He has defined the university and done a remarkable job there. You have very largely done this already, but perhaps you could give just a short response: how would you characterize your leadership style?

SJ: That I am a visionary, but a pragmatist. That I am what you would call a strong leader, that I do set a direction. I work to set it collegially, but I do believe it is important to have a notion of what one would like to do for the university as well as what one would like to help the university do for itself. I am a planner, not a plodding type, but a visionary one. I am willing to take risks, but they are calculated risks. I care an awful lot about the people in the university. I love the students and I just wish I had more time to spend with them because, again, I believe it is important to lead in ways large and small to be able to do it successfully.

FL: Now, if you don't mind, I'd like to cover some issue-oriented questions. In respect to funding, how have you managed to keep your tuition at a level that is reasonable and allows you to attract a diverse student body, while at the same time, allows you to meet the needs of your institution? What I think is least understood, especially in the public sector, is that if you have to add new programs—you mentioned biotechnology—they are very costly.

SJ: It is going to sound repetitive Fran, but we have planned very tightly. The planning has prioritization built in, it is a forced march, and as we do that, we look to get the maximal use out of each dollar. I think in some ways this is where some private institutions may have a slight advantage over public institutions, that is, it is easier to be clear when I meet with the board in retreat, as I described, what is going to drop off the plate if something new comes on to the plate. That is something that I feel is very important, that one is always prepared to say what one is not going to do and to absolutely insist, as much as one can, on balanced budgets. That is why the prioritization is important.

FL: You must prioritize in order to attain the balance you need.

SJ: Right. If you're going to have a balance you need to ask people, not tell people but ask them, what are your highest priorities? I tell people that I don't want horizontal lists; I only want vertical lists. You decide. Do not tell me to decide, you decide, but the line is going to be drawn somewhere. So what is below the line may not happen this year. In doing that and forcing that discipline, we have moderated our tuition increases. Eighty percent of our students are on some form of financial aid and we have a pretty high discount rate. That means that a lot of our budget is still tuition-driven, although the research proportion is growing as well. That is what we did.

FL: In recent years you've seen a second highly critical Knight Commission report and a major effort by the NCAA to reform Division I athletics through a committee that I chaired until I stepped down in 2003. Most of Rensselaer's sports teams are in Division III, except men's hockey, which is Division I. But there are problems in admissions criteria for athletes even in Division III schools, as Bill Bowen's book showed us. How do we handle this; how do we solve it?

SJ: I have to get my advertisement in for Rensselaer. We do have Divison 1 men's ice hockey. We're about to elevate the women's hockey team to Division I, but we have been fundamentally a Division III school. It turns out that our student athletes have higher GPAs than the students overall, not by much, but by some. Twenty out of twenty-seven of our men's ice hockey players are on the Dean's List and twenty out of twenty-seven of the women's ice hockey players are on the Dean's List. Now how does that happen?

FL: That is unusual.

SJ: We do insist that the curriculum is pretty rigorous, even for the people who decide they want to major in management and go to business school. They still have to end up taking calculus, physics, and chemistry. We do not have any math at Rensselaer that is less than calculus. So that says something about what people have to do. There are two ways that one can deal with some of this. I know Myles Brand, and Myles is a Rensselaer alum. I have talked with him a little bit about it because this past January at the NCAA convention in Nashville, Tennessee, the Division IIII President's Council had a reform proposal on the table that would have precluded Division III schools that had one Division I sport from offering athletic grants in aid to the student athletes in that division. So we fought it. I came together with Bill Brody of Johns Hopkins, Dick Celeste of Colorado College, and a bunch of other schools and we prevailed. We actually got it overturned. We put in a substitute amendment that allowed the grandfathering to continue and allowed us in fact to offer grants in aid in an opposite sex sport as well, for gender equity. I believe that two kinds of approaches are important. They actually also relate to issues of diversity and some of the questions that arise there, although one has to be careful in what one may be trying to say. If one is serious, how does one reconcile an athletic program with a university which remains a university, not a remediation program, or an institution with an athletic program filled with students who never graduate. That is where a lot of the travesty is in some of the Division I sports. Let us just face it. Why not then go in and have two kinds of approaches to recruiting and retaining student athletes as students at the universities? One is, let us identify these kids with extraordinary athletic talent early rather than having all these scandals about how one recruits athletes to college X or college Y.

FL: Through a scouting program?

SJ: Yes. Any of these student athletes, the ones that these schools recruit, have obvious talents that show up in eight, ninth, or tenth grade. Why not invest the time and the money in creating true academies for them, perhaps primarily focused in the summer, but with supplemental work during the academic year? That would tie their ability to participate in athletics to their success in a particular kind of academic curriculum. They would have to perform at a certain level to stay eligible to participate on the athletic side of the academy: that puts them in the greatest possible position for being prepared for college level work, when that point comes. People might say, "Ah it never works," but something has got to replace the travesty, the statistics, the scandals that occur. It also gives you a time with these young people to work on them from the values point of view, as you have them summer after summer, as well as in reinforcement activities. But nobody thinks about them that way.

FL: This would be in addition to their regular high school curriculum, an academy during the summer where you offer them supplemental academic work?

SJ: Yes. Even as they have so many practices in basketball and football or tennis or golf or swimming, some portion of the day is specifically devoted— and a portion means hours, not an hour—to academic work. Young kids have a lot of energy, energy to burn, so you could do that. I would love to see somebody conduct it as a pilot. The approach is, I think, that one should think more about articulation agreements between major four-year institutions and two-year community colleges, which are pretty efficient in helping students make up for background deficiencies they may have. So if the students go through a certain program and perform at a certain level, they can come into the four-year university with some standing, maybe sophomore, to preserve their athletic eligibility so that they can play at least the full three if not four years. Now that is a five-year de facto program, but universities compile statistics on baccalaureate graduation rates based on six years and there is a reason for that. A lot of kids, even at the very best institutions, do not graduate in four years.

FL: Many students double major now. At Rutgers, a significant proportion of our graduates have double majors.

SJ: Exactly. So it takes them five years. Those are my thoughts: we ought to spend the money and the time to identify these kids. Not all of them are fully blossomed when you first see them, but you end up identifying them early enough that you have at least a couple of years to put them through a rigorous academic preparation. It is too late to say that they have to meet certain standards at the point when they're leaving high school. Given the pressures and the time they are going to spend in these athletic programs, it is a joke to think they're going to make up for a lack of academic preparation.

The other piece is that, even once they are in the university, the academy concept needs to continue through the years, so that there is academic reinforcement, because anyone who has to put in the amount of time, tension, practice, travel, and effort required to play in Division I athletics, by definition is not going to have the freedom to structure his or her time that the typical student will. At Rensselaer we have students who do an industrial co-op, which is viewed as being very important interning or apprenticeship for their later careers. We offer courses in the summer that allow them to have the opportunity to catch up with their entering class, because we view the internship as important. If we view athletics to be an important part of the college experience, both for the athlete and the larger student, alumni, and other populations, then let us restructure it in a way that makes sense. Those are my two thoughts: to identify talented athletes early on and to give them the academic support they need to prepare for and succeed in college.

FL: Given the magnitude of the problem, we need innovative solutions.

SJ: I am going to be honest with you. If I were in Myles Brand's shoes, that is what I would be doing. People might not like it but if I were he, I would give speeches on this every day, because I think it can happen. It needs some group of schools, like the Ivy League institutions and the other high-end privates, to think about it and to try to pull something like that off, because they have the flexibility to see if they can do it.

FL: How has your university responded to the criticism that research universities do not care about the undergraduate teaching. We talked a little bit about that at the beginning. You may want to add more to it.

SJ: To give you a quick answer, it is first of all by having people understand that research and teaching go hand in hand and by getting undergraduates engaged in research as an extension and a form of teaching. That is number one. Secondly it is to create clear expectations among the faculty and to reward them accordingly and ensure that no one gets tenure without having a review on teaching as well as on research.

FL: How has your institution managed to make progress in improving the diversity of the student body and faculty? Of course diversity is an even bigger issue as you look over the next decade.

SJ: I think that we still have a ways to go, but we have a number of pipeline programs, some of which we had to restructure in light of the Supreme Court decision, but we believe in early intervention, starting as early as the eighth and ninth grades. So that is number one for women and for underrepresented minorities. We do, in fact, run a version of the academies that I'm talking to you about, academies focused on kids from the capital region, from the six lowest income districts. It starts in seventh grade and runs through twelfth to ensure that they persist, that they'll be eligible for college some day. Those students who do very well in the academies come to Rensselaer. We even have a residential program in the summer for a month. Then we also have articulation agreements with certain community colleges and if they go through a certain specified program and get at least a B or a little more than a B average, then they can come to Rensselaer with at least sophomore and many of them with junior standing. These students do well here. It is not just specifically the minorities, it is any student who's not totally ready to start right into a four-year college, but this collaboration with community colleges has been working quite well.

FL: We developed a strong relationship with all nineteen community colleges in New Jersey and that has worked very well for the students and for Rutgers.

SJ: The other concern is diversifying the faculty and ensuring—this is where the VP for human resources and the provost work together—that as these searches are structured, they reflect the diversity of the pool of candidates. They have to show that they have done that before they propose any candidate to come forward to be hired. We do not set any quotas or anything like that, but we say that the pool of candidates must be reflected in the group of candidates selected for consideration. The process has to be fair. And that is again where the two administrators work in partnership.

FL: What do you feel are the most critical capital investments that you've made up to now in your years as president?

SJ: We are about to open a new Center for Biotechnology and Interdisciplinary Studies, a 218,000 square foot research facility to support our activities across the spectrum in biotechnology, bioscience, biomedical engineering, etc. We are building an experimental media and performing arts center, a 200,000 square foot facility that is considered the nexus of technology and the arts, the idea being that it is both a creativity platform and a research platform. I will give you an example. It would support high-end classical and contemporary musical performances. It will also support work in areas like acoustics, as well as in simulation, visualization, and animation, so it will be a research platform as well. It will bring researchers in engineering and science together with artists and people in the humanities and social sciences. That is getting underway now. We are building a new athletic complex on our east campus, beginning with an athletic support building and the upgrade of a number of our outdoor athletic fields. Then we are going to be building out that whole complex with a new field house for indoor sports, indoor track and field, a new basketball arena, and a natatorium. We are also systematically renovating what we have. We have renovated all the freshman residence halls and we built a new freshman residence hall as well. Now we are starting the renovation of the upper-class residence halls and we'll probably build one in addition. Moreover we have actually bought properties in the City of Troy and we have renovated those. Some of them we have put to university use, particularly targeting some of the housing to graduate students and upper-class undergraduates, but also putting some of them back into the market to help some of our neighbors to have better housing. I would say that these are some of the critical investments, as well as upgrading the information infrastructure of the campus, the fiber optic backbone and so forth.

FL: At this point of your career at Rensselaer, what do you believe will be your most significant legacy to the institution?

SJ: I think that I will have strengthened significantly the financial base of the university. I think you know that philanthropic support will have increased significantly. It already has. I think it will become a full-flowered research university. We are not trying to do everything, but to have focused excellence, so that, whatever we do, we aim to be among the best if not the best. Therefore I have certain graduate programs that are highly ranked and have actually expanded the size of the graduate school as part of that, particularly focused on Ph.D.s. I think the university will have been broadened, particularly with this focus on technology and the arts. We have a new Ph.D. program in electronic arts that has just been approved. We have one of the first Ph.D. programs in architectural science that ranges across acoustics to lighting research, to IT and design, informatics and design, to building sciences. I think we will have improved the quality of student life, particularly the undergraduate experience. We have completely restructured the first year experience, assigning deans to each class and improving the physical campus and the activities. So the university will be stronger financially and will have a real research presence, and reputation, a larger, stronger graduate school, major improvements to the physical plant, and an undergraduate program that is without peer.

FL: You have been on boards of very different universities.

SJ: Yes, I am on the board of two today.

FL: In your experience what are the differences in the way in which public and private boards function? Do you see a difference?

SJ: To some extent. Private university board members know each other better, but most private university boards are self-perpetuating boards. For public university boards, the appointments always involve a political process of one kind or another. At Rutgers, you have a complicated process through which people come up from the board of trustees and, in addition, you have people appointed by the governor who form the majority of the board of governors. In Michigan, people actually run for office to be a regent. In most states, public university boards are filled by gubernatorial appointees. One could argue that it makes them answerable to the people and it is the public university that is the state university. Private universities' criteria for board membership are laid out in the charters that the universities have from the states. They have to satisfy those criteria and the board has the same kind of fiduciary and ethical responsibilities to the institution as public boards do, but there is a lot more flexibility in some ways. Public and private universities are becoming more similar. The degree of effective public support that public universities get is a lot lower than the degree of control that exists over them out of the political process. I think ultimately those things are going to come to a head because some public universities have 30 percent or less of their effective budgets from state support.

FL: For public universities with large medical centers, that percentage is often in the teens or less.

SJ: I think the big advantage that the publics have doesn't have to do with governments, it has to do with capital projects. If you look at the physical plant of most state universities, they look pretty good. People, politicians, like to build things.

FL: Especially in the athletic area.

SJ: Especially in athletics. So I would say it is a question of flexibility that is inherent in having a self-perpetuating private board. At the same time, you know one could argue that for a true public university, the accountability should be there. I like being president of a private university.

FL: What do you see as the strongest forces driving the need for change in higher education over the next ten to twenty years? What are the most important changes that you expect to see take place?

SJ: You know there is a huge demographic shift coming in this country. What is now called the underrepresented minority, if not becoming the underrepresented majority, will certainly become the underrepresented plurality. Women and underrepresented groups together today comprise the underrepresented majority, but people are not paying a lot of attention to it, though some people are beginning to talk about it. So if we want to talk about where our future will be, who will be the lawyers who work on the cases, and (a thing I worry a lot about) who will do the science of the millennium, then we'd better deal with that issue. But buried underneath is a question that has to do with the majority as well, because part of the problem we have is that men, in many ways, get lost. People have talked about it from the point of view of white males, but actually, if you looked within minority groups, minority males don't appear in as strong numbers as minority females. So I think we have some real issues there about who we are attracting to the universities and how we will accommodate them. With those shifts are other kinds of cultural shifts as well. You know this country is becoming more diverse, not just in terms of whites, blacks and Hispanics, but folks from all kinds of backgrounds, and I am not sure that the university model is prepared to do that. The second change, I think, is the need for anytime, anywhere continuous learning. That raises a question about the role of the residential college and university. What is it we expect out of them and will they be able to serve the needs of an increasing proportion of the eighteen- to twenty-four-year olds in colleges? That ties into issues of access, affordability, and accountability. I think the question of access is going to come to a head because you have forces that relate to affirmative action or non-affirmative action being driven at the same time that the population is changing before our eyes. That is why I talked about some of these intervention strategies. We talked about it in terms of athletics, but it represents a broader set of issues. I think it is a coming perfect storm that we are going to have to reckon with. I think the financing of higher education is coming to a critical point. It is a big deal. We see it with some of these issues today of what has happened to state budgets. A question that has occurred to me is whether some public universities will become private universities because of the vicissitudes they deal with. I actually believe that private universities that do not have a certain inherent strength may not survive. That inherent strength obviously has to do with financial strength, broad appeal, and intellectual capacity. I think that universities are going to continue to be expected to be engines of economic growth and development. That puts enormous pressures on what does an administrator do, what are the expectations of the faculty, how do presidents lead, and what are the kinds of ethical questions that arise when one has an economic agenda attached to the university, which started with the fundamental educational social growth agenda. And how then does one balance the focus on the student with all of these other enterprises that relate to the other things that the university is being asked to do?

FL: The issue of public education concerns me. For years now we've heard that money needs to be pumped into primary and secondary education. I'm in total agreement—inner city schools in particular are not getting as much as they need—but what has happened with this demand on resources is that money has not been given to public higher education, to the colleges and universities, and therefore they may not be as well prepared as they should be to take in the next generation and supply their needs.

SJ: That is right, and that is what I mean when I say I think these things are going to come to a head. I am trying to think of the last Secretary of Education who had any real focus on higher education. The focus on higher education has come in a very indirect way. It has come actually more through the research agendas of research universities, through the National Science Foundation, NIH funding, the role of universities in things like Homeland Security. Those areas are where the federal government attention to higher education has come. In some ways, ironically, there has been more focus on the higher education system in the states than in the federal government, at least coming out of the Education Department. So I am not sure how it is all going to play out, Fran, because I think universities are being asked to do more and more and more things on a smaller and smaller, and smaller publicly provided resource base. Now you fold into that the tightening of the markets, people feeling less wealthy because of the economy, and you could have the makings of a disaster. I think access, in the end, will be affected. We discussed it in the context of universities being prepared and able to deal with the kinds of populations that may come their way with demographic shifts, and I think that is true. At the same time, because it takes money to deal with diverse groups and kids from various socio-economic backgrounds, but frankly, because of all the things universities are being asked to do besides just teach students, the pie is only so big. I actually believe that the access questions dominate. But this business about affordability and the issue of putting tuition caps and things like that on universities, I think that is very wrong.

FL: It does not help. You really focus on the issue that is worrying me, even though I am no longer leading an institution. I remember that after the Second World War, we changed the direction of higher education forever by opening access to university education to returning veterans. We know that if people have an opportunity to be educated, they go on to do a very good job in their communities as well as for their families. But if they are not educated, it can be a tragedy.

SJ: That is right. Coming out of World War II, two things happened. A couple of forces came together. You had the GI Bill, which provided a lot of access to a lot of folks to a lot of universities, including high end universities, and it made all the difference in terms of an educated work force, productive lives, good citizens, and so on. But there was an attendant initiative that came a little bit later, starting with Vannevar Bush, Roosevelt, and later Truman: the major federal government investment in the universities. That is how the real research universities started, but coupled with that—which is what I worry about—was support for students. There were two kinds of support for students. The GI Bill provided universal access across all fields. Then, after Sputnik, there were various specific science and engineering and math oriented types of support very much focused on graduate education. Both of those approaches recognized that it is people we have to invest in. You cannot just invest in the physical plant. Even as more money and research money was being put into research universities, the federal government recognized that we had to invest in the people. The GI Bill supported people going on to higher education in the broad-based way. Things like the National Defense Education Act, and those sorts of programs invested in a focused way in people studying the sciences and engineering.

FL: My life was changed by the NDEA. I received one of the first NDEA scholarships for Ph.D. studies in French and Italian.

SJ: That is right. I misspoke, because I've always focused on it in terms of its enabling function in educating scientists and engineers, but you are absolutely right. The NDEA paid for the graduate education of many people in the languages in particular. And those are critical skills.

FL: And had we had something like that prior to September 11...

SJ: We might have known some people that spoke Arabic or Farsi or something, right? What I am worried about is whether we recognize at the national level, those linkages, the linkages of having a broadly well educated population to good citizenship, to technological advances and to having inherent capabilities that allow us to understand all the cultures and to speak to all the cultures, and therefore, first, frankly to head things off—but if we cannot, to anticipate better what may occur—and that was what we missed this time around.

Shirley Strum Kenny

Shirley Kenny has served as president of the State University of New York at Stony Brook since 1994. She came to Stony Brook from her presidency of Queens College of the City University of New York (1985-1994). Prior to that, she was the provost of arts and humanities at the University of Maryland, College Park. At Queens College, Kenny initiated a number of new curricula designed by leaders in the professions, for example, programs in the liberal arts and business and in journalism. She worked to build a foundation board and to begin private fund raising, as well as using capital funding to construct attractive facilities for the college.

Kenny earned bachelor's degrees in English and journalism at the University of Texas, a master's at the University of Minnesota, and her Ph.D. at the University of Chicago. She is a scholar of Restoration and eighteenth-century drama and has published five books and numerous articles in her area of specialization.

At Stony Brook, she has initiated a five-year planning cycle that uses task forces on which faculty, staff, students, and alumni serve. She has directed the remodeling of the campus with new and renovated facilities for research, teaching and student life, as well as improved landscaping. The Stony Brook Hospital is also being expanded. In the undergraduate curriculum, the university is implementing the recommendations of the Boyer Commission report on educating undergraduates in research universities, a national initiative that Kenny launched and chaired (1998). In 1998 the university, in cooperation with the Battelle Corporation, took over the administration of Brookhaven National Laboratory for the U.S. Department of Energy. Stony Brook launched its first major fundraising campaign in 2005.

In addition to chairing the Boyer Commission report, her national leadership positions include service as chair of the Association for American Colleges and Universities and the Folger Shakespeare Library Institute and membership on the board of the Carnegie Foundation for the Advancement of Teaching.

Francis Lawrence: It is increasingly rare to encounter a research university president who is a humanist, as you and I are. The trend seems increasingly to look for candidates whose background is in the sciences. You were the president of Queens College for nine years before coming to Stony Brook as the first woman to be named to the university's presidency.

Shirley Strum Kenny: I might mention, Fran, that I am also the first president of Stony Brook who is not a physicist.

FL: What personal attributes do you feel have contributed most to your success as a leader?

SK: In some ways I feel it's my energy and my lack of need for a lot of sleep: the presidency takes a lot of time and energy. Somebody told me that I was the most improbable college president he had ever met and I suppose that may be true. When I left college, I knew that I wanted to go into higher education, but I just happened into my career in higher education administration. We didn't have career paths in my day; we just worked.

FL: Do women in higher education need to have different or superior skills and leadership qualities than men who are higher education leaders?

SK: I think so but, at the same time, I think that is less true now, when there are more women in higher education. For example, there are more women who are the presidents of research universities, which was very rare when I started out. I think that it is sometimes more difficult for men to understand a woman not as a mother, but as an authority figure. I think we have to learn to express ourselves in the way that men express themselves—at least I did when I started out—because women tend to be gentler and more indirect in saying the same things. A woman might say in a tentative fashion, "Maybe we could try such-and-such," whereas a man would say in a very positive way, "We ought to try such-and-such." So I think, at least early on, women really had to learn that they were in a different environment. If you are working in Japan, you'd better know how to speak Japanese. You'd better speak in a way that your audience can understand you. That was the lesson I had to learn: that what I might see as courtesy could be interpreted as weakness. It did not make me believe I should not be courteous, but I did learn that I would have to adopt other ways of letting people know what I wanted them to do.

FL: Let's talk a bit about your family background and your education. I'm sure that they shaped your values and your development.

SK: I grew up in Tyler, Texas. Three of my four grandparents were immigrants, two from Russia, one from Poland. My mother was one of eleven children, a middle child. Because her parents had made enough money at that point to begin to send the children on to higher education, she went to college. Three of the younger ones were doctors. My father aspired to be a lawyer but had to quit high school in order to go out and work because his father went broke. I grew up Jewish in Tyler, a small town in Texas and went to the white public high school, which was not academically challenging. My uncles ran a furniture store next door to the Carnegie Public Library. The library was a second home for me: you could check out four books at once and I was always a reader. I have a brother who went to college before I did. When one went to college, one had a choice between the local community college and the University of Texas. I went to the University of Texas and earned an undergraduate degree in journalism and English.

FL: What do you regard as your first leadership position at any level?

SK: That's an interesting question. I think in some ways the first thing I did as a leadership position was to be the leader of the baton twirlers in my high school and at the University of Texas teaching routines to the performers. The most important University of Texas experience I had was being editor of the *Daily Texan* student newspaper. That was a fulfilling job. But I think the first time I ever did anything in which I was working with people was in that first, very curious way—leading baton twirlers—and that, I suppose, is more related to teaching than to leadership.

FL: Who were the people who inspired you and acted as your mentors?

SK: The people who most influenced me were, first of all, my parents, who never gave me the impression that I couldn't do anything I wanted to, but never pushed me to do anything. Professor Leo Hughes at the University of Texas taught me eighteenth-century studies as an undergraduate. I think that he was the reason I ended up in eighteenth-century studies. When I was fresh out of undergraduate school, Harry Ransom at the University of Texas gave me my first opportunity to teach in an experimental program in which he had people from other disciplines teach English. I was perceived as a journalist.

FL: What were the challenges that Queens College faced at the time when you became president?

SK: Money and morale most of all. I became president in 1985. The New York City fiscal crisis was in 1976 and they had never gotten over it. As it turned out, nobody actually lost his or her job, but they were so afraid they were going to that they went and sat on the lines for unemployment. That experience scarred people at Queens College and frightened them so badly that, when I got there nine years later, it still dominated their thinking. It was important that things change so we could go on with our work and get that out as a center of their lives.

FL: The challenges were money and attitude.

SK: Money, attitude, and, as there tends to be in this part of the country, there was also a kind of inferiority attached to being a public institution rather than a private institution. That was something I had not experienced before because it's not true throughout the country, but in the Northeast, for many people, the assumption is that private higher education is better than public higher education.

FL: Despite the high quality and excellent reputation of public research universities in the Northeast, belief in the traditional hegemony of private higher education lingers from here through New England.

SK: That's right, and that mentality really sort of has pervaded both CUNY and SUNY for far too long.

FL: Was Queens able to overcome that problem?

SK: I had at Queens College what I believed was the best foundation board in America, people who were CEOs of major corporations, I also had an arts board that worked with alums like Paul Simon and Marvin Hamlish. Jerry Seinfeld also graduated from Queens. The university had really given this country, and certainly New York City, a very proud tradition of leadership. People came to Queens College as immigrants or children of immigrants and this opportunity for higher education was their one shot, so it has an extraordinary history. Connecting the university with the future made a big difference in giving it a positive outlook. We also had a number of capital projects and that helped, because you do see the future there.

FL: When people see things being built, even if they're not being built for them in particular, it makes a difference in their outlook. What were the challenges that you initially faced at Stony Brook?

SK: At Stony Brook again, I suppose morale was the biggest problem because Stony Brook was so new. It was founded in 1957 and moved to the Stony Brook location in 1962. I came there in 1994, so that excitement and thrill of the early years and the pioneer spirit involved in creating this wonderful research institution had tapered off to a period in which everything was getting regularized, but in doing that, it had leveled off till there was not a lot going on. And then, instead of Rockefeller who really believed in Stony Brook as a great research university, we got administrations that did not put money into it. The plant was ugly and awful. The landscaping was embarrassing. We had a great central mall that was too much to mow, so they put concrete and blacktop over it. Undergraduates didn't matter. We had been told by the Middle States accrediting team that if we did not do something about the undergraduate program we would not get accreditation next time. They were coming back in five years to check, which happened to be great for me because it handed me a real lever. So there was not a sense of pride and direction and excitement. There was a sense that they're not giving us our full due, they're not giving us what we ought to have, and the plant had gotten terrible. The dormitories were so bad that it was hard to get people to live in them. The complaint was that it was a commuter college: students went home on the weekends. There was not the sense of being a full-grown research university, which is what we are.

FL: What effects had the role and demands of each of these leadership posts had on your family life and how do you maintain a balance?

SK: When we started out teaching, there were nepotism laws, so my husband and I, who were both academics, had to be in a city where there was more than one institution. We ended up in Washington, D.C. with him at George Washington University. I was the camp follower, I taught at Gallaudet, the college for the deaf, and then at Catholic University. Then for fourteen years I was at Maryland, where I got into administration. During that time we were living in McLean, Virginia and our children were in a small cooperative school. Our friends were the parents of our children's schoolmates, so in a way that grounded us. Socially we were very much where our kids were and we just focused on the kids. We did our work and the rest of the time we were there. We worked very hard to have schedules so that one of us would not be in class but could be there if there was a crisis. Our family is really the most important and the most enjoyable part of our lives. We had five children: four sons who were very close in age, then a five-year space between the boys and our daughter. I think that she probably felt the lack of our being there more than any of the boys because there was always so much going on.

FL: What have your internal constituencies—your governing board, faculty, students, and staff—at each of your presidencies expected of you?

SK: The governing boards have always been easy for me. In each of these cases there was a governing board for the whole system. In the case of SUNY there are sixty-four campuses in the system, so they can't really look down your neck too much, although we have some interesting board members. I have always used my foundation board as my close advisers. They have been much more like a board of trustees to me because they are focused on Stony Brook and because they are so bright and so savvy. That part has not been hard at all. I would say that the faculty are the hardest because they really need a lot of personal interest, concern, and stroking. I have sometimes thought that if we could just give all of our faculty members an A every semester they would be happier, because they all got A grades in school. It's hard to see how you're doing when you're a faculty member. You get tenure and then you've got all that time. I think that's the hardest part of being a president. If a president is going to really make differences in the institution, raise money, and be the public face of the university, then there's no time for all that stroking. Also the faculty tends to be really reactionary in many ways about change in the institution. So to make changes that may be necessary and important you have to go through the whole faculty governance structure. That is very slow and grinds exceedingly fine. Then you have SUNY Central, the SUNY Board of Trustees, and the state, so there really is a tendency not to change things, like curriculum for example. It just takes too long. And I think that's the problem. I think that there are ways to do it. There are certainly ways to recognize excellence in faculty. Students are easier. They too can be reactionary about change, but you know they are going to be here only a few years: they don't have the investment that the faculty have in the status quo. Staff I have found very easy to work with. For faculty, I think you have got to get the leadership on your side, and then things fall into place.

FL: What have you felt that you owe to these groups, given that you have demands upon you tugging in several different directions every day?

SK: When I came to Stony Brook I thought that I had lots of goals and ambitions for Stony Brook and a very clear vision of what I needed to do, but the overarching and most difficult thing I had to do or try to do was to make Stony Brook a nice place. It was a great research institution. It was not a nice place. It was not an attractive, inviting campus. That took a long time, but I think it is a nice place now and I think that makes everybody nicer. Undergraduate students had a lot to beef about because they really were an afterthought. Stony Brook was founded in 1962 when the great thing was research and how you proved that you're a great research institution. So that turnaround was very hard: to make it a place where you want to come to work, to make it a place where people are courteous, all those things I thought really mattered. The physical environment mattered.

FL: How have you managed the expectations of different groups?

SK: What I found when I came to Stony Brook—I think it was in part because it was such a young institution—was that it was the hardest place to sell change that I had ever been. You had the founders who came there with this extraordinary dream of creating a great research university out of potato fields, which is what they did. They were part of that and nothing was the way it was in other institutions. Then here we were turning it into the kind of institution that's not so rare and unusual, more like other institutions. I think that really was very hard for faculty. You had to get over that problem and sell the new vision. You weren't going to do it just by words. What I always find in my work is that you have to pick the right symbols and let the symbols do the work.

FL: What has been your greatest challenge as a leader?

SK: The money problems, which you really have to deal with. If they're not settled in the way that they used to be settled, which was by convincing the state to give you more money, then they don't go away. The more ambitious you are, the more money you need. One of the problems for me as a leader is timing. There's a disconnect between where my thinking is and where people are. You really have to have perfect timing to make something happen. If you are ahead of the game, thinking out there, but unable to sell that vision, it can be a problem. I think that's unique to me. That's the problem I have.

FL: I think there's a lot of truth to that. Let's look at the organizational structure. How have you recruited and structured your leadership teams in each post, Queens and Stony Brook?

SK: In Queens my big problem in the first year was to realize that I had to get rid of the provost, who had been acting president. He had been acting president and he knew how to do it and then he went back to being provost and this person who didn't know how to do it came in to replace him. I might not ever have solved that problem, but I had a conversation with Joe Murphy, the chancellor of CUNY in which I said that I knew the provost was not loyal to me, but he had good ideas, and Joe said, "Shirley, loyalty is everything." In a way he was right. If you don't work with administrators who are loyal to you as the boss...

FL: You're being undermined behind your back.

SK: I learned that lesson and I did get a new provost. When I came to Stony Brook, all the vice presidencies were silos to the extent that if the facilities people did something for the academic side, the academic side had to pay for it. So if you got a new light plug, they'd charge you $300. It seemed to me that the money was just going around in circles rather than anything happening, so I told them that we're going to decide who spends how much money, I'm going to put it there, you're going to do it, you're not going to charge each other. At the end of the first year, I got rid of two vice presidents: one was finance and one was facilities. The finance person thought he owned the finances and did not share with me the answers I wanted, and the facilities head was just arrogant and impossible. He was a military man who didn't have much use for a woman coming in. With both of these I said, "You know, we're going to need a change. Take six months. Find something." Fifteen minutes later one of my secretaries heard from the cleaner in the ladies' room, that one of them had been fired. They couldn't believe somebody was going to fire them, so it was immediately known I'd fired them and that turned out to be a good thing because people were relieved that they were leaving and because I was able to get somebody really terrific to take on both of the positions as one position.

FL: Can you tell me some of the specific qualities that you look for in the people you choose to work with and depend upon?

SK: Flexibility, energy, excitement about their work, loyalty, strength, courtesy, I think are important, and the ability to work as a team, because that's the way I work. If you're working as a team and having fun, it happens. And Lord knows you have to have a sense of humor.

FL: I know that in each post that you have been expected to spend a lot of time on the road. In each of your presidencies, have you had someone in your administration who has handled the day-to-day work of the university while you were gone?

SK: I haven't, but I think I should. It makes a lot of sense. I have some difficulty personally in perceiving a presidency where the president is the outside person and the provost is the inside person. To me, the inside is the big part of my job and I work very closely with the provost, but I have not perceived myself as purely an outside person and I think it would be very hard for me to do that.

FL: Actually, in this age of technology it's very easy to communicate back and forth instantaneously. Most if not all presidents have not only cell phones but Blackberries, so when they are on the road people consult them about problems, propose solutions, and get approval about handling crises.

SK: That's absolutely correct.

FL: How did you formulate a vision for the future of each university?

SK: I came to Queens College from the University of Maryland, which is a very different sort of institution. My experience was with research universities basically, but Queens College, which is a jewel, a very special place, has far more undergraduate than graduate emphasis, far more students of the humanities and social sciences than sciences. I really had to get a sense of the place, both the fact of its glorious history and the fact that it is in the Borough of Queens, which is one of the most grandly diverse places in the country. We had that tradition of immigrants, all these new immigrant populations, and we were part of the city: that's a wonderful combination. We invented some new kinds of programs that connected the students with the city in very special ways. With Stony Brook, I knew before I got there exactly what I had to do. I've often said that Queens College was the college of my heart and Stony Brook is the university of my head. I didn't immediately feel the kind of personal love of the place that I felt at Queens, but there was a lot that had to be done. The first thing was that we had to do something about the undergraduate program. Nobody wanted to think about it, but we knew that. And the place was falling apart. It had to be physically improved. My theory is that faculty morale is always the worst it's ever been, and that was certainly true here. Actually I've seen improvement, which ruins my theory. There just had to be a sense of us now being great and there had to be some ways to measure that and know that it was true. That meant improvement, that meant change, and change was frowned upon.

FL: What strategies did you use to communicate and create acceptance of your vision by the academic community and by its external constituencies, whether alumni and friends or the leaders in the town, the city, and the state?

SK: There again I think Stony Brook was harder than Queens College because Stony Brook had such a different tradition. Alumni were really tough. At that point we had one of these runaway alumni associations and very little serious contact with the alumni. Leaders in the town and the state were easier. That's not so different from any place else, except that I had gone from very Democratic Queens to very Republican Long Island: that was different. But to get the buy-in of the alumni, to start raising money (nobody had ever raised money seriously), to create a mechanism for getting the alumni tied in with fundraising was really hard. You could do it in part by meeting with people, letting them know what it was that you were going to do at the institution, and getting them excited. But it took some proving that things were getting better before we got real buy-in. It took a long time. I kept feeling it took longer than it should have.

FL: Let's get into planning. How did you translate your understanding of each university together with the external realities into a long-range plan for change and improvement?

SK: The first year I got to Stony Brook, I said we're going to have a five-year plan and we set up about ten task forces. I asked for volunteers and we got something like a thousand. We used 200-250, faculty primarily, but also staff, students, alumni and community people, and that was a very good device. I don't have a rolling plan. We did a five-year plan and we published it, showing which administrative officer was responsible for each goal. We had a committee that winnowed the task force reports down to a workable number of recommendations and an administrator responsible for each one, then a matrix of which one should be done in each of the five years: what should be finished in year one, year two, and so on. Then every year we publish a report card about what has been done or has not been done: that encourages you to get everything done during the year it's meant to be done. In the fifth year, we made the second five-year plan. The first one had a lot of fix-it kinds of things, big issues that really needed fixing. The second five-year plan I thought was less interesting because it was still dealing with fix-it issues, but they were lesser things because we had done a lot.

This year is the planning year for the third five-year plan and we're going to have six task forces on really major issues, not about fixing it, because presumably it's fixed, but about what our next steps should be to go to the next level. They are issues such as administrative, academic, and organizational structure and curriculum. We're also examining where we should be investing, what direction we ought to follow. Where is the world going and where should we be putting our money? How should we improve graduate education? Certainly across the country it needs improving. We're also looking at the student experience, because we had to do that anyway for the Middle States report. Anyway, we are looking at six major issues that have to do with the future.

Now other things have happened that were not in those plans, and one could even say that the things the plans treated are not the most important things that have happened at the university, but they did establish a process for planning and seeing whether things were accomplished or not. I believe in not having a rolling plan but in getting specific things done. Other big things have happened: we took over management of Brookhaven National Laboratories and established Stony Brook Manhattan. We couldn't have known that those opportunities were going to come up and be possibilities. Other things like that were not in that plan and may have had a greater impact, but at least the faculty could see that the things in the plans needed doing and we got them done, so I think that the planning mechanism was important.

FL: Was Queens similar?

SK: No, I didn't do that at Queens. We had an administrative council of vice presidents, deans, and the faculty leaders with regular meetings, but not the kind of planning that I did here.

FL: How did you link the changes that you wanted to make to the financial budgeting practices in each institution? It's nice to have plans, but one has to pay for those plans.

SK: I've been at Stony Brook ten years and the tax levy budget for Stony Brook is 3 percent higher this year than it was ten years ago. So I learned pretty soon that if you're going to do many things you'd better not just sit there and hope the state comes through and funds them. We went without a tuition increase for eight years; then we got a tuition increase of about 28 percent. Our tuition is now $4,350 for in-state undergraduates. You absolutely have to look at other places in order to find the money to make things happen. At this point, we have higher research expenditures than we have tax levy income to the university. Tax levy is about 10 percent of our whole budget, including the hospital, or 15 percent if you count state fringe benefits. We have better luck in getting capital money from the state than operational money. In the five-year plans, if the issues are simple things such as painting offices, you can simply allocate money in the facilities budget for that purpose. In fact we started the quality of life budget with a very minimal one million dollars a year. Then we put in two million to improve facilities like faculty and student lounges and conference rooms or faculty offices, just to give that little margin of change that shows people that things are improving. We fixed leaky roofs with that money. Those little things were symbolic. We couldn't renovate the building, but we could give them a nice place to be together and have their coffee pot. We could fix the elevator: that's expensive actually, but it certainly helps morale. It took a long time.

I started early on to improve landscaping. The Sunday after I accepted the job I went to the campus with John Belle, who is a great architect. He planned the renovations of Ellis Island and Grand Central Station. I asked him what I could do, because this was the ugliest place I'd ever seen. The buildings were built in the 1960s (we called them neo-penal), open spaces were blacktopped, and nobody was taking care of what little grass there was. John looked around and asked if the campus had a center. It really didn't. The buildings had been built with the main doors facing outside toward the parking lots instead of inside toward the mall. So the first thing we did was create a center, an absolutely beautiful, stunning mall with a fountain in the middle of the main campus. Immediately people began to gripe and complain, "What's she doing building a fountain? I need a T.A.!" But the day we turned on that fountain there was a different attitude. Then we got the best landscape architect we could find. My theory is if you're really poor you cannot afford anything but the best. You can't waste it on the mediocre: you don't have enough money. So our landscaping is gorgeous. Milton Glaser is our designer and bit by bit we have raised the aesthetic appeal of the campus. The signage was hideous. No sign looked like any other sign. They just printed them up and put them out. Now we have a signage program, which may sound silly, but it makes a difference. All of those little things helped change the atmosphere and get the faculty on board. The staff were on board well before the faculty.

One other thing I want to say about linking the changes to the budgeting process is that one of the things I did was to bring the budgeting process into my office: the budget officer reports to me, and that helps. I know where the money is. The new vice president of finance is wonderful to work with, but having the budget officer report to me makes it much closer. I think it was an important move, although an unusual move.

FL: Change can often meet more resentment than approval in universities. Can you describe one or more critical incidents, how they arose and how you dealt with them?

SK: Well I mentioned the beautification, which was greatly resented. Good thing I had a tough skin because there was a lot of animosity. As I said once it happened, people enjoyed it. It gets more and more beautiful because we don't have much money, so we can't just do it all at once. So there are always added improvements coming, which I think is not a bad thing. We have another little garden planted or another building improved.

The other thing for which that beautification has been largely responsible is that over the last four to six years, we have increased enrollments by about 5,000 students and SAT scores by more than 100 points. People now realize the fact that it's a nice place to come. Beyond that, I renovated all the dorms and we built new dorms because now people wanted to live on campus. We built a new student activity center and a new stadium with a capacity of 8,200 people. It can grow to accomodate15,000 (which I like because I grew up in Texas and even high school stadiums are big in Texas), but it's a lovely little stadium that feels like a stadium. We did a lot of things for student life. All those things helped to attract better students and attracting better students raises faculty morale. It was a long way around, but they finally got it. It took a while, but it is a better place and oddly enough, of all the things that I've done as Stony Brook's president—and I certainly have done a lot that were more important—the campus improvements are what they're going to remember, probably because it's important in their own lives.

FL: What methods have you used to assess the outcomes of your initiatives at each institution, Queens as well as Stony Brook? And how have you measured progress toward your long-term goals?

SK: For the five-year plan, every year we have an outcome assessment or what I call a report card evaluating what we've done to achieve our goals. I think that in terms of assessing the outcomes, that assessment is probably the most standardized report. A lot of the things that we've done as an institution couldn't have been predicted. They were opportunities that arose, such as taking over management of the Brookhaven National Lab, so they couldn't be part of a plan. But in my inaugural address I very rashly gave a number of goals that I was going to complete over the next seven years. Some of them were things that I had no control over. I was really an idiot to do that. I said that we were going to make X amount of money on research and that we would rise in national rank to Y. Both X and Y actually happened! For my personal assessment, I have looked back at that occasionally to see what I have not done yet, what we still needed to do. But that is not a public thing. This is my tenth year. Every fall I give a state-of-the-university message. In that message this year I focused on what has happened in ten years and what needs to happen in the next ten years.

FL: How have you reinforced and celebrated success?

SK: Every spring we have Strawberry Fest, we have Fountain Fest when we turn on the fountain, and other annual things, but we decided that for the fortieth anniversary year of being on our campus we were going to have a great celebration all over campus of everything that was going on intellectually and in student life. It was the most elaborate plan you have ever seen in your life. We scheduled it for September 11, 2001. Needless to say we did not have our celebration. We did finally have a celebration a year or so later. We used the T-shirts we had for everybody and we did all the programs we had planned. When we awoke that morning of September 11, 2001, it was the most gorgeous day in the world....

FL: Then all hell broke lose.

SK: Yes. The best laid plans. We do a lot of honoring the faculty for different kinds of achievement and honoring students too. We have a university research day in which the students show their posters. There is a big event with competitions for the best projects and a display in our new student activity center of research projects being done by undergraduates. We now have a new focus on spirit and pride. We have a new athletic director who is really bringing a lot of academic excellence as well as everything else to our athletic program, which is very small. We're Division 1 but we're very minor players so we're not running into the big athletic problems that it is possible to have. We have a new focus on spirit and pride that we're really working to foster. We also have an image campaign, an advertising campaign that is letting the world know more about what's going on at Stony Brook.

FL: What importance have you placed on the roles of Queens College and Stony Brook in their communities?

SK: A lot. In Queens, it was really easy because of the diversity of the institution. I came to Queens nineteen years ago. Then diversity was something people didn't talk about in public, but when I came there, it was absolutely splendid, so we did a lot of bragging about it and then tying in with all those diverse communities in Queens. That was a very pleasant and easy way to connect with the community. We also had a good political situation in Queens. The borough president Claire Schulman would call all the legislators together. She'd ask me what it was that I most wanted, I would give them a list, and they would all support it. So we had nice influence in Albany at that point.

At Stony Brook it is very different. We have a very diverse student body. About 50 percent are not Caucasian. About 30 percent are Asian, about 12 percent black, maybe 8 percent Hispanic. We live in a very white environment. Early on, they thought that they were getting a small New England style liberal arts college, but they got Stony Brook, which is a big research university. The locals have never realized that their economy is based on Stony Brook. We're the largest single-site employer in Suffolk County, which has about a million and a half people. They have never taken account of the fact that their neighbors teach at the university and that the university is a great asset to them. Instead, it has always been resented. That has meant a very different kind of connecting with the community. So we connect with civic groups and with the school systems: we do a great deal for high school and even for intermediate schools whose students get research opportunities on campus. We do all of those kinds of things, but there's not the sort of warm glow that one expects to surround a university in its community. We have to work at it.

FL: What are the major groups outside the university with which the institution has interacted under your leadership?

SK: We work with the churches particularly in the black community, that's very important. We work with the civic associations. We work with business groups particularly. What we're doing for economic development is the engine for the long haul because you've got to have a great research university to have the kind of economic development you need now, hi tech kinds of industries. That part of our relationship with the community goes very well. I think that I was the first person in the country to appoint a vice president for economic development. That person is very good at working with the local businesses and the local associations of businesses, but unlike Queens, Long Island has no core center or focus.

We also have a hospital and a state veterans' home on campus, so we interact with the community through those institutions as well, and that can be a plus or a minus. You know we have wonderful programming at our Staller Arts Center. We have an exciting film festival that's really grown and marvelous programming through the year. We have bicycle paths on our 1,100-acre campus and on weekends you see lots and lots of people with their kids biking through the campus. Our football games cost around $6.00, so people come and bring their children. We use our facilities for high school football tournaments and soccer tournaments. People can use our library: we offer a lot of that kind of thing. But there's still resentment. It's very odd. I think people moved out of the city and expected Long Island to be potato fields, never to change, but it has changed and Stony Brook is part of that change.

FL: Let's look at the day-to-day realities of the presidency. How have you allocated your time in your different posts, Queens or Stony Brook, and what have been your top priorities? Have you had to work differently at each institution? Clearly one institution is huge compared to the other.

SK: At Queens College I worked on getting some new and interesting programs. For example, we started a Liberal Arts and Business program which let students major in anything they wanted, then go on to take a set of business courses. Those business courses were designed by a board of New York business leaders who were interested in such a program. Then the students were given opportunities for internships and the program worked very well. We did the same thing with journalism, and again the top people from the New York newspapers got involved in designing that curriculum. I would gather an equal number of faculty and professionals to plan these programs and I focused on getting some sort of oomph into the curriculum. I also worked at building the foundation board and starting the fundraising enterprise. We had a number of buildings that we were constructing at the time so there was a lot of focus on that as well.

At Stony Brook, it was very different. There the first thing I had to do was to focus on the undergraduate program. It was because we had such a problem that I got interested in the issues that led to the Boyer Commission operations. The fundraising responsibility, of course, was huge. Then I did a great deal of work toward trying to raise our status so that we would be invited to become a member of the Association of American Universities. I also placed a high priority on taking over the management of the Brookhaven Lab. I'm working now to buy a piece of property adjacent to the university for our research and development park. The first five years were spent trying to get the campus in shape and since then there has been more expansion.

FL: Could you tell me about what you are doing on your branch campus, Stony Book Manhattan?

SK: It is quite a recent facility that opened within the past four years. We do several things with it. We have programs particularly in health technology and management with the local 1199 Health Workers Union. We have a social welfare program in Manhattan. We also have an executive MBA program in Manhattan and we do various other short courses. Students get degrees in those subjects in Manhattan and some of our students are working in Manhattan, so they can take their summer school courses there much more easily than out in Long Island. We're starting internship programs connected with the art museums and other organizations here in the city. We also offer other short courses to the public, things like the Center for Wine, Food and Culture.

If we're going to have press conferences, we use the Stony Brook Manhattan facility. We also use it for conferences, such as the humanities and medicine conference, which attracted people from all over the country. It was about narrative in medicine: we learned that the average amount of time a doctor listens to a patient without interrupting is twenty-one seconds, so they were suggesting longer narratives might be useful. This facility was important to us because we needed a foothold in Manhattan and we are able to do a lot of interesting things.

FL: Every leader experiences planned and unplanned events that escalate into time-consuming crises. Do you have any crisis management stories that you'd like to share?

SK: Oddly enough, buying property adjacent to our campus for a research and development park has ended up being a major issue because Long Island has a certain mentality of being against anything. The proposal for the property had been for a 330-home gated community on a golf course. If you're worried about cars on the road, anyone would know that proposal would have had more impact than the ten research facilities we're proposing. That issue involved having to spend lots of time talking to civic groups and working through the process. We ended up having to condemn the land, so it really has gotten very messy. The corporation that owns the land is trying to get the price up, so they tried to get it rezoned as residential, which would make it more expensive than the light industrial zoning it now has. The issue is important, but it takes a lot of time. I have not had any of those issues that came to Stony Brook earlier. At one point they had a tent city there and what people remember about Stony Brook is the drug raids in the 1960s. Thank heavens I have not had those kinds of issues.

FL: How would you define leadership?

SK: I think leadership is, most importantly, having the vision and then selling that dream to all of the stakeholders. I think that is the most important thing. From there on, people do it lots of different ways—some are hands-on, some can just let other people handle the implementation—but you first of all must have the vision. It may take you a while to fully realize what that vision is, but it has to come early and you have to be able to convince other people that the vision you propose is attractive and viable, that it is where they want to go.

FL: What are the most important qualities for university presidents today? You've served since 1985 as a president at two different institutions. Do presidents need different qualities now than they did fifteen to twenty years ago?

SK: I think that we need to reevaluate what university presidents should do and where their focus should be because we have put such emphasis on fundraising.

FL: That seems unlikely to change, given the dwindling support from the states for public higher education across the country now.

SK: But if you're the president of an institution that is hugely wealthy, that is still what you're supposed to do. I think there are some institutions that really don't need all that money; nevertheless their presidents are expected to raise huge amounts of money. I think that presidents are not these days expected to think about education as much if what institutions want in their president is a great fundraiser. I enjoy fundraising and I have not been bad at it: I got a $52 million building from one of our donors. But if that's where presidents are going to be putting not only their time and attention but their evaluation of themselves, then are we really getting the kinds of leaders that are going to make these institutions great? Will our institutions be able with that leadership to make the kinds of leaps that we will have to make in order to have the higher education we need in the future? I think we're a little bit off track. When I think of the great university presidents of the past, that's not what they were known for.

FL: Nor did they spend the amount of hours that the university president today must spend if she or he is to be a successful fundraiser.

SK: You certainly want to raise the money, but I think we've gotten a little bit off track. It's worth our thinking about it and discussing it as university presidents because that's not the vision. The other thing is that, with all the hoopla about fundraising, much of the money you raise is apt to be either not where you would put it if you were working from your vision or really funny money anyway. When people have these huge campaigns, they count everything they collect every year anyway as part of it. There's a real problem now with in-kind gifts, with software being evaluated at enormous amounts. I think that you just have to say, "No, I'm not going to be a party to that." With all the planned giving, you're not really getting money into the institution to do things now, although it may be great when you do receive it in the future, or it may be that it won't be worth so much money by the time you get it. So it seems to me we ought to get more realistic about the fundraising in the way things are counted. People do it the same way, but....

FL: Yes, there are certain professional standards that you must follow.

SK: But it's misleading, I think, and what presidents ought to be doing is to look at what education should be and lead our institutions.

FL: How have the role and demands of the presidency changed over the past decades in response to the disinvestment of the states in public higher education?

SK: That's one of the reasons that we are spending much more time on fundraising, looking for ways to raise money, I think that's been unfortunate; I think it is unfortunate for the country. I think that if states thought about it, they would know that if they want their states to prosper, they've got to invest in higher education and that is the opportunity to be great. So yes, it has made a difference. I hope we will get through that phase and they will recognize, as other countries are recognizing, that you have to invest in higher education.

FL: Asia is putting a lot of money into higher education.

SK: They're going to eat our lunch.

FL: How has the presidency changed in response to the technological revolution?

SK: Clearly we are investing more in our plant in terms of technology and that is true not only in terms of communications and computer technology, but also, for example, in the hospital. The costs are enormous for the medical technology in the laboratories, but of course great opportunities come with that. There's no doubt that we're putting much more into not only buying technology but keeping it up and replacing it. It's a burden on the budget.

FL: How has the presidency been affected by the growing roles of private support for university research and commercial application of university research?

SK: Commercial application is important because we don't have a very good handle on it right now. Stony Brook has for the last five years been ranked somewhere between tenth and fifteenth in the country in terms of royalty income. That is terrific but it's based almost entirely on a single drug and if anybody gets one that is either better or cheaper, we're out of business. That income stream is no longer with us. We have some others coming along. Universities are just now learning or trying to learn about investment, not just the royalties, but having equity in the companies where these new projects are developed and that could be a very important income stream as well.

FL: What has been the effect of the increasingly strident demands of students and politicians for high quality and accountability in both expenditures and results?

SK: I think the country is making a huge mistake by focusing on testing rather than education at every level. It is demanding that schools prove themselves by showing that their freshmen, sophomores, juniors, your fourth graders, and eighth graders can pass a certain test. It's just taking money, taking energy, taking faculty time away from teaching. Frankly I don't think there are ways that those tests can have any meaning in terms of what students are learning. Standardized testing makes no sense to me in this context, yet boards of trustees and other authorities are really thinking that's the way to go.

My own feeling is that universities ought to be accountable to themselves for making sure they're teaching those students what they should, which I think we do through the processes of judging faculty for tenure and promotion. We may not do it well enough, we may not put enough emphasis on teaching, but we could, given that responsibility. I just find that our students are wonderful. They are grateful for what they learn and really delighted that they have opportunities to work as they do in these research initiatives with our research faculty.

FL: I agree with you about standardized testing. Standardized tests only gauge a particular moment and teaching to the test guarantees only that students know the information at that particular point in time.

SK: Yes, and you're not teaching all of the other things they need to learn.

FL: What do you think may be the reason why we are seeing so many short terms in university presidencies during the past decade or so?

SK: I don't know the answer to that. You know it can be an exhausting job. I think you have to love it and I think you have to have really tough skin. If you're looking for strokes, forget about it, it's not going to happen. But if you're looking to see if things are better on the campus now and it doesn't matter who gets the credit for it, then it's really very special. I think the job is hard. I think if you're spending all your time fundraising, it's less fun than if you're engaged in the educational issues. Maybe that's why I've been at it for so long, but it's never over, you don't get a weekend off.

FL: How would you characterize your leadership style?

SK: My mother said to me, "Shirley whatever you're doing, you're just yourself," and I think that's right. I think I could not be a model president. I have to work with what I've got. I am very honest, I am very straightforward; I guess I'm not smart enough to be dishonest; it wouldn't work. I'm a cheer-leader. I get excited about where we're going. My father was in the retail women's shoe business. Maybe I'm a salesperson because he was. I have felt that the one place I had talent was to look at what needs doing at an institution, to be able to articulate that, and move that agenda forward. If you asked people on campus, you would get a lot of other views. People say I'm not consultative enough and I think that's true. But I think you can have paralysis by analysis and you really have to move on. You have to consult with the powers that be, you have to get your constituency, but I don't like waiting years while a faculty committee investigates.

When we do the five-year plan we do it in the spring in one semester, have the reports and hold public meetings so everybody can participate in that, but there are other decisions that aren't things you can consult on, such as the decision to manage the Brookhaven National Laboratory and the decision to get the land for the research park. You have to act. Those two things were not controversial at all, but there are times when you just have to take advantage of a situation and move things forward. The academic issues are faculty issues and I respect that very much. It is the faculty who have the responsibility for approving curricula and other academic initiatives. I may wish they could move faster at times because I think sometimes we move all too slowly and miss the main chance for something really exciting. But if we are talking about administrative decisions, who is going to report to whom and that sort of thing, the president has to act.

FL: What do you feel were the most critical capital investments made under your leadership, both at Queens and at Stony Brook?

SK: At Queens we built a beautiful new library and we dedicated it on the twenty-fifth anniversary of the deaths of Chaney, Goodman, and Schwerner. Andrew Goodman was one of our students and Michael Schwerner's sister was there for the dedication of the clock tower of the library to the three civil rights workers who were murdered in Mississippi during the Freedom Summer of 1964. The Queens students who attended the dedication weren't even born in 1964; it was ancient history for them, but the clock tower will always be a special symbol. We also built a beautiful music building and made the old library into a facility for the departments of Art and English. We dedicated another building for the Economic Opportunity Program. I think all of those buildings were important and really made a difference, and we started build-ing a couple of others that weren't finished by the time I left.

At Stony Brook, the first thing we constructed was a Center for Molecular Medicine. We also recognized that it was essential to do something for student life. As I mentioned, we renovated all of the student housing and built nine new apartment-style residences. Now people are anxious to live on campus, whereas before they didn't want to live on campus. As I mentioned, we built a student activity center with meeting rooms and the stadium. Our next student life project is the building of a recreation center. Now we are focusing on the academic buildings because they were all built at the same time and they're all falling apart at the same time. One that I made sure that we renovated was the humanities building, which was the oldest building on campus. (If I didn't do that, I was afraid that nobody else ever would.) Now we are working on others, such as the chemistry building and the hospital, which has a big renovation and addition project in progress. The beautification of the campus and the little projects to improve departmental lounges took a little bit of money and were probably the most important things of all. They really helped because they raised spirits and made the campus more appealing to both faculty and students.

FL: What do you believe to have been the most significant legacy that you left to Queens College and what are your plans concerning your legacy to Stony Brook?

SK: For Queens, I believe that it was the new curricula that appealed to contemporary students and employers instead of those of the past, along with the physical additions, the buildings that made it a nicer place for the students to be. We had the capital budget to do it then. I would also cite getting the foundation board involved because, as I said, it was a wonderful board and that's helped in getting alumni reinvolved.

I think my legacy to Stony Brook is moving it into its rightful place among the research universities in the nation. It once ranked very high, then it slipped to the point that no one heard about Stony Brook or knew where it was, and now it's on the rise again. It's doing very well in surveys, which doesn't mean much except that people are hearing more about it. It is giving and instilling a sense of pride that enables us to get the best researchers and the really top quality people. The quality of my appointments has been excellent. I think that the fundraising will be in a totally different place than it was and that's important because once you get it there, then it's going to stay there. That transition was a big one because alumni were not connected to the university, so many of our donations are from friends not alums. Building that alumni base up, getting the word to them and getting them involved is a huge piece of it. There is one other thing: getting the image focused with the designs, the new logo, the look of our publications has been important. Nobody was wearing our products in terms of shirts and stuff, getting all that where there is a certain consistency is important.

FL: What advice would you give to presidents as they come into office?

SK: First of all I would say have tough skin, don't expect people to say you're wonderful and don't live for that. You have to know that you are on the right path. The second is to learn to use symbols. You can't do everything all at once but you can give people hope and a sense of direction, so choose what it is that's going to give the best message and do that. The third is communicate, communicate, communicate. When you're on a large campus, in our time, communication is a much harder thing than it once was because people are so overburdened with information that you can say the right things, put them in the newspaper, send them individual letters, send them emails, and post it, but people will say, "Oh why didn't she tell us about that?" Communication is really hard and I don't know how you solve it.

I think in terms of communicating how good a place is and communicating pride in the place, you really have to send it through the outside world back to your faculty. Have the *New York Times* say it and they will believe it.

FL: What is at the core of your work in higher education and what is the underlying purpose that you want to accomplish?

SK: I realized a long time ago that I am committed to public higher education. I think that it is the most important sector of education in this country. I think it is the backbone of this country and Lord knows it's hard. That is my commitment and it really focuses what it is I am doing. I want our students to have opportunities, to have their chance to get to the top because so many of them have the energy and determination. It is the story of America and I really resonate to that story of the opportunity that comes through public higher education. I know our students. If they weren't having the opportunity here at Stony Brook, at the University of Texas, or at Rutgers they wouldn't have it. That is so exciting, so thrilling to me. If you look at the Fortune 500 companies and their CEOs you will see how many of them come from state institutions. We're doing something important in giving these kids their one chance, their shot at it, and that's what it's about.

FL: I couldn't agree more. As states reduce their funding of higher education while state legislators and governors try to cap tuition, how can institutions resolve their budget problems and continue to build access and excellence?

SK: First of all we know that you can't depend on the state any more. We have to find other ways to get things done. There are a number of other avenues, fund-raising being one of the most obvious. Another means is bringing in research funding. We've learned a number of ways to finance construction and renovation of buildings if the state will not fund our capital needs. There are several ways that you can bring in other monies: royalties and research for outside companies among them. We just have to be nimble and clever in figuring those out and learning how to support ourselves. In our, case, tuition is not going to do it and the state is not going to do it. Our tuition is decided by the board for the sixty-four campuses of SUNY and it will never be increased in an election year.

FL: Is it the responsibility of our state institutions to solve the problem of providing students from low-income families access to quality education?

SK: This year the community college sector was growing in numbers, not the universities, which were down slightly. Community colleges have a very important role to play. They are focused on it, are good at it, and know what they're doing. I think our articulation with those colleges to bring those students to the university is very important.

I believe that it is helpful to have tiers so students can go to community colleges, state colleges, or research universities. Different options are right for different people. It's not a matter of financial access because certainly we can handle that in our Economic Opportunity Program, which has great success stories. But it's not going to do a student any good to come to Stony Brook unless the student can do that level of work. There are students who do not have very good educational backgrounds who are very bright and can get there in a hurry; there are others for which it's just not the right place. It's not going to help the student to feel like a failure. Our closest relationships are with Suffolk Community College and Nassau Community College because a lot of these kids have to live at home while they attend the university, but SUNY articulation as a whole is good.

I'm a great believer in community colleges: my husband attended one because his father was a farmer and three of the children had to go to school in the same year. Without the community college, they wouldn't have gotten there, so I have always believed in them. Still I think that we've got to be intelligent about the directions in which we send those students. I don't think it's about financial issues because there are a lot of very bright kids.

The other thing that we do is to work with the schools, particularly the schools in less affluent areas, to bring their kids in for summer programs in the sciences and bring their teachers in for summer programs in the sciences. We're working with the elementary school in Washington Heights, which is heavily Dominican, so there are language issues as well. We're working with their students from the time that they're in kindergarten on up, with a donor who's helping us to support those students. I think that there are really important things you can do there. We also have high school programs in which students do research at Stony Brook. That is one of the reasons Long Island has all those Intel winners every year: high school students work with our best professors.

FL: The board of trustees of the State University of New York could probably be called one of the most activist inclined state university governing boards in the country, perhaps equaled only by the California State Governing Board. For example the SUNY board recently decreed that each of its sixty-four campuses must begin to test 20 percent of its undergraduates every three years in order to track how well individual campuses meet SUNY's educational standards.

Like you, other research university presidents I have interviewed in recent months have expressed serious concern about the prospect of standardized testing being applied to universities in the same way that has been applied to K-12 as an index of quality. They feel that one-size-fits-all testing would be damaging to higher education. From your experience, what would you say are the defining characteristics of good governing boards?

SK: Well I certainly agree with what other presidents have said about standardized testing. I think the most important thing governing boards do is pick the right president and then they should let that president run his or her institution. There is a real problem with governing boards that meddle into the day-to-day life of an institution. In fact it can be just one or two people on the board who create problems while the rest have a much saner outlook. In our system, people have gotten into the issues of what the core curriculum should be for SUNY. That's ridiculous because our distribution requirements are tougher than the requirements that were proposed. It got down to the absurdity of thinking of decreeing that students should have two semesters of American history and each semester should cover precisely half the span of years that the United States has existed. The person who was head of the academic affairs committee of the SUNY board has since resigned from that post. There is simply no way that a lay board can know as much about academic matters as the faculty can know. Another thing in which our board started getting involved was monitoring the awarding of honorary degrees. Honorary degrees are a matter for the faculty and certainly academic requirements are matters for the faculty.

If you have a board that works with the state to support higher education and takes the matter of appointing new presidents very seriously, ensuring that political issues have no part in the appointment process, that would meet my definition of a great board. I do think that it is impossible for a single board to manage sixty-four institutions. If you're a president that doesn't necessarily seem bad because you have a lot of leeway and as long as you're on track, you know it's going to be fine. But there are issues boards just should not be getting into.

FL: In recent years higher education has become more and more important to states and their citizens both as a necessary prerequisite to desirable employment for individuals and as an economic engine for the state. Governors have increasingly taken a hands-on approach to higher education policy that has not always been well advised or well received by state universities. In New Jersey for example, the governor proposed a reorganization of Rutgers and the University of Medicine and Dentistry of New Jersey that would have put Rutgers directly under control from Trenton. That was an offer that the university's board of governors and board of trustees were able to refuse because the university has a unique contract with the state. Do you think that the overt involvement of governors with higher education policy is a trend about which we need to be concerned and how can presidents deal with these political issues?

SK: I do think it's an issue. There are many ways that governors influence what happens in the state, most of all, obviously, through the budget. The governor of New York proposes a budget that the legislature has to approve. We now have a situation in which the governor has vetoed the state budget. Our budget, which begins on April 1, has not been approved yet and this has been true since I've been in New York: it happens every year. The governor in our state appoints the board of trustees for SUNY and ten of the fifteen in CUNY, the other five are appointed by the mayor. The governor can influence who is appointed in central administration and even who is placed on campus. I have certainly seen this happen. If you have a really bad situation, a governor can influence what happens in terms of contracts for facilities and so on, so there is always at least the potential danger of interference from the governor.

The legislature, if it has control of the budget, obviously can have a great deal of influence. In New York, virtually every senator has a SUNY college in his or her district, so funding can be political rather than going to the place where you can get the biggest bang for the buck. State higher education is always full of those problems. When I was at the University of Maryland, the governor's sister was in the English department and had been hired after he became governor, so that at least created the impression of political influence. But of course it can work the other way: universities can try to cater to the powerful with the expectation that they will receive more favorable treatment.

FL: Stony Brook has recently moved up to become a Division I school in collegiate athletics. As you know, that status can be a mixed blessing for any institution. According to the critics of NCAA athletics, even those Division I schools that manage to run an athletic program with an unblemished record are guilty of devoting a great deal of attention and funding to their intercollegiate athletic program that ought to be directed instead to their academic programs. How would you answer that criticism? What's your take on the current and very public and damaging perceptions of serious problems in recruiting, admission, retention, graduation, student athlete conduct, and funding of athletics, including the huge escalation in the compensation of successful Division I coaches in revenue sports? Can we resolve these problems?

SK: Stony Brook is not yet at the point where we have serious issues here, but I was the person who certainly pushed for going to Division I athletics. We were Division III when I got here. The reason we advanced to Division I is that I see athletics as a very important way to bind a community together. Stony Brook had the reputation of a commuter college which everyone left on the weekend. We don't have chapel any more. We don't have a lot of those old traditions, but athletics is very much a community builder, not just with the students, but the larger community. So I felt it was important to us to build athletic programs. They're building slowly. They are a real plus, not a minus, at our stage of the game but we don't have a stadium for 110, 000 people. It is also, of course, a way to get people involved, since they like coming to the president's box.

I do know something about institutions that have much bigger programs: I was at Maryland and at Texas. Big-time athletics can be a problem. You have to keep a balance. It's like the rest of fundraising. The money that you raise through athletics does tend to go into the athletic program and not into the academic program: it's just a fact. Then there's also the fact that the athletic program can rob the other programs of resources in order to get to the very top. Since we have a very long way to go to get to the top, I don't have those problems yet. On the positive side, I believe that, in this country, an athletic program is one of the things that bring us together.

FL: Did you want to comment on the issues of recruiting, admissions, graduation, and student athlete conduct?

SK: We are very kosher on those issues. We just got a fine new athletic director. He inherited some problems that I had not heard about from the old director, which of course showed the wisdom of changing leadership. It is, of course, possible to develop bad problems in athletics, especially problems that affect student athletes who, if they're not going on to professional ball, are wasting their opportunities.

I also wonder how fair it is that athletes get so much tutoring and so much more attention than other students. The students in the Economic Opportunity Program have access to tutoring and other support services, but students who are not in that program don't have those advantages.

FL: I know that you have been very concerned about the improvement of undergraduate education and, as Stony Brook's president, you established and chaired the Boyer Commission on Educating Undergraduates in the Research University. Could you sketch for me how the report issued by the commission has been implemented at Stony Brook— for example in the areas of removing barriers to interdisciplinary education, changing faculty reward systems, and culminating students' education with a capstone experience?

SK: I felt Stony Brook should be in the forefront on this, but we weren't because institutions that have a lot of money could do it faster. MIT, Stanford, and Harvard were able to put in freshmen seminars immediately, for example. We had to build our capacity to get there. However we have done a number of things.

The Boyer report emphasizes undergraduate research. We have a lot of undergraduates working on research projects with major researchers on campus. We have bright undergraduates, so our faculty do not feel that it is a burden to supervise them. When Paul Lautebur, who was on our faculty when he developed the MRI technology for which he just got the Nobel Prize, visited us recently, he talked about having undergraduate research assistants when he was here because they couldn't afford graduate assistants in those days. So it's not altogether new apparently, but our faculty is very responsive to that initiative and it has gone very well.

We have initiated theme-centered freshman colleges in which the freshmen are grouped so that they study together in a smaller academic community. We have initiated freshman seminars and will do them on a big scale in the spring. Those things are coming along very nicely. I think we need to do more on our writing and oral communications. We have not done that yet, but it seems to me an increasingly important thing.

The capstone courses vary. Some departments conduct capstone courses that are much better than those in other departments, but what I find is that all of these things are becoming part of the expectations.

If you read the academic press, you will notice that the people who were shocked and horrified when we published the report saying that research universities should focus more on undergraduate education and that undergraduates had a right to participate in research now talk about it as just part of the rhetoric. Things may become part of the rhetoric before they become realities, but that's a very important step to becoming a reality. I find that close to home, here at Stony Brook, not only is the focus on undergraduate education part of the rhetoric, but some of our best researchers are working with undergraduates and are really excited about it. To my great astonishment, it has had a profound effect.

The faculty rewards system is the slowest to change. We have raised some people to full professor because of their extraordinary teaching, but that happens rarely, very rarely, and I think it will always be rare in a research university. I think that sometimes in a research university mediocre research can get you rewards, particularly if the department is weak and the university-wide committee doesn't know that academic field very well but is satisfied with seeing some research. So far as faculty rewards for teaching are concerned, I think it's easier to give dollar rewards. We do have distinguished teaching professors that get monetary awards.

FL: We have just discussed one area in which you have taken national leadership. How important do you think that it is for presidents and chancellors to participate in the work done by national higher education associations?

SK: I have not done as much of that as many people. I was chair of the American Association of Colleges and Universities and I found their work with the curriculum very interesting. It's certainly important to know the other chancellors and presidents and to learn from them. The association that I have found most important is the AAU because everybody is from a major research university and we have the same issues. But if you go to ACE, for example, the meetings bring together all different kinds of institutions and their focus is not on the problems that I need to solve. So I've done less work with a variety of associations than some presidents have.

FL: How have you gone about the effort to diversify your campus in terms of the student body, the faculty, and the administration?

SK: So far as the student body is concerned, I have not had to work at diversification in either of my presidencies, though we did devote effort to it at the University of Maryland. Queens was diverse when I got there and became more so during my tenure. Stony Brook was not as diverse as Queens when I arrived but the diversity of the student body has grown because the immigrants to our shores send their kids on to college but want them to be close to home. Even though Stony Brook is in a very white community, we have great and exciting diversity in Suffolk County, so the diversification of the student body is easy.

What is much harder is diversifying the faculty because faculty members so often come and stay at an institution for thirty years. An institution like Stony Brook can have a class of incoming faculty comprising half minorities and half women and not influence its statistics by as much as one percent, particularly in tough years when the institution doesn't have a lot of money to devote to faculty recruitment. . It takes a long time to diversify the faculty because you hire such a small percentage of your faculty every year. When you introduce your incoming faculty on the stage at the fall convocation it may look terrific, admirably diverse, but your statistics move very slowly. Stony Brook's proportion of women and minority faculty has been increasing more rapidly in the last three years because we're forty years old, so we're having more retirements now. The subtraction of white men as they retire has probably made a considerable difference in our statistics.

Diversifying our clerical staff is even harder because faculty will move here in order to take a position, but if you live in Queens or in Brentwood (which is a minority community with which we work closely in Nassau), you're not going to drive that far for a secretary's job. You're going to get something close to home. We have worked with the bus company to offer free bus transportation to our employees and we have training programs in areas like Brentwood and East Islip with greater minority population, but we have not had very good results, so due to the geographical factor, the area where we look worst is in the diversity of our staff members. What you can do quickly is to change the diversity of the administration, because administrators don't ordinarily have thirty-year careers.

FL: What do you see as the strongest forces driving the need for change in higher education over the next ten to twenty years?

SK: Certainly science and technology are going to be dominant forces. In view of that fact, I am concerned that we may be in danger of losing our focus on all the other parts of the university that matter if we're going to have the kind of nation we want. I just visited South Korea, where they have a ministry position for science and technology. That minister, who happens to be one of our alumni, has recently become the deputy prime minister of South Korea.

They devote five percent of their budget to science and technology. The United States has not done that. We have an office of science and technology but it's not a cabinet position. But South Korea does, because they know, as China knows and as India knows, that a focus on science and technology offers them the way to build their future. When the United States wakes up to that realization it will add to the enormous pressure already building for the production of greater numbers of graduates in science and technology.

When that happens, universities will have to be very certain not to let the other things go. For example, given the growing importance of Asia in world affairs, one of the things that we're working on at Stony Brook is our new Department of Asian and Asian-American Studies. We already have an excellent India Studies-Center. We're trying to focus on those areas, but we've got to be sure that we don't just let the humanities sink. This country needs the arts more than ever and universities as well as conservatories are working with the arts so that people can have a strong, broad education as well as a major. Those are some of the dangers we're going to face and university presidents ought to be thinking about these challenges rather than focusing all their time on fundraising. Of course the president must listen and work with the university community, but, in the end, the decisions on where the money goes have to be made by the president.

These issues are going to weigh heavily upon us, but I think that there's going to be a natural tendency to stay where we are rather than getting ready for the next challenge. For example, although our world was different after 9/11, we did not react with the speed that we should have. Presidents have to see what's on the horizon and ask themselves what it means to them for their institution, what it means for American higher education, and how we can be prepared to meet the demands of the future. If we are responsible for deciding where we need to be twenty years from now, we must start tomorrow.

FL: Certainly science and technology will continue to be major factors at the leading edge of research and development in both higher education and economic growth, just as they were in the latter part of the twentieth century. In the twenty-first century, as countries across the globe modernize their political, economic and higher education systems, and we face greater international competition, we can expect that the importance of science and technology will be even greater. Are there other changes looming on the horizon at this point that you feel are likely to assume greater importance in the next five to ten years?

SK: One of the things about which I am concerned, particularly since the last election, is the way that Americans were influenced in this election. The direction of both sides was really scary to me because they were communicating through emotion, visual images, flash, flash, flash, repeating the same words over and over and over, and attacking. It was not about logic. It was not a discussion of issues at all and the American public seemed to accept that. It was a vicious PR battle between two sides. All I could think was that American higher education is failing if we are not creating Americans who are asking candidates "Tell me what your platform is, tell me what you're going to do and let me evaluate you on that basis."

It seems to me we need to have more focus on things like logic and oral communication because that and writing really teach you logic. We've got to get back to those basics, not just in science but in the whole of life. What am I going to accept in this world and what am I not? Consider the reality shows and other popular television programs that people are accepting as authentic. Think about what happened to the news on television or in the press during that election. People are not separating opinions from facts anymore. So at the same time we're looking forward to technology and science, we have to look back at how to improve our students' capacity for critical evaluation.

FL: A good argument for the importance of some of the skills we concentrate on developing through the liberal arts requirements. Stony Brook is involved internationally in Korea. Are there any other countries with which the university is connected?

SK: Yes, a number of countries. We have agreements with a lot of countries from Germany to Australia, to China and Japan. We exchange students and faculty with a lot of different places. We're getting an interesting connection with Kenya through Richard Leakey, who comes to our campus for a few weeks each semester. We're importing graduate students from Kenya and we're going to be doing a number of joint research projects in the area of paleoanthropology. We have a special relationship with Eritrea, teaching their medically related students and nurses.

FL: So you have a broad view at this point, having been involved with higher education internationally. Where do you see their higher education systems going and how have they changed in the last few years? What kind of competition is U.S. higher education going to encounter?

SK: I think it's going to be intense, particularly from China and Korea. The Koreans are much like us. They're aggressive, dynamic, and energetic. Americans, despite what I said about the university, are not so tradition- bound they can't move with the times. The Koreans are that way too and I think that they're moving very fast. They are focusing on science and technology as well as business training. We do a business program in Korea for mid-level executives. And as for China, when they decide to do anything, they throw themselves into it.

FL: And they put the resources behind it.

SK: That's the real thing, the resources. Look at California with its three billion dollar stem cell approach. How am I going to keep my best stem cell people?

FL: You probably aren't. This is an opportunity for California to get the top people in the country. We live on competition in this country. Institutions routinely raid one another for the best faculty.

SK: Absolutely. I hope New York says, "Ha! We're not going to let that happen. Here's, three billion dollars to build world class stem cell research capacity."

FL: For public higher education to be able to deliver everything of which it is capable, there has to be a clearer understanding of its importance. Right now it seems that public colleges and universities are viewed simply as the discretionary part of state budgets.

SK: Yes, New York thinks of us as an agency, the way the Department of Motor Vehicles is an agency. In some states, the university is not just an agency; it has a special existence. New York is tough. It puts resources in prisons before it does in higher education

William English Kirwan

William Kirwan became the chancellor of the University System of Maryland in August of 2002. He came to Maryland from Ohio State University, where he had served as president for four years. Prior to that, he was the president of the University of Maryland College Park for ten years and, before assuming the presidency, had been a member of its faculty and an administrator since 1964, serving as provost and as the acting president. As chancellor, he oversees a system of thirteen institutions, which includes the University of Maryland at College Park.

Kirwan earned his bachelor's degree in mathematics from the University of Kentucky, and his master's and Ph.D. from Rutgers University. He is co-editor of a book on advances in complex analysis and has published a number of scholarly articles in his field of mathematics.

At College Park, Kirwan fashioned a more selective and prestigious undergraduate program and worked with faculty to develop peaks of excellence in graduate education and research. He also led the university through one of the first court challenges to affirmative action, in which the university defended its scholarship program for African-American students, a battle that it won twice at the district court level, but lost in appearances before the Fourth Circuit Court of Appeals and in its bid to take the case to the Supreme Court. Nevertheless, the integrity of the university's defense demonstrated its commitment and resulted in improved recruitment of African-American students.

At Ohio State, Kirwan led the university through a strategic planning process that developed a strong sense of its focus and direction to shape its future. The institution emerged with a vision of itself as a great Midwestern university with a commitment to equity and diversity. He also worked to build the quality of the medical school and raise the research profile of the university.

Dr. Kirwan was appointed by President Clinton to serve as a member of the National Commission on Mathematics and Science Teaching for the 21st Century and he chaired the National Research Council's Commission on the Mathematical Sciences in the Year 2000, which produced the report, "Moving Beyond Myths: Revitalizing Undergraduate Mathematics," National Academy Press (1991). Kirwan was appointed by President Bush to the Board of Advisors on Historically Black Colleges and Universities. In addition, he has served as chair of the board of directors of the National Association of State Universities and Land Grant Colleges and the American Council on Education.

Francis Lawrence: Brit, if I remember correctly, you grew up on a university campus, an auspicious start for a future university president. I'm sure that you owe a great deal to your upbringing.

William E. Kirwan: Yes, I was born and raised in Lexington, Kentucky. When I was born, my father was the football coach at the University of Kentucky, the head football coach. He had gone to the University of Kentucky, was the football captain, graduated, went back to his hometown of Louisville, Kentucky, and got a law degree. When the Depression came along, he couldn't make a living practicing law, so he began teaching in high school and became the school's football coach. Because of his coaching success at the high school level, he was offered the position of head coach at his alma mater. But he and my mother had larger interests in life than just athletics and football. During the war years, when there was no football program, he went to the president and asked whether he could join the faculty if he went back to graduate school and got his Ph.D. The president probably thought, "What football coach is going to go back to school and get a Ph.D.?" So he said, "Yes." It was a very bold move by my parents. They owned a house in Lexington, which they sold to finance my father's graduate education at Duke University. Remarkably, he earned his Ph.D. in history there in two years. He came back to UK and had a long and distinguished career there, first as a historian, then as an administrator. He was the dean of the graduate school and, at the very end of his career, president of the university. He went from football coach to president. Along the way, he won Guggenheim and Fulbright fellowships and several book prizes. He was a remarkable person, and my mother was his equal in some ways. She did not have a professional career, but she worked with him on all of his books. She'd go to the library and help with the research. Then she'd organize the notes, type the manuscript, and help with the editing.

One of the things I'm sure we'll talk about is the whole issue of diversity and my life-long commitment to fairness and equity in our society. When I was growing up in Lexington, Kentucky, it was a segregated community. We lived in the white part of town. There was also a black part of town and the two never mixed. All the schools were segregated, so I did not go to school with an African American until my senior year in high school. That's when Brown vs. Board of Education came to Lexington. Three African Americans were admitted to my high school. It was the first time I had ever been in school with African Americans. I remember feeling such great empathy and admiration for those brave individuals. I also remember feeling how unfair it was that they had grown up in an environment of discrimination. Indeed, from my very earliest memories, I recall feeling how unjust life was in Lexington and how unfair it was to African Americans. I know that this sense of unfairness didn't just spring spontaneously from my brain. They resulted from the values that I learned from my parents, who were very liberal people in a very conservative community. I credit them for creating my deep feelings about inclusiveness, diversity, and equity.

But my debt to my parents is much, much larger. I grew up in an academic household where books and music were important. I learned to love opera and classical music because my mother and father listened to fine music all the time. They also were great entertainers, so our house was a focal point for interesting social events and dinner parties. This was my introduction to the academic life. Even as a very young person, there was no doubt in my mind that I was going to be an academic when I grew up.

My older brother had gone to Princeton. When I graduated from high school, I could have gone to Princeton too, but I was an athlete and thought that I was going to be a great football player along my way to becoming a professor. So I went to the University of Kentucky on a football scholarship. Eventually I became disenchanted with big time college athletics and stopped playing to devote full time to my academic pursuits. This proved to be a very good decision. I was a mathematics major and because of my academic success, I won an NDEA fellowship to pursue my Ph.D. at Rutgers University.

Just to summarize my thoughts on your first question, I have such a sense of debt to my parents. I guess many people do, but I really feel that they shaped the core values that have stayed with me throughout my life. I remember coming home from Rutgers in the summer and walking back and forth with my father to the university, where I would spend the day working on my research. Some of my most wonderful memories are of being able to spend that kind of time just talking with him. He and my mother had such a strong influence on me.

FL: That's a priceless anecdote about your relationship as a young man with your father and his impact on you. As a follow-up to that, what personal attributes do you feel have contributed most to your success as a leader? Perhaps it ties into what you've said about your parents.

WK: There are two things that I would point to. One is a strong sense of values. That may sound trite, but both of my parents were such principled people and had such incredible integrity in every aspect of their lives. They instilled in my brother and me a sense of responsibility to live by the rules. Let me give you one example of their standards. My uncle had a farm and we'd visit him periodically. When I was fifteen years old, I begged my parents to let me drive our family car on the farm. They said no because I didn't yet have a learner's permit. The parents of every other kid I knew would have let their kid drive their cars in similar circumstances, but I wasn't allowed to drive until I had a learner's permit.

I also learned from my parents by watching how they conducted their lives. They were both such warm and outgoing people. They had an incredible ability to connect with others, no matter what their station in life. They were so gracious and had such a genuine respect for people. This left a profound impression on me. I learned a lot from them and I'd like to think that I have some of their characteristics.

FL: What do you regard as your first leadership position?

WK: My first real leadership experience was being the captain of the football team in high school. It was a big thing in my life to be the captain of the team. We had a good football team but at times we had our struggles. I learned a lot from having the responsibility to bring the team together during time-outs and talk to them about what we needed to do. I did finally stop playing football, but I think that participating in athletics can be a very valuable thing in one's development. You learn so much about discipline, teamwork, and responsibility.

I think the opportunity to participate in some form of organized athletics can be a very valuable thing when people are growing up. One of the healthy things in our communities today is that there are so many more opportunities for young people. I watch my grandkids play several sports. One of them plays on a soccer team. It doesn't matter whether you're good or not, you get to play. In my day, that didn't happen. Last year, I saw him play basketball. His team lost 53 to 13, but there were four quarters and there was a rule that everybody got to play two quarters. What a great experience for him.

FL: You make a good point. I have been watching my grandchildren in New Jersey play sports. All of their leagues have rules that dictate that everybody has to play. If you don't play all of the children on the team, you lose the game. Anyone who thinks that kid's sports leagues are not good for children doesn't understand that.

WK: I certainly profited enormously by being so involved in athletics, playing three sports in high school and one in college. I think that for athletes, no matter what they do in later life, there can be a very significant residual value.

FL: Other than your parents, who were the people who inspired you and acted us your mentors?

WK: When I give a list of my heroes, I always start with my parents. To this day, I have such great appreciation for the values they imparted to me. They would be at the top of the list. But there are others. I grew up during the civil rights movement and several people made a deep and lasting impression on me during this era. One of them was John Kennedy. If he had lived, perhaps–as some suggest—he may not have gone down on the list of our great presidents. Who knows? But I found him to be such an inspirational person and to this day I have enormous admiration for him. I actually saw him at Rutgers in the fall of 1960. He came to New Brunswick when he was campaigning for the presidency. I was as close to him as I am to you now, and I heard him speak. Not only did I feel that he stood for things that I valued, but he showed me the importance of rhetoric in leadership. He was so eloquent. I still think of his inaugural address as one of the most inspiring speeches I ever heard. But I would say that I was probably even more inspired and moved by Martin Luther King, Jr. I was there on that famous day. I had just come to the University of Maryland. I went to the Mall and heard his extraordinary "I Have a Dream" speech. I still listen to that speech today. It was incredible. As you may know, he had a prepared text that he set aside when he went into his "I Have a Dream..." declaration. I still get goose bumps when I listen to it. He was a huge influence on me.

I was also inspired by Bobby Kennedy. I thought he, in a more understated way, conveyed a real sense of passion. With him, it wasn't so much the verbal rhetoric. It was the intensity of feeling that he brought. He conveyed a moral passion that I found inspiring and moving.

In my academic discipline, of course, I had mentors and professors, who had a profound impact on me. One of the things that I learned from those two or three professors is that, while in our lives we come in contact with lots of teachers, there are a few special people who see it as their responsibility to pass on something to the next generation. Without these special people, I don't know that my career in mathematics would have been what it was. They not only helped me when I was under their supervision, but stayed in touch with me in later years, making certain that opportunities were created for me. They were always there to support me when I needed help. They inspired me to try and be the same kind of mentor for young people who came under my supervision.

FL: Going on to the institutions you have served, let me ask three very general questions for your response. What were the challenges that College Park faced at the time when you became chancellor? What were the challenges at Ohio State? Finally, what are the common elements and differences in the challenges and the responsibilities of the system president?

WK: I feel that I've grown so much through my different leadership experiences. It almost makes me wish I could stop the clock, go back, and start over. When I became president at College Park, I was a very inexperienced administrator. It was also a pretty unique thing to become president there because, until that point, I had spent my entire career at College Park, from assistant professor to the university's president.

I came to the university in 1964, right after completing my Ph.D. I got tenure, became a professor of mathematics, and then department chair. After that, I was the provost for seven or eight years, and then I was appointed president. My entire career was at that institution. Ironically, when I first came to the university, I had no desire to be an administrator. In fact, if anything, I had a slight degree of disdain for administrators.

FL: We're schooled that way.

WK: I certainly was. I was a very serious academic. I came to the university wanting to be the best mathematician and teacher that I could possibly be. That's all that mattered to me professionally. But, after some years, I was asked to take my turn as the department chair. I had the good fortune to follow an extraordinary person. During my tenure as chair, wonderful things happened in the department, not so much because of the things I did, but because of the groundwork that had been laid. The experience taught me something, however. It showed me that academic leadership has its own special value and rewards. It, too, is a noble calling. Work in your discipline enables you to make a contribution to your field, but the impact is on a relatively small universe. Being a department chairman showed me that, in a leadership position, you can have an impact on the entire institution.

I actually had my baptism by fire even before I became department chairman. The chairman at the time had taken me under his wing. I didn't realize it back then, but he had decided that I was going to be the next chairman of the department. This was in the early 1970s just when the Vietnam issue was really heating up. There were lots of protests and demonstrations on the campus. The chairman was going on sabbatical. He told me that he wanted me to be the chairman for the summer. I replied that I had a research grant and didn't really want to do it. He talked me into it, assuring me that it was going to be a cushy job and I wouldn't have to worry about anything. Then, about a week before he left, when we were having one of our final talks, he said casually, "By the way, I have to tell you something. We have somebody up for promotion and it's very likely that they're going to turn this promotion down. They'll never admit it, but the reason they're going to turn it down is that he signed a letter of protest about something the president did to anti-war demonstrators." I thought, "Oh my God, what have I bought into?"

The chair went off on sabbatical and, sure enough, a couple of weeks later we got a letter saying that the promotion the chair had warned me about was denied. It turns out, however, that the president made a tactical mistake. He actually said in his letter of denial that the decision was based on the letter of protest. If he had denied the candidate on other grounds, there's not much we could have done about it. At this time, I was still an associate professor of mathematics. Now it suddenly became my responsibility to get the decision reversed, because the denial was based on such an egregious abuse of freedom of expression. My first step was to get the whole math department faculty together and tell them what had happened, why it happened, and what I was going to do about it. Then I got the campus senate and the other department chairmen involved. We wrote letters and had meetings with the provost, the president, and the board. I worked on this—all—summer—long. It was totally consuming. And (I will never forget this) at the end of the summer, the last day before I was leaving for a year's sabbatical in England—we got a letter saying the board had reversed the decision and the promotion would be approved.

FL: Fantastic. That was a real coup.

WK: It was. Five or six years later, I became the department chairman and served for four years. Then, I was nominated to be the provost. I thought that it was very unlikely that I would be selected because I had been department chairman for such a short period of time and had never been a dean. But, lo and behold, I was selected to be the provost and then the president of the university.

When I became president there were a number of challenges. Probably the biggest adjustment I had to make was to the public role of the president. I was so much of an academic and I was so internally oriented to the institution that the role of the president as an external figure and spokesperson was just something I hadn't really thought about. Perhaps this responsibility should have been obvious to me, but no one or anything in my previous experiences prepared me for this role. In those days, a lot of the external and legislative relations, and even the fundraising responsibilities, fell, oddly enough, to the head of the system. The head of the campus, even though College Park was the flagship campus, traditionally had not had that kind of responsibility. But I came to see that if the university was going to make real progress, it needed a more visible and vocal proponent. So the challenge for me was to develop the skills necessary to be an effective external voice and face for the institution, something that had never been part of my development or training or expertise up until that moment.

We in higher education do a poor job of preparing new presidents for the full gamut of their responsibilities. We just let them sink or swim with on-the-job training.

Another challenge that I faced when I became president in the fall of 1988 was the fact that, although Maryland had a handful of very good graduate programs (physics, mathematics, economics, and history), it was seen in the state as a big university that was only a decade removed from a policy of open admissions. Slowly, we had begun to move toward higher standards and more selectivity at the undergraduate level. But the university had grown too large for the available resources. I believe there was something like 38,000 undergraduates.

I realized that, if the university was ever going to become a distinguished university, we had to have a much more selective undergraduate student body. I knew we were on our way to building a strong graduate education and research program. There was no question about that. With all of the resources in the national capital area, with the potential for partnerships with well-funded federal laboratories, it was going to happen. But, if the university was going to really change its status and be viewed as a distinguished university, it had to develop a more selective and prestigious undergraduate program. So I worked with the board of regents and the state government (this was on the job training for my external role) and developed a plan to reduce the undergraduate enrollment by 20 percent, with the understanding that the state would provide general fund support to replace the lost tuition revenue from having fewer students. The board and the state bought into the plan. In short, the plan was to be phased in over a period of five or six years by decreasing the size of the entering class of students, holding at those new admissions levels until the total enrollment was reduced by the 20 percent figure.

After the state, the governor, and the board bought into this plan—this was in the early 1990s—the economy went south, as it did in many other states. So, rather than fulfilling its commitment to replace the lost tuition, the state began cutting our budget. The challenge facing me, right after becoming president and successfully developing and selling the plan, was what do we do now? Do we continue with the plan, reducing the enrollment even though the state can't meet its commitment, or do we suspend it? That was a huge challenge. We decided to just bite the bullet and keep going with the enrollment reduction plan. Although there were some very tough times—we ended up eliminating a college, seven departments and twenty-six degree programs just to support the plan—we did it. We pulled it off. Now the selectivity and the quality of the undergraduate program at College Park is extraordinary. I think this was one of the most difficult challenges I have faced as a university president, but it proved to be a very good decision.

FL: What did you face when you went to Ohio State?

WK: When I got to Ohio State, there were a whole set of challenges, but the first one I faced was not knowing anybody. It's hard to convey the feelings of leaving a university where you are a fixture, where you know everyone and going to a place where you know no one. I had been at College Park for thirty-four years. I couldn't go into a building where I didn't know the custodial people in that building. To go to a huge university where I didn't know a soul was a huge challenge. A number of academics have gone from one university to another during their careers and they learn to deal with this situation, but I was a person who'd lived in a single university community for thirty-four years and suddenly found myself in a huge place where I knew no one. I wasn't prepared for it. The first challenge facing me was who do you believe, who do you trust? You have all these people filling your ears with their opinions. In retrospect, I should have prepared myself for this. It should have been obvious to me that this would happen, but it wasn't. As a result, I felt very much alone within a community of 50,000 people. In this circumstance, not really knowing anyone and not knowing who to trust or who had talent, I had to put together a leadership team.

There were a couple of other challenges. One is that Ohio State was a wonderful institution, but it had no focus. There was no overarching vision for the university. No one had really asked, "Where is this institution going?" The struggle that Ohio State faced while I was there was, should it try to be all things to all people or should it strive to become a great Midwestern university? It was a very good university, but was it going to become a great university? So, as I entered Ohio State, that was the challenge I faced, resolving this issue. Another challenge I faced was the institution's commitment to diversity. I was shocked by the complacency around the issue of equity and diversity at Ohio State; I think that it is to some degree a reflection of the Midwest. This hit me as much as the sense of not knowing anybody. I really wasn't prepared for it. At College Park the issue of diversity was part of the fabric of the institution. It was in the air. It was everywhere. We talked about it. There was an institutional passion and intensity around the issue of diversity that was apparent to everyone. There was energy surrounding the issues and things were happening.

Now, to be fair, Maryland had been a segregated institution. It had a lot of correction to do for the wrongs of the past. And, the East Coast is much more diverse than the Midwest. At my first press conference when I went to Ohio State, when they announced me as the president and before I had moved to the campus, I said to the audience that they needed to know what my values are and what would drive my administration as president. I briefly outlined what I thought they ought to know. One of the values that I mentioned was building the excellence of Ohio State University through our commitment to diversity. Later people told me they were stunned that I would say that. Coming to grips with diversity as a personal agenda in an institution that didn't really see it as an institutional issue was a huge challenge.

Another challenge I faced was the role and the expectations of the president of Ohio State in the state of Ohio. I don't know if there's anything that's quite comparable to it. Most states have several distinguished universities. North Carolina has Duke, Chapel Hill and North Carolina State. In Maryland, there's Johns Hopkins and the University of Maryland. In New Jersey, there's Rutgers and Princeton. In Ohio there's Ohio State, and basically a lot of smaller regional universities. The focus of Ohio on Ohio State is unbelievable. In Columbus, a city of a million people, it's in the news every day. When you hire a department chairman, he or she is profiled in the paper. If there's a disturbance in a dorm or something like that, it's a front-page news story. Right after I got there, we hired Brad Moore from Berkeley as vice president for research. It was a major front-page story. One unsettling thing I faced at Ohio State is the importance that the state placed on athletics and the football team. I found this disconcerting, to be honest with you. Athletics was important in Maryland but not anything like as important as it was there. Coming to grips with that was also a challenge.

FL: What effects did the role and demands of each of these leadership positions have on your family life and how do you maintain a balance?

WK: We have a very close family, but as I look back on my career, I realize my leadership positions did take a toll. I wasn't there a lot. I was traveling all the time and out late at night, not always there for dinners and birthdays. Fortunately, Patty, my wife, is a tower of strength and has been the glue that held everything together. Also fortunately, we had children relatively young in life, so when I became president our son had graduated from college and our daughter was a student at Maryland. But the job of the provost is 24/7, just like that of a president, and, as much reward as I've gotten out of my career and my professional life, I have a real sense of regret that there wasn't more time for the family. It's interesting to compare the situation with our children to that of our grandchildren. Although I am still very busy, I was telling Patty the other day that I think I'm a better grandfather than I was a father.

I think that the time demands also take a physical toll for a lot of people in leadership positions. Most of us don't take the time to take care of ourselves. Even today, I should be exercising regularly, but I don't, because I'm always on the go. I also believe that the time demands, if anything, have grown. The expectations for these positions are greater now than they were even ten years ago or fifteen years, and certainly twenty years ago. I worry about the young presidents coming along right now, because, as I think we agree, it's even a more demanding job today than it was a decade ago.

FL: What did your internal constituencies—governing board, faculty, students, staff expect of you at different institutions, if you were to compare Maryland versus Ohio State?

WK: I think in terms of students and faculty and staff it was very much the same at the two institutions. Where there was a difference was in the expectations of the external constituency. They were much, much greater in Ohio. They were large in Maryland, but they were extraordinary at Ohio State.

FL: In Ohio, would you say there's the governor and then there is the president of the state university?

WK: People actually say the two most visible people in the state of Ohio are the governor and the president of Ohio State. They're wrong. The football coach is number one—by a wide margin. In any case, there was a real difference in the external visibility and expectations at Ohio State.

FL: If you look at all of your constituencies, what are the pressures that the system head faces in Maryland?

WK: I am asked a lot about what I think of being system head versus president of a university. My feeling about this is I would not have wanted to start out as a system head. Without a doubt, I think that the more interesting job is being the president of a campus, where you're working hands-on with the faculty and students. But, I do feel that, at this stage of my career, being a system head is both appropriate and rewarding. I have thirteen presidents who report to me. I was a president longer than any of them, so I can be helpful in nurturing them, mentoring them, and assisting them in achieving their goals for their institutions. Besides the presidents, the major constituencies I have as chancellor are the Board of Regents and the elected leaders in Annapolis. I enjoy grappling with the major policy issues facing higher education – funding, access, quality and accountability. A lot of university presidents may find those issues unattractive. But, given my long history in Maryland and the number of state leaders I know, I believe I have an opportunity to have an impact on the future of the state that a president of a single university just could not have.

FL: Your long career in Maryland would make you very comfortable in doing it.

WK: I like engaging and interacting with people, so I feel very comfortable going to Annapolis. I see my role as helping the institutions through this very difficult fiscal time. My goal is to create an environment in the state where there will be greater appreciation for the role of the universities, for higher education, and to develop a more stable funding environment for the future.

FL: How have you managed the different, sometimes conflicting expectations from your various constituencies? Speaking just in a generic way, how do you handle these things physically and mentally?

WK: In this kind of job, I'm blessed to be a very optimistic person. When people ask me, "What are your greatest disappointments," I always take a long time to answer, not that there haven't been plenty of disappointments along the way, but they don't stay with me. I always have the sense that there's tomorrow and it's going to be a better day. I do get down and depressed, but it is never for a very long time. It's just part of my nature. I feel very fortunate that's one of my characteristics.

Another characteristic I believe I have is that I am a good listener. I think that is a very much underappreciated quality for leaders. Often people who get into a leadership position think that they've got to be out in front on every single issue, showing they're in control. There is a time for that. But the ability to bring people together and hear what they have to say is very important. One of the things I've learned is that when you make a decision that goes against a certain group, if those people feel that they have had their say and you have genuinely listened, it helps. They might not be happy, and they may grumble, but having listened goes a long way toward avoiding dissent in the community. I also believe that having the patience to sit with people and listen to what they have to say is a large part of creating consensus. Effective leaders must demonstrate the flexibility to genuinely listen to opposing points of view and, when appropriate, change established positions to reflect new understandings. Patience and the ability to listen are two qualities of leadership that I believe are very, very important.

FL: What do you see as having been your biggest challenge as a leader?

WK: It comes back to something I want to say about my time at College Park. The biggest challenge that I faced, in many ways, was over the Benjamin Banneker Scholarship court challenge. Maryland was one of the states that had segregated schools until Brown vs. Board of Education. A few decades after desegregation, the Office of Civil Rights (OCR) came into Maryland, as they did to thirteen other states, and looked at the pace of integration. In effect, they said, "You folks are not getting the job done. Every one of these states has got to have a plan, and every institution has to have a plan of how you're going to integrate the institutions." I was a math professor at that time. As part of its response, Maryland created something called the Benjamin Banneker Scholarship. Benjamin Banneker was an African-American mathematician who actually did much of the master planning for Washington, D.C. This scholarship was awarded to very high-ability African-American students. There were about thirty to thirty-five of these scholarships given each year, which doesn't sound like a huge number, but it was built on a very solid premise. The idea was to get some of the best African-American students to commit to the University of Maryland. Once they did, it would send a signal to other minority students that is was o.k. to go to the university. There are many other things we did in response to the OCR mandate, but the Benjamin Banneker Scholarship was a major component of our response to the Office of Civil Rights.

Now we fast forward to the early 1990s and the Banneker Scholarship is well entrenched and hugely successful. About 18 percent of the university's entering class is African American, way ahead of universities of our type. Although racial tensions still existed, the campus had become a much healthier place. Just at the height of our success, we were sued by a student who claimed that he was not eligible for the Benjamin Banneker Scholarship because it was racially based. Although we had other merit scholarships open to all students that this student could have applied for, he wasn't eligible for the Banneker Scholarship, so he took us to court. We won in the Federal District Court.

The student appealed to the Fourth Circuit Court of Appeals. We had based our case on the fact that OCR said we had to have special programs and the Banneker program was one OCR had blessed. Since OCR had never come back and said that we had met our obligations, we asserted that we had the right to continue this program. The Fourth Circuit said, in effect, "We don't accept that argument. The University of Maryland has much more diversity than most other institutions of its type, and we don't think that you can justify this program. The fact that OCR hasn't given you a clean bill of health is their problem. You don't have the grounds for this scholarship. If you are going to keep it, you've got to make the case that there are continuing effects of past discrimination." So the case was thrown back into my lap. What were we going to do? Get rid of the scholarship or try to make the case that there were continuing effects of past discrimination at the university? Incidentally, to do this, we would have to expose our "dirty linen," and show that things were still not what they should be on the campus. There was a huge debate at the university. What were we to do? Of course, there were strong feelings on both sides. A lot of people said, "Declare a victory. You know you fought the good fight; you went to the Fourth Circuit Court of Appeals. It's over." Others said, "How can we abandon the very program that has been the key to our success?"

We decided, after taking all the input, that we were going to go back and try to make the case for the continuing effects of past discrimination. The Banneker Scholarship was too important to us. It had been a centerpiece of our success and to get rid of it would have been to walk away from it when we really hadn't gotten to where we wanted to be in terms of diversity. So I decided, and the board and chancellor supported me, that we were going to make the case and go back to the District Court. We put together an incredible case to show that there were continuing effects. We went to high school counselors who could not go to Maryland in the pre-Brown vs. Board of Education era and did interviews with them, asking, "What do you think about the University of Maryland?" They had very negative thoughts about the university because they had been barred from attending. We did interviews with grandparents: "What do you think about the University of Maryland?" Grandparents have enormous impact, particularly in the African-American community, on college-bound students. Ironically, their negative views helped to make our case. Our graduation rates weren't as good for African Americans as for our other students. We'd had racial issues on our campus. We didn't have as diverse a faculty as we should have. All of those things demonstrated that there were still problems for us to address and we were very upfront about our shortcomings. Both the campus senate and the student governing association endorsed the effort to make this case. I'm very proud of that.

We won our case in the District Court and it went back to the Fourth Circuit Court of Appeals. For a second time, the Fourth Circuit Court of Appeals reversed the District Court and ruled against us. They said, "You have to disband the Banneker Scholarship. We don't think that there's a compelling case for continuing impact of past discrimination." We appealed to the Supreme Court and the Supreme Court refused to take the case. We had now run the gamut. There was no choice but to eliminate or modify the Banneker Scholarship. So, we enlarged the scope of the scholarship and waited to see the impact on our diversity efforts.

To our great relief, an amazing thing happened. We had the best recruiting year ever for African-American students and for a very interesting reason. We heard over and over again that the African-American community had great respect for the integrity of the university's position. The fact that the university was willing to say that there were continuing effects of past discrimination and to be honest about its continuing struggles for equity demonstrated its commitment to making it a better place. So rather than damaging the diversity effort, the loss of the Banneker Scholarship actually enhanced it. I can remember being so tied up in knots over this issue and so relieved when it had this happy ending.

FL: How did you recruit and structure your leadership teams at Maryland and Ohio State?

WK: Imperfectly. I've made my mistakes. I learned early on that you really can't trust what references tell you in a search process. On a very important search, I called a reference, the president of the institution, who was a graduate of the University of Maryland, about a candidate. He just went on and on about how good the candidate was. I appointed the person and he turned out to be a disaster.

FL: He wanted to get rid of him.

WK: Precisely. You are exactly right. I guess I'm naïve and trusting and didn't understand that motivation.

In putting a leadership team together, here's what I have tried to do. I'm not saying I've always done it successfully, but here's the goal. First of all, particularly in this day and age, an institution needs a diverse leadership team. You've got to have people who see the world through different lenses. I think that's more important today than ever before and I can't imagine any leader being successful who doesn't have that. I think that the greatest trap for a president is not selecting people or not creating the atmosphere where the president's views can be challenged. I think a lot of people get in trouble as presidents because they have people around them who either aren't connected to the community or who tell the president what the president wants to hear. It takes a confident leader, and one who's got his or her ego under check, to avoid that kind of environment. The best protection from going off the deep end is having strong-willed people who can look the president in the eye and say, "You know you're making a huge mistake." The most important thing is having smart people, well connected to the community, who are not afraid to express their views and to tell you when they think you're wrong. Now obviously, sometimes they're going to change your mind, sometimes they aren't, but if you don't have that kind of atmosphere, you are not going to be successful over the long haul. None of us is smart enough to know the right thing to do all the time. If your ideas aren't honestly and rigorously challenged, you're going to get yourself in trouble. I think that is the single most important quality in putting together a leadership team.

FL: And you did that in both institutions.

WK: Yes. I certainly made some mistakes with individual appointments, but I had very strong-willed people around me who felt they could tell me when they thought I was wrong. That has been a valuable thing to me.

FL: You didn't necessarily have a structural model in mind; you were mainly trying to make sure you had the right people.

WK: Structure is also important. When I came to Ohio State, I felt they had a very top-heavy administration with too many vice presidents. The first thing I did right after I got there was to ask Frank Rhodes, the former president of Cornell, whom I've always admired greatly, to come in as a consultant. He had recently retired from Cornell. I said to Frank, "I want you to go out, talk to people, and tell me what you're hearing. Use your judgment, write me a report, and also help me think through how to reorganize this place so that it is more rationally structured for what it is I want to accomplish." I felt that people would be more likely to talk openly to Frank than they would to me. I think that worked extremely well.

One organizational thing that I feel strongly about is that I believe that the right model for the modern research university is to have a strong provost position, someone who is really the number two person inside the institution. Given the external responsibilities of the president, there needs to be a chief operating officer, to use a business term, and that has to be the provost. The more common model is to have a lot of vice presidents who operate at the same level as the provost. I believe that the provost should be, in effect, the executive vice president. The provost must be seen as a half a step above the other vice presidents. I'm even of the mind that the vice president for research should report to the provost, not the president. Now I know a lot of people won't agree with that, but I think that anytime you divide the academic enterprise between two people with equal access to the president, it sows the seeds for a lack of alignment.

FL: Let's go on to the topic of formulating and implementing a vision.

WK: This is a very good topic. It is one on which, I have to say, my thinking has evolved radically over my career. When I became president at College Park, I had certain ideas about what I wanted to achieve, a distinguished university, a more selective undergraduate program, greater diversity. But the idea of writing out some grandiose vision or strategic plan was, I thought, a waste of time. I genuinely thought it didn't have a useful purpose. I have swung completely around to the view that it is very important for an institution to have a sense of vision and values and mission that it can articulate in a very convincing way in order to more effectively align its resources with its aspirations. I've gone from being someone who had an informal sense of goals and planning to one who advocates a much more structured process. We had a very structured process at Ohio State that worked extremely well. It was helped immeasurably by Jim Collins.

FL: The author of *Good to Great*.

WK: Yes. I learned so much from him. When we started working on a strategic plan at Ohio State, we quickly became bogged down. How to proceed? How to structure the plan? How to involve the larger community? Someone finally said, "Why don't you call Jim Collins and ask him to come here and advise us?" In a rash moment, I picked up the phone, called Jim Collins, and said, "Dr. Collins, we're trying to develop a strategic plan at Ohio State. Here's what we're thinking of doing.... Would you consider coming out and spending the day with us?" He laughed and said, "I can't do it for two reasons. First I'm working on a book [which turned out to be *Good to Great*], and I just don't have the time. Second, you can't afford me. But I tell you what: I'm very impressed with what you're trying to do. If you bring your team out here, I will give you a day and a half pro bono."

We got on the plane, flew out to Boulder, Colorado and about twelve of us had a day and a half with Jim Collins. I will never forget the first session. We got into the room, sat down with him and the first words out of his mouth were, "Okay, I want to hear what the values of your institution are?" We sat there in silence and sort of looked at each other wondering out loud, "What *are* our values?" He said, "You know you can't do a strategic plan if you don't know what the core values of your institution are, what's really important to your university. What's your vision? What's unique to your academic institution?"

We studied his books and absorbed his wisdom on planning issues. It was very, very helpful.

Through this process, I came to understand the value of a strategic plan and of setting strategic directions. In this day and age, with such a constraint on resources, if you don't do that, what you have is lots of random motions, many of which are productive things, but they don't have the multiplier effect of all the energy and resource vectors pointing in the same direction.

FL: So you involved the whole community, which is the only process capable of ensuring that a strategic plan is going to work.

WK: Absolutely. We didn't appoint a team and tell them to go write a strategic plan and bring it back to us. The leadership team took responsibility for articulating the values and developing the strategic plan, but we kept putting drafts out to the larger community and getting feedback. And through an iterative process like this, we got more and more and more buy-in on the strategic plan. In the end, it was very well received on the campus. The board bought into it to such an extent that, when I left, they said to the candidates for my replacement, "We have our strategic vision for this university. We want somebody who can shape it, and make it their own, but we're not looking for someone to create a new vision and plan." One of the things that we did with the strategic plan relates to another one of your questions.

FL: How did you align the resources of the university with the goals of the plan?

WK: We had goals and initiatives in the plan and we put target dollar values on what each of our initiatives would cost. We had a projected resource base. To give the plan credibility, we identified the resources to support each of the plan's initiatives. This was difficult but it was so very important to do. It made the plan real. We also established benchmarks to measure progress and we established a real sense of accountability with the plan. I feel very proud of this document and I think it is serving Ohio State very well today.

FL: As you implemented your plan, how did you monitor and track outcomes and progress?

WK: There were two things we did. As I said, we established goals and benchmarks. Then we set a rigorous means of collecting data to measure our progress against peers. We also committed to issuing an annual report card on our progress. To my knowledge John Lombardi, when he was the president of the University of Florida, was the first to do something like this. He gathered data measuring the university's performance against peers. He had the courage to show where the university was successful, as well as where it wasn't so successful. Although this forces the institution to expose some of its shortcomings, it also gives its claims of success added credibility. I think it's a very effective strategy.

FL: And it's ongoing. In this age, when assessment and evaluation are watchwords, if you don't gather data and evaluate your own performance, you may pay a deep price, when others decide to do it for you.

WK: It's ongoing, and that kind of strategy is important because without effective means of accountability, I think that strategic planning becomes a meaningless exercise.

FL: The process of change does not always go smoothly. Could you describe any critical incidents and how you dealt with them?

WK: I gave a talk on this topic at a conference at Wake Forest. I'll describe an especially difficult change effort at the University of Maryland during my presidency. Just as I was becoming president, a new system of higher education was created in the state. The charter for this new system designated College Park as the state's flagship university, "with state funding at the level of its best funded peers." That's pretty strong language in a higher education charter. The governor made a huge commitment of funding as a result of this language. The first couple of years there was a significant increase in our appropriations. So, it looked like we were on our way. What a time to be president of the university, I thought. Then the economy in Maryland was hit hard, harder than most other states. Suddenly this flow of resources—that had been turned on with such flare—went dry. But, it was worse than that. It was the way it happened. Over the course of eighteen months we had a series of seven or eight budget cuts. Every month or so, I'd get a call from the governor's office saying, "We have to take two or three percent more, but this is it. We're not going to come back to you." Six weeks later, I'd get another call with the same message.

In the end, we suffered cuts of about 25 percent to our state funding. Now, it's bad enough to get cuts when things are moving along at the institution at a more or less normal pace of progress. It's very demoralizing. But imagine getting cuts like this on the heels of an unprecedented funding commitment. Expectations and aspirations were at an all time high. The deflation of spirit on campus was horrible to experience. The issue for me became, what were we going to do about it? Were we just going to hunker down and wait till the economy came back or were we going to try to deal with this and do the best we could to maintain our momentum with the resources available to us? We raised tuition of course, but there's only so much you can do with tuition. We eliminated positions and made other budget cuts. But these were stop-gap measures. We had priorities to support. We had aspirations to realize. We had the enrollment reduction plan I spoke about earlier to fund. We realized that if we were going to move the institution forward, we would have to eliminate whole programs and transfer these resources to our highest priorities. So we launched an elaborate planning process.

Fortunately, I had a very good provost to help lead this effort. Colleges were asked to say what their strengths and weaknesses were, what their priorities were, top to bottom. They had to identify programs central to their mission and those that were not. I appointed a committee of distinguished faculty to assess the quality of all programs. Out of this, we put together a plan that was vetted with the campus senate on several occasions. It called for the elimination of a college, seven departments, and 26 degree programs. Open hearings were held. There were demonstrations in front of my office building by constituents of the affected departments and programs. I received countless letters of protest from alumni and legislators. In the end, however, the plan we put forward was overwhelmingly adopted by the faculty senate. As a result, we created a fund of about $15 million, which may not sound like a huge sum of money but it was in that day. It became an invaluable resource to sustain the momentum of the university and the morale of our best faculty. It demonstrated our resolve to build a great university.

There were several things we learned in this process that I think could be useful to others. First, before any decisions were made, the goals for the process were stated and the procedures that were going to be followed were all laid out. We were determined not to invent the rules as we went along. That would have destroyed the credibility of our decisions. Secondly, we involved the shared governance organizations in establishing the review process. The fact that the faculty senate was a full partner in the effort made the difficult decisions possible. And, we rigorously adhered to the established procedures throughout the process.

There was an aspect of the effort that we didn't plan for adequately. Something that didn't come to me naturally, but I learned from all of this, was the importance of strategic communications. I grew up thinking of academia as a little sheltered world where arcane subjects like planning and resource reallocations would have little interest to the outside world. But this process suddenly presented a huge communications challenge for us. Because of the demonstrations, the *Washington Post* became interested in the story. Initially, the image was created of an institution in great distress, as opposed to an institution with the will and the drive and the courage to protect its priorities.

I learned from that experience. During that time, I came to understand the importance of talented communication folks. We eventually got the real story out and received kudos for what we had done. But for me it was another example of on-the-job training. When I got to Ohio State, I created a vice president for communications and was able to hire a very talented person who had been the chief communication officer for Dupont. He was an Ohio State alum and it was his dream to come back to Ohio State. Having a real professional running the communications operation was a huge blessing. When I came back to Maryland as chancellor of the system, one of the first things I did was hire a very talented director of strategic communications. That's a long way from where I was when I first became a president and thought that all you had to do was just go out, meet the media, and, say what's on your mind.

FL: You think that all you have to do is to tell them the truth and they'll believe you. I'd like you to talk about the external constituencies just a little bit more. What importance did you place on the roles of College Park and Ohio State in their communities?

WK: As I said, when I became president, I didn't really understand the importance of external relations or how much time needs to be devoted to this area. By the time I left the University of Maryland, we had launched a successful capital campaign, developed a governmental relations program, reinvigorated our alumni operations, and begun serious marketing efforts. You might say I'd gotten religion on the subject.

I think that the experience at Ohio State deepened my sense of the importance of these activities. In fact, at Ohio State, there was a group of staff that met weekly to monitor my calendar and be certain that I was spending adequate time each month with alumni, with students, with faculty, and with donors. I found this very valuable, because if you don't do this systematically, the president is drawn into a schedule that hasn't been rationally thought out. If you don't have a process that ensures that you spend time with each of the major constituencies, I think the odds are that you will overlook some important group.

FL: What expectations did each of the external groups have of you?

WK: Unfortunately, they all expect access. It's human nature perhaps, but people want to meet with the president. The symbolism of meeting with the person in charge is important. As a result, most presidents have to spend time in meetings that don't amount to a lot but are important because of the symbolism of having the institutional leader in the room. It's one of those things that have to be done. But it can be overdone. The development of the calendar should be part of the strategic thinking of the operation of the president's office and, for most, I don't think that it is.

FL: So far as the day-to-day realities of the job are concerned, how have you allocated your time in your different posts? What have been your highest priorities? You've discussed the process of scheduling the president's time, but perhaps you'd like to expand a bit on your own sense of the most important ways to spend your time and energy.

WK: I think that the question of time management has become a huge challenge for presidents, primarily because of their expanded external role. There's always tension between on-campus time and the external role. In this day and age, you can't be an effective president if you don't spend considerable time in both worlds. My observation is that, because of the external demands, there is an increasing danger for presidents in not minding the store at home. You've got to have a strong provost and chief operating officer, but ensuring that there is meaningful, visible time of the president on the campus is a must. Without the support of the community, no one can be an effective president. So, it is essential that the president be seen as visibly and meaningfully engaged on the campus. To me, that is the highest priority. Obviously, in addition to that, setting aside time to be out in the community, raising money, and building support for the institution is a huge responsibility. It just can't be done to the extent that the president neglects the internal constituencies.

FL: When you're on the road, do you delegate decision-making powers to your provost or do you communicate back and forth?

WK: If you're going overseas for a month, I think you would need to delegate some responsibilities, but if you're away for a short time, absolutely not.

FL: Are there any other crisis management stories that you'd like to share?

WK: At College Park, one crisis, which I already mentioned, was exacerbated because we didn't have a good communication strategy. That was the program elimination process. We eventually developed one, but we should have had it from the start.

Right after I got to Ohio State, I inherited a totally botched union negotiation. Many of the blue-collar workers went out on strike. They were out for ten to twelve days. When you go up against a union, they bring in the real pros. These people know how to play the politics and the media. They can say things that you can't counter. They got a lot of students behind them because, on the surface, we were seen as the fat cats, making all this money and driving around in fancy cars, negotiating with workers who are asking for a living wage. The students, of course, weren't thinking about the fact that if we went too far in the negotiations, their tuition would have to go up to pay the bill.

We did develop a crisis management approach. As I mentioned, we had a very good vice president for communications who created opportunities for me and others to go on television, talk to the media, and put our story out. During this period, the crisis management team would meet at 4 o'clock every day to review what the issues were, what the challenges were, and what the stories were that we needed to combat in the media. It proved to be quite effective for us.

FL: How would you define leadership?

WK: That's a tough question. So much has been written on leadership. I'm often asked to speak about leadership. But, trying to capture the essence of leadership in a few words is not easy. I think leadership is the art of getting a constituency to move in an agreed-upon direction. It presumes the ability to create a shared agenda, which is half of leadership. But after that, the leader must have the personal qualities to get people to do the things, make the hard decisions, and create the change necessary to move toward shared goals.

FL: What are the most important qualities a university president or chancellor today needs in order to be successful?

WK: I think it's very important for a person to be well grounded, to have a strong set of values and principles that guide their personal and professional lives. There are many pressures that come upon a president and it's easy to make what seems the expedient decision in any given situation. Having a good sense of the principles and the values that will shape decisions is important. As I think I mentioned earlier, being a good listener is extremely important, but I think an underappreciated quality. Having the ability—in some form—to motivate and inspire people through verbal eloquence, through personal commitment and integrity, by example, or through written expression is absolutely essential in my mind.

FL: How have the role and demands of the presidency changed over the past few decades in response to the many changes in environment, including the disinvestment of the states in public higher education, the growing roles of private support and commercial application in university research, and increased demands for accountability?

WK: You're right. The nature of the presidency has changed in so many ways. First of all, sources of revenue for institutions have been greatly diversified. Some decades ago, revenue for public universities came mostly from a single source: the state. Now presidents must deal with—and encourage—multiple streams of revenue: state funds, private gifts, federal grants, intellectual property, and private sector partnerships. This requires the president to be attentive to and develop strategies for support from a much broader set of constituencies.

State and federal funding is much more competitive today than in the past. University budgets are now in direct competition for scarce dollars with K-12 education, social services, and public safety. This means that presidents have had to develop more intense and effective governmental relations programs. Obviously, the need for private fundraising has had a major impact on how presidents must spend their time. Universities are also seen today as important forces in economic development. This requires presidents to be in much greater contact with the private sector, to build the kind of partnerships with corporations that university presidents could not even have imagined twenty years ago. And, as you said, there are also much greater expectations for accountability from the board, from the state, and from the public. This places the president under much more public scrutiny than in times past.

FL: One of the advantages we have as public institutions is our large role in economic development.

WK: I think this is one of the most positive developments in our relations with the external world. The public is much more attuned to the role and importance of universities in modern society. There is a better understanding of the fact that high quality universities do have an impact on the economy. People have much greater awareness of the need for a highly educated workforce and the importance of research. Finding ways to translate this public recognition into greater support for their institutions is a whole new dimension to presidents' leadership responsibilities.

FL: What do you think may be the reasons for the high rate of attrition that we have seen in the university presidency during the past several years?

WK: Definitely, there is a higher rate of presidential attrition. That's not a good thing. Institutions need stability and consistency in leadership to make real change. But there is no question that the demands and pressures, the increasingly visible role of the president has gone a long way to making terms shorter. It is such a demanding job and the need to be constantly on the go takes its toll. Not only that, but when you're in the public eye all the time, you can make a mistake and that can be fatal in ways that it wasn't when the president played mostly to an internal constituency.

FL: What have been the most critical capital investments made under your leadership or the ones in which you have the greatest pride?

WK: That's a tough question. There have been so many important capital projects that singling out the most critical is not possible. I can tell you the two that have given me the greatest sense of accomplishment. At College Park, it was an incredible performing arts center, a $120 million project that was developed during my tenure. It was a project of special interest to me. Some critics even referred to it as "Kirwan's folly." It took an enormous amount of effort to get the governor's and the legislature's support for the project and to raise the matching private dollars. But now that it is completed, the center has had a profound impact on the campus. It has not only added immeasurably to the cultural and artistic life at the university, it has become a magnet drawing people to the campus. It is now a source of enormous institutional pride. In a technological age, to have succeeded in building this magnificent facility for the arts is something I take a lot of pride in.

At Ohio State, one of my priorities was to build the quality of the medical school and the biosciences. I recruited a talented, high energy vice president and dean from Johns Hopkins. He shared my goal of raising the research profile of Ohio State. But we were constrained by the lack of appropriate facilities. He and I put together a plan to build a research tower, a two hundred million square foot building, with basically no state investment. We did it with what for Ohio State was a very innovative funding model. We had to sell the concept to the trustees, who were initially very skeptical. We patched together the resources from discretionary funds at my disposal, from private gifts, and from research overhead. The building is nearing completion now and it is already having a very significant impact on Ohio State's ability to recruit talented researchers in medicine and the biosciences. And it was all done without state support.

FL: What do you consider your greatest legacies to the institutions you have served?

WK: That's another tough question. I think one thing I have been known for at all the institutions I've served has been my commitment to diversity. I think that commitment has had a positive impact on both the University of Maryland and on Ohio State.

At Maryland, I would also cite the effort to transform College Park into the state's flagship university and a highly selective Research I AAU institution. This was done through developing "peaks of excellence" in selected areas of graduate education and research. It was also done through an innovative plan to reduce the size of the undergraduate population and by putting much greater emphasis on the quality of undergraduate education. As a result, College Park has been transformed from a "safe school" to the school of choice for Maryland's best students.

At Ohio State, I think it was the strategic planning process, which firmly established the university's direction for the future. When I left, one of the things people said was that Ohio State had resolved the long-standing question of whether it was going to be a great Midwestern university or a large, sprawling, open access institution. It had been the historical tradition of Ohio State to be all things to all people. But it was evident to me and others that, with the scarcity of resources, a university which accepted all comers could never be the great institution that every state needs. In my mind it was essential that Ohio State develop a stronger sense of strategic focus and direction. And that's what we did.

In my present position as chancellor of the University of Maryland system, I hope that my legacy will be creating a stronger commitment on the part of the state to support for higher education. One of the challenges we have in Maryland is that we will have a huge demographic surge in eighteen- to twenty-two-year-olds over the next decade. If we can't convince the state that they have to help fund this enrollment growth, all the effort to build high quality institutions will have been for naught. A true state commitment to higher education funding is the legacy that I hope I can leave in this position.

FL: As demand for higher education continues to grow and state funding for public higher education shrinks, how can state universities resolve their budget problems and continue to build both access and excellence?

WK: Given the increased demands for higher education, I have become convinced that we have to develop alternative, lower cost models for delivering degree programs. We just will not be able to have the kind of quality institutions we aspire to have if we don't do this. We're hard at work at that in Maryland. We developed a highly cost-effective educational center in Montgomery County, the state's most populous county and one undergoing tremendous growth. Eight of our institutions are offering high-demand degree programs at the center. The center operates in partnership with the local community college, which provides the first two years of instruction for these degree programs.

We are also very fortunate in having the University of Maryland, University College, which has the nation's largest number of enrollments in online education, as part of the system. University College has created a partnership with every community college in the state. We can now guarantee students enrolled in a community college that they can complete their degree from University of Maryland University College through a combination of onsite and online delivery, without ever leaving their community college.

In both of these examples, there is a significant reduction in cost to the state for delivering the degree programs. I think these kinds of innovative efforts are going to become increasingly important in higher education.

FL: Is there any hope that the federal government will assist us in dealing with the issue of access for students who need financial aid?

WK: I'm very discouraged about this possibility. The federal government has essentially walked away from the Pell Grant. And we see states focusing more and more on merit aid over need-based aid. I think merit only programs like the Hope Scholarship in Georgia are essentially morally bankrupt.

FL: It's also financially bankrupt.

WK: That's right. But what really bothers me is that, with Hope, 80 percent of the scholarship funds go to middle and upper-middle class families and 80 percent of the funds come from the poorest families in Georgia. So you've got the poorest people in the state subsidizing the education of middle class and upper middle class students. It's outrageous.

As I said, I'm also very discouraged about the Pell Grant program. Through the American Council on Education (ACE) and the National Association of State Universities and Land Grant Colleges (NASULGC), there was a huge push to try to get enhanced funding for the Pell Grant and other need-based programs this past year. Sadly, Congress ignored the effort. Clearly we need some new and creative thinking on how to get more funding for need-based financial aid programs at both the federal and state levels. We are moving toward a national crisis. The demographics tell us that there is a surging population of eighteen- to twenty-two-year-olds that is disproportionately low income and would be the first in their families to go to college. In this day and age, when a college degree is the key to a good job and a good life, imagine living in an America where large numbers of these young people just can't afford to go to college.

One idea I've been pushing with ACE and with NASULGC is to get the federal government to create a matching need-based program with the states. Perhaps the federal government would be willing to increase need-based federal financial aid if the states had to match the money.

FL: Do you think the states can do that, or are willing to do that?

WK: To be honest with you, I don't know about all states, but I think there's a lot of aid money in the states that's going into merit, non-need-based aid. In Maryland, for example, $80 million a year is spent on financial aid. Only $40 million of it goes to need-based aid. If there was a matching program, perhaps Maryland and other states would commit more of their merit aid to need-based aid.

FL: The first thing that would be helpful would be to get all the data on this. Are ACE and NASULGC going to look at it? You may find, once you get all the evidence, that it may not be a good deal, but you've got to get the evidence to find out. You're absolutely correct in trying to think of some new way to put together the funding for more need-based aid.

WK: There has to be a new way.

FL: You've had the opportunity to work with more than one governing board. Could you outline what you feel are the important characteristics of good governing boards?

WK: I have thought a lot about this issue. The major problem is a board that gets out of control and becomes too involved in operational issues, rather than setting the major policy directions. I think the natural tendency is for boards to move in this direction. One of the things that a president or a chancellor has to do is regularly find ways to remind the trustees of the difference between the roles of the board and of the CEO.

FL: Yes, and let me add that each chair has to help in convincing the board.

WK: Absolutely. The relationship between the chair and the president or chancellor is absolutely crucial. I've been blessed to have very supportive chairs who have worked with me to keep the board focused on policy issues. One thing that I think can be helpful is for presidents to ask the Association of Governing Boards (AGB), or similar organizations, to periodically offer workshops or forums on best practices for governing boards. It has been my experience that boards are usually willing to participate in such sessions.

We were talking about the demands on presidents. I think another huge time demand for the CEO is the interaction with the board members. I would recommend that a president keep a scorecard or a diary on the last time he or she talked to each board member. I try not to let a week go by where I don't have some communication with every board member, either a message I send out to all board members, or a one-on-one telephone conversation, or a social occasion. I told the board that if anything important ever comes out in the newspapers that I haven't told them about in advance, I haven't done my job. Board members need to be kept informed. It is a tremendously time-consuming but very important responsibility of the president. It's also one of the most effective ways to keep them from micro-managing.

FL: In the past few years there have been several instances in which a governor of the state has gotten involved directly with policy issues in the flagship university and/or the state higher education system. Do you think that this is a trend about which we should be concerned? How can chancellors and presidents deal with this?

WK: It is something we need to be concerned about. Historically, the strength of our higher education system has been its independence from intrusive political influence. I see that eroding. Boards are becoming much more political. Since many are appointed by the governor, we run the risk in this partisan political era that boards will become an extension of the governor's office.

I recently served as member of a site visit team to the University of Illinois. They have an unbelievably ugly issue. It involves their mascot, Chief Illiniwek. The chief is a student dressed up like an Indian who comes out at half time and does a stereotypical Indian dance. The faculty governance bodies and many student groups feel this is inappropriate and want the Chief to be retired. The governor has said, "Not on my watch." The board members, who are appointed by the governor, have sided with the governor and against the faculty. Nancy Cantor, the chancellor, is leaving the institution, in part because of this issue. Her support for the faculty position was well known. There were billboards in Champaign saying, "Cantor must go; the Chief must stay." The faculty has written letters to the board on the issue, but the board won't budge. What's going on at Illinois is just a sign of the times and it's very disturbing.

FL: Do you think that the chair of the board should also act as an intermediary?

WK: Yes. But this requires two things. First, the board chair must be a person who understands the importance of the independence of the board and its role in university governance. And second, it requires that the president and the board chair have a very close relationship.

FL: Let's go on to one of your favorite topics. You have been chairman of the NCAA board of directors, the president of two Division I schools and a leader on the national level in the academic reform movement in Division I athletics. What's your take on the current very public and damaging perceptions of serious problems in college athletics?

WK: Throughout my career, I have believed and argued that the presidents can get control of intercollegiate athletics and institute the needed reforms. But I have to tell you that I have become quite discouraged about whether that's possible. I think the effort that you and I helped lead with the NCAA is sort of a last gasp attempt to bring rationality back to intercollegiate athletics.

FL: It looks like it's going through, including the penalties.

WK: Right. I'm encouraged by that, but if that agenda and other reforms don't get implemented quickly and begin to shift the emphasis back to student-athletes as students first and athletes second, I worry that our institutions will be indelibly tarnished by the egregious excesses of our present models of intercollegiate athletics. The promise of the reform agenda has to be viewed in juxtaposition to the recent distressing series of incidents such as those at the University of Miami and the University of Colorado.

FL: What worries me is that we only know about those two because they have become very public. There may be thirty-five or forty others that are in the same situation.

WK: Absolutely. The external cultural, societal, and economic interests are so powerful that I have become discouraged about our ability to rein in this monster we call intercollegiate athletics. I do think the reform agenda we worked on is a noble effort. I just hope it has some legs and some teeth, because what's going on in collegiate athletics is really very troubling.

FL: And it's getting worse.

WK: Absolutely.

FL: We've discussed one area in which you've taken national leadership. How important do you think that it is for presidents and chancellors to participate in national associations and therefore join in the work of discussing and formulating solutions to these current problems?

WK: I think it's very important. These associations not only offer opportunities for presidents to come together and discuss common issues. They also offer an opportunity for higher education to speak with a more unified voice on the many issues where our interests align. The recent University of Michigan case on affirmative action is a case in point. The associations enabled higher education to speak with a unified voice on this crucially important matter.

I just wish we could get presidents to also rally around reform in intercollegiate athletics with the same sense of passion that we had on affirmative action.

FL: Let's continue to talk about the issues of affirmative action and diversity. How did your institutions manage to make progress in improving the diversity of their student body?

WK: This is one of those areas where leadership must come from the president. Creating a more diverse campus community is hard work. It requires a degree of institutional commitment that just won't happen without expectations set forth by the president. As I noted earlier, a sense of equity and fairness has been one of my core values since my earliest memories. Therefore, it was very natural for me to make diversity a top priority in every leadership position I have held. This priority has always been reflected in planning processes I have led. One thing I have always insisted upon is the establishment of specific diversity goals with accountability mechanisms. I think this is very important. Without accountability, diversity goals tend to become more rhetorical than real. I had a big debate about this at Ohio State. When we developed our diversity action plan, people kept insisting that we didn't need to have specific goals. My response was, "if we don't measure it, we won't do it."

FL: Which brings us back to the necessity for assessment and evaluation. I gave a keynote for a presidents' forum on lifelong learning at Excelsior University a couple of weeks ago and stayed to participate in a roundtable on outcomes assessment in an online learning environment. The participants arrived at a strong consensus that higher education must create a culture of assessment in which outcomes are measured to provide evidence of value and quality. They feel that this is particularly necessary for online providers from the non-profit sector to survive in the face of competition from other sectors of the economy that have implemented a culture of evidence in the way that we have not.

WK: I don't think higher education has done a good job of coming to grips with assessment. Assessment is becoming an accepted part of the K-12 world.

The idea that the public's demand for assessment in education is somehow going to stop, magically, at the twelfth grade seems illogical to me. I think once the assessment process is firmly established at the K-12 level, it's going to become an expectation of higher education. Public dollars are just too scarce and too precious. Governors and legislatures will demand ever-greater accountability from us. I don't think we in higher education have done a very good job of preparing for this eventuality. If we don't get our act together soon, I fear we will have assessment measures imposed upon us that we won't like.

FL: Right. Plans, goals, and assessment are the keys to progress in any area.

What do you see as the strongest forces driving the need for change in higher education over the next ten to twenty years? What are the most important changes that you expect to see take place?

WK: When I look down the road, what I see is a "perfect storm" brewing. It has three elements. One is the public's expectation that more and more young people will need to go to college, if our nation is going to prosper and if individuals are going have successful lives. We've gone from an economy built on muscle power to one dependent upon brainpower. That's the nature of the knowledge economy we have entered. The second element of this perfect storm is, ironically given the perceived importance of higher education, the public's unwillingness to invest in higher education. Over the past several decades, we've seen the public view of higher education change from a public good to a private benefit. The attitude now seems to be, if you want it, you have to pay for it. The third element of this perfect storm is the surge in demand brought on by a dramatic increase over the next decade in the number of eighteen- to twenty-two-year-olds in our population. If these trends continue, universities are going to be faced with terrible choices: keep raising tuition at high rates to protect quality and, thereby, close out opportunities for many young people, or keep college affordable, be swamped by the demographic surge, and watch quality decline. This is a huge public policy issue for our nation. Unfortunately, our elected officials won't focus on it right now. When they finally do—and they'll be forced to—I fear it will be too late.

FL: We will see a much more diverse college-bound group in our lifetime.

WK: Exactly. When you look at where the population growth is, as I noted a few moments ago, it is disproportionately low income, minority and young people who would be the first in their families to go to college. So first of all, getting these young people prepared for college is an important issue. But ensuring that there are adequate higher education opportunities for them is an extraordinary challenge. It is remarkable how many states have made a very substantial commitment to K-12 education, as if that's all they have to worry about. In Maryland, as in many other states, higher education has been cut dramatically, while the state continues to pump money into K-12 education to increase the participation rates in higher education. I keep saying that we have this irrational circumstance where the state is priming the pump and, simultaneously, punching holes in the bucket it is trying to fill.

In a more rational world, higher education would also be allocated funds so it can expand capacity to accommodate this enrollment surge. I think that the issue of the coming decade is this mismatch between the expectations for a college degree and the need for people to have those degrees on the one hand, and the absence of resources that would enable higher education to build the capacity to serve all of the people who want and need a college education. The potential consequences are huge. If we end up with a society where only the middle class and the upper middle class can go on to college, what are people who don't get a college degree going to do with their lives? We are faced with the prospect of an ever-widening gap between the haves and the have-nots in our nation.

I saw some data the other day that is very alarming. A low-ability, high-income student is more likely to go to college than a high-ability, low-income student. On our present path, we are facing a frightening future. Finding the resources and the will to change this course is, for me, one of the most significant issues facing our nation.

Francis L. Lawrence

Francis Lawrence served as the eighteenth president of Rutgers, the State University of New Jersey from October of 1990 until October of 2002. Prior to his appointment, he was academic vice president, provost, and dean of the graduate school at Tulane University. Since stepping down, President Emeritus Lawrence has taught in Rutgers' Student Leadership Development Institute and is a fellow of the Center for Organizational Development and Leadership.

Born August 25, 1937 in Woonsocket, Rhode Island, Lawrence earned his bachelor's degree in French and Spanish from St. Louis University in 1959, his Ph.D. in French and Italian from Tulane University in 1962. Before becoming academic vice president, he served as a department chair, acting dean, and deputy provost. In his research, he has focused on French classical drama and baroque poetry. Lawrence has authored or edited several works of literary criticism printed in the U.S. and abroad. In recognition of his contributions to his field, the French government has conferred on him the honorific title of Chevalier dans l'Ordre des Palmes Académiques.

At Rutgers, Lawrence led the university in reemphasizing and improving the support structure for undergraduate education, making the service mission more visible, and formulating a successful strategic plan that enhanced the university's interdisciplinary areas of academic strength and leveraged external support. He also implemented a massive broadband communications infrastructure project to support instruction, research, and outreach. He revitalized Rutgers' state and federal relations, resulting in increased federal support of science and state funding for outstanding New Jersey students, major construction projects, equipment, and renovation. With strong support for the university's efforts in encouraging respect for human dignity, Lawrence emphasized increasing minority enrollment and graduation, as well as the hiring of minorities in the faculty and administration.

On the national scene, Lawrence served on the executive committee of the Association of American Universities. He was a member of the boards of directors of the American Council on Education, the National Collegiate Athletics Association, and the Association of American Colleges and Universities. He also chaired the Big East Conference and the NCAA Board of Directors Task Force on Academic Reform in Intercollegiate Athletics. He was a member of the Kellogg Commission on the Future of State and Land Grant Universities and chaired its committee on a lifelong learning society.

I grew up in Woonsocket, Rhode Island and Franklin, Massachusetts. On my father's side, my grandparents were Austrian and Hungarian. My granddad was the landscaper for the Draper Corporation in Hopedale Massachusetts, a company town. On my mother's side, my grandmother was from Connecticut, my grandfather from French Canada. He was the superintendent of a textile mill. Neither my mother nor my father had a traditional high school education. Both went to what was then called Commercial School, a business education school, where they met. My four older sisters completed high school and certainly had the ability to go on to college, but my parents were struggling to get a business off the ground, so college wasn't an option for them. The girls went directly from high school to work. Two of them worked in the family business, the Service Sales Company, a paint, wallpaper, and hardware store in Woonsocket. The second oldest of my sisters entered the religious life as a member of the order of the Presentation of Mary and eventually earned both a bachelor's and a master's degree. She became a member of what was then known as the Business Department at Rivier College in New Hampshire and was the head of the department until her retirement.

As far back as I can remember, the clear message from my parents and my sisters alike was that a good education was of paramount importance and that I was expected to go on to college. Nevertheless, like Chuck Vest, I was probably more interested in sports than academics as a child. Luckily I had the advantage of attending an excellent school, Mount Saint Charles Academy in Woonsocket, which at the time was an all-male college prep school with a small boarding school enrollment in addition to the day school students. There I became a serious student and had my first leadership experience as a pitcher for my high school baseball team.

My parents and my sisters shaped my values by their teaching and their example; they were deeply religious and very hard working. In the summer of 1955, as I was preparing to go to college, Woonsocket was hit with back-to-back hurricanes, Connie and Diane. The Blackstone River rose to 17 feet above flood stage, drowning my parents' store. In spite of their desperate financial situation following the flood, they insisted that my college fund remain sacrosanct and that I must leave for school on schedule, while they worked to put their lives and their business back together. I felt extremely guilty about leaving. However I understood the importance they placed on my education and it was impossible to contradict their insistence that the best thing I could do for them was to go to St. Louis University on schedule and study hard, in order to fulfill their ambitions for me.

I think that I knew even then, though, that the greatest lesson I would learn that year was right before my eyes. My parents' determination to pull themselves back up from a devastating natural disaster and to do it without declaring bankruptcy, to honor all of their obligations, had a great influence on me. It showed me that it was possible to confront overwhelming odds without allowing even the most crushing circumstances to defeat you if you simply persisted on your course with the innate dignity and integrity my mother and father demonstrated all their lives. For example, my father had a large backlog of accounts on which certain customers had paid him little or nothing for months or years. When some people from Boston came around offering to buy the debts and allow my father to recoup at least a portion of his losses, he turned them down. He knew them by reputation. They were excellent collectors, but their methods—harassment, threats, and intimidation—were unscrupulous at best. He simply could not do that, even to customers who continued to abuse his good nature, especially a few professional painters who ran up large bills and failed to pay them, despite having received their compensation for the jobs.

I majored in French and Spanish at St. Louis University. I had gone there planning to take a pre-medical curriculum but the lure of the humanities was too strong for me. By Christmas of my freshman year, I had switched to the language and literature area and was engaged to an English and theatre major from North Dakota. Having gotten the whole dating thing out of the way in very short order, my future wife and I settled down to our studies, taking out just enough time to marry between our junior and senior years. The language departments were small and the teachers in both the French and the Spanish departments took a personal interest in every student's progress. Among my mentors, the French department chair, Homer Welsh, and a young instructor in Spanish, Ray Sullivant, were especially influential in mentoring me by providing challenging work and encouraging me to go on to graduate studies. As a practical young scholar, though, I hedged my bets. In those days, when it was common to take as many as six courses or more a semester, I took enough philosophy courses for a minor and all of the education courses necessary to qualify for a high school teaching certificate—just in case.

I was tremendously fortunate to graduate at precisely the time when the National Defense Education Act went into effect. For one brief shining moment, languages were viewed as essential components of our national defense and three-year Ph.D. fellowships were available in order to build up the capacity of the nation in cultural understanding. I sent applications to graduate schools across the country and was just about to take an assistantship from the one place where both my wife and I had received offers (she was pregnant, therefore persona non grata in most graduate programs during those family-unfriendly times), when I got an offer we couldn't refuse from Tulane University in New Orleans: an NDEA fellowship in French and Italian that required no teaching, simply three years of full-time study at what was then a princely stipend, with an added sum for each dependent.

At Tulane, I was guided by Bill Woods, the department chair, who earned his doctorate in medieval French studies at the University of North Carolina at Chapel Hill under Urban Tigner Holmes. The department was in transition when I arrived. It had a number of well-educated, ambitious scholars like Bill, but was still staffed in part by several wonderful women who had been hired long ago by Sophie Newcomb, the women's college. They were not published scholars or Ph.D.s, but they had attracted students because they were excellent, nurturing teachers, in love with French language and literature. Since these teachers were on the brink of retirement, they were being replaced by well-known and highly regarded faculty with impeccable scholarly credentials, some of them hired from European institutions.

My good or ill fortune was that the leading departmental authority in 17th century French literature—the area of research in which I chose to specialize—was approaching what was then Tulane's inflexible retirement age and decided to accept a position at the University of Houston, where he could stay on as an active faculty member for several more years. So there I was, without a director, on the eve of beginning my dissertation. Nevertheless, as the father of a young, growing family, I could not wait for a new hire so, with the department's blessing, I accepted as my advisor Panos Morphos, a faculty member in a completely different field and tore into writing my dissertation the moment that I finished my comprehensive written and oral exams for the Ph.D. I completed all of my requirements, racing to a photo finish with the end of my three-year NDEA stipend. The department immediately offered me an instructorship, which I gratefully accepted. With Bill Woods' gentle, nagging encouragement, I began publishing by getting into print several articles and a book, then moving on to a long love affair with the metaphysical epic of a newly rediscovered poet. That interest motivated me to go to France for a year with my family in order to do research on my poet while I directed the Tulane/Newcomb Junior Year Abroad program in France, Italy, Spain, and Germany. On my return from JYA, in spite of offers from other universities, I decided not to uproot my family again: I took Tulane's counteroffer.

My first academic leadership position was the French and Italian Department chairmanship and, as I often tell faculty, it was one of the hardest. As a department chair you have the unenviable job of keeping everyone happy and working together, including the two or more people in nearly every department who have been carrying on a bitter feud for years. I hit every rung of the administrative ladder then. I spent two very happy years filling in as acting dean of Newcomb, with Tulane president Sheldon Hackney's blessing. Then, at the invitation of my friend, Provost Frank Birtel, I went to the provost's office as deputy provost. Under Eamon Kelly's presidency, I capped my Tulane career with a long stint as academic vice president, provost, and dean of the graduate school. In spite of some interesting feelers from other institutions looking for presidents, I stayed in the top academic post at Tulane for nine years, perhaps longer than most people in my position might have done. We decided not to move until our children were older because our family took precedence over my career advancement at that point.

When I came to Rutgers in October of 1990, the New Brunswick campus had recently accepted the invitation to join the Association of American Universities, confirming its status among the nation's most distinguished research institutions, and it faced a number of challenges. Everyone was proud of the membership in the Association of American Universities, but the Board of Governors and the Board of Trustees were very concerned about the need to restore the balance between research and teaching. Rutgers was not unique in this: it was a problem that many research universities faced at the time. I think that one of the reasons that I was hired was that I was the provost of a private research university with a strong tradition and reputation for excellent undergraduate education, and it was undergraduate education that the boards and many faculty felt was in trouble.

The university was also in fiscal difficulty, with serious budget shortfalls due to cuts in state support. In fact just a few weeks after my arrival, during the Thanksgiving break, the state notified us that it was cutting $20 million from the promised Rutgers budget. Allied to this issue was the perception of the boards that Rutgers ought to be more attentive to its service to the state and the hope that, if the state recognized the university's importance to New Jersey, the legislature and the governor would realize that funding its needs and ambitions was a crucial investment in the future.

Another of Rutgers' pressing needs was the re-invigoration of the University Senate. Faculty representatives complained bitterly that they felt alienated, that they needed to be consulted and wanted to see their university-wide representative body treated with respect.

With the exception of the difficult financial situation, Rutgers' problems were minor in comparison with its strengths. It has a diverse student body that reflects the rich, multicultural composition of New Jersey, which has benefited from its cheek-by-jowl closeness to the great New York City port of debarkation for immigrants. In my inaugural address I proposed that in Rutgers, New Jersey should build the country's first major public university that recognized and rose to meet the challenges of our future by making a serious effort to transform itself. I discussed the necessity of educating a much broader, more inclusive spectrum of our society and observed that Rutgers was a twenty-year veteran in many areas of access and opportunity, but we could and should do more. Despite our financial problems, I renewed our commitment to hiring minority faculty and worked with enthusiasm to attract funding for a campaign to support minority and cross-cultural programs and scholarships. I asked that we renew and reconstitute the ways that we relate to one another, making even greater attempts to encourage cross-cultural understanding and said that it would help neither us nor our students to enroll a richly diverse student body if we were to fail to educate them, graduate them, and prepare them to live in an increasingly multi-racial and multicultural society. I talked about renewing the university's commitment to undergraduate education and about the importance of graduate education and research to the vocation of the faculty and the needs of society. I proposed that, as the intellectual nexus of our state in an era when advanced knowledge is a necessity for individuals and for society, Rutgers could be a dynamic force for the reinvigoration of the state's economy and human services. Acknowledging the importance of community within the university, I pledged to work with the University Senate, talked about the student advisory council I had formed, and asked all units of the university to include students on their standing committees. Finally, I told the university community that they did not need me to make Rutgers an even greater university: I needed them.

The move to Rutgers was exciting and challenging. I was immediately immersed in a round of meetings and outreach activities to acquaint myself with the faculty, the students, and the alumni, as well as meeting the state legislators and the new governor's staff, but the transition was much more difficult for Mary Kay. We left behind not only the three oldest children, who were married and had nearly completed their education, but also the only one of our children still living at home and our first three grandchildren. Jenny, our youngest, was a sophomore at Newcomb. Josh, Ben, and Beth, the three children of our oldest daughter, Lissy, were eight, six, and two years old. In New Orleans, Mary Kay had seen them nearly every day, so it was a tough separation, even more difficult than we anticipated.

As many of my presidential interviewees have noted, it is not easy to maintain a balanced life and keep up your energy in these demanding jobs. A presidency can easily become your entire life. I managed to maintain my exercise routine by getting up early to work out from five to six a.m. We missed the continuous family presence, but, as many empty nesters have discovered, we actually enjoyed a renewed closeness, spending time alone together. I tried to take an afternoon off on the weekend. When our daughter Naomi decided to accept an offer from Cooper Hospital in Camden and set up a practice in Marlton, our lives were enriched by the contact with her, her husband Jerry and their three boys, Michael, Mark and Lucas, the latter two born after moving to New Jersey.

When I arrived at Rutgers, I knew just a couple of people on the faculty. What I wanted to do first was to get to know the institution and become acquainted with the people, so I made no changes or additions to the administration when I came in. I preferred to take some time to evaluate the needs of a large, complex institution with three campuses spread across the state. Some of the administrators submitted their resignations, planning to return to teaching, but I asked everyone to stay on a few months longer. Over those months, I had a series of lunches and other meetings with faculty and went to the dining halls to eat and talk with students. I met with the University Senate every month and talked with the president of the faculty union frequently. I made it a practice to schedule regular trips to the Newark and Camden campuses. And

I read through a very interesting accumulation of Rutgers reports and studies that the bright, hard-working manager of the president's office, Mildred Schildcamp, gave me to look over. (When I had to change the person who took care of the affairs of the university's governing boards, Mildred took over those responsibilities as secretary of the university and, since I couldn't spare her, continued to run the president's office.)

In choosing people to work with and depend upon, I looked first for smart, experienced people. Like my colleagues at other universities, I didn't want clones of myself, people with the same strengths and weaknesses. I needed people whose strengths would complement mine, bright people who understood the issues and would discuss, deliberate, and debate the solutions with me and with the rest of the newly formed president's cabinet, then work together as a team to implement the decisions.

I was very fortunate to find distinguished professors at Rutgers who were willing to take on the responsibilities of administration in order to make the university a better institution. Joe Seneca, who became my vice president for academic affairs, was the chair of the New Jersey Council of Economic Advisors to the governor and the legislature and the co-author of the well-regarded *Rutgers Regional Report*, a series that provides periodic, comprehensive analysis of current economic issues. A couple of years down the road, we were able to simplify the many-layered structure of the university, cut back significantly on administrative expenses, and eliminate a structural overlap between the responsibilities of the provost and the dean of the faculty by combining the responsibilities of the vice president for academic affairs and the provost of the New Brunswick campus in Joe's very capable hands. He had the complete confidence and respect of the New Brunswick faculty and he knew the strengths and problems of Rutgers across the state: he was an excellent chief academic officer. He tends to be painstakingly analytical in his decision-making and to spend all the time that needs to be spent on negotiation, gradually working through things to everyone's satisfaction. Those are qualities that faculty always appreciate, so Joe was ideally suited to his post.

As vice president for research, I hired Jim Flanagan, who was a former director at Bell Laboratories and had come to Rutgers to direct the Center for Advanced Information Processing. His experience and stature made him tremendously effective in the role and, a couple of years after his appointment, I had the pleasure of seeing him awarded the National Medal of Science. Jim is the most modest, self-effacing man I know, a Mississippian who has never lost the drawl and punctilious courtesy of his native state. At the same time, he is unsurpassed in his ability to bring talent together and draw the best from it. Rutgers may have been a newcomer to the ranks of the nation's foremost research universities, but due in no small measure to Jim's leadership, our research support supervision and our services to faculty for research and sponsored programs as well as for corporate support and technology transfer were improved and strengthened. We made large incremental gains in federal grants and contracts and in licenses and options that yield income from applications of scientific research. Those gains added to the university's reputation and made significant contributions to its resources.

I had equally good fortune on the non-academic side of the administration, where I found that Rutgers was blessed with people who really understood the primacy of the academic mission of the university and cared about our students. Joe Whiteside, who was the senior vice president and treasurer and the administrator to whom the whole facilities operation reported, immediately tendered his resignation when I came in, saying that he knew presidents want to have their own team, but he was such a good person, so knowledgeable, respected, and liked by everyone from the boards to the cleaning crews that I asked him to do the university and my administration the favor of staying on as long as he wished. The boards knew him and had complete trust in him, in his absolute integrity and his ability, so I never had reason to be concerned about any of the major construction projects the university undertook during my administration.

Marvin Greenberg, the chief budget officer, also an excellent person, retired the year after I arrived, but his deputy, Nancy Winterbauer, who took over the post, was equally good or, as Marvin promised, even better. I could rely on her skill in explaining the abstruse intricacies of the university budget in terms so clear and compelling that the whole complex topic became transparent to whomever her audience might be, students, faculty and administrators, as well as reporters, legislators, and members of the governor's staff. In addition to her responsibilities as university vice president for budgeting, I asked Nancy to assume the supervisory responsibility for other important administrative areas: admissions, financial aid, the registrar's office, and human resources. She did a splendid job of caring for those important services.

I hired one of the important members of my administration away from my former institution. Christine Haska (now Cermak) was pivotally involved in the formation of the successful strategic plans, technological plans, and accreditation studies at both institutions. At Rutgers, she headed not only the area of institutional research and planning but also our university communications division and our computing area. I asked her to take on the planning for our $100 million RUNet 2000 project, in which we wired our campuses in Newark, New Brunswick, and Camden for voice, video, and data (with a campus cable television network in New Brunswick). For that project, she persuaded the tri-state authority constructing the toll highway automatic pass system to give Rutgers two strands of fiber, providing us with a hard-wired broadband connection among our own campuses and the potential for connections to public schools across New Jersey.

My number-two person in command was Joe Seneca, but on a day-to-day basis, all of the members of the president's cabinet had the authority and the responsibility to act on vital issues. The Newark and Camden campuses had felt somewhat neglected, so I made a point of visiting them regularly and including provosts Norman Samuels of Newark and Walter Gordon of Camden in my cabinet in order to ensure that they were active partners in university deliberations. Modern communications gave us the ability to stay in touch with one another whenever necessary and everyone understood, of course, that I would have to know all there was to know about any issue on which I needed to communicate with the Rutgers Board of Governors, Board of Trustees, and Board of Overseers of the Rutgers Foundation.

The first vital task we tackled was the strengthening of our support structure for undergraduate education. Undergraduate education is always in need of periodic renewal, but in the late 1980s and early 1990s, research universities were particularly singled out and accused of a lack of balance between their high expectations for faculty research and their lack of interest in the quality of undergraduate teaching. There was some truth in the allegations, however overdrawn the attacks of the more sensational critics may have been. The Board of Governors took the problem seriously and so did many of our Rutgers faculty. We made the evaluation of teaching a much more important formal part of the procedure for our tenure and promotion reviews as well as our hiring criteria. There was no objection from any quarter to doing that. It was useful because it brought the importance of good teaching forward into the light and kept it there. When faculty under tenure review had their support materials sent back for supplementary evidence to demonstrate their teaching abilities or were turned down for tenure on the basis of poor teaching, teaching came into sharp focus as a vital professional skill.

At the University Senate's recommendation, we set up resource centers that offered teaching support to our faculty on Rutgers' three regional campuses and charged the centers with implementing university-wide student evaluations of courses. We set up several learning centers for our students as well, offering study skill workshops, study groups, individual or group tutoring, and supplemental instruction for difficult courses. They were envisioned as partnership ventures between the faculty and the center staff. The learning centers were extremely well received by students and many faculty, but a few saw them as eroding elements of control that had traditionally been vested solely with the academic departments. For some faculty, this also signaled a growing focus on a service orientation, a development that they felt equated students with consumers.

A curriculum study is the traditional pièce de résistance of every undergraduate education reform effort and we were fortunate to have leading ours Barry Qualls, one of Rutgers' faculty members most devoted to education. I also issued a report on undergraduate education and created two new posts in the central university administration—the Vice President for Undergraduate Education and the Vice President for Student Affairs—in order to bring strong focus to the concerns of undergraduates. We funded an annual Award for Programmatic Excellence in Undergraduate Education that encouraged departments to provide innovative curricula and scholarly communities that included undergraduates. One of the most visible projects launched by our creative and enterprising Vice President for Undergraduate Education Susan Forman was a very successful effort to honor our undergraduates who do research under faculty supervision by giving them the opportunity to present their projects to the university community during undergraduate research weeks at the end of the academic year. With this and the undergraduate research fellows program, we were able to raise the proportion of students who undertake ambitious research projects significantly over a relatively short time, to a self-reported level of 60 percent of our graduating seniors.

Improving undergraduate education was our greatest concern, but the bureaucracy of Rutgers' huge organization, with its geographically dispersed campuses, also needed attention. In my conversations with people in the university community, I discovered that the difficulty that faculty, staff, and students alike experienced in getting things done was a very sore point. In fact the problem had its own somewhat vulgar name: "The RU Screw." We put together a task force of faculty and staff from all three campuses to examine procedures for fulfilling routine requests and they set to work with enthusiasm, finding ways to make the university more efficient and responsive to all its constituencies. The task force became known as the red tape committee and, with a couple of other studies on administrative efficiency and university communications, we worked to streamline our operations and improve our efficiency in every area, including admissions, financial aid, external affairs, and computing.

Then, because I know that cutting red tape is not a one-shot success but a perpetual necessity and have always been a great believer in using the rich internal expertise of the university to diagnose and address its needs, we asked Brent Ruben, a distinguished professor of communication who is an internationally reputed expert on organizational development, to put together a program that would encourage continuous improvement in the university's operations. He founded a Center for Organizational Development and Leadership that has helped departments throughout the university to assess themselves and develop plans to measure service satisfaction, analyze and refine their procedures, plan improvements, and assess their achievements. Brent took the project much further than I had expected or envisioned. He translated the Baldrige criteria into academic terms, and wrote several authoritative books on educational excellence. Over the past decade, he has worked with academic as well as administrative units at Rutgers and provided professional consultation on organizational improvement not only to major corporations, but also to a number of universities, among them the University of California-Berkeley, the University of Wisconsin-Madison, MIT, and the University of

Pennsylvania. Thanks to his scholarly and professional work, Rutgers has become an internationally recognized center of thought and practice in organizational assessment and improvement in higher education.

We were also concerned about assessing and improving the regard for Rutgers within New Jersey in order to advance both its reputation and its financial support as New Jersey's flagship public research university. We formed a task force to review university communication policy and practices, both within the university community and directed outward, for public advocacy. On the recommendation of the task force, we commissioned a university marketing study aimed at assessing public perceptions and understanding of the university among the members of the legislature, the corporate community, and other stakeholders in order to glean insights on how to present the many virtues of the university in the most effective way possible. We may have been a bit ahead of the curve, but such studies are now an increasingly familiar practice in higher education. Predictably, there were some faculty who were troubled by the idea of a marketing study. They argued that a focus on students, external stakeholders and their perceptions, as well as adopting the ideal of a service orientation, would make the university too much like a business.

The $20 million cut to our operations that we learned about at Thanksgiving time in my first year at Rutgers left the university with $20 million less in state funding than we had the previous year. Since the state also refused to fund $20 million in contractual salary increases for our employees, we had an effective budget shortfall of $40 million. I persuaded the boards to take the unusual expedient of funding a reasonable faculty raise from our reserves, despite the tight budget, and we were able to settle our contract negotiations. While we cut costs, we made sustaining the quality of instruction our highest priority. The standard joke about faculty morale is that it is always described as being at the lowest point in the institution's history, but it was true that morale at Rutgers had suffered under a succession of blows from the withdrawal of state support. When money is that tight, it affects everyone: faculty lines can't be filled and retirees can't be replaced. It seemed to me and my cabinet members that the best way to revive hope and ambition throughout the university was to launch a counter-intuitive action, a bold strategic planning project that would include as many faculty members as possible. We involved the whole community in formulating the vision for the future. Self-studies began on the campus levels in 1992, the Newark, Camden and New Brunswick plans were incorporated into a university-wide plan in 1994, and the university plan was approved by the Board of Governors in June of 1995.

We took a risk by involving a very large number of people in handling the actual implementation of the plan. We asked 250 people—roughly a tenth of the Rutgers faculty on all three Rutgers campuses—to serve on the university-wide implementation groups that represented our twelve academic priority areas and I phoned a number of the implementation committee chairs to persuade them to accept the responsibility. The implementation committees set to work with enthusiasm, formulating and soliciting hundreds of proposals, and sent the best forward to a distinguished university-wide selection committee. Not all of the proposals could be funded, of course, but the plan drew upon the ideas of the majority of the faculty involved, energizing and mobilizing their efforts.

Achieving buy-in to the strategic plan from the university community was easy, in fact virtually automatic, since the vision was created by, for, and with the community as a whole. We used all of the avenues available in order to keep the alumni and our external constituencies in the state informed. I met with newspapers' editorial boards and submitted op-ed pieces that a good cross-section of New Jersey newspapers carried. We also initiated regular alumni gatherings to meet and talk with alums across the state and I traveled to spread the news to alumni from Florida to California. We issued several progress reports on the strategic planning initiatives and continued to measure the benchmarks of our achievement.

One of the biggest, most difficult battles we waged was undertaken in connection with the strategic plan's ambitious goal of making Rutgers one of the top public research universities in the nation. Accountability is more than a popular watchword; it is a practical requirement for higher education in our time. In 1994, the new chair of Rutgers' governing board, Carleton Holstrom, proposed that we ought to require something beyond the customary reviews performed for tenure and promotion in order to ensure that our faculty members remain productive as teachers and researchers throughout their professional careers. It can be argued that faculty are in fact continuously reviewed by their deans and departments for the purposes of allocating teaching and recommending salary, as well as promotion in the professorial ranks, but it cannot be denied that nothing equaling the review for tenure is ordinarily performed again and, on that basis, a more formal, periodic post-tenure review is not a bad idea, at least in theory.

Of course theory is one thing; reality is something else. As Nils Hasselmo characterized it in his interview with me, anything to do with tenure is the third rail in academe. When, at the insistence of his board chair, Nils broached the idea of tenure reform, including post-tenure review, at the University of Minnesota, the resulting uproar was so wild that he described it as "a nightmare…one of the worst things I've ever been through in administration."

We conceded that post-tenure review was a reasonable concept, so Joe Seneca and I set out to sell it to the faculty. Singly and together Joe and I visited faculty bodies and held a series of open forums in Newark, New Brunswick, and Camden, making many converts as we explained the rather strict rules of the review: it was to be undertaken every five years, was to be conducted by the department chair, was to be kept as a private matter among the chair, the faculty member, and the dean to whom they report, and was not to have even the whisper of an effect upon tenure. It would consist in a review of the faculty member's teaching and research over the past five years and a plan for the coming five years. We were pleased and a little surprised at how easy a sell it proved to be, once the parameters of the review were set out. When they understood precisely what was being proposed, most faculty members had no objection to it.

Nevertheless, there were a few die-hard opponents who were dead set against it. They were primarily individuals with a mindset of us-against-them. One such individual followed us around with a cassette tape machine, patiently recording our every word in the hope of catching us in a faux pas. When they saw that things were not going to their taste, they made a formal demand for an extraordinary assembly of the entire Rutgers faculty to thrash out the matter. There they expected to secure, if not a universal vote of no confidence in the administration, at the very least a resounding vote against the post-tenure review proposal. It would be an understatement to say that when the assembly voted in favor of post-tenure review they were shocked and displeased: appalled and furious would be closer to the truth.

The real nightmare began less than a month after that assembly. Ironically, during that university-wide information campaign for post-tenure review, it was in one of the areas of my deepest personal conviction that I made a misstatement diametrically opposed to all of the values and actions at the core of my career in academe. During a meeting with faculty and students in Camden on November 11, 1994, while I was in the midst of explaining that higher education is being called upon to be more accountable and arguing that our over-reliance on the results of standardized tests poses a danger to equal access and affirmative action, I jumbled together several subjects in an awkward verbal stumble that implied I believed the arguments of Charles Murray (author of *The Bell Curve*) that intelligence levels vary based on ethnicity and that minorities are genetically inferior.

The tape of the meeting was duplicated and sent out to 100 faculty members more than two months later, timed just before the beginning of Black History Month and brought to the attention of a local newspaper. It spawned a media storm in New Jersey. The story was published on January 31, 1995. It stunned and mortified me to be misunderstood, particularly on a subject about which I care so deeply, but there was no choice but to address the misperception forthrightly. On the same day, in a public apology, I told the world that I could not be sorrier for the damage and pain I had caused with those wounding words.

The members of the Board of Governors and the Executive Committee of the Board of Trustees issued a statement in which they expressed their concern about the distress the misstatement might cause. The statement also indicated that they felt it was their responsibility to judge me not just by three badly articulated words but by deeds and cited my "established record of commitment to an aggressive program for admitting and graduating student minorities, as well as…the recruitment, hiring, promotion, and tenure of minority faculty." Rutgers was at the time setting new benchmarks for minority access and advancement among its peer AAU institutions in terms of its total minority enrollment, the number of African-American students graduating, and its employment of African American faculty. The university's minority students and faculty have always been and continue to be among the nation's most accomplished individuals, honored for their outstanding achievements. Over my tenure as president we appointed six highly qualified minority candidates to undergraduate college deanships, one to a professional school deanship, and two to vice presidencies.

I sent my apology out to the university community and repeated it at a press conference where a number of Rutgers faculty, administrators, and board members, both minority and white, appeared at my side in order to talk about what they termed my exceptional track record on the issue of diversity and minority inclusion. They were joined by my friend, Paul Robeson, Jr., the son of Rutgers' most celebrated alumnus, who stood by me, literally and figuratively. Eamon Kelly, my president at Tulane, when contacted, told the press that the record at Tulane showed that I had worked to increase black student enrollment from 1 to 10 percent and total minority enrollment from 5 to 27 percent and had been a moving force behind curriculum development that included an African studies program and a multicultural studies program.

When Rutgers students staged a sit-in at a nationally televised basketball game on February 7, the story quickly went national. Throughout this period, I conducted meetings with small groups of students, faculty, and staff, as well as minority members of the New Jersey Legislature. I apologized in person, explaining that the remark was completely opposed to my deeply held beliefs. I held open public forums on the campuses in order to give students the chance to express their feelings and to allow me to answer their questions. Those sessions were painful for me and for the students who addressed me, but it was necessary to go directly to the university community in order to apologize in person to those I had offended.

On February 10, at the regularly scheduled public meeting of the Board of Governors, people again had the opportunity to voice their feelings and opinions. Board members were disturbed by the discovery that so much was still wrong with the university in the eyes of students who belonged to minorities and they wanted to improve the university atmosphere, but they did not believe that my departure was the way to accomplish that.

After listening to those who wished to speak, the board retired briefly to craft its reply. It emerged to proclaim its commitment to remedying the deficiencies in the university environment perceived by minority students, to charge the administration with proposing a blueprint for improving multicultural life, and to reaffirm the board's support for my continued service as president. In a situation that was an emotional public maelstrom of overwhelming proportions, the board steadfastly reaffirmed its commitment.

I don't think that many boards are as courageous or as principled as the Rutgers Board of Governors of 1995 chaired by Carleton Holstrom. I believe it was because they knew my character so thoroughly and were so familiar with what I had done at Rutgers, with my principles, with every policy we had put in place together and every action I had taken with their blessing, that they had no doubt that the misstatement was a clumsy mistake, not a racist manifesto.

It is a common cliché that our perception of time expands to such lengths in times of crisis that we can review a lifetime in a few seconds. Those eleven days from January 31 through February 10 certainly seemed a lifetime. My wife was at my side through the ordeal. My daughter Naomi and her family, who live in New Jersey, as well as my entire family, were a strong support, as they have always been. My son Chris dropped everything and flew to New Jersey with his three-year-old, Jeffrey, to be with us at the height of the fury.

There was a powerful irony to the entire affair since I misspoke about something on which I have strong convictions that are precisely opposed to the sense of the words I uttered. In fact, right around the same time as I made the misstatement, months before it became public, I read several reviews of *The Bell Curve.* In a televised appearance that aired in December, I spoke against its public policy implications, which would limit access to education based on the scientifically and morally indefensible concepts of genetic inferiority. In another program televised about that time, I expressed my strong views on the urgent need to educate all of America's children because higher education is now a requirement for a quality life for individuals. I had for a long time argued there, and elsewhere, that a greatly expanded effort to educate and use the talents of our entire population is absolutely necessary to the future of our nation. The other theme that I broached in these televised appearances was my longstanding opposition to the overuse and misuse of a single standardized test such as the IQ or SAT, which has the power to stigmatize students, sap their confidence; and, tragically, sometimes to bar them from access to opportunity and prevent them from undertaking the efforts they must make to succeed.

The other ironic aspect of the furor was that, despite the way that media attention magnified my shortcomings to gigantic proportions and created what some might term a feeding frenzy in which I was the object of intense scrutiny by reporters, editors, and cameras, it ended by instilling in me an even deeper and stronger respect for the freedom of the press in all its glory. Like everyone who undergoes such an experience, I was subjected to all of the media's most unattractive attributes of intrusiveness and obsession. Nevertheless, major newspapers from coast to coast, after examining my life under their pitiless lens, ended by publishing opinion pieces or editorials that said, in essence, "He is being judged on the basis of a sound bite. He has apologized for what was essentially a stumble in words. We ought to be big enough to forgive a mistake." One or two went on to add, "Lawrence has an impressive record at two institutions on matters affecting minorities. It would be a loss to the university and its minority students if he were to leave." (Among the newspapers publishing supportive editorials and opinions were the *New York Times,* the *Daily News,* the *Wall Street Journal* the *Philadelphia Inquirer,* the *Chicago Tribune,* and the *San Francisco Chronicle,* and, in New Jersey, the *Press of Atlantic City,* the *Hunterdon County Democrat,* the *North Jersey Herald & News,* the *Times* (Trenton), the *News Tribune,* the *Asbury Park Press,* and Newark's *City News.*)

In unexpected acts of courage and generosity some prominent individuals also came out publicly to urge forgiveness, among them Reginald Jackson (head of the Black Ministers Council of New Jersey), Joe Williams (Chair of the New Jersey Commission on Higher Education), nationally syndicated columnist Carl Rowan, and Stephen Jay Gould, who, in the midst of the turmoil, told a Rutgers audience, "Three words don't amount to a hill of beans. Remember it says, 'By their fruits you shall know them,' not 'by their sound bites you shall know them.'"

I got an avalanche of mail from people in New Jersey and across the nation. My friends at Tulane and Rutgers and my colleagues in the Association of American Universities, people who knew my principles and my record, were shocked and supportive. Those voices of support meant a great deal to me and my family during this period, as such generous acts must to all who find themselves in similarly difficult situations of public scrutiny. People who didn't know me were about evenly divided between those who felt that my record proved that I was not a racist and those convinced that my words were evidence enough that I was. Then there were some who thought the entire thing was a disgusting orgy of political correctness (among those were conservative pundits who felt that I merited my fate because I myself was among the p.c. people). And there were others who believed that I ought to slink away into the revolting morass of hateful prejudice that was obviously my native environment. A few saw the dark side of academic politics at work. Finally, there were letters from the people who were true believers in genetic inferiority and thought that I was their new champion—the unkindest cut of all.

What was the effect of the entire firestorm on me? Like the members of the board, I was saddened by the racism that many of our students told us that they encountered at Rutgers and touched by their pain. The university community had worked for a long time, since well before I arrived, in order to display and to encourage respect for human dignity, but despite its best efforts, it was evident that we still had a long way to go. And it will probably surprise no one to hear that the problems our students saw were not simply a matter of aberrant acts by thoughtless individuals; there were institutional areas in which we needed to make much greater efforts to remedy the widespread sense of racial inequity. The multicultural plan that the board asked us to formulate was directed toward the investment of substantial resources in the areas of greatest need. The experience made me not just more aware of inequity but more determined than ever to do everything in my power to remedy it.

As an institution we continued to focus on communication and implementation of the strategic plan (of which the strengthened multicultural plan was now a part). We worked on communicating the plan to all of our constituencies, on integrating its implementation with the university's financial planning, and on making it the basis of our administrative responsibilities and reviews. The senior administrators discussed it with the internal academic community. It became the framework for Joe Seneca's discussions with the deans about the progress of their schools. We made the deans partners in our fundraising efforts, responsible for soliciting gifts that would support the schools' strategic planning goals. As we recruited deans during the campaign, one of the key qualifications for candidates was the willingness and ability to raise funds for the support of their school's role in the strategic plan. The plan provided the basis for our fundraising, the structure for planning our major fund campaign. We monitored the achievement of our goals closely through strategic plan implementation reports as well as the president's annual report. We communicated our progress through all of our contacts with the alumni and friends of the university. We also made formal periodic reports to the three boards, the Governors, the Trustees, and the Overseers of the Foundation. In each reporting format, we tracked our outcomes, reporting data on our progress, and noting our successes in working toward our goals. We celebrated stages in our success, publicly thanking everyone involved and encouraging their efforts. For example, we instituted formal installations for endowed chairs in order to honor both the donor and the distinguished faculty member installed in the chair. The plan permeated all of our communication to the public.

Funding the implementation of the plan was, of course, far from easy. Even in the best of times the amount of slack in a university budget is marginal, since most of the money is committed to faculty and staff salaries. In order to jump start our progress we reallocated $4 million from administrative operations and created an annual fund (the Strategic Resource and Opportunity Analysis or SROA program) dedicated to providing seed grants, strategic investments in the plan's twelve academic priority areas. Special initiatives in undergraduate education, graduate student support, and minority recruitment were funded. We put particular emphasis on using the internal awards to develop research projects that would generate external grants and contracts, including federal, state, foundation, corporate, and private support. The chairs of the twelve priority area implementation committees, the vice president for academic affairs, and the provosts of the Newark and Camden campuses served on the award committee. We gave priority in the award process to initiatives that were multidisciplinary, cut across school or campus lines, and had potential for leveraging significant new resources. Over its seven cycles, the university invested a total of $26 million in support of innovative projects proposed by almost 200 faculty members. The faculty who received this funding brought in approximately $300 million in external funding associated with the projects for which they originally received SROA funding.

Eventually, when happy fiscal times came back in the state, we enjoyed modest improvements in state funding that allowed us to devote more than $40.9 million over a six-year period to a program we called Reinvest in Rutgers. We directed the money to strengthening the university's core academic functions: graduate student support, faculty salary packages, library resources, multicultural initiatives, and academic infrastructure improvements. Our enhancements to the library deserve special mention. Taking advantage of the RUNet project and the resources provided by Reinvest dollars and regular budget support, University Librarian Marianne Gaunt led the transformation of our huge, widely dispersed library system into a full-scale digital library with a strategic plan that involved faculty and students as well as librarians.

Good times are always wonderful, but the strategic plan kept us going and improving through bad times as well as good. We were able to increase our research and development expenditures by more than 70 percent, making Rutgers one of the top public institutions in its rate of growth.

Governor Whitman put state resources into several higher education infrastructure improvement efforts: a Technology Infrastructure Fund, a Scientific, Engineering, and Computer Equipment Leasing Fund, a Higher Education Facilities Trust Fund, a fund for installing fire suppression (following a disastrous fire at Seton Hall), and a Higher Education Capital Improvement Fund.

Once the board had approved the strategic plan, we invited the respected consulting firm of Grenzenbach Glier to assess our readiness for a new major fund campaign. Initially they recommended a goal of $400 million at the most. Based on their advice, there were a number of things we needed to do to prepare the Rutgers Foundation to undertake a campaign far larger than the successful prior campaign for $166 million that concluded in 1990. As part of that process, we hired Michael Carroll to head the foundation. Both he and I wanted to set a more ambitious goal.

When we had strengthened the foundation to the point of readiness to undertake a substantial campaign, we sought the approval of our consultants and the board to set a higher goal. We increased the public goal to $500 million, hoping to raise even more than that. Of course the point of any campaign is not just to achieve its goal or more but to raise the bar for the next campaign, to prepare the way to raise twice as much—in this case a billion dollars—the next time.

The campaign was one of the most enjoyable and memorable experiences of my tenure as president. We were very fortunate to be able to persuade Jim

Cullen to be our national campaign chairman. I had met him during the first months following my appointment, while he was CEO of Bell Atlantic (now Verizon), and had stayed in touch with him. It is always important to have someone of that stature to lead a major fundraising effort; his leadership played a significant part in our success. Campaigning for Rutgers was pure fun. It was my job to go out and brag about what Rutgers was doing and what it planned to do in the future with the right kind of support. Rutgers is a wonderfully rich university in every way that counts in academe. The quality of its faculty is superb and the research they conduct is at the leading edge of their disciplines. Its student body is not only bright and ambitious, it is almost ideally diverse: Rutgers is one of the top three Association of American Universities institutions in African-American enrollment, one of the top six in total minority enrollment.

I have always felt that the quality of students' education depends very largely on what they learn from one another, both in class and outside it. College is the first place that many of our students come into close contact with people of other cultures. As Shirley Jackson observed in her interview, "There is a huge demographic shift coming in this country. What is now called the underrepresented minority, if not becoming the underrepresented majority, will certainly become the underrepresented plurality...the population is changing before our eyes." Rutgers' student body makes it a highly superior learning environment for young people who are growing up in a nation that is fast becoming much more diverse. Rutgers' education, research, and service have a tremendous impact on New Jersey and the nation. My job of explaining the university's many virtues, cultivating Rutgers alumni and friends, and asking that they help their university to become even greater was easy and rewarding. In the end, the campaign exceeded its goal handsomely, bringing in more than $600 million.

I was fortunate in having tremendously knowledgeable, devoted, and actively involved boards at Rutgers. Rutgers' boards are structured in a way that allows their members to educate themselves about the university in a comprehensive, well-designed fashion. The fifty-nine member Board of Trustees was the governing board of the university when it was a private college. Its members come to it from the alumni associations and by individual nomination. It is from the Board of Trustees that five of the eleven members of the Board of Governors are chosen (the other six are appointed by the governor). Trustees serve on committees that advise the deans of the schools and colleges on all three campuses of the university. They also serve on important university-wide committees with members of the Board of Governors, so any trustee who becomes a member of the governing board is thoroughly familiar with the university. The Board of Trustees is the party to the agreement that made Rutgers an instrumentality of the state through the Act of 1956. As the university counsel, David Scott, told each new group of trustees, their stewardship of that agreement is an important responsibility that, in essence, gives them the power to review and to have a strong voice—a decisive voice—on any issue in which the state suggests a material change in the terms of the original contract.

The Board of Governors and the Board of Trustees, as well as the Board of Overseers of the Foundation, want to be well informed about the current issues of the university, fiscal and academic. They also want to be actively involved in finding solutions to the university's problems. Presidents must spend a good deal of time keeping their board(s) up-to-date, ensuring that members, and especially their board chairs, are fully informed about issues of policy and current news. If at all possible, you do not want your board members to wake up to see in the morning news anything that they do not know about the university. The board will return your diligence with interest. Rutgers' boards did the hardest things with as much devotion and good will as the easiest. For example, following several years when the spring protest marches took the size of the annual tuition increases as their theme, the Committee on Educational Planning and Policy of the Board held annual public forums where they invited students to discuss the issue of tuition with them. The policy-makers were able to listen to student opinion and, in turn, to inform students about the reasons for proposed tuition increases. Thanks to their faithful attendance and hard work on their committees, board members were thoroughly informed on university finances, understood the key budget issues, and wanted students to understand them as well.

What the faculty want of the president—in addition to excellent compensation—are the best possible conditions under which to do their work. They need to be involved in setting the priorities for the university and to participate with the administration in putting into action what the university is doing in order to enhance its strengths. Through the campus and unit plans, we involved as many faculty as possible in the planning process, from the ground up. Then we were able to make certain that the faculty was an integral part of the plan's execution by persuading a tenth of the entire faculty to participate in the broadly-based interdisciplinary, intercampus strategic plan implementation committees.

Students too want an environment in which they can do their best work. From my contacts with students (my meetings with student leaders, my encounters with students and their parents around commencement time, and our senior student surveys), I have found that the vast majority of Rutgers students are happy with their education and proud of their university. However, as I mentioned to Bob Berdahl, one of the university's affectionate nicknames is the Berkeley of the East. Rutgers has a tradition of activism and protest that is part of the culture, stretching from the Vietnam War and civil rights protests of the late 1960s and early 1970s to the tuition protests of the late 1980s and early 1990s. I wasn't a complete stranger to student activism. Tulane had its share of Vietnam-era protests. At their climax, the old ROTC building, a World

War II Quonset hut was burned down (a loss it was hard to mourn), and when the protestors sat in at the student center overnight, I came out with other young faculty members to patrol the campus and talk with the students.

The concept of protesting over tuition was new to me, but the Rutgers protestors had a point. Tuition had more than doubled from fall 1980, when it was $940, to fall 1990, when it had risen to $2,856, an average increase of 11.75 percent a year. There was a generous amount of theatrical flair in the protests. Among the unforgettable images from my inauguration are the students with wrists bound and mouths taped who lay down on the path that we took to the ceremony in the old Rutgers College gymnasium. Our Board of Governors meetings were held in an increasingly siege-like atmosphere. Protesting students were crammed into the meeting room equipped with signs and banners and shouted demands from the floor to address the board. Every meeting saw the board members assailed with accusatory rhetoric. One meeting ended with a protestor seizing a pitcher of water in order to drench the last person to exit, Joe Seneca. Nevertheless there was a good deal of sympathy for the idealism and activism of the students and our response was to hold the meeting in a bigger place in order to accommodate more students. In the larger venue, which, as I remember it, was another college gym, several protestors came in huge papier mâché masks, with towering signs fastened to substantial staffs, and stood behind the board, rhythmically pounding their staffs on the floor as board members tried to be heard above the din. Then a couple of the protest leaders grabbed a microphone from a board member and announced that they were taking over the meeting. The university police urged us to leave the gym, so we exited. On the way out, an especially aggressive female protestor elbowed me in the stomach.

After that, I told the board that I thought that we were at the point where it was becoming impossible to conduct the business of the board. We were going to have to set limits on the protests. They agreed, and we established some reasonable conditions that allowed the board to conduct its meetings without disruption. At the same time, we decided that, despite their tactics, we needed to heed the primary grievance advanced by the protests. Although the nearly 12 percent annual tuition increases may have been critical in supporting Rutgers as it climbed to prominence as a distinguished research university, they were excessive and burdensome to students and their parents. Between fall 1991 and fall 2002, tuition increased from $3,114 to $5,770, a markedly lower rate of 5.76 percent annually.

Staff members at Rutgers are an uncommonly devoted and effective force. As the late great Joe Whiteside, who signed their paychecks, used to tell them, the university would come to a grinding halt without their good work. What they want from the president and the university is the guidance and opportunity to do the best job possible for students and faculty.

Recognition is an important part of encouraging improvement and celebrating accomplishment. Among the steps we took to strengthen our efforts to acknowledge the work of the university's most dedicated people were our annual service recognition luncheons that celebrated the years of service that faculty and staff have devoted to the university, beginning with ten years and proceeding in ten-year increments. We also wanted to find a way of recognizing sustained and exceptional service to the university, the academic profession, the state or the nation by a faculty member at the full professorial rank. At Joe Seneca's suggestion, in 1999 we proposed and gained the board's approval to establish the Board of Governors Distinguished Service Professorship, which gives special honor to individuals for their service.

Like all universities in urban settings, Rutgers plays a special role in the cities where it has campuses. In Camden, Newark, and New Brunswick, Rutgers contributes to the economy and offers community outreach services in business, education, legal services, and health care. Our student volunteers are busy in the schools and in service to nonprofit organizations. In fact, CASE, our citizenship and service education program, which integrates community service with classroom learning, is a national model recognized by President Clinton when he visited Rutgers in order to announce his voluntary national service program in early 1993. Our faculty perform research on public policy issues important to the state and the nation. Our libraries are open to all of the state's citizens. Our facilities are used for school athletic events and k-12 summer camps. Beyond that, the university plays an important role in employment and spending in each community. Its greatest contribution is, of course, the more than 10,000 bright, capable young people Rutgers graduates every year.

All three of the cities in which our campuses are located are working to bring about their renaissance and Rutgers' senior administrators have worked with the cities. Newark Provost Norman Samuels was involved in the planning for the New Jersey Performing Arts Center (NJPAC), which has become one of the major factors at the heart of Newark's revival. The Center for Law and Justice, the new law school building, is a beautiful contribution to urban renewal.

In New Brunswick, Vice President for University Budgeting Nancy Winterbauer represents the university on New Brunswick Tomorrow, the private non-profit organization orchestrating the city's revitalization. Despite the fact that state budget cuts limited our ability to take on new building obligations, we continued to initiate major projects, with the encouragement and support of State Senator John Lynch. Rutgers built a modern twelve-story student housing facility with 168 two-bedroom apartments and a health club, parking, and retail space in downtown New Brunswick. Our second major New Brunswick construction effort was the Civic Square Project with two new facilities for Rutgers: the Edward J. Bloustein School for Planning and Public Policy and the Mason Gross School for the Visual Arts. For that $40 million project, thanks to Governor Whitman's help, more than half the obligation was funded by state authorities. We also planned a new public safety building and a home for the Bloustein School's Heldrich Center for Workforce Development.

In Camden, we constructed additions to the student center and the library and renovated the science building. The state built Campbell's Field, a minor league baseball park on the river, and handed its ownership over to Rutgers. Under the excellent leadership of Roger Dennis, Camden's provost since 1998, the university has bought row houses, renovated them, and converted them to university uses.

As my colleagues have noted, the demands on a president's time can become all consuming if they are allowed to run rampant. One of the essential functions of the president's top staffers is to put together a long-term and short-term calendar, prioritizing requests and keeping in mind the fact that there will always be more demands than time available. Mildred Schildcamp who was the secretary of the university, the key person in the care of the boards, and Carol Koncsol, my invaluable executive assistant, together with people from the Rutgers Foundation, handled my schedule. They knew that I needed to book regular visits to Trenton and Washington to talk with key representatives. I wanted to make every effort to attend the meetings of the University Senate and its Executive Committee as regularly as possible. I also put a high priority on annual trips to some of the major urban areas where we have large alumni clubs and on meetings with alumni around New Jersey. I felt that all of the university's key constituencies on campus and off campus deserve and appreciate attention. At certain times, especially when we were in full campaign mode, I needed to spend a lot of time on donor relations. The tried and true formula for success is that all fundraising is really friend-raising. The trips to alumni who were potential donors were journeys of discovery, re-connecting with people, many of whom we had neglected to contact for years. They enjoyed recalling warm memories of their Rutgers education and were happy to learn what the university was currently doing in their areas of interest. They were fascinated by Rutgers' metamorphosis into a top-flight research and teaching institution. And many were interested in the opportunities they might have to support our contemporary students and faculty.

One of the greatest crises Rutgers experienced during my tenure as president was 9/11. The whole country was devastated by the attacks, and the New York area had an especially personal, visceral connection to the disaster. My executive assistant, Carol Koncsol's daughter-in-law was pregnant with their first child and working in one of the Twin Towers that day. Her co-workers helped her down the stairs and throughout their flight from the area, encouraging her to keep going for her baby's sake. It seemed that everyone at the university knew or was related to people who worked in the Twin Towers. Our faculty, staff, and students lost colleagues, friends and relatives. Thirty-eight Rutgers alumni died in the attack. It was hard to know how to respond to a horror of these dimensions, but everyone did what they could. Rutgers people formed lines that stretched for blocks in order to donate blood. The Newark campus offered its facilities for triage and ended by furnishing a depot for relief supplies. Students loaded trucks with materials donated for the relief effort. Our public safety staff provided police, fire protection, and emergency medical assistance in New York City.

We wanted to offer a meaningful institutional response to the tragedy, something of lasting value, in addition to the hundreds of compassionate acts by individuals and groups in the community. With the support of our board of governors chair, we decided that the best thing that the university could offer was access to a Rutgers education. At the University Senate meeting on September 21, in the annual state of the university address, we announced that Rutgers would provide full tuition undergraduate scholarships to the dependent children of all the New Jersey residents who lost their lives in the September 11 attack on the United States, should they attend the university. As part of the campaign, we set up a 9/11 endowed scholarship fund. Even at that early moment, we knew that we had at least two students who had lost a parent in the attack and would be immediately eligible for the scholarships. We got a flood of immediate responses from alumni in New Jersey and around the country who wanted to convey their pride and gratitude for the scholarship initiative.

The presidency of a major research and teaching university like Rutgers is a wonderful job. I think that among the greatest privileges and obligations of such a presidency are the chances it offers to become engaged in the national dialogue on higher education. It has been immensely satisfying to me to have the opportunity to contribute, however modestly, to working with other presidents and chancellors in national organizations in order to discuss problems and opportunities in higher education and formulate policy recommendations on current issues. I owe thanks to Peter McGrath, the head of the National Association of State Universities and Land Grant Colleges, for having recruited me to serve on the Kellogg Commission study on the future of state and land grant institutions. The series of studies produced by the commission have, I think, had an influence on the course of higher education nationally. I was especially privileged to have been able to chair the committee that produced the report on lifelong learning.

My work on the board of directors of the American Council on Education was also very satisfying and, as part of the ACE special interest group on international education, I enjoyed and learned a great deal as I attended the biennial conferences with chief administrators of institutions around the world, planned and supported by the superb work of the ACE international initiatives staff led by Madeleine Green.

Working with the NCAA board of directors and, most recently, having the opportunity to chair the Division I Task Force on Academic Reform at its inception was extraordinarily fruitful and satisfying. The reform measures that we sent up to the board of directors for their approval were thoroughly researched by the excellent NCAA staff and a distinguished group of consultants, then well aired and debated. I believe that they will be effective in improving athletes' preparation for success in college and their progress toward degrees, goals that have been elusive in the past.

I have attended the meetings of the Association of American Universities for many years, first as a graduate dean and provost, while I was at Tulane, then as the Rutgers president. As many of my colleagues have remarked, it is the group of presidents with whom, as a rule, research university presidents have most in common and the meetings always treat matters of absorbing interest. When we are being very frank, we usually admit that the presidency of a large university can be a rather lonely job and it is especially refreshing to have the chance to meet and exchange stories with people who have been dealing with similar problems in their institutions.

I have enjoyed working with all of Rutgers' constituencies, both internal and external. It has been a particular pleasure and honor to work with Rutgers faculty. Their research is transforming our environment and our understanding in ways that affect our view of the world and our lives and it is ultimately the knowledge of these accomplishments that makes the work of a university president so meaningful. It has been a rewarding experience to work closely with Rutgers' board members, who are deeply committed to the institution and spend themselves generously for its sake. Our students are enthusiastic and idealistic. I left every meeting with student leaders energized and almost as ready to change the world as they are. Now, as a teacher, I have confirmed my impression that, while Rutgers has a tremendous diversity of cultures and a wide range of opinions, our students are capable of working together, and of conducting civil exchanges of views on controversial subjects and that imbues me with great optimism for the future. At the same time, the deaths of students are the most terrible events that campuses must face. It is against nature. I don't think that anything is more heart-wrenching than the loss of young people who should have had an entire life before them.

In the 1990s, crisis management became part of the job description for a public university president, in part because we were a bit slow on the uptake. It took us a little while to realize that state support was never going to return to former levels; instead it would continue to dwindle as the states' mandatory spending in areas like public safety, pensions, and health care increased and the discretionary part of their budgets shrank. Of course it wasn't entirely our obtuseness that was to blame. In the yearly legislative appropriation process, a certain amount of support was promised, but during an economic slowdown, that sum would fail to materialize. Instead we would be notified that our budget had been cut at least once, sometimes twice during the year. We learned that no matter how cogent and persuasive our arguments were, we couldn't count on consistent and adequate funding from one year to the next—or, in tough times, even within a particular year. In the process, we learned not to look to tuition alone to solve our problems but to hold our tuition increases down to the minimum raise that we could manage. Because most of our budget was devoted to salaries, it was challenging to find economies. We already had a backlog of deferred maintenance that in bad years had been allowed to grow. Private fundraising couldn't be devoted to it. Nobody is interested in funding repairs to a leaky roof. We had to plan to work within the budget to reduce the backlog and keep up with the repair of aging buildings until the economy improved and a Higher Education Improvement Fund was passed during Governor Christie Whitman's administration.

Salary negotiations with our employee unions were sometimes drawn-out and contentious. The faculty union had during its entire existence insisted that nearly the entire amount of salary increases be across the board, with very little reserved to be awarded for merit. The board and I agreed that a much larger proportion of salaries ought to be given for merit determined by a peer process. It took enormous effort and persistence—we went almost three years without a contract to get it accomplished—but, in the end, the faculty contract was settled with 50 percent of the increase in salary determined by merit. We were also successful in getting consideration for merit into the staff contracts and having salary increases determined by merit for non-union employees. Those were major accomplishments, and so was our success in initiating mutual gains bargaining procedures to replace the old, high-tension labor-versus-management style of negotiation, which relied on dramatic oppositional tactics and the creation of crises.

I asked my colleagues what they considered the most significant capital investments during their tenure. Like Bob Berdahl, I have to cite an essential infrastructure improvement as our largest and most important capital project. The greatest single investment that we made during my tenure as president was RUNet 2000, the $100-million-dollar-plus project that wired all three Rutgers campuses for voice, video and data from Newark in the north, through New Brunswick in central Jersey, to Camden in south Jersey. It was inspired by the two-year process of strategic planning, when unit after unit made it clear that greatly expanded broadband capacity was a sine qua non in order to advance to the highest level of excellence. Before RUNet, easy instant access to the full resources of the Internet was unevenly distributed, now it is ubiquitous, available throughout the offices of faculty and residence halls of students. It has had a huge impact on learning and research, as well as services at Rutgers. Among the other significant investments, all with a combination of state and private funding, were the new law school building in Newark (the Center for Law and Justice), the Civic Square building in New Brunswick and the completely rebuilt football stadium, and soccer-lacrosse facility, along with the playing fields for student recreation on the New Brunswick-Piscataway campus. We also expanded the library and the art museum and completed or initiated some important teaching and research facilities, such as the Biomedical Engineering Building, the Center for Advanced Infrastructure and Transportation, the Allison Road Classroom Building, the Center for Cancer Research, and the Life Sciences Building. Again, most were constructed with a combination of funding from the state and private gifts.

I didn't hesitate to ask my colleagues what their legacy to their institutions would be, so I am obliged to answer the same question, with the caveat that Chuck Vest very appropriately added: nothing that is accomplished in a university is the work of a single person. Everything has to be accomplished with the cooperation and hard work of many. The success of the strategic plan is certainly a case in point: it is a major accomplishment that the university owes to the Rutgers faculty, the Board of Governors, the Board of Trustees, the Foundation's Board of Overseers, Provost Norman Samuels of Newark, and Provosts Walter Gordon and Roger Dennis of Camden, as well as Vice President for Academic Affairs Joe Seneca and Vice Presidents Christine Haska Cermak and Nancy Winterbauer.

The technological plan, RUNet 2000 is also the work of all the people I have just cited, as well as the administrators who saw it to its completion. Christine Haska Cermak was in charge of shepherding the project from beginning to end. Kim Manning-Lewis was the point person of the management team that led the planning phase of the mammoth undertaking. Mike McKay, the Vice President of Information Technology, and Joe Sanders, the project supervisor, together with many others, were the people who made it all happen.

Rutgers' major fundraising campaign, Creating the Future, owes its success to Jim Cullen, who was our campaign chair; to the boards; to the chairs of the Rutgers foundation board of overseers, Alvin Rockoff and Kevin Collins; to Mike Carroll, the superb head of the foundation and his excellent staff; to the current president, Richard McCormick, who saw the campaign through its final months; and, above all, to the thousands of alumni, faculty, and friends who gave so generously in order to ensure Rutgers' bright future. Thanks to all of those good people Rutgers had steady, sizeable increases in research grants and contracts, in student quality and diversity, and in private giving to the university during my tenure, all solid accomplishments on which the university is building an even better future.

Our understanding of leadership has changed today. We no longer look on it in a narrow sense as the work of a succession of great men, CEOs and generals, molding history to serve their own ambitions, but as a process of building that depends upon gathering people together to accomplish good work. People lead in many different ways and in a variety of situations, with or without a formal position and title. In most contemporary organizations, leadership does not consist primarily in telling people what to do, but in interaction between leaders and followers, an exchange of views in which leaders carry out the wishes of the community by developing a principled vision that people support, empowering the community by involving it in setting goals and effecting necessary change, and sustaining ethical standards with consistent commitment to moral behavior.

If that answer sounds premeditated, it is because I am now teaching leadership in classes on both the New Brunswick and Camden campuses. This rediscovery of the classroom in the new style of teaching that allows students to engage in active learning has been a lot of fun. We're teaching students the concepts and skills of leadership through their assignments. They work together with classmates who come from a variety of backgrounds and collaborate to build consensus on the problems and opportunities in the areas they investigate. Then they improve their writing and public speaking skills by writing papers and giving presentations. In the process, we try to supply them with opportunities to grow in their ability to identify ethical issues.

My advice to those considering a university presidency would be to use the presidential search interview not simply as a chance to let the committee know you, but an opportunity for you to find out everything you can about the institution: its people, its challenges, and the directions that it is taking. Then, when you take office, you owe it to yourself and the institution to spend at least six months conducting your own due diligence examination of the institution. As you make decisions, you ought to be aware of the fact that, as Bob Berdahl puts it, "You start these jobs with a full bank account and you spend it down with every decision you make because you never replenish the account by creating goodwill. You only draw it down by creating ill will with decisions. And the fact that many constituencies now have much more claim on the university simply means that you spend it down faster." Your slightest gesture is magnified, as though you are living under a microscope, especially in public institutions.

You need to act out of your own deep commitment to higher education and your understanding of its crucial importance to our society. If you do that, you will not please everyone all the time, but you will do what needs to be done and will have no reason to regret it, whatever it may cost you. For example, I accepted Governor Whitman's request to serve on the Governor's Advisory Panel on the Restructuring of Higher Education, which recommended that the Department of Higher Education be abolished and replaced by a Presidents' Council and a Commission on Higher Education. The Governor was pleased and Rutgers benefited, but everything I did and said from that point forward was viewed with a hostile eye by a major media outlet that prided itself on having championed the creation of the DHE. Personally you may often pay a price for doing what you believe is the right thing for your institution and for higher education, but at the core of your work must be a kind of integrity, a compass that keeps you going in the direction of what you truly believe to be the best course for the institution and the broader community it serves.

Certainly, as my colleagues have said, some of the key issues in the shortened tenure of university presidents are the increasing complexity of the job, the multiple roles a president or chancellor must play, the growing number and involvement of constituencies, and the ever-increasing expectations for colleges and universities as they become more central to the economic, political, and social advancement of nations and their individual citizens. However I have an additional theory on the reason that tenures in presidencies have become so much shorter. I think that we owe it, at least in part, to the peripatetic style of academic career adopted by the faculty some time ago. It took a while for that style of career building to catch on in higher education administration, but it seems that it is now here to stay. Faculty members, deans, vice presidents, provosts and presidents used to settle down at a college or university and spend their entire professional lives there, but making a long commitment to a particular institution has become an old-fashioned way of functioning. A career in the presidency can span two or three institutions, more than that if we count the individual's moves from place to place as a faculty member, then up through the administrative ranks.

We also have to take into account the facts that some moves take place for idiosyncratic, personal reasons: some because the fit between the president and the institution isn't good, others because the person wants to move on to a more prestigious post, and still others because the person feels that she has accomplished everything that she could in that particular institution. There are also a few candidates who find that the job is simply not what they thought it would be. It can be difficult to understand in advance how much your life will be changed and what reserves of energy will be required in order to stay fresh and vigorous, all day, every day.

The role of the presidency has changed over the past few decades in response to several powerful trends. The disinvestment of states in higher education has obviously made the role of the public university president harder. If, as seems likely, this challenging trend continues and grows, it will have extremely negative results, especially on access, and may be the greatest problem we will face over the next decade.

The technological revolution can make learning more exciting and is having a huge impact on research. It also offers opportunities for distance learning that allow people to continue their education who otherwise might not have had that chance. On conventional campuses, the asynchronous communication of e-mail allows students and professors to communicate freely outside the classroom. Online library resources give them access to reserved readings and allow them to scan library resources from their rooms. Online laboratory exercises are engaging, safe, and, according to Rutgers' Mellon grant-funded studies of instructional technology, the voluntary use of online laboratories improves student learning.

The growing role of private support and commercial applications for university research is more than a trend; it is a flood that is nearly irresistible, especially in this time when universities are striving to develop new streams of revenue. At the same time as private support and commercial applications are encouraged, they need to be carefully monitored by universities in order to keep both the individual researcher and the institution on the path of scrupulously ethical behavior by avoiding conflicts of interest and preserving the necessary freedom of scholarly exchange of information.

Demands from the public and from our students for high quality and accountability are going to increase as higher education becomes more and more important to individuals and our society and as our students advance in their sophistication about learning. We need to do a much more comprehensive and better job of informing the public on a regular basis about issues of importance to them. The better our critics understand the issues, the more likely it is that we and they will be able to come to a resolution.

Cost is also an issue that is not going to go away. The availability of lower cost, more convenient access to higher education through community colleges at the entrance level and through distance education at advanced levels will give students choices that fit their ability to pay. Private institutions like MIT will be able to keep reasonable access to their institutions open through financial aid funded by their endowment and continuing private support. Public research universities will depend on state and federal aid, along with private giving, to help students to pay for their college education. The majority of students at Rutgers also work from ten to twenty hours a week to help to support themselves, just as my wife and I did in undergraduate school.

New Jersey has large programs of need-based student aid that it regularly cites as evidence of its generous support of higher education, but I have no great hope that the states or the federal government will take on more of the responsibility of providing low-income families access to higher education. I do feel that, even in difficult times, it is important for the institutions themselves to find new ways to address the problem of access. For example, when we realized that Rutgers was receiving many more applications from qualified students than we could possibly accommodate, we worked with the 19 New Jersey county colleges to develop what we called the Dual Degree program. It offered Rutgers applicants the opportunity of enrolling in their local community colleges with the guarantee that they could transfer smoothly to the university in their junior year upon completing the approved prerequisites and earning a grade point average of B or better.

At the policy level, good governance of a university relies on the relationship between the governing board and the president. The quality of the governing board depends very largely on the time and care that good people who value the mission and integrity of the institution, people like Michael Tuosto and Dean Paranicas, are willing to commit to becoming knowledgeable enough and active enough to make solid contributions. Like any job, the first requirement for good board membership is just showing up, being there for all of the meetings of the board and serving as an active member of the board committees. The institution is responsible for making its best effort to orient new board members. They need to hear from the president and from experienced board members about the issues the institution faces and the way that the board has worked with the president to address the university's ambitions and solve its problems. A weekend retreat for new board members would be a good formal orientation, if it could be arranged.

The role of the chair is crucial in keeping the board on track. Under a weak or easily led chair, wild card board members can wreak havoc, but even a board that has members with private or political agendas can be effective with a strong chair guiding their work and firmly keeping their focus on the central priorities of the university and the board's policy-making function. The quintessential example of a devoted and effective board member for me is Anne Thomas, who is an alumna of Middlebury College but served for many years on the Rutgers boards, faithfully attending innumerable committee and board meetings. She served three years as chair of the Board of Governors (1995-1998), a tower of quiet strength and excellent counsel to me and her fellow board members.

Political pressures are a fact of life in public institutions. In our state, the University of Medicine and Dentistry of New Jersey (UMDNJ) is now under investigation for having contributed generously to politicians over a number of years and having contracted with politically connected consultants whose services to the university produced no reports or records of any kind, save the large, regular payments issued to them over the years. Rutgers is fortunate and, I believe, unique in its relationship as an instrumentality of the state under the Act of 1956. It has been able to retain the kind of quasi-independent status that allows the university, even under political fire, to refuse on the grounds of academic freedom to fire a faculty member, as President Mason Gross did in the case of Eugene Genovese in 1965, or to reject a strong bid by the governor to merge Rutgers with UMDNJ and put both under the power of Trenton, as President Richard McCormick, the Board of Governors, and the Board of Trustees did in 2004.

Every major university in the country has been working hard to diversify its student body. Rutgers and the state of New Jersey have been in the forefront of well-planned and well-supported initiatives to attract, retain, and graduate young people from economically and educationally disadvantaged backgrounds. The New Jersey Educational Opportunity Fund was proposed in 1967, following the summer riots in Newark, and was passed by the legislature in 1968. EOF is described by the New Jersey Commission on Higher Education as "a leader and a linchpin" in the state's effort to increase diversity, but participation in EOF is not limited to minority students. The program is designed to identify and assist low-income, educationally disadvantaged students who, as the Commission puts it, "demonstrate the commitment, motivation and potential for success…but lack adequate preparation for college study." It offers participants supplemental financial aid, in addition to their Tuition Aid Grants, as well as academic help in the form of campus-based outreach and support services at both public and private New Jersey colleges and universities. The goal for New Jersey's public higher education institutions is to enroll EOF students as 10 percent of the New Jersey freshman class of each of their colleges. That can be a challenging objective, but we have been remarkably successful, thanks to the good recruitment work of the colleges and the admissions office. Our Rutgers EOF college programs provide excellent academic support, including pre-college summer programs, counseling, tutoring, study skills, supplemental instruction, career services, and leadership development.

Rutgers' Newark campus is consistently singled out as the most diverse national university in the county. The Rutgers School of Law-Newark, which regularly ranks among the most diverse in the nation, boasts a large number of prominent minority graduates. For several decades, the school practiced a bold affirmative action preference system called the Minority Student Program, under which it was very successful both in attracting underrepresented minorities and giving them support in their studies. These distinctions drew a legal challenge to the law school's admissions procedures in 1996. It was unsuccessful because the complainant had qualifications below those of all other students accepted in the year that he applied, but the dual track system of admission was challenged. In order to fend off the possibility of future challenges, the school has, since 2000, offered students a choice suggested by Professor Paul Tractenberg: they can ask to be judged for admission based primarily on their test scores and undergraduate grade point average or to be evaluated on a more broadly based assessment of their experiences and accomplishments. The system is still dual track and has not been tested by a legal challenge, but both students and faculty are pleased with the new policy.

My least favorite subject among all of the topics involved with higher education is that Dr. Jekyll and Mr. Hyde of the American university, Division I college athletics: a juggernaut difficult to keep on the straight and narrow path of righteousness, a voracious consumer of resources, and a volatile potential source of embarrassment for everyone concerned and/or a brilliant display of fiercely competitive talent, an attractive showpiece that continually renews the place of the university in the hearts of alumni and friends, and a source of pride to the university community. In January of 2005, NCAA President Myles Brand appointed a second NCAA task force, chaired by University of Arizona President Peter Likins, to grapple with the next stage of athletics reform. The Presidential Task Force on the Future of Division I Intercollegiate Athletics is charged with examining "the alignment of Division I athletics with the mission, values and goals of higher education in such areas as fiscal responsibility, presidential leadership, and student athlete well-being" (*NCAA News*, vol. 42 , no.13, June 20, 2005, pp. 1, 19). Both President Brand and committee chair Likins are careful to avoid the rhetorical excesses of the sky-is-falling school of athletic reform, framing their approach instead as a work of vision and long-term planning, based on sound evidence, and intended, in Likins' words, "to protect something we value...rather than to fix something we perceive as broken." Nevertheless, it is a tall order to rein in the thorniest problems, such as the huge increases in athletics budgets which, at the most competitive programs, are now paying multimillion dollar salaries to head coaches, and the rich potential for disagreement among boosters, faculty, presidents, and board members when athletic interests come into conflict with academic priorities. I am afraid that the task force is undertaking the work of Sisyphus, but theirs is a necessary and high-minded labor. We must hope that they meet with all the success that their difficult task deserves.

Charles M. Vest

Charles Vest was president of the Massachusetts Institute of Technology from 1990 until December of 2004. He came to MIT from the University of Michigan, where he was the chief academic officer.

Born in Morgantown, West Virginia on September 9, 1941, he earned his bachelor's degree in mechanical engineering from West Virginia University, his master's and Ph.D. from the University of Michigan. In his research, he has focused on the thermal sciences and the engineering applications of lasers and coherent optics.

At MIT, Vest has encouraged and supported the OpenCourseWare project and used the power of his office to draw attention to and advocate for the status of women faculty and professionals in science and engineering. He has built the brain and cognitive sciences at MIT to a new level, created a stronger international emphasis in the university's programs of teaching and research, worked with leaders of industry to create an environment in which collaboration could flourish, and increased the diversity of the student body, faculty, and administration.

On the national level, Vest has worked with government leaders to create a level of understanding and collaboration favorable to rebuilding the system of federal funding of research in private and public universities. In that effort, he chaired the President's Advisory Committee on the Redesign of the Space Station, served as a member of the President's Committee of Advisors on Science and Technology (PCAST), and the National Research Council Board on Engineering Education. He chaired the U.S. Department of Energy Task Force on the Future of Science Programs and served for ten years as vice chair of the Council on Competitiveness. He has served as chair of the Association of American Universities. In February of 2004, he accepted the invitation of President Bush to serve as a member of the Commission on the Intelligence Capabilities of the United States Regarding Weapons of Mass Destruction.

Vest is now president emeritus and professor of mechanical engineering at MIT and a life member of the MIT Corporation.

Francis Lawrence: I have admired your work, not just as president of MIT, but as a national leader in higher education. You have articulated important issues with style and grace. The whole education community owes you a debt of gratitude for your role as a public spokesman. I'm sure that your family background and education contributed to shaping your values and development. Could you tell me something about your early life?

Charles Vest: I grew up in a small college town in West Virginia, Morgantown, which is the seat of West Virginia University and a very open kind of community. There I went to public schools with the children of professors, doctors, farmers, and coal miners all mixed together. I can't help but believe that environment has colored my view of life to some extent. Both of my parents were from West Virginia. They grew up in the small town of Elkins and both attended a small Presbyterian College, Davis & Elkins. We moved to Morgantown when my dad (after having been a power company lineman, a high school science teacher, and the principal of a high school with two teachers) decided to get a master's degree in mathematics and ended by staying at the university as a mathematics professor. He earned his Ph.D. at the University of Michigan by going there in the summers, starting before the war, but interrupted by service as a civilian teaching radar technology to military folks. He finished his Ph.D. after the war, when I was five or six years old. I grew up in an academic household in typical middle class, small town America. I think I learned a lot from my father about the love of science, disciplined work and thought, and a strong work ethic. My mother stayed at home and raised her children. She was well read, had an artistic temperament, and a great interest in history. Most of our vacations when I was young consisted of going up and down the great old battlefields of the Civil War and tramping through graveyards. She was also a very good genealogist of the family. I think that in many ways my outlook on life, to a surprising extent, reflects both of my parents' temperaments. We were fortunate in having a close family. I have a brother almost seven years older than I am who is also a mechanical engineer. He spent his career here in New England at Pratt and Whitney Aircraft. It was a wonderful time to grow up in America, at least if you were a white male, and I had a very enjoyable youth. I was probably more interested in football than I was in science and mathematics, but those academic interests grew through my high school years. I went to a good public high school that benefited from being in an academic community. There were always faculty—wives or spouses of graduate students—who were involved. It probably kept things on a little higher plane than they might have been otherwise. It was a halcyon period in which it was fun to grow up. I did have a little more than my share of illness as a young child, a terrific number of allergies which caused problems with asthma and bronchitis, but I outgrew that, and I've been healthy as a horse ever since. When I was sick I would stay home and draw all day long; I believe that had something to do with becoming an engineer. Everything balances out.

FL: What was your first leadership position?

CV: I was vice president of my class when I was in high school, but I never saw that as a particular goal. When I was an undergraduate at West Virginia University, I was the president of what was referred to as the ranking men's honorary. That was a little unusual because normally law students or graduate students served as president. Then I decided, halfway through my undergraduate years, that what I really enjoyed was teaching. After graduation I moved on to the University of Michigan and earned my Ph.D. in mechanical engineering. I joined the faculty and really was fully absorbed in being a faculty member, uninterested in being a department chair, trying to stay away from committees, doing my teaching and research and working with my graduate students. I always enjoyed teaching immensely. About 1981, Jim Duderstadt as a thirty-eight or thirty-nine-year-old became dean of the Michigan College of Engineering and convinced me to serve as his associate dean. With a combination of reluctance and an attitude of oh, why not, I agreed to do it for no more than two years and no more than half time.

FL: Were there certain people who inspired you and acted as your mentors?

CV: There were actually quite a few, but as I think about the question, I begin with my father and mother. We were very close. We did not often express our feelings, but we learned a lot from each other, and I certainly considered my father a mentor. I took two classes from my father as an undergraduate. People told me that if I wanted to take the second course in applied mathematics, which was a mixture of graduate and undergraduate work, I wouldn't really be prepared for it unless I took my dad for the first course: so I swallowed hard and did it. In the classroom, he was disciplined and hard-nosed, so much so that the other kids hardly raised an eyebrow about my being in the class. I too didn't ask a single question for two semesters, but when I think about mentorship, I remember my dad. I lived at home while I was an undergraduate and he would come home before exams, plunk an envelope down on the table, and say, "Well, there are the exams for tomorrow." He wouldn't say another word, but I knew what he was teaching and I appreciated that. I also owe a lot to my mother, who I think gave me a sense of history, a sense of place, and a sense of art. Another person who had a lot to do with my career was Bob Slonneger, a mechanical engineering professor at West Virginia. The year I was a freshman, he convinced me to become a mechanical engineer. I had actually intended to be in electrical engineering or physics. The field of mechanical engineering was undergoing a rapid shift: it was the beginning of what's referred to as the engineering science revolution. Bob taught heat transfer and thermodynamics. He got me very interested and took me under his wing. I owe him a lot. It was a big thrill to have him come to my inauguration at MIT in 1990. Then, of course, there is my thesis adviser for my Ph.D., Vedat Arpaci, who was a wonderful mentor in a broader sense. He grew up in Turkey and was educated there as an undergraduate, then came here to

MIT for his doctoral degree. We spent enormous amounts of time together, mostly concentrating on technical issues and very much in a partnership mode, yet I learned a lot somewhat more broadly from him about how to pose, formulate, and think about problems and problem solving. I think that psychologically, he branched out well beyond the technical things that we dealt with. He was a person totally uninterested in administration, but I learned things from him that I value in what I've done administratively. Then the fourth person I would note was again a professor, and ultimately a faculty colleague, named Gus Yih. His real name was Chia-Shun Yih. He was an applied mechanics professor at Michigan, a very well-known scholar in hydraulics and fluid mechanics. I spent a great deal of time with Gus and learned a lot about academic values, as well as about mathematics and mechanics. Those are the four people to whom I would point as my most influential mentors

FL: What were the major challenges of MIT when you became president?

CV: Beyond the challenges that every institution faces, there were a few very identifiable issues when I came to MIT in 1990. One was that the relationship between the federal government and the research universities was in serious disrepair. It was an interesting time because we were at the end of the Cold War and the military rationale behind the enthusiasm in congress for physics and engineering had dissipated. At that point we were also in the midst of a couple of very high profile issues. One had to do with the alleged scientific misconduct at MIT of a scientist who worked with David Baltimore. It was one of several high profile cases involving accusations of scientific misconduct that had raised the hackles of many in Congress. I point out very quickly that, in the end, after a long and very trying affair, David and his MIT colleagues were totally exonerated of those charges, but the accusations did a lot of damage in the meantime. On the heels of that, we were facing challenges about indirect cost expenditures and the Dingle hearings regarding Stanford University. Congressman John Dingle from Michigan is the constant link through these matters because he drove the Baltimore issue and the indirect cost issue. Stanford, along with other research universities, was also exonerated after several years, when the accusation of improper charges of indirect costs proved to be false, but of course the exoneration received far less coverage than the original charges had attracted. The results were a combination of damage to MIT and the other universities attacked, along with what were, frankly, some worthwhile reforms. MIT as one of the major research universities and recipients of federal research funding was deeply concerned about those issues.

The other hot topic here in 1990 in the scientific area was that, despite the fact that MIT had operated the Francis Bitter National Magnet Laboratory since 1950, NSF had decided to reopen competition for it and gave the award to a consortium centered around Florida State, despite the fact that both review panels had recommended that the lab stay here at MIT. All of these factors created a swirling of issues that rose very suddenly, creating a strained, even alienated relationship between research universities and the government, especially Congress. Those were the big issues that had a lot to do with the way that I spent some of my time here. When I came to MIT, there was also a civil investigative demand from the U.S. Justice Department over financial aid practices among a group in which MIT participated with other private universities and colleges that had overlapping admissions pools. It had been the practice of our group to meet once a year in order to compare how individual colleges and universities had measured the ability of applicants' families to pay for a portion of the tuition and expenses of any student who was admitted to more than one of these institutions. The goal was to see whether we all measured it the same way. If we didn't, we would discuss the reasons and arrive at a compromise. Everybody would use that as a uniform base on which they could apply their own formulas and decision-making for the financial aid. The philosophy behind this procedure was that these schools were all pledged to admit students without paying any attention to their financial status, then to disburse their financial aid according to need. Shortly after I came here, literally in my first term, the Justice Department brought suit against the members of the Overlap Group, i.e., the eight Ivy League institutions and MIT, claiming that our financial aid practices violated the Sherman Antitrust Act. The eight Ivy League institutions settled by signing a consent decree, basically saying that they didn't do anything wrong, but they would never do it again. I decided that MIT would fight this in court. We lost the first round and immediately appealed it to a three-judge panel in Philadelphia. There were three points of the law at issue: in two of them the justices decided unanimously on MIT's behalf; on the third one, two sided with MIT and one sided with the government, so the case was remanded back to the lower court. At this point, the damage to the Justice Department's case was so great that they negotiated a little face-saving with us and we won a good moral victory, if nothing else.

The other two things that were major issues when I came here are quite different. One is not a problem, just an issue. MIT had long been focused, to a large extent, on the physical sciences, engineering, architecture, and the school of management. The school of humanities, arts and social sciences had become quite strong, but the big change was the growth of the life sciences. The role of biology as clearly in the core of MIT was relatively recent and there was an intellectual readjustment going on in dealing with that. Finally, there was a lingering issue around the nature of the housing system at MIT. In those days and, in fact, until a couple of years ago, our freshmen during their first two or three days on campus were all rushed by the fraternities (or what we call independent living groups), as well as by individual parts of the dormitory system. They made their decisions about where to live in those first few days. In many people's view this distorted the way in which students were introduced to the institution and to their university life. There was a lot of concern about the lack of diversity and large chunks of the fraternities were in independent living groups. I hasten to add that those groups are almost uniformly very diverse today, but there had been a report during the previous administration suggesting that this rushing process should be changed, that freshmen should have to live in the first year at campus residence halls and become acclimated to MIT as a whole in a different way. It was a very complicated issue that has actually played out over the last fourteen years and is still continuing to play out. These were the big issues of the day when I took office.

FL: What effects have the role and demands of the presidency had on your family? How have you maintained a balance and kept up your energy?

CV: As you well know, being president of a major institution is a life, not a job. Becky and I were fortunate in that, when this incredible opportunity came along, two things allowed us to consider it seriously. One is I had been for almost a decade involved in pretty heavy administration, having been dean of engineering and provost of Michigan, and was somewhat used to the lifestyle. We also were fortunate in that our daughter graduated from the university that previous spring, in 1990, and our son was in his second year at the University of California-Berkeley, so they were out of the nest. It was a time when we didn't have the same constraints we might have had at an earlier part in our life. I still marvel at how smooth the transition was. I felt as though one day I was sitting at a desk in Ann Arbor, the next day I was sitting at a desk at MIT. It went extraordinarily well because people worked so hard to welcome us and make it smooth.

It was a much more difficult thing for Becky. As you know, you go through a period in life in which most of your deep friendships are formed with other couples while you are raising children together. Although Becky was not working in a full-time job, she had been involved with a couple of small businesses, had a huge circle of friends, and did a lot of gardening. It was a real uprooting for her, but it was a family decision to take this on. There were a tough couple of years for her when we moved here, primarily because of what she was leaving, not because of what she was going into. I think that she has enjoyed her time here. People couldn't have been nicer and more accommodating to us, but it was a very abrupt change. Happily, both of our children have ended up on the East Coast. Our daughter was married about a third of the way through our tenure here. She, her husband, and our two grandchildren are in Washington, D.C. Our son transferred as a junior to Harvard, so he was here a couple of years, then went to medical school at Columbia, and is now doing a cardiology fellowship at Columbia Presbyterian Hospital. He too is married. With our daughter in Washington and our son in New York, everybody is within an hour and a half trip on the shuttle. We're very fortunate that we get to see a good bit of each other. In that sense, our family life has remained intact and close. So the transition to MIT was a smooth one for me and a more complicated one for Becky.

As for maintaining energy and balance, I don't know if I maintain a balance or not. I try to. I make no pretense of maintaining a balance in my time because MIT has been my life for fourteen years, but I do two things. One is that, when I'm here, I religiously get up and run two miles every morning about 6:00 or 6:30. I take this marvelous route along the bank of the Charles River and sometimes I think that, without that run, it would really be tough. It gets the cobwebs out of my mind and I enjoy the sights and the relative quiet. That gets my day started and I think it has a lot to do with keeping my energy up. We also are fortunate that we've bought a home up on the shore of Lake Winnipesaukee in New Hampshire, where our goal was to spend a weekend a month, but it's sometimes more like a weekend a semester. At least it's there, and, if we can, we get away and go up there. Even if I sit at my desk and work all day, it's different to look out the window at the lake. We like to go there in the winter, when it's snowy and quiet. All of these things help. Although in Ann Arbor we managed to be reasonably faithful in attendance of concerts, and I don't think we missed a home football game in our twenty-seven years there, I'm ashamed to admit that, although in the first few years we were here, we bought concert tickets, the time just disappeared. We gave up on that, but Becky and I sneak off and go to the movies when we can on a Friday or Saturday evening, then go out to dinner, and, as I say, these days, at every opportunity we have, we get together somehow with the kids and the grandchildren. That's what keeps us going now.

FL: How did you recruit and structure your MIT leadership team?

CV: When I came here in 1990, I was an outsider at MIT. I had two or three friends in the faculty and that was about it. I have no degree from here and never spent any time here. I asked Paul Gray, who was president at that time, and John Deutch, who was provost, if they would stay on an extra month after they had planned to step down. That allowed me to take almost two months before I started work as president. I kept an office in Ann Arbor, but would come up here early every Monday morning, stay until Friday night, then go back for the weekend at Ann Arbor. With the guidance of some of the people who had been involved in the search process, I met an hour at a time with a very large number of faculty, administrators, and various other people. During that period, I asked each person who I met two questions. First, what are the issues, that is, what does the new president have to think about here, and second, who do you think would be a good provost? I knew I needed a provost who was thoroughly familiar with the institution. Through that process I learned a lot about MIT. I would go home, put what I had learned together on my computer, and make a little outline. When I was finished, I gave it to Paul Gray and asked him to take it home and tell me what he thought about it. He told me that I hadn't missed anything. Paul has a mind like a steel trap and an unbelievable understanding of the institution, so I knew that I had indeed learned a lot.

Through this process, I also selected Mark Wrighton, who was the head of the chemistry department, as provost. Mark started the same day I did. I like to think that we were a good team. He was an excellent provost and virtually everybody else in the administration stayed in place. Then, through evolution, that changed somewhat. One of the hardest things for me in keeping the institution structured during the first half of my tenure was that three members of the academic council, the senior administrators of the institution, died, all far too young. Each loss was traumatic and each time I ended up doing a lot of restructuring because I tend to think about what has to be done and what people's talents are, then shape the jobs around the people, rather than the other way around. Through about two-thirds of my time here, the administration continued to evolve. First Mark served as provost, then he left to become the president of Washington University in St. Louis, and Joel Moses, who was the dean of engineering, became provost.

In 1998, I saw that a lot of stars were aligning, the economy was getting strong, and there was a chance for a new beginning. We had assembled a terrifically powerful group of young faculty. We had been through difficult times with some process reengineering and we had executed a massive retirement incentive program that reduced our staff head count and brought about a major turnover in the faculty. As new young faculty came in, we were getting up a full head of steam: a lot of good things started happening. I rebuilt the administration to take advantage of this momentum. I brought John Curry in from Caltech to serve as our executive vice president after a national search conducted by a blue ribbon committee of faculty and staff here. I knew exactly the person I needed to be our provost during this period; I recruited Bob Brown, who is a chemical engineer and has turned out to be the most talented academic administrator I have ever observed anywhere. He's just been terrific. We also hired Alice Gast as vice president for research. At this time, of course, I had matured in my understanding of the institution. I knew where our strengths were and what we needed, so I'd like to think that we were able to build a dream team. We also developed a new senior position that we called chancellor, because I felt that the position of provost in our rather centralized system was becoming an undoable job, particularly if we were going to bring about the major changes that we all thought that we could accomplish. The chancellor's post was occupied first, quite admirably, by Larry Bacow. As chancellor, Larry was in charge of all the cross-cutting things that have a tendency to get lost in the cracks and also supervised our international relationships. I asked him to spend at least 50 percent of his time on a set of issues around student life—back to the housing issues that we talked about—and a number of things of that nature. Larry had been the elected chair of the faculty the year before becoming chancellor, had gotten to know everybody, and was deeply respected. Then Larry became president of Tufts and Phil Clay, who had been the head of urban studies and planning, became chancellor. He has carried on very much in that tradition. Summing up, my first effort when I arrived was to pick a provost whom I deeply trusted and felt complemented my capabilities in a variety of ways and then to let the rest of the administration evolve, but later on there came a point when I made a more sweeping set of changes in both structure and people.

FL: What are some of the specific qualities that you look for in the people you choose to work with and depend upon, such as the individuals you named both in the early stages and in your later restructuring?

CV: The first thing I look for at the highest level of administrative positions is somebody who complements me. Knowing that the two of us will have to talk and wrestle with things, I try to complement myself, and if you look at my three provosts, I think they all fit that profile. I have a sense of what I can do and where my weaknesses are, so I look for people who will complement those qualities. No matter how you organize the university, the president and the provost have to be a team. There's just no other way to get everything done. I tend to take a pondering kind of approach to problem solving. Despite the fact that I'm an engineer, I sometimes focus more on qualitative aspects and people aspects than the financial and business aspects. I always look for people who are quantitatively oriented and who may have a different kind of decision-making mode, in particular people who make decisions a little faster. But beyond that, the first qualities I look for in senior administrators, even in areas like the executive vice president, are people who truly understand and care about academia. They have to have that in their blood and cherish it as a value. They have to know what faculty really do and what faculty care about. That is fundamental. Then I expect people to have the highest levels of integrity. Any hint that is not the case and I would totally lose interest. Those are the three things I would put first: academic values, integrity, and complementarity. Finally, I have to be honest: I look for real commitment and hard work. Maybe I look too hard for that; I always expect people to work long hours as needed to get the job done. I have found that if you put these characteristics together, you generally end up with people who can work together as a team. Those are the things I have looked for and been fortunate to have found.

FL: Hard work is certainly a sine qua non. University presidents have to spend a lot of time on the road. Did you have someone in your administration who stood in for you, handling the day-to-day work of the university or were you in communication on a constant basis?

CV: This has varied over time. I have been a bit of a chameleon and each of my provosts has had particular talents, so I pretty quickly figure out what they really like to do, what they don't like to do, and sometimes I switch around what I'm doing to match that. In some periods, I was much more a hands-on president internally than I have been in the last few years, but the fact is that I have always structured things so that the provost is both the chief academic officer and chief budget officer.   He is the person who primarily interacts with the deans. After thirteen of my fourteen years, I finally learned to delegate a bit, so the last part of my presidency has focused more on the larger issues and a few key decisions, less on the day-to-day operation. But the fact is that, for all of its faults, electronic mail ties us together. We are all in constant twenty-four hour a day, seven-days-a-week communication by e-mail. People like the provost, the chancellor, the executive vice president, and Kathryn Willmore, who is the vice president in this office, have quickly developed a good sense of when we have to touch base with each other. We have as much face-to-face meeting as we can and talk a good bit on the telephone, but the fact is that it is email that constantly chains us together.

FL: How did you formulate the vision for the future of the institution?

CV: If you talk to people around here, you will find that in my early years I may not have articulated a clear vision. Some people may have thought I had no vision and maybe I didn't. I will always remember the day that Gerhardt Casper called me, totally exasperated, and said, "Chuck, if just one more person asks me what my vision for Stanford University is, I quit!"   To be honest, I always had the view that an institution like this is sufficiently complex and important in all its myriad dimensions that I had difficulty boiling it down to two or three sentences that I could state as my vision. I hated to be asked that question and I never answered it. Then in 1998, which was the culmination of this period when we realized that we were going to have—both financially and in other ways—the opportunity to make some serious changes, I spent a year, along with the provost and others, talking a lot about the future and listening as much as I possibly could to what the faculty thought were the important issues. We also had the report of the Task Force on Student Life and Learning that had worked for two years to make recommendations about the future of the learning community at MIT. That task force had given us some very good guidance. They told us to stop thinking about the institution as resting on two pillars of research and teaching and to start thinking about *three* pillars, as they put it, academics, research and community. We began to build on that community theme and think about it. We had opportunities for campus expansion. When I sat down and wrote my annual report that year, my essay was called "The Path to Our Future." It articulated a vision for MIT and what we were going to try to accomplish together. It was a reflection of what I had heard and what I thought the aspirations were, modulated by the fact I spent a lot of time outside of the institution, with industry and in Washington, thinking about the opportunities, as well as getting ready to launch a capital campaign. I also listened a lot to alumni as preparation for starting the capital campaign. "The Path to Our Future," while it by no stretch of the imagination originated in a classical, disciplined strategic planning process, was an articulation of what we were going to do. We built our budgets and, to some extent, the structure of our administration around it. So, while I always thought I didn't have a particular vision, I'm going to end my answer with something that still surprises me. During these last several months, since I announced I was stepping down from the presidency, I have done lot of looking back. Two weeks ago, I looked at the tape of the remarks I gave the day I was elected as president of MIT, and also my inaugural address. Then I compared them with "The Path to Our Future" and found that they are absolutely consistent. So there was a set of things within me, principles that I probably viewed more as values than I did as vision, which have been consistent through the whole time.

FL: What strategies have you used to communicate and create buy-in with the university community and your external constituencies, such as alumni and leaders of the city? When you had worked out the direction that you felt MIT should take, did you have specific strategies to bring people down that path with you, or did they embrace it immediately?

CV: When I was interviewed for the presidency here, there were two committees, of equal size, one of the trustees, and the other an advisory committee of the faculty, which always met together, as a single committee. After the decision had been made, I met with the faculty group, and asked, "What would you like me to do?" One of the things they said was that they would like to know what the president thinks about important issues. They said, "We would encourage you to commit in writing, or however you want to do it, your views on some major issues from time to time." I translated that into writing an essay once a year that is published as part of something called the Reports of the President. Every summer I have sat down and written such an essay, sometimes about national topics, and twice very specifically on MIT topics. They were subjects that I thought I had some responsibility to think about and to let my colleagues know what I thought. I don't know how many people actually read them, but the act of writing them has been important because it has been very helpful to me. I enjoy writing and that discipline helps me to shape messages.

When we started the work for the 1998 essay called "The Path to the Future," it had some very substantial budget implications. The provost, the chancellor, and I went to every single department to spend an hour with the faculty talking, answering questions, and reshaping. Open Courseware, which is an incredibly brilliant idea, came from a faculty committee thinking about the role information technology can play here. Again we went out as a small team to every single department in the institution to discuss the idea of Open Courseware and try to achieve buy-in. When big changes have been made internally, we've done a lot of that kind of discussion. One of the joys of MIT is that it is sufficiently modest in size that department heads meet together for lunch three times a semester. There is also a group of mid-level managers and administrators that meets two or three times. Generally I am at all of these meetings, sometimes having other people speak, sometimes doing much of it myself. Then, for each of the fourteen years that I've been here, every semester

I visited two departments in each of our five schools just to talk about whatever they wanted to discuss. There is a lot of that kind of informal communication. I personally have tried to have a lot of that sort of contact. The provost, as I indicated, has made the same kind of effort. There is also a lot of e-mail traffic when decisions are coming about. We have tried to be as transparent and as open about big changes as possible, but the kind of things that I try to get across as president often do start either as this annual essay or as speeches. It's as much a discipline of putting that together as anything else. As every institution does, we continually try to improve our communication here and get some coherence among the different schools and departments in fundraising. Then, like every president, I am on the road a good bit talking to people in alumni clubs and as individuals. It is a long process of communication, not terribly disciplined, with the exception of the writing that I do once a year.

FL: As you know, it is not possible for a president to be all things to all people. You have to pick your battles. How have you made and carried out some of those decisions that were very difficult for you?

CV: There are probably two planes on which to answer that question. We have internal groups that are important to making major institutional decisions. One is the Academic Council, which I chair. It has all the deans and provost, the vice presidents, both from the academic units and from the service, finance, business, and human relations end. That's a senior policy-making group. Most major issues get kicked around, not necessarily decided, but simply discussed deeply in that venue. The other group, the provost, the chancellor, the executive vice president, and the vice president / secretary of the Corporation, Kathryn Willmore, and I, meet every Tuesday morning at 8:00 for an hour and I generally set the agenda for that. That's when we talk about anything that's tough, make sure we're coordinated, and bring up any problems that we have. That's an important mechanism. Then the executive committee of our Corporation, which is what we call our trustees, meets monthly except for July and August. The really big decisions that involve financial moves and so forth have to come to that group. These are the three groups that problem solving and major decision making generally work their way through. Of course there are things for which there's no script: a student death, an unexpected discipline problem of some magnitude, a national issue on which an institution like MIT should have a position. Those things, if I choose to go after them, are an individual decision, just something that my gut and my value system tell me either that I should say something about or that the buck stops here. Those you just have to know when you encounter them.

In any president's career, a few really difficult situations are going to occur. It is inevitable. That's why I said, earlier on, that when you hire other senior officers, you have to understand what their values are and have to expect integrity, because they will have their own values and will end up largely acting instinctively.

FL: I think that you have explained quite well how you have strategized translating your understanding of the institution and the external realities into a long-range plan for change and improvement. Is there anything you would like to add to that?

CV: The only thing I would add is a variant on the instinctive action that you sometimes have to take. There have been major decisions that we've decided to take and just go out on a limb. I'll give you two examples. One is the decision to bring some very bold new architecture to the campus in buildings that were designed by Frank Gehry and Steven Holl. Another is the moves that we made in changing the financial structure of how we support our graduate students, plus the changes we're bringing about in the nature of the housing system. These are all big institutional decisions. I have to admit that, once my mind was set on a few of those things as being really important, my personality changed and I became sort of a snapping turtle, grabbed on to the trustees' ankles and didn't let go until I got the job done. That was necessary because, if such large projects are delayed, economic ups and downs can intervene and—you know how these things go. Most of what I do, since I am highly consultative, tends to be evolutionary rather than revolutionary. But to get a few of the big things done on a campus, particularly if they bring substantial change or simply involve large expenditures and play out over a period of time, you really do have to aggressively grab on to them and not let go until they're done.

FL: How have you linked the changes you wanted to make to the financial budgeting process in the institution?

CV: In terms of financial things, I just have to tell you I'm a big picture guy; I'm not a detailed financial type. So first of all I have to have really good people like our treasurer Allen Bufferd, my executive vice president, John Curry, and the provost, Bob Brown. They do virtually all the detailed things, but I try to pay a lot of attention to the big structure. During these last five years, building on the fruits of a very strong economy and the maturation of a lot of new faculty working in really hot areas, we've been able to accomplish a lot. We did have to put together a financial plan and that plan involved some expenditure beyond what we would normally be spending out of endowment. We had to have that well justified and fully understood in a very disciplined way with our executive committee and the entire Corporation. It has been a topic of every single meeting of our executive committee for five or six years now. We have produced documents with the now traditional red, green, and yellow lights on them and we have graphs whose evolution people follow. This is the sort of thing that was on my mind when I said that you have to grab on and cling for the ride, because it's not going to be easy. Projects of this size and importance require a lot of continual selling, a lot of discipline, a lot of deciding when it's worth taking risks, because there are things much more important than financial indicators that guarantee or make possible the future strength of the institution. We all have to work together, but it has been a very concerted effort, with a lot of trustee interaction.

FL: Finally, making change often is not synonymous with making friends. Can you describe one or more critical incidents and how you dealt with those? Not every decision that a president makes is necessarily one that everyone approves and supports.

CV: The first example that comes to anybody's mind around here was the long-standing sense that we needed to change the nature of housing in the first year and the significant way it affected the way we introduced students to the institution. The system we had in place probably worked wonderfully twenty-five years ago, when MIT was still dominantly white male engineers with somewhat similar worldviews. Today, we have an enormously diverse place in every dimension, starting with the fact that we have 42 or 43 percent women students now and women do not have equal access to a fraternity-dominated housing system. We also have lots of micro communities that are, in a sense, separate from the institution. Based largely on the work of the task force on student life and learning, and following a lot of discussion, I made one of my few unilateral decisions: that we were going to change this. That was very hard for a lot of our alumni to accept, particularly our alumni who came up through the fraternity system and quite correctly felt that that system had served them very well in a variety of ways in the1940s, 1950s, 1960s, or 1970s. Changing the traditional first year housing system was a very controversial, hard decision that led to two years of intense heat and still hasn't totally died down, but I knew we had to do it. After receiving a lot of advice in town meetings and other gatherings, I moved ahead with it.

This got associated in people's minds with a terrible tragedy: the drinking death of Scott Kruger. Scott Kruger was a fraternity pledge in his fifth week of classes at the Institute who died following a fraternity event, the only such death MIT has had in its entire 140-year history. All of these things converged at about the same time. After that tragic death, we held a number of town meetings and various discussion groups about how to deal with alcohol on the campus. That was a bit ironic, in one sense, because every survey shows that our students drink about half as much as they do at most schools, but nonetheless we had this terrible death. I noticed that, at every one of these meetings I attended, or led, the discussion began with what you do about alcohol and, within thirty seconds, people were talking about the housing system. I knew that the time had come to make the change that the institution had talked about for ten or twelve years. Legends arose that this was a deal with the parents of the young man. That was not the case. It was a very controversial, tough decision, but we just had to stick to it in good MIT fashion. We put together a group to implement the change in which Larry

Bacow played a key role. We had a housing system design competition. We allowed any team that wished to do so to enter it and didn't require any particular makeup of a team. A team could consist of a single faculty member, but it was usually a group of students, faculty and alumni. Then we took the best plans, put them up on the web, and let people comment. We had a massive program (which everybody has forgotten about now, by the way). It played out over almost two years and helped us to redesign the system. We tried to involve everybody, but at the end of the day, it still came down to sticking to some important things, doing a very tough selling job, and knowing that we weren't going to get everybody convinced. That's probably been the hardest issue that I've had to deal with although, on one plane, one might think, "Well, what's the big deal?" However it was so deeply embedded in the culture that it was and is a big deal.

The other issue I might point to is something that I did not do well. In the early to mid- nineties, like most institutions in the country, our budgets got a bit out of whack and we knew that we had to do some restructuring of our processes. I swallowed hard and decided to use the terrible R word, re-engineering, so we deployed a lot of teams. Frankly, we used too many external consultants. I wanted this to be MIT's re-engineering not somebody else's. There's still some bitterness around about the work that a lot of people did and about the fact that this happened simultaneously with trying to bring ourselves into the modern era in terms of administrative and business computing and financial systems. As I mentioned earlier, we also had a retirement incentive program, which in and of itself, by the way, was very well received. Everybody who volunteered thought they got a fair deal. The re-engineering ended up being very spotty, done well in some places, not done well at all in others, with some bitterness lingering around the community. The fact is that something had to be done. If you look around at the people who are emerging into administrative leadership positions today, you will find that during the period of re-engineering, many of them became engaged and learned about other parts of the institution. We reaped some benefits from it, but many people felt that the cost/benefit ratio was not good. That was a tough one. In retrospect, I think that I did not exert enough day-to-day, hands-on leadership. It might have been done better, more smoothly, and still have gotten us to the same point. I think that most people would bring those two issues up as the toughest ones for large numbers of people.

Then, frankly, the most difficult thing I faced the whole time was dealing with all the ramifications of Scott Kruger's death. That was just a terrible trauma and something that weighed on me horribly. In that personal sense, it did not begin to go away until I finally succeeded, after over two years, in actually sitting down in a room with the parents. We worked things out, and I'm not talking about finances, I'm talking about coming to an understanding and respect for each other. There was a criminal grand jury along the way before which I had to appear as a person who might be indicted for manslaughter. In every way, it was a very, very difficult thing to deal with. And yet I think, in some way, the institution came out a little stronger and we brought some peace to our relationship with Scott's parents.

FL: We all felt deeply for you and the institution in that heart-rending situation.

CV: I know you did. You let me know.

FL: Returning to the issues of progress and success, how have you monitored and tracked outcomes and progress on goals? As you know, this is the hot new issue; everyone has to have their outcomes lined up for public inspection.

CV: For me, the outcomes are what the faculty are accomplishing, how they feel about their lives, that they are able to do first rate work and that we are getting great students. These are the things that count at the end of the day. Of course, there are some things we look at. Certainly, as I mentioned earlier, we track our finances in certain ways. We are delighted at the moment because we made a huge leap, and for us an all time record, in our yield rate. This year 67 percent of the students we admitted chose to come to MIT. These are good things. So we watch these things and we watch the obvious metrics such as achieving our goal for the capital campaign, which was, with huge hesitation, set at a billion and a half dollars, when most people thought we couldn't raise a billion. With three years to go, we had raised a billion and a half and we increased the goal to $2 billion. Now we're at $1.97 billion and absolutely determined to make it in the next few months. There are some things we track like that, but at the end of the day, what I care about is the quality of people here and about whether we are enabling them to do their best and to feel that they have a good quality of life. In an intense institution like this, the latter issue is always hard. You asked about my balance. I worry much more about the balance in the quality of the lives of our faculty. It's very hard to achieve, but it is quality that counts at the end of the day. I'm infinitely more interested in that than I am in some of the goals that may be more easily accomplished.

FL: Looking at constituencies and cultures, what does each of your internal constituencies expect you to do for the university and for them?

CV: That's a hard question to answer. Because we're sitting here talking when I am probably in the last two or three months of my presidency, I may have a different perspective on it than I had a year ago. I think that everybody has the right to expect that the institution is seen to be progressing and enabling them to meet their individual or group goals and aspirations. The governing board cares first and foremost about quality and secondly they quite properly see themselves as the long term financial stewards of the institution, so those are the two primary things that they look for. Faculty members want the conditions to do their job well. They want the best colleagues and infrastructure they can possibly get. Students—give or take trends that flow through things—want access to good faculty. They work hard here and they need a decent place to live. I think expectations are fairly basic, but every group does have its own perspective. I think that the president's job is very much to explain to group B what group A thinks and why that's important, and then to tell group A what group B thinks and why. The president has to rationalize the internal and external roles of the university. I have no simple answer to that, but you do have multiple constituencies. You have to divide your time and effort among them. Again, at the end of the day, simply speaking for MIT, if you talk with any one of these groups, what they really care about is quality. When I'm able to stand up with great pride and say that MIT faculty won seven Nobel prizes in the sciences in the last fourteen years, people like that.

I often tell people the following true story. About the second year I was here I spoke at the luncheon at what we call Technology Day, which is a big alumni gathering right after commencement. This was when *U.S. News and World Report* rankings—the bane of our existence—were just getting a lot of popularity. Here I was, the neophyte president, addressing hundreds of alums of all ages. I said that we were very proud of our faculty achievement because the *U.S. News and World Report* ratings had come out saying that we were number one in engineering and everybody cheered. That year they also ranked science, so I said that if you add across the five elements of the school of science, we were number one in that and we were number one in economics. Everybody cheered. Then I said that, even looking at us as a broad undergraduate university, the only schools ahead of us were Harvard, Princeton and Yale. There was dead silence. So I knew then and there where MIT people expect you to be. They expect you to be number one.

FL: What importance have you placed on the role of your institution in the community? Did you feel obligated or even pressured to undertake any urban renewal building projects?

CV: We think first and foremost about Cambridge in the sense you are asking. We also have enough hubris to think of the nation as our community. I'd like to answer that both ways. We have wonderful people here who have worked on our community relations. One might argue that we have not been as visibly aggressive as some schools around the country have been, but we do a lot. If you track back far enough, well before I came here as president, we've actually been responsible for construction of a lot of low income housing in the city. We have had huge positive influence on economic development here, building the biotech industry and so forth: people look to us for that. The political environment of the city of Cambridge, as you would suspect, is quite complicated. We have a proportional voting system. We have a lot of community activism. One of the things that I think has helped us is that around 1993-1994, I managed to settle a long-standing controversy with the many of the active elements of the community by building immediately adjacent to our campus a modest facility called CASPAR (Cambridge and

Summerville Program for Alcoholism and Drug Abuse Rehabilitation), which is a center for alcoholics right adjacent to our campus and, despite dire predictions, we've never had a problem with it. I think that helped a lot of people through difficult times in their lives. We feed huge numbers of our undergraduates into the school system, both public and private, but particularly Cambridge public schools, where our volunteers number in the hundreds every year. We have a very active community service program here. There are a whole lot of little things that involve many people, particularly students.

One of the things that has probably built our community relations more than any other event or than any other thing is an annual award Becky and I give but was a brainchild of wonderful colleagues Paul Parravano and Sarah Gallop, who co-chair our community and government relations office locally. It is a community service award that we celebrate at the president's house once a year. We give two awards, one to a member of the MIT community and one to a member of the Cambridge community who is not directly associated with MIT. You never leave that room with dry eyes. It brings together a wonderfully dedicated group of people. I would never have believed how much good will this has elicited. That recognition of people who do great things in public service to the community and the sense it engenders of all being in it together have been extremely important. The public service awards and the number of students who go out to do volunteer work in the community, particularly helping out in the schools as mentors in science, athletics, computer skills, and so forth, are the primary things that we have done in recent years. We have helped to build the economy of the city and its future together. There is a broad recognition that MIT has made important contributions.

FL: Can you describe a little bit about how you've allocated your time? Or do you deal with the problems as they come to you, one by one?

CV: One of the things that allows us to keep going in jobs like these is the fact that every day you are around great people and, no matter what you do, that interchange is interesting and exciting. When you talk to your colleagues, they agree that what leaders do in many other parts of our society sounds pretty dull and boring by comparison. I think the variety and intensity of our jobs tend to go together. My first few years here, we did analyze my calendar every year or two to track what fraction of my time I was spending with various constituencies in retrospect. It's a discipline I've lost, but I probably shouldn't have given it up, because it would be interesting to see how it has changed over fourteen years. The one area that I have disciplined is the way we deal with apportioning my travel time in advance. We begin by asking a combination of the resource development people and the alumni association to tell us, almost a year in advance, how much time they will need next year and for what purpose. Then my assistant, Laura Mersky works with them to boil that down, for example, into a one week trip to the west coast, a week and a half in Asia, one day here locally, two days in New York, half a week somewhere else. After we have the requests outlined in that form, the two of us sit down well in advance, at the beginning of the school year, take all of the fixed commitments, and try to fit everything in. We start with the obvious things—the corporation meetings and the various standing committees—then we work the core travel requirements around it, and that gives us a pretty good matrix. After that, it's a little bit more of a free-for-all. We just try to make those decisions in real time. Getting me to focus on answering yes or no to requests is probably the worst thing Laura has to put up with. I'm honestly not very good at disciplining my own allocation of time. As I look back, I started working every evening, every Saturday, and half a day on Sunday when I was a graduate student, and I've never stopped, so there's nothing new about that. I must admit that I kind of take things as they come. When I am forced to make something a priority I will, but I don't have a very disciplined approach to it, beyond those fundamentals.

FL: What part of your work have you enjoyed the most?

CV: Without question, the most enjoyable thing about this job is the incredible people you get to know. For me that includes, first and foremost, the MIT faculty. Sometimes, even after fourteen years, though I know some of these people inside and out, I still pinch myself when I realize that so-and-so, a Nobel Laureate, is a good friend of mine and that we value each other. That means a lot. And through fundraising, through interaction with the government and industry, I have gotten to know a tremendous number of interesting and accomplished people and have learned from them constantly. That's what really drives my enthusiasm for the job. The number one thing I have enjoyed is really the people. Having grown up in an academic household and been in universities my whole life, I also still enjoy some of the ceremonial things that go around that. Greeting the new freshmen class is the most thrilling thing that happens in any year. I get to do it one last time in about two weeks. I've never had a commencement I didn't enjoy. Now maybe next year, when I'm sitting in the audience, I'll feel differently about it. I enjoy the ceremonial aspects, but the best things are really the people that you get to know and having the sense that what you're serving is really important. I don't think that you could do these jobs if you didn't believe that what a university like this accomplishes is truly and absolutely important. Those are the things from which I get enjoyment.

FL: We have had wonderful jobs. We spend a lot of time on tough issues that can test our fortitude, but when you look back, being in the presidency of a great university is an incredible opportunity. Of course it is also true that every president experiences planned and unplanned events that escalate into time consuming crises. Do you have any stories along those lines that you would care to share?

CV: Two kinds of things happen. One is that in any organization, there are some 1 percent of the people out there who take around 80 percent of the time of long-suffering administrators. We've had very few of those, but they exist. There you do have to learn there has to be a process in place and you must extricate yourself. I didn't used to be able to do that very well because I care about people and I want to see their problems solved, but you do have to avoid getting totally unreasonably sunk into things like that. I've also been very fortunate here to have worked with a wonderful attorney named Jeff Swope, with Palmer and Dodge in Boston, who has been enormously helpful in working through difficult problems. He has a wonderful facility for knowing all the technicalities and all the boring details, but also knowing what's important and what's not, helping to draft things and knowing what to do, not from an overly legal point of view, but in a way that respects the law and what's going to have to happen. His help has been a real godsend to me and to others around here on problems that could otherwise be vexing.

Crisis issues are a little different in my view. Crises are things that escalate and demand your time. We have evolved an approach that has tended to work well. Whenever almost any kind of an event occurs that I would tag as a crisis, we call a group together. It's not always exactly the same people, but there are few stalwarts who are really good. I rely enormously on Kathryn Willmore, whose title is vice president of the Institute and who works in one sense as an extremely high level staff person with me. She also has a pretty big management portfolio. She manages all of our communications and public relations and has credibility with the non-academic staff as well as with 90 percent of the faculty. She is a very experienced, wise person who has been around here for quite a while. When almost anything occurs that escalates to crisis proportions, the first thing that happens is that Kathryn and I talk on the phone and decide on the group we need to pull together, depending on what the issue is. If this is really serious business, I will be there. Sometimes I'll make a judgment that things will go better if I'm not in the room, but usually I'm there, at least at the beginning. Most of the people who would be involved in such things have gotten to know and work with each other. When I show up, my usual role is to begin by saying that we'll worry about the public relations and legalistic aspects afterward. First we have to do what's right. We'll outline the things that have to happen, then we'll talk about the communications piece. We have had two good directors in the news office since I've been here and we use an external consultant on crisis communication. Depending on the issue, we may very well have either an in-house attorney or Jeff Swope in the room. Kathryn is always a terrific leader in that process. The main goal is to get the constituencies pulled together so we can get all the perspectives on the table, do our best in real time to figure out what's right, line the process up, and attempt to follow it.

FL: Presidential tenure was once measured in decades. Some of our former colleagues were in their jobs for twenty years or more, but now terms of four or five years are more common. Do you think that the much shorter average tenure of contemporary presidencies is due to changes in the role in the last few decades or are there other reasons for it? You have had a fourteen-year tenure. That's unusual.

CV: We have some strong relationships with the University of Tokyo. They have had five presidents since I've been here. I think to truly understand the answer to that question, I'll have to look back as a historian. First, I believe the data will show that there is some distinction between the public and private institutions. So many of the presidents of the public institutions (for a period which I hope is waning, but I'm not sure) have had to deal with highly politicized boards that have some single-issue members. I suspect that that's been the primary reason that public presidential tenures have, as you say, been shorter. Presidential tenure in private universities has been a bit longer because you tend to have a different kind of board, generally people who are there only because they love the institution and want it to succeed. Private institutions' boards usually don't have many one-issue members, although they're not unheard of. I think there is also a different sense of continuity. The funding of private institutions, particularly the older, highest quality ones, is more continuous. Having lived in and deeply valued both public and private higher education, I've always pointed out that both sectors are subject to exactly the same pressures, but they tend to be more volatile in the publics and tend to be smoother in the privates, to some extent because a fair chunk of the bills in private institutions are paid out of the endowment. I think that some combination of the economic volatility, but more importantly, the politicization of boards may be the largest reason that tenures have been brief, especially in public institutions. It's hard for me to believe that the answer in the private university context is just simply burnout because, when I look around, everybody works hard around here—not only the president.

I think that the recent abbreviated tenures have gotten too short for increased value, but you should only stay as long as you feel that you're bringing the right freshness and energy to the institution. I couldn't do that for twenty or twenty-five years. I sensed, starting a couple of years ago, that from the institutional point of view, it was time. We accomplished a lot of things. I had a particular style, a particular way of operating and relating to people. I knew that, starting downstream, we're going to see the natural occurrences of deanship turnover and the retirement of some of the senior officers. A new president should be making the decisions about replacing them at the beginning of his or her tenure, not at the end. It would be a good time for some rethinking and renewal of the institution. That basically is the reason I decided to step down. Having now committed to it, I also realize that I am getting a little tired, but I think about a month will fix that. You do need some refreshing in an institution, but I certainly would like to think that after at least ten years, when things are going well, is the right time.

Then I think there are other issues. I'm not thinking of any particular people and I haven't run into this much in the Association of American University institutions such as those you and I have been fortunate to serve, but the death knell in a good university is for a president try to operate by cult of personality. That goes back to my view that most of the institutional vision has to come up from within and be collective. You can't run a group of first-rate people based on ego. If presidents attempt to do that, almost by definition their tenure will be short. Ten years, twenty years from now, somebody is going to have to look back, do a real historical analysis and figure out what it is that changed. Some years ago, another of my mentors, Harold Shapiro, got tired of all the editorials complaining that university presidents of today are pygmies and asking where are all of the great presidents resembling those of the past, so he had some graduate students examine five or six great presidents from early in the last century in order to find out what they did day-to-day. Their lives weren't much different from ours—Woodrow Wilson was getting on the train and going into New York to raise funds—but I do think that society in general has picked up the pace. CEOs of corporations don't stay around very long either. Some of it is probably endemic to the speed, the pace, and the constant expectation for new visions and change, but I think we need some balance.

FL: What are you planning to do after the presidency—after that one-month rest?

CV: I have been so consumed by my current work, I have defined myself by this job for so long, that I really don't know what the answer is. The trustees were kind enough to give me a year's leave, whenever I am replaced. I laughingly call it a sabbatical because my last sabbatical was thirty years ago, not seven years ago. We're going to stay here. In fact we've rented an apartment recently so that, in a more leisurely way over the year ahead, we can look for a permanent place to live. I've already picked out an office. I hope to do some thinking and writing. I'm involved with two major corporate boards, which of course are increasingly time-consuming, and for the next nine or ten months, I will be active on the Commission on the Intelligence Capabilities of the United States Relative to Weapons of Mass Destruction. This is a very serious undertaking and I expect to devote a lot of time to it. And during the year, I have some travel lined up. I'll visit two other universities in this country and one outside. I hope to reconnect with myself in a different way and come to some conclusions about what I would like to do next. I have ruled out in my own heart and mind going to another university. If I'm in a university, I'll be right here. If the right kind of thing somewhere in the nonprofit sector that I thought I could contribute something to for four, five, or six years came along, I might do that. But I think at the end of the day, the most likely thing is I'll be here at MIT, at least as home base.

FL: I wish you well. It has been a great change. My sabbatical is up, but it has been productive and has renewed my energy. What do you feel have been the most critical capital investments made at MIT under your leadership?

CV: I'm going to talk about buildings and, in the university, buildings shouldn't be very important, without people and ideas. But I learned long ago at Michigan from observation that there is nothing like some steel going up to make people feel confident and strong about the future. I came to the conclusion, with quite a bit of help from our then dean of architecture, Bill Mitchell, that at the beginning of this new century, MIT had to have some bold architecture. Looking back at the beginning of the twentieth century, when the building we're sitting in was built and thinking about how grand in scale and how unusual and effective these buildings were, I honestly felt it was time to do that sort of thing again and to do it in a way that helped to build the greater sense of community that our task force on student life and learning had asked for in 1996. We needed to create some of the exciting spaces that we just didn't have enough of around here, yet do it in a way that fully respected the way our faculty like to work and our students want to learn. We needed more communal space for the undergraduates, but things that would make people think a little differently. This is a philosophical point on which a lot of good people, smart people disagree, but I felt that we should have some buildings here that reflect more of the enormous creativity and energy that we have inside. So we took some big risks, to some extent a financial risk, but really more of a spiritual and perceptual risk, in building the Stata Center that Frank Gehry designed and in creating a somewhat different kind of dormitory, Simmons Hall, that Steven Holl designed for us. We also constructed a remarkable new building to house the area that has been the biggest investment we've made going forward, intellectually and financially, the area of brain and cognitive sciences. It will house the McGovern Institute for Brain Research and the Picower Institute for Learning and Memory. I hope you have a minute to walk over to the Zesiger Sports and Fitness Center, which is a facility of a quality that MIT has never before enjoyed. It's a place where students, staff and faculty mix and it has had a transformative influence on the campus.

In making my departmental rounds last year, I visited one of our smallest units, in the School of Humanities, Arts and Social Sciences. I suspect that, if we were to look at its budget, it might be the smallest budget we have in our academic departments. We had just announced that we were going to have a salary freeze for a year and had some very tough budget cuts to take. I sat down with this faculty and said here are the issues, here's what we're going to have to do. We have had three years of bad performance on the endowment. We are going to really tighten our belts for one year instead of nibbling away at ourselves for the next three or four years. I went through the whole thing and stopped, petrified, worrying about what the comment would be. After a brief pause, the department head said, "Every morning I drive in and I park my car in the new parking structure under the Stata Center. I come up and walk down Vassar Street, which now has nice pavers and trees growing on the side of it (and lighting if you're there early). I go to the Zesiger Sports and Fitness Center, swim, then come back to my office, and I just feel completely different about my life." That was the end of the discussion. Nobody mentioned anything else. I think it is starting to have that effect on people. I never thought that buildings would be the most important investment we've made, but I think the nature of these facilities that are bolder, riskier, more exciting, and yet provide the right kind of infrastructure for teaching and research, have made a huge difference.

FL: What do you regard as your legacy to MIT, of what are you most proud?

CV: I'm really hesitant to use the word legacy because it implies that one person did it, but I can tell you some of the things that happened while I was here that I think are really important and that I'm very proud about being part of. It's quite a mixed bag. There's no question that I'm enormously passionate about our OpenCourseWare project which, as you know, is putting the basic teaching materials for all 2000 subjects that MIT teaches on the World Wide Web for use by anybody who wants them anywhere for free. I think this is a very exciting undertaking and I have to put it right up there.

I am confident we will look back with enormous pride at building the brain and cognitive sciences here to a new level because, again listening to a lot of faculty and a lot of outside people, it is quite clear that understanding the human brain is very likely to be the great scientific adventure of the next twenty or thirty years. It also has the potential for improving communication and learning and beginning to attack some large classes of mental and emotional diseases in the same way that biology has helped with more physical kinds of diseases over the last thirty years. That has been a major investment and one on which I am confident we'll look back with great pride.

Another initiative in which I feel very privileged to have played some role is advancing the status of women faculty and professionals, particularly in science and engineering. It was not something that I started at all. It began with the very critical report that biology professor Nancy Hopkins and her colleagues put together about the status of women in our school of science, but I was able to publicly support that and advocate for it in a way that helped create an enormous resonance around the country and around the world. I think that has turned out to be something very important that MIT helped to spearhead in this era.

One effort that will always be an ongoing battle, but I also feel pretty good about, is the many, many hours that I devoted in Washington, together with some very talented colleagues, especially Vice President Jack Crowley. Going back to what we talked about at the beginning of the interview, in the environment that existed in 1990, we really were in peril of throwing out one of the most important advantages the United States has: this wonderful system of federally funding research in our public and private universities, from which the nation could reap great social and economic benefits. I decided in June of 1990, actually before I formally started this job, that to work to rebuild that sense of partnership and to convince all of our colleagues to spend a little less time pushing specific projects for institutions and all to speak with a common voice about the fundamentals. As soon as I knew I was coming to MIT, I have spent one day every month in Washington, talking to whoever will listen, getting involved through the Association of American Universities and serving on PCAST (the President's Council of Advisors on Science and Technology). That has been very important. I've had a great colleague and mentor in Jack Crowley, who has expertise about Washington, yet couples it with a deep understanding of what the real values of our universities are. I'm pleased with what we've done working together. It could all disappear and the next generation of university leadership may have to fight it all over again, but it is very important that we keep explaining to the government and to the public exactly why what we do in universities is so important.

FL: You are absolutely correct. The issue of tuition, for example, never ceases to resuscitate and to demand comprehensive explanation and correction of garbled information all over again every few years. What advice would you give to new presidents? What's the most critical set of skills that you think that they're going to need in the future to succeed?

CV: One person can't do everything. That's the main piece of advice I would give to anybody. When I look back at what has enabled me to do my job here, I always come back to the two-month period I spent at the beginning listening to everybody. I believe that it's important to listen because great ideas in the university seldom come from the president. They may come from the provost or other administrators, but they really come out of the faculty. Those are the bright people and that's where the intellect is. For example, why did we invest so much in brain and cognitive science? It goes back to the fact that several years ago, in the early 1990s, a foundation approached me and said that it might want to fund a "big thing" in science and, if it did, what would MIT want to do? I pulled together a group of first-rate faculty from science and engineering, because that was to be the theme. They argued for a bit and then unanimously said that research that advances our understanding of the human brain and mind was the most important thing we could do. It's important for biology; it's important for computer science; it's important for a variety of disciplines. That really was the origin of our efforts to build up the area of brain and cognitive science; I didn't dream it up. I didn't dream up Open Courseware. I can advocate, push, and help to make these things happen, but I think that the number one skill for a president is listening. I'll step on toes here, but I find that the most important people to listen to are very young faculty and very old faculty. I always want to know what is it that the young people want to do. That's why we do nanotechnology, not because it's a buzzword, but it's what these young men and women want to do. And some of the older folks, who have been great scholars all their lives, have a lot of wisdom and are not quite so invested in what's going to happen next year, so their perspective is well worth hearing.

Another thing in which presidents have to play an important role is interfacing the university to the outside world. When I look back, a lot of what I've done to help MIT is just been relationship building. It's a soft kind of term, but it means that the president works with leaders of industry, leaders of government, and others to create the environment in which support and collaboration, synergy and understanding, can then be built by the faculty, who have the ideas and do the work. If the president develops an interest in how people view universities and an understanding of how our opportunities and strengths look from both sides, it can go a long way to helping the university accomplish what it wants to accomplish.

Finally, I think it's less an issue of what the specific skills of the president are than it is of understanding what skills are going to be required and then building a team that has them. These jobs are just too complex to do alone. Building a team that has the right skill set and abilities to bring some coherence and get things done is extremely important. And the last thing may be arguable, but as I indicated, what I enjoyed most about the job is just getting to know and working with such smart and interesting people. Unless you do value people and are interested in them, your job is going to be a lot harder. Those are some of the qualities that I think would be most valuable in a president.

FL: What would you say has been at the core of your work in higher education? What has it been your underlying aim to do or to facilitate?

CV: My first aim has been simply to try to create the infrastructure, the wherewithal and the environment with which the faculty of MIT and the students of MIT could meet their aspirations. Among those aspirations at MIT is that people here like to work on the really big, important things. Sometimes people think that's arrogance but that's not what it is. It's that people want to make a difference. This is a very outward-looking institution. If our faculty want to do something important, like develop courses, they want to share it with the whole world in Open Courseware. Helping to facilitate and create the infrastructure for faculty work and also helping to build those bridges that create opportunities for influencing the larger world are certainly things that have been at the core of what I've tried to do. Then, in addition, I would suggest that anyone who is president, particularly president of a major institution like MIT, should pick up one aspect that has import beyond his or her own campus that they really want to emphasize. Without question, for me that has been trying to contribute to reestablishing the sense of partnership and trust with the federal government and, along with that, a better public understanding of science. I felt that there was a natural bully pulpit for the president of

MIT and it was the right time to deal with that. For other presidents, it might be something totally different. It might be literacy, or improvement of the community around the campus, as you mentioned. It might be advocating visibly and vocally for the role of humanities. It could be a number of things, but I think that each president will have a more satisfying time if, in addition to the total commitment to the institution, he or she has one broader thing to contribute personally and work on with a particular passion.

FL: I found on your website a very good talk that you gave in 1995 to an alumni conference on leadership. You offered a comic rundown on the expectations of the university president today (unfortunately not too far from the reality), but I was especially interested in your sketch of the societal and organizational nature of leadership in the future, which was very much like the concepts and skills of contemporary leadership that we're now teaching our students in classes at Rutgers, that is, working in teams with people from a wide variety of different backgrounds, collaborating with their peers to build consensus, improving their public speaking ability, and growing in their ability to identify ethical issues. In your 1995 talk you cited a 1994 survey that you felt showed that MIT could and should do more to develop in students the skills needed to become leaders. What has the university done along these lines?

CV: Whenever I am asked to think about or talk about leadership, I like to broaden the definition. I worry that most people have a very narrow perspective of what leadership is and immediately think of either a CEO or a general. I think that's wrong because it implies that leading just means telling a big group of people what to do. To me that isn't what it's about. I like to think about the fact that we can lead in a lot of different ways and one of the examples I like to use is the era in the 1970s and 1980s, when recombinant DNA technology first came about. There was great angst about what this would mean, what the dangers were, and whether we would inadvertently create strange mutants. There were a number of people involved, but I point particularly to David Baltimore, who was a faculty member here long before I came to MIT. David gathered several of his colleagues and they established a moratorium on doing recombinant DNA work. They had a famous conference out at Asilomar in California and engaged political activists, religious leaders, politicians and all kinds of people, in addition to the scientists themselves, and hashed these things out till everyone had a better understanding of them. Out of that came not only a better understanding of DNA research but also the NIH guidelines on what kind of containment facilities you need to do this work. To me, putting together that conference was a monumental example of leadership, even though it doesn't fit the mode of running a big organization. I think we can lead in lots of different ways and we serve our students best if we point that out.

Your question alluded to a survey we took some years ago that showed that our students felt that, while they were gaining fantastic analytical skills, their communications skills had not advanced the way they thought they should during their education. We have worked hard on that. A few years ago, our faculty established a new communication requirement that every undergraduate has to meet. It involves four different subjects, a couple of which are communication classes on writing and speaking, but the real core of it is building communications into other subjects using team teaching. It is now pretty difficult for a student to leave MIT as an undergraduate without having some substantial experience in having to communicate ideas in writing and speaking. We continue to improve that and we fight a sort of guerilla warfare by building it into other things. We've done very specific curricular things like that with a lot of faculty leadership. We do a lot of things that really run the gamut. We've created opportunities for students to do things in the summer or during spring break. Kids go into Central China, they wire schools and get them on the Internet, and do other service activities. A wonderful woman named Amy Smith has taken the students all over the developing world to think about local problems and create technologies that can ameliorate or solve them. We put a lot of emphasis on such experiential learning which, while most people might not call it leadership, I think actually teaches a lot about leadership. At the other end of the spectrum, we offer things like our 50K entrepreneurship competition. If you want to talk about learning how to communicate effectively, that is probably the most effective thing we do. Our entrepreneurial kinds of activities teach discipline in making business plans, learning to get teams to work together, bringing together multiple talents, and communicating ideas clearly and succinctly. A variety of these things have improved the situation. If you come back in six months, and some of our current fundraising activities are successful, I may have a different and exciting kind of a leadership center on the campus to tell you about.

The other part of your question, about growing in the ability to identify ethical issues, troubles me. I do not think we do that very well and that's an absolute statement. I don't know enough to say how we do relative to other universities but I don't think that we do enough in ethical education for the incredibly talented science and engineering oriented kids who make up a large part of our student body. Most of them can leave here without having been in the situation of having to think deeply about societal and ethical implications of the kind of things they'll likely to be doing. There are, of course, many opportunities to do that here. There are seminars on science, on technology in society, and lots of similar subjects. There's a lot going on, but still it is easy for students to go through here and never think deeply about the ethical dimensions of the work they're being trained to do. We have just started a task force on what I call the undergraduate educational commons, the things that are common to the education of every student here, starting with our general institute requirements, our core curriculum. Ethics education is one of the issues I have asked them to think about and I am sure they will. We have many individual faculty members in areas of science and engineering who routinely build ethics into their subjects in marvelous ways, and of course the Sloan School of Management has formalized approaches to business ethics, but we still need to do more of that.

FL: I think we'd find that every institution, public or private, could do a lot better on it and I hope that in Rutgers' leadership program area we're getting there. I know that you have thought deeply and spoken at the National Association of State Universities and Land Grant Colleges (NASULGC) meeting about the problems that higher education, especially our research universities, have faced since 9/11. We're committed to the American and scholarly values that traditionally have motivated us, to maintaining open access to our campuses for international students and scholars, and to preserving openness in scientific dialogue. At the same time we want to cooperate with our government in protecting our country and the world from terrorism. How are we doing in achieving both goals? Is the dialogue with all of the federal agencies handling the new security measures going well, or is this a dilemma for which it is extremely difficult to find a resolution?

CV: It is a dilemma to which the full resolution is always going to be difficult. I believe we face two specific categories of problems. One is just the process of issuing visas for students and even more importantly for visitors, visiting scholars and scientists, and moving out in fairly short spaces of time. At the highest levels, I believe the dialogue on this issue, given the depth of legitimate concern, following 9/11, is actually going rather well. In terms of getting students in and out of the country to our best institutions, we've done better each year and the process is slowly but surely getting better. It has to improve further on visitors coming in and out. As you know, we have all kinds of horror stories. Some of these issues play out at the local level, a particular guy at the airport zealously checking something. We have created ill will for ourselves around the country and I think we're still in danger of being damaged by it, but I don't think it's because people at the highest policy levels in the White House and Department of Homeland Security don't care. I think they do care. I think they understand. I think that they're trying, but there are not enough resources in our embassies and consulates to fund the technologies that could help to smooth some of this. We have to keep on the pressure in order to keep it improving. Even though I think there's a pretty good understanding at the top, like all human organizations, as you go down deeper, you encounter people so risk averse that they make their own decisions. So we're not out of the woods, but I feel that there is some understanding and some progress has been made.

The other component is less visible and not broadly known. There have been far too many attempts to put restrictions on grants and contracts to universities since 9/11 such as restricting the access of foreign nationals to equipment and to certain areas of research and study as well as requiring that people who were not born in the United States undergo a special kind of security review in order to work on a certain project. There is also a lot of implicit classification of information by government agencies that insist on prior review of papers before publication. This is a slippery slope. At one end of the spectrum, I feel that this is very dangerous. Science is an international undertaking. It thrives only in an environment of openness. In a sense, this is much harder to work on than the visa issue because a much smaller number of people understand it or care about it. Again, it's less an issue of policy at the top than it is a matter of the way that things are implemented and interpreted down through the system. I'm very worried about this. I don't think that we've made a lot of progress on it, but we all have to understand what's happening. We have to be very visible about it. We have to try to work with the government to solve the problems: that's the only way to do it. I worry about over-classification and about the use of categories like "unclassified but sensitive" as well as new, tough, unreasonable approaches to export controls and deemed exports, which means that a graduate student born in another country who can walk down the hall, look through a window, and see a certain kind of machine tool has to be licensed. It's going to unjustifiable extremes, and I'm not at all confident that we are making a lot of headway in solving that one. So it's a mixed bag. We are going to somehow work our way through the visa problems, but we've done a lot of damage to professional relations and public relations. It is critical that we remain the magnet for the world's best and brightest.

FL: Through Open Courseware, MIT has led the way in a creative use of the worldwide web in order to open a new door to democratizing and transforming the power of education. You have received very positive comments from around the world on this generous initiative. In 2000-2001, you reported that faculty engaged in using educational technology say that they believe that they've become better teachers, mainly because the process of designing the program forces them to rethink their teaching in fresh ways. I agree with your comments toward the end of the report that we need to focus on the real objective, learning, and to evaluate new approaches to make certain that they actually do improve learning. At Rutgers we undertook several such studies with Mellon Foundation funding and found some positive results. What has MIT found from its studies evaluating use of electronic technology in teaching?

CV: There are a lot of aspects to this. Open Courseware is an idea that came from a faculty committee and I've been very passionate about it. We don't think of it as electronic teaching. We think of it as putting the books on the library shelf. This is democratizing. It is providing materials and ways of organizing knowledge and learning that other people can use, picking and choosing. It's more like a publishing activity than it is literally teaching, although its goal is to improve teaching around the world. It is going like gangbusters. There is a group of twenty-seven Chinese universities that are networked together, translating the MIT materials into Chinese, and using it. In one country, there is an underground university based on MIT's Open Courseware. It is educating around a thousand kids who, because of their religion, are not allowed to go to college in that country. Just marvelous things are happening. We're very proud of Open Courseware but it's more a matter of sharing and publishing than literally teaching.

We have a variety of activities that involve information technology in teaching. We took ideas originally developed at Rensselaer Polytechnic Institute, and adopted a studio kind of teaching that we've been using particularly in physics. We have built facilities where students work in an atelier style, in small groups at tables, with tabletop experiments and computers. The teacher can get the attention of the whole room and talk back and forth, creating more of a mentoring and coaching situation than traditional lecturing. That particular experiment is very well instrumented and we find that there is a clearly measurable positive difference in how much and how well students have learned concepts compared to the traditional lecture subjects.

We have one major distance education program in Singapore, the Singapore-MIT alliance, which does masters level engineering education where the metaphor is a classroom that's half in Cambridge and half in Singapore. That is done through an Internet II video link with live teaching. That has been enormously effective and was actually what I was referring to when I said that faculty almost uniformly talk about how it has improved the way they think about their teaching. We also have totally different innovations like the WebLab program that Jesus Delalamo in Electrical Engineering and Computer Science developed. It was set up for students to be able to run experiments in fields like electronics from their laptops in their dorm rooms. It has evolved now to heat exchanger experiments in chemical engineering and, very excitingly, with a little help from the Carnegie Foundation, he has now set up two or three universities in sub-Saharan Africa that are running experiments here from computers there. There's a lot going on, but no grand philosophy. We're feeling our way. I think most of us believe that information technology is the pencil and paper of our era, so we should not get too fixated on it, but figure out how it works as an adjunct and a communication and learning mechanism. We're learning a lot here and there, but I don't know that there are any giant lessons to be drawn yet. I'll end just by pointing out what went on when we kicked off the marvelous fund that two of our alumni, Alex and Brit d'Arbeloff, established for excellence in education here. They created a $10 million endowment because they were interested in improving the quality of education in a residential university and because they had a particular interest in what the role of instructional technology would be. We had a kick-off symposium workshop for a day with students and faculty in idea sessions. At the end of the day, I looked around and realized that nobody talked about computers the whole day. So we keep focused on teaching and learning and try to figure out how it serves that purpose.

FL: Tuition, especially the relatively high sticker price of the best private universities continues to be an issue in the media and a subject of congressional attention. How have you managed to keep your tuition at a level that is reasonable and allows you to attract a diverse student body and at the same time continues to meet the needs of MIT?

CV: MIT's ability to do this now and our future ability to do it are based on maintaining the approach of need-blind admission, admitting kids based on their merit and regardless of their financial circumstance, and distributing our undergraduate financial aid on the basis of need. If we can maintain the level of endowment and gifts that it takes to do that, we will continue to be able to build powerful, diverse undergraduate student bodies and keep MIT education affordable. If we should ever lose the ability to have sufficient financial aid and to distribute it on the basis of need rather than on other measures, we'd be in a bind. So that is our approach to it. Pure and simple, it is really keeping the ratio of the financial aid here to our tuition that makes the system work.

FL: You have seen the Knight Commission report, noted the recent NCAA academic reform measures, and I'm sure you are also familiar with Bill Bowen's books on Division III sports at highly selective schools, *The Game of Life* and *Reclaiming the Game*. Has MIT considered taking any steps to examine or change its intercollegiate sports program?

CV: We are real outliers. We are a Division III school. We give no athletic scholarships. We do very little athletic-based recruiting. The coaches will sometimes spot a bright kid who they know is a really good player of soccer or some other sport and they'll keep reminding the admissions office of this, but basically, we believe that sports here should be highly participatory. We mount more teams than we could begin to afford in a higher NCAA division. We have some superb athletes, but also sometimes get kids playing varsity sports who didn't even play them in high school, so I think we've kept a pretty good balance and we intend to continue to do that. It comes under pressure. There's always great pressure to try to move our crew teams into Division I. We have not done that, with the exception of women's crew, which is a complicated issue. What we really want to do is stay participatory, no athletic scholarships, all scholarships funded through our need-blind, need-based approach. If we can do that and also maintain a strong club system, we'll be happy.

FL: I know that you have worked hard to increase the diversity of the student body and the faculty. In reading your remarks at MIT's February 5 Martin Luther King celebration, I noted that MIT is to be congratulated on increasing underrepresented minorities to 14 percent among its undergraduates. Do you feel that the percentage of minorities in the administration is an important index of inclusion? How do you think MIT measures up in hiring individuals who are minorities as part of your administration?

CV: It is important in the sense that I believe that leadership should be diverse. We talked a lot earlier today about decision making, priority setting, goal setting, I believe that's always done best when you bring multiple experiences and perspectives to the table, and of course we all know that there is importance for virtually every field in having good role models, as well as good performance in a diverse leadership. The easy answer to what you ask is that I could tell you that when I came here, there were no minority members in the senior administration and I now can tell you that, when the academic council sits down, there are two African Americans present: our chancellor and our dean of graduate studies. I appointed the first woman vice president MIT ever had and the next five as well. So we do have more diversity than we used to. We have done much better with women in a relatively short period of time. Several of our major laboratories are now headed by women. We have the first woman department head in the school of science this year. We have our first African-American department head in the school of engineering. There are a lot of individual things I could point to, but the fact is it still isn't good enough. Frankly I am much more worried in terms of building racial diversity in our faculty. Other areas will change naturally once we do that. I can show you a few answers that look great. I could tell you that we've increased the number of both women and minority faculty by about 75 percent and 60 percent, respectively, but minorities are still present in the MIT faculty in very small numbers.

I'm proud to say that the MIT faculty, not the administration but the faculty, this spring passed a resolution indicating that they intend to play a national leadership role in building the diversity of the faculty. They decreed that there was going to be an annual report issued by the provost that will look at this. This is in addition to the work we've done as the administration and what our faculty diversity council has done. We've made much more progress with women than we have with minorities. I will tell anybody who asks that, in my view, the biggest failing during my time is that we didn't make more progress in hiring minority faculty.

FL: It's a lot of work and it's not easy. We talked earlier about a committee of women faculty who reported on gender discrimination in the school of science. You and your top administrators not only accepted the report without argument and took immediate action to remedy inequalities, you also insisted that the report be made public and praised the courage and leadership of the women who compiled the report. This had an impact at not only at MIT but coast to coast. Your reaction, in turn, drew a great deal of well-deserved praise. More recently an MIT follow-up study released in 2002 pointed out that even though unequal salaries had been remedied, women still feel marginalized and in some fields still are not hired in proportion to their numbers in the pool of candidates. Was it possible to take any action to address this or is the new effort by the faculty also dealing with the issues cited in the follow-up report?

CV: There were three people who played critical roles in the original study. First and foremost credit has to go to Nancy Hopkins, whose story is very interesting. She never thought of herself as a feminist. She thought her career was going swimmingly and all of a sudden one day she realized that everything wasn't so great. She talked to the other women in the school of science and then went to Bob Birgeneau, who was the dean of science at that time, and somebody you know. Bob is a very particular hero in this. He called me and said you know they want to have this committee and they want to look at salary information and so forth and I said to Bob, "Just do it." He did in a really smart way, pulling just the right committee together and involving all the women who wanted to be involved, but also putting on it some male department heads who knew how things worked. They generated an extraordinary confidential report. We did a public version of that report and I wrote a brief preface to it, just a couple of paragraphs. In a public sense, that's what sparked everything, because Bob and I and others who had been involved said that we weren't going to shove this under the table. I only partly facetiously tell people that we don't have a general counsel so I didn't ask any lawyers about this before I wrote the preface in its support, but I felt it was a convincing study. The resonance to that was unbelievable. We were getting a hundred messages an hour for a couple of days. They just piled up and they weren't just from the United States, they came from all over the world. While not all but most of the things Nancy's report said were not different from a hundred other reports sitting out there, (you'll have to excuse my institutional arrogance here) I think the fact that it came out of the school of science at MIT and that the women who wrote it were really world class scientists, some of whom are in the National Academy of Science, followed by the fact that Bob and I said that it was right, gave this report a kind of gravitas that had not occurred before. It just had a marvelous impact and we continue to work at it.

Bringing it up to the present, what you're referring to is a study that was done at one school with five departments, the school of science. Most of the salary issues had been fixed long before that study was done. Every year Mark Wrighton and I would sit down to make sure that we were actually reasonably balanced in terms of salary. So this report was much more about decision-making, lab space, and things like who ran what committees. It involved not feeling part of the real leadership, the decision making. It was more qualitative in that sense than quantitative in terms of things like lab space and resources for the work. It addressed a lot more than just salaries. We had all of the other schools at MIT do similar studies. They came out and, in varying degrees, said that they had problems too. When those came in under the provost's leadership, Nancy and Wes Harris, a distinguished African-American faculty member who is now head of Aero Astro, put together a faculty diversity council. That council has been trying to work with groups in each of the five schools in order to come up with implementation strategies to improve the situation. We have some pretty astounding stories to tell, particularly in the school of engineering where Dean Tom Magnanti and some of the department heads have been enormous leaders in this. After years of hearing that there were not there enough women out there, all of a sudden we have had an unbelievable influx of world-class women faculty who are just setting the place on fire. It demonstrates that you can never let your guard down. You have to think about it, keep it in the forefront of your mind, and try to build the same level of commitment and concern on the minority hiring, where I think the big problem, more than anything else, is that people just get tired. It's been such a difficult problem through your career and my career, with such deep historical and societal roots, that the biggest fear is that people are just getting tired of trying. I think the way to deal with that is to be sure you bring along the younger generation, who care and will go at it.

FL: I have one last question. Do you have anything that you want to say about the strongest forces driving the need for change in higher education within the next twenty years?

CV: I think that there are four very important forces. I don't know where any of them are going to lead. First, I think that globalization is going to be an enormous force in higher education. I don't know how that's going to play out, but I will tell you it's going to be important, just as it is in every other aspect of society. Information technology is going to be an important force. I believe that it will be really important, but I'm not a true believer in the sense that I think we have found precisely how it will be important. I think there are surprises around the corner. One of these days, cognitive science and information technology are going to come together in some marvelous way that will really improve learning, but it already is a big force. At minimum, it is an increasingly dominant factor just in how we store and access information. Whether it will take the next step to really improving the quality of education remains to be seen. On a somewhat more negative side, I worry a great deal about maintaining the societal commitment to higher education. We have this strange bifurcation, where we have terrific problems on average in K-12 education, and terrific quality on the average in higher education, yet I see a lot of the same arguments and forces that have kept K-12 education from being what it should be starting to descend on higher education. I think that we really need to worry about that. The final thing that, tired though we may be, we just can't stop and talking and acting to maintain is the diversity of kinds of institutions of higher education. That is extremely important. To the extent that things cause us to start homogenizing our colleges and universities, we will have made a horrible mistake, because it's this richness that encompasses big Midwestern public institutions and specialized places like Cal Tech, and MIT, small liberal arts colleges, public and private institutions—it is that mix, and the competition within that mix, that I think keeps us strong. We have to be sure that the forces line up to allow that diversity to continue. Those are the four things that I believe will have an enormous effect on the future of higher education.

David Ward

Chancellor Emeritus of the University of Wisconsin-Madison David Ward became the president of the American Council on Education in 2001. The ACE, founded in 1918, includes members from all sectors of higher education, approximately 1,800 accredited, degree-granting colleges and universities, as well as many associations, organizations and corporations related to higher education. The association serves its members in articulating their consensus on issues in higher education, coordinating their efforts to influence public policy, and disseminating information to members and policymakers on higher education concerns. Its areas of focus include: access, success, equity, and diversity; institutional effectiveness; lifelong learning; and internationalization.

Ward was born in Manchester, England on July 8, 1938. He received his bachelor's and master's degrees from the University of Leeds, came to the United States on a Fulbright award in 1960, and was awarded a Ph.D. by the University of Wisconsin in 1963. After teaching at Carlton University and the University of British Columbia, he joined the faculty of Wisconsin-Madison in 1966. Before becoming chancellor, he served as associate dean of the graduate school (1980-1987), as vice chancellor for academic affairs and provost (1989-1993), and as interim chancellor (January 1993). He was appointed the twenty-fifth chancellor of the University of Wisconsin-Madison in June 1993, and stepped down in January 2001. Ward's academic specialty is historical urban geography: he has authored two books, edited two more, and contributed numerous scholarly articles.

Both as provost and as chancellor, he led the university in the development and implementation of a strategic plan that improved the quality of undergraduate education and encouraged creative combinations of public and private support. It also provided a new framework for the expression of the Wisconsin Idea, the philosophy underlying the university's public service, with partnerships between the university and the public and private sectors for efforts ranging from economic development to K-12 collaboration.

Ward has chaired the Board of Trustees of the University Corporation for Advanced Internet Development (the Internet2 organization) and the Government Relations Council of the National Association of State Universities and Land Grant Colleges. He has served on the Science Coalition and the Kellogg Commission on the Future of State and Land Grant Universities.

Francis Lawrence: David, have you found virtually from childhood that being a leader in various ways is something that has come naturally to you? Or is it a skill that you decided to cultivate and worked hard to develop over time?

David Ward: I would say the first observation fits me very clearly. It may have been the fact that I was born right before World War II and my two sisters right after World War II, and I was more like an uncle to my sisters. When vacations became a possibility for my family in the 1950s, they would all go on vacation and leave me in charge of the business. In some ways, being 16 years old and running even what was admittedly a very small business was an enormous level of responsibility. It also gave me an opportunity to innovate in the business in very minor ways. I think that having the self-confidence to take actions on behalf of the family business is a kind of leadership. My skills came that way, rather than from some professional development like an MBA program or being made a dean and deciding, "Well I'd better figure out what leadership is." It really was a much more experiential kind of thing with me.

FL: I would like to hear more about your family background, your education and how they contributed to shaping your values and your development.

DW: I was born in Manchester, England, a commercial and industrial metropolis of the nineteenth century, but all my family came from a textile town, Blackburn, about twenty miles north of Manchester. I have done a little genealogy and I found that everybody in my family in the 1890s were cotton weavers. My parents moved from Blackburn to Manchester during the Great Depression. That was the first migration; mine was the second, and much longer one. My parents started a small business in a classic working class neighborhood. If anything drove my values, it would be growing up behind a shop that was a mom and pop store in which my two sisters, my parents, and I basically ran the enterprise. It was a general store—newsagent, tobacconist, candy, paperback books, ice cream—a sort of a corner store without the pharmacy. I think two influences came from that experience. One is that success is a curious combination of energy and imagination. The imagination helps, but ultimately there's a lot of groundwork. My father placed greater emphasis on energy than imagination and that's not meant to be critical of him, because I learned so much from him about the power of good works and bringing energy to the job. Since he left school at 11 he insisted that his children complete their education.

I was the first kid in my family to go to high school, the first kid eventually to go to college. Once I was in high school, I became aware that the world was bigger than a small business and realized what my parents had missed. It was not just a matter of access to professional employment but that his frame of mind in dealing with the business was much more steady state, much more risk averse than mine. So I think that his insistence on my formal education was not just to open opportunities but also to engage a different mindset. I value that commitment because he always said that the thing he valued most in his retirement was being able to read, to think, and to do those things that he never had an opportunity to do until he was sixty. So he knew that he was not just giving me the chance to be a doctor or a lawyer, but a chance to have a different view of the world. The second is that nothing was achieved unless you worked at it and were responsive to the client or customer concerns. There was no free ride: if they didn't come in the shop there would be no bread on the table.

Those two influences came from growing up behind the store. Obviously I was also part of a small pioneer cohort that took advantage of a small expansion of college access in the 1950s and constituted a new group of first generation students. The degree to which I was the pioneer is very interesting. Most of my family and contemporaries went to teacher training colleges. Very few of them actually went on to a university. So I was very unusual not only in going to college as the first in my family, but, even in that generation, only one other of my cousins actually went to university, as distinct from a technical school or a teacher training college.

FL: What do you regard as your first leadership position at any level?

DW: I think at the University of Leeds I felt very comfortable and confident as an undergraduate. I was very active in the Youth Hostel Association, partly because I was a geographer, but partly because of my aesthetic appreciation of the English landscape and the visible past. Participation and leadership in a student association is, I think, an enormously engaging experience. It took a fair amount of organizational skill to have a good program and bring people together. That might have been my first leadership encounter in how to engage people, how to make sure they all got there and that they returned on Sunday evening to be undergraduates the next day.

FL: Were there people who inspired you and acted as your mentors along the way?

DW: In my early days, my mentors were more in the scholarly end of things. I don't think they were necessarily concerned about leadership, except to the degree that everything I've been able to achieve as a leader has been more legitimate because most people respected me as a scholar. To the degree that academic life respects leadership, it usually is a kind of hybrid respect. In higher education it is important to have been a craftsman before becoming a leader. My early academic mentors were my instructors in geography both at high school and college. I corresponded with Leonard Body, my high school geography teacher, until his death. Glanville Jones, my undergraduate tutor at Leeds, and my Ph.D. dissertation adviser at Wisconsin, Andrew Clark, both demanded high standards and stretched my abilities. I think I was privileged academically to have a succession of three broad-ranging, not just narrowly defined geographic teachers. All three of these men encouraged me to range far beyond any stated curricula. Geography is a broad discipline to start with, if indeed it is a discipline in the usual sense, and they allowed me, in the case of my high school teacher, to cross-fertilize with geology, in the case of my undergraduate mentor, to cross-fertilize with history and, in the case of my mentor as a Ph.D. candidate, to cross-fertilize really with intellectual history, social theory, and anthropology. So all of these mentors encouraged my cross-disciplinarity and all of them, however different they were, had a strong empirical streak which, particularly for somebody like me who was always interested in ideas, succeeded in giving me methodical discipline as well. I could have had advisers who just let me be an essayist and avoid the grunt work of accumulating data, picking up statistics, and generally appreciating how to deal with information. My ability to manage a large university and know whether to trust or not trust data, I think, goes back to the fact that they all kept me honest, just like my father kept me honest because of his work ethic.

FL: What were the challenges the University of Wisconsin-Madison faced at the time that you became chancellor and how did they change over your tenure?

DW: My chancellorship and my experience as provost were almost seamless. I have a Ph.D. from Wisconsin. Incidentally, I came as a foreign student in 1960 and became a citizen in 1976. I started as a TA and I rose through the ranks at Wisconsin, so I am a pure creature of that institution. Of course I went on leave many times, and after my Ph.D., I taught for three years in Canada, in part because I had the wrong visa. It is unusual, I think, to start as a TA and end as a chancellor at one institution. Donna Shalala was the very assertive and effective chancellor before me. Much of what we did was as a team. John Wiley is now my successor, but was also my provost, and we were also a team. As provost, Donna gave me broad responsibility to develop a change agenda and she was without question an extraordinary mentor. This agenda was sustained when I became chancellor, so there was considerable continuity.

I want to stress that really the diagnosis of what needed to be done at UW-Madison goes back to the self-study prepared for the accreditation process in 1989. That continuity persists today! John Wiley, when asked what his agenda was when he became chancellor in 2000, said "consolidation." He asserted that he was following two chancellors who had a consistent drive for what might be described as not short term but midterm change and as part of that team he wanted to consummate many of the unfulfilled parts of that agenda. So a very ambitious change agenda was developed after 1989 based on the somewhat critical accreditation review of UW-Madison that also captured the reasons why there was considerable public ambivalence about the university at that time.

With respect to undergraduate education, there is no question that the accrediting team recognized that we were Darwinian in style and that, while we had a great graduate school and a superb faculty, the way that this manifested itself in our undergraduate program was unclear, unplanned, and negligent. The second thing that they pointed out was that while we were indeed an enormously successful graduate school, facilities were falling behind those in many of our peers. We needed capital reinvestment to address a backlog of almost twenty years. Thirdly, there was extensive criticism in the newspapers and from the legislature when Donna Shalala met them and from citizens when she had town meetings. The relationship with the state seemed to be broken. This problem was partly based on a sense that undergraduates were not treated well and partly a perception that the research of the university did not have an impact on the state. This was a much less articulate kind of criticism than that coming from accreditation. The fourth criticism, at which we might all smile, was about athletics. We had a football program that experienced years of losing seasons and a basketball team that was less than ambitious. The only compensations for these sports were an outstanding track team, outstanding oarsmen and an outstanding ice hockey team, but those successes didn't seem to matter. And the final issue, of which I was very aware as a faculty member, was lagging salaries. That complaint naturally came more from the faculty side. There was quite an agenda. From our outside peer review, from our faculty and staff, and from our friends in the legislature and the press, we were aware in our first few weeks that it was a tall agenda. We realized that we couldn't pick them off one at a time: that was where strategic planning came in. We had a list, but the list needed priorities and interconnections. I think that's why we were so ambitious and why what we did lasted and therefore, when I became chancellor, there was much still to be done that had been defined four or five years earlier.

FL: How did Wisconsin manage to make progress in improving the diversity of its student body and faculty?

DW: In the undergraduate student body despite ambitious goals and much investment, we achieved only small successes. Whatever our intentions, I would have to judge our outcomes to have been decidedly modest. I believe we did improve the campus environment, but the numbers of some under-represented groups were low. With faculty and staff we did a better job. In a state with small populations of minorities, we needed a national recruiting process that worked better for faculty, staff, and graduate and professional students. Of course, some areas did better than others: the school of education was probably the most successful.

We were more successful in the recruitment of females and certainly the appointment of Donna Shalala as the first women chancellor energized our efforts to diversify the campus. Undergraduate recruitment was also affected by the upward rise in entrance standards as the campus became attractive as one of the best values in U.S. higher education. During the 1990s UW-Madison became a highly selective state university rather than an open admission state university. We did provide enhanced advising to assist students who were at risk despite their admissibility, and it was critical to avoid high drop-out rates amongst under-represented groups.

FL: What effects did the role and demands of being chancellor have on your family life and how did you maintain a balance?

DW: The main issue was how to handle the conflict of interest of two professionals working in the same system, since our kids were grown and we were empty nesters. Judith was a professional administrator, first at the UW System and then as associate director at the Waisman Center. The demands on a professional spouse were of course considerable, but I believe we managed and indeed enjoyed our public and social obligations. Donna had shared so much of the public agenda of the university with me that Judith and I felt that we were living not in our own house, but in a very nice and attractive house. We had many events, but we had served a very successful apprenticeship. There was no major event in Donna's chancellorship that we had not been invited to as guests, so we were already well exposed to the ritual. In terms of the theater and the drama of being chancellor, it was an easy transition.

It was much harder becoming provost. When I moved from the faculty into being provost, I was, I think, much less prepared for my public role. I remember Donna coming up to me at one of my early events, taking my arm and saying, "Circulate!" I was spending too much time with one person, obviously. I think my ability to deal with the press and television also developed as provost. So when I was appointed as chancellor, I felt a comfort level with my public role in part because Donna had both protected me and mentored me.

I may well have had a very easy transition to chancellor. It was my own university and I'd been a successful provost. I think that it must be a very different transition for those coming from the outside into an unfamiliar institution. What then was the new challenge of becoming the chancellor? I think I underestimated the responsibility of being accountable for all key decisions. As provost, I was involved in most decisions, but in fact I didn't make the key decisions. As Harry Truman once said, you know the buck stops right here with me. I had underestimated that responsibility as provost. We did love the house that the university provided and we enjoyed the vast extension of friendships with faculty, alumni and the community. I think both of us, in the end, thoroughly enjoyed that side of the job. I think if we had not, I would not have lasted as long. We left still enjoying much of what we were doing.

FL: What did each of your internal constituencies expect of you when you came in?

DW: In a way, the self-study associated with the 1989 accreditation publicized a broad range of concerns and once we developed a responsive strategic planning process, many of the issues raised earlier in this dialogue—undergraduate education, facilities, competitive faculty-staff salaries, improved relationships with state and community—were all part of a set of rising expectations.

The governing board was definitely influenced by the accountability movement of the 1980s and there was a lot of legitimate pressure on how to be more effective and how to make cost savings. It was also the beginning of the Thompson era after a period of overlapping Democratic and Republican governors. We didn't know at the time that he would be a four-term governor. As provost and chancellor I encountered only one governor—a governor who appointed the board. In Wisconsin, the governor is very powerful and really sets the tone for higher education. As a new Republican governor, Thompson wanted to make the system more effective, more efficient, and reasonably priced. The board became very much an instrument of that agenda.

From the faculty and alumni we had demands for higher salaries, demands for new buildings and from the board, demands for cost efficiencies, and demands for specified outcomes for undergraduate education as well. So they were pulling against each other in some ways, but they repeated much of what we had already heard. Soon after my appointment one member of the board said that unless I was successful I could be the last academic to be chancellor of the university, since a private sector CEO would likely be much better prepared to do this job—and I'd better succeed. So by the time I became chancellor some board members speculated about the benefits of what was described as "professional management." The word leadership is interesting here because the board was unclear about the distinctions between management and leadership. One of my responses was that "I'll give you leadership: I can hire a manager." Overall, however, the Board was extremely supportive.

FL: There have always been questions along these lines. Many people who have not been connected to universities feel that universities can be run precisely like businesses.

DW: My answer to that is they can be, as long as the person understands the creative product. If you have people who don't know what the advancement of knowledge is about and who have no sense of the challenges of engaging the brain cells of the young, it doesn't matter how good they are at management or marketing, they can't do it. In fact universities are no different than any other enterprise in wanting their leadership to have deep knowledge of the product. I don't think businesses that are smart are any different. In the end, all of the successful business people I have talked to have said that 90 percent of their competency at the time of appointment was knowledge of the product.

FL: If you talk to people who are interested in leadership positions, be it provost or chancellor or president, questions arise about how you manage the different, sometimes conflicting expectations of the university's many constituencies. Would you like to say something about that?

DW: Yes, I think that's the other mistake in this corporate analogy. Knowledge of product and the client are important, but we're really not a pure enterprise. I view our role as a cross between an enterprise and a polity, that is, a little city-state. The skills of a CEO need to be complemented by those of a mayor of a complex city. The role of the mayor is frequently to deal with the adjudication of differences within the polity and between the polity and interest groups. People who think about the role of a mayor and use that as a model will come to the job with more tolerance for the fact that it involves this adjudication of differences.

I think that one of the big mistakes that boards commit in interviewing new presidents is in stressing the command structure of an executive of a not-for-profit enterprise rather than being the mayor of a complex polity. I think that boards err by not raising expectations about this issue in the interview, particularly where the faculty governance is very powerful or where the governor is very powerful and can pull strings through the board. In that situation, the president is sandwiched between a very influential faculty and a very influential governor and his board. If you don't see that as your reality on entering the job, then I think you will fail. In Wisconsin I encountered a powerful governor with a determined board and an activist and powerful faculty senate and that tug-of-war is something you have to be prepared to deal with. I would say that I underestimated the potential for conflict embedded in that situation. The need to coax the faculty and ameliorate the board in dealing with what could have become a civil war was an enormous challenge. I'm not quite sure whether there is an easy solution, but if you don't go into the job knowing that the governance "sandwich" is a large part of the job, then you won't like it.

I think that your question raises what, to me, defines one of the most indispensable skills of the presidency - real diplomatic skills. You need to be able to convey to all sides that you hear everything they have to say about the university. With the board, it's easy to rely on your superior knowledge of the university; in dealing with the faculty, your advantage is your knowledge of the larger picture of the university. Your intermediate role allows you to develop a little moral power in the calculus. I think that's the toughest and most consistently difficult part of the job. Some weeks it goes well and some weeks it doesn't go well.

FL: As you pointed out earlier, you came up the administrative ranks through that culture. It could have been more difficult for someone coming from the outside.

DW: Donna Shalala certainly proved that an astute and experienced outsider could do the job, but I think she would agree that she created a team including several insiders to facilitate her agenda. I was one of those insiders. When I was appointed, it was a bit of a surprise because two years earlier I had left an associate dean's position and returned to my department full time. I completed a book and was elected president of the Association of American Geographers. I had in short resumed my scholarly career. But this may have the attribute most needed to move a new agenda. The most immediate priority was the improvement of undergraduate education and the best kind of leadership would be derived from an individual with a well-recognized research agenda and an ability to avoid a conflict between the needs of research and teaching. Donna made the decision because she understood the politics of change.

FL: This leads perfectly into the next set of questions having to do with organizational culture. Coming into the chancellorship of the University of Wisconsin-Madison from the outside, Donna Shalala began the recruitment of her leadership team by choosing as her provost the ultimate insider, a distinguished scholar who had earned his degree from Wisconsin, to be her intermediary with powerful faculty—and then you became her successor. How did each of you construct your administration?

DW: Donna's first organizational initiative was to create a powerful vice chancellor and provost. At Wisconsin deans were very powerful and the vice chancellor's influence varied from chancellor to chancellor. The chief budget officer reported to the chancellor and the deans triangulated the provost, the chief budget officer, and the chancellor. The provost handled tenure cases and other academic matters. With the departure of the previous budget officer, the new budget officer reported to me. That elevated my post as the provost to be unambiguously Donna's deputy. She changed the organizational culture of the university. There was now a triangular team of chief administrative officer, chief academic officer, and her, but there was no question in the eyes of the deans that she had delegated a great deal of authority to the provost. Partly because of accidents of demography, there was also considerable turnover of deans.

When I became chancellor, I inherited a fair number of deans whom I had helped choose with Donna and they were in a sense an inherited team. John Wiley, who became my provost and is now the chancellor, was appointed as dean of the graduate school, with Donna's approval. Another big change we made was to create a more centralized function for activities like instructional technology and international studies. Many of the areas that were important to the 1990s—interdisciplinary activities, undergraduate education, advising— needed stronger leadership and, without denying the deans their role, we had to give the directors of at-large functions more influence in decision making.

I was so involved in the managerial restructuring while I was provost that in moving to chancellor, I needed only to do some fine-tuning. In fact I retained the chief budget officer, John Torphy, whom I had appointed, so the team of Torphy, Wiley, and Ward actually ran the university, first with Donna, and then with me, for thirteen years. We were personally compatible, very similar in outlook and no dean and no director ever felt that they could go to one or the other and get a different decision. It was a triangulation of mutual confidence that I think helped to get rid of some of the tension of decision making. When one of us made a decision, almost everybody knew all three of us had made it.

FL: What would you describe as the qualities that enable a good leader to find and keep the best people and draw the best performances from them?

DW: Well, it's quite simple. You look for future growth not current achievement. You choose people who still have the energy to grow and change. You don't want somebody who is becoming a provost because they have completed a term as dean. You want somebody who is going to grow into being a chancellor. You must empower your team. You don't micromanage. And you set large scale strategic goals with great energy and conviction.

FL: Were there any changes you made in the administration other those you described? You pretty much had it set.

DW: Donna was so able to facilitate public relations by the power of her personality and I felt the need to systematize what had been a very distinctive personal role. I actually appointed a chief of staff, not in the sense of creating a very influential filter but rather to provide coordination, especially in external communications. I appointed Henry Lufler, an associate dean from the school of education and a former alderman of the city of Madison. He very quickly created an information-communications nexus around me so that the filtering of federal relations, legislative relations, city and county relations, and press relations was aligned. We created an effective communications team. It included people from the alumni association, press relations, political liaison and fundraising, so that when we were dealing with decisions, events and my schedule, the chief of staff really had full responsibility for effective communications. Consequently, everything ran smoothly, without my needing to be accessible twenty-four hours a day.

Donna was able to use very effectively the power of her presence and an aura of celebrity to sell her agenda. Her style is different than mine. Mine is more cerebral. We were a very effective team, but obviously when she moved on to a cabinet position, I had to develop my own style and my communications team made that possible. I think the change was a matter of style and personality. I recognized these differences despite the continuity of agendas and in my case a communications team with astute leadership was essential. When I stepped down, I believe the relationships between the state, the legislature, and the community were at an all-time high.

FL: How did you formulate a vision for the future of the institution? You have described some of this, so perhaps you could just focus on the process.

DW: We talked earlier about the fact that Donna and I felt we were aware of negative feedback, almost a bill of indictment, from a variety of sources. Donna had invited Mike Williamson, an assistant to the mayor and a committed quality management disciple, to be her legislative liaison. He had helped the mayor use quality management techniques to improve delivery of public services in Madison and now works for the governor of North Carolina doing similar things. He approached me one day in 1990 when we were trying to figure out how we were going to address our problems. He said, "You know you've got to do this with systems, you've got to do this with priorities, and you've got to do this with data." My scholarly temperament was immediately aroused by this approach, which was coming not from a corporate executive but from someone who worked with the city. He suggested that we develop a strategic plan which at UW- Madison was almost unthinkable at that time. At about that time, I became aware that John Wiley, then dean of the graduate school, had appointed a quality management professional, Maury Cotter, and she quickly became a key driver and staff support for all university efforts.

For several months, we worked together on how we might develop a plan and how we might introduce it. We speculated on how to approach faculty governance and I concluded that if I responded positively to the idea of systems, data, and priorities, why wouldn't my colleagues? I also sensed that the self-study associated with accreditation would provide an environmental scan by the faculty and staff with a broad range of proposals suitable for a strategic plan. So we developed a very crude process to develop a strategic plan and there was little opposition but much skepticism. What I detected was a critical but not an oppositional culture. We began by creating working groups to address the most obvious issues like undergraduate education. We decided to address our admission process, advising, class access, and raise the priority of undergraduates within the university. The working groups using material available in the self-study were energetic and creative. I felt that we could make singular advances but needed a more robust framework to connect and publicize the reforms. That's when we had ignition!

Two years later we had a well-defined strategic plan and some early successes. As provost, I organized retreats with senior administrators and deans, worked closely with faculty, staff, student government, and with any department or unit that would listen to me. I made the plan my only non-negotiable policy. Eventually, the local business community, the alumni association and the UW foundation found out about it. They were all delighted. The plan proved to be robust inside and outside the university. We had the beginnings of a set of priorities rather than a limitless "wish list." Donna gave me a lot of freedom to develop the plan. She was very supportive and left me free to manage the engine room.

Finally we had what I would call a prototypical plan ready to be formally launched just as I became chancellor. So I had the good fortune of having done a lot of the grunt work for four years. I could be announced as a new chancellor and say simultaneously, "Now we have a five-year plan!" I couldn't have done that had I not been provost. I was able to hit the road running with this plan that had been nurtured for four years. While I do think that there was skepticism, in the end we had enough early successes that all I needed was the energy of those who supported it.

FL: What strategies did you use to communicate the plan and engage the university community in its implementation once you had completed it? How did you deal with the internal community and the external community after the plan was approved and launched?

DW: The first strategy was to publicize our early successes. Sometimes these early advances were modest. I remember one success that was very powerful because it basically connected the strategic plan to a tactical approach by which the university could leverage itself better.   State support was constantly negotiable, constantly being nibbled away.   How could we use the strategic plan to influence state policymakers?

To stimulate innovations in undergraduate education we had used endowment funds to support a research experience for students between the junior and senior years. Faculty members could nominate a student or a group of students to work in the lab on a project or to join them in the field, including I might add the South Pole. The outcome might be jointly authored papers or simply an experience of value in applications to graduate schools. The amount of money involved was quite small.   The students each received a stipend of $3,000, which would hopefully discourage them from working in the summer while the faculty member received $1,000 and much virtue. I planned for 200 summer fellowships and received almost five times that number in applications. The faculty, who allegedly were not interested in undergraduates, responded enthusiastically.   Many undergraduates later reflected that they not only received their B.S. at Wisconsin but had a joint publication with a distinguished faculty member. Of course, for many faculty members, these projects were integrated into research that they were doing anyway, while the competition attracted the best undergraduates who, as several people pointed out to me, were as good as some of the average graduate students.

Our success prompted us to place publicity in the hometown newspaper of every undergraduate recipient. The story went out with a picture of the faculty member and the student. About a week after this publicity campaign, a legislator called me and said, "I'm just reading about this undergraduate research fellowship in my local newspaper and I think the state should support this too." In the next budget round, the state put in a very significant budget line item to support this. The faculty recognized the power of leverage and that was real success.

Our other early success was to persuade the state that, if we could raise private money for buildings, we should be free to build the buildings faster. State regulations and processes almost always involved a ten-year building cycle after formal approval and the approval process could also take years. When we needed to construct a new business school that was jointly funded privately and by the state, we were able to speed up the entire procedure and at the same insist on some aesthetic and quality standards that were rarely possible in a structure built with state funds. This procedure became a model that later sustained a facilities building boom on the campus. These early successes and the various astute ways of doing them gave the plan an operational integrity. The private and the public support for the university was also beginning to be integrated and that was exactly what the plan intended to do. It was also a means to bring both kinds of support together.

FL: How did you link the changes you wanted to make to the financial budgeting process of the institution?

DW: We recognized that there had to be some financial incentives attached to the strategic plan. Early on, rather than creating a zero sum game between existing commitments and new commitments, we tried desperately to find new money or, on non-controversial projects, to create the means to support it. We moved gradually, rather than rapidly. Initially much of the plan was funded without new funds. I think that because we had done phase one with new money, it was easier to do the second phase within clear budget priorities. I was simultaneously paying a lot of attention to the competitiveness of our salaries and especially faculty recruitment and retention. I realized that solutions to these issues were far more demanding than program innovations. As long as this larger concern was visible, it was possible to reallocate to the priorities of the plan—improved advising, research opportunities for under-graduates, and enhancement of international studies and programs abroad among others. What amazed me was how far small reallocations went. The faculty recognized that their salaries were among my highest priorities; the amount of money I needed to drive change in areas other than salaries struck me as quite small. So, while budget management was very important, the magnitude of what was required was much lower than I had anticipated.

FL: Everyone who initiates change soon finds that Machiavelli was correct in warning that the innovator can be sure of making enemies of all those who did well under the old system but can count upon having only lukewarm defenders among those who may profit under the new. Can you describe one or two critical incidents of this nature, how they arose, and how you dealt with them?

DW: Yes. We had a very old system of manual registration. It was evident to me that we had to move into the late twentieth century with a computerized registration system. I realized that the major impediment was the fact that most departments and faculty preferred to wait until the last minute to set their curricula for the next year. Programs liked to wait until April or May before they set their courses for September. There was no planning to avoid courses being offered either at times that weren't appropriate or at times when the courses in two departments were clearly competing with one another, although the students needed both. I thought that computerized registration could solve both problems, so I pushed very aggressively to put in place the kind of program that other universities were using.

When the departments discovered that they needed to, first of all, consult more completely on scheduling and, second, meet the challenge of setting up the curriculum by March rather than by May, some faculty regarded this as an intrusion on their autonomy. My response was to ask a question at a meeting of department chairs, "How many of you have children who are freshmen in college?" A fair number responded affirmatively. I asked them to tell me about their children's difficulties with registration and they related horror stories not necessarily just from Wisconsin. I said, "You know, it seems to me that if, as parents, you have these kinds of expectations for better treatment of your children, we've got to think our way through this problem." I added, "The whole issue of the content and quality of the undergraduate curriculum is already under university-wide discussion and you are all examining your undergraduate programs in connection with periodic department reviews, so, in many ways, you're already thinking about these issues." Eventually we were able to get the parental faculty on board. The second thing was to provide some data. We produced some data on enrollment patterns and then we retrieved some parents' letters on the topic, and slowly we worked our way through to a solution. But it was initially seen as an issue of intrusion on departmental autonomy by the university administration. I was surprised by how hot that was. It took ingenuity and patience to work my way through that heat. It is perhaps a trivial example, but it was a challenging moment.

FL: You've alluded to your interest in data. In what ways did you monitor and track outcomes and progress on goals and how did you reinforce and celebrate the success of what you were doing?

DW: We asked the deans and program directors to issue an annual report and connected the review of deans and directors to their annual reports. The foundation, of course, liked this process because they needed this information for advocacy. An annual report forces programs to set goals and to declare what they've achieved. We also developed some survey data on how many students received what kind of advising and monitored complaints on matters such as foreign teaching assistants. We tried not to be formulaic. We let the deans recount their unit's achievements in relation to their mission. We relied very heavily on the deans, who were in the driving seats, to produce their progress reports as part of the larger strategic plan.

FL: What importance did you place on the role of your institution in the community?

DW: A very high importance. I would say that we were, if not the first, possibly the second largest employer in Madison, even though it was the state capital. Madison had grown rapidly in the 1980s and had reached a population of about 175,000. As a university with over 35,000 students and probably 15,000 employees, we were the behemoth and could have inadvertent negative impacts on our neighbors. The once vibrant city center had been decimated by retail decentralization from the downtown area. The city still had memories of the student riots of the 1960s. The real question was why the university was not more of an engine of development as well as a participant in local public issues like the school system or land use and redevelopment.

We developed a calculated effort to reach out to the city. Relations with the mayor's office were very good because in part because of the aldermanic experiences of my chief of staff. If the university is collaborating with the city, it is headline news, because most news is local. The university had already developed a research park on land previously used by the College of Agriculture and during the 1990s it became a symbol of high-tech small-cap job growth in the city. The city loved it. I think the research park became almost an emblem of the effect of the university on the region. It was so visible, it was aesthetically designed and it just took off in the 1990s. We also developed a master land use plan for the facilities on the campus. We consulted with the city because we were located right up against the downtown businesses and the student rental areas, as well as some attractive inner suburbs. We even became involved with the issue of the homeless and connected concerned students with the city and voluntary organizations. Community connections were a high priority.

FL: Were there any other specific external groups that you worked with, other than the city?

DW: Obviously we connected with the state business communities and other groups. They too were interested in how the university influenced the state economy. They were increasingly worried about human capital development. While they were often very supportive, higher education was always a little bit of a political challenge for them. There were always political issues about Madison having the research university that leveraged state support in contrast to UW-Milwaukee, and of course Madison as the state capital and leading center of high-tech jobs attracted the jealousy of less favored parts of the state.

The relationship with the business community was a complicated one, but on the whole a very positive one. I tended to work through the UW alumni association and the UW foundation to reach the business community in order to focus on people who already had some connection and loyalty to Madison. With the active support of the alumni association, we created a Badger political action network. We organized for every seat within the state legislature a group of three or more people who were contacted by either e-mail or telephone on any issue and, depending on which committee or subcommittee of the House or the Senate was treating the issue, we would have them do the third party advocacy for us. They need not be in business.

Another kind of connection was based on the athletic programs. During this period football and basketball went from being mediocre to seriously competitive and that involved a new challenge for me. First of all, now we had a sold-out stadium. You'd say that's a good problem. No, because people can't get tickets. People feel entitled to tickets. Then the prices went up. Parking became a big problem. Behavior of the students became a problem. In fact there was a stadium surge at the end of a Michigan football game in which many students were injured. This was probably the biggest crisis I had to handle in all the time I was chancellor. We also had to build a brand new hockey and basketball arena because the old basketball facility built in the1920s could only hold 8,000 people and had very poor views, inadequate facilities and had been declared basically unacceptable by the State Health

Department. Yet I had a whole set of academic buildings that needed to be built. This was a political challenge with the faculty. What was I supposed to do? Fortunately, we built the entire facility with private gifts and revenue bonds. Once we had the funds, the location became an issue: should it be on campus? Should it be on the edge of the city? Should it serve the city's needs? Would it threaten the business of the new convention center? So it became a complex set of decisions. We had to manage relationships with the city, state, business community, and legislature. During this process my communications team served me extremely well.

FL: How did you allocate your time? How did you decide your priorities? You can't be all things to all people every day, because you eventually just wear down from overwork.

DW: I think I was protected from the initial demands for multiple connections with people and agencies because of my visibility as provost unlike, for example, when I came to Washington and had to make many new connections. Another advantage I had in terms of time is that I'm very disciplined about meetings. I usually know what I want out of it and, if it's dragging, I just stop it. One example of this I myself don't remember but it was recounted at my retirement by a leader in the development learning communities in our dorms. That was an initiative for attaching faculty and graduate students to floors of dorms and trying to run programs that enhanced the quality of student life in the dorms. We were trying to scale up some of these learning communities in the dorms. They needed additional funds. They had developed a proposal and had held numerous planning meetings. They came in for a meeting with me and had requested two hours with me. It was a worthy and creative proposal and after five minutes, they left with their money (which was far less than I imagined they would need). Some were a little surprised at my haste because they wanted to tell me more about what they were doing but, since they got their money, it was hard to be too agitated. Especially since I ended the meeting with a suggestion, "Let me come down to the dorm and have dinner with you two weeks from now, but today is the day from hell. The regents are meeting this afternoon." They understood that.

In some meetings there are no objectives, all people are doing is venting, but in meetings in which you know there's a decision to be made, my view is move them to focus on the decision. I also used to phone a lot. I would use gaps in my schedule to phone people who I knew were going to ask for an unnecessary meeting. Spending three minutes on the phone allowed problems to be solved without loading up my schedule. Increasingly e-mail served the same purpose as long as the response was prompt and decisive.

FL: A university chancellor travels frequently, sometimes only within the state, but sometimes out of state for four to five days, or out of the country. Did you have an assigned deputy, a second-in-command, who could make those decisions that needed to be made or was a consultation with you required?

DW: Donna had traveled widely as chancellor and I basically had a well-defined deputy role. She was the one who created a powerful deputy. She made that clear; my style made that clear. Many people finally got used to it and I did the same thing once I had appointed John Wiley as provost. Once I became chancellor and empowered John, we were very disciplined about keeping connected. The provost in Madison in that period was truly empowered to do 90 percent of what needed to be done, so nothing was ever really held up by the chancellor's absence.

FL: Do you have any crisis management stories that you'd like to share?

DW: I think there would be two. One would be that the university hospital, with virtually no state support, was being drained of reserves in a new competitive environment of HMOs. There were too many hospitals in competition in Madison to boot. Most revenues were derived from either grants or patient insurance. Donna had recognized the problem but I was to inherit the debate about solutions. I had also observed similar problems at the University of Minnesota two years earlier. We had decided to convert the hospital to a public authority with a CEO free to manage it in a way that was unencumbered by state regulation and with its capital needs met by its own bonds. Then we needed to think of a governance structure that would be appropriate and this issue was complicated by union concerns about the change from state employees to authority employees.

The governor and the legislature were necessarily deeply involved, but eventually a new independent public authority was created by an act of the legislature. At the same time it also became clear that the faculty of the medical school needed to become an HMO and, that once it became an HMO, it would need to buy other HMOs to balance primary and specialty care. So as we were developing a public authority status for the university hospital, the medical faculty was not only organized as an HMO but also merged with another local HMO creating a mixed organizational culture. I thought this would be fine because they would need the primary care physicians in order to feed patients into that bicultural merger. I personally spent much of my time with the dean of medicine dealing with sensitive issues of governance and compensation.

Another crisis was one that I referred to earlier: the crowd surge of students during the final seconds of the Michigan football game. Many students were injured, including fifteen very seriously, and of course the "who to blame" issue came up. Anybody connected with the university administration and the athletic program was fair game. I was sued for five years following that event and resolution only came from the Wisconsin Supreme Court. A more immediate issue was how to create a legitimate public inquiry. The inquiry exonerated individuals of personal culpability but suggested that the stadium needed major design changes as well as improvements in crowd management, so we redesigned the stadium. The short run public relations and the long-term litigation were extremely challenging.

FL: With so many competing demands on your time, how have you succeeded then and now in finding something that helped you stay focused on
what was important and keep your balance. You spent two years on the hospital issue and more than two years on the athletic issue.

DW: I am unsure. While there were days in which these problems were
dominant, I never felt in the seven and a half years that there were any consuming problems that actually engaged me for long periods of time. There was a
student sit-in that was a big problem. It had immediate impact on the day-to-
day management and on my support staff, but the intensity tended to be short
term.

I think two things probably helped me. Firstly, temperament: if I can see my
way to a solution, I am able to be very patient. My emotional stamina is highly
correlated with the feeling that I have a solution. It's usually when I have no
concept of a solution, when it's like a meeting with no outcome, that I find it
difficult. Secondly, I understood personal therapy. Judith and I had this
cottage about two hours north of Madison. We could canoe, we could enter-
tain close friends, we could talk. I think we were very good at just suspending
the stress. And I think if you can just take a time-out in some way, that's
important. Problems don't disappear, but you've got to figure out some way to
get some distance from them.

FL: How would you define leadership?

DW: I think having a horizon of achievable goals. Leadership must lead to
something. Leadership in my view is direction. You must have direction and
you must know what the direction is. Then it seems to me there are secondary
attributes of how to develop enthusiasm, buy-in and so on. This capacity still
depends on the desired goals and outcomes. Unless there is a destination with
some shared desire to get there, then it doesn't matter what kind of leader you
are. So I've always stressed where I want to go.

You know people laugh at this, but there's this evocative quote from Wayne
Gretzky of all people. He says, "I skate to where I think the puck will be." I
believe that statement is one of the most powerful metaphors for everything
I've ever done, because if I'm sitting here today, the thing that most matters is
where will I seek to be at some future time? I think that's the key to leadership,
knowing where you want to go. If you don't know where you want to go, it's
pointless.

FL: What are the most important qualities for a university president or
chancellor today?

DW: They're probably multiple, aren't they? I would actually go back to
my last answer. I think it is knowledge of where you want to go. I think that's
the navigational skill. As I look at deans who failed, as I look at many presidents who struggle, I believe that they really saw it as a position, not as an
action agenda. Of course, some people have unrealistic agendas that don't
work out and your goals do have to be feasible, achievable, but the key,

nevertheless, is to have defined goals. I was asked by the provost at Miami, when Donna Shalala was appointed, to reflect on my own experience as provost and my answer was, "I would go and talk to her and find out two of her immediate goals and achieve them."

FL: What kind of advice could you offer new presidents as they walk into their offices and size up some of the issues?

DW: My advice is to show that you are a very good listener and understand what people who may differ with you have to say. On one hand, you want to make sure they know that you have determined goals and committed values, but you can also hear the other side. I think one of the best compliments is, "You're a good listener." I remember one encounter with a newly appointed conservative board member. She was concerned about the "liberal" reputation of the faculty and the university. She was clearly interested in political thought and I revealed that I was currently reading a biography of Edmund Burke. We started talking and I think the idea that I knew the origins of British conservatism, if not of Reagan's American version, redefined her concerns. I think she felt that I knew where she was coming from, even if I didn't always agree. I think that's very important.

FL: How have the role and the demands of the presidency changed over the past few decades

DW: I think that when people say that in the past there were great presidents who were like priests or archbishops, it's a matter of cause and effect. They had status and they could in fact view their position as the priest. My colleague at Wisconsin, Professor John Cooper wrote a book on Theodore Roosevelt and Woodrow Wilson entitled *The Warrior and The Priest.* In simple terms, there is a kind of an activist energy to Roosevelt and a more priestly academic style to Wilson. College presidents have to be more like Roosevelt than Wilson today. Today you are more likely to be engaged in a wider range of social and political issues, whereas I think that formerly you could have been a reflective academic priest. Wilson was a college president and in many respects typical of an older style of college leadership. I think college presidents were able in the past to reflect on higher education in a very altruistic and idealistic way and were rarely engaged in entrepreneurial issues of the modern presidency.

Over the last fifty years our responsibility for budget and accountability to the public or their representatives has grown. I think that this shift has proceeded much further in publics than privates. People in the press have asked me several times, "Where are the great presidents?" I have said, "What do you mean by a great president?" They refer to those who made memorable moral pronouncements of a kind that no longer attract much media attention. I think we should continue the priestly tradition and offer appropriate sermons, but in fact our engaged and activist role is often the means by which we express our values. To return to the metaphor, we're expected to be warriors rather than priests.

FL: Presidencies used to be measured in decades but now are more typically no more than four or five years in length. What do you believe is the reason for that relatively high, rapid turnover?

DW: The reason is that the respect for leadership in the late twentieth century is much diminished and in this media-driven world no mistakes are hidden. The transparency of leadership and therefore its potential vulnerability has greatly increased. Therefore the emotional stamina to be a leader has become especially demanding at a time when the positive vibes of appreciation, whether obsequious or not, are quite rare. Unless you are extraordinarily tough, there's a point in an eight to twelve year cycle that you recognize the need to question your own longevity in the job. I think many people now anticipate that moment when the board, the faculty, and other groups create questions about the actual or perceived success of your leadership. Perhaps the real insight is to move on before this realization occurs! I think I had the good fortune to do that. I think it may have happened, but I didn't wait to find out! I just came to the conclusion that I had one more job left in me and if I didn't step down at that time, I would deny myself one more interesting job.

FL: What do you feel are the important characteristics of good governing boards and what are the problems that one can encounter in dealing with governing boards?

DW: I think the best way to come at this issue is to imagine that you are a mayor with limited powers with a very difficult council. If you are a public university president, you need to be aware that boards do not see their role to make you look good, but rather that they are appointed by the governor to represent interests in the state. You have to view this whole encounter as a political experience. By having that political framework, you limit your expectations. Board members have their own specific loyalties and you need to be a very good ethnographer of regional, ethnic, and economic interests. You have to determine the most likely supporters or advocates on the board so that you can focus your energy on compatibilities and eventually trust. Of course board members turn over very fast, but I think it's crucial to identify a person or two with some simpatico, who can then be your representative, your speaker, in a way, in this group. I felt able to do that. I also was protected from an immediate relationship with the board since it served the system as a whole. UW-Madison was the 600 pound gorilla, and on many issues, like health sciences or athletics, it was I, rather than the system president, who was in the hot seat, but I was protected from many difficult encounters with the board by a system president.

The idea that you can meet all the needs of all board members is an illusion. You can most effectively relate to a board by means of prudent bilateral connection with those few members whom you know understand the institution. In fact, the highly charged political character of most public governing boards means that a classic business CEO would find leadership in higher education frustrating and anarchic. We had a board that in no way resembled a corporate board, and yet some members of that board wanted a corporate CEO. The board behaved more like the city council and the leadership of the university needed the astute skills of a successful mayor and certainly not a corporate CEO command structure. The key to the relationship with the board is to have in mind the right model of what the board is about.

FL: In the past few years there have been several instances in which the governor of the state has gotten involved directly with policy issues in the flagship universities. Any advice on how presidents can handle this kind of thing?

DW: I would say that as the primary advocate for your institution, you need to be very firm, and independent on those occasions when you believe that the interests of higher education are in play. I know that this sounds suicidal! But I think that with governors you have to be very respectful and lose gracefully rather than capitulate. I was always passionately committed to raising faculty salaries because, unlike your faculty salaries at Rutgers, ours were not competitive at that time. This commitment placed me in opposition to many members of the board, and of course the governor, who realized the challenge that my proposals placed on the state budget. My position brought a variety of pressures from many directions and although I did not prevail, the press reported on my position favorably and eventually we did better than I had anticipated. The governor was doing exactly what he had to do – influence the board that he had appointed. On other occasions we bonded on issues of economic development, and the governor was a key leader in making possible a major building boom on the campus. But I think the real fatal thing would be for the chancellor to seem to be part of the cabinet. I think that, as graciously and as effectively you can, you've got to be your own person and recognize the degree to which the board may be indebted to the governor. You might lose your job of course!

FL: How did you make your decision about what you would like to do after the presidency?

DW: Initially I really felt that I wanted to stay in Madison and return to the faculty. I had been there most of my professional life; our family had roots there. I felt that, if I could be gone for a year, my successor, John Wiley, would have the space to establish his style. An opportunity to be a visiting fellow at the University of California-Berkeley provided me with the option of a sojourn and indeed the possibility of a longer relationship, but that experience raised some questions about my future. Once I actually did step down and moved off to Berkeley, I realized that maybe what I planned to do was not going to be quite right for me. I began to explore at Berkeley what I would have done in Madison, which was to run a center for the study of higher education. Leading a center is like running a department, with all of the immediate personal issues that, as a chancellor, you step back from. Small-scale management didn't appeal to me. I needed something bigger than the center, not as big as the university but a place where higher education issues were at the forefront.

Then, I had a gift from heaven when somebody—probably you—nominated me for the presidency of ACE. The interview engaged me and I realized that it was a good fit and eventually so did the committee. The issues were all of the issues that I would have liked to deal with if I were at a center for higher education studies. I just feel enormously privileged to have this job, where all of the higher education issues that engage me are a matter of daily discussion. I may have been lucky that I stepped down before I got into real trouble, and that I found a spot that fit my aspirations.

FL: I know that we have already touched on this question many times, but perhaps you could sum up your views on it in a sentence or two. How would you characterize your leadership style? You said earlier that you are a good listener.

DW: Yes, but I think also that I try to be thoughtful and engaged in what we're trying to do. I like to manage effectively so that there is time to reflect on where we're going or why we're going there. Many people have said to me, "You bring intellect to the job." I thought, "My God, I would hope most people do."

FL: What do you feel are the most critical capital investments that were made under your leadership at Wisconsin?

DW: Capital investment, you mean in terms of mortar and bricks?

FL: If I were asked that question, the example I would give wouldn't be a building.

DW: I think my choice would be the Center for Biotechnology, because it became a symbol of the multiple implications of the strategic plan. Whenever I wanted to sell the strategic plan to the business community, I talked about the biotech center, which had already assisted old and new companies. It had links to some companies in the research park. It was also linked with a strong interdisciplinary department, genetics. So it symbolized the links between basic and applied research, the links between the university and business, and the interdependency of several departments. The building also reflected the new and fast process of constructing facilities that rested on a combination of public and private revenues.

FL: What would you consider your most significant legacies to Wisconsin ?

DW: I think it would be that it is unquestionably able to compete with very best public research universities. There was doubt about that in the late 1980s in terms of undergraduate quality, quality of the professional schools, faculty retention, and the quality of facilities. In a state of four and a half million people, with a very modest tax base, you wouldn't expect to have a university as highly ranked and regarded as UW-Madison and to maintain that stature with only local resources would always be a challenge. But with national stature, came national resources from both the federal government and the philanthropy of our alumni and friends. In 1989, I think we had doubts about our future stature, but I think that when I left, there was no question that UW-Madison would weather future problems with a stronger institutional capacity and resource base.

FL: Now you're in a very different sort of post as president of the American Council on Education, but there are undoubtedly a number of commonalities as well. During your presidency of ACE, what have been the areas essential to higher education where you think that the ACE has been able to make the greatest contributions or to head off the most egregious potential problems?

DW: I think that ACE was effective in the handling of the whole range of post-9/11 issues for higher education. I believe we moderated and rationalized a lot of spontaneous, legitimate, but excessive responses to uncertainties about security, whether it was the student visa system, the security of biological hazards, or in forging alliances with other constituencies that have interests in these matters. I arrived in Washington two days before 9/11 and my first testimony to the Congress was on the post 9/11 concerns about student visas. We have continued to promote a balance between legitimate security concerns and the value of foreign students to our universities.

Another immediate issue was referral of the University of Michigan affirmative action case to the U.S. Supreme Court. ACE was without question the lead coordinator, working with Michigan, to connect the military academies and the business community and to make the case an issue of the national interest and of social justice. The third major issue in which ACE is in a continuing leadership role is in the co-ordination of the responses of higher education to the Higher Education Reauthorization Act. Since there is very little money available to fund new programs or to increase the capacity of established programs, there is a tendency for Congress to turn to policy matters. With the "No Child Left Behind Act" as an example, we were apprehensive about proposals to increase federal regulation of colleges and universities. One proposal did include the regulation of tuition by means of "price controls" at a time when many states were substituting tuition for state support. Other proposed regulatory intrusions will need our attention.

I would, however, say that a difference between the role of university chancellor and president of ACE is that I am spending much more time in the political prevention business. I am more frequently engaged in stopping bad things from happening rather than in getting good things done. The nature of congressional politics is, as I'm sure the founding fathers wished, to make change difficult and much of what we do with little recognition is to dissuade people from doing bad things rather than persuading them to do what we would like them to do. Those would be the three big issues that we faced in the two and a half years I've been here.

FL: In both your former role as chancellor of a great research university and now in this post, you've worked with some highly intelligent professionals who are themselves leaders. In ACE, how have you addressed some of the issues of external and internal challenges, forming a vision, planning, all of those particular issues that you also encounter within the university?

DW: When I arrived at ACE, the board was fully aware of the need for a strategic plan. I had just spent twelve years first as provost, then as chancellor, thinking strategically about how to change an institution. My immediate predecessor, Stanley Ikenberry, had made several changes that were very important. He had repositioned ACE with respect to other higher education associations and he had upgraded the facilities, but the organizational culture of ACE had not really experienced an integrated strategic change.

I think in some ways the board felt that ACE was now ready for integrated or systemic change since Stan Ikenberry had solved some of the most immediate operational challenges that he faced when he came on board. What hit me was that the culture of a university and of ACE had many similarities. It was surprising to me how ACE lagged behind so many of its members in the way it was managed as distinct from what it did. In some respects ACE was effective in spite of itself and I devoted a lot of time to try and develop a plan that would also engage us in a change of culture.

We needed to change from an organization that relied very heavily on traditional systems of communications (commissions and publications) to one more in tune with the speed of electronic communications and the human touch of programs on the road. We also needed to set priorities. ACE was thought by some to be all things to all people and I think the process of determining our priorities was the key to our strategic planning process.

FL: I was on the board when you came in and announced you wanted to do a strategic planning process. I can tell you that all the colleagues sitting next to me were not only impressed but found that highly unusual. Most people wait to launch a strategic plan, but sometimes, if you wait, you can't have the impact you need. Strategic planning was a terrific idea. People are now saying that things have changed.

DW: I would say that we're about half way to where we need to get, but I think we're over the hump. Ellen Babby served as a key point person in the planning process and the appointment of Ben Quillian as senior vice president for business and operations means that I am no longer engaged in what initially had been a need to micromanage many aspects of our operations. I am now in a better position to guide the larger strategic objectives of the association.

FL: What would you say are presently the highest priorities of ACE?

DW: To make it clear to our members and all interested in higher education what the value added of ACE is. It's very difficult being an umbrella organization, where every member belongs to one if not two of the other presidential associations. You can argue that ACE is everybody's second organization and most members are likely to have a primary loyalty to their niche organization. So ACE needs to be especially clear about its value added. We appeared to be doing so many things that we obscured the things we did best. That lack of specificity or priority was the main reason for a plan, to create a "funnel" out of what was a "delta." That metaphorical reversal of process was very important for my first and second year here. A funnel is the means to narrow priorities. If a proposal doesn't test positive for our priorities, it is not in the plan, whereas ACE's culture before was if other people didn't do it, ACE probably would. And I think the key to our funnel was federal relations in the broadest sense, whether the courts, the executive branch or the Congress. Everybody recognized that strength and whatever else we do we need to make that focus clear.

FL: Certainly one can never predict a 9/11, but it was clear that ACE under your leadership was taking a leading role in dealing with the fallout from that, as well as the Michigan issue, and tuition concerns. Because ACE represents a great variety of institutions you can speak with a strong voice for the broad range of higher education.

DW: You can, except the difficulty for ACE is that frequently small policy differences among these various groups cloud broad areas of agreement. It is up to ACE to work through those differences, if possible, before they become a problem. Sometimes, without any malevolence or any negative intent, other organizations will, from time to time, need to run contrary to ACE to establish their visibility or separate identity. Deep down we all believe that we are stronger when we speak with one voice.

FL: How important do you think it is for presidents and chancellors to participate in national organizations and join in their work on issues in higher education? I always felt that I learned something by going to meetings and that when I talked to my colleagues, all of a sudden my problems looked smaller.

DW: Yes, I would say that if you're a professional academic you need this face-to-face communication. There were times when the Association of American Geographers didn't exactly meet my academic or professional needs, but I went anyway. I think it is an indispensable role of associations to create a community larger than the local bonds of each member. You need these external connections so that you have a means to make peer comparisons. For a university leader, effective federal relations with your own congressional delegation are critical, and it is very likely that you will need some third party help. I don't know any president who is able to do this without the assistance of the Washington higher education associations. An institution-specific need is always better represented as a national policy priority.

FL: I mentioned earlier the term assessment, an extremely important issue for academe in areas ranging from how you assess what students learn in their freshman year to assessment of teaching. Is this an issue on which ACE is focusing?

DW: Really it's a subset of accountability. Accountability is often a bureaucratic form of outcome measurement and assessment is usually a more
specific programmatic evaluation. ACE emphasizes the current role of accreditation in meeting most needs for accountability and assessment. Last
year I chaired the regional (or institution wide) accreditation of the University
of California-Berkeley to see in what way accreditation was responding to the
growing demand for accountability and assessment. The comprehensiveness
of the required self-study, often directly linked to a strategic plan, and the
specific examination of outcomes of recent changes in programs and procedures cover many of the issues of accountability. However there is no question
that what accreditation is currently doing would not satisfy what the leaders of
the accountability and assessment movements would like.

ACE and the Council for Higher Education Accrediation (CHEA) need to
encourage institutions to accept more a more demanding and transparent process of accreditation. At ACE we have also examined issues of assessment in
collaboration with the Business-Higher Education Forum, since the business
community needs more confidence in our current practices so that they will
support us in our efforts to avoid federal intrusion in these areas.

FL: What is your take on the increasing problems that public universities
are encountering as states reduce their funding of higher education? How can
institutions resolve their budget problems and continue to build both access
and excellence?

DW: This is a key issue for ACE. We have functioned under a social compact developed between 1945 and 1965 designed to expand accessibility by
keeping tuition low and providing grants to those in need. During the seventies, expanded access and multiplication of institutions of post-secondary
education outran state tax resources. The shift was very gradual but tuition
was slowly substituted for state subsidies and loans slowly replaced grants.
Over the past decade and especially over the past two years, the magnitude of
these changes has redefined the social compact. Tuition has increased quite
dramatically and debt burdens have become a source of concern.

It is now clear that the individual beneficiary of higher education will pay
higher tuition and rely on loans. Of course there is considerable choice of
institutional type and tuition levels and a wide array of financial aid, but the
calculus of the new social compact has been obscured by efforts to blame the
entire problem on alleged willful increases in tuition. We need to ask ourselves what part of the new proportionate contributions to the total cost of
higher education should come from individuals, institutions, and from government. In particular, we need to conduct the debate on the basis of actual
tuition payments rather than sticker prices of the most expensive independent
universities. If individuals and society are joint beneficiaries of higher education, how should they share that cost? That will require discussions of a new
social compact which may well conflict with current efforts to set taxation at

extremely low levels. The current tuition issue owes its immediate magnitude to the recent downswing in the economy, but it was a gradual process over almost three decades during which the proportionate share of college cost borne by individuals and their government was fundamentally altered.

Most states have created tax structures (as has the federal government, but it can legally function with deficits) resulting in tax levels that are about one-half those of most of Europe. So at some point we have to ask the public what is the threshold minimum of public services they want and then to be honest about the tax levels necessary to sustain them. So I think there are two debates that have to be raised to a national level: one is the respective contribution of individuals and government to higher education and the other concerns the level of state investment and services the public wants for a level of taxation half that of Europe. We must make the strongest possible arguments to increase public awareness of the social costs of diminished public investments in higher education and test whether they are open to specific levels of taxation directly linked to opportunities in higher education. I don't think we've done that.

FL: It might be worth trying, but university presidents and higher education policy experts have certainly worked hard at making the argument for consistent and adequate funding of higher education—to little avail. Private institutions also have their budget problems. When I was at Tulane, I remember Eamon Kelly once characterizing Tulane's tuition policy as a Robin Hood approach: taking from the rich to give to the poor.

DW: I think that is what financial aid has become for public institutions now. It's a means-tested redistribution of revenues. You could argue that this system is better than having uniformly low tuition. Since our best institutions enroll predominantly upper-middle-class students, in a way, you could argue that low tuition is an income and benefit transfer to the wealthy. We do our best to enroll students from less affluent circumstances, but most of our students are from families for which low tuition is an attractive tax subsidy. So, in some ways, the Robin Hood notion may be a fairer system than an entitlement of everybody to extremely low tuition. We have to make a better case for a new social compact.

FL: Do you think it's the responsibility of the state to try to solve this access problem or is it the federal government's responsibility to take this on so that students from low-income families have access to a quality education?

DW: I think this question of responsibility is another great challenge in American higher education and therefore of great importance to ACE. Discussions of the changing social compact and of fiscal policies will necessitate a much better coordination of state and federal policies. In many respects the states have defined higher education policies and the federal government has been a major banker. Because the federal government now provides a high proportion of both student financial aid and research funding, the federal government will necessarily engage in more regulatory policies. This creates problems of redundancy of regulations at different levels of government and the federal government often creates one-size-fits all policies that fail to recognize the variety and choices available in higher education. Perfectly legitimate standards when applied with little sensitivity to this variability may injure the best and fail to confront the worst. In some respects this may be one of the lessons of "The No Child Left Behind Act."

I think we need a blue ribbon panel to examine and develop strategies to confront the changing composition of revenues and responsibilities of different levels of government. This dialogue is given urgency not by issues of cost but concerns about capacity. Largely because of the huge influx of legal immigrants during the last decade, Florida, Texas, the East Coast corridor, and California will not have the capacity to serve eligible students, but other parts of the country may well have excess capacity. We're going to have to decide whether we need some flexible national guidelines to deal with capacity quite apart from the issue of cost. It may not happen soon but out-of-state tuition policies may well need better coordination with each other. A new role for ACE will be to support improved connections in policy discussions at the federal and state level.

FL: When I came in, Rutgers' total student body was somewhere around 47,000. When I left it was 52,000. The way in which I dealt with that issue in my last two years, when we had no more room, was to work with community colleges to establish a dual degree program to which we would admit qualified applicants with a guarantee that if they took certain core courses and had a B average in their community college, they would be admitted to Rutgers in their junior year.

DW: That is one solution. But the California system is turning away qualified applicants in all three levels. You can use the system to stretch out capacity if the system has capacity, but if, as in California, you have tax policies that no longer sustain the ideal of segmented access, then we are back to the social compact discussion again.

FL: Capacity is the issue that deeply concerns me. No one wanted to listen, in fact I was criticized not only by politicians but by the press when I told them that capacity was a tremendous looming problem back in the year 2000. Without marshalling the resources of the state, you can't unilaterally solve the issue. You can't build the new buildings, you can't hire all the faculty you need, deal with the parking issues and so on, statewide, even if you were able to build some capacity on a few individual campuses.

DW: I think there will be some real and necessary pressures from Congress and governors to improve capacity through improved management. Time to degree, year round use of facilities, seamless transfer policies are clearly issues we need to address before they are addressed for us.

FL: Recent years have seen a second highly critical report by the Knight Commission, a major effort by the NCAA to reform academic regulations in order to improve student athletes' preparation for college and progress to a degree as well as graduation. What else can universities and their organizations do about the problems of intercollegiate athletics?

DW: The theater of athletics—bowl games—regional rivalries - the Final Four—are part of a complex bond between a university and its students, alumni, legislators and the community. In Wisconsin athletics were a key part of tribal pride in the state. This wide-ranging engagement is of course the source of commercialization. This complex relationship of commercialization to local and popular culture does create many challenges. I do believe that the reinvestment of the revenues of athletics in an "arms race" needs to be restrained and perhaps some stronger links between athletic revenues and academic mission of our institutions would help. I do think there is a need to continue efforts to ensure appropriate academic standards are applied to all student athletes. Ultimately this may result in a greater acceptability of high school athletes moving directly to professional athletic careers. Of course, the vast majority of student athletes do not become professionals and it would seem to me more appropriate for those with professional potential to be free to choose that course without any necessity of attending college immediately after high school. The indifference to college performance is usually based upon an expectation of becoming a professional, and we need to break that connection. It is also critical that we recognize the non-athletic professional successes of so many student athletes—but that does not make news!

FL: Some have suggested that the development of semi-pro leagues might be a solution.

DW: It is unlikely to happen, but it would certainly address the problem by attacking its roots. Universities could also act directly by connecting athletic directors more directly to the academic enterprise and connecting alumni with hyper-athletic interests to the broader alumni agenda. Largely because of the unusual change in the fortunes of our football and basketball programs, the university benefited from a reservoir of public goodwill, and I now feel that I didn't do as much as I should have done to support reform.

SL: The last question is the look into the crystal ball. What do you see as the strongest forces driving the need for change in higher education over the next ten to twenty years and what are the most important changes that you expect to see take place?

DW: The global knowledge economy will, I am sure, become a major driver. This knowledge economy is based on advances, often at our research universities, in the information and life sciences. The dominance of transatlantic connections has been changed by remarkable economic advances in India and China. There is a new post 9/11 geopolitics in which the United States is changing its world posture, but the exact outcome of that change has become less certain since the invasion of Iraq. Certainly, higher education is facing great uncertainty in the recruitment of foreign students and we need to be alert and responsive if it appears that our dominant role in attracting the best and brightest worldwide is threatened.

From an international perspective, U.S. higher education has achieved a great deal over the past fifty years. What will we do in the future? I think that we need a post 9/11 strategy and vision that recognizes the different and changing positions of the U.S., not in a military sense, but rather in a cultural and political-economic sense. For example, I think that the time at which China will be geopolitically influential is already on us. How we can cope with that and what it means is a big question.

Another issue is that higher education is still largely organized in terms of the advancement of knowledge along the disciplinary lines of the late nineteenth century. So our intellectual division of labor remains very much one with which an Edwardian or an American Progressive reformer would be familiar, with the exception, perhaps, of computer science, maybe genetics. And the academic department remains the dominant unit in our changing enterprise. I am not sure what those changes should be, but we do need to ask questions about what is the right way to organize ourselves. We need some scenarios of different kinds of structures that will enable us to advance and disseminate knowledge as successfully in the twenty-first century as we did in the twentieth century. Over the long history of universities, I think we can recognize that change is sometimes slow and occasionally late, and that too may lie behind our institutional survival.

Conclusion: Lessons in Leadership from Higher Education

Their Families

The least controllable aspect of leadership—but possibly one of the most influential—is the leader's background: the family of origin and the social situation from which he or she comes. What emerges as an almost universal circumstance in these stories of leadership development from university presidents is that the parents of nearly all of them had a tremendous influence, not just on their educational preparation but on their conviction that higher education is a domain of unique value. The choice of the area in which they were to concentrate their achievement seems, to a great extent, to have been guided by the deep reverence for higher education that almost all report that they learned as children. That is true not only of Kirwan, Coleman, and Vest, who, having grown up on a university campus, might have been expected to see higher education as a desirable career, but of presidents like David Ward, Norman Francis, and me, whose parents didn't have the opportunity to complete a traditional secondary school education. In some instances, these leaders in higher education were singled out as youngsters through an early use of academic ability/academic achievement testing. Shirley Jackson benefited from academic tracking and the mentorship of exceptional teachers brought to Washington D.C. to teach in the newly integrated schools. John Casteen's academic progress was closely monitored by University of Virginia professors and administrators. Mary Sue Coleman's interest in science was encouraged in the laboratory school that she attended on the University of Northern Iowa campus.

First Leadership Experiences

Self-confidence and the ability to inspire collaboration in a common cause are qualities that seem to have been developed consistently, and, in some cases, quite early in the careers of these university presidents and chancellors. Looking through their stories, I realized that most appear to have been singled out by teachers or peers for leadership positions by the time that they were in secondary school. They report having been elected to class offices and organization presidencies as some of their earliest leadership posts (Hasselmo,

Francis, Berdahl, Vest) and, as might be expected in an American setting, some cite their first memorable exercise of leadership as an experience connected with high school athletics: Kenny taught baton twirling routines; Kirwan was a quarterback; I was a pitcher.

In their academic careers, most of these leaders moved in an orderly progression through a number of varied responsibilities, developing their skills steadily. Shirley Jackson mentored young colleagues, was elected to office in her professional society, and served on the New Jersey Commission on Science and Technology before becoming the Chairman of the Nuclear Regulatory Commission and, later, a university president. Mary Sue Coleman headed a center for cancer research at the University of Kentucky, was first the associate provost, next the vice chancellor at UNC Chapel Hill, and then the provost at the University of New Mexico before becoming the president of the University of Iowa. Two presidents were singled out for advancement because they were successful in difficult assignments as faculty members. Nils Hasselmo was a faculty senator when he wrote a strategic planning document and suddenly found himself appointed as vice president of administration and planning. Brit Kirwan, on assignment as acting department chair during the summer, was confronted with the denial of tenure to a department member (tantamount to firing) by the university president over a freedom of speech issue. He managed to get the decision reversed by the summer's end, a coup that demonstrated to his department chair that he had found his successor. Bob Berdahl, lured by his dean's promise of summer salary into an assistant deanship, had his first experience of academic administration leading a curricular reform.

The Necessity of Teamwork

Command and control leadership has never been the key to success in the university presidency. Long before the arts of building leadership abilities among one's colleagues, encouraging teamwork at all levels of the organization, and achieving buy-in for goals and plans from the entire organization became matters of interest to leaders outside of academe, they were the means that successful administrators in universities employed to shape and accomplish their work. It is striking how often these university presidents observe that they kept many of the members of the former administration in place for some time because they were excellent people who were flexible enough to work well with a new president.

Every leader interviewed gave an important role in their administration to the absolute necessity for teamwork. Norman Francis has steadily improved his own university and conducted an amazingly large and impressively successful program of outreach to the New Orleans public schools by turning over to faculty and staff the ownership of the programs he wants to initiate. John Casteen organizes and reorganizes administrative teams to deal with all of the standard university functions and with issues as they arise, sitting in even on teams that he does not lead. Myles Brand emphasizes the need for individual initiative and responsibility, but at the same time requires that administrators be mutually supportive of one another, loyal to the team and the university. Molly Broad uses a system that she calls "interchangeable parts," meaning that it is open, collaborative and relies on a consultative style.

Involving the Institution in Leadership Responsibilities

In universities, the teamwork approach extends to the planning process and involves a broader range and higher proportion of the entire organization than is customary in most other sectors of society. Even when it is the president's leadership group that articulates the values and writes the plan, as Brit Kirwan's team did, the plan is disseminated to the university community and reworked, taking into consideration the commentary on it and gathering added support in the process. Shirley Kenny plans on a five-year cycle, using task forces on which faculty, staff, students and alumni serve. Shirley Jackson outlines a tightly organized process in which she laid out a vision and wrote a document with her leadership team, sent it out for discussion in workshops, in "portfolio areas" (schools and departments), and for a critique by external experts, then distilled all of the commentary into a series of key strategic issues and finished the first draft of the plan in the first semester of her administration. The first draft was put out for sixty days to gather public commentary by students, alums and others and the second draft, which incorporated changes suggested during the public review, was approved by the board in April of Jackson's first year. At Rutgers, the planning was first done by schools and campuses, then the directions derived from those plans were incorporated into a university-wide document. The implementation planning was put into the hands of faculty committees and a Committee for the Future composed of the faculty committee chairs, the provosts, and the vice presidents for academic affairs, for research, for budgeting, and for institutional research and planning. The plan provided the structural basis for the university's major fund campaign as well as the organizing principle on which administrative responsibilities were defined and reviews conducted.

Leadership in universities, and in other institutions as well, becomes more powerful when it is widely distributed, its goals are universally understood, and its accomplishments become the responsibility of the entire organization.

Intelligence, Humility, Integrity—and Listening

It is almost a reflex action in politics for a leader to claim piously that a variety of viewpoints is not only welcomed but sought out in choosing the members of the inner circle of advisors and the cabinet. Given the aspects of a university that resemble a polity, perhaps we might expect to find the same kinds of declarations from university presidents. However the tone and the context go beyond political inclusiveness when Mary Sue Coleman, Brit

Kirwan, and I talk about the need to have administrative colleagues who will discuss and debate issues. Like all leaders of complex organizations, we look for associates who can help us to avoid the mistakes that we as individuals may fail to see, giving us a broader, better informed basis for decision making.

No one will find it remarkable to learn that university presidents mention intelligence as one of the top qualities they seek in hiring, but it is interesting that these very able people are, at the same time, quite conscious of their own limits and the limits of others. Chuck Vest knows his own weaknesses and looks for people who will complement him. Brit Kirwan warns that "none of us is smart enough to know what to do all the time." Bob Berdahl repeats and has confirmed through experience his colleague's insight that you need to look for people with humility because "a person without humility at twenty-five is going to be a person without ideas at forty."

As one might expect, the ability to listen is also high on the list for leaders of institutions that depend so heavily on teamwork. Nearly all of the presidents interviewed for this book mentioned having used their first months in office to listen to people in an institution new to them. David Ward offers being a good listener as his most important piece of advice to new college presidents. The truth is that at any institution with excellent, hard-working faculty, staff, and administrators, the lion's share of the credit for the accomplishments of the institution belongs to them, not the president, and it is only fair that Chuck Vest, Norman Francis and I frankly acknowledge that fact: the president and the top administrators in excellent universities are first and foremost excellent listeners.

Integrity, which in this case can be defined as understanding of and devotion to the values of higher education, is central in importance for presidents and the administrators they depend upon. It is cited as a key requirement in choosing administrative staff by several of my colleagues, among them Nils Hasselmo, Norman Francis, Molly Broad, and Chuck Vest. I would be surprised if it were not high on the list of qualities that leaders in other fields feel are very important for people in their organizations.

Balancing the Mission

Visionary leadership is a sine qua non of success in the turbulent, challenging conditions that higher education, like many other sectors, has faced in recent times. When their universities were under considerable stress, each of the presidents whose stories we have recorded was able to call on the institution's strengths and traditions and to mobilize the members of their academic communities to think strategically, to plan a way to take the university forward, and to act on that plan.

In the early 1990s, restoring mission balance through the improvement of undergraduate education was one of the overriding concerns of research universities. In institutions that had traditionally maintained open access, such as the University of Minnesota and the University of Maryland College Park it was vital to reduce the enrollment in order to raise the quality of undergraduate instruction, as well as making other investments in order to provide additional support. Even in universities like Rutgers, where admissions policies were selective and graduation rates were over seventy percent, it was necessary to renew the focus on undergraduate instruction, increase academic support, and encourage undergraduate involvement in research.

The Funding Crisis in Public Higher Education

Public higher education's funding crisis developed slowly but inexorably over the past couple of decades as college-going rates increased, states' entitlement programs, along with their efforts to fix K-12 grew, and the proportion of every state's budget devoted to mandatory funding soared to hitherto unimagined heights. In Oregon, a taxpayer revolt created a particularly drastic change of circumstances: a 75 percent reduction in funding over three years for the University of Oregon. Myles Brand made the hard decisions on selective cuts based on faculty recommendations, then succeeded in turning the situation around with a new stream of revenue from the recruitment of out-of-state students. When university presidents and system heads finally came to grips with the fact that public funding for state universities was not going to return to the fondly remembered 50 percent levels of yore, it was not so much a question of achieving a vision as it was of taking stock of the new order of priorities in state funding.

At that hard place, as John Casteen points out, it was necessary to imagine what the alternatives might be. On one hand, it would have been easy to reduce their universities' character and ambition in order to fit the public funding available, in short to give up the claims of public insitutions of higher education to excellence as internationally known and respected centers of research and teaching and to scrape by instead as mediocre public utilities. The other alternative was risky: it exposed the presidents to the possibility of public failure and meant that all of the people who worked with them—administrators, faculty, staff, alumni, and friends of the university—had to be convinced that, in order to keep the academic enterprise moving ahead, they would have to find new sources of strength and take on additional responsibilities.

At the University of Virginia, at Rutgers, and at universities across the country, presidents explained the new facts of life in public higher education to sitting deans and candidates for deanships. There was no hidden treasure in state coffers or in the university's budget that could be tapped to finance their schools: it was the deans' responsibility to raise the funds to advance to the next level.

Faculty increased their efforts to bring in funding to support their research and their graduate students and those efforts received better support from their universities. Offices that help faculty to secure corporate funding, protect intellectual property by patents, copyrights and other agreements, and promote technology transfer and commercialization were also strengthened in order to produce increased streams of revenue for their institutions.

Alumni and friends found that their public institutions were, of necessity, launching major fund campaigns of a size and intensity never before imagined in order to support the high quality that their states and their alums wanted to be able to continue to expect of them. It was a tough crisis, but like many difficult conditions, it forced everyone to work harder, smarter, and with much greater shared responsibility for the success of the enterprise, to be more conscious of their high performance goals, and more focused and determined in the actions they took to reach them.

Building Diversity in Higher Education

As America became increasingly diverse, universities confronted the need to diversify their enrollment, their faculty, and administration and to increase the respect throughout the academic community for human dignity, while legal strictures on affirmative action and tensions in their communities made their goals increasingly difficult to attain. Ultimately we reached a point of crisis in the affirmative action suits against the University of Michigan. In the Michigan cases, the Supreme Court ruled that the use of a point system for racial preference in undergraduate admissions was impermissible, but found merit in the nuanced arguments for the educational benefits of diversity.

Vision is indispensable, but vision is only the first step and perhaps the easiest. The actual accomplishment of a complex goal like building a just and supportive diverse society requires changing hearts and minds. It is a process that takes not simply good will and nice words but iron determination and tireless efforts to advance toward an ideal that seems continually to recede into the distance.

Access

In the problem of ensuring access to higher education, we are at a much more difficult juncture than the traditional rock and a hard place. We are in the path of a flood of young people, a cohort both more numerous and more diverse than we have ever seen before, who are coming of college age and are eager to enter higher education. Of course increased public higher education access is only one part of the problem. Access is meaningful only if it is affordable and, as Shirley Jackson observes, "It takes money to deal with diverse groups and kids from various socio-economic backgrounds, but frankly, because of all the things universities are being asked to do besides just teach students, the pie is only so big." This is a problem too large and too important to the future of the nation for individual institutions, private or public, to solve on their own. Nor can we count upon our state governments to grasp the full dimensions of the need to ensure access and to devote the resources necessary for its solution, since the states now enjoy only intermittently an exceptionally good budget year or two in which they can bestow largess on their institutions of higher education. We must look to the federal level, where now the bulk of student aid is devoted to loan programs geared to middle class debt tolerance. The hard truth is that John Casteen is precisely correct in declaring, "Educational debt is a great mechanism for the middle income class, but it makes no sense at all for the poorest Americans." The only viable solution capable of offering meaningful access to all academically qualified students is one that is not yet even under discussion: large increases in need-based federal aid to students in the form of grants.

If we, the American public, our politicians, and our universities, are very quick, very clever and incredibly generous, the oncoming flood of college age students could create the greatest intellectual flowering, produce the largest skilled workforce, and provide the best global model for human development in a diverse society ever conceived. But if we are neither quick, nor generous, nor clever—if we procrastinate; if we seize this opportunity to aggrandize the status and the "quality" of our individual institutions by narrowing access; if we fail to improve the college preparation our schools give their students; if we abandon as too difficult and controversial the effort to increase the proportion of underrepresented minorities in our college and university enrollment; if we see access as someone else's problem—then we may be guilty of creating the kind of societal nightmare foreseen by some higher education policy analysts: a nation split in two, with an unbridgeable chasm between the top and the bottom levels: one side well-educated with high expectations, the other minimally educated with little hope for the future. That would transform our country into a stark and inhospitable landscape where none of us would want to live.